THE WH
F

THE WHICH? GUIDE TO
FRANCE

CONSUMERS' ASSOCIATION

Which? Books are commissioned and researched by
The Association for Consumer Research and published by
Consumers' Association, 2 Marylebone Road, London NW1 4DF

Distributed by the Penguin Group:
Penguin Books Ltd, 27 Wrights Lane, London W8 5TZ

First edition 1982
Second edition 1985
Third edition 1987
Fourth edition 1989, revised reprint January 1991
Fifth edition 1994

Design: Tim Higgins
Illustrations: Peter Byatt
Cover illustration: Lucinda Rogers
Cover design: Paul Saunders
Maps: Perrott Cartographics

For this edition
Editors: Anna Fielder, Andrew Leslie
Contributors: Fred Mawer, the *Holiday Which?* team
Additional research: Liz Piccin
Wine section: Andrew Jefford
Index: Marie Lorimer

British Library Cataloguing in Publication Data

'Which?' Guide to France
5 Rev. ed.– ('Which?' Travel Guides)
I. Ruck, Adam II. Series
914. 404

ISBN 0 85202 530 0

Typeset by Tech-Set, Gateshead, Tyne and Wear
Printed and bound in Great Britain by
Clays Ltd, St Ives plc

CONTENTS

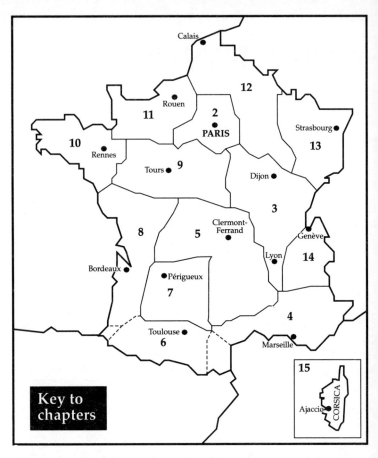

Key to chapters

Regional maps of France, designed to help situate most of the places mentioned in the text, and the hotels recommended in the Hotels sections, are included at the beginning of each chapter. The numerical sequence follows the order of the regional chapters after Paris (map on pages 50–1):

Introduction

Like two neighbouring families in a long-running soap opera, the French and the Anglo-Saxons gaze at each other across their watery garden fence with a mixture of suspicion, envy, admiration and frustration. They have known each other for a long time, so there are few inhibitions on either side of the Channel when it comes to commenting on the incomprehensible failure of the other to perceive what really matters in life.

The French take it for granted that France is the finest country in the world, and see no reason why others should think otherwise. In matters of style, culture, cuisine and *savoir vivre*, the natural order of things suggests that they should lead and others follow. The French are happy to trumpet their own virtues, for prestige and glory have never become a debased coinage in France. The love of world-beating projects, such as the TGV network or the redevelopment of the Louvre, is typical of the French desire to be in the front rank – penny-pinching on big ideas is not something the French go in for.

It is easy enough to be seduced by a people with self-confidence, and today more and more of us are taking our holidays in France. It has now outstripped Spain as the most popular holiday destination for the British and the number of British people who choose to buy property in France shows little sign of diminishing. Like a magic emporium, it has almost everything the holidaymaker could desire (though careful choice is needed, for some resorts, hotels and restaurants are past their sell-by date). The active, the indolent, the cultured, the greedy, the impoverished and the self-indulgent need choose only what suits their tastes and pockets best. The only qualification needed to enjoy France is a willingness at least to attempt the language and to appreciate the French and their way of life.

The way of life is easy enough to appreciate. After all, a nation which believes in the virtues of the extended lunch hour, the village market, children having the right to eat out with their parents *and* that an efficient railway system is a top priority cannot be doing everything wrong. The elaborate bureaucracy becomes easier to bear when you realise that the French happily disregard the parts they do not believe are relevant to them; there is even, arguably, a linkage between motorways blockaded by tractors and the unspoilt beauty of so much of the French countryside. Only when behind the wheels of their cars or when, for whatever reason, they cannot be bothered to be polite to you, do the French become intolerable. But for every instance of rudeness, most holidaymakers will find a dozen or more courtesies.

INTRODUCTION

Getting the best out of France means taking your time. Many of the small Romanesque churches, for example – among the country's great glories – are hidden in tiny villages well off the beaten track. So too are romantic châteaux, sunny market squares, working mills and friendly vineyard owners. Rushing from one major tourist sight to the next is not the way to enjoy the country.

Parisians would argue that you need go no further than Paris for the best that the country has to offer, but, while it is true that no one who loves France can ignore its capital, the city is merely an island – though a civilised and beautiful one – in what is still a rural nation. The distinctive faces and accents of the French regions, from the nationalistic Bretons to the laid-back inhabitants of the Languedoc (who believe that they are the genuine French and the rest merely Johnny-come-latelies), provide more variety and fascination than all the pleasures of the Louvre or the Champs-Elysées.

Knowing where to go for what – whether a good meal, a quiet village or an uncrowded beach – is made extra difficult in France by the sheer breadth of choice. This is where *The Which? Guide to France* will help. The guide covers all of France, from the Pyrenees to the Channel Coast, and aims to point you to the best things to see and do in each region – not so much in the field of the exclusive, the luxurious or the fashionable as in the simple pleasures. We shall also try to steer you away from the mediocre.

In each region we have selected the hotels which we believe are the best-value places to stay at, and these you will find clearly marked on the maps. Many of them are off the beaten track, for the best of France is to be found in small, sunny villages left undisturbed since medieval times. As the French themselves are increasingly coming to realise, the glamour of a beach at Deauville or a prestigious Cannes restaurant is not necessarily preferable to a leisurely lunch in a country inn or in a well-run family *logis*. Here, as you may witness in many of the villages of, for example, the Dordogne or Normandy, French and Anglo-Saxon tastes coincide.

Hotel choices

One of the great delights of travelling through France is making the discovery – or the rediscovery – that comfortable friendly hotels with efficient staff and good food still exist, and that they are still prepared to charge sensible prices. The disappointment and bitterness of paying out extravagant sums in exchange for pretentious décor, surly staff and inadequate food is a less common sensation in France than in most other European countries. This is partly because the best French hotels are local institutions of the kind not seen in Britain since the days of the coaching inn. They have a dependable year-round clientele for the restaurant; they are family-owned, family-run and have not felt the need to call in either the marketing men or the interior designers.

Knowing that such places exist is one thing, finding them is another. The march of standardisation and of internationalisation (or at least of Europeanisation) is no slower in France than anywhere else, and it is becoming quite a task to find hotels that manage to remain character-istic of their region, or even of France. In particular, the growth of the chains of budget business hotels on the outskirts of French towns is in danger of knocking the traditional town-centre inn out of the market altogether. These chains (*Formule I*, *Primavere*, *Novotel*, *Ibis*, to name but a few) are cheap, convenient and often comfortable, but bland beyond belief. Bland too, but in a different way, are increasing numbers of luxury hotels, particularly those in châteaux. The need to encourage foreign visitors used to having their widely varying tastes satisfied has meant the ironing out of joyful French eccentricity, the provision of English-speaking staff and English-version menus where the transla-tion is often more interesting than the food. Alas, too many simple family-run hotels appear to feel that they must imitate to compete, and begin by imitating the prices. Choose wrongly, and it is as easy to feel in French hotels, as anywhere else, that, to quote Pope: 'Nor public flame nor private dares to shine; Nor human spark is left nor glimpse divine.'

In the belief that our readers care enough about France to wish to stay in hotels which could be found nowhere else, and in the virtual certainty that they would rather do this at a cost which allows the satisfactory sensation of money well spent, we have taken care to select hotels for this edition of the *Guide* which are both good value for money and French to the core. We have seldom included hotels, however good, which do not have at least one double room for 500FF or less, and we have deliberately preferred the comfortable, peaceful, family-run enterprise with simple, regional menus to the expensive palace-hotel with its international restaurant. We have also looked for well-located hotels outside big cities rather than in the heart, in the knowledge that prices are usually lower, parking charges and security less of a problem, and the atmosphere usually more pleasant.

For those who want their choice widened, there is no lack of guidance. Many British visitors to France still carry their copies of the *Red Michelin*, or the *Logis de France* list, and while both are useful if you have no idea where you will be by nightfall, the large numbers of hotels listed means that the mediocre is sometimes garnered in with the good. Those who are confident of their French should try *chambres d'hôtes* – the French equivalent of the British bed and breakfast. As in this country, some of these easily rival the most comfortable hotels, although there is not usually the same difference in price. *Gîtes de France* produces the most extensive yearly listing, called *French Country Welcome*. Château Acceuil is an organisation of château-owners offering B&B (and sometimes an evening meal), often using the income to renovate their homes. Standards may vary wildly, but the experience is usually interesting. At the other end of the market, Relais et Châteaux includes among its members some of the most prestigious historic hotels in France. For country hotels, we have found our tastes shared by the excellent *Guide des Auberges et Hôtels de Charme en France*, of which there is now an English version (*Guide to Hotels and Country Inns of Character and Charm in France*, Rivages, 1993–4). The booklet produced by hotel-owners based in converted mills, called *Moulin Etape* (available in tourist offices), will lead you to some interesting and isolated spots.

If food is a chief concern, we recommend the *Gault Millau* or *Bottin Gourmand* guides. Both are weighty tomes whose lyrical descriptions will tax your French vocabulary, but they will ensure that you do not eat badly (an all-too-common experience if you take pot luck over where you go).

French hotel-keeping differs from that in Britain in several respects, and it is worth remembering a few simple points. Chief among these is the fact that washing facilities rather than size usually govern the room price, and if you choose a shower rather than a bath, or can manage with a basin and WC, you will often save disproportionate amounts of money. Second, the price you are quoted rarely includes breakfast – and the local café may provide cheaper and better morning fare. Third is the fact that many hotels will have family rooms (usually three, but often four beds) and that these usually represent better value and more space than booking two separate rooms for parents and offspring.

Happily for the traveller, the habit of taking credit card numbers with every telephone booking is catching on only slowly in France and most hotels will trust you to turn up when you say you will. The down side of this is that the hotel will feel free to re-let your room if there is no sign of you by 6.30 pm. Always telephone if you are delayed – it saves tears.

Most hotel restaurants take last orders at 9.30 pm, and it is wise to reserve a table when you book your room, especially on Friday or Saturday nights. Bear in mind, too, that many hotels still insist that you take half-board, particularly in high-season seaside resorts; others charge room supplements if you do not eat in-house.

Hotel fire safety

Consumers' Association has long campaigned for an EC Directive on fire safety in hotels. At the moment there are agreed standards throughout the EC, but they are not legally binding, and standards vary from country to country.

One of the biggest dangers in a fire is smoke. When you arrive at a hotel, always:
- find out where the nearest exits to your room are and check that the exit doors will open easily
- find out where the nearest fire alarm point is and read the instructions
- find out how to open the windows in your room and look for ledges and balconies that might help you escape
- read any emergency information available.

If a fire breaks out:
- do not panic
- report fire or smoke to reception immediately
- never use the lift
- never try to go through thick smoke.

A useful leaflet, *About Hotel Fire Safety*, is available free with an SAE from the Fire Protection Association, 140 Aldersgate Street, London EC1A 4HX.

History and architecture

HISTORY

Celts, Gauls and Franks France during the last thousand years before Christ was gradually occupied by tribes of Celts from the east. In the 6th century BC Greek traders established themselves in Mediterranean sea ports and, in the 2nd, the Romans arrived. Southern France became the Provincia Romana, three-quarters of a century before Caesar conquered all Gaul in seven years (58–51 BC). Even when Gaul was Roman, the old southern Provincia was much more thoroughly colonised and the influence of Romans, Roman law and Roman buildings has survived in the language, customs, way of life and style of architecture of southern France.

Several centuries of Roman peace were brought to a bloody end in the 4th and 5th centuries AD by another succession of invaders from the east, the most destructive among them being the Huns. In the late 5th century the originally German tribe of Franks established control over what is now roughly France, and later rulers extended their control over most of Europe; Charlemagne was crowned Holy Roman Emperor by the Pope in Rome on Christmas Day 800.

These empires were personal ones and did not survive the conqueror, for inheritance was divided. What did survive was the concept of united throne and altar, symbolised in the coronation ceremony at Reims, which went back to 496 when King Clovis was baptised by Saint Remi. The moral and material support of the church was of great importance to the later medieval monarchs of France in their struggle to establish true control of the lands and minds of the French people. The story of this struggle, long and bloody, is the political history of France throughout the Middle Ages and beyond, not really concluded until the time of Louis XIV.

Feudalism and war The feudal system has been described as everybody belonging to somebody else and everyone else belonging to the king. In practice, royal control over lands outside the royal domain around Paris was negligible, and resisted by local lords who behaved like kings in their own realms. As long as it worked, the social contract – the lord's protection in return for the subject's economic and military support – bred no particular enthusiasm for the monarchy, whose main interest was revenue.

In the king's favour was time, and the weariness engendered by long periods of fighting. In the 14th and 15th centuries one particular feudal conflict took on national dimensions and did much to awaken national spirit in France. The warring parties were the kings of France, and the kings of England in their capacity as French landowners – English kings up to and including Edward III spoke no English. In the 12th century the Plantagenet kings of England had built up a mighty empire in France and lost most of it thanks mainly to the weakness (always called pusillanimity) of King John. In the 14th century the renewed power struggle was given a new dimension by the extinction of the ruling dynasty of France. Edward III's claim to the French throne and Philippe de Valois's resistance to his claim began the Hundred Years' War, wherein the French and English sides were repeatedly swollen and depleted by other French factions (notably Brittany, Burgundy and Orléans) whose main interest was to ensure that neither side could win. The English seemed to have won in 1418 when, in an alliance with the Burgundians, they forced the dauphin Charles to flee Paris; in 1420 Henry V of England married the French king's daughter and was recognised as regent and heir to the throne of France. Then the almost contemporaneous deaths of the kings of England and France were followed by the appearance of saints to a peasant girl in Lorraine, conveying a divine mission to rid France of the English. She managed to halt for ever the advance of the English, and made the dauphin, Charles, the undisputed king of France. Saint Joan is the patroness of France, the outward and visible sign of an inward and spiritual birth of French national consciousness.

Crusade and pilgrimage The Middle Ages were ages of faith as much as ages of warring nobles and land disputes. A majority of the nobility had no land, for shared inheritance had been discarded in favour of primogeniture (leaving everything to the eldest son). Younger sons could join the church, they could fight for land or a cause far from home, or they could do both by going on a crusade. Crusading is a leitmotif of medieval Europe, begun in defence against invading Saracens in 8th-century Spain, and in the late 11th century becoming a Holy War to recapture Jerusalem and then defend it against the infidel. In the early 13th century, a crusade was launched to stamp out heresy in south-western France. The religious issue cloaked nothing more edifying than a lust for blood and land, and the war which destroyed the power and civilisation of Toulouse to the benefit of the crown illustrates how the church helped the monarchy.

The peaceful version of the crusade was the pilgrimage. In the Middle Ages people travelled far and often: throughout the land there were miracle-working relics and venerated tombs which brought pilgrims and prosperity to a religious community. The pilgrims were not content to pay their respects and make their requests simply at the nearest shrine. The great journeys were to Jerusalem, to Rome and to the tomb of Saint James at Compostela in the north-western corner of Spain. Four major pilgrimage routes led across France to converge in the Atlantic Pyrenees on the way to Compostela, and were marked by important secondary pilgrimage churches on the way and by monasteries and hostelries for the accommodation of pilgrims. The international security of the pilgrim was in the hands of two orders of knights which were founded to defend the Christian kingdom in the Holy Land and which were granted lands all over Europe (the Knights Templar and Hospitaller).

Consolidation and reform The Messianic appearance of Joan of Arc was one sign of a new France: there were many more practical ones in the late 15th century. Charles VII was the first king to have a permanent or standing army, and he had recourse for his war-waging to the funds of a brilliant merchant banker, the bourgeois Jacques Cœur, who made his fortunes from the spice trade with the Orient. Louis XI saw the sense of surrounding himself not with his peers, as feudal monarchs had to do, but with men who owed all their success to the king's pleasure – civil servants. By subtle manoeuvring (he was often called the spider), bribery and alliance with the Swiss, Louis overcame the last of the great representatives of the age of chivalry, Charles the Rash of the noble house of Burgundy.

The 16th century throughout Europe was the century of religious reform, an issue which in France gave the nobility a chance to stand and assert itself again. Religion became a pretext for civil war, involving the crown, the nobility and towns, both of the last trying to recover some of their lost freedom. On St Bartholomew's Eve 1572, 2,000 Huguenots (Protestants) were massacred in Paris, setting the tone of the religious wars which were as bloody and unprincipled as only religious wars can be, and having a similar effect on the countryside and population of France as the endemic warfare of the Middle Ages. In 1589 the crown fell to Henry IV, but the gates of Paris would not open to him because he was a Protestant. Having weighed the moral and political considerations carefully, he renounced his faith in 1593 with one of the most famous throw-away lines in the history of Catholicism: 'Paris is well worth a mass'.

Royal supremacy The 17th century saw the great consolidation of royal power. By the Edict of Nantes, the far-sighted and tolerant Henri IV attempted to enforce religious compromise by guaranteeing Huguenots freedom of religious practice – allocating them several towns in the south-west – and the wars subsided. Religious wars of a different complexion, but similar savagery, so devastated 17th-century

Alsace that the province looked to the French King Louis XIV for protection.

The most glorious period of the French monarchy, the *Ancien Régime*, is the century and a half when the throne was occupied by three Bourbon kings, Louis XIII (1610–1643), Louis XIV (1643–1715) and Louis XV (1715–1774). It is the period of the great civil servants – after Henri IV's Sully came cardinals Richelieu and Mazarin under Louis XIII, and Colbert among others under Louis XIV; of the destruction of medieval fortresses; and of the installation of provincial governors and *intendants* to strip the nobility of their local power.

Louis XIV's accession at the age of five gave the nobility the chance once again to attempt to win back lost influence over the crown. This meant civil war (the *Fronde*) between noble factions, and the king grew up in a humiliating climate of being a refugee in his own kingdom – an experience which made him determined when he finally took full possession of his powers in 1661 to establish the absolute nature of royal authority. Versailles was the appropriate context for king worship and the place where the aristocracy of France could be kept under control – and under-employed except with questions of courtly protocol. The provinces became merely the place for disgrace, exile or poverty; as a result, rural France suffered neglect and economic stagnation.

Louis's own comparison between himself and the sun is irresistible. It was a brilliant, heroic period for the arts and philosophy and thanks to the administrative achievements of the civil servants Louis was able to take war abroad and extend the frontiers of France to the east and north-east. But it is in the nature of the sun not to remain at its zenith; the evening of Louis's reign is more notable for lengthening shadows than glorious sunset. After the revocation in 1685 of Henri IV's Edict of Nantes, over 400,000 Protestants took their skills to other countries – the decline of the Aubusson tapestry manufacture is just one example of the effect of emigration. The wars of the early years of the 18th century against a network of European allies were disastrous for France and Louis left his realm in much more of a mess financially than he had found it.

Royal decline Like his great-grandfather, Louis XV came to the throne at the age of five; unlike him he was never strong enough to take for himself full kingly control. The reign of Louis XV was a period of *distractions*, to keep courtiers deprived of political utility and amused. A special Ministry of Lesser Pleasures for Versailles entertainment was the recipient of a lavish endowment of state funds. The nobility's lack of power in the realm was exceeded only by the extent of its privilege, for aristocratic acquiescence in the robbery of its power had been dearly bought in terms of tax exemption. In such a climate it may seem surprising that a revolution took so long to come. It was only in the reign of Louis XVI, when attempts were at last made to improve the lot of the mass of French society, that serious objection to the *Ancien Régime* was articulated in line with the enlightened ideas of 18th-century philosophers. Demands for social and constitutional reform came to a head all over France. Meetings of the three estates (nobles, clergy and commons) were followed by the first meeting for nearly two centuries of the Estates General of the realm. At Versailles, with the famous tennis court oath, the third estate declared itself a national assembly and swore not to disband until France had a constitution. On July 14th 1789 a Paris mob in search of arms went to the Bastille – a once notorious prison for political subversives – stormed it, and liberated the seven remaining prisoners. Bastille Day is celebrated with fireworks all over France.

Republic and Empire The idealism of the Revolution – a longing for freedom – was greeted in intellectual circles throughout Europe and especially in England with the same ecstatic euphoria as it was in France, but soon revealed itself to be above all destructive. Religion and the established church was the main target; churches all over France were sacked. The Revolutionaries even changed the calendar, starting history again at the year 0 and giving the months of the year naturally inspired names – Thermidor for the hot period, Ventose for the windy one and so on. The old order was replaced not by liberty (nor equality and fraternity) but by savage mob rule (the Terror), of which two inevitable victims were the king and queen, guillotined within a few months of each other in 1793. The French soon longed for servitude under an absolute order again.

The architect of the new order was to be Napoleon Bonaparte, a brilliant and daring commander who led the forces of Revolutionary France to conquest all over continental Europe, and met even less resistance in his adoption of imperial powers and status in France. Consciously attaching himself to the tradition of Charlemagne and Christian monarchs of medieval France, in 1804 Napoleon made a humiliated Pope watch him place the crown on his own head. Napoleon's ambitions were not just military. Under his rule, and after it under his influence, France was subjected to more social, administrative and legal reforms than ever before. He confirmed the peasants in their land and freedom, restored the Catholic state, created authoritarian government and established a new system of civil, criminal and rural law – the civil code was known as the Code Napoleon. The Anglo–Austrian alliance finally broke Napoleon's power in 1814 (and again in 1815 when an attempted comeback failed at Waterloo). Several attempts to revive the monarchy all proved unsatisfactory; a Second Republic was even more short-lived than the first and was followed in 1851 by another Empire and another Bonaparte, Napoleon III. France grew fat and industrial as nephew followed uncle's social and economic reforms, but not his military exploits. After a series of defeats the bourgeois Second Empire finally succumbed to Prussian might at Sedan in 1870. Paris spent a winter under siege, and Alsace and much of Lorraine were ceded to Germany. The Third Republic, proclaimed after the débâcle at Sedan and confirmed by one vote after the *communard* uprising in the capital had been suppressed, was to last until the Second World War.

The World Wars By the turn of the century, the balance of power in Europe had unmistakably changed in favour of Germany. France allied herself with Britain and Russia. When Russia resolved to risk a European war in the name of the Serbian cause, France was dragged into the First World War by her obligations, as Britain was by hers to France. By November 1918 France was an exhausted victor, her richest departments had been devastated, her most valuable industries ruined and almost 1,400,000 men lost. The feeling of relief that the war was over – and the need to believe that it must have been worthwhile – was naturally greater in France than anywhere else; it helps to explain the fervent pacifism of French government policy in the inter-war years. When in May 1936 Hitler tested the temperature of the water by occupying the Rhineland, France, to his great surprise, made only token protests. Despite belated rearmament, France was inadequately equipped to resist the German invasion of 1939. After only a few months, marshal Pétain, something of a folk hero from the First World War and the head of government, asked for an armistice which was granted on terms which included surrender of two-thirds of France. France withdrew from the War and the government adjourned to Vichy, which became the capital of non-occupied France. From November 1942, however, the Germans occupied the whole country. A resistance movement, known as the Maquis, was gradually organised to fight the occupiers and given a lead by Charles de Gaulle. From his base in England, de Gaulle recruited for the Forces of Free France and sent them with the British and Americans to land on the Normandy beaches on D-Day, 6 June 1944. A little less than a year later, the last German outpost (Bordeaux) was liberated. General de Gaulle was recognised as the head of provisional government of the French Republic.

Post-war politics After disengaging herself from the war in Indo-China France had to face the civil problem of Algerian nationalism (the country was constitutionally part of France), which took on the status of a war of independence after a coup d'état in 1958; de Gaulle was called back from retirement to deal with the crisis. With popular approval for a new constitution (the Fifth Republic) de Gaulle became president with virtually dictatorial power and led France through a decade of renewed confidence and economic boom. The growing complacency, and de Gaulle himself, were broken in 1968, when student riots in Paris and other towns escalated to a general strike.

The influence of the Second World War on French political loyalties has been a lasting one. Such was the bitterness of the years of occupation, when resistance Frenchmen hated collaborating Frenchmen even more than occupying Germans, that a politician's war record is still an important part of his manifesto. Valéry Giscard d'Estaing was the leader of a new generation of technocrat politicians; his record was a financial rather than a military one. Repeatedly, Giscard and the Gaullistes called on the French bourgeois fear of communism to keep socialists out of power (socialists and communists have been formally allied since 1972), and it was assumed that as long as the alliance lasted that fear would keep it out of power. In the 1981 Presidential Election the French showed, contrary to all expectations, that they wanted a change not from the old order, but from the new. President Mitterrand is one of the last of the resistance heroes in French politics.

ARCHITECTURE

Prehistory The earliest evidence of man's architectural impulse in France is the wealth of large stones or megaliths that he raised all over the country but nowhere in such numbers and in such arrangements as in Brittany. These alignments appear to have had mystical significance, oriented like embryonic temples according to the sun's axis.

Roman Gaul There are marvellous Roman amphitheatres, theatres and other civil monuments: Nîmes has one of the most perfectly preserved Roman temples anywhere, built according to pure classical principles. Provence is the fortunate possessor of most of the surviving Roman remains; here invaders from the east penetrated less thoroughly and used Roman amphitheatres for their own fortifications, and old Roman cities were developed much less in later centuries. In other areas Roman buildings were used unscrupulously as quarries by later builders: in Le Puy cathedral you can see Gallo-Roman relief carvings incorporated at random in the fabric of the medieval walls.

Medieval churches There are treats for the lover of churches in almost every area of France. The south is mostly Romanesque (11th to 13th centuries), the north mostly Gothic (13th to 15th centuries). The five centuries preceding the year 1000 were troubled and dangerous times of barbarian rampage and arson; most early Christian buildings were replaced in the new wave of church building which followed. The new era was one of relative order; travel by pilgrims, crusaders, merchants, kings and masons led to the exchange of ideas and artistic influence. It was also an age of faith and economic growth, and powerful monastic orders played a major role. The most important was the Benedictine order of Cluny, which spread from Burgundy all over Europe, pushing back forests and putting up churches.

The style of these churches has since the last century been termed **Romanesque** (*Roman*) to express its derivation from the Latin style, in the use, for example, of the round arch. Compared with classical architects, Romanesque church builders were free from the shackles of theory; styles evolved from the nature of materials, the tastes of patrons and the functional requirements of buildings – abbey, pilgrimage or parish church. As a result Romanesque churches are fascinating in their local variety, their liveliness and their personality. In the north the warlike Normans evolved a powerful and undecorative version of the Romanesque which they exported to England. Because of its sobriety, a familiarity with Norman architecture in England gives no hint of the richness of French Romanesque south of the Loire, where influences from further south and east penetrated along trade and pilgrim routes. North Italian masons took their style and their elegant arcaded belfries to the cosmopolitan and economically precocious Mediterranean area of Catalonia, where monastic builders also drew inspiration from Islamic and Byzantine *objets d'art* and manuscripts to produce marvellously decorative carving in local marble to adorn their churches. The sculptural style spread, not without modification, throughout south-western France; its examples remain the greatest artistic heritage of the area. In Poitou, fresco painting in a similar style was particularly popular; in Provence, Roman remains were the inspiration for a very classical local style of sculpture and architecture. Arab influence is to be observed in architectural features of the Massif Central, and – with less certainty – in the domes which proliferate in a limited area around the Dordogne. No better reason for the existence of these churches in this area has been found than human contacts; for example, the bishop of Cahors went to Constantinople and when he returned ordered domes like those of Constantinople's church of the Apostles for his new cathedral.

Other developments were practical. The system of a passage or ambulatory around a central shrine, with subsidiary radiating chapels for little shrines, was first hit upon to cope with the crowds at the great pilgrimage church of St-Martin-de-Tours – the victim, like so many churches, of the Revolution. Another victim was Cluny, the greatest Romanesque church of all, whose builders were highly adventurous with vaulting to achieve optimum acoustics for their chant.

The **Gothic** style, which dominated Christian church building from the late 12th until the 16th century, was an engineering revolution; still more it was a spiritual, intellectual and even a political one. It spread across France from Paris and the north in step with royal control and influence – the style for a new era of monarchy. In contrast with the charm and invention and sheer decorative exuberance of Romanesque architects and stone carvers, the Gothic cathedral is programmatic and intellectual. The cathedral as a whole represents heaven, so lofty that it seems to exist as much in the sky as on the ground, and bathed in an unearthly coloured radiance by stained glass. The main doorway or gateway to heaven reminds the visitor of the requirements of entry with a representation of the Last Judgement. The Virgin also features prominently as the period's favourite intermediary between man and a remote God. Stained glass illustrates the scriptures, not just as a picture book for the illiterate but for symbolic reasons – the light of heaven shines through the scriptures to illuminate the faithful.

The new style was made possible by the development of the pointed arch, reducing the outward thrust of round vaults which had a tendency to make walls collapse. The use of ribs in a vault conducted weight to specific points instead of all along the wall, and the flying buttress enabled the vault to be supported not by reinforcing the wall itself, but by using pillars isolated from it. With these techniques, it was possible to build enormously high vaults above slender pillars. Instead of vast areas of masonry requiring frescoes and carvings for decoration, with small openings in the thick fabric for light, the stonework became a mere skeleton for the enormous expanse of stained glass.

Gothic cathedrals of northern France produce a phenomenal impression of verticality. Architects and patrons often overreached themselves – it was standard practice before the scaffolding was removed to say a mass imploring divine support for the building. The vertiginous isolation of the choir of Beauvais, to which no nave could successfully be attached, is the most striking example of the excessive ambition of Gothic architects and episcopal patrons.

The great Gothic century was the 13th. In the 14th century everything went wrong – France was torn apart by the Hundred Years' War, the monarchy was humiliated at Crécy and Poitiers, and plague reduced the population of Europe by a third. Confidence was not unreasonably shaken, church building interrupted, and people looked to their faults and those of the church: religious feeling turned inward. Artistic achievements became those of individual works of painting and sculpture; one admires not the *élan* of the whole, but the fineness of the decorative detail. General pessimism seems to be expressed by the flame-like form of stonework which has given the name *flamboyant* to the late Gothic style.

Medieval secular architecture From the Romanesque age of faith, few non-religious buildings of distinction survive: all aesthetic architectural effort seems to have gone into church building. Later centuries brought prosperity, and town houses began to be built with pride, as at Cordes near Albi. In the wealthy north, town councils spent large sums on the building of magnificent town halls and belfries, monuments of civic spirit.

Most non-religious Gothic buildings are fortified. Such was the war-torn tenor of medieval French life, and the remote nature of royal control in many areas, that castles, fortified churches and monasteries, and complete fortified towns covered France; their ruins remain. Almost every area was strategically important for somebody, from the kings of France and England to local lords who defied anybody from rocky strongholds. In the border zones of English and French territory in south-western France, rival powers tried to secure footholds in an under-populated landscape by founding new fortified towns called *bastides* and attracting loyal subjects to inhabit them. The popes forti-fied themselves on the edge of their territory in Avignon; the kings of France responded by fortifying a hill on the other side of the Rhône. As royal power was extended, fortresses were frequently maintained to buttress the central authority, or (if appropriately situated) to defend France. Development of artillery forced a major revision of the style of fort building, from the high and dominant to the low and massive. Many other refinements to the style of military architecture (including the use of round towers and concentric plans) had been learnt from crusading experience.

Medieval architecture – destruction and restoration Many medieval fortifications presented a threat to law and order and were destroyed, notably by cardinal Richelieu in the 17th century. Some fortifications have survived because places lost their importance: one example is the old crusading port of Aigues-Mortes where the sea retreated, and the town never grew. In other places, what remain are not survivals but restorations, after centuries of destruction in the religious wars when puritanical Protestants stripped statues – idols – down from niches in façades, and during the Revolution.

The Middle Ages came into fashion in the 19th century. There was a rapid Catholic reaction after the Revolution: in a climate of romantic nostalgia for mossy, overgrown and tenebrous medievalism, Prosper Mérimée was appointed Inspector General of Historic Monuments in 1933. He engaged the young and brilliant architect Viollet-le-Duc to restore churches and fortresses, Romanesque and Gothic, all over France. Without these two, scores of France's greatest medieval monu-ments would not have survived. Much of Viollet-le-Duc's work has been criticised partly because, as at Carcassone, he imposed a strictly regulated uniformity of style. Carcassone, having evolved over many centuries, had never had this; what we see today has been described as a puristic concoction. At St-Sernin in Toulouse, Viollet-le-Duc took out all post-Renaissance works of art from the pilgrimage church – where they have since been reinstated. Another aspect of many restored churches which tends to shock the visitor is the garish re-painting of pillars and capitals and vaults; it is clear that in some areas, at least, a taste for the gaudy painting of church interiors accompanied the taste for frescoes. What to do about restoring the work of the restorers is still an open question in France.

Renaissance to Revolution The 16th century was a period of relative peace. Together with the spread of royal power and refinements in the technique of war-making, this produced a change from fortress to château. From their military campaigns in northern Italy in the late 15th and early 16th centuries the French brought back a taste for extravagant, classically inspired ornamental detail applied to Gothic architectural forms. In the Loire Valley, where the kings of France hunted and held court, châteaux were built with many of the characteristics of medieval fortresses – such as machicolations and round towers – preserved and transformed for their decorative value, giving the buildings a quality of playful fantasy. Later in the century architects became more serious students of theory, and directed the French Renaissance into a more classical phase.

At Fontainebleau, François I built the first great royal palace of the Ile-de-France, importing Florentine artists to take charge and give his royal palace the grandeur and Italian pedigree appropriate to his imperial pretensions. In the same way that François's image and ideas are thus reflected in the 'Fontainebleau' style, later trends in French architecture throughout the 17th, 18th and even most of the 19th centuries reflect the personal style of the ruler as well as the trend of taste throughout Europe (Baroque, Rococo, neo-Classical). It is not merely convenient abbreviation that has led to the different styles (which do not exactly coincide with the individual reigns) being called after kings Louis XIII, Louis XIV, Louis XV and Louis XVI. 'Louis XIII' is a style of sobriety and restraint, in contrast with the excesses of the Fontainebleau school.

The long reign of Louis XIV, the Sun King, was marked by military conquest abroad, and at home by the extension of autocratic royal control over an anarchic and constantly bickering nobility. For such a period, the imposing, rich but ordered grandeur of the Louis XIV style was made to measure – exemplified by the architecture, to an even greater extent by the interior decoration, and even by the regulated order of the park, at Versailles. Characteristics of French might at this time are the fortresses built in an uncompromising geometric way all along France's frontiers by Louis XIV's military architect and engineer Vauban.

The 18th-century age of the Rococo and Louis XV was one of elegance and refinement of manners. It was accompanied by a taste for less formal gardens, more intimate rooms on a smaller scale, and an architectural and decorative style where emphasis was placed on delicacy of detail rather than on the grandeur of the whole.

The second half of the 18th century saw the development of a new moral climate. At first it was a sentimental kind of morality, exemplified by romantic ideas of nature and the noble savage; later, a heroic republican consciousness that built up to the Revolution was accompanied by a return to the strictest classical principles in art and a new interest in the Greeks and the Romans, leading on in turn to the Empire style of the Napoleonic age. The spirit of revolution inspired radical projects from the neo-classical architects but few of the plans for new Utopian cities – built for a new society glorifying neither God nor king – were ever put into practice. In general, the Revolution was a period of destruction on a far greater scale than construction.

The 19th century Napoleon stepped into the ruins of the Republic and replaced it with Empire; Republican classical art became Imperial classical art. Napoleon did not build new royal palaces, but redecorated old ones in what is now known as the Empire style, drawing heavily (and ponderously) on ancient Egypt for inspiration as well as Rome. Napoleon's monumental ambitions were not confined to individual buildings. He wanted to fashion Paris in his image, and did so, thanks to later rulers who carried out his plans. It is to Napoleon that we owe the great perspectives of Paris – including the Champs-Elysées with a triumphal arch at each end.

Napoleon's urban planning for Paris was completed and extended under his nephew Napoleon III in the style known as Second Empire. All the restraints of classicism were abandoned in the new taste for an overload of luxury and display – the tastes of a bourgeois age of money-grabbing and materialism. Baron Haussmann ploughed up insanitary old Paris, drained it and laid 85 miles of new streets lined with façades whose architecture was dictated with no less rigour than Versailles 200 years before, but with considerably less aesthetic success.

The deluxe style of the Second Empire was well suited to the casinos and Riviera resorts which sprang up at the end of the century; since this was the age of the railway, it was also the style of the railway station façade. In other fields the late 19th century was merely eclectic – churches were built by antiquarians in more or less faithful Romanesque and Gothic styles, thermal baths were built in the exotic Oriental manner. Restoration of medieval buildings was undertaken on an unprecedented scale.

The builders of railway stations and department stores exploited steel, and soon learnt not to hide its use. Gustave Eiffel engineered prodigious bridges of cast iron, and for the Paris Exhibition of 1889 designed the 984-feet tower which dominates Paris. The Eiffel Tower – like Beauvais Cathedral – has an enormous element of sheer virtuosity, but as well as being a feat of engineering it has many decorative elements which foreshadow the development of Art Nouveau, or modern style as the French called it, in the 1890s. This style, which owes much to a taste for Japanese art and English ideas (William Morris) is essentially one of interior decoration. Its profusion of arabesque and vegetable forms, in paint or more characteristically in metal, can transform a simple staircase into an exotic hothouse dream world. Paris is full of splendid examples of this *fin de siècle* style; a few of the original Métro signs still stand, as does Maxim's restaurant and the Petit and Grand Palais exhibition halls.

Modern France Even before the First World War architectural fashion was swinging back to economy, extreme simplicity of form, and emphasis on structural features. The most influential architect of 20th-century France, Le Corbusier, described his work in the 1920s as the construction of *machines à habiter*; and this is the impression, cheerless and functional, made by most of the urban reconstruction after the enormous damage inflicted by two World Wars. But Le Corbusier's commemorative chapel of Notre-Dame-du-Haut at Ronchamp, built in the 1950s, is a work which points in a completely different direction – anti-rational and expressive, like an abstract sculpture yet inspired partly by its surrounding landscape. The concern to fit into a context rather than express a general stylistic ideal has characterised much of the most ambitious and recent development – in many cases new holiday villages in severe natural settings of high mountains or flat coastal sands. There has been no lack of daring in these projects; nor a shortage of failures.

Food and drink

Eating and drinking in France means eating and drinking well. Raw materials are of the highest quality, and varied regional styles of cooking make the most of them. French food is equally suitable for appreciation in restaurants and around picnic tables. The traveller who crawls around from restaurant to restaurant misses food shopping, hardly less enjoyable than eating. The ideal balance is one meal a day in a restaurant; another, more simple, in a field, campsite, flat or *gîte*.

Food shopping

French food markets are a delight to the eye and nose. There are nearly always good cheese, fruit and vegetable stalls; and, depending on location, shellfish, fish, poultry or game (sometimes brought live to market). *Boulangeries* (bakeries) offer a wide variety of long French loaves, from the tiny *ficelle* to the regular *baguette* and the larger *gros pain*. Smaller loaves go stale quickly; there are several bakings daily, so bread purchases should be delayed to the last possible moment. Longer-lasting loaves include the large *pain de campagne*, brown *pain complet*, or *pain de seigle* (rye bread). Bakers sell *croissants*, *brioches*, and *pain au chocolat* (buns with a chocolate heart). *Pâtisseries* also sell these and more exotic cakes, fruit tarts, and usually speciality sweets.

Charcuteries sell a much wider range of food than the pork-based products from which the name originates. As well as cooked meats and pâtés, there is a variety of salads and cooked dishes: vol-au-vents, quiches, pies, pizzas, sausage, cooked chicken and fish, and delicacies in tins and jars. These are among the most enticing of food shops, their produce often expensive.

There are relatively few specialist cheese shops. Dairy products are most often sold in *épiceries* (grocers), *alimentations* (general food stores), and in supermarkets and hypermarkets, which have far more to offer in terms of variety and quality than the average UK supermarket.

Poissonneries (fishmongers) often sell cooked as well as fresh fish. If you are not equipped to open oysters, ask the fishmonger to do it for you.

Boucheries (butchers) usually sell poultry, game, and *abats* (offal), as well as meat. The cheapest mince is not usually intended for human consumption.

FOOD AND DRINK

Cafés

Snacks are not part of French life. In most cafés it is possible to eat something, but rarely anything imaginatively or carefully prepared. A *sandwich* consists of a lot of French bread, and a little pâté, cheese or ham, usually without butter. *Croque monsieur* (grilled ham and cheese sandwich) is a staple but very variable. Cafés are for passing the time of day over a drink. *Un café* is small, black and strong, *un café crème* is the same with a little hot milk, *un grand crème* is larger; *café au lait* is very milky. Tea comes without milk or lemon unless specified. Beer comes in bottles or *à la pression* (draught); the usual measure is *un demi* (about half a pint). Cafés serve wine (occasionally a selection) by the glass, all sorts of alcohols, fruit juices, *syrops* (fruit-flavoured syrups), fizzy drinks and mineral water. Drinks at the bar are cheaper. Payment is made on departure, not after every drink. Some cafés are *tabacs* (tobacconists), and sell a wide range of tobacco, cigarettes and cigars, and also stamps. French cigarettes are much cheaper than foreign ones.

Restaurants

Most restaurants offer *à la carte* and fixed price meals. *La carte* is the menu, *le menu* is a fixed-price meal. The simplest *menu* usually consists of three or four courses – a starter, a meat dish of the day accompanied by *frites* (chips) and perhaps a green salad, cheese and/or a dessert. In simple restaurants, little more is to be expected than *crudités* (raw vegetable salad) or soup to start with; ice cream, tart or fruit for dessert. Sometimes the *menu* includes a quarter litre of house wine (*boisson compris*). There is usually a range of different *menus*, most offering better value than *à la carte*. Cheap *menus touristiques* (tourist menus) and restaurants which advertise them are generally to be avoided. Prestige restaurants often have a *menu* described as *gastronomique* or *dégustation* (gastronomical or tasting), which includes some of the great specialities of the house. The first usually means a huge blow-out, the second a long sequence of small portions designed to show off the chef's expertise. In all but the most expensive restaurants you can eat for well under £20 including wine. Food but not wine prices are displayed outside restaurants.

Many French eating customs differ from ours: table-cloths are often disposable paper; bread is provided, but butter or side plates only in more expensive places; vegetables are often served separately from the main course (salad always is) and need to be ordered specifically if you want a 'selection', as in England; cheese is eaten before the dessert. Meat is usually served rarer than here (fish, too, in some restaurants). If you like 'medium' steak, ask for *bien cuit*; if you like 'rare' meat, ask for *à point*. 'Rare' for the French is *saignant* (bleeding), or still rarer *bleu*.

Brie de Meaux

Bleu d'Auvergne

Camembert

Fourme d'Ambert

Livarot

Excelsior

Maroilles

Pont l'Evêque

Munster

St-Nectaire

Port-Salut

Tomme de Savoie

Roquefort

Reblochon

27

For most French (especially outside the large cities), lunch is the main meal of the day. This starts at around noon, and popular restaurants fill up by 12.30. If you arrive after 1.45 pm, you may be turned away, even if there is room. Sundays and holidays are days for large family lunches, so booking is advisable. In the provinces tables are hard to find after 10 pm. Dinner is eaten at about 7.30 in most family hotels and resorts (later in the south and in big towns). Few people eat out on Sunday evenings.

Trends in cooking

The 'revolution' of *nouvelle cuisine*, at its height in the seventies, has had a profound effect on French cooking at all levels, but especially on the more expensive places. Its emphasis on presentation and lightness is still felt and it allowed French cooks, normally very conservative, to be more inventive. However, in the eighties the fresh approach of *nouvelle cuisine* was harnessed to *cuisine traditionelle*, *cuisine du terroir*, or *cuisine grandmère*, all ways of stressing an apparent return by chefs to the roots of peasant, bourgeois and regional cooking, with a definite modern tilt. Expect to see re-interpretations of old favourites involving a lot of offal, cheaper cuts of meat and slow-cooked dishes. More creative chefs are also using new (i.e. old) ingredients such as wild flowers and hedgerow herbs.

Modern French cooking is also less chauvinist than it was. Oriental spices, Chinese cooking methods, Japanese influence on arrangement, even American chillis are met with in adventurous kitchens. Ethnic cuisines, once limited to North African couscous houses, are also making a new mark: Vietnamese of course, but Chinese, Indian and Japanese restaurants are now to be found in unlikely spots. French cooking is still on the move.

REGIONAL SPECIALITIES

No less a characteristic of French food than its general excellence is the regional variety of food produce and styles of cooking. Norman cooking is based on the excellence of its dairy products, provençal on its olives and herbs. Local styles and a few of the most important specialities are listed in the sections below. Inevitably the selection misses out as much, more even, than it includes, because such is the local gastronomic pride that every town has its specialities – often sweetmeats such as Toulouse's candied violets and Agen's stuffed prunes. Nor can this selection include all the local names applied to dishes like *coq au vin* or fish stew (there are at least 14 different varieties, from *bouillabaisse* in the south to *marmite Dieppoise* in the north).

Nowhere perhaps is French regionalism more obvious than in its cheese. Nearly all French cheeses are the products of very small areas, and nobody, as de Gaulle observed, can unite a country which has 265 speciality cheeses. Some cheeses travel, and these are the ones we know at least by name – Bleu de Bresse, Roquefort, Munster, Camembert. Even the most familiar can be rediscovered in the locality of their production, and in speciality cheese shops which offer only the very best. Other cheeses, such as the little Azay-le-Rideau of the Loire or the infinite different goats' cheeses of Poitou, travel hardly at all, and discovery of them is one of the great joys of travelling in any area in France. Many French believe that the cheeseboard is the best sign of whether a restaurateur is serious about his business or not; if it looks good, be sure to ask not just for names, for they will surely baffle, but for advice.

Burgundy, the Rhône Valley and the Jura

Beef from the Charolais region; *boeuf bourguignonne*, beef stew with red wine, onions and mushrooms; mountain ham from the Morvan, often with a cream sauce; *jambon persillé*, jellied ham flavoured with parsley; *pochouse*, a fish stew; corn-fed chicken from Bresse; *escargots*, snails; sauces based on Dijon mustard; *oeufs meurettes*, eggs poached in red wine with bacon and mushrooms; onion soup in Lyon; *quenelles de brochet*, pike dumplings, classically from Nantua; Brie, Coulommiers, Chaource, Epoisses and Bleu de Bresse cheeses; blackcurrants in sorbets, or used for *cassis* liqueur.

The South

Provence Olive oil is used in all dishes which require fat; *bouillabaisse*, fish stew: the classic version contains *rascasse*, scorpion fish, red gurnet and conger eel, seasoned with (among other things) saffron, fennel and orange peel, usually served with *rouille*, a paste of chilli peppers; *bourride*, a creamy fish soup; *aïoli*, a garlic mayonnaise; fish including *rouget*, red mullet and *loup*, sea bass – often grilled with fennel; *brandade de morue*, creamed salt cod with olive oil and garlic from Nîmes; lamb grilled with herbs and garlic; *pissaladière*, anchovy tart; rice dishes in the Camargue; *ratatouille*, vegetable stew; olives (from Nyons); herbs including rosemary, thyme, and basil; *soupe au pistou*, a garlic-flavoured soup; *ravioli* in Nice; *salade Niçoise*, with French beans, olives, egg, and sometimes tuna; *pan bagnat*, a salad and anchovy roll; *pieds-et-pacquets*, a kind of tripe, from around Marseille; almond sweetmeats; fruit and glacé fruits.

The Languedoc *Cargolade*, snails stewed in wine; *bouillinade*, a variant of *bouillabaisse*; fish including sardines, tuna, mackerel and squid;

pickled anchovies from Collioure; *langouste à la Sétoise*, spiny lobster in tomato and wine sauce.

The Massif Central

Tripoux, mutton tripe with stuffed sheeps' feet; cured mountain ham; dry sausage; trout; salmon from the Allier; *aligot* or *truffade*, a potato and cheese dish; green lentils from Le Puy; Cantal, St-Nectaire and several blue cheeses including Roquefort, Bleu d'Auvergne, Bleu des Causses and Fourme d'Ambert; *clafoutis*, a sort of cherry flan.

The Pyrenees

River fish including trout; mountain ham; snails; ewe's milk cheese (*fromage de brebis*); Basque dishes (see the Atlantic Coast) and Mediterranean (see the South) in the west and east respectively; *cassoulet*, stew of haricot beans and mixed meats (sometimes including potted duck or goose) in the area around Carcassonne.

The Dordogne

Foie gras, goose liver (sometimes made into a pâté or terrine); *confit*, potted and preserved meat (usually duck, or goose); *magret* or *maigret de canard*, fillet of duck served rare; truffles; mushrooms (especially the large *cèpes*); *pommes sarladaises*, potatoes with goose fat and truffles; prunes from Agen; walnuts (used in walnut oil for salad).

The Atlantic Coast

The North Fish and shellfish, particularly mussels (used in *mouclade*, mussel stew with white wine and cream) and oysters; sardines from Royan; *chabichou*, and many other goat's milk cheeses, from Poitou; melons from the Charentes.

Bordeaux and the Landes *Agneau de pré-salé*, salt-marsh lamb, from Pauillac; *lamproie*, lamprey eel, in Bordeaux; ortolans and *palombes*, wood pigeons; oysters from Arcachon; cured ham from Bayonne; sauce *à la bordelaise*, with bone marrow, shallots, tarragon and red wine.

Basque Country Tuna from St-Jean-de-Luz; sauce *à la basquaise*, with garlic and onion; *ttoro*, Basque fish stew; *chipirones*, little squid usually cooked in their own ink (*à l'encre*); sardines; *pipérade*, scrambled eggs with tomatoes, peppers and onions.

The Loire Valley

River fish (carp and salmon; *brochet*, pike; *alose*, shad) with *beurre blanc* – sauce of butter, shallots and vinegar – or *à l'oseille*, with a sorrel sauce; *rillettes de porc*, potted pork; *rillons*, braised breast of pork; pork with prunes; game and wildfowl from the Sologne; mushrooms; *crémets*, fresh cream cheeses; goat cheeses; mushrooms; asparagus; fruit.

Brittany

Fish and shellfish of all kinds, particularly *homard*, lobster, *langoustes*, crayfish and *langoustines*, scampi; *araignée*, spider crab; *palourdes*, clams (*gratinées* or *farcies* means in half-shells, buttered, breadcrumbed, grilled, and usually with garlic); *coquilles*, scallops; oysters (the best from the Belon river); *moules*, mussels; *cotriade*, fish stew; salmon from the Aulne and Elorn; trout; *agneau de pré-salé*, salt-marsh lamb; strawberries from Plougastel and artichokes from Roscoff; *crêpes* or *galettes*, pancakes (wheat or buckwheat, sweet and savoury); cakes (*Kouignaman* and *gâteau breton*) and biscuits (especially *crêpes dentelles* from Quimper).

Normandy

Sauces using butter, cream, apples and *calvados*, apple brandy (dishes usually described as *Vallée d'Auge*); tripe, especially *à la mode de Caen*, stewed in a spicy sauce; sole in various sauces (the most famous is *Dieppoise*, with white wine, cream and shellfish); mussels; mackerel from around Dieppe; oysters from Courseulles and the eastern Cotentin; *andouille*, tripe sausage from Vire; Camembert, Livarot and Pont L'Evêque cheeses.

The North

Picardy and Artois Soups (particularly vegetable) and stews (*hochepot*, mixed meats with vegetables; *potée*, with cabbage); vegetables (artichokes, leeks, haricot beans, cauliflowers); *flamiche*, leek tart; pâtés (duck, woodcock, eel); herring (particularly pickled herring in Boulogne), mackerel, sole, turbot, shellfish (particularly mussels); Maroilles cheese and *flamiche* (tart) *au Maroilles*.

Ardennes Game (venison, wild boar) as main dish or made into pâtés; river fish including trout and pike; ham.

Champagne *Andouillettes*, tripe sausages; *tarte aux raisins* (with grapes).

Alsace, Lorraine and the Vosges

Alsace and Vosges Foie gras, poultry and river fish *au Riesling* (with white wine sauce); pork (smoked or in sausages); *choucroute*, sauerkraut; game (venison, wild boar, hare, partridge); *baeckeoffe*, hotpot of mixed meats; fruit tarts, onion tart and *tarte aux vigneronnes*, potato pie; *kugelhopf*, *brioche* cake; Munster cheese.

Lorraine *Quiche Lorraine*; *potage Lorraine*, potato and leek soup; *potée*, cabbage and pork soup; *charcuteries*.

The Alps

Lake fish such as *omble-chevalier* – like salmon trout or char – *féra* and *lavarat*, like salmon; trout; *gratin dauphinois/savoyard*, potatoes cooked with local cheese and cream; *fondue savoyarde*, melted local cheese with wine, kirsch and garlic, eaten with cubes of stale bread; *raclette*, grilled cheese scraped on to hot potatoes with garnish of mountain ham and gherkin; French Gruyère, Emmenthal, Beaufort and Reblochon cheeses.

Corsica

Charcuterie from chestnut-fed pigs – *lonza, coppa, figatelli*; pâtés from game of the *maquis* including blackbirds; seafood, especially lobster and spicy fish soups; meat stews of pork, mutton, kid, wild boar; pasta, often eaten with *brocciu*, the most versatile of many goat and sheep cheeses; chestnut-flavoured biscuits and puddings; honey, fruit preserves.

WINE

In the last quarter century, the world of wine has expanded beyond previous imagining. Wine is now produced everywhere from Argentina to Zimbabwe; connoisseurs fight as eagerly for the best wines of Australia or California as ever they did for top burgundies and clarets; internationally recognised grape varieties have taken over from European placenames as the main signposts to flavour.

And yet ... when Australian wine-makers decide to work their way out of the squalls of a Southern Hemisphere winter, where do they go? When Californians want to see how their Cabernet Sauvignon matches up, which country ships the bottles they buy for comparison? When the big international competitions come around each year, which country produces the wines everyone wants to beat?

The answer is France. For several hundred years, France has filled the world's cellars; it remains the world's wine benchmark. No country, even today, comes close to producing the range of wines France can manage, nor to matching its stylistic polish. France's new generation of *vins de pays* (country wines) offers some of the most exciting yet inexpensive flavours in the world; at the very highest level, France's finest wines remain unbeaten.

We may ask why. France's geography is one reason. The country sits squarely between 40° and 50° north, that band of privileged earth which, when subject to maritime influences, provides the ideal conditions for vine growing. (Almost all wine is produced between 30° and 50° in both hemispheres.) Yet look at the wine map on page 37 to see how scattered France's main wine-growing areas are. The spots where everything comes good (soils, slopes, microclimate) are, even in France, uncommon.

The second reason is the French themselves. British visitors to France will scarcely need a lecture on *l'art de vivre*: the French flair for making everyday life as pleasant as possible. Food and drink, sources of thrice-daily pleasure, naturally figure prominently; and of all drinks wine is best adapted to partner and embellish food. Moreover, the French, having discovered something sensually appealing, rarely leave it at that: they tease it, polish it, take it to pieces and put it back together again in a different and usually better way.

BUYING WINE

Buying wine is, for many visitors and particularly those travelling by car, one of the main reasons for visiting France. This may be for the low prices – though, remember, only the cheapest wines are cheaper in France than in Britain. Indeed, the most expensive wines are often *more* expensive in France than in Britain, due to the fact that the French wine trade is less intensely competitive than the British. In France you will, though, enjoy an unrivalled choice of local wines; and, of course, you will have a chance to meet the producers, should you wish.

Supermarkets and shops

For most French people, a bottle of wine is about as exciting a purchase as a pot of jam or a slab of cheese. They often take little interest in wine, though they may drink it twice a day, seven days a week. They buy on price.

Most French supermarkets, therefore, compete with each other in getting the cheapest price for certain well-known *appellations* (such as Muscadet, Côtes-du-Rhône or Beaujolais-Villages). Quality matters less. When it comes to more expensive wines, such as those from different villages in Burgundy, very often every wine will be bought from the same wholesale merchant (*négociant*). Not only will these wines be almost identically labelled, but their tastes may not differ as much as they should.

Despite these cautions, good wine can certainly be bought from French supermarkets; one way to give yourself a sporting chance of finding such wines is to look for mention on labels of medals and awards given to wines at wine fairs or regional agricultural shows. Better still, try a number of different wines, and only buy in quantity when you find one to your taste.

Wine shops in France are often the reverse of French supermarkets: luxuriously fitted boutiques where the finest wines are sold at high prices, alongside small tins of foie gras, jars of truffles and beautifully packaged boxes of confectionery. By all means buy a souvenir bottle or two, but you will usually get a better price for larger quantities of such wines on your return to Britain by contacting specialist wine merchants.

Visiting producers

Visiting a wine producer in France can be an enormously rewarding experience: the beginning of a cross-cultural friendship, rather than simply a commercial interlude in your holiday.

Wine producers come in all shapes and sizes. Some are large companies, well equipped to receive visitors with multilingual host-esses, audio-visual displays, even small laser-guided 'trains' to shuttle you around their cellars. You are most likely to receive this kind of treatment in Champagne (Reims and Epernay), Burgundy (Beaune) and Cognac. A small fee may be charged for the visit, which will conclude with a tasting. You should feel under no obligation to purchase anything afterwards, though you will usually be offered the chance. Some of the grandest and most visited Bordeaux châteaux, by contrast, offer guided tours, but do not stoop to the mercantile depths of permitting visitors to buy bottles afterwards. Instead, you will have to buy the château's wine through the normal commercial channels, such as wine merchants.

Most French wine producers, of course, are not like this at all. They are farmers. Like most farmers, they have an endless round of jobs, and never enough time to carry them all out. If you want to visit, you should phone for an appointment first. (Sometimes appointments can be arranged via an English wine merchant.) If you speak no French at all, check that the producer speaks some English; many do, but not all. Try not to take up too much of his or her time, and be prepared to buy at least half a dozen or a dozen bottles at the end of the visit (which should always include a tasting).

Bearing this protocol in mind, it is sensible to try to visit producers whose wines you have enjoyed in the past, rather than the first one whose roadside invitation (*Dégustation – vente*) draws your attention. The paperwork the producer will give you as you conclude the purchase permits you to transport the wine home; you should keep it with you until the journey is over. You are now allowed to bring back up to 90 litres of table wine (of which 60 litres may be sparkling) if bought in an EC country, provided it is for personal consumption only (you must not re-sell it).

Wine in restaurants

It may come as something of a shock to discover that mark-ups on wine in French restaurants are just as high as they are in British restaurants. Usually, too, the selection will have a strong regional bias, so there is little point in attempting to order a good bottle of burgundy if you're eating out in Bordeaux, nor should you hope for a range of Muscadets when you sit down to lunch in Provence.

The place of origin is, however, almost always where a wine tastes best, thus quite ordinary, inexpensive wines, such as a half-litre *pichet* (jug) of dry rosé wine in Provence, will taste far better on a sunny terraced restaurant in Antibes or Arles than ever it will back home in Manchester. The pleasure of wine in France is a democratic one, and drinking cheap, local wines can be just as much fun as drinking expensive ones. A good restaurateur, moreover, should always be able to choose good cheap wines.

FRENCH WINE LAW AND LABEL TERMINOLOGY

The basic unit within French wine law is the *appellation d'origine contrôlée* (or AOC: name of controlled origin); certain foods such as, for example, Crottin de Chavignol cheese also enjoy an AOC.

This piece of legislation controls the exact area where a wine can be produced and specifies its grape varieties, alcohol levels and maximum harvest yield; sometimes wines also have to be approved by a tasting panel before they are permitted the AOC. Within AOC legislation, there may be further quality hierarchies. This is particularly true of Burgundy, whose complex pyramid of AOCs (regional, village, *premier cru* and *grand cru* wines) is best explained by a specialist wine reference book.

Beneath AOC lie the *vins delimités de qualité supérieur* (VDQS). This category tends to be used for apprentice AOCs, and the regulations are similar in outline to those for AOC wines, though less demanding.

Next come the *vins de pays* (country wines). These have been one of the great success stories of French wine in recent years. They are produced in areas previously unfancied for wine growing (sometimes quite wrongly), or are used for wines produced in classic AOC areas but without following classic AOC rules – usually in regard to grape varieties. This freedom from regulatory interference, at a moment in history when technical advances in the winery and vineyard are finding exciting layers of flavour in fruit of humble origin, is the reason for the excitement. The best *vin de pays* can be as good as AOC wines of high quality.

The *vin de table* (table wine) is, in France, usually a commonplace and often nasty wine, made cheaply and sold cheaply, according to alcohol level. It is usually best to avoid these wines.

Other information may be included on labels, such as (in Bordeaux) the fact that a wine is a *cru classé* (classed growth) – in other words a château listed among the top 61 (divided into five tiers) by the brokers of Bordeaux in 1855. (Ignore the term *cru classé* in Provence and elsewhere.) *Premier cru* and *grand cru* are other label terms of varying significance in different areas: if you feel you want to understand such terminology fully, buy a wine reference book and take it with you on holiday. Hugh Johnson's *Pocket Wine Guide* (Mitchell Beazley, 1994) is a handy size for travelling.

French wine regions

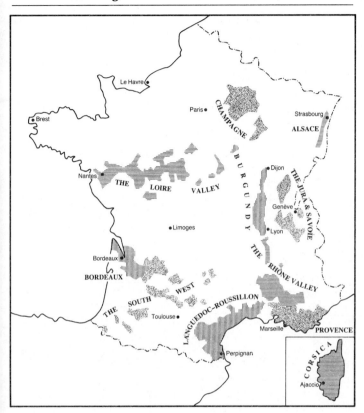

ALSACE

Alsace, where vineyards cut like a long ribbon into the foothills of the Vosges mountains, is a white wine region. There is a little Pinot Noir red made, but it seldom matches the quality of the whites. Most of these are labelled by grape variety: Pinot Blanc (which includes Auxerrois), Pinot Gris, Riesling, Gewurztraminer and Sylvaner; blends are called Edelzwicker, Gentil, or sold under brand names. Vineyard names may be mentioned on labels and, if the vineyard is a designated *grand cru*, this will form part of the AOC description. After particularly warm later summers, richer-than-usual wines are made called *vendange tardive* (late harvest) or *séléction de grains nobles* (wines made from specially selected grapes affected by noble rot or *botrytis cinerea* – a mould which concentrates a grape's sugars and provides a distinctive, bitter-edged flavour of its own). Such wines are generally sweet, though on occasion *vendange tardive* wines are made in a dry style.

The taste of Alsace wines varies according to grape variety. Riesling (dry here, in contrast to many German examples) provides the most severe, deep and assertive flavours, and makes excellent wines for food, particularly fish. Pinot Blanc is softer and grapier, while Pinot Gris can be fat, slightly smoky and full – it is Alsace's answer to Chardonnay (which is now grown on a small scale in Alsace). Sylvaner is fresh and earthy, without a great deal of personality, something which makes it an amenable match for a wide range of dishes. Gewurztraminer, finally, is the extrovert of the bunch, its heavy, heady aromas managing to conjure up everything from roses to gingerbread, lychees to lemon verbena, depending on who has made it. It is often very strong, too: a Gewurztraminer of 13.5 per cent alcohol by volume (abv) is not uncommon, while much claret is 12 per cent.

Alsace is, broadly speaking, a region of small growers. There are also a number of high-quality, family-owned *négociants* (such as Hugel and Trimbach); both growers and *négociants* usually welcome visitors. Those living in Alsace, with its bilingual birthright, are often good linguists, and English is more commonly spoken here than in many regions.

ARMAGNAC

There could be no greater contrast to the international urbanity and formal elegance of Cognac (see page 42) than Gascony's Armagnac. This area, encircling Condom and Eauze, remains something of a forgotten region, buried in the depths of the countryside. There are a few large armagnac houses, chief among them Janneau, but this is overwhelmingly a region of farmer-distillers who guard their vintage stocks of spirit, in old casks and demijohns, with all the pride and protectiveness of family heirlooms.

Armagnac differs from cognac in that it is made by a different distillation method. The actual grape varieties used are similar: Ugni Blanc accounts for almost all cognac and over half of armagnac (the balance being provided by Baco and Folle Blanche). Whereas cognac is distilled twice on a pot still to high strength (70 per cent abv), armagnac is distilled once in a continuous still (of local design) to lower strength (50–60 per cent abv). This gives a young spirit of greater impurity, but greater flavour too, since impurities equal flavour in the spirit world. The drawback is that young armagnac can be very rough; smoothness (and expense) comes with age.

Fine, well-aged armagnacs are wonderfully warming, complex, robust spirits, full of the flavour of prunes, smoke and leafy autumn earth. Restaurants in Gascony often stock a wide range of vintages, and there can be few better ways to terminate a meal based on local specialities (which include wild mushrooms, truffles and foie gras) than with a glass of one of these dark, aromatic spirits.

BEAUJOLAIS

Beaujolais is fun. Its red wine, made from the Gamay grape variety, is softly fruity, exuberantly scented, and incites you to gulp rather than sip. Its people are warm and much given to passion and intrigue. The model for Gabriel Chevalier's *Clochemerle* is Vaux-en-Beaujolais, one of the villages whose wine is sold under the Beaujolais-Villages *appellation*. Ten individual villages sited in the north east of the region provide its finest wines (they are known, collectively, as the Beaujolais *crus*); at their best, as in Moulin-à-Vent or Morgon, aged for five or six years, they can acquire near-burgundian depth.

BORDEAUX

Bordeaux is, in vineyard terms, enormous – it includes everything, more or less, between Cognac and the high country of the Pyrenean and Auvergne foothills. How does the visitor make sense of it all?

First of all, decide what you are most curious to see. If you want to enjoy pretty, rolling vineyard scenes, choose St-Emilion (for red wines) or Entre-Deux-Mers (for white). If you want to make a pilgrimage to the great, historic châteaux of Bordeaux, the 'classed growths', then choose the Médoc. If time is at a premium and you want to dart out of Bordeaux and back again within an afternoon, the Graves is closest at hand. If you are an admirer of sweet wines, then Sauternes and Barsac are essential stops. And if you just want to find plain good value, then try one of the outlying districts, such as Bourg and Blaye (Blaye's citadel is architecturally interesting and encompasses vineyards), Bergerac (not technically a part of Bordeaux, but it uses the same grapes to much the same effect), Ste-Foy-Bordeaux, Bordeaux-Côtes-de-Francs, or the St-Emilion 'satellite' appellations. Tourist offices in Bordeaux can supply maps showing these zones within the *appellation* area.

In flavour terms, Bordeaux is complex, since most of its wines are blended from a number of different grape varieties. It is, though, by the seaside, and Bay-of-Biscay freshness and elegance usually leave their mark. Bordeaux's reds (collectively called claret in Britain) should never be heavy or soupy, Bordeaux's dry whites never fat and buttery.

The grandest part of Bordeaux is the Médoc – the eastern side of the long tongue of sandy, stony land which runs north of Bordeaux and up between the Gironde estuary and the Atlantic coast. This is the home of assertive, blackcurrant-flavoured Cabernet Sauvignon, softened by smaller amounts of Merlot, Malbec and Petit Verdot. The grandeur of the Médoc lies largely in the château architecture (most châteaux welcome visitors, though always try to make an appointment first) and the sheer density of the vines. Otherwise, the landscape is one of soporific monotony.

Merlot is the grape variety which dominates St-Emilion and Pomerol, giving red wines of meaty warmth (St-Emilion) and deep-driven plummy fruit (Pomerol). St-Emilion itself is the Bordeaux region's most charming town. Fronsac is where the Cabernet Franc grape takes over, to chunky effect.

The main white grape varieties used in Bordeaux are Sauvignon Blanc and Sémillon. The former produces fresh, crisp, grape-and-gooseberry flavoured wines; the latter is broader-hewn, providing a firmly structured base in blends, and taking well to the flavours of oak (from wooden casks) and of botrytis (see Alsace). White wines are, increasingly, being produced right across Bordeaux, though the main *appellations* remain Graves and Entre-Deux-Mers for dry whites, and Sauternes, Barsac, Cérons and Loupiac for sweet whites.

BURGUNDY

Burgundy is, in one sense, the most complicated of all France's wine regions to understand. Its delicately structured pyramid of AOCs can take even the brightest student of wine weeks to understand in theory, and years in practice. Yet, in another sense, Burgundy is simple enough. Almost all its red wines are made from Pinot Noir, and almost all its whites from Chardonnay.

Burgundy is usually understood to stretch from Chablis in the north to the southernmost tip of the Mâconnais in the south, where it meshes with Beaujolais. In between Chablis and the Mâconnais lie two other sub-regions, the Côte d'Or and the Côte Chalonnaise. The appeal of the scenery, as a rule, is in inverse proportion to the quality of the wines, and the unremarkable appearance of some of the world's most precious vineyards (Chambertin, La Romanée-Conti) has left many ardent pilgrims nonplussed.

Self-contained Chablis (between Auxerre and Tonnerre), where the world's stoniest, most mouthwatering Chardonnays are produced, is unusually easy to visit and to grasp. As throughout Burgundy, its wines are graded by vineyard of origin – into plain Chablis, Chablis Premier Cru and Chablis Grand Cru. (There is also a fourth, bottom-grade wine called Petit Chablis: its wines are rarely exciting.) Loire renegade Sauvignon de St-Bris is produced nearby, as are some sylph-like reds (Bourgogne-Irancy).

Serious red wine begins at the northern end of the Côte d'Or, just outside Dijon. The stretch of land between Dijon and Corgoloin is known as the Côte de Nuits (after its capital, Nuits-St-Georges); the stretch from Ladoix-Serrigny to Santenay is called the Côte de Beaune (after its own capital, Beaune). The Côte de Nuits produces red wines almost exclusively – seldom the heavy, rich, red wines mistakenly associated with the word 'burgundy', but wines which, at best, burst with such pure, fine-grained fruit that they succeed in suggesting a depth far in excess of what sober analysis would reveal. Fine red burgundy, from villages like Gevrey-Chambertin, Volnay or Nuits-St-Georges itself, seems to make an almost emotional appeal to the senses. The best is rare, though, since both weather and heavy-handed wine-making can pitch it off-balance easily.

White burgundy from the Côte d'Or (in practice almost exclusively from the Côte de Beaune) is more reliable. At its best (Montrachet) it combines enormous wealth and concentration of flavour with limitless elegance and poise; it can also run to buttery richness (Meursault) without ever slipping over into clumsiness or monotony.

The Côte Chalonnaise seems destined to be the eternal bridesmaid to the Côte d'Or. Its wines, both red and white, are built along the same lines and are often generously flavoured, yet never seem quite to achieve the same degree of finesse as those of Beaune or Nuits.

The Mâconnais, finally, produces large quantities of white, Chardonnay-based wine at high prices; its reds, though, are often light and disappointing.

CALVADOS

Calvados is the apple brandy of Normandy. It is also the name of a *département* centred on Caen, though calvados itself can actually be produced in three entire Normandy *départements*, as well as parts of some neighbouring ones. The best calvados comes from the pays d'Auge *appellation*, which covers an area of woods and hills around the Touques valley (Lisieux to Trouville); this also happens to be the cheese heart of Normandy.

Good calvados starts life as good cider. In France (in contrast to Britain) this is always made using cider apples; sometimes a smaller quantity of perry (based on pears) is used in addition to cider. The spirit itself is produced by distilling the cider (or perry) twice in a pot or cognac still (pays d'Auge) or continuous still (other calvados). Like armagnac, calvados needs long ageing in wooden barrels before it tastes at its best.

This, one of the most ardent of spirits, was once the northern French working-man's daily tipple; in recent years it has seen its market decline rapidly in quantity but increase in quality. Abandoned apple orchards, their branches laden with mistletoe, become a familiar sight as you wind your way through the Normandy lanes. Like armagnac again, calvados remains essentially a farmer's product; large companies are still the exception here rather than the rule. As in Armagnac, too, local restaurants make an ideal setting to enjoy one of possibly 20 or 30 examples stocked; enjoy it either as a *trou normand* (a glass of neat spirit taken midway through a meal to excavate a 'hole' for further food) or, more conventionally, as a *digestif* at the end of the meal.

CHAMPAGNE

Champagne is France's most northerly wine region. North means cool; cool means high acidity; and high acidity is one of the prerequisites for great sparkling wine.

Of course, things aren't quite that simple. Champagne is a region of chalky soils, and chalk yields piercing wines of great finesse. In Reims, nearly two thousand years ago, the chalk also provided building stones for the Romans, and the caves left by their quarrying work (*les crayères*) furnished perfect cellaring space. These cool, deep cellars have proved particularly propitious for the slow second fermentation in bottle which puts the sparkle into sparkling wine. The region of Champagne is the nearest to Paris, and its nobility and wealth – and wealthy patronage – permitted the development of what was, initially, an insanely expensive luxury, far pricier than it is today. It is this complex of factors which made Champagne the home of the world's first, and still its finest, sparkling wines.

The large champagne houses are almost all sited in Reims and Epernay and most offer good facilities for the visitor. Best of all perhaps are those houses sited in the *crayères* area of Reims, such as Pommery. Their sepulchral chalk vaults, sometimes carved with bas-reliefs, taper away to high, ivy-covered skylights on the surface; it is hard to avoid seeing them as subterranean cathedrals in the service of pleasure and its sophistications.

If you are touring the vineyard areas, most villages will be full of growers' cellars offering *dégustation – vente*. Champagne is made from three grape varieties, and growers in villages in the main vineyard areas of Champagne will tend to emphasise one of the three in their champagnes: Chardonnay in the Côte des Blancs (from Cramant to Vertus); Pinot Noir on the horseshoe of vineyards surrounding the Montagne de Reims; and Pinot Meunier in the Vallée de la Marne (stretching eastwards from Epernay). Maps showing these areas are available from tourist offices in Reims and Epernay.

COGNAC

Vigorous arguments rage between hot-blooded Gascons and the more phlegmatic Cognaçais as to who produces the finest brandy in the world; on the evidence of sales, at any rate, Cognac wins emphatically. As with the finest burgundies, it is the combination of extreme power and depth of flavour with fingertip delicacy and complex perfume which makes the best cognacs so enticing. It is their age, and world-wide demand, which makes them so fearsomely expensive.

Big, multinational producers dominate cognac production. Yet they neither harvest the grapes nor distil the raw spirit; that is still the farmer's task. What they do is buy spirit, age it and blend it: blending plays as important a part in the creation of fine cognac as it does in champagne. Most of the large cognac houses in Jarnac and Cognac itself (a town which combines sleepiness with elegance as only France can) welcome visitors, and the blending process will be explained to you then – in the most theatrical terms.

If you want to meet the wine-growers of the region you can gener-ally do so via Pineau des Charentes, a silky-sweet mixture of fresh grape juice and cognac which the local grape farmers take great pride in making and selling. Well-chilled, it is as good before a meal as a glass of cognac is afterwards.

JURA AND SAVOIE

These two districts in the eastern marches of France produce wines as distinctive as those of any other part of the country, yet because production is small and most of the wine is consumed locally, they remain little known. In the Jura, indeed, the wines are so distinctive as to prove shocking on occasion: whites in which oxidation (exposure to air, frowned on in most vineyard regions) is used as a way of adding complexity of flavour; reds so pale and light ('coral' is an enticing description) that they barely seem deeper than rosés. The Jura's great speciality, *vin jaune*, is a wine made from the capricious Savagnin variety, aged for six years in part-empty barrels (a scummy film of yeast grows over the wine's surface), then bottled in 62cl bottles called *clavelins. Vin jaune* needs long ageing, even after it has been bottled, to emerge eventually as a powerful wine with a scent of dried ceps and very high acidity, perfect as an accompaniment for the local speciality of cock in cream sauce.

Savoie produces more conventionally styled wines, some of them based on burgundy's grape varieties (Chardonnay, Pinot Noir and Gamay). Yet when local grape varieties are used, the whites (based on Jacquère and Altesse/Roussette) can be unusually delicate and racy, with hedgerow scents and mineral flavours; while the reds (from the Mondeuse) can be surprisingly deep and vigorous.

THE LOIRE VALLEY

The Loire is, in some ways, the mirror image of the Rhône. While the Rhône rises among Switzerland's glaciers, the Loire begins life with one toe in Provence. Both rivers' banks quickly become vine-decked, yet the southward-flowing Rhône attracts predominantly red grape varieties and the northward-flowing Loire mainly whites. In both cases, the greatest wines are produced roughly half-way along the river's course.

The first commanding wines produced on the banks of the Loire come shortly before it makes its abrupt turn westwards towards Orléans, at Sancerre and Pouilly-sur-Loire. Here, Sauvignon Blanc makes its most flamboyant appearance in France, with a series of vital, pungent, green-leafy white wines. In Touraine, the vineyards begin to grow more diverse; Vouvray and Montlouis are where the Chenin Blanc grape variety comes into its own, producing a dazzling spectrum of wines of every shade of sweetness, from knife-edge sharp (sec) to intensely sweet (moelleux or liquoreux). At Chinon and Bourgueil, the fount of Rabelaisian excess, red wines take over, made from the curranty, rain-fresh, iron-edged Cabernet Franc grape. Saumur and Anjou, too, produce everything from the driest of white wines (there is no finer dry Chenin Blanc than that of Savennières outside Angers) to heady dessert wines, red wines and sparkling wines. The sparkling-wine cellars of companies such as Gratien & Meyer are well worth visiting in Saumur since, like the cellars in Reims' *crayères*, they occupy former stone-quarries, this time running deep into the tufa hillside, with the vines which produce the wine growing directly above the dark, bottle-filled vaults. Afterwards, you could visit a mushroom cellar or two; the same caves make the perfect environment for silent fungal procreation.

Wine runs with the Loire to its mouth. The area around Nantes (the Pays Nantais) is where Muscadet hails from. Muscadet is, in many ways, the white Beaujolais: a fresh wine best consumed as young as possible, in situ, with abandon, over a *plateau de fruits de mer* or a fillet of pike-perch (*sandre*). Look for the term *'sur lie'* on the bottle; this indicates that the wine was bottled directly off the lees in the bottom of the tank, giving extra freshness and a slight fizz.

THE MIDI AND CORSICA

The Midi has gone from being French wine's dustbin to French wine's research laboratory in under a decade. Once, the plains of Languedoc were factory vineyards for the *gros rouge* with which French city workers would coast through the day. Those vineyards are now being uprooted; serious wine-makers have taken to the hills in the back country. There, under a bewildering variety of *vins de pays* names, some first-rate wines are being produced using both local grape varieties (Cinsault, Grenache, Mourvèdre) and internationally known star-turns (like Chardonnay, Cabernet Sauvignon, Merlot and Syrah). Existing *appellations*, most notably Corbières and Minervois, are producing red wines more pungently plummy, stony and herby than anyone dreamed possible ten years ago. White wines still struggle to match the interest of the reds, as is generally true in southern France away from the Atlantic seaboard, yet even this problem is unlikely to prove insuperable, especially for some of the Australian-trained wine-makers working in the south.

The traditional wines of the Midi which have survived the changes of the past decade are the *vins doux naturels* – in other words the sweet, fortified, mainly Muscat-based wines usually drunk as dizzying aperitifs in the region. Sparkling white Blanquette de Limoux and the chiefly red Côtes du Roussillon grown near the Spanish border are two other long-standing *appellations* of worth.

Corsican red wine, from its own native varieties Sciacarello and Niellucio, can be tangy and herby; Corsican whites, from the Italian Vermentino grape variety, often have the faint flavour of aniseed so appreciated around the Mediterranean basin.

THE RHONE VALLEY AND PROVENCE

The first wines grown on the banks of the Rhône are those of Switzerland's Valais, and the first French *appellation* on the river's route south is Seyssel in Savoie. The Rhône's major contribution to the wine world, though, begins south of Vienne, and continues discontinuously as far as Avignon, with a big break north and south of Montélimar. This break divides the Rhône into northern and southern sections.

The Rhône's finest wines are found in the north, at Côte-Rôtie (behind Ampuis) and Hermitage (above Tain l'Hermitage, with Tournon across the river). Here the Syrah grape variety reaches heights (both metaphorically and literally, since these are famously steep vineyards) attained nowhere else in France: perfumed, penetrating, smoky wines of hugely exciting style and character. Crozes-Hermitage can offer superb quality at a lesser price, as can the very best of St-Joseph.

The southern Rhône produces much larger quantities of wine over a much wider area. Its prototype red is Châteauneuf-du-Pape, a much softer, sweeter wine than the muscular giants of further north. Syrah no longer dominates; other grape varieties, like Grenache and Mourvèdre, come into prominence. Côtes-du-Rhône is the catch-all *appellation* for red and white wines grown throughout the whole region, north and south; it varies from superb to thin and poor. The better villages of the hills west of the river in Vaucluse sell their wine as Côtes-du-Rhône-Villages, and the leaders among those (such as Vacqueyras or Cairanne) can add their own name to the *appellation* formula. *Vins de pays* from within the Rhône region can be very good, too: look out for the *vins de pays* des Collines Rhodaniennes, often Syrah-based, from the north. Despite the worldwide renown of the best Rhône wines, this remains very much part of *la France profonde*; wines served in the finest restaurants in New York or Tokyo may well have been made in a poky cellar entered through a trap door in its grower's living-room floor.

Provence, so fortunate in many respects, has sometimes struggled to keep up with other French regional competitors in terms of wine quality. Perhaps the steady and undemanding market provided by tourists has acted as a disincentive; perhaps it's the fact that the best wine-growing sites, such as the stony fastness of les Baux, have yet to be fully explored for high-quality (and therefore high-effort, high-price) viticulture. The wines of Domaine de Trévallon show the astonishing potential of les Baux.

What Provence has always done, though, is to produce large quantities of good-time wine, much of it simple, dry rosé: pretty wine in a pretty bottle. It's fun to drink, even if the memory it leaves fades quickly.

In general terms, the most consistent red-wine *appellation* of Provence is Bandol, where the Mourvèdre grape comes into its own, producing dark, spicy, sometimes chocolate-edged wines. The *vins de pays*, as ever, can be good: look out for Cabernet Sauvignon from the Bunan family's Mont Caume.

THE SOUTH-WEST

South-Western France is a kind of archipelago of wine. Little islands of vineyards are dotted here and there about the landscape; curious, half-forgotten grape varieties provide original, startling flavours. This is France's most rewarding sector for the wine explorer and pioneer.

The region's best-known red wines are Cahors and Madiran; Jurançon is its leading white. Cahors is dark in colour, full of plummy, mineral fruit, but softer, finally, than the colour suggests it will be; Madiran is its opposite: a tough wine which needs a good stew to see it down. Jurançon comes in both dry and sweet guises; either way, it is a fresher, slighter wine than the latitude suggests, yet one brimming with strange, exotic fruit scents and flavours.

Other AOCs, VDQSs and *vins de pays* abound, all the way to the last Basque outpost of French wine-making: Irouléguy. If you find wines you like down here, bring as much as you can back to Britain with you, since they are still difficult to locate in shops at home.

Pompidou Centre

*Fickle in everything else, the French have been faithful in one thing only –
their love of change*

[Sir Archibald Alison]

PARIS

The heart of France pulsates with life and pumps life – economic, political and cultural – to the rest of one of the world's most centralised nations. The capital, where every aspect of French life except its essentially regional culinary excellence is concentrated, distils many of the qualities of the French people: their exhibitionism, their excitability, their charm, and their sense of their own importance – and especially their importance in civilising the world. Victor Hugo said Paris was the synonym of cosmos.

Paris is a notoriously trying place to inhabit but a marvellous place to visit – as full of modern life and as pacy as New York, as full of historical and cultural interest as Rome, as compact and picturesque as Oxford. It is a city which earns a special place in the heart of every visitor not because of its art treasures but because of its atmospheres, its smells, its noises, its inhabitants and its landmarks, shown off as skilfully as a woman's most seductive features.

First on the list of natural advantages is the curvaceous Seine, which carves a gracious sweep through most of central Paris. It was the Seine, flowing past an island or three, which defined the original settlement of Lutetia (meaning marsh) which, as Caesar reported, was inhabited by the Parisii and joined to the boggy terra firma by a couple of wooden bridges. Today the Seine – still the heart of the city – has banks planted with chestnut groves where it is so delicious and fragrant to idle in Paris's famous spring; the embankment pavements are lined with stalls of old books and prints; and artists plant their easels by the most picturesque of Parisian scenes.

Paris shows off nearly all its great monuments along the river, so a stroll along the *quais* (embankments) or a boat trip along the river are the best and most delightful ways to get a first feel for the layout of the city, and by following the river you cannot get lost. The styles of the two banks are different, but the Seine does not divide Paris as the Thames divides London. Bridges are numerous, in many cases very

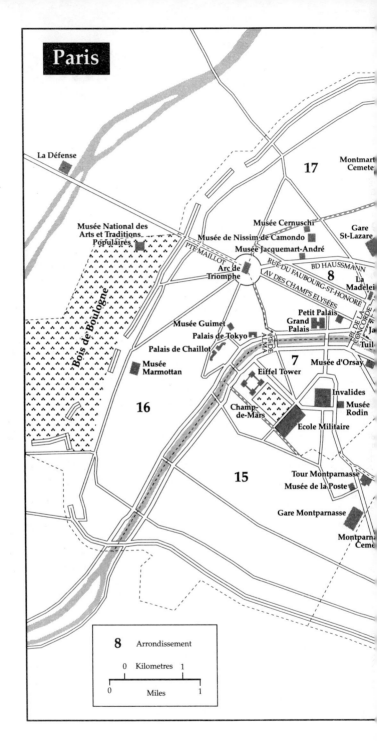

Paris

La Défense

17

Montmart
Cemete

Musée National des
Arts et Traditions
Populaires

Musée Cernuschi

Gare
St-Lazare

Musée de Nissim de Camondo

Musée Jacquemart-André

PTE MAILLOT

RUE DU FAUBOURG-ST-HONORÉ

BD HAUSSMANN

Arc de
Triomphe

8

La
Madelei

AV DES CHAMPS ELYSÉES

Petit Palais

Musée Guimet

Grand
Palais

Ja
Tuil

Palais de Tokyo

AV DE L'ALMA

PL DE LA CONCORDE

Palais de Chaillot

7

Musée d'Orsay

Musée
Marmottan

Eiffel Tower

Bois de Boulogne

Invalides

Musée
Rodin

16

Champ-
de-Mars

Ecole Militaire

15

Tour Montparnasse

Musée de la Poste

Gare Montparnasse

Montparna
Ceme

8 Arrondissement

0   Kilometres   1

0   Miles   1

50

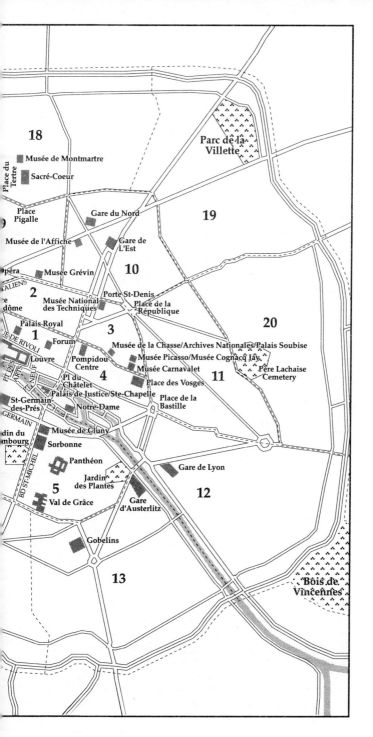

18

Place du Tertre

Musée de Montmartre

Sacré-Coeur

Place Pigalle

Gare du Nord

19

Musée de l'Affiche

Gare de L'Est

péra

Musée Grévin

10

ALIENS

2

Porte St-Denis

re dôme

Musée National des Techniques

Place de la République

Palais-Royal

1

3

20

Forum

Musée de la Chasse/Archives Nationales/Palais Soubise

Louvre

Pompidou Centre

Musée Picasso/Musée Cognacq Jay

4

Musée Carnavalet

Père Lachaise Cemetery

Pl du Châtelet

11

St-Germain des-Prés

Palais de Justice/Ste-Chapelle

Place des Vosges

GERMAIN

Notre-Dame

Place de la Bastille

din du mbourg

Musée de Cluny

Sorbonne

BD ST-MICHEL

Panthéon

Gare de Lyon

Jardin des Plantes

5

12

Val de Grâce

Gare d'Austerlitz

Gobelins

Bois de Vincennes

13

Parc de la Villette

decorative, and crossing them on fóot is no more of an expedition than crossing a main road.

Many of the city's monumental perspectives span the Seine: the colonnades of the Madeleine and the Chambre des Députés deliberately echo each other across the river on either side of the Place de la Concorde; and Notre-Dame enjoys the most picturesque setting of any French cathedral, on an island in the river, beautifully shown off and reflected in its waters.

Although long vistas are one of its great visual characteristics, Paris did not grow according to a plan but spread naturally in all directions from the Ile de la Cité, and had a semblance of order imposed upon it only by demolition and reconstruction in later periods. Not content with nature's thoroughfare, Napoleon created another through central Paris – arrow-straight and running just to the north of the river: from the Bastille in the east through the Louvre, the Tuileries gardens and the Place de la Concorde, along the Champs-Elysées to the Arc de Triomphe. For most of its course it is an imposing axis and, like the river, very convenient for purposes of orientation. Its arrangement changed the balance of the city westwards: until the 19th century the Ile de la Cité and the Louvre were the centre of town, and today's Champs-Elysées fields on its western outskirts; now the Place de la Concorde is the centre. Later in the century many miles of long wide boulevards were laid down with Germanic thoroughness and uniformity by the prefectorial Alsatian baron Haussmann, who moved bridges so that roads could go geometrically straight across the Ile de la Cité. Haussmann's façades, regulated in architectural style and size, are among the most characteristic and least attractive aspects of the capital; but although much was destroyed to make way for them, much was left standing in between – including labyrinthine *quartiers* and the monuments with which earlier monarchs had embellished the city.

In contrast to Haussmann's heavy-handed approach, the turn-of-the-century monuments, which rarely win much applause for architectural merit, are light and ornamental, in tune with the not too serious spirit of the time, and of Paris. The Pont Alexandre III, with its gilt metal statuettes, and the greenhouse-style Petit and Grand Palais lighten the grandeur of Louis XIV's Invalides in a way which should, no doubt, be deplored but which is rather fun and very Parisian. The Eiffel Tower was put up as a feat of virtuosity – a 300-metre flagpole for the World Exhibition of 1889 – and was greeted with howls of horror from all remotely serious Parisians, but it has become the defiantly cheeky symbol of Paris, looking down on the Louis XV elegance of the Ecole Militaire. From the hill of Montmartre, all Paris is overlooked by the no less derided mock-oriental white domes of the pilgrimage basilica of Sacré-Coeur, now an accepted and essential part of the city skyline.

The second half of the 19th century did as much to fashion Paris's image as it did to change its physical appearance. It was at this time of accumulation of wealth that Paris became the frolicsome fun city of Europe – 'gay Paree'. City dwellers acquired a taste for pleasures: they rode out to play in the Bois de Boulogne – newly laid out under the inspiration of Hyde Park – or to socialise at the Longchamp races. The musical note of the age was the light comedy of Offenbach, and the new, sumptuously over-decorated Opera House was adorned with wonderfully lively sculptures called La Danse. Parisians danced in the Tuileries, and they flocked to watch the high-kicking dancing girls of the Moulin Rouge at the foot of Montmartre, the picturesque hill village of windmills and Bohemians – the hard-up artists and poets of Puccini's opera. The turn of the century was the 'Belle Epoque' – the high life of *haute couture* and high spirits, of cafés filled with the noise of popping corks and clinking glasses. It was also the time of the low life reality behind the façade – the heavy make-up, the premature lines shown up in the mirror under the harsh artificial lights, the humourless smiles that scowl, the absinthe drinkers staring sightless – as recorded for ever by Manet, Degas and Toulouse-Lautrec. The visitor seeking too literally the image conjured up in the painting and literature of the era is bound to be disappointed. The Moulin Rouge and other traditional cabarets are still there, with dancing girls still going through the ritual can-can, but the audience is no longer Parisian, and the show has lost its earthy vitality. Now nocturnal Parisians are to be found in throbbing discothèques all over town, and for those who want to do more than just dance, there are places to cater for all tastes and proclivities, most notoriously the Bois de Boulogne and the Rue St-Denis, just round the corner from Beaubourg and the Pompidou centre, the very lively new focus of Parisian tourism. The contrast of gaiety and sleaze is every bit as evident in the Paris of the early 1990s as it was a century ago.

There is a willingness to brave outrage, indeed a positive relish for controversy, with new architectural projects for the adornment and transformation of the capital. Considering how crowded Paris is and how few empty spaces the Second World War created, it is remarkable that the city centre should have become the scene for new building and redevelopment projects on an ambitious scale unmatched anywhere.

The reasons for the sudden explosion of building activity are not hard to find. Presidents able to take and impose bold decisions, and keen to initiate monumental projects by which they will be remembered (Pompidou and Mitterrand, both committed modernists); having as mayor of Paris one of the protagonists in a presidential election campaign (Chirac); the 1989 bicentenary of the Revolution, a marvellous opportunity for the French to indulge their love of grandiose abstractions, and no time to be over-respectful towards the past; a willingness to reinforce the dominant position of Paris in the cultural life of the nation at a time when other countries would concentrate on taking culture out into the provinces; and the simple need to improve the operational efficiency of the city.

A large area at the heart of Paris has been transformed by the separate but adjacent projects of Beaubourg and Les Halles. After a relatively brief period of relaxed planning rules in the '60s and early '70s, certain sectors of the Parisian skyline now bristle with tower blocks, most notoriously Montparnasse and the high-rise western suburb of La Défense, whose dark silhouette looms behind the Arc de Triomphe at the end of the great perspective from the Tuileries gardens. Or did, until the construction of a new arch large enough to shelter Notre-Dame, which houses 5,000 working people inside its structure. At the other end of the axis, tremendous works have been undertaken to reorganise not only the Louvre palace and museum, but its whole surrounding precinct. Beyond Bastille into the east end of Paris where few tourists or fashionable Parisians care to tread, a huge complex of sports centre and government offices has been built on the banks of the Seine. In the north-east, still inside the all-embracing Boulevard Périphérique, La Villette has a vast new park full of leisure palaces and cultural supermarkets. The whole of down-at-heel eastern Paris, in fact, is a redevelopment project.

Various phases can be identified. The Pompidolian style was confident and the results are among the least attractive – the Montparnasse tower and the creation of a motorway along one of the banks of the Seine, apparently symptomatic of a time of headlong Americanisation when the Boulevard St-Michel, high street of student Paris, and the once elegant Grands Boulevards became anonymous avenues of burger bars, drugstores and denim shops. Reaction came with a more environmentally aware president and the end of a long period of rapid economic expansion. President Giscard d'Estaing called a halt to high-rise building in the city and cancelled the plan for a second riverside *autoberge*. The redevelopment of the old market, Les Halles, was arrested, leaving a hole for Parisians to argue about for years.

Giscard was eventually persuaded not to insist on a major scaling-down of his predecessor's greatest and most original project, the Pompidou Centre itself – monument, museum, meeting place and Centre of Cultural Creation designed, in the words of one of its co-architects, 'to bring down the wall of mistrust that separates the great public from official culture'. Giscard's own legacy to central Paris is the transformation of the Gare d'Orsay, a disused railway station on the left bank, into a magnificent new museum of late 19th-century art.

On becoming President in 1981, François Mitterrand immediately set his sights on 1989 and launched competitions for not one but three monumental new projects, at both extremities of the Napoleonic axis and at the centre of it: La Grande Arche (home of the International Foundation for Human Rights and Human Sciences), Le Grand Louvre and Opéra Bastille. The grandeur of this conception takes the breath away. The French still think big.

All these projects, with the possible exception of the Orsay museum, occasioned furious controversy, fuelling the pens of traditionalists and self-styled defenders of Parisians in the street. The Pompidou Centre was loudly derided as a refinery, a steamship (both insults that the architects would probably welcome) and attracted the usual criticism levelled at any modern building erected in an older quarter. The fuss died down when it became clear that the public loved the place. Conceived as the centrepiece for the redesign and resuscitation of a whole area, the Pompidou Centre has been a huge success. Beaubourg lives. There are already signs of similar revival in the once depressed Bastille quarter, although it is unlikely to become a tourist attraction.

Parisians are no less reactionary than inhabitants of beautiful old cities the world over. They simply do not have Prince Charles to speak up for them, and their leaders have tended to side with imaginative innovation. The result is that modern Paris resembles neither a show-case museum nor Manhattan-sur-Seine, but a fertile breeding ground for new creative ideas, which almost brings the city to its cultural position at the turn of the century.

While the grand designers concentrate on purity and transparency and the erection of monumental windows open to the future (the cube's slogan, coined by its Danish architect), the hard work of cleaning up the old city, restoring its old buildings and providing its inhabitants with a better quality of life continues; these are the tasks to which Mayor Chirac has applied much of his prodigious energy. In the circumstances, his former boss Giscard's nickname for him, *le bulldozer*, seems less than appropriate. *Le décrotteur* might be more suitable, after the force of sanitary motorbikes that patrol the streets sweeping canine deposits from the pavements of the capital.

In such a city the job of restoration is never complete, but the achievement has been enormous. At least as much was done in the '80s to return a beautiful old city to the Parisians as to build the new one most claim not to want. The Marais, capital of pre-Revolutionary Paris, looks more beautiful and becomes livelier every year, with more of its magnificent palaces rescued from dereliction and restored to their former splendour, like the Hôtel Salé, home of the Picasso museum, the entire Place des Vosges, and the Pont des Arts, beloved of the Impressionists.

We ape the French in many of our fashions and the French borrow from us and from America many of theirs. Kilts, tweeds, labradors and American brogues are perennially popular, and Marks and Spencer and C&A (hideously unpronounceable in French) have tremendous cachet; C&A does wedding lists and W H Smith's tea room is the height of fashion. Kids out on the town go to McDonald's and Love Burger, which has been voted top of the burgers by the great arbiter of taste, Gault-Millau, and has a branch on the Rue St-Denis.

The fast food industry flourishes but too much can be made of it as a symbol of disposable, characterless style of modern city life. It is not even very relevant to the serious matter of the capital's gastronomy, for the Parisian palate has survived the onslaught and continues to demand high standards in true French tradition. It is not difficult to find good, enjoyable and characteristically Parisian restaurants at various price levels – we recommend a selection on page 80. A remarkable feature is the care that has been lavished on the beautiful restoration of many of the interiors of the most celebrated and traditional restaurants, brasseries and cafés, from Chez Francis to Les Deux Magots.

A traditional part of Paris's image is the café where, once upon a time, intellectuals discussed the human condition in a fog of *caporal* tobacco over coffee in St-Germain-des-Prés, and idle rich Parisiennes discussed their extra-marital affairs in a haze of Virginia cigarettes, also over coffee, on the Boulevard des Italiens. Few Parisians have the time to sit around in cafés these days, and even in the university quarter a hard-working, library-bound realism has replaced the lazy radicalism of the '60s. But the cafés are still there, seats facing the street so that the customer can watch the world go by and be watched by the bypassing world, and the coffee is still the same – strong and sharp and taken in after-dinner quantities. Visiting Paris invariably means spending most of the time on foot. The cafés are a godsend.

In many other ways Paris continues to oblige by living up to the image we have of it. For contemporary art it still has the most adventurous and varied selection of private galleries, even though the throughput of today cannot compare with that of the half-century between 1870 and 1920 when Paris hosted Impressionist and Cubist revolutions. There may have been a gastronomic revolution, or at least a renaissance, in France over the last few decades, but Parisians still crowd into their unchanging neighbourhood brasseries for Sunday lunch and the scurrying waiters still find time to address elegantly turned compliments to their most elderly regular customers.

The distinction between business and residential areas does not exist in Paris. Every quarter has its inhabitants, and many (even in the city centre) retain their village atmosphere with pavement oyster stalls outside the best brasseries. *Concierges* still rattle their keys and complain, red-faced men in track suits (or *joggings*, as they are now called) still play *boules* on the very uneven gravel of the Tuileries gardens, where children still hire toy boats, and touts with Polaroid cameras still pester tourists. The chestnuts still bloom in the spring and romance is still in the air.

Nor has Parisian *haute couture* declined from its traditional pre-eminence. The presentations of the annual collections are still the biggest events in the world fashion calendar and the shop windows make mouth-watering sightseeing, with streets of fabulous *couturiers* and bootmakers whose standards and prices have remained unshakeably high despite all pressures for economy and standardisation. Parisians, too, remain much the same: extrovert, demonstrative and short-tempered, closer to a Mediterranean temperament than Paris' geographical position would suggest, always in a hurry to work or play hard; the streets of the city stay busy late into the night – much later than London and anywhere in provincial France.

Undeniably, though, wandering the streets of Paris by night is no longer an unmitigated pleasure. Vice is no nicer in the world's fun capital than anywhere else. Transvestites trawl the rush-hour traffic jams in the Bois de Boulogne like children selling evening newspapers. Drug rings operate in tandem with prostitution. Parisians will warn you not to hang around the Champs-Elysées late at night. The Rue de la Paix, always featured on the Paris By Night bus tours, is full of riot police vans and its famous jewellers' windows are empty and barred. The Métro was notorious for crime before commuters on the London Underground fell prey to gangs of steamers. There is international terrorism, too, with political assassinations and bombs lobbed into supermarkets from passing cars. It may come as a shock to see fresh-faced *agents de police* with machine guns directing traffic.

These afflictions of the age have not deterred tourists from visiting Paris. Nor should they, although striking out into Belleville or the Bois de Boulogne by night for a glimpse of the seamy side of Parisian life is probably not advisable. On balance Paris in the 1990s is an even more fascinating and a more beautiful city than it was in the 1980s. One of the reasons for its continuing vitality, and for its problems, is the fact that most Parisians prefer an urban to a suburban life. The city has for centuries been the most densely populated in Europe and has twice as many people per acre as London. Most people live in apartment blocks, there are few private or public gardens (mainly dusty gravel with trees) and hardly any parks – except the Bois de Boulogne, the Bois de Vincennes and the new park at La Villette, all of which are on the periphery and do nothing to ventilate the centre. The density of cars is no less a problem than that of humanity. Traffic on the terrifying Périphérique (the complete circular motorway around Paris) is either at a standstill or nose-to-tail at sixty; while the road helps keep juggernauts out of the city, at rush hours it seems only to ensure that all traffic going in or out of Paris is travelling in the same direction. Weekend exits and re-entries are horrific, and solid traffic jams in the Champs-Elysées and around the Opéra at midnight are common. In cramped Paris, which outgrew a series of confining town walls, there is no more room for any new roads. As elsewhere, planners have recognised the folly of attempting to solve the capital's traffic problems by building new roads and inviting more cars. The Métro has been extended to serve suburban new towns and is working hard to brighten up its image, with video entertainment on the platforms and much talk of going out into the community and winning customers.

Parisians, who barricaded their streets in so many revolutions and welcomed with equal unanimity so many dictatorial rulers, still love to do things *en masse*. They know it doesn't make sense, but with a Gallic shrug they accept city life, with all its stresses, as being preferable to a more sensible but oh, how boring provincial existence – as long as they can escape to the country. As well as a mass movement at weekends, there is an even greater exodus from the city in July and August. It may sound attractive to be able to enjoy the picturesque townscape and museums without all the traffic jams and the horn blowing, but it isn't. Paris without the Parisians seems pointless. Large numbers of shops, restaurants and even some museums are closed. To visit at this time is to learn that Paris is not what you see on postcards but a living city where, as Balzac wrote, '*tout fume, tout brûle, tout brille, tout bouillonne*'. Many shops and restaurants in residential *quartiers* also close at Easter.

GETTING AROUND

It is easy and inexpensive to get to Paris by plane, train or bus, so there is no need to attempt to see Paris by car. Parking is usually a major problem, and driving habits take some getting used to: Parisians believe that bumpers, no less than horns, are made to be used – in spite of the fact that the law forbids the use of the horn throughout Paris.

From a fairly central hotel you will find most essential places from the tourist point of view within manageable walking distance. It is much the most enjoyable and indeed the most relaxing way to get around, although dodging traffic often calls for some agility – pedestrians are not respected by drivers and if you try the favourite tourist game of reaching the Arc de Triomphe on foot overground you have only yourself to blame for the consequences.

When the feet give out, you are never more than a few hundred yards from a Métro station (underground, mostly). The Métro system looks very complicated on a map because there are so many different lines, but it is fast (15 minutes from Châtelet in the centre to the Porte Maillot, or 5 minutes from L'Etoile to La Défense), generally efficient and easy to use. Many stations have maps which light up to indicate the route you should take to a given station. The trick is to remember the name of the station at the end of the line you need, in the direction you need, and follow signs to it, either headed *Direction* or *Correspondances* (connections). Lines close at 12.30 am. Most trains are modernised and smoothly cushioned on rubber tyres. Doors have to be opened by releasing a catch. There is no smoking, no spitting and some seats have to be given up to pregnant women and those wounded in the war. You can go anywhere on the Métro for one standard price ticket which when bought individually is nearly double its price as part of a book (*carnet*) of 10. Métro tickets are valid on Paris buses, and

1-, 3- and 5-day tourist passes for unlimited use of both systems and the RER are also available from major Métro stations.

In recent years the RER (Réseau Express Régional) has been grafted on to the Métro system, initially extending it into the suburbs (including La Défense) and beyond, now crossing Paris. It has a ticket system of its own and is only of relevance to tourists who want to get out of the city – to St-Germain-en-Laye, to Charles de Gaulle Airport or to Euro Disney. It is also a convenient way to get across the city centre quickly.

Paris buses are more expensive than the Métro (journeys of more than a few stops require two tickets and if you change you pay again) and less comprehensive in coverage, especially on Sundays and public holidays when many bus routes are closed; it is, however, a much more attractive way of travelling around town. Because of the one-way systems, buses often take different routes back and forth. Books of tickets cannot be bought on buses.

There is nothing strange about Paris taxi drivers except that they are taciturn by comparison with those of London or New York. They wait in ranks with telephones, they display fares on the meter, they expect a tip and they charge extra at night.

One of the nicest ways of seeing central Paris is to take a boat (*bateau mouche* or *vedette*) from the Pont de l'Alma, Pont d'Iéna, or the Pont Neuf. There are covered sections for rainy days, and commentaries in English. At night, some boat trips include a meal.

Another good way of getting your bearings is to take a bus tour around town by day and/or night (particularly recommended for illuminations); some night tours include cabaret stops and a meal. Be prepared for over-diligent translations – the Elysian fields, Peace street and so on. You can obtain information from your hotel or a tourist office (the main one is at 127 Avenue des Champs-Elysées). They will also have information on coach excursions out of Paris – a great variety, from half a day to a château in the Ile-de-France to several days in the Loire valley.

The map on pages 50–1 shows the major sights and landmarks, and the different districts (*arrondissements*) numbered 1 to 20. Michelin produces a Paris atlas with street maps in book form, and some useful information including bus and Métro maps.

PARIS AREA BY AREA

Paris is divided into administrative districts (*arrondissements*) which spiral clockwise from the centre (the Louvre) from numbers 1 to 20. The inner twist of the spiral from the 1st to the 8th *arrondissements* contains most of the museums, the sightseeing and the shopping.

The Right Bank

The Arc de Triomphe crowns Paris's most famous processional perspective, the gentle climb of the **Avenue des Champs-Elysées** from the **Place de la Concorde** to the starfish **Place Charles de Gaulle** (ex-Etoile), its course interrupted in the middle by the fountains of the Rond-Point des Champs-Elysées. On the Concorde side, the Champs-Elysées has kept its gardens, with theatres, exhibition halls and the presidential palace. On the Etoile side it is a broad and uninteresting avenue of car showrooms, airline buildings, cinemas and department stores: no longer a very appealing place to sit in a café and spectate, although the magnificent Fouquet's, the King Canute of cafés, survives protected from excessive contamination by a barricade of foliage. The area to the south and west between the Champs-Elysées and the **Avenue George V**, particularly the **Avenue Montaigne**, is a select one for hotels, *couturiers*, food shops, embassies and cabaret. The further you penetrate westwards into the 16th *arrondissement* the more drearily residential Paris becomes. To the north and east of the Rond-Point, the best streets for well-established art galleries (**Avenue Matignon**) and *haute couture* (**Rue du Faubourg St-Honoré**) lead towards the Palais du Louvre.

The central area around the **Louvre** and the **Place de la Concorde** is the least residential in Paris. It has most of the luxury hotels (the occupying German commander in the Second World War had his headquarters in the Meurice) along the arcaded **Rue de Rivoli**, and set quietly back from it, like the Ritz on the **Place Vendôme** – the 17th-century square which is probably the most beautiful in Paris, spoilt only by the outrageously oversized column of Napoleon as Caesar. Shops and restaurants vary from the most exclusive (the **Rue du Faubourg St-Honoré**, the **Rue de la Paix** and Maxim's restaurant) to the merely expensive (the Rue de Rivoli itself which specialises in clothes for export and also has an English bookshop and tea-shop). It is an area for the theatre and opera, the Louvre, and perspectives – up the Tuileries to the Arc de Triomphe, up the Rue Royale to the Madeleine, up the Avenue de l'Opéra, now lined with travel agents, to the Opéra itself – the most extravagantly brassy of all the buildings of the Second Empire. It is also an area where resting your feet in a café will cost you dearly, so it's better to pause in the **Tuileries** gardens, partly dusty with a few feeble fountains and ponds popular with model boat enthusiasts, partly arranged with lawns and statues and the diminutive pink marble Arc de Triomphe du Carrousel. To avoid being pestered by eternally hopeful Polaroid camera touts, you could repair to the quieter and more elegant central backwater of the **Palais-Royal** gardens surrounded by 18th-century arcades with fascinating off-beat shops and the beautiful Grand Vefour restaurant, well worth a glimpse even if you can't afford a meal. North of the Palais-Royal, the neighbourhood of the Bourse (stock exchange), the Banque de France and the Bibliothèque Nationale is a quiet and untouristy area, with some very fashionable *couturiers* and a purveyor of fresh crustaceans on the circular **Place des Victoires**. The statue is Louis XIV and the church is one for pilgrims.

The *quais* (embankments) are particularly attractive and amusing to the east of the Louvre: booksellers' stalls on the river side, noisy petshops on the land side, and delightful views. The famous pedestrian **Pont des Arts** gives the most picturesque views of all.

To the east of the Palais-Royal is the wide and still somewhat desolate open space in place of **Les Halles** – the central food market, the stomach of Paris according to Zola's celebrated formula. The market has for practical reasons been removed to the suburbs, and in its place fountains, modern sculptures and metalwork not yet overgrown by creepers do less to enliven the open space than a very entertaining and imaginative children's playground, which has supervisors and separate sections for under-7s and under-11s. Other attractions for children include deep-sea adventures in the Centre Océanique Cousteau and the holography museum – both in the **Forum des Halles**, a vast underground shopping centre. The Forum is one of the less interesting facets of modern Paris and does not really live up to its name, although young people do sit around on the steps and fondle the pink sculptures that adorn the open floor of the pit. In the old days Les Halles was the place for all-night restaurants and the tradition lives on. Between Les Halles and the other major development scheme of modern Paris, Beaubourg, the **Rue St-Denis** runs north/south up to the Porte St-Denis. The Rue St-Denis has become synonymous with pornographic entertainment and shops, and you do not have to wait until nightfall to see what is for sale around here. Thousands of tourists and Paris-By-Night coachloads crowd the area, too; the atmosphere is not threatening, although hardly refined, and spectating is a popular pastime.

Beaubourg is the name of the area redeveloped in the early '70s which includes the Pompidou Centre. The idea, as President Pompidou conceived it, was to provide not only a museum for modern art but also a focus for contemporary French culture. Inside the building, extraordinary and controversial in itself, there is lots to see and do. The piazza in front is a bit bleak but usually animated by all sorts of pavement artists. Selling anything on the piazza is forbidden but the cap-bearers hustle relentlessly, especially if they spot you taking photos. The whole area has benefited from the redevelopment, commercially at least; some eight million people a year visit, and new arty shops and restaurants are springing up all the time in what used to be an unsavoury part of town. (Renovations are due to take place in 1995/6 and parts of the area may be closed during that period).

Between Beaubourg and the river, the seedy end of the **Rue de Rivoli** is the place for the most inexpensive department stores, and the **Place**

du Châtelet for popular theatre. The Hôtel de Ville, on the old execu-
tionary Place de Grève, was rebuilt completely in the late 19th century
in imitation Renaissance style, and is a building of no aesthetic
distinction. Along the north of the central area from the Madeleine to
the Bastille, the so-called **Grands Boulevards** (the only wide ones there
were in Paris before Haussmann's time) occupy the site of the city
walls knocked down by Louis XIV in the 17th century (Paris fortifications were thought to be more likely to be used against him than by
him). Louis also put up a couple of handsome arched gateways – the
Portes St-Denis and St-Martin – at what is now very much the popular
end of the boulevards. Around the Opéra there are still some reminders of a grander and even more fashion-conscious style of living when
dandies, beaux and many others paraded along the **Boulevard des
Italiens** – the centre of Parisian elegance throughout the 19th century.
Many of the succession of famous cafés and restaurants have now
disappeared. The **Boulevard Haussmann**, which joins the Grand Boulevards behind the Opéra, has many of the bank headquarters and the
biggest and best-known of Parisian department stores (Galeries Lafayette, Au Printemps).

To the east of the Hôtel de Ville – between the river, the Bastille and
the easternmost Grands Boulevards – the area called the **Marais** (like
Lutetia meaning marsh) is the former 17th-century heart of the city. It
was later abandoned by fashionable residents and left to crumble, until
a major campaign of restoration was started in the '60s. Now the old
palaces, from the medieval Hôtel de Sens to the 18th-century Palais
Soubise, and the delightful 17th-century **Place des Vosges** (formerly
Place Royale), have been cleaned and restored to all their former
resplendence; the area has come to life in an attractive way, with
galleries, restaurants and a number of quiet and comfortable hotels. It
is a fascinating area to explore – the only part of central Paris which
does not bear the scars of botched 19th-century architectural surgery.
The vast crossroads of the **Place de la Bastille** marks the boundary
between busy central and seedy eastern Paris. A few lines on the
ground are the only remains of the stormed fortress and Bastille is
neither interesting nor picturesque, save for the opera house, opened
on 14 July 1989 – the biggest in the world. Napoleon proposed the
erection of a huge bronze elephant on the site, but instead there is a
column commemorating a second generation of July revolutionaries,
those of 1830.

The islands in the Seine – once three, but since the 17th century only
two – are joined by a footbridge; they come into the 4th and 1st
arrondissements and so are more 'right' than 'left' for administrative
purposes, but fall between the two in style. They are moored to the
banks by no fewer than 13 bridges; the **Pont Neuf**, despite its name, is
the oldest (16th-century) and finest of Parisian bridges. The **Ile de la
Cité** – the oldest part of Paris – is dominated by Notre-Dame, one of the

Place des Vosges

finest Gothic cathedrals in France. The imposing Palais de Justice hides most of the Ste-Chapelle – Saint Louis' royal chapel in what used to be his royal palace. One splendid part of the palace, complete with medieval round turrets, has not been destroyed and is open to the public – the Conciergerie, an infamous Revolutionary waiting room for condemned prisoners, including Marie Antoinette. Between Notre-Dame and the Palais de Justice is a flower market and in the angle of the bow of the ship (a comparison to which the *cité* lends itself irresistibly) the secluded, elegant **Place Dauphine** is one of the best addresses in Paris. There are interesting antiquarian shops all around the island's *quais* and very good views from both main banks of the river.

The **Ile St-Louis** was not inhabited until the 17th century; since then it has been endowed with some of Paris's most magnificent *hôtels*, which you cannot easily visit. It is still quiet, although hardly the residential backwater it once was – there are restaurants and hotels all along its main street – and it is one of the best places of all to stay as long as you don't have a car to park.

The Left Bank

The Ile de la Cité and Ile St-Louis are moored to the Left Bank and the **Quartier Latin**, so called because of the common language of medieval Europe's most excellent and international university. The **Montagne Ste-Geneviève**, which climbs from the *quai* giving the best views of Notre-Dame to the domed churches of the Sorbonne and the Panthéon, is a genuine student quarter with academic bookshops, cheap oriental restaurants, cheap accommodation and cinemas for *cinéphiles*. The two main axes – the **Boulevard St-Germain** and especially the **Boulevard St-Michel** – are now thoroughly characterless, with pubs, fast-food restaurants and knick-knack stalls. The narrow streets around the beautiful church of St-Séverin, between the Boulevard St-Germain and the river, are colourful and very lively in the evening, with dozens of cheap ethnic (that is to say, not French) restaurants. The dominant Panthéon, a ponderous, domed neo-classical temple dedicated to the heroes of republican liberty, stands on top of the hill on the site of the former abbey of Ste-Geneviève, patron saint of Paris and its protectress against 700,000 Huns in the 5th century. The building is so badly cracked that it has been largely closed to the public – except the crypt. Its dome is best seen from down a sandy avenue in the **Luxembourg Gardens**, a traditional and very attractive context for student idleness. The Luxembourg is a mixture of formal and informal gardens: there are terraces, lawns, statues, a puppet theatre, tennis courts, and fountains – one of which, the 17th-century Fontaine de Medicis, is beautifully shaded and impressively monumental in proportions, with the sculpture of a cyclops about to squash some unlucky victims. The gardens originally belonged to the massive Luxembourg Palace, built for Marie de' Medici in a style to cater for her Florentine nostalgia, drawing heavily on the Pitti Palace. The palace is now the home of the French Senate (Upper House) and only occasionally opened to visitors.

The Montagne Ste-Geneviève's history goes further back than the university: the hill was the main Roman settlement (the Gauls were on the Ile de la Cité). There isn't much left of Rome in Paris – certainly nothing to compare with Provençal remains of towns which were of greater importance than Lutetia – but there are remains of the Roman arena to the east of the hill, and the Roman baths can still be seen in the Hôtel de Cluny.

The **Jardin des Plantes** (botanical gardens), with a small zoo and a natural history museum, is a favourite park for children and old folk alike. This neighbourhood is a corner few tourists bother with. But it is of interest to those who realise there is more to Paris than the picturesque and the exclusive central areas: old, poor Paris, women in grey, men in berets, Algerian immigrants and all sorts of artisans struggling against the overwhelming tide of technological progress. There are cobbled courtyards and mysterious dingy half-open doorways, washing hanging out of windows, communal water fountains and Paris's

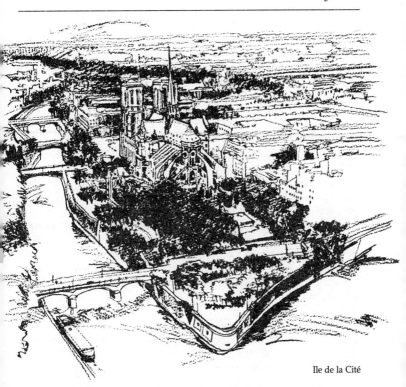

Ile de la Cité

mosque (which you can visit) – all in a labyrinth of alleys and court-yards and peeling façades that the wide Second Empire thoroughfares pierced, crossed, but failed to reach. This aspect of Paris is not immediately attractive – indeed quite the opposite – and it is hard to know what to look for. Rather than for the tourist, it is for the longer-stay visitor and native Parisians to discover. One part of this area which until recently combined the most colourful charm and a real, old, unaffected Parisian vitality was the immediate vicinity of the **Rue Mouffetard**. However, these very qualities, especially its lively street market, have brought great change: there are pizza parlours, trendy boutiques in the style of the more fashionable Rive Gauche and even *un bowling*. Despite all this, the Rue Mouffetard is still great fun.

Fashionable Rive Gauche means **St-Germain-des-Prés**, named after the most important of the abbeys of the Left Bank, whose noble church still stands at the heart of the *quartier*, looking down over the Cafés de Flore and des Deux Magots, the two melting pots for radical artistic and philosophical ideas of the first half of this century. Nowadays the cafés are expensive, and fuller of expectant tourists than intellectuals, and the tone of the area is set more accurately by the modern Drugstore across the road. All the same, the areas either side of the **Boulevard St-Germain**

65

are full of very attractive, trendy and youthful shops, restaurants and art galleries. Leading down to the Ecole des Beaux-Arts by the river, the **Rue Bonaparte** is full of fascinating antique and antiquarian shops and there is a colourful market in the **Rue de Buci**. St-Germain-des-Prés is perhaps the most fun of all areas to stay in, and there is a wide selection of reasonably quiet hotels.

Between St-Germain-des-Prés and the Invalides, the **Faubourg St-Germain** was the favoured aristocratic residential area of the 18th century, and although ministries occupy much of it now, it is still an area of some elegance and little excitement. One *hôtel* to visit is the Hôtel Biron, now the beautiful setting for the Rodin museum. The Hôtel des Invalides, the majestic architectural complex that was Louis XIV's greatest legacy to Paris, was originally built to lodge war veterans, and now houses the Musée de l'Armée; the neighbouring Ecole Militaire is another of the finest examples of French 18th-century architecture. The approaches to these great military institutions from the river enclose another area much favoured as a place to live, quiet and well situated but without particular attractions for tourists.

Facing the Ecole Militaire, the **Champ-de-Mars** and the Eiffel Tower are about as far as most tourists will want to go downstream on the Left Bank.

To the south of the Invalides, **Montparnasse** was the Bohemian quarter of the early 20th century. Now it isn't even particularly squalid, just lively and popular as a nightlife area, whose atmosphere (or lack of it) fits in with the bare modernism of the great Montparnasse tower.

Out of the centre

Of the outlying inner-city areas, the hill or *butte* of **Montmartre** is the one that all tourists want to visit, to admire at close quarters the basilica of Sacré-Coeur, whose domes pop up at the end of street perspectives all over the capital (even irreverently crowning the Madeleine from the Concorde). The Butte's other attraction is its past as the Bohemian village of the 19th century, with its narrow, steep cobbled streets and staircases. Utrillo's Montmartre is still a picturesque place to explore, and a couple of windmills have been preserved. Among the trees beneath the silhouette of the basilica, the **Place du Tertre** is the dense forum of snap-happy tourists and aspiring artists, who prop up their canvases but never seem to do much painting. It is a place to watch your pockets, and very lively at night, with crowds of young people around guitarists, and boisterous cafés and restaurants. Away from the small over-run area immediately around Sacré-Coeur, the slopes of Montmartre live up to their reputation as a good place for traditional bistros.

Clichy/Pigalle, at the foot of the Butte, lives off its reputation for traditional Parisian nightlife. Coaches still tip their loads into the eager

portals of Clichy cabarets for music-hall *dîner-spectacles*. By day, the area teems with popular Parisian life, with lots of cheap markets on the main boulevards.

On the western edge of the city, the **Bois de Boulogne** was laid out like Hyde Park when Anglomania was at its height. The Bois became the place to be seen horse-drawn, and still has style, with lakes for boating, paths for jogging or sporting a saluki, elegant open-air restaurants, race courses and *the* Paris sports club. There is also a less salubrious aspect to the Bois, and it is traditionally the place where Parisians abandon their pets before leaving the capital for a month's sunbathing in the traffic jams of the Autoroute du Soleil.

The **Bois de Vincennes**, like that of Boulogne, was made into a park in the late 19th century, and included within city limits half a century ago. You can visit the very impressive keep of a medieval royal fortress, France's largest zoo, exotic gardens, and several museums, including a good one devoted to the arts of ex-colonial Africa.

SIGHTSEEING

So many of Paris's great monuments border the river, or like Notre-Dame float on it (*fluctuat nec mergitur* – she is tossed but not submerged – is the town's watery motto) that to walk along the banks of the Seine and over the bridges is the most agreeable introduction to Parisian sightseeing.

Viewpoints

Arc de Triomphe Massive triumphal arch planned by Napoleon but not finished for many decades (Napoleon put up a canvas version for a triumphal procession), crowning the view from the Louvre. Of the sculptures, one of those facing the Champs-Elysées is Rude's masterpiece of Republic ardour (the Marseillaise). Tomb of the unknown soldier beneath; splendid view of radiating avenues (commemorating Napoleonic victories) and most of Paris from upper platform. Métro: Etoile.

Eiffel Tower The appropriate symbol of Parisian lightness and exhibitionism (its 7,000 tons are only the equivalent of 57 lbs per square inch dead weight, and it was built for the 1889 World Exhibition) gives the highest (nearly 300 metres) view – which does not mean the finest, to most eyes – of the capital and beyond. You can walk up as far as the second floor (about 700 steps) but the top viewing platform is now accessible only by lift. Restaurants at stages one and two. Métro: Trocadéro, Ecole Militaire.

La Grande Arche Known as *le cube*, this arch is a monumental focus to the high-rise business/shopping precinct of La Défense. It completes the great perspective westwards from the Louvre past the Arc de Triomphe. Lifts take visitors up to the rooftop belvedere to admire the view and the building itself. RER: La Défense.

Montparnasse Tower Very good views; on the 56th floor an observatory with orientation frieze, and a bar and restaurant. Métro: Montparnasse-Bienvenue.

Notre-Dame Climb the towers for very good views, not least over the spine, statues and gargoyles of the cathedral herself. Métro: Cité.

Pompidou Centre Roof terrace with café; no charge for access. Splendid views over central Paris, the building itself and the non-stop entertainment on the piazza below. With its colourful, Meccano-like appearance, the building looks none too serious, a typically Parisian bagatelle. It may indeed mark a deliberate move away from conventional functional modern architecture, but there are coherent principles at work. The inside-out idea, with all the bits and pieces that are normally hidden away inside being on the outside, has the effect of liberating space inside, ideal for a building such as this. The colour system is also systematic, with an explanatory purpose as in an anatomical drawing, in line with the general theme of the centre to make art more accessible. White identifies the structural elements of the building, red stands for lifts and stairs, yellow for electricity, green for water, blue for air-conditioning. The white funnels around the piazza ventilate the basement. Métro: Rambuteau.

Sacré-Coeur Good views of eastern Paris from the terrace in front of the basilica, and from the walkways around the domes. Métro: Abbesses, Lamarck-Caulaincourt, Château-Rouge.

Samaritaine Department Store Free and beautiful, although modestly elevated, view over the *cité* from the roof terrace – the Belvedere, on the 10th floor of shop 2. Métro: Pont-Neuf.

Museums

From bread to cigarettes and meteorites, there is a museum for it in Paris. For art lovers there are the museums of world-wide celebrity – the Louvre and the Pompidou Centre – and also private collections bequeathed to the nation, less exhausting and in some ways more satisfying. Everyone can enjoyably sample a few of the less obvious Paris museums: the Musée Guimet for Oriental Art, or the Museum of Posters; and those with some knowledge of French history and literature may enjoy a visit to famous Paris cemeteries. Some museums are of specialist interest, notably those devoted to particular artists – Moreau, Delacroix, Balzac. All those we have chosen offer exceptional collections of their kind; some are better displayed than others.

Most national museums in Paris close on Tuesday, while those run by the Municipality of Paris generally close on Monday. Outside the capital, Versailles is shut on Monday too.

Musée de l'Affiche The poster as art, and the history of advertising and thereby society – fascinating stuff. Closed Tuesday. Métro: Château d'Eau.

Musée de l'Armée In the Hôtel des Invalides, this museum has splendid collections of arms and armour, Napoleon's greatcoat, battle models and film shows. The domed church, France's masterpiece of Baroque church architecture, seems made to measure for the huge porphyry tomb of France's greatest soldier, surrounded by symbolic victory figures. In the upper part of the church there are more tombs of French martial heroes (Foch, Turenne). Métro: Ecole-Militaire, Invalides.

Musée d'Art Moderne de la Ville de Paris Near the Palais de Chaillot, this is the municipal modern art museum, with choice works from Paris's great arty period at the beginning of the century. Free Sunday; closed Monday. Métro: Iéna, Alma-Marceau.

Musée des Arts Décoratifs In the Louvre Palace (entrance Rue de Rivoli), the evolution of French taste in applied art down the ages.

Fascinatingly displayed; reopened 1985 after years of large-scale reorganisation. Closed Monday and Tuesday. Métro: Palais-Royal, Tuileries.

Musée National des Arts et Traditions Populaires On the edge of a children's amusement park in the Bois de Boulogne; rural French life and folklore past and present, attractively displayed. Closed Tuesday. Métro: Sablons, Porte Maillot.

Musée Carnavalet A beautiful partly Renaissance *hôtel* with formal gardens in the heart of the Marais, containing a municipal museum mainly devoted to the history of Paris: old prints and paintings, models, a collection of inn and shop signs and a series of reception rooms decorated as in the days of Madame de Sévigné, who held her famous salon here. Free Sunday; closed Monday. Métro: St Paul, Chemin-Vert.

Musée Cernuschi A private collection of oriental art, including terracotta funerary statues of great antiquity. Closed Monday. Métro: Villiers, Monceau.

Palais de Chaillot Four museums and a theatre, in the curved wings with gardens and fountains which were built on the Trocadéro Hill for the 1937 Exhibition, to crown the monumental perspective that stretches from the Ecole Militaire up the Champ de Mars to the Eiffel Tower. The **Musée de la Marine** has model ships, old maps and navigational instruments; maritime history from Christopher Columbus to Jacques Cousteau. Children love it. Closed Tuesday. The **Musée des Monuments Français** was based on Viollet-le-Duc's scholarly initiative: plaster-cast highlights of French architecture and sculpture and reproduced frescoes, often very much more easily admired than in dingy country churches. A fascinating place if you like that kind of thing (children usually don't). Closed Tuesday. The **Musée de l'Homme** (ethnography and anthropology) has displays of art and artefacts from civilisations all over the world – Easter Islands to Greenland – and of the evolution of man. Closed Tuesday. In the basement is the **Musée du Cinéma** – closed Tuesday. Métro: Trocadéro.

Musée de la Chasse Hunting museum including animal paintings, in the splendid 17th-century Hôtel Guénégaud; a favourite with children. Closed Tuesday and Friday. Métro: Rambuteau, Hôtel-de-Ville.

Musée de Cluny Housed in one of the few surviving medieval *hôtels* in Paris. An exceptionally fine collection of medieval works of art, including the famous series of tapestries The Lady and the Unicorn; and remains of Roman baths dating from the 3rd century AD. Half-price Sunday; closed Tuesday. Métro: St-Michel, Odéon.

Musée Cognacq-Jay Another private collection, of mainly 18th-century furniture and works of art. The museum is now housed in the Hôtel de Donon in the Marais quarter. Free Sunday; closed Monday. Métro: St-Sébastien-Froissart, St-Paul.

Conciergerie The Law Courts' prison dates from the 14th century, but its historical interest is of the time of the Revolution when it was the antechamber to the guillotine. You can visit the Prisoners' Gallery, the Women's Court, Marie Antoinette's cell and mementoes of her kept in the Girondins' Chapel museum. Half-price Sunday. Métro: Cité.

Les Gobelins A chance to see tapestries being woven in the old-fashioned way, in the state factory by royal appointment to Louis XIV. Visits afternoons only, Tuesday, Wednesday and Thursday. Métro: Gobelins.

Grand Palais The principal location for art exhibitions (always worth checking), near the Place de la Concorde. The Grand Palais also houses the **Musée de la Découverte** – a science museum which has been pushed out of the limelight by La Villette, but is still worth visiting – and the **Planetarium**. Closed Monday. Métro: Champs-Elysées-Clémenceau.

Musée Grévin A Madame Tussaud's of France: disappointing compared with the London version, but always popular and open every day. Further exhibits (illustrating the Belle Epoque) are displayed in an annexe in the Forum des Halles centre. Métro: Richelieu-Drouot, Rue Montmartre.

Musée Guimet A national collection of arts from the Orient, from India to Japan. Closed Tuesday. Métro: Iéna, Boissière.

Musée Jacquemart-André A very fine private collection, with many beautiful French 18th-century paintings, and some from the Italian Renaissance. Closed Monday and Tuesday. Métro: St-Philippe-du-Roule, Miromesnil.

Le Grand Louvre Speculation as to the world's richest museum usually ends at the Louvre; there can be few rooms in the world to beat the Salle des Etats, where the Mona Lisa is just one among many masterworks of the Italian Renaissance. The Louvre is a vast and magnificent royal palace beside the Seine, built first as a fortress by Philippe Auguste in the late 12th century and not finished until the late 19th century in the stodgy architectural style of the Second Empire. The oldest and most distinguished part of the exterior is a section of the closed court (Cour Carrée) dating from the late 16th century, and the colonnade of the east end designed by Perrault for Louis XIV. The museum itself is of daunting size. It cannot possibly be visited all at once (imagine trying to do the National Gallery, British Museum and V & A in a day), and you should plan the route carefully to satisfy particular interests. If you just want to see the world-famous masterpieces, make sure that you do not get side-tracked and exhausted on the way.

The Louvre has been undergoing a vast redevelopment programme, begun in 1981 and due to be completed in 1997. The main objective is to improve the quality of the museum, with a simpler arrangement of galleries and easier access to different sections from a vast central reception area which has cafés, restaurants and shops. This is a subterranean zone, with the 60-foot glass pyramid in the middle of Cour Napoleon acting as a skylight and window on to the flanking pavilions. Two mini-pyramids surmount the passages leading to different sections of the museum. The latest phase in the development – the conversion of the north (Richelieu) wing – has recently been opened and lives up to the standards of the rest of the project, with its exciting style of architecture. The final phase will see the provision of much-needed parking space underneath the Tuileries gardens.

Because François I persuaded Leonardo da Vinci to spend his last years in France, the Louvre is richer than anywhere else in the world in the works of one of the greatest and least prolific of painters. You can follow the Louvre's supremacy in French painting from the 14th century to the middle of the 19th, with two particularly good rooms containing many 19th-century masterpieces. Other countries, with the notable exception of Britain, are also very well represented. There are also large and very distinguished collections of Oriental, Egyptian and classical antiquities (stars in the last category being the Venus de Milo and the Winged Victory of Samothrace), European sculpture (Michelangelo's Slaves) and *objets d'art*, including the French crown jewels displayed in the magnificent Apollo Gallery, designed by Le Brun. There are tours in English three to six times a day, according to season. Closed Tuesday. Métro: Palais-Royale, Louvre.

Musée Marmottan In a sedate residential quarter on the edge of the Bois de Boulogne, a connoisseur's private collection (furniture and works of art from various periods) was given much wider appeal by two important bequests of works by Monet, including the 'Impression – Sunrise', which christened the Impressionist school, and endless water lilies painted at Giverny. Relatively expensive but uncrowded; closed Monday. Métro: Muette.

Musée de Montmartre A small museum of the history of the hilltop village and its Bohemian villagers, among Paris's only vines. Open each afternoon and from 11am on Sunday. Closed Monday. Métro: Lamarck-Caulaincourt.

Musée Nissim-de-Camondo Next door to the Cernuschi, in the patrician residential area on the edge of the Parc Monceau; an outstanding collection of 18th-century furniture in an elegant and period context. Closed Monday and Tuesday. Métro: Villiers.

Orangerie This pavilion in the Tuileries gardens houses a large formerly private collection of Impressionist (over 20 Renoirs) and post-Impressionist paintings, including a remarkable series of works by Soutine. Downstairs is the *'bouquet de fleurs'* that Claude Monet left the nation, eight vast mural canvases of water lilies, painted in Giverny for these rooms, between 1918 and Monet's death in 1926. Across the gardens, the twin matching pavilion of **Jeu de Paume** is now used for temporary exhibitions of contemporary art. Closed Tuesday. Métro: Concorde.

Musée d'Orsay Built at the turn of this century (1898–1900) in a relatively old-fashioned style, out of respect for the buildings across the Seine, Orsay is a station, complete with huge clock. The Gare d'Orsay has a theatrical grandeur that makes it a fitting home for a museum of French art of its time, at least in the sense that it is a major exhibit in its own right. The structure is not immediately suitable to the purpose: a huge vaulted hall, 32 metres high, 40 wide and 138 long. The museum's architects have attempted to break up this enormous space without destroying its unity. The contrast between the style of the old building and the sober new articulation of the interior is deliberate and extreme.

The station fell into disuse gradually from 1939 and was sold by the SNCF in 1961. Idle for many years and narrowly saved from demolition in 1971, it served as an occasional film set (for Orson Welles's version of *The Trial*, among others) and as temporary home for Jean-Louis Barrault's theatre company. Orsay opened in 1986.

The museum represents far more than the transfer of the Impressionists from the old Jeu de Paume, where they were not happy, to a more spacious setting. Orsay is devoted to French art from revolution year of 1848 to 1914, and thus includes much that came before Impressionism – Daumier (the artist of 1848), Millet, Courbet, late Delacroix and Ingres – and after. With sections devoted to sculpture, photography, the decorative arts and architecture (Paris was redesigned by Haussmann during the second half of the century), masterpieces from one of the greatest periods in the history of French art are shown in context. The museum is always full and queues build up well before opening time. It is worth the wait and there is a very good café, too. Closed Monday. Métro: Musée d'Orsay (RER), Solférino.

Petit Palais Another of the municipal museums which come into their own when national ones close. This is a fun art nouveau palace in itself, and its art collections are varied, beautiful and not too big. Paintings, especially of the 19th and early 20th centuries; tapestries, *objets d'art*, furniture, some temporary exhibitions. Closed Monday. Métro: Champs-Elysées-Clémenceau.

Musée Picasso The magnificent, restored palace (known as the Hôtel Salé) of a 17th-century collector of the salt tax is a neatly appropriate place for Picasso's personal collection of his own and other artists' works, presented to the state in lieu of death duties. Picasso's practice was to keep five paintings a year, a copy of every print and all his sculptures, so there is no shortage of material. The collection, well furnished with photographs and explanatory notes, makes a fascinating and illuminating chronological journey through the changing periods and recurrent themes and obsessions of Picasso's life and work. As well as works by his contemporaries, Picasso's collection includes primitive works of tribal art, a rich source of inspiration for him. There is usually a temporary exhibition related to some aspect of Picasso's work or examining an individual work in detail. Closed Tuesday. Métro: St-Paul, St-Sébastien-Froissart.

Centre Georges Pompidou (Beaubourg) Among many other cultural workshops, libraries and reading rooms (which it was hoped would make Beaubourg into the engine-room of living French culture) is the **Musée National d'Art Moderne**, which is as good as it should be here in the most important centre of early 20th-century art. Free Sunday morning; closed Tuesday. Opposite, in a basement in the Rue Beaubourg, is the small **Musée Français de l'Holographie**, where three-dimensional images are created from diffracted light. Fascinating for children. Métro: Hôtel-de-Ville, Rambuteau, Châtelet. (Parts of the Beaubourg area may close in 1995/6 for renovations.)

Musée de la Poste History of communication and rare stamps. Closed Sunday. Métro: Montparnasse-Bienvenue, Pasteur, Falguière.

Musée Rodin A great favourite among the lesser known and less visited museums, and the best endowed of those museums in Paris devoted to individual artists. The works of this 19th-century sculptor are displayed inside and around a beautiful *hôtel* near the Invalides. Half-price Sunday; closed Monday. Métro: Varenne.

Musée National des Techniques France's national science museum; very interesting and enhanced by the setting in the old abbey of St-Martin-des-Champs, with a magnificent 13th-century refectory, and very early Gothic church housing old planes and cars. Half-price Sunday; closed Monday. Métro: Arts et Métiers.

La Villette Three canals were built on the north-eastern perimeter of Paris in the early 19th century as a reservoir to feed the fountains of the capital. For over a century from the 1860s, the land around them was the site of abattoirs and a vast meat market. In 1977 President Giscard d'Estaing initiated the conversion of an unfinished slaughterhouse building into a museum (referred to as a city) of science, technology and industry. In 1982 President Mitterrand extended the scheme to include the creation of the largest park in Paris, with a theatre, concert hall, exhibition centre (the 19th-century market hall) and a 'city of music' whose main ingredient is the Paris Conservatoire.

The Science and Industry building, reflected in the waters of its moat, is clearly related to the Pompidou Centre, with lifts giving views out over the park. The emphasis inside (where light is provided by two computer-controlled mobile domes) is on individual discovery by the visitor. There are audio visual displays, computer terminals to fiddle with and two special hands-on sections for children (3 to 6 and 6 to 12 year-olds). The main permanent display (Explora) is divided into four sections – life, the earth and space, raw materials and work, language and communication. There is also a planetarium and a very high-tech library (*le Médiathèque*).

The trade mark and star attraction of La Villette is La Géode, a polished steel sphere 36 metres in diameter, set in its own pool of water beside the Science and Industry building. The orb mirrors the surrounding skyscape and buildings, and houses in its top half a film projection chamber with a hemispherical screen and sound system that combine to produce an intense sensation of being enveloped by the projected image for a *'voyage spatio-temporel'*. Fortunately the film displayed (once an hour) is not of a disturbing nature. *Séances* are often sold out well in advance. Closed Monday. Métro: Porte de la Villette.

Churches

With a few notable exceptions, Paris is not a city that you remember for its churches – as you do Rome or Florence. Most visitors will want to see Notre-Dame – you can hardly avoid it – and the Sainte-Chapelle; and Paris has the best examples in France of church building after the Renaissance – which means little more than a few splendid domes, the most splendid of them all sheltering Napoleon's tomb. Several of the churches listed below close at lunchtime, and on certain days of the week; some are undergoing restoration. Enquire at the tourist office for up-to-date information.

Madeleine Built like a Greek temple with the Last Judgement on the pediment. According to the grand design of Napoleon, the Madeleine's colonnade is an admirable finish to the perspective which crosses the Place de la Concorde to the similar colonnade of the Chambre des Députés across the river. The domed interior is sumptuously decorated. Métro: Madeleine.

Notre-Dame A great Parisian landmark, and one of the great Gothic cathedrals in France. Superlative early Gothic sculpture around front and side doorways, atmospheric warm lighting within. It's well worth admiring the east end from the gardens behind. Frequent organ recitals. Métro: Cité.

Sainte-Chapelle After Notre-Dame, the church in Paris that everyone wants to visit. It's a Gothic chapel on the site of an old royal palace, now in the middle of the law courts; very small and often extremely crowded. The crypt-like lower floor for servants is distinguished by 19th-century repainting of glistering unpleasantness; the upper chapel is slender and uncomplicated, just a framework for stained glass of exceptional beauty. Entrance charge. Métro: Cité.

St-Denys-du-St-Sacrement A not very beautiful early 19th-century church in the Marais, but Delacroix's very powerful altar-piece of the *Pietà* is well displayed. Métro: St-Sébastien-Froissart.

St-Etienne-du-Mont A very unusual church with a jumbled classical façade dating from the early 17th century, and inside an exceptionally delicate Renaissance rood screen with spiral stairways around its pillars. Métro: Cardinale-Lemoine.

St-Eustache On the edge of the old Les Halles market, renamed the Temple of Agriculture in the Revolution. One of Paris's most impressive churches, a 16th- and 17th-century giant, built in the conventional Gothic way – with rose windows and flying buttresses – long after the style breathed its last vital gasp. Very good recitals. Métro: Halles.

St-Germain-l'Auxerrois Gracious Gothic and Renaissance royal parish church opposite the classical façade of the Louvre. Unwittingly, St-Germain bell ringers triggered off the massacre of St-Bartholomew's Day (24 August 1572) which started the wars of religion. The interior is much damaged and diminished in works of art but still of interest. Lovely Flemish altar-piece in the chapel on the left-hand side. Métro: Louvre.

St-Germain-des-Prés Paris's oldest surviving church, once part of a large abbey in the fields, now at the heart of one of the most colourful and attractive areas of the city. Romanesque tower and parts of the nave; varied works of art inside. Métro: St-Germain-des-Prés.

St-Gervais-St-Protais A late Gothic church built mostly in the 16th century with the first systematic classical façade in France. It was hit by a shell on Good Friday 1918 by a long-range German gun (Big Bertha); 50 people were killed. Very varied works of art inside. Recitals. Métro: Hôtel-de-Ville, Pont-Marie.

St-Julian-le-Pauvre Tiny, very old and charming, with an appropriately small garden giving a favourite view over Notre-Dame. Métro: St-Michel, Maubert-Mutualité.

St-Louis-en-l'Ile. A beautiful and harmonious late 17th-century gilt interior adorned with contemporary sculpture. Older works of art around the chapels. Métro: Pont-Marie.

St-Paul-St-Louis Built in the domed Jesuit style in the mid-17th century, a tall and imposing classical façade and some beautiful works of art inside including a 16th-century marble Virgin by Pilon. Métro: St-Paul.

St-Séverin A very Parisian Gothic church in that it grew in width because there was no land available for lengthy extension. There is an unusual, very pleasing double ambulatory, and a famous organ. Métro: St-Michel.

St-Sulpice Large and somewhat ponderous classical church containing exceptionally fine mural paintings by Delacroix in the first chapel on the right. Beautifully decorated Lady Chapel at the east end, and another famous organ. Métro: St-Sulpice.

Val-de-Grâce Architecturally distinguished domed mid-17th-century church built for Anne of Austria in thanksgiving for the birth of Louis XIV after 23 years of waiting. Inside, a museum of military medical history – the former abbey became a military hospital at the time of the Revolution. Métro: Port-Royal.

Cemeteries

Père-Lachaise A favourite and moody place for reflective Parisian perambulation, in a particularly gloomy part of town: lots of famous tombs (Abelard and Héloïse, Oscar Wilde, Edith Piaf) and a common one for 147 anonymous defenders of the Commune, whose resistance came to an end in the cemetery on 28 May 1871.

The **Montparnasse** and **Montmartre** cemeteries have other famous artists' and poets' tombs.

SHOPPING

Haute couture The most famous names are in the 8th *arrondissement*, around the Champs-Elysées – avenues Marigny, George V, Montaigne, Victor Hugo, and Faubourg St-Honoré. Don't assume that they're all inhospitable to the casual shopper – small items and accessories are sold too.

Prêt-à-porter Famous names (but slightly more accessible to the average consumer) are scattered throughout Paris, but several (Cacherel, Benetton, Ted Lapidus, Micmac) have boutiques in the new Forum des Halles centre, or in the Claridge centre in the Champs-Elysées. Another good hunting ground is the Boulevard St-Germain.

Jewellery The famous names are mainly around the Place Vendôme, Rue de la Paix and Faubourg St-Honoré; also Forum des Halles.

Boots and shoes Several good shops in Rue François Ier; also Forum des Halles, Boulevard St-Germain, and Rue du Faubourg St-Honoré.

Books Particularly numerous bookshops (of all sorts) in the 6th *arrondissement* (around the Boulevard St-Michel and Boulevard St-Germain).

Antiques Many in the 6th and 7th *arrondissements*, including Rue du Bac and Rue Bonaparte.

China, porcelain and glass The big names – including Christofle, and Lalique – can be found in the 8th *arrondissement* (Rue Royale); and the Rue de Paradis (10th) has no fewer than five good shops, including Baccarat for crystal.

Department stores Two of the largest and best are in the Boulevard Haussmann: Galeries Lafayette, and Au Printemps. La Samaritaine is by the Pont Neuf.

Food and wine The big names – including Fauchon, Fouquet, Hédiard and Michel Guérard's Comptoir Gourmand – are treasure troves of goodies, selling almost anything including foie gras, honey, cakes, chocolates, mustard, wine; they are concentrated in and near the Place de la Madeleine (8th *arrondissement*), where you will also find La Maison de la Truffe, and specialist cheese and wine shops. The Rue St-Louis-en-l'Ile has a good cheese shop, and one of Paris's best ice-cream makers, Berthillon. L'Herbier de Provence has several branches of its herb shops, including one in the Forum des Halles. For year-round (and daily) oysters, try Boutique Layrac in the Rue de Buci, which also has produce from several French regions.

Markets Eight different flea markets in the St-Ouen area around the Porte de Clignancourt (open Saturday, Sunday and Monday); others at the Porte de Montreuil, Porte de Vanves, Porte de Lilas, and Porte de Pantin. Popular and colourful food markets in the Rue Mouffetard (5th *arrondissement*) and the Rue de Buci (6th), and a large flower market on the Ile de la Cité.

INFORMATION

The main tourist office, Office de Tourisme, is at 127 avenue des Champs-Elysées, tel (1) 47 23 61 72.

RESTAURANTS

Most of the places recommended below offer a chance to see Paris at its most charming and traditional; in many the décor is particularly attractive (in some cases unchanged for decades). They are not the cheapest places that you can find to eat in the city, but they have been chosen because we feel they offer good value for money at their level. Unlike many other Parisian restaurants, most are open in August.

Key: prices are estimates for a three-course meal *à la carte*, excluding drinks. Most offer fixed-priced menus too, which may be available for lunch, late nights or weekdays only – these are much cheaper.

◆ = under 200FF
◆◆ = 200–300FF
◆◆◆ = over 300FF

The major credit cards are accepted in all the restaurants listed.

Brasseries

Something of a Parisian institution, these are places where you can eat (as well as drink) throughout most of the day and, in many cases, night. Brasseries are to be found on every street corner; some offer very simple fare (*croque-monsieur*, omelettes and *tartes*), others specialise in hearty stews or oysters. If you chance your luck, you may find yourself very disappointed in the food. Our selection features places where you can have a full meal, with a good selection of dishes, and above-average cooking; it also includes a few of Paris' most famous meeting places.

Le Boeuf sur le Toit

34 rue du Colisée, 8e
TEL (1) 43 59 83 80

Wonderfully atmospheric 1925 art deco décor – vast mirrors, lugubrious lighting, potted palms, brown seats and white cloths. Specialities are oysters, foie gras in various forms and *cassoulet d'oie*. Carafe wines and lots of half-bottles. Good service.

OPEN All year, daily, until 2am, exc. Christmas Eve METRO Franklin D. Roosevelt

Bofinger

5–7 rue de la Bastille, 4e
TEL (1) 42 72 87 82

Mirrors, stained glass and art deco lampshades characterise the interior of this restaurant, which lies on the edge of the Marais district. The menu is good value, especially at lunch when it stretches to three courses and a carafe of house wine. You'll find the service is professional and the ambience relaxed. An ideal place to recover from a morning's sightseeing.

OPEN All year, daily METRO Bastille

Brasserie Flo

7 cour des Petites-Ecuries, 10e
TEL (1) 47 70 13 59

See La Coupole for details. Brasserie Flo serves beer from the barrel.

OPEN All year, daily, until 2am, exc. Christmas Eve METRO Château d'Eau

Chez Francis

7 place de l'Alma, 8e
TEL (1) 47 20 86 83

A celebrated and long-established brasserie on the busy riverside crossroads where the brass of the Avenue George V meets the elegance and culture of the Avenue Montaigne. Chez Francis is at its best at midday, when journalists and editors, publishers and authors, pressurised businessmen and their lunchtime ladies come together to discuss animatedly their various affairs while bow-tied old gentlemen occupy their daily tables in dignified solitude. The décor has been restored to marvellous effect, with intimate bedside lamps on the tables and butterfly lights overhead casting a warm golden glow over the interior and receding towards infinity in the smoky looking-glass walls, which are ideal for not-too-obvious spectating. Should you prefer to watch street life, there are also tables on the front terrace. The army of black and white uniformed staff is attentive, friendly and very efficient, and the place positively hums. Expect impeccably prepared dishes as classically simple as a starched white shirt. There are plenty of tempting wines, but few bottles for under 100FF.

OPEN All year, daily, until 1am METRO Alma-Marceau

La Coupole

102 boulevard du Montparnasse, 14e
TEL (1) 43 20 14 20

This is one of Paris' largest brasseries – it seats 600 people – and part of the Flo group, whose hallmarks are wonderfully atmospheric décors, seafood special-ities, house foie gras and *choucroute*. They are extremely popular – you may have to queue for a table and you should not expect peace and quiet. Look out for the good-value fixed-price menus. See also Le Boeuf sur le Toit, Brasserie Flo, Julien and Le Vaudeville.

OPEN All year, daily, until 2am, exc. Christmas Eve METRO Vavin

Julien

16 rue du Faubourg-St-Denis, 10e
TEL (1) 47 70 12 06

Under the same ownership as Le Boeuf sur le Toit, and with similar food but with a very different style – authentic art nouveau décor dating from 1890 (tiles, murals, mirrors), and a very Parisian atmosphere. The clientele is largely local and sedate, and the brasserie with its formally dressed waiters seems a haven of respectability in this seedy street of shops and kebab houses at the edge of the 'red light' area. Specialities include oysters, foie gras and *cassoulet d'oie*.

OPEN All year, daily, until 1.30am, exc. Christmas Eve METRO Strasbourg St-Denis

Lipp

151 boulevard St-Germain, 6e
TEL (1) 45 48 53 91

Perhaps the most famous brasserie of them all, Lipp is an institution which does not need to re-create its décor or its style, for these have resolutely stood the test of time: the clock here stands at 1900, the (mostly) elderly waiters have impeccable haircuts and are courteous, and among the many faded notices exhorting you to do this, that and the other, you might reasonably expect one requesting you not to spit. Specialities include *cervelas rémoulade, harengs 'Bismarck'* and *choucroute garni*; there's a dish of the day (if it's Tuesday it's *blanquette de veau*), and simple desserts including *tartes* and *crème caramel*. There are few frills, but the cooking is wholesome and portions are hearty.

OPEN All year, daily, until 2am, exc. Christmas and 4 weeks Jul/Aug METRO St-Germain-des-Prés

Lutétia

23 rue de Sèvres, 6e
TEL (1) 49 54 46 76

On a major Left Bank crossroads, this air-conditioned modern brasserie – all chrome and glass, echoing the traditional brasserie style – forms part of the Hôtel Lutétia. It's a bustling place, popular at lunch, with a central bar and covered pavement-terrace area. Specialities include *terrine de lapereau en gêlée, andouillette*, American-style rib-eye steak, and some fine tarts and other desserts; there are plenty of fish and meat dishes, and several *plats du jour*.

OPEN All year, daily, from noon to midnight METRO Sèvres-Babylone

Le Muniche

5–7 rue de la Bastille, 4e
TEL (1) 46 33 62 09

This stalwart of the Parisian brasserie scene moved in 1991 to new premises. The décor is more appropriate to its reputation – Belle Epoque, with mirrors everywhere. It specialises in wonderfully fresh oysters and in hearty country dishes, including *choucroute*. There is a good three-course menu for 140FF.

OPEN Daily, until 2am METRO St-Germain-des-Prés

Le Pavillon Baltard

9 rue Coquillière, 1er
TEL (1) 42 36 22 00

A former butcher's shop by the old Halles market, this brasserie has been completely revamped – as indeed has the entire neighbourhood. There's a pavement terrace area with sunshades, a bar, and stylish and jolly modern 'farmhouse' décor inside. This place specialises in all sorts of fine *choucroutes*, including one made with three types of fish; you can also have *confit*, *andouillettes* and, of course, oysters.

OPEN All year, daily, until 1am METRO Les Halles

Le Petit Zinc

11 rue St Benoît, 6e
TEL (1) 47 34 01 13

Like Le Muniche (q.v.), this brasserie is in the heart of St-Germain-des-Prés and is run by the Layrac family, specialising in oysters and seafood. The décor is wonderful turn-of-the-century. It is popular with the after-theatre crowd – you should always book.

OPEN All year, daily, until 2am METRO St-Germain-des-Prés

Le Procope

13 rue de l'Ancienne Comédie, 6e
TEL (1) 43 26 99 20

This claims to be the oldest café in the world – it was opened in 1686 – and has been a haunt of famous figures for three hundred years. A list of Procope's regulars doubles as a manual of required authors for literary study – La Fontaine, Racine, Voltaire (his desk remains), Rousseau, Diderot, Balzac, Hugo, Verlaine; and Robespierre, Danton and Marat are said to have hatched a few ideas here. The décor is partly authentic and delightful, with painted wood panelling, mirrors and gilt. There are a couple of bars where you can wait for a table (it's heavily booked) and read a paper while listening to a jolly duo, or a lone pianola. With all the activity, it comes as something of a surprise to find that the food is good – straightforward classic dishes, well prepared.

OPEN All year, daily, 8am to 1am METRO Odéon

Le Vaudeville

29 rue Vivienne, 2e
TEL (1) 40 20 04 62

See La Coupole. Le Vaudeville is opposite the Bourse and has Egyptian-style décor.

OPEN All year, daily, until 2am, exc. Christmas Eve METRO Bourse

Restaurants

L'Amanguier ◆

110 rue de Richelieu, 2e
TEL (1) 42 96 37 79

This is the most central outlet of this chain of straightforward, inexpensive, ungimmicky, efficient modern restaurants (the others are at 51 rue du Théâtre, 15e; 43 avenue des Ternes, 17e; 12 avenue de Madrid, 92200 Neuilly). Set back on a courtyard off one of the main axes in the businesslike *quartier* between the Opéra, the Bourse and the Bibliothèque Nationale, l'Amanguier occupies two floors, with a sub-tropical decorative scheme of jungle greens and ocean blues. There is nothing exotic about the food but it is mostly good and well priced. If you reserve, remember to specify which Amanguier you mean – the telephone number is a communal one.

OPEN All year, daily, until midnight METRO Pyramides

Armand

6 rue de Beaujolais, 1er
TEL (1) 42 60 05 11

The golden columns echo those of the Palais Royal just in front, the low stone-vaulted ceiling is lit to perfection, the closely packed tables are beautifully dressed with creamy-gold linen and fine table ware; add to this an elegant clientele, and you have a fine *ambiance*, particularly at night. The short *carte* offers some light and creative dishes (*soufflé de légumes et son coulis aux poireaux, émincé de saumon mariné au gingembre*), which average 130FF a dish; there's a three-course fixed-price menu for less than 170FF, as well as a fuller lunch menu with several choices for under 250FF.

OPEN Daily exc. Sat lunch and Sun; closed last two weeks Aug; dinner until 10.30pm METRO Pyramides

Le Belier

13 rue des Beaux-Arts, 6e
TEL (1) 43 25 27 22

This eccentric restaurant is in fact a hotel dining-room – that of L'Hôtel, made famous by Oscar Wilde. It's enormously atmospheric – with a décor which incorporates a fish pond and fountain, vast flower arrangements and an enormous brooding owl; there's a piano bar to one side. While tables are well spaced, it's not meant to be intimate – you come here to be seen (or if you don't, at least you should be entertained by everyone else). In this atmosphere, you hardly expect the food to be good value – but it is, particularly on the fixed-price menu at 170FF, and *carte* dishes are much less expensive than in many restaurants of its class. The cooking is reasonable enough: some dishes are not wildly exciting, but others are flavoursome (*filet de rascasse en bourride, gigotin de lotte aux épices, le rôti d'agneau en crépine*).

OPEN All year, daily; dinner until midnight METRO St-Germain-des-Prés

Le Bourdonnais

113 avenue de la Bourdonnais, 7e
TEL (1) 47 05 47 96

In a dull residential and business quarter near the Invalides, this quietly elegant and sophisticated place – decorated in salmon tones with *objets* and flowers – is in fact a hotel dining-room. It has long had a name for good service, and for the charm of its owner, Micheline Coat; but the reason for coming here is for the excellent cooking of young Philippe Bardau. If your gastronomic aspirations are at a higher level than your finances, come to lunch – where there is a very good-value three-course fixed-price menu for 220FF (including wine). If, on the other hand, you are feeling expansive, go for the seven-course *menu dégustation*, or perhaps simply a couple of dishes on the *carte – mille-feuille de saumon au cerfeuil*, or *gêlée de joue de boeuf*.

OPEN All year, daily; dinner until 10.30pm METRO Ecole-Militaire

La Bûcherie

41 rue de la Bûcherie, 5e
TEL (1) 43 54 78 06

From the front tables here you'll have a superb view of Notre-Dame. The décor is sophisticated – tapestries by Lurçat, contemporary paintings and a blazing fire in the hearth in winter. The cooking is good and classical with no frills. A set menu at 220 FF includes wine. The selection of Bordeaux wines is huge.

OPEN All year, daily, until 12.30am METRO Maubert-Mutualité

Le Caveau du Palais

19 place Dauphine, 1er
TEL (1) 43 26 04 28

There are few better addresses in Paris than the Place Dauphine, a haven of residential calm at the sharp end of the Ile de la Cité, as easily walkable for shoppers and sightseers on the right bank as it is for those staying on the other side of the river around St-Germain-des-Prés. Le Caveau is a friendly and straightforward local *bistrot* with beamed rooms on two rather cramped floors, the upper one with a pronounced list. There is no fixed-price menu, merely a wide-ranging *carte* of familiar classical dishes and grillings.

OPEN All year, exc. two weeks end Dec; weekdays only, plus Sats June to Sept until 10.30pm METRO Pont Neuf

Aux Charpentiers

10 rue Mabillon, 6e
TEL (1) 43 26 30 05

Hidden down a side street near St-Sulpice church, this little bistro is a gem. You'll find no pretensions here – substantial meals are efficiently served in a yellow-painted dining room by aproned waiters. Diners sit on simple wooden chairs pulled up to white-clothed tables. Through double doors, you can see the cooks preparing wholesome dishes of the day like *veau marengo* (a hearty stew). The no-choice menu changes daily.

OPEN All year, daily, exc. Sun and public hols, until 11.30pm METRO Mabillon

Dodin-Bouffant

25 rue Frédéric Sauton, 5e
TEL (1) 43 25 25 14

An elegant and comfortable *Rive Gauche* restaurant where the set menu at 200FF (lunch and dinner) is very good value indeed. The carte dishes include foie gras, fish, fresh seafood (oysters, mussels and others wait in large tanks in the cellar), and game in season.

OPEN All year, daily, exc. Sun, until 11pm; closed Aug and last week Dec METRO Maubert-Mutualité

La Ferme St-Simon

6 rue de St-Simon, 7e
TEL (1) 45 48 35 74

A stone's throw from the Assemblée Nationale, this elegant small establishment serves as a lunchtime canteen for politicians, and a more lively gathering place in the evening. The décor is a mixture of mock-rustic and sophistication – beams and mirrors, Flemish-style still-life paintings, trailing greenery and trellises in the tiny 'garden room'; the lighting is amber and mellow, tables packed very closely together. It's not the place for an intimate *diner à deux* or a family row. The cooking is very good – combining light and inventive creations with 'old-style' dishes. The desserts are particularly innovative. The damage to your pocket will be less if you choose to join the politicians at lunch – there's a fixed-price menu for 170FF.

OPEN All year exc. first 3 weeks in August, Sat lunch, and Sun METRO Rue du Bac

La Guirlande de Julie

25 place des Vosges, 3e
TEL (1) 48 87 94 07

Now that the social hub of 17th-century Paris has been restored and is once more a fashionable place to be seen, one expects to pay for the address underneath the arches of the Place des Vosges. But there is no question of falling into a well-laid tourist trap in what is the most modest of a trio of distinguished restaurants (the others are Coconnas, also on the Place des Vosges, and the famous Tour d'Argent) under common ownership. This is a cheerful and informal pink and green place, with a playful décor of arbours and trellises and painted brickwork.

In the division of responsibilities Coconnas handles *nouvelle cuisine* and the Tour d'Argent unalloyed grandeur, leaving the Guirlande to look after *la cuisine du terroir*, which means honest country cooking.

OPEN All year exc. Christmas to late Jan, daily until 10pm METRO Bastille

Jamin

32 rue de Longchamp, 16e
TEL (1) 47 27 12 27

To quote our last edition: 'This is Joël Robuchon's place, and his name is engraved on the hearts of every true gastronome'. As we went to press, the news broke out that Robuchon has left Jamin.

OPEN All year exc. July, Mon to Fri only METRO Trocadéro

La Fermette Marbeuf 1900

5 rue Marbeuf, 8e
TEL (1) 47 23 31 31

In an extraordinary, authentic Belle Epoque décor (discovered only in 1978, when the 1950s plastic cladding was disturbed) this is a restaurant which is extremely popular, partly because of the charm of the art nouveau surroundings – cast-iron pillars, stained glass windows, tiles – and partly because the food is good. There's a small *carte*, with standard dishes such as grills, steak tartare, bouillabaisse, *andouillette* and sweetbreads, and fancier dishes. Best of all, there's a very good-value fixed-price four-course menu for 160FF.

OPEN All year, daily, until 11.30pm METRO Franklin D. Roosevelt

Pharamond

24 rue de la Grande Truanderie, 1er
TEL (1) 42 33 06 72

The Halles are no more, but Pharamond soldiers on. Now surrounded by the innumerable cafés and bars, brasseries and restaurants that vie for tourist custom in this newly created pedestrianised shopping area, Pharamond remains true to its ideals, and the faithful continue to come. There is no better place in Paris for *tripe à la mode de Caen*, accompanied by a fine *cidre Vallée d'Auge*, perhaps; and other dishes are good, too. The décor is authentic Belle Epoque (fine ceramic tiles, mirrors), the atmosphere jolly (bench seating around the smallish room). There is a terrace in front.

OPEN All year, daily exc. Sun, and Mon lunch METRO Châtelet-Les Halles

Thoumieux

79 rue St-Dominique, 7e
TEL (1) 47 05 49 75

Opened in 1920, this restaurant has changed little in its style – not so much in terms of décor, but in the type of cooking, which is hearty *bistrot* fare, specialising in Corrèze dishes. It is understandably a popular place, and the bustling atmosphere is reminiscent of a brasserie; yet it is in fact a hotel dining room. You can take a simple three-course fixed-price menu for 60FF (*carottes râpées* or *pâté, côte de porc grillée flageolets* or *poulet rôti*, cheese or pudding), you can choose similar dishes off the *carte* for little more, or you can opt for slightly more expensive fare, including plenty of good country dishes such as *gratons 'maison'*, *rillettes de canard* or *raie au poivre vert*. The house wines are cheap and good. This is a thoroughly well-run establishment, where the cooking is well above average in its class.

OPEN All year, daily METRO La Tour Maubourg

HOTELS

> Key: ◆ = 0–250FF, ◆◆ = 251–450FF, ◆◆◆ = over 451FF; prices are per double room without breakfast, which costs around 35–60FF extra. Some hotels may insist on half-board during high season, some hotels or restaurants may close at specific times during the week – it is always worth checking. Most hotels accept the major credit cards; we have indicated where a hotel takes no credit cards.

Agora St-Germain

42 rue des Bernardins
75005, 5e
TEL (1) 46 34 13 00; FAX (1) 46 34 75 05

On a side street close to Maubert-Mutualité métro stop this is a small functional hotel within easy reach of the *quais* and the Panthéon. Bedrooms are reasonably small but neat, with muted colour schemes. Breakfast of fresh orange juice and warm croissants is served in the basement breakfast room, with high-backed tapestry-effect chairs and exposed stone walls. The small reception lounge is more of a waiting room than a restful space, with a TV and magazines to pass the time.

OPEN All year ROOMS 39 (all with bath or shower) METRO Maubert-Mutualité

Des Arènes

51 rue Monge
75005, 5e
TEL (1) 43 25 09 26; FAX (1) 43 25 79 46

This substantial 19th-century building is in a suburban street a little way away from the activity of St-Germain-des-Prés. Rooms to the rear are spacious and some have views over the ancient Lutetia amphitheatre. Provençal-style prints in dull pinks and a mix of brown and orange décor are the style in bedrooms, whilst the limited public areas are more flamboyant. Package prices through tour operators can be reasonable.

OPEN All year ROOMS 50 (all with bath) METRO Cardinal-Lemoine/Monge/Jussieu

Bastille Speria

1 rue de la Bastille
75004, 4e
TEL (1) 42 72 04 01; FAX (1) 42 72 56 38

A small modern hotel in an excellent position at the eastern end of the Marais, just a couple of minutes from the Place de la Bastille and beside the well-known

Brasserie Bofinger. The open-plan ground floor, incorporating the reception, a lounge area and breakfast tables, is in light greys and blacks, partitioned by pot plants and with a tropical fish tank and lots of modern prints and photos to provide interest. Rooms are well equipped and functional with geometric designs on curtains and bedcovers co-ordinating with colour scheme⸱.

OPEN All year ROOMS 42 (all with bath) METRO Bastille

Beaubourg

11 rue Simon Le Franc
75004, 4e
TEL (1) 42 74 34 24; FAX (1) 42 78 68 11

As its name suggests, this hotel is very convenient for exploring the Georges Pompidou centre and Beaubourg, and the Marais area is close by too. It is a neat town-house hotel dating back to the 1600s, but only traces of that period remain. Beams and exposed stonework contrast with soft settees and glass-topped coffee tables, and the bedrooms are reasonably sized with stylish, floral décor.

OPEN All year ROOMS 28 (all with bath or shower) METRO Rambuteau

Hôtel du Bois

11 rue du Dôme
75116, 16e
TEL (1) 45 00 37 96; FAX (1) 45 00 90 05

Close to Place Charles de Gaulle, this small, good-value hotel is on a quietish pedestrianised side street off the busy up-market shopping area on avenue Victor Hugo. The attractive white 19th-century building has colourful window-boxes, and a flight of steps leads up to the entrance. The small seating and breakfast area has simple pine furnishings and Paisley wallpapers; the overall effect is light and cheerful. Bedrooms are spacious and airy with floral fabrics. The atmosphere is relaxed and friendly.

OPEN All year ROOMS 41 (all with bath or shower) METRO Etoile/Kléber

Hôtel de la Bretonnerie

22 rue Ste-Croix-de-la-Bretonnerie
75004, 4e
TEL (1) 48 87 77 63; FAX (1) 42 77 26 78

In a lively street at the western (Beaubourg) end of the Marais, with a café-théâtre and plenty of cheap *bistrots*, this 17th-century house has been skilfully transformed into a hotel of charm and character. Sturdy old beams (mind your head) and rough stone walls set the tone; solid period furniture and gentle lighting add to the atmosphere. Your bedroom may be split-level, or tucked under sloping eaves; a process of refurbishment ensures rooms are prettily decorated, and there's nothing antique about the bathrooms. Breakfast is taken in the handsome vaulted cellar. No restaurant.

OPEN All year exc. August ROOMS 30 (all with bath) METRO Hôtel de Ville

Des Célestins

1 rue Charles V
75004, 4e
TEL (1) 48 87 87 04; FAX (1) 48 87 33 26

Set on a quiet corner in the Marais district, this small family-run hotel feels personally welcoming. There's no lounge, bar, or restaurant room (though soft drinks, tea and coffee are available) – only a small reception area; there's no lift, and the ancient staircase is gently sloping. The characterful house, with its many beams, dates from 1623; many of the bedrooms have tiled floors and are small. This little hotel is good value – as British visitors have already discovered.

OPEN All year ROOMS 15 (all with bath or shower) (Credit cards not accepted) METRO Sully-Morland/Bastille

Hôtel des Deux Iles

59 rue St-Louis-en-l'Ile
75004, 4e
TEL (1) 43 26 13 35; FAX (1) 43 29 60 25

Anywhere on the Ile-St-Louis is a prime location for visiting Paris, and this stylish hotel is well placed on an attractive road with lots of boutiques and restaurants around. The 17th-century house is imaginatively decorated with antiques combined with tiled floors, hessian-covered walls, soft lighting and fresh flowers. The bedrooms are cosy too and, whilst space is limited, provençal fabrics and smart blue-and-white tiled bathrooms make them an attractive choice. Book early.

OPEN All year ROOMS 17 (all with bath or shower) (Credit cards not accepted) METRO Pont-Marie

Ducs d'Anjou

1 rue Ste-Opportune
75001, 1e
TEL (1) 42 36 92 54; FAX (1) 42 36 16 63

On a pedestrianised street within the Les Halles shopping area the Ducs d'Anjou is ideally placed for a weekend shopping or visiting exhibitions in the nearby Georges Pompidou Centre. The décor is fresh and modern with a marble floor, and aluminium and leather-like 50s-style chairs and uplighters in the uncluttered reception lounge. Bedrooms are less distinctive but modern, bright and comfortable. Breakfast is taken in the vaulted basement room.

OPEN All year ROOMS 38 (all with bath or shower) METRO Châtelet

Esméralda

4 rue St-Julien-le-Pauvre
75005, 5e
TEL (1) 43 54 19 20; FAX (1) 40 51 00 68

This small Left Bank hotel, opposite a green square near Notre-Dame, dates from the 17th century, but is smart outside. The interior is slightly eccentric – the reception area is a delightful cluster of antiques, worn velvet and riotous plants. There is no lounge, but a small light breakfast room. Bedrooms have an old-fashioned *boudoir* flavour – low hanging lamps and plush velvet – but they're rather small and dark. Bathrooms vary from good modern to tiny. Some street noise filters up. There is no lift or restaurant.

OPEN All year ROOMS 19 (16 with bath) (Credit cards not accepted) METRO St-Michel

Hôtel des Grandes Ecoles

75 rue Cardinal Lemoine
75005, 5e
TEL (1) 43 26 79 23; FAX (1) 43 25 28 15

Well worth searching out, this delightful garden hotel is in a quiet position along a lane behind wooden gates in the area between the Panthéon and the Sorbonne. The attractive creamy pink house, with shutters and a terrace and garden shaded by mature trees, is a perfect retreat from midsummer heat. A simple, old-fashioned hotel with wooden floors, it has a small breakfast room, where tables have lace cloths. Bedrooms are fresh and pretty with lots of floral-design fabrics and wallpaper. Some rooms are in the annexe across the garden.

OPEN All year ROOMS 34 (all with bath or shower) METRO Cardinal Lemoine/Monge

Hôtel de Lutèce

65 rue St-Louis-en-l'Ile
75004, 4e
TEL (1) 43 26 23 52; FAX (1) 43 29 60 25

The quiet but central Ile St-Louis is one of the best places to stay in Paris, and the Lutèce lies near its sister hotel, the Deux Iles, among enticing shops and boutiques. Since there is no outside courtyard to enjoy in good weather, this hotel is better as a cosy retreat when the weather is chilly. The interior exudes charm – flagstoned floors, large open fireplace and beamed ceiling – and the bedrooms are small but welcoming and cheerfully co-ordinated in bold colours. Ask for a room at the back, since those at the front can be disturbed by high-spirited revellers in the early hours, despite double-glazing.

OPEN All year ROOMS 23 (all with bath or shower) (Credit cards not accepted) METRO Pont-Marie

Des Marronniers

21 rue Jacob
75006, 6e
TEL (1) 43 25 30 60; FAX (1) 40 46 83 56

Set back from the road in the heart of St-Germain-des-Prés, this popular small hotel needs to be booked well in advance. Reasonably priced, the rooms here are quite basic with old-fashioned furnishings and some signs of wear and tear. Public rooms, though, are cheerful with a breakfast room overlooking the garden and an interior salon, all overseen by an easy-going proprietor.

OPEN All year ROOMS 37 (all with bath or shower) (Credit cards not accepted) METRO St-Germain-des-Prés

Molière

21 rue Molière
75001, 1e
TEL (1) 42 96 22 01; FAX (1) 42 60 48 68

This immaculately kept hotel is close to the Opéra. The spacious rooms have period charm, though public areas, which are smartly decorated, lack atmosphere. The ground floor breakfast room is done out in pinks and greens with a window overlooking a courtyard.

OPEN All year ROOMS 32 (all with bath or shower) METRO Pyramides

Hôtel de Noailles

9 rue de la Michodière
75002, 2e
TEL (1) 47 42 92 90; FAX (1) 49 24 92 71

This is a high-tech designer hotel in a commercial side street near to the Opéra. Matt black and aluminium, leather sofas and smoked-glass tables reflect the style in uncluttered rooms, where a youngish clientele in designer clothes predominate. Bedrooms have all modern comforts and are equally stylish.

OPEN All year ROOMS 58 (all with bath or shower) METRO Quatre Septembre/Opéra

Hôtel de la Place des Vosges

12 rue de Birague
75004, 4e
TEL (1) 42 72 60 46; FAX (1) 42 72 02 64

On a pretty street close to one of the most attractive squares in Paris and in the midst of the Marais, this is a reasonable budget choice. Rooms may have seen better days but are clean, if a little scuffed. An L-shaped room on the ground floor, with heavy wooden beams and dark striped wallpaper, is the setting for breakfast.

OPEN All year ROOMS 16 (all with bath or shower) METRO St-Paul/Bastille

Hôtel Prima Lepic

29 rue Lepic
75018, 18e
TEL (1) 46 06 44 64; FAX (1) 46 06 66 11

Cheap and cheerful, the Prima Lepic is a 15-minute hike to Sacré-Coeur and the artists' haven at Place du Tertre. Lively street scenes are daubed on the wall of the small lounge and a rose arbour mural plus white wrought-iron chairs and tables in the windowless breakfast room give the impression that you are in a verdant garden. Bedrooms are of the high-ceiling, flowery wallpaper and mismatched furniture type – perfectly adequate but far from luxurious.

OPEN All year ROOMS 38 (all with bath or shower) METRO Blanche/Abbesses

Hôtel Prince Albert

5 rue St-Hyacinthe
75001, 1e
TEL (1) 42 61 58 36; FAX (1) 42 60 04 06

In spite of its proximity to the bustling shopping street of rue St-Honoré, this is a surprisingly peaceful position. Unmodernised and with a mix of generally dated furnishings, the hotel has an old-fashioned feel, though this is reflected in the price.

OPEN All year ROOMS 30 (all with bath or shower) METRO Tuileries/Pyramides

Récamier ◆ ◆ ◆

3 Bis place St-Sulpice
75006, 6e
TEL (1) 43 26 04 89

Squeezed into a corner of one of St-Germain's leafy squares, the Récamier is an intimate, genteel hotel with well-priced rooms. There are two small reception rooms on the ground floor – one doubling as a breakfast room with goldfish tank and flowery wallpaper. Breakfast comes included in the price, although you might prefer to opt for a hot drink and snack at one of the corner cafés nearby as the hotel fare is plain. Bedrooms are simple and clean; they have candlewick bedspreads, old-fashioned plumbing and more of the ubiquitous flowery wallpaper. Those overlooking the square are the nicest.

OPEN All year ROOMS 30 (23 with bath or shower) METRO St-Sulpice

Regent's Garden

6 rue Pierre Demours
75017, 17e
TEL (1) 45 74 07 30; FAX (1) 40 55 01 42

Set back from a quiet residential street a few minutes' walk from the Arc de Triomphe, this fine 19th-century townhouse was built for Napoleon III's physician. Rear windows open on to its pretty garden with tall trees, flowers and statues and scattered tables for summer breakfasts. Inside, handsome public spaces are furnished in-period, though some freshening up of paintwork and soft furnishings was planned on our last visit. Bedrooms vary (some are enormous) and though a few have been redecorated others require attention.

OPEN All year ROOMS 39 (all with bath) METRO Ternes/Etoile

Résidence du Globe

15 rue des Quatre-Vents
75006, 6e
TEL (1) 43 26 35 50

This is a 17th-century St-Germain house, where all the rooms are small, personal and completely charming. Past the discreet reception desk the ground-floor lounge is adorned with antiques, massed paintings and a suit of armour; the tiny bedrooms and bathrooms under the old beams have rugs and hangings, assorted pretty furniture and more paintings. Breakfast and drinks are served in your room, and a thoroughly intimate atmosphere prevails. No restaurant.

OPEN All year exc. Aug ROOMS 15 (14 with bath or shower) (Credit cards not accepted) METRO Odéon

Hôtel Résidence Lord Byron

5 rue de Chateaubriand
75008, 8e
TEL (1) 43 59 89 98; FAX (1) 42 89 46 04

This elegant hotel is in a quiet street about ten minutes' walk from the Arc de Triomphe. With a garden terrace, salon and breakfast room it has a little more public space than most comparable small hotels in this price range. Junior suites have swathes of fabrics framing windows and dramatic colour schemes. Other bedrooms are less elaborate with simple furnishings, but bathrooms are all modern and a good size.

OPEN All year ROOMS 31 (all with bath or shower) METRO George V

Riboutté-Lafayette

5 rue Riboutté
75009, 9e
TEL (1) 47 70 62 36; FAX (1) 48 00 91 50

Off the rue Lafayette in an area convenient for department stores, nightlife and the main railway stations, this hotel has been recently refurbished inside. The small reception and lounge area is light and bright. Bedrooms are generally reasonably sized (those on the top floor are smaller); they are friendly and colourful, with new modern bath and shower rooms. Quiet and good value. No restaurant.

OPEN All year ROOMS 24 (all with bath or shower) METRO Cadet

St-Germain

88 rue du Bac
75007, 7e
TEL (1) 45 48 62 92; FAX (1) 45 48 26 89

On a lively street with delicatessens, cafés and restaurants and some good shopping nearby, this hotel has an appealing reception lounge with white walls hung with tapestries, antiques and soft lighting, combined with cleverly placed mirrors, which give an impression of space.

OPEN All year ROOMS 29 (all with bath or shower) METRO Rue du Bac

Hôtel St-Louis

75 rue St-Louis-en-l'Ile
75004, 4e
TEL (1) 46 34 04 80; FAX (1) 46 34 02 13

This small welcoming hotel is on the island's high street. Reasonably priced for the location, it has a small sitting space in the attractive reception area with tiled floor and hessian-weave wall-coverings and a pretty vaulted breakfast room. Bedrooms lack individual charm but are well kept.

OPEN All year ROOMS 21 (all with bath or shower) (Credit cards not accepted) METRO Pont-Marie

---

Key: ♦ = 0–250FF, ♦♦ = 251–450FF, ♦♦♦ = over 451FF; prices are per double room without breakfast, which costs around 35–60FF extra. Some hotels may insist on half-board during high season, some hotels or restaurants may close at specific times during the week – it is always worth checking. Most hotels accept the major credit cards; we have indicated where a hotel takes no credit cards.

Hôtel Solférino

91 rue de Lille
75007, 7e
TEL (1) 47 05 85 54; FAX (1) 45 55 51 16

Convenient for the Musée d'Orsay, this hotel is comfortable and clean, but a little bland. The pretty breakfast room with lots of French china displayed on the walls has a cheerful air. Bedrooms are well equipped and comfortable, with fitted reproduction Regency-style furnishings.

OPEN Early Jan to mid-Dec ROOMS 32 (28 with bath or shower) METRO Solférino/Assemblée Nationale

Tiquetonne ◆

6 rue Tiquetonne
75002, 2e
TEL (1) 42 36 94 58

In a narrow street between Les Halles and the Marais, this is a well-placed budget option. The family-run hotel with exuberant marble-effect paintwork throughout has a collection of dated furnishings, with some curious items amongst them. Bedrooms are fairly basic, and most have showers only, but the price is good value for such a central position.

OPEN All year exc. Aug & 1 week Feb ROOMS 47 (32 with shower) (Credit cards not accepted) METRO Étienne-Marcel/Réaumur-Sébastopol

Château de Versailles

La gloire est le soleil des morts
[Balzac]

THE ILE-DE-FRANCE

The Ile-de-France, original land of the Franks and cradle of the monarchy, is one of the sightseeing treasure grounds of France; yet few visitors to Paris bother to venture beyond the gates of the capital which it surrounds. From the point of view of the tourist, the Ile-de-France may be compared with the Loire valley. It may not have the river, nor the wine, nor the regional identity; but it does have châteaux great and small. Although these don't look like illustrations in a book of fairy stories, they're more rewarding to visit, for in general their contents are more lavish and their historical interest more varied.

After a short half-century of royal château building in the Loire (something of a playful period of recuperation after the long suffering of the Hundred Years' War) the kings of France inevitably moved back to the Ile-de-France, whence they had been banished by the English and Burgundians. At Fontainebleau, François I created a court for himself in a new style, and later kings added St-Germain-en-Laye and eventually Versailles, Compiègne and Rambouillet to the list – all royal palaces within range of and not too close to Paris, a compromise between hunting pursuits and administrative convenience. In these royal châteaux and in the no less interesting ones built by royal servants and the nobility, the full development of French history, architecture, painting, furniture, garden and park design – in short, taste – from the middle of the 16th century until the late 19th century is on display as nowhere else. In addition to this wealth of châteaux, the Ile-de-France has some of the finest examples of the Gothic style of architecture, first convincingly put into stone and glass by Louis VI's versatile adviser, Abbot Suger, in the church of St-Denis. Chartres and Beauvais can claim perhaps the most beautiful and certainly the most extreme realisations of the style.

The countryside of the Ile-de-France is attractive, and to the beauty of the landscape is added the pleasure of seeing it through the eyes of 19th-century painters. It was then that landscape painting became fashionable, and artists abandoning Paris found the rivers, poplars and

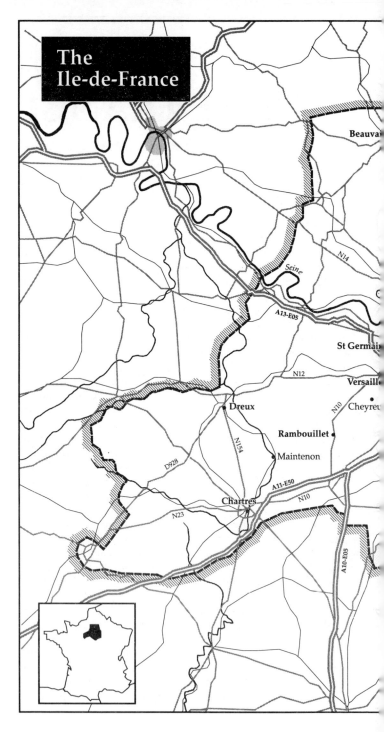

The
Ile-de-France

Beauvai

Seine

N14

A13-E05

St Germai

N12

Versaill

N10

Dreux

Cheyreu

Rambouillet

N154

Maintenon

D928

A11-E50

N10

Chartres

N23

A10-E05

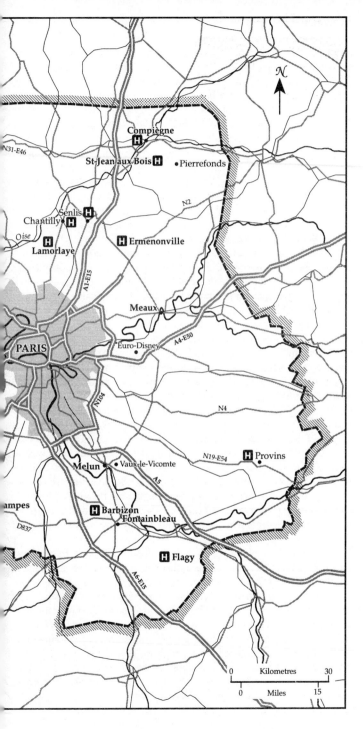

forests of the Ile-de-France waiting for them. Impressionists loved to paint Parisians at leisure in the then countrified surroundings of the Seine (now swamped by the westward growth of Paris). Monet – who was more interested in pure landscape – went to the Epte, others to the Oise. The Barbizon school has even stronger links with a particular area: the Fontainebleau forest. More than the Impressionists who came after them, Fontainebleau artists were landscape painters in the tradition of the Dutch 17th-century masters, relishing the chiaroscuro light effects of the forests and the images of everyday peasant life. The forests of Chantilly, Fontainebleau, Compiègne, and Rambouillet – which attracted the French kings (and more recent rulers) as the forest of Chambord did in the Loire – have now been preserved from destruction, and count among the Ile-de-France's greatest attractions.

The Ile-de-France has changed, of course; some would say it is becoming Greater Paris. But by comparison with London at least, it does not give this impression. The city of Paris is very densely populated, and commuting from the Ile-de-France happens on only a relatively small scale. Recent decentralisation has resulted in a few industrial new towns on the edge of Pontoise and Meaux, for example, and the extension of the Métro (the Réseau Express Régional, RER) has been accompanied by the growth of a few new residential communities in the countryside; but these remain fairly isolated and the Ile-de-France is – apart from weekend tourism – remarkably little affected by Paris. The area is in no way neglected by Parisians, however. Nowadays, nature, fresh air and healthy outdoor pursuits are seen as an antidote to the stresses of modern city life, and especially Parisian life, and have become a serious and indeed worrisome preoccupation of the city dwellers. The gates of Paris on Friday evenings, Saturday mornings and Sunday evenings are the scenes of such horrific traffic jams that Parisians on their way to weekends in the country must wonder whether a weekend in Paris would not after all be more relaxing. At weekends the woods, rivers and châteaux are packed with day-trippers. But during the week the area is comparatively empty, and you can visit the sights – including the great royal palace of Fontainebleau – without having your enjoyment spoilt by overcrowding.

Our description of the Ile-de-France divides the area into sectors which can be visited in separate excursions from Paris, although a number of them cannot reasonably be attempted in a single day. Many of the sights feature in organised coach excursions from Paris, and most of the towns and some of the villages can easily be reached by train or by underground. But the Ile-de-France is certainly not to be discounted as a region to tour, and in which to stay – there is plenty of accommodation, mainly catering for the needs of Parisians (prices are relatively high as a consequence). Barbizon is outstanding for the quantity and variety of its hotels; here, as elsewhere in the region, most are comfortable but may seem rather artificial with their studiously rustic style.

South and south-west of Paris

The **Château de Versailles** is France's most popular tourist attraction outside Paris, visited by some four million tourists every year. You will get your wings burnt if you pay less than a full day's homage to its creator, Louis XIV, the Sun King; and a full day will leave you, though not Versailles, exhausted. For this is not just another château where you do the interior, perambulate briefly in the surrounding gardens and continue on your way. There are various guided tours around different sections of the palace including, occasionally, the fascinating royal kitchen garden, as well as a large part of it where your visit is described as 'libre' – unguided but not free. The park and gardens are large (although one-tenth of their original size) and varied and even contain a couple of out-châteaux to visit.

Louis said 'L'état c'est moi'; but he might with no less truth have said 'L'état c'est Versailles'. Versailles was the *Ancien Régime*, the gilded prison which kept the most important element of the French nobility busy with petty intrigues far from their provincial power bases. It also provided the appropriately magnificent and rigorously ordered image of Louis' monarchy for public consumption. The personality which is expressed by the place is not that of the artists who created it but of Louis XIV; the great triumvirate achievement (Le Vau succeeded by Mansart for the architecture, Le Brun for the interiors and garden sculptures, and Le Nôtre for the gardens) is a team effort of individual talent subordinated to the effect of the whole. Louis' own role he likened to that of the sun – his bed was sited at the exact centre of the château, on the east-west solar axis.

But Louis did not create his egocentric universe in six days. The marshy land on which his father's small brick and stone château stood had to be drained (and paradoxically water had to be supplied to feed 1,400 fountains). The vast palace and gardens themselves had to be constructed in several campaigns spanning decades. Eventually over a thousand members of the French nobility and their servants lodged in the palace itself – in notoriously insanitary conditions. Louis also saw to it that Versailles town, which had to grow rapidly to accommodate all the courtiers, did so in appropriate style. He granted land for nothing except a promise to follow strict architectural guidelines, to ensure that the town should not rival the château but show it off with a degree of architectural unity. The town retains this severe classical unity today despite its growth into an important residential suburb, with the N10 passing right round the spacious Place d'Armes in front of the château.

To the west of the palace, terraced gardens and park represent the strict order Louis XIV imposed on Nature as he did on his country. There is a formal section with crisp gravel, pools with splendid river gods, and an orangery; and there is a spacious area with imposing avenues, intimate arbours, a beautiful marble colonnade where Marie-Antoinette listened to concerts, and fountains and sculptures rising from the waters of their basins. In the park beyond there are more waters and an artificial Grand Canal, where Louis XIV had a troop of Venetian gondoliers running a fleet of boats (you can still hire boats). From here there is a splendid view of the palace from a distance of just over 3km. The great event in the gardens is the so-called Grandes Eaux, when all the remaining fountains are activated for an hour or so on Sunday afternoons in the summer. It is crowded of course, but memorable.

The interior of the château has been changed even more than the exterior, much of it having been transformed in the 19th century into an historical museum dedicated 'to all the glories of France'. But the central section of the building has kept many of its original Louis XIV decorative schemes and these are being restored, slowly but to magnificent effect. After the superb chapel, you visit the most impressive rooms, the Grands Appartements. Although not all furnished (many of them never were, being reception rooms) they are sumptuously decorated, with paintings and stucco-work, all with predictable themes related to Louis, triumph, and the sun. You visit too the apartments of king and queen – the Queen's Bedroom, where royal births were watched by crowds, has been the object of particularly beautiful restoration. The fabulous 75-metre Galerie des Glaces (mirrors not ice-creams) which looks out over the gardens was where most important festivities and receptions took place, as did the signing of the Treaty of Versailles in 1919. To the south of the Queen's Apartments is the even longer but architecturally uninteresting Galerie des Batailles, constructed in the 19th century to house dozens of huge paintings of French victories. Other parts of the museum are devoted to French history from the 16th to the 19th centuries. Most visitors find the Grands Appartements quite enough. Those who want to see more can visit the Petits Appartements of king and queen with a guide. Not surprisingly, they are smaller and more intimate. Louis XV preferred this style and some privacy, and took up residence in the king's Petit Appartement, now a marvellous example of the decorative style of his reign, a delicate contrast to the monumental grandeur of the Louis XIV style.

Another masterpiece of restoration is the opera house, which was built at the end of Louis XV's reign to celebrate the marriage of Louis the Dauphin with Marie-Antoinette of Austria. It was here, in the alcoholic and smoky aftermath of a banquet where Versailles body-guards entertained Flemish officers on 1 October 1789, that a toast to the nation was refused and tricolour rosettes were trampled underfoot. When the news of this insult reached Paris the queen was blamed – as she was for everything else – and the great march on Versailles followed.

On the north-west edge of the palace, on land bought from the monks of the parish of Trianon, Louis XIV commissioned a small pavilion, called the Porcelain Trianon after its Oriental-style décor. In 1687 Mansart built in its place the much more magnificent Grand or Marble Trianon. Its manageable size affords a pleasant contrast with the main palace, but it is no less sumptuous inside; now it is used for the most prestigious of state visitors. Most of the furniture is in the Empire style of the early 19th century. Nearby there is a carriage museum and the sober classical Petit Trianon, like an elegant town house, built by Louis XV for Madame de Pompadour. Marie-Antoinette, who couldn't stomach the minutely regulated etiquette of court life, spent weeks on end here in what were construed by the poisoned tongues of jealous courtiers to be extravagant orgies. But there is no evidence that the queen indulged in anything more shocking than amateur drama at the Petit Trianon, which has also been recently restored and contains some late 18th-century furniture and *objets d'art*. The gardens are appropriately informal, a Rousseau-inspired idyll with a curious pseudo-rustic hamlet around a lake where Marie-Antoinette and her friends liked nothing more than to play at being peasants, until the peasants decided to play at being royalty.

The area south-west of Paris cannot, even excluding Versailles, be seen in a day. If no more time is available, one of the châteaux in the **Chevreuse** area may reasonably be combined with the town of Chartres. Dampierre is the most beautiful of them, but Breteuil and Rambouillet are of more varied interest.

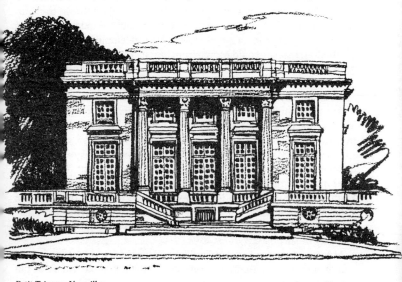

Petit Trianon, Versailles

This is a particularly green and intimate region of river valleys and sandy woods (**Les Vaux de Cernay**), good for picnics and walks, and frequented at weekends. **Chevreuse** lies on the river below feudal ruins, but has no particular charm. **Senlisse** has a choice of restful accommodation. The **Château de Dampierre** is a moated brick and stone building of impressive and sober elegance, mostly built in the late 17th century. The interior (with guided tour) contains some beautifully furnished and decorated rooms in the styles of Louis XIV and XV, as well as much from the 19th century in a more ponderous vein – nowhere more ambitious and less successful than in the remarkable Salle des Fêtes upstairs, where the ageing Ingres tried to do for Dampierre what Raphael did for Rome. There is a large and well-maintained park with swans.

Realising that their château is not going to pull crowds for reasons of architectural or decorative distinction, the enterprising proprietors of the **Château de Breteuil** have filled its rooms with well-dressed wax models of those prominent people whose paths members of the distinguished Breteuil family have crossed. A gouty Louis XVIII sits in his very own chair, Marcel Proust reclines in a lacquer bed, and the Prince of Wales (Edward VII) and French prime minister discuss the Entente Cordiale over a drink with cigars. There are temporary exhibitions in the old kitchens, concerts in summer, and a snack bar which is open on Sundays.

The **Château de Rambouillet** has been a presidential residence for the last 100 years. The building itself (with guided tours) is no beauty outside or in, but the park is of interest. Here, as at Versailles, Marie-Antoinette is thought to have employed the landscape painter Hubert Robert to create gardens in the English style, with rare trees and rhododendrons. Her pastoral tastes are commemorated by a classical temple-like dairy which was built so that she could escape from the château which she hated and drink milk, which is about as far as her involvement with the dairy process ever went. Nearby there is a thatched cottage whose round main room is entirely decorated with sea shells and mother of pearl. Louis XVI's agricultural interests were more serious than those of his wife: to improve the quality of French cloth he bought a flock of merino sheep from the king of Spain, and had them shepherded on an epic journey. On 15 June 1786, 334 ewes, 42 rams and 7 leading sheep left Segovia to begin the crossing of the Pyrenees at St-Jean-Pied-de-Port; all but 16 ewes and one ram safely reached Rambouillet on 12 October. The National Sheep Farm is still flourishing, and you may be guided around it by one of the young and enthusiastic students of ovine genetic engineering and other related topics. If you've never thought of sheep as magnificent beasts, you may be surprised.

At the northern end of Rambouillet forest (which has lakes and cycle and walking trails), **Montfort l'Amaury** is a delightful old village at the foot of a ruined fortress. The ruins themselves are less interesting than the elegant Gothic-Renaissance church which has a beautiful series of 16th-century windows.

Between Rambouillet and Chartres you may pause at **Maintenon** to admire the unfinished aqueduct whereby Louis XIV hoped to feed Versailles with water for its fountains. To divert the river Eure a three-tiered aqueduct of nearly 5km in length was planned, but unfortunately Louis' funds were diverted instead of the river, human resources were eroded by malaria, and after over 100,000 man-years of work – by which time the short bottom register of arches had alone been accomplished – the project was abandoned. The **Château de Maintenon** is a composite building of medieval, Renaissance and 17th-century elements. It was bought by Louis XIV in 1674 for the young and beautiful Françoise d'Aubigné, later Madame de Maintenon, who took charge of the king's children by Madame de Montespan and gradually supplanted their mother in the king's affections. Soon after the death of the queen in 1683 Louis XIV secretly married Madame de Maintenon, who became a major force beside the throne for the last 30 years of the king's reign, occupying the difficult position of king's wife (but not queen) with great humility and tact. The château contains many souvenirs of the good if disingenuous woman, but little of great beauty. Most of the gardens are out of bounds, for the château is still inhabited by Madame de Maintenon's descendants.

Chartres is the principal market-town of the flat cereal-growing Beauce Plain – not really part of the Ile-de-France, and different from it in its spaciousness. The town is well situated by the Eure, from whose banks and hump-backed old bridges there are beautiful views of the cathedral, one of the great treasures of France and perhaps her best-loved church. Chartres is well worth the journey from Paris, and is also well placed beside the motorway for visits in transit. Its accommodation is, however, not very attractively situated – around the station or on the busy ring-road.

Sights in Chartres

• **Cathedral** The glorious pale golden church is world-famous thanks to its stained glass and its asymmetrical western façade whose twin towers dominate the surrounding cornfields. Apart from the elaborately carved Gothic spire which crowns the north tower, the façade dates from the 12th century, and the famous south tower is the tallest of the Romanesque period in France, sober, solid and elegant. Around the west doorways there are marvellous examples of the elongated figure sculpture of the period, contrasting sharply with the more realistic later sculptures – hardly lesser masterpieces of their period – around the south and north doorways. Once inside the widest nave in France, you may be dazzled by the 13th-century stained glass, whose

famous blue is so brilliant that sun seems to be pouring through it on the dullest days. The screen around the choir is decorated with a wealth of remarkable carving, most of which dates from the last days of the Gothic style and is full of fascinating detail and great vitality. There is an abrupt change to vapid posturing and fluttering draperies in the scenes executed in the 18th century to finish the series (Lives of Christ and the Virgin). On the floor of the nave there is a rare labyrinth, a spiral pattern of black and white stone (usually obscured by chairs) around which pilgrims advanced on all fours. Those interested in giving the cathedral more than a cursory glance will find the daily guided tours in English rewarding. There are also official guided tours, in French, around the 11th-century crypt, the largest in France, which has some interesting frescoes.

● **Fine Arts Museum** An interesting collection of glass, furniture, tapestries, paintings, and an exceptional series of Limoges enamels, all housed in the elegant 18th-century archbishop's palace in gardens behind the cathedral.

● **St-Pierre** A large Gothic church in the lower town beside the Eure near the best viewpoints for the cathedral. The church itself has a splendid array of flying buttresses and its own distinguished stained glass from the 14th and 16th centuries.

At the **Château d'Anet** just about enough remains to give you an idea of the architectural beauty of what was once the finest of all French

From the cathedral's west door a carving of Aristotle, the Greek philosopher whose logical writings formed one of the pillars of medieval scholarship; cathedral schools like the one at Chartres played a major role in the education of the period

Renaissance châteaux, built by the highly original Philibert de l'Orme for Diane de Poitiers around 1550; very little is left of the splendour of its decoration, which included the enamels now at Chartres. The most interesting surviving elements are the circular domed chapel and the entrance gateway, featuring a cast of Cellini's famous bronze of Diana. South of Anet, **Dreux** is an important old frontier town (between France and Normandy) on the edge of a magnificent forest. Its best known monument is a fine belfry – part Gothic, part Renaissance.

The châteaux of Malmaison and St-Germain-en-Laye are both accessible by public transport from Paris and can be visited together in a suburban excursion. In the ugly suburb of Rueil-Malmaison, the **Château de Malmaison** is externally unexceptional and very little of the gardens remain. The inside, however, is a rich and fascinating Napoleon museum. Malmaison was bought by Josephine Bonaparte in 1799 and became Napoleon's favourite resort in pre-Imperial days. Although the château was emptied of its contents in the 19th century it has been thoroughly restored, and now contains many more interesting and beautiful works of art and pieces of furniture than it did when the Bonapartes were in residence. There are many personal mementoes of interest, something of the atmosphere of a residence if not a home – the decorative schemes of the rooms, in many cases characteristically pretentious and eccentric, have also been restored – and an ensemble of decoration, furniture and works of art which forms one of the finest collections of the Empire style.

The old royal **Château de St-Germain-en-Laye** is situated in a more attractive suburb and stands on a hill above the Seine with what must once have been a splendid view as far as the Arc de Triomphe nearly 24km away. The château is a sombre red-brick pile built for François I, but incorporating some elements of an older fortress (notably the early

13th-century chapel which is rather like the Sainte-Chapelle in Paris without the stained glass). Until Louis XIV moved to Versailles, St-Germain was the most important residence of king and court; however, it shows little sign of its royal past. Although the gardens are not what they were in St-Germain's 17th-century heyday, it is worth wandering as far as Le Nôtre's famous terrace, whence the view reminded the exiled James II of Richmond.

Just outside the western edge of the forest of St-Germain – but sadly robbed of all its park and gardens – the **Château de Maisons** in Maisons-Laffitte is one of the masterpieces of French classical architecture, built in the 1640s by François Mansart, and intact apart from the grounds. There are occasional guided tours (take counsel before setting off) around the richly decorated but unfinished interior.

North and north-east of Paris

Most of the interest in the wide area between the right banks of the Seine and the Marne falls along or near the valley of the Oise. There is too much to see for one day; the two main centres of interest, Chantilly and Compiègne, deserve separate excursions.

Isolated in the north of the region, **Beauvais** is, like Chartres, best situated for transit visits on the road from Boulogne to Paris. Like Chartres too it is the large centre of a wide agricultural area which is dominated by the soaring silhouette of an astonishing cathedral. From 1664 to 1940 Beauvais was one of the greatest centres of French tapestry-making, but bombs destroyed the tapestry manufacture and most of the old town.

Sights in Beauvais

• **Cathedral** Architects and their patrons in the early days of the Gothic style strove to outdo each other in terms of sheer height. The trend reached its dizzy climax at Beauvais where an early 13th-century bishop and chapter commissioned a new church to rival Amiens, Paris and the rest. The vaults of the choir were built over 45 metres from the ground, but had inadequate foundations and collapsed 12 years after completion. Today the reconstructed choir is the highest Gothic vault in existence. The transept was built in the very elaborate style of the early 16th century, and an ambitious attempt to erect a 135-metre spire over the crossing caused another collapse. The project of adding a nave was eventually abandoned, leaving just a part of the 10th-century cathedral (a very rare example of the period) dwarfed by the immense Gothic greenhouse to which it is attached. Despite the damage the building has suffered, the south and north transept doorways (Renaissance and Gothic respectively) are full of delightful carvings. As well as being architecturally remarkable, the interior has some very fine tapestries and stained glass in the transept. Near the north door there is a 19th-century astronomical clock of great complexity.

● **St-Etienne** A very interesting church with a late Gothic choir, and a late Romanesque nave and transept. There are very beautiful 16th-century windows around the choir, including a celebrated one depicting the Tree of Jesse.

● **Tapestry Museum** Next to the cathedral. Tapestry-making explained and demonstrated, with some beautiful finished works on display.

The **Château de Compiègne** has been an important place in the history of France and a royal residence from the days of Pépin the Short to those of Napoleon III, with whom the château is mainly associated. Its magnificent forest which attracted hunting monarchs is still the finest natural feature of the area, and a restful place to stay – there are a number of simple hotels deep in the forest.

The interior of the château (with guided tours) is mainly decorated and furnished in the styles of Louis XVI, and Napoleon I and III. The best that can be said for it is that it may help you to answer the interesting question posed by the historian Alfred Cobban: 'whether the official art of the Second Empire was, or was not, more boring, pretentious and vapid than that of the First'. Many visitors will find more entertaining the magnificent collection of old cars, bicycles and historic carriages housed in another part of the château.

Other buildings of interest in **Compiègne** include the early 16th-century town hall, where wooden soldiers are set in motion on the striking of the quarter hours, and the Vivenel Museum, which has a very distinguished collection of Greek vases as well as a variety of medieval *objets d'art*.

Near the left bank of the Aisne to the east of Compiègne a railway carriage stands in a clearing; it is not the one which hosted the signature of two armistices, on 11 November 1918 and on 22 June 1940, but a commemorative replica. Inside, more is understandably made of the earlier of the two occasions.

Napoleon III and Eugénie liked nothing better than to take their guests through the forest to the village of **Pierrefonds**, which became something of a spa and resort, romantically overlooked by the ruins of a once magnificent medieval fortress which had been bought very cheaply by Napoleon I. In 1858 the emperor instructed Viollet-le-Duc to restore the fortress to its original condition. The result of over 20 years' work is the fortress you can visit today, a massive quadrangular building with solid round towers and conical roofs. However vulnerable to criticism some of the details of reconstruction may be it is tremendously impressive as a whole.

Pierrefonds

South of Pierrefonds, the hamlet of **Morienval** has a large and very splendid church dating from the 11th and 12th centuries, also much restored in the 19th.

The area around Chantilly is one of the best for excursions from Paris, offering a variety of fascinating monuments, a wealth of historical and literary associations, and very pleasant countryside (although the Oise valley is rather industrial around Creil).

Chantilly is a smart little town famous for lace, aerated cream and some of the classiest race meetings in France (the Prix de Diane and the Prix du Jockey-Club) which take place in a magnificent setting every June. Spacious turf is bordered by what must be the most noble stables in the world (which now house a museum dedicated to the horse). Next to the race-course is a château which completes the scene perfectly with its fairy-tale pinnacles and domes and swans idling on the water. The château is in no sense an architectural masterpiece; of its two sections the smaller (Petit Château) dates externally from the 16th century, the rest is no more than about a hundred years old. The magnificent 17th-century Grand Château was destroyed during the Revolutionary period. Inside, the extremely precious Condé collection of works of art is presented not museum-style but as a private collection, arranged by its great accumulator, the Duc d'Aumâle. There are magnificent medieval manuscripts including *Les Très Riches Heures du Duc de Berry* – too fragile to display in the original; Renaissance portrait drawings; and Old Master paintings from Raphael to Ingres. From the decorative point of view the old section of the château is the most interesting; it was redecorated at the end of the 17th century to commemorate the Great Condé, a towering hero and villain of 17th-century France. He distinguished himself on the battlefields of northern France and the Low Countries and even the streets of Paris both for and against France with devastating energy and boldness, and eventually retired to Chantilly which he embellished and where he surrounded himself with the foremost intellects and writers of his day. Condé entertained on a lavish scale; in April 1671 the king and thousands of courtiers descended on Chantilly and such was the strain on the catering corps that its commander-in-chief, the great Vatel, veteran of many such campaigns and hardly less of a key figure in the creative aspect of

Louis' court than Le Nôtre or Le Brun, slept not a wink for days. When the fish failed to arrive one morning Vatel preferred to end it all rather than face his master's wrath.

Senlis is an attractive old town on the edge of the forest near Chantilly, one of the best preserved in the Ile-de-France. It has a very fine, weather-beaten, lichen-encrusted cathedral of mixed Gothic styles with particularly fine examples of the styles of architecture and carving of the 12th and 16th centuries (west and south façades) and a beautiful 13th-century steeple. Near the cathedral within the substantially surviving Gallo-Roman wall there is an interesting hunting museum.

The only reason to visit the large village of **St-Leu-d'Esserent** – whose quarries provided the stone for Versailles – is its disproportionately large and very elegant church which looks out from a dominating position over the wide Oise valley. As in so many cases the oldest and most curious part of the church is the west end (mid-12th-century tower and porch). The interior is bright and uncluttered – a beautiful and pure example of the early Gothic style, with modern stained glass. Very little remains of the cloisters.

The **Abbaye de Royaumont** is one of those abbeys which may not feature in text-books on the history of architecture, but is much more rewarding to visit than many churches which do. There are delightful shaded gardens, and an interesting series of monastic buildings to visit, including a very beautiful cloister and refectory. Of the church itself very little escaped revolutionary demolition. The monastery (guided tours) is now occupied by a cultural foundation which lays on occasional concerts and exhibitions.

The **Abbaye de Chaalis**, though less interesting than Royaumont, enjoys an even more privileged position deep in the forest of Ermenonville. There are a few attractively overgrown abbey ruins in the grounds, but the main part of the visit is a guided tour around the sober 18th-century abbey building turned into a private château in the 19th century and left to the nation as an art museum by the last owner. The works of art displayed are diverse and uneven in quality. Just at the gates of Chaalis, one of the natural curiosities of Ermenonville Forest, the so-called Sea of Sand – which is indeed a surprising expanse of bright white sand in the middle of the woods – has been turned into a mini theme park, good for small children and much cheaper then its rivals. **Ermenonville** itself is proud of its associations with Jean-Jacques Rousseau, the radical and sentimental philosopher whose feelings were of paramount importance in the development of European taste (and thus art, fashion, literature, social behaviour) and whose thoughts, at least according to Napoleon, were the single greatest cause of the Revolution. Rousseau died at Ermenonville in 1778 when living as a guest in a pavilion in the Marquis de Girardin's park which was, and remains, a splendid example of Rousseau's principles in landscape put into practice, with numerous thought-provoking symbolic monuments and inscriptions dotted around. Rousseau's empty tomb, classical in style and inscribed 'Man of Truth and Nature' stands on an island in the lake.

Ecouen and St-Denis lie on the main road from Paris to Chantilly and can be included in an excursion there. **St-Denis**, which lies beneath a splay of motorway junctions at the busiest northern gates of Paris, is accessible by Métro. It is a seedy suburb whose basilica, necropolis of the kings of France, is about as congruous as Westminster Abbey would be in Wapping. The basilica itself is neither enormous, nor architecturally very interesting except as being in part one of the earliest systematic applications of the Gothic style (porch and apse date from about 1140). Its contents are, however, of the greatest interest, although not always easy to appreciate under the regime of guided tours which applies. All but a very few French kings since the 10th century are buried here. The remains of most of them were scattered to the winds during the Revolution, but the tomb sculptures were saved and many of them are superb, from the simple 12th- and 13th-century statues to the elaborate Renaissance monuments for Louis XII, François I and Henry II and their queens.

The imposing **Château d'Ecouen** is a thoroughbred building of the classical phase of the Renaissance in France, contrasting with the decorative, still Gothic fantasy of Loire château architecture; it is an appropriate place for a museum devoted to the interior decorative style of the Renaissance. As well as collections of furniture from the period there are some Brussels tapestries of the highest quality and elaborate painted and carved chimney-pieces. The nearby church of **St-Acceul** has a notable series of Renaissance windows.

The Oise curves pleasantly between some wooded and other merely green hillsides from near Chantilly to Pontoise and its junction with the Seine. This is Impressionist country – not what it was, of course, but less spoiled than other of the painters' haunts nearer to Argenteuil. When Seurat painted at **Asnières** there was a factory in the background, which didn't stop the summer weekend exodus from the metropolis. It still doesn't, at least to **Boran-sur-Oise** and **L'Isle-Adam**, which are lively and attractive little riverside resorts. Apart from Asnières, the painters frequented **Auvers**, where Van Gogh committed suicide in 1890, and the old capital of the area, **Pontoise** – now with a new industrial neighbour, **Cergy-Pontoise** – which is well situated beside the river but without any monuments of outstanding interest.

East and south-east of Paris

The wide open area around the Marne valley east of Paris is more distinguished for creamy cheese (Brie, classically from Meaux, and the variant Coulommiers which, when just so, runs as well but travels less) than for sightseeing interest, although the numbers now heading into this region to visit Euro Disney probably outnumber visitors to other parts of the Ile-de-France. **Meaux** itself has an interesting though grubby Gothic cathedral (though it is hardly exceptional by the standards of northern France) and attractive old precincts (gardens designed by Le Nôtre, old chapter house and bishop's palace). One of the more interesting towns east of Paris on the borders of the Ile-de-France and Champagne – more importantly situated for trade in the Middle Ages than for tourists now – is **Provins**, whose upper town is well preserved and surrounded by massive medieval ramparts on two sides. The great landmark of the town crowning it like a 12th-century warhead is the splendid Tower of Caesar.

The **Château de Champs** is one of the great examples of the Louis XV style, still very much of a piece architecturally and decoratively (there are guided tours). It was built in the first years of the 18th century with a new concern for comfort in the design, and lightness and gaiety in the decoration; it later belonged to Louis XV's mistress, Madame de Pompadour. There is a particularly fine room decorated in the Chinese style, and beautiful formal gardens. The **Château de Gros Bois** (which is accessible from Paris by RER to Boissy-St-Léger, and then on foot) is a century older and presents inside some rare decorative schemes from the early 17th century, with ceilings of painted beams. Other rooms contrast with a lavish collection of Napoleonic Empire furniture.

A day's outing to Fontainebleau and around is perhaps the most satisfying of all to be made from Paris, a perfectly balanced diet of châteaux royal and private, forested landscapes of exceptionally varied beauty and interest, and charming forest villages made famous by 19th-century landscape painters.

The **Château de Vaux-le-Vicomte** lies a few miles north-east of the large and not very interesting market town of Melun. It is a magnificent château which quite literally prepared the way for the building of Versailles, and which is in no way except sheer size overshadowed by it. The glory of Vaux is not architecture alone but the whole effect of moated château and gardens, by no means small but appreciable in one superb vista. Little wonder that it is a favourite subject for tourist office posters. This harmonious ensemble was created with astonishing rapidity and at enormous expense between 1657 and 1661 for Louis XIV's superintendent of finances Nicolas Fouquet; there have hardly been any additions or alterations subsequently.

Before the château was quite finished (the oval salon still lacks its

Theme parks

Euro Disney

About 15km east of Paris, close to the sprawling new town of Marne-la-Vallée, stands the Euro Disney resort – the European outpost of American cartoon culture and high-tech entertainment. Designed to draw crowds from all over Europe, and made easily accessible from TGV and RER networks as well as from the A4 *autoroute*, the resort is self-contained to the extent that there is no need ever to set foot outside the complex of theme park and hotels. The very design of the place seems to imitate the circles formed by wagon trains to ward off the inhabitants of the hostile prairies, and there is little inside which has anything to do with France – one of the reasons why the park is suffering heavy financial losses as we go to press. The other reason could be the prices – they are definitely not in the bargain basement, and you will find stolid Dutch families eating picnics outside the park.

The park is a close copy of those in the United States. A railway, complete with mournfully whistling locomotives, circles the perimeter, passing the various 'lands' into which the park is divided. In Frontierland, the Thunder Mountain rollercoaster is a big draw. Elsewhere, pirates of the Caribbean and Peter Pan's ride are popular with different age groups. At the centre of the park, Sleeping Beauty's Castle contains a very life-like and scary dragon. In addition to the static attractions, a constant round of parades, staged Wild West fights and wandering cartoon characters ensure that there is always something going on. Restaurants, snack bars and souvenir shops are thick on the ground.

For all the unashamed razzmatazz, the high technology of the rides and the touches of genuine creativity make a visit a satisfying, if expensive, experience. The chief hazards are high-season queues and the uncertain climate. There is a lot of walking, and small children can wilt fast. Avoid visiting on French public holidays.

Parc Astérix

Just off the A1 *autoroute* to the North of Paris, this is a less expensive alternative to Euro Disney, perhaps more suitable for small children. The famous Gaulish village and its inhabitants form the centrepiece of the park; there are several gentle rides and an imaginative climbing frame disguised as a Roman fort. The entertainment is fleshed out by more conventional roller coasters and by performing dolphins. The park lacks the glamour of Euro Disney, but is much loved by Parisian families and can become quite crowded on fine weekends.

ceiling paintings) Fouquet entertained the young king and his court at Vaux on 17 August 1661. A magnificent repast was served on 36 dozen gold platters (Louis had had to melt his gold down to pay for war) and an alfresco musical entertainment was laid on by Molière. Louis could hardly fail to be provoked to jealousy and anger by the splendour of the occasion, which far outshone events at Fontainebleau and St-Germain-en-Laye; by Fouquet's style – his motto 'Quo non ascendam?' (what heights will I not reach?) and his emblem, the squirrel, were evident all over the decoration of the château – and by this example of the hugely extravagant use of public funds. The story goes that Louis was so incensed that he had to be restrained from arresting the superintendent that very night. Although the king and his prime minister Colbert had certainly been plotting Fouquet's downfall for some time, the fact remains that he was arrested 19 days later; Louis and Colbert then appropriated for Versailles Fouquet's entire team – not only Le Vaux, Le Nôtre and Le Brun, but also the tapestry factory, the poets, composers, caterers, and even the pick of Fouquet's statues and rare trees. Inside the château (notes in English available) the rooms open to the public are not great in number but magnificently decorated.

Fontainebleau is a smart and busy international town with one of the most important and interesting of royal châteaux. The forest was a favourite hunting resort for French kings but it was not until the mid-16th century that the hunting lodge became a palace for François I. For the **Château de Fontainebleau**, the king imported Florentine artists to create a new style appropriate to his grand ideas of himself. Rosso's richly complex Michelangelesque decoration of the François I gallery and Primaticcio's painting of the splendid ballroom represent the greatest achievement of what became known as the Fontainebleau style. Here at its best, it is dense and wonderful art, far removed from the usual French château decoration in the styles of Louis XIII to XVI. There is much more to the château than this, for subsequent kings added and altered. The interior takes you swiftly and superbly through the evolution of French decorative style from the Renaissance to the Empire; there are some rare painted ceilings from the late 16th century; the gracious and famous snaking double staircase at the entrance to the château dates from the early 17th; Louis XIV redecorated some apartments including the imposing Throne Room; the Council Chamber is a beautiful example of the Louis XV style; Marie-Antoinette's boudoir is decorated in the neo-classical style; and inevitably there is much that is the work of Napoleon, who was at Fontainebleau when he decided to abdicate in 1814. For most people the unguided tour round the major apartments will suffice, though other sets of rooms of lesser interest can be visited with a guide. There are some delightful gardens and a fine forest with marked trails for walkers and riders (horses are for hire at various places). Near the village of Barbizon on its north-west edge are

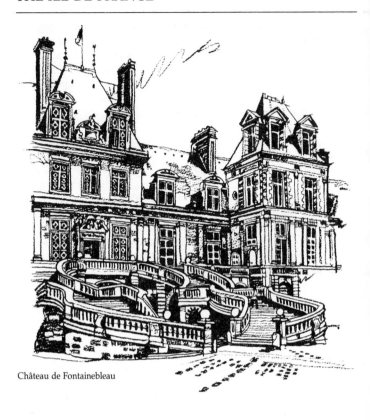

Château de Fontainebleau

some of the remarkable and desolate hills and valleys with piles of huge and often grotesquely shaped grey boulders which have made the forest famous (the **Gorges de Franchard** and **Gorges d'Apremont**); some of the rocks are challenging and large enough for real climbers.

Barbizon itself is a delightful and fairly peaceful village which exploits its mid-19th-century luck: it attracted landscape artists and gave its name to their school of painting. This might reasonably be called the Fontainebleau forest school but for the role of Jean-François Millet, who was more interested in the peasants labouring in the fields around Barbizon and Chailly than in the broken light effects of the forest itself. Like Pont-Aven in Brittany and St-Paul-de-Vence in the south, Barbizon's popularity with the painters had much to do with the presence of an enlightened and sympathetic and no doubt non-profit-making inn-keeper, in this case Père Ganne. Nowadays the village is full of hostelries; they are run on less charitable lines but nevertheless make it a good place to stay. There are several galleries and you can also visit the studios of Théodore Rousseau (the master of the forest painting) and Millet, which both contain a few minor works. Their tombs are at Chailly where Millet painted his famous Angélus, the painting of rural piety that hangs at the head of countless French beds.

Another very attractive and less commercialised village on the western edge of the forest is **Milly-la-Forêt**, with waterways and many old buildings including a splendid 15th-century market hall. The poet and artist Jean Cocteau decorated the interior of the 12th-century chapel of St-Blaise in 1959. Nearby **Courances** has a majestic Louis XIII château which can be visited on summer weekends.

On the south-east of the forest **Moret-sur-Loing** is beautifully situated on a wide stretch of the river shortly before it joins the Seine; there is an old bridge, a number of little islands overlooked by a fine Gothic church, and the single tower remaining from the old royal fortress. The English Impressionist Alfred Sisley lived and painted here for 20 years and died, as he had lived, in extreme penury.

Between Milly-la-Forêt and Paris the quiet rural village of **St-Sulpice-de-Favières** has an important late 13th-century Gothic pilgrimage church sometimes referred to as the most beautiful village church in France. It has damaged sculptures round the doorway, some interesting stained glass, and amusingly carved choir stalls.

HOTELS

Key: ◆ = 0–250FF, ◆◆ = 251–450FF, ◆◆◆ = over 451FF; prices are per double room without breakfast, which costs around 35–60FF extra. Some hotels may insist on half-board during high season, some hotels or restaurants may close at specific times during the week – it is always worth checking. Most hotels accept the major credit cards; we have indicated where a hotel takes no credit cards.

BARBIZON

Hostellerie de la Clé d'Or

73 Grande Rue
77630 Seine-et-Marne
TEL (1) 60 66 40 96; FAX (1) 60 66 42 71

In this artists' village, with galleries and museums a stone's throw away, the Clé d'Or is a village inn with added smartness. This is mostly to be seen in the reception area, cocktail lounge and restaurant – the first two are perhaps a little too like a town-centre hotel, but the restaurant is quiet and pleasing with space in the courtyard for outside dining. The bedrooms have been very attractively done up – the new attic suite is perhaps the best. Service is formal but friendly and food is tempting, though you will not eat at bargain rates.

OPEN All year ROOMS 15 (all with bath or shower)

THE ILE-DE-FRANCE

CHANTILLY

Château de la Tour

Chemin de la Chaussée
60270 Gouvieux
Oise
TEL 44 57 07 39; FAX 44 57 31 97

Set in a large area of woodland, this turn-of-the-century château offers style and elegance in a beautiful and tranquil spot close to Chantilly. The rooms in the modern building are smart and comfortable but if you are seeking somewhere with more character, stay in the château itself. The public rooms are grand and spacious with parquet floors and stone fireplaces and the bedrooms have autumnal colour schemes and lovely views.

OPEN All year ROOMS 41 (all with bath or shower) FACILITIES Outdoor semi-covered heated pool, tennis, billiard room

COMPIEGNE

Hostellerie du Royal-Lieu

9 rue de Senlis
60200 Oise
TEL 44 20 10 24; FAX 44 86 82 27

Originally part of the Forest of Compiègne (as its name suggests), this beautiful half-timbered country inn maintains a strong air of tradition. The inn itself houses the splendid Louis XIII dining-room, whose large windows look out on to the rear gardens. The breakfast room/bar area has low beams, a stone fireplace and some lovely stained-glass windows. Bedrooms are in a modern annexe that resembles a row of cottages; each is individually styled with furniture representing a different period of French history – comfortable and elegant with only the sound of the birds outside to disturb your morning slumber.

OPEN All year ROOMS 15 (all with bath)

ERMENONVILLE

Le Prieuré

Chevet de l'Eglise
60950 Oise
TEL 44 54 00 44; FAX 44 54 02 21

The creeper-covered priory right beside the church of this attractive village (birthplace of Rousseau) has been turned into a small and very charming hotel with an exemplary garden and a degree of peace and quiet, although some of the rooms suffer from some traffic noise. A salon with round-back chairs and squashy sofas, and a lovely breakfast room in the old kitchen with an enormous *cheminée* are to be found on the ground floor; furnishings throughout are in excellent taste with simple, pretty, antique furniture. Bedrooms are on the rudimentary side for the price, but the friendly owners and the excellent position to the east of Paris compensate for the comparatively high prices. There is no restaurant.

OPEN All year exc. Feb ROOMS 11 (all with bath or shower)

FLAGY (near Montereau)

Hostellerie du Moulin

77940 Seine-et-Marne
TEL (1) 60 96 67 89; FAX (1) 60 96 69 51

Tucked away in a small village on the edge of rather barren countryside, this is an excellent family-run hotel, very popular with visitors looking for tranquillity. Flagy is a small village of ochre houses running down to the river Orvanne, at the bottom of the slope on which the village stands. The old mill by its banks looks unchanged from previous centuries and only the cars in the courtyard detract from the rural idyll. Inside, among millstone coffee tables and comfortable chairs, peace and quiet reign; there are a few alcoves for the romantically inclined. The dining-room is bright and pretty and the food extremely good, but fairly plain. If you need the patron for any reason you may have to delve into the kitchen in search of him. There are steep stairs to some of the bedrooms but they are very comfortable when you reach them – rustic, wooden and without pretension; some have pleasant views of the river. The welcome is warm and genuine.

OPEN All year exc. 2 weeks mid-Sept and 1 month Christmas ROOMS 10 (all with bath)

LAMORLAYE

Hostellerie du Lys

63 7ème Avenue
60260 Oise
TEL 44 21 26 19; FAX 44 21 28 19

At the centre of a small network of tree-lined avenues, a short drive along the N16 from Chantilly, the Hostellerie du Lys provides a tranquil sightseeing base. Of its four two-storey buildings the 1930's main building has a white-washed, stone-clad exterior and a pleasant terrace. Inside there is an unforced country ambience in the dining-room and breakfast room which also extends to the gaily-coloured bedrooms. The rooms in the newer annexes tend to be rather drab and institutional.

OPEN All year ROOMS 35 (all with bath or shower)

THE ILE-DE-FRANCE

PROVINS

Aux Vieux Remparts

3 rue Couverte
77160 Seine-et-Marne
TEL (1) 64 08 94 00; FAX (1) 60 67 77 22

Right in the centre of the medieval *ville haute*, this rambling hotel could hardly be better placed for enjoyment of Provins' leisurely lifestyle, although you must drive around the back of town and through a series of narrow medieval lanes to find it. Basically, the hotel consists of an old restaurant with a modern block of rooms built alongside in a harmonious combination of the old and the new. The restaurant is a good, beamy, dark place, fairly formal in tone and with promising menus. The bedrooms are soothing in shades of blue and grey or rose, and are comfortable without being in the least flash. The same goes for the bathrooms. The establishment is run with style and enthusiasm by Xavier Roy.

OPEN All year ROOMS 25 (all with bath or shower)

ST-JEAN AUX BOIS

Auberge à la Bonne Idée

60350 Oise
TEL 44 42 84 09; FAX 44 42 80 45

Right in the middle of the Compiègne forest, this village inn with hunting lodge overtones is now something of a rural retreat for weekending Parisians. It makes an excellent overnight stop from the nearby motorway or, alternatively, a good base for exploring Beauvais and the surrounding area. There's plenty of sitting space, a bar down by the reception desk and a large, rather grand restaurant decked out with starched white napery. The very quiet bedrooms are commendably comfortable with a good range of extras. The food is not quite as good as the prices on the menu might lead you to expect (likewise the wine list), but service is ultra-slick.

OPEN All year ROOMS 23 (all with bath or shower)

Key: ♦ = 0–250FF, ♦♦ = 251–450FF, ♦♦♦ = over 451FF; prices are per double room without breakfast, which costs around 35–60FF extra. Some hotels may insist on half-board during high season, some hotels or restaurants may close at specific times during the week – it is always worth checking. Most hotels accept the major credit cards; we have indicated where a hotel takes no credit cards.

SENLIS

Hostellerie de la Porte Bellon

51 rue Bellon
60300 Oise
TEL 44 53 03 05; FAX 44 53 29 94

Good accommodation is scarce around the historic centre of Senlis, which makes this hotel a couple of minutes' walk from the ramparts worthy of a recommendation. The small bar and restaurant have the attraction of a small country inn, while the pretty rear terrace is a good spot for lunch. The bedrooms also tend towards the rustic – many have wooden crossbeams – but the standard of décor and furnishings is not consistent throughout the hotel.

OPEN All year exc. Christmas and New Year ROOMS 19 (16 with bath or shower)

Aloxe-Corton

To happy convents, bosomed deep in vines,
Where slumber abbots, purple as their wines
[Pope]

124

BURGUNDY, THE RHONE VALLEY AND THE JURA

Not one landscape but many, among whose changing colours the greenest green in France plays harmonies with fields of brilliant mustard, villages of warm ochre and roofs of red and geometrically multi-coloured tiles. Burgundy, wedged heart-shaped between the unlovely Saône and the transitional Loire, has many of the ingredients of the Dordogne's rural charm. Although it has no river to match the beauty of the Dordogne, there is a network of canals, some still used for commercial communication, others reserved for non-commercial traffic; Burgundy, where a leisurely water-borne pace is most appropriate for savouring the beauty of the countryside, is a favourite place for canal holidays.

The Burgundian table is one of the best in France; the finest beef comes from the white Charollais cattle which are such an attractive component of the landscape throughout western Burgundy. To the east the vineyards of the Côte d'Or, the most expensive agricultural land in France, produce the world's most expensive wines, which have given the word burgundy its association with blood-red velvet luxury. The wine is the single most potent reason for breaking a journey south, and the vineyard capital Beaune is the perfect place to admire, taste, learn and inwardly digest. Along the different *routes du vin* you can roll the great names sonorously round the palate, sample humble wines more liberally, and stay in attractive vineyard villages.

There is great splendour and ceremony to the Burgundy wine industry; because of the quality of the produce and the sums of money involved – around Vougeot, land changes hands in units of one-tenth of an acre – *vignerons* are no mere labourers of the earth, but citizens of standing. They are also likely to be *chevaliers* of the confraternity of

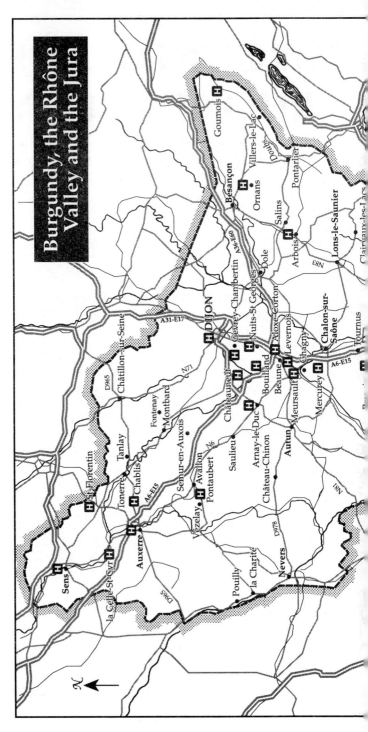

Burgundy, the Rhône Valley and the Jura

126

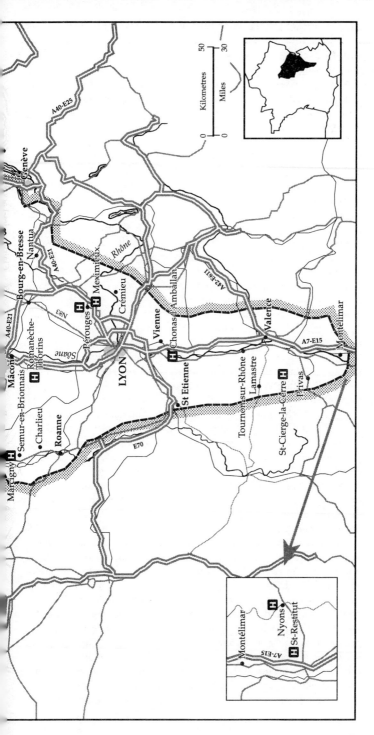

Tastevins, whose year reaches a climax every November with the celebration of the *Trois Glorieuses*. There are banquets at Clos de Vougeot
and Meursault, and another at Beaune after the world's most famous
and influential wine sale, the annual Hospices de Beaune auction
which takes place in the town's splendid medieval market building,
decorated with ancient tapestries for the occasion.

All the ritual, the sumptuous costumes, the banqueting and the
medieval halls set the Burgundy wine trade firmly in the glorious past
of the province, whose power and brilliance in the late Middle Ages are
of much more than merely academic interest. Burgundy's great period
started when the French king awarded the duchy of Burgundy to his
son Philip, known as the Bold, in 1363. By a bold and brilliant marriage
policy, Philip gained control (in principle for France but, as it later
turned out, for Burgundy) of large areas of the industrially powerful
Low Countries, and made diplomatic alliances all over Europe. He was
the most powerful nobleman in France. His successor John the Fearless
disputed, and mostly achieved, control of mad king Charles VI and his
revenues, and did very little to advance the French cause against the
English in the Hundred Years' War (he was absent from the field of
Agincourt). His assassination in 1419 by agents of the dauphin Charles
threw young Philip the Good firmly into the arms of the English.
Together, English and Burgundians (who controlled Paris) forced the
king to recognise Henry V as his son and heir, and Henry and Philip as
co-regents. Philip captured Joan of Arc and sold her to the English;
then when England sank into the depths of civil war, he neatly abandoned those whom he no longer needed (and no longer needed to fear)
and dictated his terms for support of Charles VII, which included even
greater – virtually sovereign – authority. At this time, Burgundy was a
power unrivalled in Europe, its ruler – self-styled Grand Duke of
Occident – lacking only a royal crown.

The wealth of 15th-century Burgundy was the envy of all Europe, and
the taste of the dukes for surroundings of dazzling luxury was part of a
deliberate policy to outshine their rivals. Philip the Good was in the
habit of wearing a sash decorated with balas rubies and pearls, worth a
hundred thousand crowns. The order of Tastevins recalls his foundation
of the chivalrous Order of the Golden Fleece, which survived in the
noble houses of Austria and Spain until the 1930s. Greatest among the
surviving buildings of this period is the Hôtel-Dieu in Beaune, the
hospital founded in the 1440s by chancellor Rolin for the benefit of the
poor on earth, and of himself on the Day of Judgement. Van der
Weyden's Last Judgement polyptych inside the Hôtel-Dieu is one of the
greatest masterpieces of 15th-century Flemish art, which in its golden
age was Burgundian court art. Philip the Bold brought artists from the
Low Countries to embellish his capital, Dijon; in the Dijon museum there
are marvellous ducal tombs, and at the Chartreuse outside the town
some of the most monumental and vigorous of medieval sculptures.

The mid-15th-century ascendancy was not to last, though; King Louis XI set his mind on the destruction of Burgundian power, and although Charles the Bold, the fighting Téméraire, pulled off a few military successes, he had not, in the words of the historian Comines, 'enough sense or malice', and he behaved more and more wildly as Louis wove a spider's web of bribed alliances against him. Trying to unite Burgundian dominions north and south, Charles met his death outside Nancy on 5 January 1477.

Earlier Burgundy had been the cradle of medieval monasticism. In 910 Duke William of Aquitaine founded a Benedictine abbey at Cluny. Under the leadership of a distinguished series of abbots, Cluny established order in monastic Europe, and hundreds of dependent priories sprang up. At Cluny itself Abbot Hugh started, and his successor Peter the Venerable completed, the greatest Romanesque church in Christendom – so beautiful, it was said, that if it were possible for the inhabitants of heaven to be happy in a building constructed by man, it would be the ambulatory of angels. Of the enormous abbey church all but a tower of the south transept has been destroyed; but all over Burgundy there are superb examples of the Romanesque style, from the great pilgrimage church of Vézelay, where kings of France and England took the cross in 1187, to the most humble village church.

The Cluniac order was never particularly rigorous in its discipline. Its churches were magnificent, and it grew ever more prosperous. Criticism of the order and its lifestyle was vigorously expressed by one of the great orators and church politicians of the Middle Ages, Saint Bernard of Clairvaux, who sneered that the welfare of the order was held to consist in the magnificence of its feasts and its buildings. Speaking of the carved Romanesque capitals, Bernard asked 'what are these monsters doing in cloisters under the eyes of monks occupied with their reading? What are these filthy apes, monstrous centaurs doing here? If not ashamed, one should at least regret the expenditure of money'. A new order, the Cistercian, was founded a few years before Bernard joined it in 1111 at Cîteaux near Dijon; its goal was a return to the original Benedictine spirit sharing the poverty of Christ. Under Bernard's leadership, the order enjoyed enormous success, which inevitably compromised its founding principle of worldly renunciation. Needless to say, Cistercian architecture is stripped of all decorative elements; the surviving monasteries are simple, harmonious and elegant, and usually set in remote valleys. They are ideal for contemplation of the tranquillity of both rural French and medieval monastic life. Fontenay, near Montbard in northern Burgundy, is one of the best preserved of all the representations in stone of Cistercian spirituality.

In its many ways, cultural, scenic and gastronomic, Burgundy is one of the most completely satisfying of all French areas. It lacks only the sea – which means that except for Beaune, and the motorway, it is never crowded. It is an ideal area for a short visit, conveniently situated on the way to or from the south, Italy, Switzerland or the Alps. Have a few meals, do some wine tasting, see a few churches – in all categories, you will have sampled the very best.

At Lyon the Saône, a dull river of medium stature, joins the Rhône, a great river which has always been one of the major thoroughfares of Europe. Around Lyon, and further south, the river itself is industrial and unattractive; but the motorway at least avoids the factory-lined river banks, so travellers by road don't see the Rhône corridor at its worst. In fact it is an impressive drive, with the Massif Central dropping abruptly down to the river on the western side and the higher massifs of the Alps rising further away to the east. If you are driving south there is the appetising change of landscape as you approach Provence – the pleasure of spotting the first poppy-fields, and very often the even greater joy of seeing a first break in the clouds south of Lyon as the valley widens around Montélimar. Along the Rhône there are some towns of very ancient importance, but they do not compare in sightseeing terms with places further north or south. You can take panoramic detours along winding roads up above the vineyards on the western side of the valley, but these routes are not as spectacular as the drive along the Ardèche gorges – the most powerful reason for a diversion (see the chapter on the Massif Central). Another good reason for a halt is the fact that the Rhône valley is an area of renowned culinary excellence, and bristles with Michelin rosettes.

The Jura is approximately the old Franche-Comté, or free county of Burgundy which, unlike the duchy, was outside France until the time of Louis XIV. The word Jura means forest, and the mountainous region has a very different kind of appeal from Burgundy. In complete contrast to the civilised thoroughfare area, it is an out of the way land of lakes, rivers, farms, and wooded mountains which, although they rise to no great height by continental standards (1,723 metres), are so structured that communications have always been difficult. The mountain range drops steeply down to Lake Geneva, whose crescent shape it echoes. On the French side, the mountains descend like a staircase towards the plains of Burgundy and Belfort in a series of ridges and plateaux. The ridges are thickly and monotonously covered with evergreen at the top, with a more interesting variety of woodland lower down. The highest part of the Jura near Geneva is bleak and very snowy in winter, and popular for cross-country skiing – for which it is the best area in France. In summer it attracts tourists who like the woods, the lakes, and the uncommercialised rural mountain life which is still based, as it has been for centuries, on the cutting of wood and the making of cheese. On its lower slopes, the Jura has more of the wealth and variety of the Burgundian landscape: there are orchards and golden stone villages, and vineyards producing small quantities of a little-known golden wine (*vin jaune*) which commands respect and high prices.

One of the great admirers of the landscape of his native Jura was the 19th-century painter Gustave Courbet, of Ornans. The shady river valleys, waterfalls and the grassy escarpments all around Ornans are an enormous Courbet gallery. He was a character larger than life, stubborn, iconoclastic but very canny, fully aware of the publicity value of posing as a rough-cut peasant when everyone else was posing as an intellectual, and loving nothing better than doing exactly the opposite of what was expected of him. In all this he was a typical product of a region which, until the 17th century, was independent of the French monarchy and, for all practical purposes, of any outside control; and which fiercely defended its independence against campaigns of French devastation for nearly 200 years after the death of Charles the Bold of Burgundy.

Northern Burgundy

Sens and Auxerre are two northern gateway towns to Burgundy. Somewhere between the two, near Joigny, the southbound traveller goes over the brow of a hill and looks down over a wide and pleasant, swollen landscape chequered with brilliant yellow mustard fields; this is the **Auxerrois**, and it is Burgundy – warm and welcoming. Of the two towns beside the Yonne, **Sens** has a less attractive old centre, but a more distinguished cathedral; St-Etienne is the oldest of all French Gothic cathedrals, and his statue on the pillar of the central doorway of the west façade is particularly beautiful. Inside there is a splendid array of medieval stained glass; one of the 12th-century windows on the north side of the choir tells the story of the murder of Thomas à Becket, who had spent years of exile at nearby Pontigny. The north and south transept doorways are very fine examples of intricate Flamboyant decoration, and the treasury has an exceptional wealth of precious vestments, goblets and reliquaries.

Auxerre should be admired from the east bank of the river Yonne. The *quais* are planted with trees, and above them three great churches on the hill turn their shapely backs to the river. The centre of town has cobbled streets, a Gothic clock tower, and timbered houses.

Sights in Auxerre

• **Cathedral**   Damaged but richly decorated façade with a wealth of story-telling around the doorways; exceptional 13th-century stained glass.

- **St-Germain** The abbey church of this once celebrated Carolingian monastery is of no particular interest, but there is a series of underground sanctuaries of great age beneath it, with 9th-century frescoes.
- **St-Pierre-en-Vallée** Not much to admire inside, but a rich mixture of an exterior, with a late Gothic tower and a laden 17th-century façade.

Auxerre is where Burgundian exploration most conveniently begins, whether by canal or by road. The motorist heading in the direction of Beaune has two main choices: to the east of the motorway lie beautiful Renaissance châteaux, perhaps the most satisfying Cistercian monastery of all, the provincial capital Dijon, and the great vineyard *côte*. To the west lie the wilder wooded mountains of the Morvan, and just a couple, but among the very finest, of Romanesque churches.

Starting clockwise, the northernmost Burgundian vineyards produce wines of distinction, best-known among them from **Chablis**, which is not as attractive as little **Irancy** on the Yonne, whose very good red and rosé wines enjoy less widespread fame. Like Chablis, the Cistercian **Abbaye de Pontigny** grew up beside the river Serein. Of the monastery only the church survives: the stark white simplicity of its interior contrasts with the elaborate 17th-century choir stalls. All around Auxerre, the Yonne is delightful, still as Walter Pater described it in the last century: 'bending gracefully link after link through a never-ending rustle of poplar trees, through lovely vine-clad hills ... the child's fancy of a river like the rivers of the old miniature painters, blue and full to a fair green margin'.

Beyond the small market town of **Tonnerre**, Tanlay and Ancy-le-Franc (both 16th-century) are two of the finest châteaux in Burgundy. The sober classical Renaissance **Château d'Ancy-le-Franc** is built around a richly decorated closed courtyard. Inside there is a magnificent ensemble of Italian Renaissance furniture and decoration, the work of Fontainebleau artists. Sadly, it's in sore need of restoration. The **Château de Tanlay** is more interesting from the outside, for its round towers and bell-shaped domes, and the wide, flattering mirror of its moat. There are many treasures inside.

Châtillon-sur-Seine is a small town with lawns and avenues of chestnuts and limes beside the young river. The only reason for a visit is the museum, which among many Gallo-Roman finds has the huge and magnificent 6th-century BC Greek bronze vase ('crater') and other treasures found in a princess's sepulchre at Vix.

The **Abbaye de Fontenay**, founded by Saint Bernard in a softly wooded vale among well-kept gardens, is the most perfect surviving example of a Cistercian monastery. In the 19th century, the abbey was used as a paper factory by the ballooning Montgolfiers. The 12th-century church that stands beside the cloister and abbey buildings is intact but completely stripped of its fixtures and fittings – even its stone floor. The forge is also worth seeing, its bellows and hammers once powered by the river running alongside.

Near Fontenay, there are a number of minor but rewarding visits for the unhurried tourist. The **Château de Bussy-Rabutin** was mostly built and entirely decorated by its 17th-century lord Roger de Rabutin, a general who wielded the pen with such witty, penetrating and tactless facility that he was exiled from court and spent years of nostalgia adorning his rooms with portraits and allegorical scenes about Versailles. **Alise-Ste-Reine** is a small village on the flank of the natural fortress of Alésia, where Vercingetorix failed (but only just) to resist a Roman siege in 52 BC. You can visit the excavations of a Gallo-Roman town and a small museum.

Semur-en-Auxois is old and picturesquely set, with roofs of mottled tiles beneath the round towers of its castle which surveys a bend in the river Armançon. The fine Gothic church has the story of Doubting Thomas carved above the transept door. **Flavigny-sur-Ozerain**, famous for its aniseed sweets, is a smaller fortress village hundreds of metres above its almost encircling rivers, with well-preserved and restored houses.

Dijon, Burgundian capital medieval and modern, is a railway junction city of heavy industry though it is best known for its mustard and *cassis*. After the decline of Burgundian power Dijon remained an important regional capital and most of the public buildings date from the 17th and 18th centuries: the semi-circular Place de la Libération and façade of the old Grand Dukes' palace form a splendid late 17th-century ensemble. There are, however, a few medieval parts of the palace left, and behind it some attractive medieval streets and squares.

Sights in Dijon

• **Musée des Beaux-Arts** In the ducal palace, a very rich and varied collection of sculptures and paintings of many periods, of which the masterpieces are grouped in the 15th-century Salle des Gardes. The tombs of dukes Philip the Bold and John the Fearless, their recumbent statues supported by wonderfully lively cortèges of grieving mourners, are among the most beautiful works of art to be seen in Burgundy.
• **St-Michel** An imposing and richly decorated façade, Gothic in plan, but Renaissance in style.
• **St-Bénigne** Once one of the greatest Romanesque churches in France, with a circular choir. The cathedral is now Gothic, but its crypt, also circular, has been excavated.
• **Notre-Dame** A beautiful early Gothic church, with three rows of gaping gargoyles on the west façade.
• **Chartreuse de Champmol** Now an unlovely suburban asylum, the dukes' purpose-built necropolis has kept two masterpieces of late 14th-century sculpture which will be shown on request: the hexagonal base

for a calvary, called the Well of Moses, by Claus Sluter, surrounded by six magnificent prophets, and the group of statues around the chapel doorway.

To the south and west of the motorway lie the **Morvan** hills – a land of woods, rivers and reservoirs, with little cultivation and few inhabitants. It has become popular for watersports (the river Cure is good for canoeing), riding (marked rides and a number of equestrian centres around the periphery of the **Morvan Regional Park**), and walking. A hiking trail crosses the Morvan from top (Vézelay) to toe (Autun). Other bases around the park are **Château-Chinon**, which has little character, and **Saulieu**, a busy market town with a long-established gastronomic reputation and a Romanesque basilica with beautifully carved capitals.

French motorway builders take a teasing delight in putting notices beside the carriageway telling you what you are paying to avoid. One pointing upwards and westwards at nothing very obvious says simply *'Vézelay, collin éternelle'*. The description is hardly adequate, but does express the fact that **Vézelay** is not just a most beautiful and beloved Romanesque church; it is also a place, a pilgrimage village on a hill,

Vézelay

looking out over the most opulent Burgundian countryside. The village is often packed with coaches; it is worth staying nearby (the choice of good places at Vézelay, Avallon, and the leafy Cousin valley is extensive) and waiting to make the pilgrim's climb in the evening or early morning.

The abbey of Vézelay was a starting point of one of the medieval routes to Compostela. The church has a beauty to which few are insensitive; its glories are the majestic relief sculptures above the inner doorways, the chocolate and ochre bands of the arches supporting the main vault, and the capitals all around the nave. You can spend hours studying the details: Saint Anthony watching a victim being pulled every which way by monsters, a giant grasshopper, a tiny David beheading Goliath. A detailed guide is recommended.

The nearby village of **St-Père** also has a beautiful Gothic church, with the tomb of its founders in the porch. **Avallon** is more than just a town with good hotels near Vézelay; the old centre has cobbled streets and ramparts above attractive terraces leading down to the wooded Cousin valley.

At the southern edge of the Morvan, **Autun**, as Roman Augusto-dunum, was capital of Burgundy and one of the most important Gallo-Roman cities; it has kept two splendid town gateways, and fragmentary remains of the largest theatre in Gaul. The Romanesque cathedral of St-Lazare is surmounted by an elegant Gothic spire; the carving of the main tympanum is a Last Judgement of grimacing devils, howling damned souls and trumpeting angels. Many of the most beautiful capitals inside are grouped together in the chapter room – do not miss the one of the sleeping Magi, one of them being woken by an angel touching his finger. In the Musée Rolin, there is Gallo-Roman archaeology, and medieval works of art including a very beautiful Nativity by the Maître de Moulins. Between Autun and Beaune, you can admire only the outside of the splendid moated Renaissance **Château de Sully**. Madame Sévigné said its walls enclosed the most beautiful courtyard of any château in France.

The Nivernais Loire divides Burgundy from the Berry; south of the best Loire vineyards (Sancerre and Pouilly-sur-Loire), the Burgundian bank is overlooked by the 12th-century abbey church of **La Charité-sur-Loire**, once the second largest church in France after Cluny. The church has suffered much damage from the town's importance as a Loire bridgehead (the handsome 16th-century bridge has weathered better) but although some of the nave has been destroyed, leaving a single tower of the original façade, the beautiful choir and transept have survived more or less intact. Little is left of the old abbey buildings, but a gallery of the old cloister leads around behind the church, giving a splendid view.

Nevers is a large through town, famous for glass and porcelain since the 16th century when a Gonzaga prince took over the Nivernais duchy and imported talented Italian artists. The manufacture of Nevers' faience flourished until the Revolution, and there is a good collection of it in the town museum. There is a variety of other monuments – the Renaissance ducal palace and its gardens, a very picturesque 14th-century town gate (Porte du Croux), and two contrasting churches – the cathedral with an interesting variety of architectural styles and works of art, and St-Etienne, a very pure late 11th-century church of surprising interior grandeur.

Southern Burgundy

Beaune is the centre of the local wine industry, at the heart of the most prestigious vineyards. It is a beautiful historical town, full of art treasures and a very good place to use as a base for the region. The centre of the town is still surrounded by old ramparts and plane trees, and there are many fine 17th-century buildings, now the offices of the wine trade establishment. For most tourists the first priority will be a visit to one or more of the many wine cellars (see page 138).

Sights in Beaune

• **Hôtel-Dieu** Medieval hospital, founded in the 15th century by the Burgundian chancellor Rolin, run as a charitable hospital until a decade ago and still functioning as a home for the aged. It is staffed by nuns, and funded by the proceeds of the annual auction of wines produced by the 52 hectares of vineyards it owns. The auction, which takes place with great pomp and circumstance, no longer in the Hôtel-Dieu itself, is the central event of the Trois Glorieuses (3rd Sunday in November) and sets the trend for burgundy prices. The sombre grey exterior conceals a cobbled courtyard with wooden galleries and the most brilliantly colourful of Burgundian roofs. The guided tour of the interior reveals a medieval ward with double beds curtained off from the chapel, medieval kitchens still in use, an old pharmacy with jars for herbal and more exotic medicaments, and a museum with beautiful tapestries and Van der Weyden's superlative Last Judgement polyptych which is displayed behind a mobile magnifying glass for the study of individual detail.

• **Notre-Dame** A mostly Romanesque church, with a series of 15th-century tapestries depicting the Life of the Virgin (currently being restored).

• **Musée du Vin** Set in a handsome old *hôtel* near Notre-Dame, where you can see how the shape of the local wine bottle evolved and how barrels were made.

Hôtel-Dieu, Beaune

The greatest Burgundian vineyards extend a short way south of Beaune, but principally north to Dijon, along the lower slopes of a continuous hillside which looks south-eastwards over the main road and the motorway. This is the **Côte d'Or**, over 60km long by less than 2km wide from Dijon to Chagny, covering only 4,000 hectares, not very much more than a large farm. It is split up into the **Côte de Beaune** in the immediate neighbourhood of the town, and to the north the **Côte de Nuits**, which produces what are considered by most fortunate consumers to be the greatest of all burgundies, and by many of those who carry their taste for hierarchy even further to be the greatest of all wines. Certainly, they are among the most expensive. The vineyard drive is not perhaps the most attractive in France, but the villages have their golden Burgundian beauty. Along the Côte de Nuits (not on the main road), the village signposts read like an exclusive wine list – **Gevrey-Chambertin**, **Vougeot**, **Chambolle-Musigny**, **Vosne-Romanée**, and **Nuits-St-Georges**. There are wine cellars all along tempting you indoors, but do not expect free gulps of a great and aged burgundy (some of the finest do not merit their price or reach their prime until they are over ten years old). **Clos de Vougeot** is one of the most picturesque wine châteaux, and one of the few to visit. Vast expanses of rust-coloured tiles drop almost to the famous vines of the walled Clos, now the property of the confraternity of Tastevins, who hold a famous banquet in the château on the day before the Hospices de Beaune sales. There are guided tours, revealing splendid vaulted chambers and some magnificent old wine presses. On the Côte de Beaune, **Aloxe-Corton** produces a white wine of great distinction (Corton Charlemagne); so too does **Meursault**, to the south of Beaune.

137

Wine tasting

One of the most convenient places for sampling burgundy is Beaune, where most of the big wine merchants have their headquarters. The tourist office has a guidebook entitled *La Bourgogne de Vignes en Caves* which lists over 250 places (vineyards, wine merchants and cellars) that can be visited – English is frequently spoken. Not all, however, are good to visit. Some offer free tastings of small quantities of decidedly uninteresting wines, followed by a hard-selling exercise; others are geared to French tourists, with amusing anecdotes in colloquial French. You may find it just as easy to find places yourself by following the signposted *routes du vin* in the various areas, and by enquiring locally or looking out for signs announcing *dégustation*. Safari Tours (details from tourist office) run escorted tours to various vineyards, including tastings. The tours, in French and English, take about two hours and are very informative.

Marché aux Vins, Beaune is one of the best places to give yourself a taste of what burgundy is all about. You can choose from two lists: either the whole region of Burgundy, or the wines of the Hôtel-Dieu (or both) – for a relatively modest fee. The cellars are lit by flickering candles, with bottles arranged on barrels. Prices tend to be about twice as much as buying direct from the producer. You are left to yourself, with help and advice offered by sales staff if you want it.

The area south of Chagny produces wines of lesser distinction than the Côte d'Or, but the vineyard landscapes – where land and produce are less expensive – have in many ways a more attractively rural charm, and not surprisingly *vignerons* are much more liberal in the dispensation of their wine. As well as the vineyards, there is a wealth of beautiful churches, a few major ones, but mostly small and simple parish churches in small and simple country communities.

Chalon-sur-Saône is no Clochemerle: it is a commercial and industrial river port without appeal, unlike the nearby vineyard villages of **Rully** and **Mercurey**, which produce very good wine and offer accommodation. **Tournus**, hemmed in between motorway and river, is an old town in the shadow of its fortress-like 10th- and 12th-century basilica of St-Philibert – one of the finest churches in the region. It was built in a massive and austere style, beautifully enhanced by its soft pinkish stone. The nave is vaulted by a series of transverse barrels.

At **Cluny**, high point of medieval monasticism and post-Revolutionary vandalism, little remains (just one lonely transept tower) of the greatest Romanesque church of all – nearly 180 metres long, with two transepts and five naves. The route is confusing, leading from the remains of the abbey church through the 18th-century cloisters to the 13th-century flour store. Call in at the museum first to pick up an outline guide and admire some of the stone carving.

Throughout the Mâconnais and the green pastures of the Brionnais (west of the vineyards) Cluny's influence has left countless Romanesque churches. There is a marked tourist route in the **Brionnais** which includes some of the following selection, which is not exhaustive. **Brancion** is a tiny picturesque rampart-encased village on a rocky spur, with a fortress, overgrown houses, streets of earth, and a squat, harmonious 12th-century church with very faded medieval wall paintings inside. **Chapaize** has a very old (11th-century) church with a splendid, disproportionately large bell-tower. **Berzé-la-Ville**, near Cluny, has a small chapel which was part of Abbot Hugh's summer retreat; frescoes originally covered the whole of the interior. Only the apse paintings survive, with a Christ in Majesty (of Byzantine inspiration) which is indeed majestic, and beautifully preserved, having been protected by whitewash for centuries.

At **Paray-le-Monial**, well situated by the waters of the Bourbince, the basilica of Sacré-Coeur is the closest approximation on a smaller scale to what the church of Cluny must have been, with a splay of semicircular chapels around the east end, a trio of pointed towers, and an interior of sober elegance. In many ways, the Romanesque style of architecture is better suited to smaller churches, like the one at charming **Semur-en-Brionnais**, with lively relief carvings. At **Anzy-le-Duc** there is another early Romanesque church, built of a stone which is exceptionally golden even by Burgundian standards, with an octagonal belfry and carvings of men pulling each other's beards, or Daniel being licked by lions.

The small market town of **Charlieu**, in the **Charollais** – another area of golden villages, green pastures and white cows – had an important abbey; enough remains of it to reward a visit. There are guided tours around the surrounding buildings, many of them like the elegant cloister dating from the 15th century; but the glory of Charlieu is the very densely decorative carved doorways (12th-century) which can be seen from outside.

The **Mâconnais** is a hilly vineyard and farming region, whose finest wines – dry, fruity and white – come from the neighbouring villages of

Pouilly and **Fuissé**. **Solutré** too makes good wine, but is better known in a prehistoric context: at the foot of the great rocky cliff which flanks the village like a petrified wave, some 100,000 skeletons of horses were discovered, and the place is thought to have been a kind of prehistoric abattoir. Finds (not only equine) are displayed in the museum at **Mâcon**. Apart from this, and omnipresent reminders of the Mâconnais origins of the Romantic poet Lamartine, there is nothing memorable about Mâcon, a busy wine-trading town on the Saône.

The north of the **Beaujolais** vineyards adjoins the south of the Mâconnais, but the Beaujolais is usually considered to be outside Burgundy. Its wine, unlike burgundy, should be drunk cool and young. Indeed, so young has it become fashionable to drink Beaujolais that every autumn Beaujolais Nouveau is flown to eager imbibers in London wine bars within hours of the season being declared legally open, amid fanfares of publicity, and with unparalleled (and to many minds undesirable) speed. The Beaujolais landscape is inviting, with hills rising to over 1,000 metres, pine forests above and behind the vineyards, pretty villages with simple accommodation and excellent restaurants, and plentiful wine-tasting opportunities at the village co-operatives. **Oingt** and **Ternand** are among the best villages.

To the east of the Saône, the flat **Bresse** plains were in the past divided between France and Empire. As a whole, it feels neither Burgundian nor part of the Jura. To the French, the Bresse means the tastiest of chickens, a local speciality. Visual treats for the tourist are two architectural features which could not form a greater contrast – brick farmhouses with outside staircases and wooden galleries supporting huge overhanging (occasionally thatched) roofs, and on the edge of the market town of **Bourg-en-Bresse**, the monastery church at **Brou** – one of the most brilliant and extreme examples of the luxuriant virtuosity of late Gothic art. The building was carried out in the first decades of the 16th century by Margaret of Austria, duchess of Savoie, ruler of the Franche-Comté and the Low Countries; it is, like so much in Burgundy, the work of artists brought in from the north. The main doorway is a richly decorated hint, no more, of what is inside, enclosed by a stone screen of great beauty: the tombs of Margaret of Austria, her husband Philibert and her mother-in-law Marguerite de Bourbon; carved oak choir stalls; and stained glass windows – all miraculously preserved, perfect.

The Rhône Valley

The Rhône runs west from Lake Geneva to Lyon, then, like most tourists, it charts a purposeful southward course. Between Lyon and Valence the vegetation on the steep slopes of the west bank gradually changes from spruce and oak to the pines and scrub typical of the Mediterranean area, a sight uplifting to travellers in search of sun and heat. Much of the Rhône Valley is industrial, but on either side there are detours to be made through the valleys running up into the Massif Central or through the lavender fields and vineyards on the east bank. Apart from one or two half-forgotten medieval villages, there is less of interest to sightseers than to those in search of good food – for this is one of the great gastronomic areas and the valley abounds with very good restaurants. The area around the source of the Loire, and the Ardèche gorges, both within easy range, rank among the most beautiful parts of the Massif Central (and are described in the chapter on that region).

Lyon has grown up economically powerful, thanks to the natural passage of international trade and to the favours granted in the late Middle Ages to encourage trade fairs. Merchants were given a monopoly of the silk trade, originally imported from Italy, and its manufacture became the great speciality of the city. In recent years a tendency among French companies to migrate to the 'Sun Belt' of France has given Lyon added commercial weight, to the extent that it begins to rival Paris in prosperity and influence in some areas.

Lyon occupies both sides of the confluence of Rhône and Saône, and the long peninsula between the two. The meeting of the two broad rivers gives the town an impressive setting, with terraces of houses stacked above the waters, but it is not as a whole a very charming place; Lamartine called it a 'sombre, austere, monastic town', and few tourists will feel the urge to do more than pay cursory homage to its major sights.

Sights in Lyon

• **Fourvière** You can drive, walk, or catch a funicular up the steep hill on the west of town, crowned by a great 19th-century pilgrimage basilica, with no more aesthetic distinction and considerably less charm than Montmartre in Paris. Nearby, there are substantial but nevertheless fragmentary remains of two Roman theatres and a museum devoted to Gallo-Roman Lyon.

• **Old town** A mostly Renaissance area at the foot of Fourvière, with many beautiful *hôtels* (one of the finest, the Hôtel Gadagne, houses an international puppet museum) and the only church in Lyon of any particular distinction, St-Jean – mostly Gothic, but with a beautiful Romanesque choir and particularly fine carving around the doorways of the main façade.

- **Musée Historique des Tissus** Not just Lyon silk and its history, but stuffs from all over the world; a museum of exceptional interest.
- **Musée des Arts Décoratifs** A rich collection of furniture, tapestries and faience, from many periods.
- **Musée des Beaux-Arts** More like a national than a regional museum, large and extensive in its coverage of different styles, periods and places of origin. Housed in the old nunnery beside the Place des Terreaux. The only local artist particularly well represented is Puvis de Chavannes.

To the east of Lyon, either side of the Rhône, two very different medieval towns are well worth seeing: **Crémieu**, with its old gateways and towers, and its 14th-century market buildings, is less visited than **Pérouges**, which was originally colonised by immigrants from Perugia. Pérouges was identified long ago as special, preserved from demolition, brought to the notice of tourists, and restored. Many a film maker has resorted to Pérouges for local colour – ramparts, cobbled streets, late-medieval houses, and a central square with a single bicentennial lime tree.

South of Lyon the Rhône is at its most industrially ugly. **Vienne** is a riverside town of no particular beauty, but it has the greatest concentration of sightseeing interest of the whole Rhône valley. From the early days of the Roman conquest until the early Middle Ages, it was a more important city than Lyon.

Sights in Vienne

- **Roman remains** A Corinthian temple, less perfect than the Maison Carrée in Nimes, but very like it; a huge theatre often used for summer drama; and an elegantly decorated archway. On the southern edge of town, there is an isolated pyramid, once the centrepiece of the chariot race track.
- **Churches** Two very early Christian churches, with late Romanesque additions (St-Pierre, now a museum of Gallo-Roman statuary; St-André-le-Bas, with a beautiful cloister), and a large and handsome cathedral, part Gothic, part Romanesque, with beautiful carving on the façade and inside.

The main roads follow the east, or Dauphinois, side of the Rhône. From Vienne, tourists in no hurry can take minor roads through the vineyard hills on the Massif Central side of the river. The most impressive drive climbs from behind Tournon to St-Romain-de-Lerps, giving extensive views down over the river valley and down to Valence past the ruins of the **Château de Crussol**. **Tournon** shows an attractive aspect to the river, with a castle on granite rocks, and a gracious promenade of plane trees. **Tain-l'Hermitage** is dominated by the steep slopes which produce the virile Hermitage, finest of all Côtes-du-Rhône wines. Another attractive diversion is the valley of the Eyrieux, where riverside camp-sites and bathing pools are backed by steep slopes with tiny villages hidden in the hills.

Valence is a large thriving commercial town, with something of an old centre around the Place des Clercs, including a few Renaissance *hôtels*. The museum in the archbishop's palace has a collection of late 18th-century chalk drawings of Rome by Hubert Robert, a reminder of how the Rhône once carried Grand Tourists towards the treasures of classical antiquity. The artists were impatient to hurry on, and Valence does not delay many tourists now; neither does **Montélimar**, the world nougat capital. South of Valence, the Rhône, despite the occasional embellishment of a ruined fortress on its western wall, becomes characterised chiefly by hydro-electric and even atomic power stations. In this area you should wander the eastern side of the river, where lavender fields are intermeshed with vineyards. The road to Die among the steep hills which seem to have broken away from the Vercors plateau is worth exploring, as is the town of **Nyons**, with its micro-climate suitable for olive trees and its crumbling old town on the edge of the mountains.

The Jura

The southern Jura mountains have none of the gentle gradations of the centre. Relatively high peaks, like the Grand Colombier, are crowded together and drop abruptly down to the Rhône. Villages along the river produce cheerful sparkling wines (Seyssel), but have no great charm, and there is little except the hills themselves to tempt you up into the **Bugey**, as this region is known.

The highest mountains are to the north of Geneva, and attract most of the active summer tourists. Unpretentious **Les Rousses** is the region's liveliest resort, with riding and board-sailing; it is a good place to stay, with a variety of hotels; the dairy is well worth a visit. From the **Col de la Faucille**, there are ski lifts up to the Mont Rond for impressive views across Lake Geneva to the Swiss and French Alps. You can drive down from the mountains to the wholly Swiss-seeming lakeside spa of **Divonne-les-Bains**, with its casino and very clean streets, without leaving France. Further north, the Franco-Swiss border cuts into the heart of the mountains, so there is a large area (above Lake Neuchâtel) of Swiss Jura. **St-Claude** is a real town, not particularly beautiful, but dramatically situated – cramped high above two rivers in a bowl of mountains – and a convenient base for excursions. Its cathedral is austere, but curiously fortified and amusingly decorated with 15th-century choir stalls; in front of it an elaborately wrought pipe made of flowers indicates St-Claude's traditional industry of pipe making. The **Gorges du Flumen** to the south of town offer a particularly impressive excursion for motorists.

To the north of St-Claude, the **Ain** valley has been dammed to create long, sinuous reservoirs banked with pines; it is a favourite area for camping and nautical sports. So too are the natural lakes around the villages of **Clairvaux-les-Lacs** and **Doucier**, which offer simple accommodation. For walkers, the best excursion is the shaded woodland trail beside the Hérisson, which drops through a series of magnificent waterfalls accessible from Bonlieu, Ilay, or Doucier. Between Lons-le-Saunier and Arbois, the lower and very attractive vineyard slopes of the Jura are broken up by a series of beautifully symmetrical dead-end valleys, eroded from the plateaux, flanked and abruptly terminated by vertical escarpments of limestone. The most impressive and shapely of these *reculées* is the **Cirque de Baume** near Lons-le-Saunier; the valley floor has grottoes, cascades, and (at the open end) the old **Abbaye de Baume-les-Messieurs** (the title added by noble canons in the 16th century) whence 12 monks set out in 910 for Cluny. The golden abbey buildings are mostly ruined but the church remains – powerful, simple, and harmonious. Other *reculées* are the **Cirque de Ladoye,** the **Culée de Vaux,** the **Reculée des Planches,** and the **Cirque du Fer à Cheval**; and far to the north-east, the **Cirque de Consolation**. There are caves to visit in most of these.

The small town of **Arbois** is one of the most attractive holiday bases in the Jura; the golden stone of its domed church belfry and the russet tiles of its roofs are beautifully set off against the surrounding greenery; there is good fishing all around. It lies at the heart of the finest Jura vineyards, which produce the unusual *vin jaune*, of which the best – and this is very good – comes from **Château-Chalon**. The origins of the Savagnin grape are obscure; the wine-making process is eccentric. The end product tastes like nuts, prunes, fino sherry or what you will, but in fact like nothing else; it has a bottle life of centuries.

The Jura's salt-rich springs have been exploited since prehistoric times. **Lons-le-Saunier** and **Salins-les-Bains** were both salt towns, and at Salins you can visit the mines where salt is still extracted. Quite apart from this, Salins is an attractive place, with casino and gardens beside the river Furieuse, and a very handsome 18th-century Hôtel de Ville and domed chapel. The salt-processing establishment of **Arc-et-Senans** is of even greater interest. It was planned and built in the 1770s by the visionary architect Ledoux, whose plans for a Utopian city – iron foundries in Babylonian style and public buildings like temples – were inspired by the industrial revolution. Models are exhibited in the halls of the elegant and classical buildings of the salt factory; elsewhere there are temporary exhibitions on appropriately futuristic philosophical and aesthetic subjects.

To the north of Arc-et-Senans, **Besançon**, the main town of the Franche-Comté, fills a deep bend in the river Doubs and is dominated by one of the largest, most imposing and best preserved citadels left by Vauban – having expended so much effort to establish control of the Franche-Comté, Louis XIV was clearly anxious not to lose it. There are no less than four museums inside the citadel, two of them devoted to local traditions and crafts. At the foot of the citadel, there is a very dirty Roman gateway, and beside it the cathedral which contains beautiful works of art including a very well-displayed masterpiece by the Renaissance Florentine artist Fra Bartolommeo. The good fine arts museum, housed in one of the finest *hôtels*, includes several works by Courbet.

Rather than go into the city, many tourists will prefer to trace the river Loue from Arc-et-Senans through beautiful wooded hills and valleys to the ramshackle but touristy town of **Ornans**. Old houses hang over the shallow, swift-running river, and rocky cliffs provide a splendid backdrop to Courbet's home town. There is a very good museum devoted to the artist. The rivers Loue and Lison and the cascading springs at their sources, both deeply sheltered beneath a canopy of lush vegetation, were beloved by the artist, and have lost none of their beauty.

The most attractive feature of the northern part of the French Jura is the **Doubs** valley. Near its source, **Malbuisson** is a quiet resort beside the Jura's largest but scenically rather unexciting lake, good for fishing and boating. Below the dull market town of **Pontarlier**, the river follows a peaceful meandering course, which may be abandoned to visit the old **Abbaye de Montbenoît**, with its Renaissance choir stalls. Downstream the Doubs enters a more dramatic phase, as tight gorges alternate with broad natural reservoirs; boats can be taken from **Villers-le-Lac** offering the best opportunity to admire the river. The Saut du Doubs is a particularly impressive tumultuous waterfall, below the Barrage du Chatelot. The Doubs is the national frontier, and runs between thickly evergreen gorges, which, if you are car-bound, can best be seen around **Goumois**, a good and extremely quiet base for walking, fishing, and doing nothing.

HOTELS

> Key: ◆ = 0–250FF, ◆◆ = 251–450FF, ◆◆◆ = over 451FF; prices are per double room without breakfast, which costs around 35–60FF extra. Some hotels may insist on half-board during high season, some hotels or restaurants may close at specific times during the week – it is always worth checking. Most hotels accept the major credit cards; we have indicated where a hotel takes no credit cards.

ALOXE-CORTON

Hôtel Clarion

21420 Côte-d'Or
TEL 80 26 46 70; FAX 80 26 47 16

This 17th-century stone farmhouse with dormer windows, near the church in the tiny village of Aloxe-Corton, is surrounded on all sides by vineyards. Being only five minutes from the main A6 motorway, the Clarion makes a good overnight stop but is comfortable enough to stay for longer. Bedrooms are large with stylish décor and modern bathrooms – some with rafters and antique furniture, all with character. There's no restaurant in the hotel, but your host can recommend five restaurants within 2km. Breakfast, when the weather's fine, is served under the lime trees, and includes your host's home-made jams.

OPEN All year ROOMS 10 (all with bath)

ANZY-LE-DUC

Auberge du Prieuré

Face Eglise Romane
71110 Saône-et-Loire
TEL 85 25 01 79

Opposite the 11th-century church for which this village is famous, Auberge du Prieuré is popular with people popping in for coffee, having an inexpensive meal or staying overnight. Simply furnished rooms, with large modern bathrooms, are excellent value, as are the menus which include Charollais beef and local fish in hearty portions. After the tourists have gone home your hosts will help you plan a stroll through the surrounding fields.

OPEN Feb to Dec ROOMS 5 (all with bath or shower)

ARBOIS

Auberge du Moulin de la Mère Michelle

Les Planches
39600 Jura
TEL 84 66 08 17; FAX 84 37 49 69

This hotel has one of the best locations in the Jura – right under the cirque of limestone cliffs behind Arbois. On its own at the end of the road, with its own waterfall and deep natural spring, and with two pretty villages and nearby caves to visit, it makes an ideal spot for a sunny day or two. It is quite a smart hotel, although everything possible has been done to preserve the character of the red-tiled mill, and the modern style is confined to the calm formal restaurant where plate-glass windows gaze on to the waterfall and to the terrace surrounding the swimming-pool. A beautiful hanging wooden staircase leads from the reception up to the bedrooms in the main building. Rooms are attractive, heavily furnished, and a little on the dark side, as is so often the case in old mills. The food is competent and smoothly presented without being stunning; the wine list is comprehensive but on the expensive side. On inspection, the service was a little off-hand and the hotel was charging a supplement for those not wishing to eat in-house. But these are small disadvantages to set against the beauty of the surroundings.

OPEN All year ROOMS 22 (all with bath or shower) FACILITIES Outdoor heated pool, tennis

De Paris

9 rue de l'Hôtel-de-Ville
39600 Jura
TEL 84 66 05 67; FAX 84 66 24 20

The buildings of this old Carmelite convent in the centre of Arbois are only one of the attractions of M. Jeunet's hotel-restaurant. The menu and wine list remain as splendid as ever – but one can be forgiven for suggesting that the bedrooms are the real *tour de force* of the place. Spacious, atmospheric and very carefully decorated in soothing fabrics, each has a strong individuality, and although the hotel is right in the centre of this busy town, peace reigns throughout. Add the friendly welcome, and you are well set up.

OPEN Feb to end Nov ROOMS 18 (all with bath or shower)

ARNAY-LE-DUC

Chez Camille

1 place Edouard-Herriot
21230 Côte-d'Or
TEL 80 90 01 38; FAX 80 90 04 64

There are over 10,000 different wines in the cellars of Chez Camille, which gives you some idea of the Poinsots' main interest. You can choose wine from practically anywhere to go with one of the pricey but good-value menus in the pretty conservatory-style restaurant. Accommodation isn't neglected, and bedrooms are good-sized, with smart, modern décor and immaculate bathrooms. Despite its unfortunate location on a busy road junction, Chez Camille makes a pleasant halt, 16km from the A6 motorway.

OPEN All year ROOMS 11 (all with bath)

AUXERRE

Le Parc des Maréchaux

6 avenue Foch
89000 Yonne
TEL 86 51 43 77; FAX 86 51 31 72

Rescued from demolition by the current owner, this Napoleon III mansion, peaceful in its own mature gardens, makes a refined and luxurious bed and breakfast hotel. The bedrooms are furnished with antiques, and are well equipped, while the public rooms, with their huge potted plants, oil paintings and marble fireplaces, are grand as well as comfortable. When it's fine, Madame's generous breakfasts are served on the terrace – more than one guest has commented on the delicious pastries.

OPEN All year ROOMS 25 (all with bath or shower)

BOUILLAND

Hostellerie du Vieux Moulin

21420 Côte d'Or
TEL 80 21 51 16; FAX 80 21 59 90

This hotel is an old mill built in stone, which sits on the edge of a quiet village surrounded by fields – although it doesn't have much in the way of olde worlde charm. Instead, you'll find modern, comfortable rooms and well-equipped bathrooms – with lots of space but strange décor in the rooms in the modern annexe, and rather less space in those in the main building. The emphasis is probably on the restaurant, where game and fish dominate the menus.

OPEN All year exc. 3 weeks early Jan ROOMS 26 (all with bath or shower) FACILITIES Indoor heated pool, sauna, gym, billiard room

BRANCION

La Montagne de Brancion

Tournus
71700 Saône-et-Loire
TEL 85 51 12 40; FAX 85 51 18 64

Bedrooms, dining-room, garden, even the swimming-pool of this modern, hilltop hotel is positioned to take best advantage of the superb view of undulating

Burgundian countryside. From the terraced gardens you can enjoy a grandstand panorama of vineyards and villages – best seen in the golden light of evening. Bedrooms are unremarkable but comfortable, decorated in pastels with green cane furniture and equipped with mini-bars. The restaurant is cool and airy, serving good food – although service can be slow. When our inspector visited the hotel was bathed in an unpleasant smell of drains but this, the management assures us, was a one-off occurrence.

OPEN Apr to early Nov ROOMS 20 (all with bath or shower) FACILITIES Heated outdoor pool

LA CELLE-SAINT-CYR

La Fontaine aux Muses

route de la Fontaine
89116 Yonne
TEL 86 73 40 22; FAX 86 73 48 66

In the north of Burgundy, 10km west of Joigny, La Fontaine aux Muses is a small family-run hotel that makes a good base for exploring the region, mostly due to its flexible, friendly staff and the facilities they lay on – bicycles, golf, swimming and tennis as well as musical evenings to entertain you. In a quiet rural spot (follow signs from the D943), the hotel is a creeper-covered farmhouse with comfortable rooms divided between the house, converted granary and a new annexe, where rooms are larger and smarter but less good-value. The à la carte menu has a good range of fish, including trout from the hotel's own pool.

OPEN All year ROOMS 17 (all with bath or shower) FACILITIES Heated outdoor pool, tennis, golf

CHABLIS

Hostellerie des Clos

rue Jules-Rathier
89800 Yonne
TEL 86 42 10 63; FAX 86 42 17 11

You wouldn't guess that this hotel was created from a former almshouse and chapel: it has lost all signs of former usage and is now a thoroughly modern, comfortable refuge with fresh, well-lit bedrooms and flower-filled public rooms. The restaurant is the focus of the establishment and, although on the pricey side, is slick and professional. In a large conservatory-style room with ruched curtains overlooking the garden, you are likely to find many Chablis-based dishes on the menu: *filet de canard au ratafia de Chablis* or *nage d'huitres pochées au Chablis*, for example. The wine list sensibly includes reasonably priced bottles of Chablis, too, also served by the glass.

OPEN Early Jan to end Dec ROOMS 26 (all with bath or shower)

CHAROLLES

De La Poste

place de l'Eglise
71120 Saône-et-Loire
TEL 85 24 11 32; FAX 85 24 05 74

Charolles is a pretty market town dissected by canals, and the Hôtel de la Poste is conveniently located opposite the church, near shops and within an easy stroll of the ramparts. On the minus side, however, church bells and traffic make some rooms noisy (although you should find the furore dies down at night). Because room standards are reasonable and prices are low, you may feel like splashing out in the Daniel Doucet restaurant – a convivial dining-room on the ground floor – where food is tasty and efficiently served.

OPEN All year exc. 2 weeks early Dec ROOMS 10 (all with bath or shower)

CHATEAUNEUF

Hostellerie du Château

21320 Côte d'Or
TEL 80 49 22 00; FAX 80 49 21 27

This charming hotel neighbours the 12th-century château high on the hilltop of Châteauneuf, with views of ruined ramparts and green hillsides. Both the ancient town and cosy hotel make a good stop-off if you are heading down the *autoroute de soleil* from Paris on your way south. Antiques, beams, chunky stone walls and large fireplaces give the public rooms a medieval atmosphere in keeping with the surroundings, although bedrooms tend to be modern and plain. A pretty courtyard garden is a calm place to relax after exploring the town and castle, and the restaurant, in an airy conservatory-style extension at the front of the hotel, serves well-presented tasty dishes.

OPEN Feb to end Nov ROOMS 17 (all with bath or shower)

CHONAS-L'AMBALLAN

Domaine de Clairefontaine

38121 Isère
TEL 74 58 81 52; FAX 74 58 80 93

It is not advisable to try to arrive here from the Rhône valley – you may become lost in the network of lanes and villas that cluster on the hillsides south of Vienne. Come by the N7, however, and the place is easily found; it is well worth finding. A lovely 17th-century peaceful manor house in white stone, roofed in red tiles, awaits. The owners and staff are very friendly; the food (modern cooking, well presented) is without any flaws, except, perhaps, for those who like their cheese under-ripe. Bedrooms are big and solid, very much in French country-house style. Given the quality and position of this hotel it is surprising it is not three times the price – currently it is excellent value.

OPEN Early Feb to early Dec ROOMS 16 (13 with bath only) FACILITIES Tennis

DIJON

Hôtel Le Jaquemart

32 rue Verrerie
21000 Côte-d'Or
TEL 80 73 39 74; FAX 80 73 20 99

Ideally sited for exploring Dijon, Le Jacquemart lies in the old quarter, a short stroll from the Palais des Ducs (which houses the popular Musée des Beaux-Arts) and the Place de la Libération. Free, on-road parking is available in front of the hotel – a real plus-point in this busy city. Decked with flags and gera-niums, the exterior of the hotel has a jolly, welcoming look which is less true of the dingy public rooms. The lounge, particularly, is somewhat drab – domi-nated by a large television and ancient easy-chairs – but the bedrooms are quiet and respectably decorated with decent bathrooms. You can opt to have break-fast served in your room, rather than in the small but serviceable breakfast room. There's no restaurant but you'll find plenty of good places locally.

OPEN All year ROOMS 32 (23 have bath or shower)

GEVREY-CHAMBERTIN

Hôtel Les Grands Crus

rue de Lavaux
21220 Côte-d'Or
TEL 80 34 34 15; FAX 80 51 89 07

Well situated for an overnight stay if you're touring the Route des Grands Crus, this large modern house with geranium window boxes offers good-value comfortable rooms without special flair. Being well away from the busy N71, the hotel's small pretty garden is peaceful and you can have breakfast here or in the rustic, café-style dining-room. No restaurant.

OPEN Mar to early Dec ROOMS 24 (all with bath)

GOUMOIS

Hôtel Taillard

25470 Doubs
TEL 81 44 20 75; FAX 81 44 26 15

On the slope of the hill above the tiny border village of Goumois, this large chalet looks straight across into Switzerland, and five minutes' walk will get you to the stone bridge and sleepy customs post in the valley below. This is a middle-of-the-range hotel; it is very comfortable but is without a great deal of character. The views are a big advantage, and the public rooms are smart and pleasing. Bedrooms and bathrooms can be on the small side for the price, but are well decorated. There is a swimming-pool for balmy days.

OPEN Mar to Nov ROOMS 17 (all with bath or shower) FACILITIES Outdoor pool

Auberge le Moulin du Plain

25470 Doubs
TEL 81 44 41 99; FAX 81 44 45 70

Approximately 5km along the bank of the River Doubs from Goumois at the end of a tiny road, this old mill is primarily a fishing hotel for those taking advantage of one of the best stretches of trout water in France, but it is also an excellent family hotel, rather less posh than the Taillard (though beware young children and the fast-flowing river). There is a small meadow with a play area, a tiny beach and a millstream containing fat trout in front of the old mill. Behind you will find a modern block of bedrooms with a small terrace in front. The bar and restaurants are atmospheric, crowded at summer weekend lunchtimes, with a good melting pot of locals, tourists and fishermen. Bedrooms are good value, plain and simple. Much the same could be said of the menus.

OPEN Mar to end Oct ROOMS 22 (all with bath or shower)

IGE

Le Château d'Igé

71960 Saône-et-Loire
TEL 85 33 33 99; FAX 85 33 41 41

Given its history as a feudal lord's manor, Château d'Igé's huge dark beams, inglenook fireplaces and stone spiral staircase come as no surprise. On the edge of a small village surrounded by vineyards and the forests of the Mâconnais, the hotel is peaceful as well as characterful. Bedrooms are well furnished with luxury fabrics and have large modern bathrooms. The dinner menu includes an extravaganza of cheese and puddings and a wine list that concentrates on the region. When it's fine, you can have breakfast out on the terrace overlooking beautiful mature gardens. Service is friendly and attentive.

OPEN Mar to early Dec ROOMS 13 (all with bath)

LEVERNOIS

Le Parc

Beaune
21200 Côte d'Or
TEL 80 24 63 00; FAX 80 24 21 19

Hotels in Beaune are pricey – if you are prepared to stay 5km out of town you'll save a significant sum. Le Parc is good value and an excellent base for exploring both the town and the Côte d'Or heartland. It's a large, two-storey building covered in ivy creepers and backed by a shady garden. Bedrooms are simple and neat with candlewick bedspreads and small bathrooms. Breakfast is the only meal served (the proprietor can recommend restaurants if you wish to eat locally) and can be taken outside in the gravelled courtyard if the weather is too good to stay indoors.

OPEN All year exc. early Dec ROOMS 25 (all with bath or shower)

MARCIGNY

Les Récollets

place du Champ de Foire
71110 Saône-et-Loire
TEL 85 25 05 16; FAX 85 25 06 91

Grand plaster-relief ceilings and parquet floors characterise this 17th-century former convent on the edge of Marcigny. Bedrooms vary from small and fussily pretty to large and functional, while immaculate housekeeping is the norm throughout. What lifts this hotel out of the ordinary is the paraphernalia which fills every nook and cranny – old prints and a collection of hats on the stairway, for example – as well as the wonderful hospitality of Madame Badin and her staff. Guests eat breakfast around one table in the farmhouse kitchen and though there's no restaurant other meals are served on demand. An excellent base for exploring Burgundy.

OPEN All year ROOMS 11 (9 with bath)

MERCUREY

Le Val d'Or

Grande Rue
71640 Saône-et-Loire
TEL 85 45 13 70; FAX 85 45 18 45

Though the village is dull with a main road cutting through it, and the bedrooms are unexceptional – though well equipped and a good size – this hotel is worth an overnight stay for the friendliness of the staff and the excellent cooking. There's a modern pink breakfast room or, alternatively, you can eat outside on a small terrace. With its beamed ceiling and huge cartwheel light-fittings, the restaurant is more rustic, and the set menus are good value, including perhaps *foie gras en terrine cuit à la maison, coeur de Charollais poêlé au jus de truffe*, and Burgundy cheeses.

OPEN All year exc. 1 week end Aug & early Sept, 1 month mid-Dec to mid-Jan ROOMS 13 (all with bath or shower)

MEURSAULT

Hôtel les Charmes

10 place du Murger
21190 Côte-d'Or
TEL 80 21 63 53; FAX 80 21 62 89

In a small residential square near the centre of Meursault, Hôtel les Charmes is one of a row of smart 18th-century mansions with decorative stonework. The inside is immaculately kept, with rugs on polished parquet floors and fresh flowers. The bedrooms, with names such as *amoureuses* and *chevalières*, are large and comfortable. Five in the main house are furnished with antiques while a further nine in a stable block across the courtyard are more modern. Danielle Flamant happily serves breakfast in your room, or you can sit outside on the terrace if it's sunny. There is no restaurant.

OPEN All year exc. 1 week at Christmas ROOMS 15 (all with bath) FACILITIES Heated outdoor pool

MEXIMIEUX

Claude Lutz

17 rue de Lyon
01800 Ain
TEL 74 61 06 78; FAX 74 34 75 23

On the main street of this rather boring village, M. Lutz's hotel is primarily a good stopping place with first-class food. He has re-done some of his rooms since our last edition, and these are interesting places, with curious internal pebble-dash and Japanese-derived ideas, such as black paper strips embedded in the walls (the effect is much more pleasing than it sounds). The restaurant has a beamed ceiling and high-backed patterned fabric chairs. The menus remain excellent value and the food is still highly reputed – the concentration is rather more on fish than was previously the case, but there is a good variety.

OPEN Early Nov to mid-Oct exc. 1 week end Aug ROOMS 13 (11 with bath or shower)

NUITS-ST-GEORGES

Hostellerie la Gentilhommière

route de Meuilley
21700 Côte-d'Or
TEL 80 61 12 06; FAX 80 61 30 33

La Gentilhommière is more of a restaurant with rooms than a hotel, though its wonderful rural setting makes it a good enough haven for more than just a stopover. You can work off the calories from one of the well-priced menus, which concentrate mainly on game and fish, by taking a stroll along the stream where a millwheel silently turns and flocks of geese graze. Inside the décor is smart-rustic with beams, stone walls, tapestry-upholstered dining chairs and lots of fresh flowers. Bedrooms are in a separate stable block and are simply furnished with small modern bathrooms.

OPEN All year ROOMS 20 (all with bath or shower)

NYONS

Auberge du Vieux Village d'Aubres

route de Gap
26110 Drôme
TEL 75 26 12 89; FAX 75 26 38 10

This is a wonderfully located hotel, perched like a falcon's nest high above the stream of traffic heading east into the Alps. So steep is the hillside that the rooms (in a sequence of cottages) tumble downwards, linked by steep staircases lined with flowering shrubs. A secluded swimming-pool and shady terrace are squeezed in. The main building mostly houses the restaurant, and it is built to take best advantage of the view. There is also a small lounge and breakfast room, joined by narrow passageways lined with bookshelves. Rooms are expensive but beautiful, well fitted-out with pine panelling and pine furniture, and also have balconies overlooking the valley. This is a smart place, but still has all the feel of a family-run hotel, although its obvious desire to move upmarket may put it beyond the pockets of British travellers before long. Get here while you can.

OPEN All year ROOMS 23 (all with bath) FACILITIES Outdoor pool, sauna, gym and games room

ORNANS

Le Moulin du Prieuré

Mamirolle
25620 Doubs
TEL 81 59 21 47; FAX 81 59 28 79

Very close to Ornans, but in an isolated, peaceful side valley under a steep, wooded hillside, this is a most attractive hotel, somewhat removed from a private guest house, but with much of the same feeling. The small mill is surrounded by five cottage chalets laid out in a semi-circle with lawns and flowers, and the bedrooms here are simple but well furnished. The main building (reception and restaurant) is big, dark and rather splendidly formal, with high-backed chairs and equipment from the old mill. Masses of fresh flowers add charm. Menus are not elaborate but promise some fine eating. Reports would be welcome.

OPEN Early Mar to mid-Nov ROOMS 8 (all with bath or shower)

PEROUGES

Hostellerie du Vieux Pérouges

place du Tilleul
01800 Ain
TEL 74 61 00 88; FAX 74 34 77 90

Right on the main square of this medieval village, with an annexe across by the ramparts, this lovely hotel makes an ideal place for a day or two's relaxation. It is a 13th-century building, very much in the centre of village life. The ground floor is given over to a huge restaurant with scrubbed oak floor and long wooden tables where plain but delicious regional cooking is presented without formality – the home-made *galette* is not to be missed. Rooms have masses of character, with old wardrobes, wooden floors (some noisy plumbing too) and good views of the village or of the steep slopes beyond the ramparts.

OPEN All year ROOMS 28 (all with bath)

PONTAUBERT

Hostellerie du Moulin des Ruats

Vallée du Cousin
Avallon
89200 Yonne
TEL 86 34 07 14; FAX 86 31 65 47

Next to a stream 4km south-west of Avallon, this hotel looks like a ranch building, with its wooden verandahs and dormer windows. It's a peaceful spot which attracts a surprising number of people for lunch in particular, which you can have outside on the river banks. Some bedrooms have antiques and beams, while others are less characterful – those overlooking the stream are the best value, and those with new bathrooms worth the extra money. The restaurant has much improved in recent years and now has a strong reputation.

OPEN Early Feb to mid-Nov ROOMS 27 (all with bath or shower)

ROMANECHE-THORINS

Les Maritonnes

Près de la Gare
Romanèche-Thorins
71570 Saône-et-Loire
TEL 85 35 51 70; FAX 85 35 58 14

If you are seeking a base from which to explore the Mâconnais villages and wine-growing areas of Pouilly-Fuissé look no further. Located in the outskirts of an ordinary village, les Maritonnes is a comfortable hotel with well-maintained gardens and an inviting outdoor pool. The peace is disturbed occasionally by fast trains which tear through the local station nearby. Bedrooms are sizeable with good bathrooms – although it's as well to avoid those above the kitchen as cooking smells, enticing enough in the early evening, become a problem later on. The restaurant is popular: the large dining-room accommodates a crowd of diners who tuck into home-made soups and steaming casseroles. Breakfast, too, is commendable: fresh fruit, maybe a peach or a handful of cherries, comes with croissants, brioche and baguettes.

OPEN Early Jan to mid-Dec ROOMS 20 (all with bath or shower) FACILITIES Outdoor Pool

ST-CIERGE-LA-SERRE

Grangeon

07800 Ardèche
TEL 75 65 73 86

Lost in the hills south-west of Valence – indeed so lost that the last part of the drive is on a kilometre of rough track, just passable by car – this little farmhouse lies deep in a wooded valley. It is not a place for overnighters, for you will need at least 24 hours to relish the setting and to enjoy the maison d'hôtes that Paule Valette has created. The style is green, perhaps slightly alternative, but in the best sense, with fresh vegetables from the garden, home-cooking and an informal and friendly atmosphere rather than any idea of discomfort and cold lentils. Rooms have plenty of space, solid country furniture and lots of character. You could hardly wish for more peace, or more comfort to go with it. Paule asks guests to arrive by 6.30pm, to enable them to relax before the 7.30 dinners.

OPEN Early Apr to early Nov ROOMS 7 (all with bath or shower) (Credit cards not accepted)

ST-FLORENTIN

La Grande Chaumière

3 rue des Capucins
89600 Yonne
TEL 86 35 15 12; FAX 86 35 33 14

Near the centre of an uninspiring town, La Grande Chaumière nevertheless makes a good overnight stop. Smart, modern bedrooms with well-equipped bathrooms and lots of space overlook either a quiet side road or the Italianate gardens. Under canvas sun umbrellas and surrounded by flowers, you can have breakfast on the terrace, where dinner is also served on warm evenings.

OPEN Mid-Jan to end Dec exc. 1 week early Sept ROOMS 9 (all with bath or shower)

Key: ◆ = 0–250FF, ◆◆ = 251–450FF, ◆◆◆ = over 451FF; prices are per double room without breakfast, which costs around 35–60FF extra. Some hotels may insist on half-board during high season, some hotels or restaurants may close at specific times during the week – it is always worth checking. Most hotels accept the major credit cards; we have indicated where a hotel takes no credit cards.

ST-RESTITUT

Auberge des 4 Saisons

place de L'Eglise
26130 Drôme
TEL 75 04 71 88; FAX 75 04 70 88

Close to the Rhône Valley motorway in distance, but miles from it in the lack of urgency which infects the place, this is a comfortable village inn in a tiny medieval village. It consists of two small houses, certainly with medieval origins, in cool white stone. A first-floor patio provides sitting space, otherwise there is just the restaurant in the rustic old stables, which serves surprisingly good food for a small establishment – nothing flash, but excellently cooked rabbit or chicken and fine cheese. Bedrooms are tortuous to get to (narrow stairs) but some are surprisingly sizeable and all are furnished with good old country furniture. The atmosphere is homely and the price far from ruinous.

OPEN Early Feb to end Dec ROOMS 10 (all with bath or shower)

SAULIEU

La Côte d'Or

2 rue d'Argentine
21210 Côte-d'Or
TEL 80 64 07 66; FAX 80 64 08 92

The excellent restaurant is the main reason for staying at this hotel. Staff who park your car, carry your bags and bring tea to your room with impeccable politeness are an added bonus. Rooms are plain, good sized and well furnished rather than luxurious, but you're in no doubt that this place is a real treat once you embark on dinner. Frogs legs in garlic, and snails with nettles are amongst Bernard Loiseau's specialities.

OPEN All year ROOMS 19 (all with bath or shower)

SENS

Hôtel de Paris et de la Poste

97 rue de la République
89100 Yonne
TEL 86 65 17 43; FAX 86 64 48 45

Now in the hands of Best Western, this fine 19th-century *hostellerie* has become just a trifle institutionalised. However, standards remain reasonably high and its location, near the cathedral and a short walk from the town centre, is as convenient as ever. Chairs and tables are set out on the front terrace and there's a pretty courtyard behind – both preferable in fine weather to the dingy *salon* with its brown, leather-look chairs and flickering electric candles. Bedrooms vary considerably from small pretty rooms with cosy, tiled bathrooms to grander, more expensive options with lots of facilities. The restaurant has a baronial atmosphere and serves a choice of *à la carte* or *menus du jour*.

OPEN All year ROOMS 25 (all with bath or shower)

Promenade des Anglais, Nice

There was sun enough for lazing upon beaches,
There was fun enough for far into the night

[Sir John Betjeman]

THE SOUTH

The 'South of France' has a distinctive ring. To announce you're off to the centre or west, still less the east or the north, just won't impress your friends in the same way. The image is one of holidays in style on the coast, where others spend whole seasons, lives even, of millions won and more often lost at the wheel of gambling fortune, of shoulders rubbed with film stars, rock stars, writers, painters and royalty. Seventy years ago the South of France conformed to this image: the Riviera – a small section of the coast between Cannes and Menton – was the playground for the mostly British rich. Now it is only a small part of what the South of France means to tourists, and irrelevant to many. As the British have lost their wealth, the Riviera has lost the British, or at least the atmosphere of a decadent imperial colony. The mild winter climate which brought the first visitors to the most sheltered parts of the south coast has lost its importance as an attraction compared with the midsummer sun about which there is nothing mild, and which beats down on the whole coast. For in the Midi (as the French call the south), the sun is king. Its light, so harsh at midday that you repair to the shade of a eucalyptus to drink, talk and sleep, so luminous at each end of the day that it seems to paint the landscape in colours of a new intensity, alone gives unity to the area we call the South of France.

The original Provincia Romana covered most of southern France. In the Middle Ages the region became known as the Languedoc, an area characterised by the provençal language of the medieval troubadour poets of the court of Toulouse, which is closer to Latin than is the French of northern France. In the Languedoc they said '*oc*' for 'yes' whereas in the north, the Languedoil, they said '*oil*' for '*oui*'. The heart of the Provincia was the area around the Rhône delta, now known as Lower Provence. The Roman influence on the area is profound and provides the main attraction to tourists. Though perhaps not uniquely endowed with great buildings, its monuments remain intact as nowhere else in France – particularly in Arles and Nîmes; many are still used.

However, sightseeing need not be confined to Roman remains, for there is far more to see in Lower Provence. Aigues-Mortes and Les Baux are two of the most extraordinary old towns in France, the one

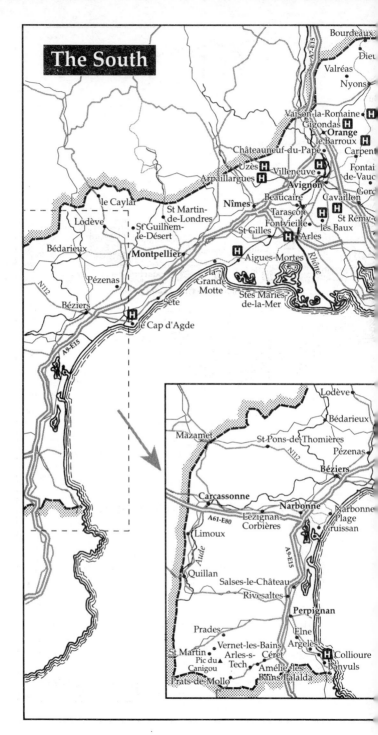

The South

Savines-le-Lac

Barcelonnette **H**

Auron •
Isola 2000   Col de Tende
Beuil •
St Martin-Vesubie •   Tende

Buis-les-Baronnies

Sisteron

Mt Ventoux
Sault

Château-
Arnoux

Digne-les-Bains

Sospel

Reillane **H**

H Saignon
Montagne du
Lubéron

Manosque

Moustiers-
Ste Marie

Castellane

Peillon **H**
Roquebrune
la Turbie

Menton

Point-Sublime **H**

Vence **H**
St Paul

Monte-
Carlo-Monaco

Grand Canyon
du Verdon

St Paul

Beaulieu

Cagnes **H**

Villefranche-s-M.

Fox-Amphoux **H**

Seillans **H**

Grasse

Nice

St Jean-Cap-Ferrat

Cotignac

Callian

Mougins

Biot **H H**

Draguignan

Cannes

Antibes

Barjols •

Juan-les-Pins

H Aix-en-
Provence

Beaurécueil

le Luc

les Arcs-sur-Argens

A8-E80

Roquebrune-s-A. **H**

Plan-de-la-Tour **H**

Agay

St Raphaël

H MARSEILLE

Ste Maxime

Fréjus

Aygulf

Cassis •

la Cadière
d'Azur

Grimaud **H**

St Tropez

Bandol
Sanary

Toulon

Hyères

Ramatuelle **H**

Cavalière

Cavalaire

le Lavandou **H**

Giens

Iles d'Hyères

M E D I T E R R A N E A N

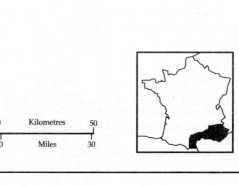

0   Kilometres   50

0   Miles   30

163

intact within its walls on the salt flats, the other partly ruined on one of the sudden lonely rocky outcrops that characterise Provence. Avignon has the magnificent palace where the popes resided under the protection and control of the kings of France for 150 years. Arles – the capital of Roman Gaul – is a beautiful town with monuments from all periods and like nearby St-Rémy is rich in artistic associations, notably with Van Gogh. Aix is the glory of the post-Renaissance classical period, a mellow and harmonious town seemingly rebuilt all of a piece in the 17th and 18th centuries. South-west of Arles in the Rhône delta lies the Camargue, land of shifting coastline, salt marshes, wild horses and bulls, leather-clad cowboys and flamingoes.

With the exception of a few rocky and dramatic crags and peaks, the landscape of Lower Provence is relatively flat, and swept by the *mistral* wind which howls dry and cold down the Rhône valley. Much of its natural scrubland has been turned to profit, with olive and almond groves, cherry orchards, vineyards and lavender beds. It is not an area, however, to come to for a relaxing holiday. The towns are very busy with commerce as well as tourism and their outskirts tend to be grim and traffic-riddled. Sightseeing can be hard work therefore, though tempered by great numbers of good hotels and restaurants – the better hotels tend to be in the countryside.

Behind the Côte d'Azur – the stretch of coast between Marseille and Menton – lies Upper Provence, a mountainous region of great natural beauty, still little frequented by tourists. On almost every one of its hills there seems to perch a village. Some of the most strikingly situated, especially those looking down over the coast, have become tourist traps – which doesn't detract from the beauty of their situation but will disappoint many visitors. In general, the hill villages further inland are much less frequented and even though the views they command may be less dramatic they reward more greatly a thirst for authenticity.

At the foot of the hills and mountains, the coast has grown apart from the interior because of tourism. Nearly all those who go to the coast go *for* the coast, and venture very little inland (in high season the density of traffic makes it very difficult to venture anywhere). Those who go to visit Roman Gaul or just to relax in a sleepy inland hideaway turn back in horror if they set out for a day on the beach, and sink gratefully back into the quiet shade of their village plane trees or into contemplation of a classical pediment.

The Riviera began with the British. The writer Tobias Smollett spent 18 months in Nice in the early 1760s because of his asthma; in many ways his experience is typical of the Riviera as it was to develop in the 19th century. In all his time in Nice he hardly associated with any non-visitors (perhaps not surprising for Nice had its own Italianate local patois); he aroused curiosity by bathing in the sea; and although he stayed through the year he describes the summer in such a way as to explain why the Riviera developed as a winter resort: 'The heat is so violent that you cannot stir abroad from six in the morning till eight at night. We are pestered with incredible swarms of flies, fleas and bugs but the gnats are more intolerable than all the rest.' It was not just that the sun was not fashionable – the place was downright insanitary. Smollett published his letters and 20 years later an English visitor was 'disgusted by the gross flattery paid to the English in particular...the whole neighbourhood has the air of an English watering place'. The coast east of Nice, which is sheltered from the north wind by the Alps, became an increasingly popular place to spend the winter. To the west of Nice, Cannes became popular in the mid-19th century by accident: a travelling English peer was prevented from leaving France because of an outbreak of cholera and fell in love with the small fishing port where he had to stay in quarantine. Following his example the English moved into Cannes; they annually brought turf for their lawns, and introduced croquet, cricket, tennis, and acacia and eucalyptus trees. In the 1820s the English visitors were responsible for the construction of a long coastal promenade at Nice, the Promenade des Anglais.

In the tiny Principality of Monaco, Prince Florestan decided to set up gaming houses (forbidden in France) as a way of raising some revenue, for all the family estates in France had been confiscated at the Revolution, and the expedient of extra heavy taxation and customs duties had already been tried. By the end of the decade the railway had reached the Riviera, and so sudden was the growth of its popularity that in February 1869 gaming revenue was sufficient for the prince of Monaco to abolish all taxes and rates (residents still pay no income tax). A young traveller of 1861, Augustus Hare, came back over 30 years later to write a guide book to the Riviera and described what had happened in the intervening period: 'Up to 1860 Menton was a picturesque town with a few scattered villas let to strangers in neighbouring olive groves; now much of its lovely bays is filled with hideous and stuccoed villas in the worst taste...pretentious paved promenades have taken the place of the beautiful walks under tamarisk groves by the seashore. Menton is vulgarised and ruined but its climate is delicious, its flowers exquisite and its excursions for good walkers inexhaustible and full of interest.' Monte Carlo, 'a wild spot covered with heath and rosemary until the 1860s', he now found to be 'a snare, never more plainly set'. Exotic gardens, the finest orchestras, and lavish reading rooms were all laid on free, but *'faites le jeu, messieurs* is heard from noon till midnight and the faster people ruin themselves and send a pistol shot through their heads the faster others take their place'. Queen Victoria came to Cimiez, and Edward Prince of Wales came to Cannes. Luxury trains came from Calais, St Petersburg and other European capitals, and an English newspaper announced the new arrivals, as if the winter Riviera was one enormous ball, which it was. Nice is estimated to have received 25,000 winter visitors in the 1880s, but only one hotel of standing stayed open in the summer.

The Riviera was aristocratic (British and Russian) but even more than that it was rich, and whereas there may originally have been a coincidence between riches and titles, by the 1920s there was not. Katherine Mansfield, one of the many tubercular visitors to the Riviera described Nice (in 1920) as a bourgeois paradise and life on the Riviera as 'ignoble. It all turns to money'. Americans played an even larger part in the seaside society and being used to the heat started the fashion for summers on the Riviera; in the late '20s they launched the summer resort of Juan-les-Pins. Perhaps the last great representative of the Riviera's golden age was Edward VIII; when the war was over Edward and Mrs Simpson did not go back to the Riviera for long, for it was becoming a mass destination for French summer tourists. Its winter attractions remain, and have even been increased by the development of well-equipped ski resorts close to Nice; but those with the means and inclination to winter on the Riviera are a select few.

Considering the tourist revolution that has taken place, the look of the Riviera is remarkably little changed. Everything still turns on money, and the Principality of Monaco's crop of high-rise tax-free international banks are quite in keeping with the atmosphere of gambling Monte Carlo. Architecturally the Riviera is still dominated by exotic villas and overblown neo-baroque palaces – although many of these have been institutionalised. Along the Riviera there has simply been very little space for development: the seafront from Menton to Nice was heavily built up before 1900 and the mountains come right down to the sea. To the west of Nice there is a little more space and some striking modern architecture in the new beach and marina resorts that have been built to accommodate the crowds.

The coast is hardly a relaxing place for a midsummer holiday; it is Paris-on-Sea with many of the qualities of the capital – flashy, self-conscious, exciting, an absorbing spectacle, where people come to see and be seen. The season reaches a peak of intense crowds in July and August, when the coast roads come to a standstill (as does the motorway south from Paris on peak weekends). At no time of the year is it empty, as a ski resort can be in summer or a pure beach resort in winter, but somehow when it isn't full it seems rather sad – like a fast car being driven at 30 miles per hour. You may enjoy the landscape more, but that isn't the point.

When Parisians took over the coast they did not confine themselves to the Riviera – strictly the stretch of coast east of Cannes. Now the coastline between Cannes and Marseille, which had been more or less ignored by visitors and in parts bypassed by the railway, is hardly less frequented than the eastern stretch, and although the resorts press less closely one against the other the crowd factor is no less marked. The obvious difference between the two parts is the absence on the western stretch of Riviera-style architecture, which barely extends beyond Cannes and finally expires at St-Raphaël with a few cheap and nasty imitations of what is at its best an imitative style. Another difference is the landscape: the west lacks the distant snowy backdrop of the Alps but instead has rocky mountains – which are related not to continental France but to Corsica and the Balearics – and long beaches with pines. But the most important difference is harder to express clinically; it is a difference of style. It is not simply a question of wealth: there are infinite gradations of atmosphere. Just as a Cap Ferrat person would not be confused with a Cannes person, still less with a Menton person, a Ste-Maxime person would not be seen dead in Le Lavandou, still less St-Raphaël or Hyères-Plage. Paris-on-Sea is as class-ridden as Paris, and on the coast the different ingredients of the metropolitan social mix have separated. The exception is St-Tropez, no less potent in its image-conjuring power than Monte Carlo, and classless. The arty bohemian resort where topless sunbathing started in the 1960s, St-Trop' has retained its hold on the public imagination, and its own inimitably laid-back exclusiveness. It is the radical chic (still chic in France) of denim and leather and Harley Davidson, of the Left Bank and the ever-youthful Johnny Hallyday. At St-Tropez, in complete contrast to the Riviera, you can recognise the smartest people by the scruffiness of their clothes.

West of the bay of St-Tropez are small family resorts – with holiday homes rather than hotels and more emphasis on practicality than style. These resorts have grown to receive tourists where barely a community existed before; few of them are large or exciting or hideous or noisy, and most of the coast is very beautiful. Around the important ports of Toulon and Marseille, the landscape is rather spoilt by industry and ill-thought-out development.

Between the Rhône delta and the Pyrenees the coast of Languedoc and Roussillon (Catalonia in France, centred on Perpignan), is characterised by two things: red wine, produced in greater quantity than anywhere else in France, usually described as unpretentious; and a flat, straight, sandy coast broken up by lagoons and marshes, only recently drained for development. Except at the extreme south there are no hills immediately behind the beaches. Until the 1960s there were few people except Sunday sunbathers from Montpellier, Béziers, Narbonne and Perpignan – cities of France's greatest rugby players and bullfighters. Now the Languedoc/Roussillon coast bristles with what were heralded in the '60s as the resorts of the future. Here the architects and the planners have asserted themselves, working hard to build with themes and styles, more often around marinas than beaches. Naturism flourishes in many. Holidaymakers here can sail to and from their backyard and everyone owns or rents flats and yachts. The style varies from the futuristic geometry of La Grande Motte, the first and most ambitious of the new resorts, to the subsequently more fashionable borrowing of inspiration from the simple rustic architecture of southern France. In contrast to the Riviera these resorts are almost devoid of life outside the midsummer months.

The coast from Menton to Marseille

Between Nice and the Italian border just east of Menton the Maritime Alps descend steeply into the Mediterranean, giving some of the most beautiful coastal scenery in Europe, and sheltering the shore from the north wind. This is the area for summer flowers and lemons in winter, and is the original winter resort for those too fragile to withstand the northern cold. Very little of the coast is not built up.

There are three roads along the coast. The **Corniche Inférieure** runs right along the coast serving all the resorts, inadequately. The **Grande Corniche** is the most exciting; it's the far from straight old Roman road from Nice to Genoa, reaching a height of nearly 450 metres above the sea. It passes behind some coastal peaks and gives a mixture of views down over the bays of the Riviera and up into the barren Alps, snow-covered for most of the year. One of the few villages the road passes is **La Turbie** which was the point of division between the Roman Empire this and that side of the Alps. The great monument (Alpine Trophy) which was erected on the site in 6 BC to commemorate the conquest of the Alpine regions, which united the Empire and heralded three centuries of *Pax Romana*, must have been very impressive, to judge from the model in the museum. The huge fragment that remains is arresting.

The **Moyenne Corniche** gives the most consistent sea views and access to **Eze**, the most astonishingly perched village of all. The view from it is one of the classics of the Riviera. Eze is one of the most popular excursions from the coast, so do not expect an unspoilt old village. At the top, on the site of the old castle, there is an exotic garden with cacti.

Menton has a reputation for being the best resort for health, and the new town on the western bay has something of an atmosphere of a spa as many of the imposing old winter palace hotels have been taken over by French institutions for holiday colonies. The mostly 17th-century town between the two bays is still attractively Italianate with ochre painted houses and dripping laundry strung across the narrow streets beneath the baroque belfry of St-Michel, whose little square is a delightful setting for summer evening concerts. Like many of the Riviera resorts, Menton has its winter carnival – here celebrating the lemons and oranges for which it is most famous. Above Menton and its adjacent resort of Roquebrune-Cap-Martin, the village of **Roquebrune** remains intact, medieval and perched, or rather clinging to the side of the hill. Its narrow and often vaulted passages are all confined within the precincts of a 10th-century fortress built for defence against the Saracens.

Between Menton and Roquebrune, roads lead back up the hillsides to the finely situated villages of **Gorbio** and **Ste-Agnès**, both of which are old and panoramic. Ste-Agnès, the highest of the villages immediately behind the coast, occupies such a commanding position that it was endowed by German occupiers with blockhouses, which remain.

You don't need a sign to announce the tiny **Principality of Monaco**, which occupies less than a square mile of ground, but the surface area of whose buildings must be many hundred of times larger. On the French side of an imaginary line down the hillside there are old houses and small villas, on the other side soaring tax-free international banks. The Principality, unable to grow on land, has grown upwards, down into the ground (underground car parks) and even into the sea in the form of conference centres and tourist developments. **Monte Carlo** is the new town of banks, some occupying modern skyscrapers, others in the old, that is to say 19th-century, villas which have all the grace and beauty of elephants dripping with diamonds. The neo-baroque style surpasses itself in the sumptuously plush Hôtel de Paris and the adjacent casino, the work of the architect of the Paris Opera House. If you want to chance your arm in the casino, there are gaming rooms (all glitz and no style) with no entrance fee and no need for ID. If you are over 21, for a small fee and with passport and smart apparel (jackets for men) you can swan around in the main gambling rooms, admire the panoply of chandeliers, paintings and frescoed ceilings and absorb the sound of clinking chips as bets are made and fortunes lost (or won).

Beyond **La Condamine**, the antique port of Hercules and now a berth for colossal yachts, the old settlement of **Monaco** stands on a natural fortress, with 45 metre cliffs down to the water on three sides. The small town (tourist access on foot or by bus only) is old and painted, and has one building of substance, the princely palace of the Grimaldis, very heavily restored when wealth came to Monaco and architecturally uninteresting. It is open June to October when the family is away, and contains a surprisingly impressive mostly 17th-century courtyard of honour with distinguished frescoes and a marble staircase. As well as the stagey square in front of the palace with its crenellations and cannons, Monaco has a 19th-century cathedral with two beautiful altar-pieces of Nice's Bréa school, and a celebrated aquarium in its oceanographic museum.

Though many interests are now vested in its continued existence, the tiny principality owes its survival largely to luck and the tenacity of the Grimaldis. The family probably came from Genoa to defend the harbour against the Saracens and bought control of Monaco in the 14th century, later adding Menton and Roquebrune. Napoleon incorporated the principality into the Alpes Maritimes, but surprisingly the Allied Powers gave it back to the Grimaldis in 1814. The sporting British started a number of famous competitions, of which the most celebrated are the Monte Carlo rally, the Grand Prix, and the tennis tournament, the first of the international clay court season.

Grimaldi Palace

Back in France, **Beaulieu** is a very sheltered resort, not unlike a version of Menton. The **Cap Ferrat** peninsula remains one of the most exclusive villa communities on the Riviera, which makes it one of the most exclusive places anywhere. At the little port of **St-Jean-Cap-Ferrat** there is a large marina which is good for yacht spotting. Near St-Jean you can visit the delicious villa and gardens built round the very precious art collection of the early 20th-century Rothschild heiress Madame Ephrussi (the Ile-de-France Museum). The French 18th century is particularly well represented. On the western side of the Cap, **Villefranche** guards one of the finest, most enclosed bays of the Riviera; however, its shingle beach is rather narrow. The old town of tall houses, narrow streets and stairways climbs up from the fishing port and 16th-century citadel and is pleasantly unspoilt. Beside the quay the small chapel is decorated by Jean Cocteau. The next twist in the coast leads round to the sweeping Baie des Anges at whose head stands Nice with its long, wide and graceful Promenade des Anglais.

Nice is the big city of the Riviera and one of the most important in southern France. Its inhabitants go quite mad for a fortnight before Lent at carnival time. With its long beach of shingle backed by a six-lane promenade highway with palm trees and ornate hotel façades, it looks like an enormous resort; but there is more to Nice than its seafront. The old town is still very much a living part of the city, with colourful flower and vegetable markets and pungent smells by day and dining at night on the Cours Saleya. There are several baroque churches, the most interesting being St-Jacques and St-Augustin. The new town, which extends to the west beyond the promenade, has very good shopping, the showy salons of the Belle Epoque Negresco hotel, a number of museums and a Russian Orthodox cathedral.

Sights in Nice

• **Masséna Museum** A splendid 19th-century palace whose interior is mainly devoted to the Napoleonic period and the memory of Nice's two most famous sons: Masséna and Garibaldi. There are paintings of the 15th- and 16th-century Nice school, the stars being the Bréa family whose works are to be found in churches and chapels all over the Alpes Maritimes and whose limited fame is largely attributed to the deep gloom in which most of the paintings hang.

• **Chéret Museum** (Fine Arts) Paintings featuring works by the local artists Fragonard (born in Grasse) and Van Loo.

• **Cimiez** The old resort hill of Cimiez, behind the centre of Nice, has its villas and turn-of-the-century hotels (Queen Victoria stayed at the Grand, now turned into apartments) and also has the city's best sights. Cimiez was a Roman settlement – the ruins of a Roman villa and the best-preserved baths in France can be visited, as well as the archaeological museum, which traces the history of the ancient province. With much hype, the Matisse museum has finally reopened in the Arena Villa; a Chagall museum lies some way down the hill near the station; see Modern Art, page 179, for both. Across the public gardens from the Arena Villa, the abbey church has three paintings by the Bréas, including a particularly affecting Virgin – an early work of Louis Bréa, and one of his most beautiful.

Excursions from the coast

From Menton and Nice a number of roads lead back into the Maritime Alps, where the enclosed valleys – with cascades and gorges – and numerous perched villages are the main attractions. For the winter (and spring) visitor, ski slopes are only a couple of hours or so from the sea. In the summer there's high mountain hiking in cool thin air, with snowy peaks still visible well into the season. The mountains have little cultivation or pastures and their relatively bare rocky slopes have become progressively depopulated, which adds to the desolate beauty of the half-empty hilltop villages. Such are the difficulties of communication that the main road linking Nice to Grenoble has to climb to well over 2,500 metres to get through – by the Col de la Bonette which boasts the highest road in Europe, although strangely not the highest pass.

• **Peillon/Peille** This short excursion behind Nice can be extended round to La Turbie or Ste-Agnès and Menton. Peillon and Peille are two finely set hill villages, both looking down over steep-sided valleys. Peille, set beside a relatively frequented road, is less atmospheric than Peillon whose setting on a high sheer rocky spur above the river far below is beautifully admired from the approach road which zigzags through the olive trees up the side of the valley. The carefully restored rough stone village itself is nothing much: steep alleyways, a few tasteful craft shops and a comfortable hotel (see 'Hotels' page 203) on the terrace outside the village. In the early 19th century the area around Peille and Peillon was terrorised by the notorious band of brigands who eluded all attempts at capture until they set upon the Marchioness of Bute and drank the contents of a bottle which she was carrying and which they assumed to be full of alcohol. It was in fact opium and they all collapsed. To everyone's embarrassment they were discovered to be members of the leading families of Nice.

• **Roya Valley** This is a busy road into Italy via the Tende tunnel. The Roya cuts through impressively tight gorges below the extraordinary situated village of **Saorge**, on a horseshoe balcony above the river (access from Fontan). **Tende** is hardly less picturesque in its tiered setting below strange spiky ruins of an old fortress. **La Brigue** has a Romanesque church with the Italianate belfry typical of the old county of Nice, and two Bréa paintings. Beyond it the isolated Chapelle-Notre-Dame-des-Fontaines is decorated with some of the most vivid (and gruesome, in the case of the hanging of Judas) of 15th-century frescoes. The key may be obtained from the town hall or several bars in La Brigue. The high mountain areas west of **St-Dalmas** (the Vallée des Merveilles) are excellent hiking country with refuges, lakes and 2,500-metre peaks. Curiously there are thousands of Bronze Age graffiti carved on the rocks. The crossroads resort of **Sospel** has an attractive old arcaded central square and the statutory Bréa in the church, and gives access to the upper Roya valley and to the less frequented, steeply enclosed Bévéra valley, which also has its gorges; there are high mountains and dark forests to be explored from the recent resort of **Peïra-Cava**.

• **Vésubie Valley** Just before it joins the Var the Vésubie cuts through a narrow rocky gateway. In its pastoral upper valley **St-Martin-Vésubie** is the centre for many excursions on foot and by car. There are mountain refuges, fishing in the lakes and an Alpine game reserve beyond Le Boréon. Mountain roads link the valley with those of the Tinée and Bévéra. From St-Jean-la-Rivière a narrow road winds up to a 19th-century pilgrimage chapel beyond Utelle.

• **Tinée Valley** An important through-route serving the most popular of Nice's mountain resorts, **Auron, St-Etienne-de-Tinée** and the more recent **Isola 2000**, built high up (at 2,000 metres) by a British property company. The Route de Restefond or de la Bonette over to Barcelonnette and the once very isolated Ubaye valley rises to 2,802 metres at the foot of the Bonette peak, which can be reached from the top of the road by a short but breath-taking climb; the landscape has its own very desolate beauty. At the top of Europe's highest road (usually closed until June) there is an appropriate shrine to Notre-Dame-du-Très-Haut.

• **Cians/Daluis Gorges** Two very impressive sequences of gorges cut by the rivers Cians and Var through fiery red rock. The old Grimaldi stronghold of **Beuil** is now an attractive and peaceful summer and winter resort, sharing its mountainsides with **Valberg**, which is more frequented.

Just west of the old national frontier of the Var – whose lower valley is industrial and unattractive – the long **Baie des Anges** is dominated by the sinuous blocks of the modern marina development – also called Baie des Anges – and the resort of **Cros-de-Cagnes**, site of the Nice race-course. The coastline itself is less worthy of note than the villages set some way back from it, and the fertile hillsides are full of prosperous villas among cypresses, mimosas, oranges, eucalyptus and vines.

Vence is one of the more important hill towns; in the old centre the Place du Peyra has great charm and the cathedral amusing choir stalls. More unusual is the Chapelle du Rosaire to the north of town, designed and decorated by Matisse.

St-Paul-de-Vence (or just St-Paul) crowns a ridge which commands excellent views. The village itself is very handsome – golden stone and russet tiles, the 16th-century ramparts around which you can walk, narrow pedestrian streets, and an interesting church with a painting by Tintoretto. Not surprisingly, St-Paul teems with day-trippers and its streets are lined with tourist shops. In all these respects it is not exceptional but its style sets it apart from other frequented perched villages. St-Paul has long attracted painters as well as tourists and its houses have been restored and converted with unusual care and restraint. There are as many galleries as knick-knack shops and the Hotel Colombe d'Or beside the shady *boules* pitch is also something of a modern art museum thanks to the enlightened proprietor's willingness to accept distinguished paintings in exchange for his distinguished fare (you are likely to be shooed away if you are wandering round to look at the art, rather than a client). There is a fine modern art museum (see page 180), and numerous hotels on the surrounding hills, many enjoying marvellous views of the village. Staying in or near St-Paul gives you the chance to wander around when the village is at rest.

Behind Vence, roads climb quickly (such as by the Col de Vence) into an area of wild rocky landscapes and steep-sided river valleys (*clues*) which contrast with the more fertile coastal slopes. The **Gorges du Loup** pass beneath **Gourdon**, an example of a splendidly perched village which has become merely trippery.

Grasse is the famous capital of the world famous scent industry, its factories producing the essence for three out of every four bottles. At the turn of the century it was an important spa and winter resort, but dozens of factories have changed that. The more attractive aspects of the industry are the fields of brilliantly colourful cultivated flowers all along the coast between Nice and Cannes, as well as all the generally more fragrant wild flowers favoured by the industrialists of Grasse. When you learn (as you can by visiting several of the factories, or the International Museum of Perfume) how many tons of petals it takes to make a litre of essence, and how many blooms to make a ton of petals, you will appreciate why the fields are so extensive, and scent so expensive. Much of Grasse is new and it cannot be considered as a whole a very attractive place, but there is an old part in projection from the hillside with an imposing cathedral which contains paintings by Rubens, and a religious painting by Fragonard which is quite out of character with his better-known style.

Cagnes stretches down in three separate communities from an old Grimaldi fortress to the sea. The fortress which dominates the enclosed perched village of **Haut-de-Cagnes** is mostly a 17th-century conversion, and is well worth visiting. Some rooms are devoted to the olive, others to modern art. The villa in which Renoir spent his final years can be found in the suburbs of Cagnes-Ville (see page 180).

The attractive hill village of **Biot** should be pronounced to rhyme with pot, which is what the locals have made for centuries. Now Biot is famous for glass-making too, and pulls in the crowds, for it is a delightful old village, and, on its outskirts, has an excellent museum (see page 180) of the works of Fernand Léger, painter and ceramic artist inspired by Biot and responsible for its success.

Where the road to Biot meets the coast there is a large family entertainment complex and a marine and aqua park. Antibes and Juan-les-Pins lie close together either side of the base of the **Cap d'Antibes**, and merge into a large built-up area, cutting off the greenery of the Cape which has some quiet unpretentious hotels and a small beach far from the madding crowd. **Antibes** is a port of great antiquity, called Antipolis by the Greeks. The old town, solidly walled on its seaward side in the uncompromising style of Vauban, is full of life (with one of the best and most colourful markets on the coast) and beautiful when admired from the small beach just along the shore towards the Cape. In the old town the cathedral, like so many others, has an ill-lit Bréa; of greater interest is the Picasso museum in the old Grimaldi château (see page 180). The rest of Antibes is a modern and bustling resort. **Juan-les-Pins**, young and very lively at night, had a *raison d'être* untypical of the Riviera – a long, sandy pine-backed beach now divided into immaculate private allotments. It extends to Golfe-Juan where Napoleon landed in 1815 on his return from Elba.

Picasso and **Vallauris**, another old pottery village on the clay soils behind the Cap d'Antibes, interacted in the same way as Léger and Biot, with an even greater impact on artist and village, now one of the world's most productive centres of artistic, and not so artistic, pottery manufacture.

Cannes is the last extravagant flourish of the true Riviera, and flourish it does thanks in no small measure to the post-war initiative of an annual international film festival, which must be the best advertising for any resort in the world. This was the small fishing port which enchanted Lord Brougham in the 1830s and which became a winter favourite among the rich British, who first covered the hills with villa estates, constructed large harbours, and built up the seafront for 8km. They cared little that Cannes enjoyed few of the climatic advantages of the coast beyond Nice; Cannes depended upon society for its attractions, and it still does. It is the most obviously smart resort of the coast, with a much greater feeling of being a resort than towny Nice. Its face is the gleaming seaside Boulevard de la Croisette which stretches from the Festival and Conference Centre by the port to the summer casino on the point. Behind its palms and gardens is a succession of very exclusive jewellers, art galleries, couturiers and hotels. The marinas are full of palatial yachts, but the port and old town of Le Suquet above it do have some life of their own though not much sightseeing interest. The beach is long and sandy. Boats cross daily to the two wooded **Lérins** islands; on Ste-Marguerite you can visit Vauban's fortress, long used as a prison; on St-Honorat there are the remaining monastic buildings of a community which in the dark days of the collapse of the Roman Empire kept alight the fires of civilisation and Christianity.

The hinterland of Cannes is much less mountainous than further east and there are no fewer than nine 18-hole golf courses; one of them is at **Mougins**, an old hill village which has become a prestigious and pricey gastronomic suburb.

Between **La Napoule**, a small beach resort squashed beside the railway and the sea with a heavily restored old fortress, and St-Raphaël the corniche road is at its most beautiful. It is cut into the rocky hillsides of deep red porphyry which drop into a clear sea from the peaks of the very ancient **Esterel Massif**, now only 500 metres at its highest point, beautiful, wild and desolate and explorable (on foot) by forest tracks with splendid viewpoints. The coast road is not an old one, and the small row of resorts along it have no particular character. From the road you can clamber down to numerous rocky coves and swim among colourful reefs. **Agay** is one of the larger resorts on the sea, and has a good sandy beach.

St-Raphaël and **Fréjus** spread round the mouth of the Argent which divides the Maures Massif from the Esterel. It is the site of the first important port and colony in Roman Gaul. Ancient Forum Julii was actually bigger than modern **Fréjus** which is no Arles or Nîmes, but does have a number of Roman remains (aqueduct, amphitheatre and theatre) and a very interesting cathedral. The 12th-century two-storey cloister is delightful with its well and oleander, the octagonal baptistry survives from the 5th century, and there are interesting works of art within the church. In the museum next to the cloister there are some local archaeological finds; more, found in the sea (scuba diving flourishes around this part of the coast), are displayed in a museum of underwater archaeology in **St-Raphaël**, a resort which participated in the boom of the late 19th century and which is still very animated, though not very attractive – its looks were spoilt by bombing in 1944. Adjoining **Fréjus-Plage** is plain and functional, but has a nice beach. **Valescure** (inland) and **Boulouris** (by the sea) are more relaxing leafy villa resorts.

Although less immediately striking than the Esterel, the larger and more wooded **Maures Massif** is hardly less beautiful. Its coastline is indented with splendid bays, of which the finest are those of St-Tropez and Le Lavandou, which attracted artists before tourists. Trees characteristic to the area are chestnuts, cork oaks – whose stripped trunks can be seen all over the hills – and umbrella pines, which look as they should. There are many more good long sandy beaches with shade than there are further east.

Ste-Maxime is an old town and busy resort facing south across the St-Tropez gulf. The palmy prom and port consists not of grandiose late 19th-century façades, but simple ochre-painted houses. **Port-Grimaud** has been constructed at the head of the gulf between Ste-Maxime and St-Tropez. Built in 1966, it is one of the earliest and the most aesthetically successful of the new marina resorts with bridged canals and warmly painted houses, the prototype for the Languedoc resorts. Set back from the sandy vineyards behind Port-Grimaud, the old hill village of **Grimaud** is quiet and unspoilt, with arcaded houses, a lovely Romanesque church and the remains of a ruined castle sprouting from its top.

St-Tropez is the old port of the region, and the harbour – where a few fishing boats fight for survival among all the yachts and motor cruisers – is still very picturesque. In the early morning before all the promenaders are out, fish are sold on the quay and the place seems unspoilt.

Port-Grimaud

For the rest of the time in season the port cafés and boutiques are crammed with people; the back streets are full of trend-setting shops and galleries. As well as the people to look at, there is a very fine modern art museum (see page 180) recalling the many painters who followed Paul Signac to St-Tropez in the 1890s. With its studiously relaxed atmosphere, lively focal port and little shingle beach below open-air restaurant terraces, St-Tropez has something of the air of a Greek island, overlaid with a patina of sophistication.

In summer, buses ferry tourists to the main beaches on the Ramatuelle peninsula, which are excellent – spacious, sandy and shady – but further than walking distance from St-Tropez itself. Most are some way from the main road and are private, requiring a hefty entrance fee. Each has its own devotees – the St Tropez high-life set. The peninsula itself has only restrained development and is delightful; its old villages of Gassin and Ramatuelle have lovely views across wooded slopes and vineyards.

The resorts beyond lack the human interest of St-Tropez and few of them are much to look at in themselves, typically with functional blocks of flats behind the beach and villas around the hills. **Le Lavandou**, an old cork industry centre and fishing port, is the most important of them. The port/marina is large and busy, as is the beach. Colourful and old **Bormes-les-Mimosas** occupies a fine vantage point high above the bay, and has as many flowers as the name suggests.

Hyères was once a popular resort, originally on account of its winter climate; now it's a large town with a medieval quarter, which has its tame resort of Hyères-Plage. 'Plage' added on to the name of a town is usually a reliable warning of a rather dreary beach resort outpost and this is no exception. From Hyères-Plage two spits of sandy land frame salt pans: one is a very popular though not attractive camping territory.

The three Hyères islands are very beautiful. The main service to **Port-Cros** and the **Ile du Levant** goes from Hyères-Plage, and to **Porquerolles** (and the other two in summer) from the Giens peninsula to the south (access also from Toulon, Le Lavandou and Cavalaire sur Mer). The Ile du Levant is a naval base and also the South of France's most famous nudist colony (the two halves are kept separate). Porquerolles and Port-Cros both have accommodation; Porquerolles has a small port and good beaches.

Between Hyères and Marseille the coast mainly serves the populations of Marseille and Toulon, the two most important ports of the French Mediterranean. Particularly characteristic are the fjord-like inlets called *calanques* which can be explored by boat from **Cassis**, the most picturesque little resort west of St-Tropez. Like St-Tropez, it was a fishing port much favoured by painters early this century; but there the similarity ends. **Bandol**, which like Cassis gives its name to wine of some local distinction, is the other unsophisticated, lively resort on this stretch of coast. **Bendor** (a quick boat ride from Bandol) is a popular amusement centre and resort island.

Toulon, like Brest in Brittany, is a fortified military port with memories of slave labour (in this case galley slaves) which owes its importance to Louis XIV, Vauban, and its magnificent situation on a deep sheltered anchorage. There are fine panoramic drives to be made up in the fortified heights behind the city (the Mont Faron, the Gros Cerveau, and the eerie ruined village of Evenos) but Toulon itself is unattractive – it suffered heavy war damage.

The name of **Marseille** has become associated with pastis, gangs, corruption in high places and the French Connection, that is to say drug running. It is a port of great antiquity – Greeks came in the 6th century BC – but its atmosphere today has little to do with history, except the Second World War, which destroyed much of the city, and the Algerian War, which ended with large numbers of immigrant *pieds-noirs* going no further than this their port of arrival. The colourful down-to-earth bustle of the old port may provide a welcome antidote to the pretensions of the other coast resorts. The most popular sights are the towering basilica of Notre Dame de la Garde and the formid-able prison island of **Château d'If**, which sits prettily in the bay, reached by regular boats. But all this is unlikely to prove adequate reward for coping with the traffic.

Excursions from the coast

• **Ste-Baume Massif** A bare grey theatre of mountains encloses Marseille – hardly less arid than those that surround Athens. Behind it, the massif is surprisingly green and bright, with beech forests and a panoramic peak (St-Pilon). On the northern side of the massif, the sight of **St-Maximin** can be appreciated from all directions. The great Gothic basilica is one of the few of any importance in Provence; it is no lofty greenhouse like the northern cathedrals, but does contain some inter-esting works of art.

• **Verdon Gorges** Alone among southern French gorges, these have earned the title of Grand Canyon. It is a title not unreasonably bestowed for this is one of the natural curiosities of Europe. Though their existence was almost unknown until the beginning of this century, the Verdon gorges have recently been made easy to admire from roads engineered along the heights – but they have not been tamed. A good starting point is the village of Moustiers-Ste-Marie – itself an astonishingly set village built on a hillside on both sides of a rocky crevasse.

Two roads lead south of Moustiers and reveal the incomparable spectacle of the swiftly running Verdon, in some places over 500 metres below. The recently built **Route des Crêtes** along the north side of the river follows more of the canyon than the **Corniche Sublime** to the south, including the deepest section whose walls are twice as high as the Gorges du Tarn. It is possible to walk down into the (→ page 181)

Modern art

The South of France is one of the most rewarding areas for anyone with an interest in late 19th- and 20th-century art. In Provence there is the pleasure of seeing landscapes through the eyes of artists who have made them famous – Van Gogh and Cézanne, sadly not well represented in local museums. Along the fashionable parts of the coast there are a large number of museums housing the collections of wealthy Riviera dwellers and works left behind by the artists who settled among them.

Although surprisingly neglected by the thousands of classically educated 18th-century artists who travelled through Provence on their way to Rome, the South of France was discovered by artists as it was by society in the late 19th century. While intellectuals argued about the nature and role of art in the turmoil of post-1870 Paris, real observations were made in the South. Paul Cézanne was a native of Aix-en-Provence who spent much of his active life contemplating the Mont Ste-Victoire, taking it apart and reassembling it on canvas in his attempt 'to revivify Poussin in front of nature'. Cézanne was not only interested in form, and in 1876 wrote from the coast near Marseille, 'the sunlight here is so intense that it seems to me that objects are silhouetted not only in black and white but also in blue, red, brown and violet'. The realisation 'that sunlight cannot be reproduced but must be represented by something else – by colour' was to be of the greatest importance for the development of art away from Impressionism, the aims of which were essentially naturalistic. It was shared by Monet and Renoir on the coast in the 1880s, by Van Gogh around Arles in 1888/90, and a few years later by the artists (notably Paul Signac) who settled in the old fishing village of St-Tropez and moved from a scientific approach to colour (Pointillism) to a much freer and richer one. Signac's work and ideas, as well as the southern light, were in turn influential on the young Matisse who, working with Derain in Collioure in 1905, made further strides away from naturalism in a manner known as *fauve* (literally, wild). Derain wrote from Collioure of 'a new conception of light – negation of shadow. The shadow is a whole world of clarity and luminosity which contrasts with the light of the sun. I am learning... to rid myself of the whole business of the division of tones... it injures things that derive their expression from deliberate disharmonies'. Collioure remained an important artist's colony, and so too did the Riviera. Some artists drew inspiration from their surroundings, other simply found the coast an agreeable place to live. Fernand Léger, for example, lived at Biot, and his work is better admired there than anywhere else; but apart from a sideline interest in ceramics which was inspired by the local industry at Biot, Léger's artistic contribution as the greatest interpreter of the machine age could hardly be further removed from the Côte d'Azur.

Aix-en-Provence The Vasarély Foundation contains a number of works by this contemporary colourful cubic illusionist. Cézanne's studio (open to visitors) has been left as it was when the artist died in 1906.

Antibes The curator of the castle in the old town complained about the emptiness of the building and Picasso offered to fill it – which he did with his usual astounding facility in paint, pencil and clay. If not specifically related to the South of France, many of the works in the Grimaldi Museum have as their theme the Mediterranean classical mythology.

Biot The Fernand Léger museum traces the development of the artist with huge and very powerful industrially inspired paintings, drawings, tapestries and ceramics.

Cagnes The villa in which Renoir lived his final years (1909–19) in Cagnes-Ville, surrounded by an olive grove, has works by him and of him in rooms furnished as they were when he was there. The château in **Haut-de-Cagnes** houses a varied art museum.

Collioure Works by locally inspired artists in the town hall.

Menton The Salle des Mariages in the town hall is decorated by the artist and poet Jean Cocteau. By the port there's also a small museum which contains his works in various media.

Nice Matisse lived for many years at Cimiez. A superb collection of his work in many media – drawings, bronzes, tapestries, canvases – is exhibited in new sunken concrete galleries joined underground to a fine rust-coloured villa beside the Roman arena. Closer to the city centre, a museum was built to house 17 canvases by Marc Chagall, illustrating in his poetic and colourful way the Bible message; it also contains many of his other works. In the heart of the new town, a bold modern construction houses the Museum of Modern and Contemporary Art, a small but important collection of French and American avant-garde art.

St-Paul-de-Vence Just outside the village the Maeght Foundation is an architectural curiosity, and contains a wealth of works by greater and lesser 20th-century Post-Impressionist painters and a number of sculptures.

St-Tropez The Annonciade Museum is an exceptional collection of mostly early 20th-century paintings, many of them related to St-Tropez.

Vence The Chapelle du Rosaire is the work of Matisse – architectural design and decoration.

Villefranche The Chapelle St-Pierre is decorated by Cocteau.

gorge from the Chalet de la Maline on the northern side, or down a very steep path from the Restaurant des Cavaliers on the Corniche Sublime, to walk along the Martel path for some 15km to the Point Sublime (it takes about eight hours). Provisions, a torch and some adder repellent should be taken.

The bottom of the gorge is in places no more than six metres wide, and the path does not follow it all the way. An attempt to investigate it should not be undertaken lightly, and requires specialist experience, equipment and guides, and up to three days. Both refuges at the end of the Martel path provide accommodation in summer.

The route south from the Verdon to the coast around St-Raphaël and the Maures crosses peaceful and attractive Provençal countryside with unexceptional market towns. **Bargème**, one of the most atmospheric of hill villages in all the south, is well worth a visit (it lies only a few kilometres north-east of Comps-sur-Artuby). It is peaceful, and you can clamber around the substantial ruins of its old fortress.

Other attractive hill villages in the region include **Seillans, Bargemon, Fayence, Cotignac, Fox-Amphoux, Saignon** and **Ares sur Argens**, which all have some accommodation.

Lower Provence

Aix-en-Provence is the old Roman spa and capital, at whose gates 100,000 Teutons were slain in 102 BC by the Roman Marius. Aix was originally a spa (Aquae Sextiae), and remains one. As well as the thermal establishment, there are moss-covered fountains in the Cours Mirabeau which spout curative water. Aix has also long been an intellectual and cultural centre, particularly brilliant in the 15th century when René d'Anjou – absentee king of Naples and duke of Provence – held his civilised Renaissance court here, and in the 17th and 18th centuries when the local nobility transformed Aix, capital of Provence and seat of the local parliament, into a town of ordered Classical elegance and dignity. In the centre at least, Aix has changed relatively little. It is still relaxing and refined, an important university centre popular with foreign students, and the host every July of an internationally famous music festival. Aix's focus and evening parade-ground for strollers is the Place du Général de Gaulle, formerly de la Libération, and the Cours Mirabeau – a majestic creation of classical *hôtels* and four rows of venerable planes providing an unbroken lofty canopy. Along the Cours there are banks, cafés, and shops selling the local marzipan speciality, *calissons* (Aix is the centre of an important almond-growing area), and along the south side splendid examples of the town architecture where muscular caryatids frame doorways and support balconies. The whole area to the south of the Cours Mirabeau is a model of 17th-century planning, with many beautiful houses around the playful Fontaine des Quatre Dauphins. To the north of the Cours, the old centre of town is a fascinating and endlessly surprising maze of old streets, also with an abundance of beautiful buildings from the 17th and 18th centuries. Highlights are the little 18th-century Place d'Albertas, and the Place de l'Hôtel-de-Ville, where there is a very colourful flower market.

Sights in Aix-en-Provence

- **St-Sauveur** A composite cathedral resulting from the incorporation of a delightful 12th-century church into a later and larger edifice, of which it now forms most of the south aisle. There is a 5th-century baptistry and hole-in-the-ground font, and a small but beautiful 12th-century cloister. The church's treasures include a painting of the Burning Bush showing King René as donor, and the Renaissance carving on the central doors of the façade.
- **Tapestry museum** A resplendent collection of 17th- and 18th-century Beauvais tapestries in the old archbishop's palace beside St-Sauveur.
- **Museum of Old Aix** A relatively interesting folklore museum, with local figurines called *santons* (which feature particularly in Provençal Christmas cribs), costumes and pottery.
- **Ste-Marie Madeleine** A 17th-century church containing a very fine 15th-century triptych of the Annunciation and a large painting by Rubens.
- **Granet Museum** Named after the local painter and generous collector, whose fame is assured by the superb portrait of him by his friend Ingres, one of the great treasures of this very rich museum. A collection of antique and local pre-Roman sculptures, and French, Flemish and Italian paintings.
- **Vasarély Foundation** A spacious museum devoted to the modern geometric artist, beside the motorway on the western side of Aix (see page 180).
- **Cézanne's Studio** Preserved as it was when he died in 1906, but the furniture of the studio does not include paintings by the artist who has done more than most to make Aix famous. Cézanne devotees should explore the land to the east of town, around the long ridge which is the **Mont-Ste-Victoire**, especially surrounding **Le Tholonet** on the D17.

To the north of the Durance, the **Lubéron** range of mountains do not compare with the Mont-Ste-Victoire or the Mont Ventoux, between which they lie, but there is a road along the highest crest (the Mourre Nègre) and there are some attractive hill villages to the north of the mountains. The area was long a fashionable rural retreat for the French before Peter Mayle wrote his now famous account *A Year in Provence*.

The most noteworthy villages are **Ménerbes, Oppède-le-Vieux** (carefully restored with arts and crafts activities), **Bonnieux, Gordes** and **Roussillon**. The last two are particularly fine. Roussillon is a village of brilliant red ochre in the middle of a region of red cliffs and ochre quarries of which the largest and most impressive near Rustrel has earned itself the name of Rustrel Colorado. At Gordes, the château in the village houses a small collection of the works of Vasarély. Near Gordes, towards Cavaillon and the Abbaye de Sénanque, there are many interesting primitive dry-stone shepherds' dwellings (*bories*). The **Abbaye de Sénanque** is a beautiful example of simple, unadorned, Cistercian monastic buildings, well-preserved and unspoilt in a wild, isolated valley setting. In summer there are occasional concerts.

Not far from Sénanque, waters well up from enormous natural underground crypts into the great cavernous **Fontaine de Vaucluse**. This, one of the most powerful springs in the world, is a natural curiosity not at its most impressive in the summer, and very trippery. Part of the attraction of the village and spring is its associations with the 14th-century Italian poet Petrarch, who lived at Fontaine de Vaucluse for many years, the fountain of his love for the unknown Laura pouring out lyric poetry.

The small village of **Venasque** is the unlikely capital of the area known to history as the Comtat Venaissin, conceded by the French king to the papacy in the 13th century, with the important indirect consequence of the popes moving from Rome to Avignon shortly afterwards. In the village is a Merovingian (7th-century) baptistry, and a short distance to the north of it the small chapel (Notre-Dame-de-Vie) which has a richly carved Merovingian tomb.

The most impressive of the gorges of the Vaucluse plateau are carved by the Nesque, between Sault and Villes-sur-Auzon. They can be incorporated in a long but worthwhile detour from the road between Carpentras and Vaison-la-Romaine, through the heart of fragrant lavender country, and back over the mighty Mont Ventoux. **Carpentras** is the most important market town of the well-irrigated Comtat; the fertile surrounding plain produces large quantities of grapes, almonds, melons, tomatoes, garlic and herbs, and the commercial streets of the town are colourful and busy. There are no monuments of great importance, but an unusual synagogue in the Jewish ghetto. You can also visit the 18th-century hospital (Hôtel-Dieu) and the cathedral, a handsome mostly late-Gothic building.

The **Mont Ventoux** is one of the great landmarks of Provence, rising in isolated symmetry to its summit of 1,909 metres It is appropriately named: the top is often extremely windy, and the expanse of bare rock on the south face makes the Ventoux look snow-capped all the year round. The panorama on the clearest days reaches from the Pyrenees to the northern Alps. The road is not usually difficult, but you are unlikely to beat the record up the 22km from Bédoin which has been covered in nine minutes at an average speed of 140km an hour. Walking up takes about four to five hours; the best starting point is Brantes, steeply below the summit on its north-eastern side. The gentlest ascent is from Malaucène, which is the way Petrarch went up on 26 April 1336.

Vaison-la-Romaine is a town of great interest and charm built in three parts on both sides of the River Ouvèze, still spanned by a single-arched Roman bridge. In the floods of 1992 the river broke its banks, part of the bridge was washed away and 42 people died. The new town is not special, except for the Romanesque cathedral which stands incongruously on its edge. Part of the walls of the building rest on the fragments of old Roman columns and complete ones support the arcade around the inside of the 6th-century apse. There is a small 12th-century cloister with a collection of archaeological fragments. From the tourist office you can get a key and walk northwards to the small chapel of St-Quenin, which also dates mostly from the 12th century and is decorated in a most unusual style inspired directly by the antique.

Sights in Vaison-la-Romaine

- **Roman Town** For grandeur, Vaison-la-Romaine cannot compare with the great monuments of southern Provence; its attraction lies in the evocation of the complete layout of an important town. In the two areas which you can visit there are streets, colonnades, gardens, mosaics, courtyards, fountains, and a small museum containing the best fragments.
- **Medieval Town** In the troubled times of the Middle Ages, the inhabitants of Vaison deserted the vulnerable right bank of the Ouvèze for the steep hill across the river, where ruins of a 12th-century fortress still stand above the medieval upper town. Its steep and narrow cobbled streets, which climb from fortified gateways towards the fortress, are exceptionally attractive and have been bypassed by the development of modern Vaison.

The pre-Alpine mountains of the **Baronnies** region east of Vaison are cut by deep valleys full of vines, olives, fruit and herbs. The picturesque arcaded market square of **Buis-les-Baronnies** is the setting every July for a very important herb market. Still further east, **Sisteron** is a busy road junction on the Route Napoléon. Although it suffered heavy damage from bombs in August 1944, there are still narrow and attractive old streets beside the Durance. The citadel has been restored to its original massively imposing grandeur on the site of an old fortress high above the town centre (a long staircase climb up). Seasoned observers of the frontier lands of France may recognise the hand of Louis XIV's military architect Vauban, but in fact the citadel is mostly the achievement of one of Vauban's unsung predecessors, Jean Erard. There are very fine vertiginous viewpoints from the citadel walls.

The domed former cathedral of **Notre-Dame** (12th-century) is a fine example of Provençal Romanesque, dark and powerful and simple in its lines.

Like Sisteron, **Orange** is a gateway to Provence, and there could be no more appropriate gateway than the magnificent Roman triumphal arch which arrests your progress from Montélimar and the north. The third largest such arch in existence, it is also one of the most richly decorated with sculptures despite having been turned into a fortress by the lords of Orange. Orange was an important Roman city of over 80,000 inhabitants in its day and is now a large market town for the surrounding region – though it does not get its name from the fruit. Surrounded by the Comtat Venaissin, Orange was a separate principality in the Middle Ages, and came into the possession of the northern European Nassau dynasty, which provided England with William of Orange. In 1713 Orange was given to the French, but the Nassau family kept the title. The Roman theatre is one of the finest in existence. Here, as nowhere else, there remains the massive façade wall, over 30 metres high and 90 metres long. Inside, there is a stage wall with columns and doorways and a statue of Augustus in a niche, and tiers which originally held 11,000 spectators. The acoustics are renowned. There are also remains of Gaul's largest Roman temple, a gymnasium and the old capitol dominating the town. On the square opposite the theatre, there is a museum of local history, paintings, and very interesting archaeological finds.

Châteauneuf-du-Pape gets its name from the summer residence built there by Pope John XXII, who was also said to have planted the vines which are now the most prestigious of the Rhône valley. Since 1944 the only remains of the château are a couple of walls and some fragments of vaulting. There is a small wine museum above some cellars in the village and plenty of places to taste.

Avignon owes its unique place in medieval history and its exceptional interest to the modern sightseer to Pope Clement V, who installed the papal court on the banks of the Rhône in 1308. It was only intended to be a short stay but successive French popes found good reasons not to leave Avignon, best of which was the war-torn state of 14th-century Italy. In 1377 Gregory XI returned to Rome, but a breakaway group of cardinals came back to Avignon the next year with their own antipope, thus initiating the great schism of Christendom – a shameful chapter in the history of the Church. The city of Avignon was not French territory but part of Provence, and surrounded by the papal lands of the Comtat Venaissin. In 1348 the pope bought Avignon from the first lady of Provence in exchange for a free pardon for all her sins, which included the murder of her husband. The Avignon popes established themselves in conditions of magnificence unmatched by any royal court in Christendom. The palace they built for themselves was described by the French chronicler Froissart as the strongest and most beautiful house in the world. Popes slept on pillows trimmed with fur, cardinals were described by Petrarch as 'satraps mounted on horses decked with gold and champing golden bits whose very hoofs will be shod with gold if God does not restrain their arrogant display of wealth'. Papal Avignon became a notorious refuge for the undesirables and outlaws of Europe and the town was summed up by Petrarch as 'unholy Babylon thou hell on earth, thou sink of iniquity, cess-pool of the world'. Avignon today is a busy modern city which extends far beyond the restored medieval ramparts; but because of its riverside situation it has not sprawled in all directions, and seen from across the Rhône it still looks almost as impressive now as when papal and royal fortresses menaced each other in the 14th century. However, the ramparts no longer look quite as high as they did, the ditches having all been filled in by the construction of surrounding roads. The famous 12th-century Pont d'Avignon (on which one never used to dance all in a circle – it was *sous le pont* on a grassy island in mid-stream) is now reduced to a few arches which jut out into the Rhône.

Sights in Avignon

• **Palais des Papes** Still dominant, strong and severely beautiful. One of the most important and impressive of all Gothic buildings, covering nearly 15 square kilometres. When Stendhal went to Avignon in the early 19th century he noted the ingenuity of the inhabiting soldiers – for the Palais des Papes was long used as a barracks – in chipping off bits of fresco and selling them locally. The interior of the palace has been much restored and there are still a large number of extremely beautiful frescoes, some religious but others in a style more familiar from tapestries whose function they took on the walls – for example in the papal bedchamber. Apart from these there is no impression of a palatial residence but many large beautiful chambers whose emptiness underlines the fortress-like impression of the exterior. The palace was mainly built in two campaigns in the 1320s and the 1330s but in two completely different styles – one simple and Romanesque, the other Gothic. Guided tours in English.

• **Cathedral** The main features of the mostly 12th-century building beside the papal palace are the lamentable 19th-century Virgin who stands on top of the tower and the damaged but splendid tomb of John XXII, greatest of the Avignon popes. Between the cathedral and the river there are some beautiful gardens giving views across the Rhône to Villeneuve.

• **Petit Palais Museum** An exceptionally rich collection of Medieval and Renaissance paintings (Italian and Avignonese), and sculptures

Palais des Papes

housed in the old archbishop's palace across the square from the papal fortress.

● **Calvet Museum** A beautiful 18th-century *hôtel*, with peacocks in the gardens, housing several different museums including a notable collection of ironwork and post-Renaissance paintings, mostly French. Many big names represented.

● **Old Town** Avignon *intra muros* is all old and the *muri* are nearly 5km round. The town is split by the main commercial and traffic artery, the wide plane-lined Cours Jean-Jaurès/Rue de la République, which runs from the station towards the Palais des Papes at the other end of town. To the west of it there are a number of beautiful 18th-century *hôtels* in the Rue Vernet, of which the Calvet Museum is one example. On the other side of the Cours the old dyers' quarter – though not as attractive as some other restored old town centres – has many houses dating from the 15th to the 18th centuries on the Rue du Roi René and the Rue des Teinturiers, beside which there are still some mill-wheels in the waters of the little Sorgue.

Villeneuve-lès-Avignon, Newtown-by-Avignon, grew after a clever initiative by the French kings who did a deal with the abbey of St Andrew which stands on a hill opposite Avignon. They built fortifications around the abbey which are in fact no less than a royal fortress, echoing the majesty and might of the papal establishment and reminding the popes of the ever-present reality of French royal pressure on papal policy. The new town itself was established by means of the kind of incentives which are still used today to take people to development areas. Villeneuve became a favoured place for Avignon cardinals to build themselves luxury villas and remains to this day a quiet, peaceful and elegant residential suburb of Avignon with a number of good hotels which makes Villeneuve-lès-Avignon a very good base for the surrounding area. Of medieval Villeneuve there remains Philip the Fair's tower which once stood at the end of the bridge and now stands alone on the bank. The powerful fortifications on the top of the hill are worth visiting especially in the evening for the view across the Rhône to the honey-coloured walls and palace of Avignon.

Sight in Villeneuve-lès-Avignon

• **Chartreuse du Val de Bénédiction** A very large and romantically dilapidated monastery which has only been restored as townsfolk have moved out of its buildings. It was founded in the 14th century but much of it is classical in style. A guided tour reveals the tomb of Innocent VI in the church and 14th-century frescoes in Innocent's chapel.

Only a very few kilometres west of Villeneuve-lès-Avignon stands one of the wonders of Roman Provence, the **Pont du Gard**, hiding its beauty in the wooded landscape of the Gardon. This is just the bridge part of a long aqueduct which brought water to Nîmes from near Uzès. It consists of three tiers of arches, the upper one over 270 metres long and over 45 metres above the river. It is a tremendous engineering feat, achieved without the use of any binding agent for the enormous blocks of stone which were lifted by pulleys powered by men in cages operating a treadwheel. It is also very beautiful and the architect's obvious

Pont du Gard

aesthetic concern in this purely utilitarian construction is extraordinary. Tobias Smollett, the 18th-century traveller, described the bridge as 'a piece of architecture so unaffectedly elegant, simple and majestic that I will defy the most phlegmatic and stupid spectator to behold it without admiration'. Smollett also considered the bridge an ideal place on a summer's evening for a cold collation under an arch. Large numbers of tourists and the inhabitants of the local towns followed his advice and the Pont du Gard is a beauty spot appreciated by a much wider public than most Roman remains. There are campsites, boats, bathing areas and hotels nearby.

The water flowed across the river to Nîmes in a covered channel supported by the small upper register of arches. It is dry now and you can walk along it; the courageous can walk along its roof, and get truly vertiginous and extensive views. It is some 3 metres wide, which may sound a comfortable width for a path, but with the sheer 45-metre drop to the beckoning waters of the Gardon the effect can be extremely uncomfortable especially when the *mistral* is howling. In the 18th century a carriage road was built beside the top of the lower register of arches and is still used by traffic. The best viewpoint of the bridge is from upstream near the Château St-Privat.

Uzès, supplier of water to Nîmes, is a splendid old town which stands above the *garrigue* – dry scrub and herb-covered limestone plateaux and hills that lie along the southern flank of the Massif Central. Although very close to the great Roman towns of Provence, Uzès is off the beaten track of Provençal tourism and has the atmosphere of a different region. From afar the town looks surprisingly Tuscan, with its three medieval towers dominating the sky-line – one for the king, one for the bishop and one for the ruler of Uzès. All that remains of the cathedral is the cylindrical bell tower called the Tour Fenestrelle because of the Romanesque arched openings in its walls. You can visit the ducal palace which has a fine Renaissance façade; but the main attractions of Uzès are the old streets and restored central square – sleepy and shady with a fountain and substantial arcaded houses. On Saturdays the square comes to life with a busy market.

In complete contrast to Uzès, Nîmes is a big city of no particular attraction in itself, but with monuments of the greatest importance. It would be nice to be able to avoid Nîmes and all its traffic, especially in hot weather; but the fact that one cannot advise doing so is a reflection of the quality of its two great Roman buildings, the amphitheatre and the Maison Carrée.

Sights in Nîmes

● **Amphitheatre (Arènes)** Not the largest but by far the best-preserved of all Roman sports grounds. Complete with vaulted galleries and arcades around the outside and accommodation for over 20,000 spectators inside, it has survived because it was transformed into a fortress and later a lodging for over 2,000 people and has never been used, as so many other monuments have been, as a quarry for later builders. On summer days when it is packed with *aficionados* of Spanish-style bullfighting, the amphitheatre lives again in the true spirit of antiquity. In the old days too, it was the arena for fights between men and beasts.

● **Maison Carrée** This small temple is not in fact square, but as its original dedication is unknown no better name for it has been thought of. Built on the purest Greek principles in the 1st century BC, Maison Carrée is not as well shown off now in the middle of the town as it was once on the edge of the Roman forum. But it is remarkably preserved, having been spared the fate of being transported brick by brick to Versailles by Colbert.

● **Jardin de la Fontaine** Around the old magic spring of Nemausus, which was the origin of the city of Nîmes, beautiful gardens and artificial lakes were constructed in the 18th century. The gardens lie at the foot of a tall wooded hill with a Roman tower (Tour Magne) on top. You can climb up for long views over the surrounding *garrigue*. Within the gardens there are substantial ruins conjecturally called the Temple of Diana.

For modern administrative purposes Nîmes, being on the west of the Rhône, is part of Languedoc. The most impressive point of the watery

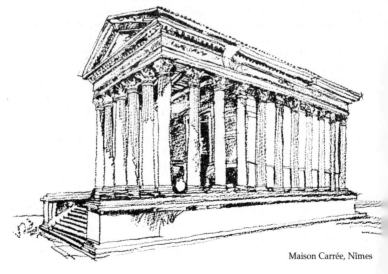

Maison Carrée, Nîmes

boundary between Languedoc and Provence – which for a time in the Middle Ages was the boundary between France and Empire – is the point where two mighty medieval fortresses stand facing each other across the river – **Beaucaire** on the Languedoc side, **Tarascon** in Provence. Having effectively deterred any fighting, the Château de Tarascon is exceptionally well preserved; but at Beaucaire, much of the fortress was destroyed by Richelieu in the 17th century. There remain a fine triangular keep and ramparts on the high rock above the river.

Tarascon is no beauty of a small town, but its riverside is dominated by its massive fortress which rises like a monolith from the rocky bank of the Rhône, and by the next door church of Ste-Marthe in memory of the saint who came and tamed the ferocious monster Tarasque that had terrorised the region, specialising in devouring women and children. It had the head of a lion, the bones of its spine broke through its skin like a hundred iron spikes, its six twisted paws had claws of a bear which furrowed the ground and its tail would have resembled an asp had it not been thick as a man's waist and long as the trunk of a cedar. Saint Martha waved a cross and sprinkled some holy water on the Tarasque which dropped the remains of an unlucky individual from its mouth and allowed itself to be led meekly to the Rhône, in which it has remained ever since. The church has a very fine Romanesque south doorway, and a beautiful tomb at the top of the stairs leading down to the crypt, the work of the early Renaissance Italian sculptor Francesco Laurana. The **Château de Tarascon** is the very model of a late medieval fortress; inside (guided tour) there is a courtyard and an impressive but empty series of Gothic chambers, and fine views from the battlements.

The area to the south and east of Tarascon, Provence by anyone's definition, is one of the most beautiful and interesting in southern France. Its main focus for sightseeing is Arles, the capital of late-Roman Gaul. Arles is a good centre for excursions – especially for those without a car, but it is a big town, with industry and over 50,000 inhabitants. For those in search of a more rural base, **St-Rémy**, the small market town of flowers, fruit and vegetables, the painters' village past and present, set against the impressive backdrop of the rocky Alpilles, is a more pleasant and relaxing place to stay. From here you can easily go into Arles of an evening, to look at the stars from a street café, and think of Van Gogh; and you can also go up to the haunted village of Les Baux at sunset or by moonlight.

St-Rémy and Arles share the memory of Van Gogh, who came to Arles early in 1888 and spent most of the last two years or so of his life here. At first he painted his lonely room, sunflowers, the Alyscamps, starlit townscapes and Arles people. After the arrival of Gauguin, months of extreme turbulence within Van Gogh's never tranquil mind climaxed with the bizarre affair of the artist's severed left ear and his application for asylum at the convalescent home at the edge of St-Rémy. Van Gogh was well looked after there, and no less productive than he had been in Arles, turning out scores of brilliant landscapes – of golden corn, silver olive groves, and black cypresses.

St-Rémy is attractive and popular with artists and British expatriates. There is a small folklore museum in an old 16th-century *hôtel* with courtyard, which includes some items commemorating the 16th-century astrologer and prophet Nostradamus, who was born in St-Rémy, and whose speculations have not lost their thrall. There is also an archaeological museum, with finds from the very important Roman site of Glanum, which lies just over a kilometre out of St-Rémy.

On the one side of the road out of St-Rémy into the Alpilles and Les Baux stand two superb Roman monuments, **Les Antiques**; on the other the only recently excavated remains of the important settlement of **Glanum**. Les Antiques originally constituted a gateway to Roman Glanum. There is a triumphal arch, by no means intact but well enough preserved to show the influence of Greek art on this the oldest of Roman triumphal arches in Gaul, and beside it a Cenotaph in a quite extraordinary state of preservation. It is an elaborate and elegant memorial to the two grandsons of Augustus, Caius and Lucius. Unlike so many Roman monuments in southern France, Les Antiques stand in an attractive, isolated rural setting. Across the road, Glanum to many people looks like a lot of rubble and a few fragmentary columns, but to the initiated, or those prepared to study the literature, Glanum has remains of three different settlements. There was a town here as early as the 6th century BC, and already excavations have revealed dwellings from the pre-Roman period of the 2nd century BC. There are also Roman remains in two different styles. Just beside Glanum the old monastery of St-Paul-de-Mausole still stands in the attractive vegetation that Van Gogh depicted when he was an inmate here. You may visit it and admire its Romanesque church with a small overgrown tower and a charming cloister.

From Les Antiques and Glanum it is only a short drive up into the completely different world of the desolate heights of the rocky Alpilles. On a natural fortress just under a kilometre long by a couple of kilometres or so wide stand the ruins of the old citadel of **Les Baux**, which so impressed Louis XIII's destructive minister Richelieu that he demilitarised it, as was his uncompromising wont. Richelieu called Les Baux 'the eagle's nest' long before the expression lost power through overuse. It was the right description, for not only does the rocky spur on which the city stood command a birds' eye view, it was also the home of a ruling family who were notoriously proud and rapacious, claiming descent from one of the Three Wise Men, and incorporating the Star of Bethlehem in their emblem. The lords of Les Baux – which means rocks in Provençal – and their ladies held one of the most celebrated and brilliant of troubadour courts of love in the early Middle Ages, and in less poetic mood pushed people off the cliffs of their rocky stronghold for sport. For a time they were amongst the most powerful lords in the south, and Les Baux numbered several thousands of inhabitants. Now there are only a few hundred, who live on a flank of the outcrop, among elegant ruins of mostly Renaissance town houses. On top of the rocks above them, the heart of the old city is even more ruinous – empty shells which look down sheer cliffs over a colourfully contrasting landscape. It is no surprise that these evocative scrub-covered ruins are overrun with tourists who never seem to feature in the tourist office photographs and who make it very difficult to imagine Les Baux as anything other than a tourist attraction. To savour its atmosphere, you must go out of season or preferably late in the day when the sun sets on the ruins and gives life to this so-called *Ville Morte*. At the foot of the outcrop, a new Les Baux has sprung up, consisting of a number of smart hotels surrounded by spacious and luxuriant gardens. It is a good place to stay for those who seek peace and quiet away from the main towns.

Between Arles and Les Baux, **Fontvieille** is another good place for a base, with several hotels, generally simpler but also peaceful. Just outside the village stands a windmill – the Moulin de Daudet, where the 19th-century novelist did not write his *Lettres de Mon Moulin*, or even stay. It is however the *moulin* about which he wrote, and has been restored and turned into a Daudet museum, probably to the chagrin of the man himself, for what he liked about the mill was its ruined state, 'its limbs broken, useless as a poet, while all around mills are prospering'.

Standing on the junction of the Rhône and the Aurelian Way from Italy to Spain, **Arles** was the capital of late Roman Gaul, and also of the medieval (9th to 11th centuries) Burgundian kingdom of Arles. Thanks to the exploitation of the surrounding countryside for rice growing, and to tourism, Arles has recently resumed importance after a long period of stagnation. It is a premier example of what the French call an 'art town', offering not only Roman monuments – some at its very heart – but also medieval ones and museums of the greatest interest. It is also a very attractive town, in the centre at least. The only disappointment here, as at Aix-en-Provence, is that the artist who has done most to make the town famous – in this case Vincent van Gogh – is unrepresented. The hospital where he was treated has now been converted into a cultural centre – Espace Van Gogh – though none of his art was on display when we visited. Most of the main monuments listed below can be visited on a global entrance ticket which can be acquired at any of them.

Sights in Arles

- **Amphitheatre (Arènes)** By no means as intact as the one at Nîmes, but well preserved nevertheless, thanks to its transformation into a fortress (three medieval towers remain) and later a complete village of 200 houses. Like the Nîmes amphitheatre, it is still a setting for bull-fights.
- **Theatre** The remains are incomplete but substantial enough for shows and festivals to be put on.
- **St-Trophime** One of the most beautiful and fascinating churches in southern France. The west doorway, slapped on to the otherwise unadorned façade in the late 12th century, contains an abundance of beautiful carving and reveals everywhere the influence of classical architecture and sculpture. The cloister – not accessible through the church – is one of the finest in France, a mixture of Gothic (west and south galleries) and Romanesque (north and east galleries) and like the west doorway has enough carving to absorb you for hours. The cloister also gives the best view of St-Trophime's splendid three-tiered Romanesque tower, again with classical elements incorporated. Inside the church there are fine early Christian sarcophagi.
- **Museon Arlaten** (Arles Museum in Provençal) This is perhaps the most famous ethnographic museum in France, itself something of a monument to Frédéric Mistral, hero of linguistic separatists, and the great champion of Provençal life and culture, who founded the museum and donated the proceeds of his Nobel prize to its enrichment. Set in a beautiful 16th-century *hôtel*, it is particularly rich in furniture and costumes, and also has sections devoted to folklore, local history and Mistral himself.
- **Musée Lapidaire Chrétien** A collection of early Christian fragments especially sarcophagi (mostly 4th- and 5th-century) unrivalled outside Rome, and housed in a 17th-century Jesuit chapel.
- **Musée Lapidaire Païen** Also set in a 17th-century church, opposite St-Trophime and curiously built in the Gothic style. Local archaeological finds and mosaics from pre-Christian times. There is a 17th-century cast of the famous Arles Venus which is now in the Louvre.
- **Les Alyscamps** Even if, as is thought probable, the Alyscamps does not mean the Elysian Fields, it should; for this is the legendary burial ground of the heroes of medieval French epics. Since Gallo-Roman times, the road into Arles from the south-east was lined with funerary monuments, and the fame of the Alyscamps and its legendary inhabitants grew until the townsfolk of Arles took to giving its monuments away as presents. Now only one avenue remains, and that has been truncated by the railway. For those susceptible to the atmosphere of burial grounds, this remains a moody place, overhung and shaded by the foliage of trees weighed down with illustrious memories. The few remaining tombs have been assembled in the Romanesque church of St-Honorat at the end of the avenue.

Just outside Arles on an isolated hill above the paddy fields stands what remains of the important old Benedictine **Abbaye de Montmajour**. It is a building which looks more like a fortress than an abbey, machicolated and unadorned. The 12th-century cloister however is full of fascinating carvings on the capitals, including depictions of Tarasque, the *mistral* and many animal-related Old Testament stories.

Due south of Arles lies the **Camargue**, an area of about 800 square kilometres, around the two arms of the Rhône delta. The highest point of the Camargue is some four and a half metres above sea level, the lowest point one and a half metres below it. The Camargue is made of deposits from the Rhône, and the coastline is constantly moving. To the east, the land is winning and an 18th-century lighthouse now stands several kilometres from the sea. Around the Petit Rhône the sea is advancing and Saintes-Maries-de-la-Mer, which used to be an inland town, if only by a few kilometres, is now lapped by the waters of the Mediterranean. Until recently much of the Camargue was lagoon, but large tracts in the north have been given over to rice growing.

The Camargue has enormous romantic appeal. Its image is of wild horses, stampeding bulls, exotic birdlife, cowboys, cabalistic gypsy pilgrimages and folk music festivals. None of these components are imaginary, but inevitably the Camargue has changed greatly over recent decades, and the unique way of life and wildlife have only survived thanks to careful preservation measures which have themselves subtly changed the character of the area. The Camargue has been a national park for over 20 years and the largest lagoon, the Etang de Vaccarès, has been made into a nature reserve to which tourists without naturalist credentials have no access, lest the extremely shy flamingo population be frightened away. The gypsy pilgrimage to Saintes-Maries-de-la-Mer has taken on something of a pop festival atmosphere and the town itself has grown into a commercial and unattractive seaside resort (the closest one to Arles). Times being what they are, the *gardians* – as the Camargue cowboys are called – want money to drive cars instead of horse-drawn caravans, and to get it they guide tourists on horseback. The *gardians* ride their white horses of mysterious descent to control the herds of local bulls which wander around the marshes. They are kept purely to fight, not once in their lives like Spanish bulls, but in the Provençal *courses à la cocarde*. These contests are to be seen all over the area around Arles, in small makeshift arenas, the more dramatic setting of the amphitheatres of Arles and Nîmes being reserved for the altogether more ceremonious Spanish bullfights. The *courses* can be recommended as a tourist attraction without fear of offending taurophiles, for Camargue bulls – which grow small, fast and agile – are not hurt in the sport, where *gardians* compete with one another to snatch a red cockade from between the bull's horns without themselves being punctured. Bulls fight again and again and grow as expert as the nimbly evasive *rasetteurs*.

There are three main roads across the Camargue. The least frequented, and most rewarding for bird-watchers who cannot get into the reserve itself, is the one that runs down the east of the great Etang de Vaccarès to the wide empty dunes of the Plage de Famarin. There are a number of good viewpoints (binoculars advisable) over the lagoon with its protected birdlife. Apart from the flamingoes, the migrant winged visitors to the Camargue – one of the most important areas of passage in Europe – are to be seen in greatest number and variety in spring and autumn.

The road from Arles to Saintes-Maries-de-la-Mer is the main tourist route. This is where you will find ranches where *gardians* offer accompanied rides through the Camargue, and there are information centres, small local museums and amusement areas. Near Méjanes, you can also get a view over the Etang de Vaccarès and follow a dirt-track between the lagoons to **Saintes-Maries**. This is one of the few places in the Camargue which has been allowed to develop into a resort, serving a long, though disappointing, beach. The resort is architecturally unattractive, but in season it has a lively and young atmosphere. Its one interesting building is the extraordinary church – crenellated and almost windowless like a battleship. If, like the Palais des Papes in Avignon, it looks more military than religious in function, this is because it was a fortress: to withstand Saracen besiegers there was even a well inside. In the crypt is the graven image of the venerated patroness of the gypsies: Sara, the black servant girl who landed at Saintes-Maries-de-la-Mer with the Holy Marys themselves (Marie Salomé and Marie Jacobé). The great event which has made Saintes-Maries is the pilgrimage of 24–25 May when gypsies come from all over Europe to pay their respects to the figure in the crypt, and when the little boat containing two figures of the Marys is lowered from the roof and carried down to the sea for a benediction, accompanied by *gardians* on horseback. In the evenings before the pilgrimage day, as the gypsy population builds up, flamenco guitarists lead dancing in the street, and after the ceremony is over there are bullfights.

The eastern route across the Camargue leads to Aigues-Mortes and the Languedoc coast beyond. On the northern edge of the Camargue **St-Gilles** was once an important pilgrimage monastery on the way to Compostela, and an important port for pilgrims, crusaders and incoming exotic goods. Now its population is only a fraction of what it was, and of the monastery the only noteworthy remnant is the very fine west façade of the church – the most obviously Roman in construction of all Provençal Romanesque works of art, with a wealth of sculpture between the columns, mostly depicting the life of Christ but also with picturesque Old Testament stories and animals. In the crypt, which is really a vast underground church with a groined vault, there is Saint Gilles' tomb.

Aigues-Mortes at the edge of the Camargue

Aigues-Mortes, meaning dead waters, is one of the best-preserved and most evocative of fortified medieval towns in France. Its rectilinear streets of low houses are all still enclosed within the four sides of its ramparts and there are practically no signs of modern growth of the town. The 13th-century King Louis IX (Saint Louis), having no Mediterranean port, negotiated the purchase of Aigues-Mortes from a sympathetic religious establishment. He built the splendid Tour Constance (which is the best part of the fortifications to climb up for a view over the Camargue), encouraged the growth of the town and set off from it on two crusades. His heir, Philip the Bold, completed the fortifications of Aigues-Mortes in the late 13th century, concentrating the points of defence on the one side which could be approached by land, for in those days Aigues-Mortes was, if not exactly on the sea, surrounded by a lot more water than today. Now the landscape is one of salt marshes and is the home of producers of Listel wines whose cellars you can visit just outside Aigues-Mortes.

The Languedoc-Roussillon Coast

The end of the Petit Rhône today is marked by the first cluster of new resorts, which have grown in four groups over the last three decades or so along the barely interrupted sand which stretches from the Camargue to the Pyrenees. In some places the beaches are wafer thin, separating the sea from lagoons where lately oysters and mussels have been farmed. **La Grande Motte** was the first of the series and the most aggressively modern in style, with honeycombed pyramidal blocks which can be seen for miles round the coast. The contrast with Roman Provence and with the Mediterranean coast between Marseille and Menton could hardly be more striking. This, like the other resorts of this part of the coast, is a place for flats and flatlets, water-sports and private boats, for which there is extensive accommodation. Like so many other aspects of French life, La Grande Motte and the resorts of the Languedoc coast have not just grown naturally and gradually but have come into being as a result of a planning decision in Paris. In the early '60s it was decided that the empty sands of the Languedoc coast were to be developed, and the architects who were given a free hand set about their task of building villages from nothing, in a flat and empty landscape, with a positive and uncompromising confidence typical of the decade. The architect at La Grande Motte said of his aims, 'to start the resort a hard core (the pyramids) was necessary to mark the countryside with its virile presence'. Needless to say, the thorough French planners didn't neglect the practicalities of seaside resorts, and summer residents of La Grande Motte and the others are well served with facilities for all sorts of leisure activities, particularly sailing and other water-sports. Since the early days of La Grande Motte a less virile architectural style has been preferred – low-rise villas with more personal access to the marina facilities. The most important of all the modern developments is **Le Cap d'Agde** on a cape near the mouth of

La Grande Motte

the Hérault, between Béziers and Montpellier. It has a large yachting port but is a somewhat bewildering place, spreading without apparent focus. There is a large naturist area – Port Nature – and there are plenty of facilities (and people, but only in July and August). The other main resorts are **Gruissan-Plage, Port-Leucate, Canet-Plage** and **St-Cyprien**. Canet-Plage is the best of the bunch, with a degree of sophistication.

One of the few older communities along this stretch of coast is the commercial port of **Sète**. It owes its greatness to the creation by Louis XIV and Colbert of the Canal du Midi which links the waters of the Atlantic to the Mediterranean, ending in the Etang de Thau behind Sète. More recently the Canal du Rhône à Sète has been constructed with the same terminus. The animated centre of the town is the canal which cuts through it from the Etang to the sea, flanked by tall old buildings and the setting on many summer days for the nautical jousts which are so characteristic of the Languedoc coast. The sport, second only in importance to rugby, consists of two crews propelling the two jousters each standing on a raised platform at the back of the boat and bearing a long pole and a shield – the winner is the one who doesn't get his nice white suit wet. Sète has no particular sightseeing interest but a lot of character and very good fish restaurants all along the port. **Agde** is an older port than Sète, standing on the banks of the Hérault a few kilometres from its mouth. Its origins are Greek (the name is derived from Agatha) and there is a small archaeological museum. Beside the waters of the Hérault the crenellated walls of the cathedral, built of sombre unweathered local volcanic stone, have an even more formidable aspect than most of the fortified churches of this part of the world.

Of the towns which have grown up behind the mosquito-ridden wasteland of the coast, **Montpellier** is the most important. It is one of the oldest and most distinguished university towns in France, whose intellectual excellence as early as the year 1000 stemmed from the town's contact with the Orient through the spice trade. Those who knew their spices and herbs knew medicine too, and this was the discipline of Montpellier when Rabelais came to qualify in the 16th century. Montpellier remains more of a pen-pushing than an industrial town for as well as having an important university, it was from the time of Louis XIV to the Revolution the administrative capital and seat of Parliament of the whole of south-west France. Like so many towns of the south-west, cosmopolitan and intellectual Montpellier welcomed ideas of religious reform both in the Middle Ages and in the 16th century. Its reward was almost total destruction in the wars of religion; Montpellier's architectural beauty is that of the 17th and 18th centuries. All around the city centre, which is animated and attractive with gardens (the oldest botanical gardens in France) and narrow streets, there are large numbers of substantial *hôtels* built by the wealthy lawyers and financiers of Montpellier. Typically

Montpellier *hôtels* are simple on the exterior and do not make the streets a joy to walk down, but have richly decorated interior court-yards. The great architectural centrepiece is the Promenade de Peyrou, built at the end of the 17th and in the early 18th centuries. It is a splendid monumental achievement with a triumphal arch, an equestrian statue of Louis XIV and an elegant hexagonal water tower at the end of the Promenade, where an esplanade gives a marvellous view over the coast and mountains behind, and the aqueduct which brings water to Montpellier. Within the city the most important sightseeing destination is the Musée Fabre which has, among many treasures, a particular wealth of French 19th-century paintings (Courbet and Delacroix) and sculptures by Houdon.

From Montpellier there are easy excursions into the southern Massif Central with its grottoes and rocky circuses. **St-Guilhem-le-Désert** and **St-Martin-de-Londres** are peaceful and beautiful places to stay, well within range of the coast. Unlike Montpellier, **Pézenas** has lost most of its importance except as a wine market town. Three hundred years ago it was an elegant and aristocratic place where Molière came to entertain the court of the Prince de Conti. **Béziers** is a large town of wine industry, rugby mania and Spanish bullfights, which was victimised by the Crusaders of 1209 (see page 274). Apart from a long series of locks engineered to allow the Canal du Midi to climb – and considered by Arthur Young to be one of Louis XIV's greatest achievements, a verdict with which it is hard to concur – Béziers has only a fortified cathedral and a wine/local history museum to detain you.

Narbonne, capital of the original Roman Provincia, is another wine town, more rewarding to visit because of the cluster of religious buildings at its heart. These include one of the most beautiful (among few) Gothic cathedrals in the south (which was never completed because it was not allowed to take priority over town fortifications) and the archaeological (mostly Roman) museum in the Archbishop's palace which is unusually attractive and informative. On the road south towards Catalonia and the Pyrenees the small ancient city of **Elne**, once the capital of Roussillon, is grouped around its 11th-century cathedral. This is a pure example of the Romanesque style with a particularly entertaining wealth of sculpture in the south gallery of the cloister.

The capital of the Roussillon – as the French part of Catalonia is called – is now **Perpignan**, which is proud of the ethnic individuality of its region. In and around Perpignan the people speak Catalan and like to dance the *sardana*, Catalonia's national dance, whose pace quickens like a bolero. For a period in the 13th and 14th centuries Perpignan was the capital of the kingdom of Majorca – a temporary offshoot (which included Montpellier) of the ruling house of Aragon. The kings of Majorca built their palace in Perpignan and it has been restored within the later citadel constructed by Vauban. Other buildings of interest include the Castillet, part of the town fortifications originally built in the 14th century; the late Gothic cathedral, simple in architectural lines, but rich in heavy gilt wooden altar-pieces; and the Loge de Mer which, in the days when Perpignan was a sea port, housed maritime commercial transactions. Appropriately enough it has a rather Venetian look about it. The Place de la Loge is the lively centre of town life.

The Roussillon coast differs from that of the Languedoc in that it is not predominantly the creation of the last two decades. The flat sandy coast finishes at **Argelès-sur-Mer**, which is built up without style, and whose buildings are heavily outnumbered by tents; it has become in its own words the camping capital of Europe. To its south the Pyrenees tumble into the Mediterranean producing a completely different coast, without the long beaches but with much greater scenic attraction and fishing ports on the coves which have long brought tourists. **Collioure**, the most picturesque (though very touristy and full of craft shops), attracted the artistic avant-garde several decades after St-Tropez (Picasso, Matisse, Juan Gris – see page 180). Down by the pebble bathing beach stands a church with an Arabic-looking pink domed belfry. Inside there is a very sumptuous collection of carved altar-pieces, dating from the end of the 17th century. Like Perpignan, Collioure has its castle, built by the kings of Majorca and later strengthened by Vauban. The last resort in France is **Banyuls**, famous as the home of the finest of the sweet dessert wines in the area.

Collioure

Excursions from the coast

● **Abbaye de Fontfroide** A beautiful old Cistercian abbey among the Corbières vineyards, which has been carefully and not too extensively restored by its private owners, and adorned with colourful gardens. More than most places, Fontfroide breathes tranquillity, and makes the attractions of monastic retreat in troubled medieval France thoroughly understandable.

● **Carcassonne and Cathar Fortresses** The medieval city of Carcassonne is one of the most popular excursion places in France, and its aspect one of the most famous (see page 274). On the way to Carcassonne there are a number of romantic fortress ruins built in a chain along the old frontier between the Languedoc and the Roussillon, which became refuges for heretics and the object of 13th-century siege. These fortresses are so inaccessibly situated that they could not be attacked, merely reduced to starvation – for which the ascetic Cathars were well prepared. The most accessible of these fortresses is **Puylaurens**, the most spectacular **Peyrepertuse** and **Quéribus**. If you are fit enough to climb over 300 metres to reach **Peyrepertuse**, and then the vertical and vertiginous staircase up its keep, you will be rewarded by a marvellous view and an understanding of why this was the one castle that was never taken. Quéribus, which is hardly less impressively set, received some of the last Cathars and only fell through treachery in 1255.

● **Wine Tasting** The drive from the coast to Carcassonne gives the opportunity for a leisurely wine tour. This is not the area for tasting prestigious vintages, but rather for admiring the vineyards and sampling good-value wines at small outlets and co-operatives. **Lézignan-Corbières**, the main centre of the **Corbières** wine region, stands on the edge of the hilly area on the plain. Between Béziers and Carcassonne the Minervois vineyards produce very drinkable wines and the small village of **Minerve** enjoys a magnificent setting, its rocky citadel isolated between two rivers. It is no surprise to learn that Minerve was a Cathar stronghold which enjoyed a reputation of being impregnable and to which the Crusaders' leader Simon de Montfort duly laid siege in June 1210 – he cut off Minerve's water supply with the use of six mighty war engines, and the fortress capitulated. No fewer than 150 heretics preferred the flames to a denial of their faith. At Minerve there are still the remains of the fortifications to see and an attractive Romanesque church. South of Carcassonne, **Limoux** is another attractive wine-growing centre and its product, the Blanquette de Limoux, is one of the most acceptable of all champagne substitutes. The inhabitants would no doubt object to the term, for Limoux has been making bubbly for much longer than Champagne has.

HOTELS

> Key: ◆ = 0–250FF, ◆◆ = 251–450FF, ◆◆◆ = over 451FF; prices are per double room without breakfast, which costs around 35–60FF extra. Some hotels may insist on half-board during high season, some hotels or restaurants may close at specific times during the week – it is always worth checking. Most hotels accept the major credit cards; we have indicated where a hotel takes no credit cards.

AGDE

La Tamarissière

34300 Hérault
TEL 67 94 20 87; FAX 67 21 38 40

Right at the mouth of the river Hérault on a quiet quayside, not far from the beaches of Agde, this hotel is something of a local institution. It is not a pretty building from the outside, but a shaded garden and a swimming-pool give it charm. There is a two-part restaurant, its rather bland décor brightened by paintings; the food retains its reputation for excellence. Bedrooms are medium-sized with good modern furnishings, some with balconies overlooking the river. The friendly owners are long accustomed to British visitors, and you can be sure of a warm welcome.

OPEN Mid-Mar to end Nov ROOMS 27 (all with bath or shower) FACILITIES Outdoor pool

AIGUES MORTES

Les Arcades

23 boulevard Gambetta
30220 Gard
TEL 66 53 81 13; FAX 66 53 75 46

It should come as no surprise that the main feature of this restaurant-with-rooms, within the ancient walls of Aigues-Mortes, is an arched arcade, used for table settings which continue, bistro-style, inside. The mainly fishy cuisine has a reputation for quality and value. The few comfortable bedrooms, with washed stone walls and some interesting bits of furniture, hide behind the mullioned windows of the 16th-century house. Our inspector found service cool when staying on the first night of the season.

OPEN Mid-Mar to mid-Feb ROOMS 6 (all with bath or shower)

THE SOUTH

AIX-EN-PROVENCE

Le Manoir

8 rue d'Entrecasteaux
13100 Bouches-du-Rhône
TEL 42 26 27 20; FAX 42 27 17 97

This is a converted 14th-century cloister in a quiet residential area close to the historic centre of town. Bedrooms are traditionally furnished, with good bathrooms. Breakfast is taken under the cloister ogives; there's a small terrace and courtyard parking. An excellent peaceful city-centre hotel without parking. There is no restaurant, but there are plenty in the city nearby.

OPEN End Feb to early Jan ROOMS 42 (32 with bath or shower)

Hôtel des Quatre Dauphins

54 rue Roux-Alphéran
13100 Bouches-du-Rhône
TEL 42 38 16 39; FAX 42 38 60 19

This elegant old town-house in a quiet quarter of Aix has been converted into a stylish hotel. Bedrooms can be on the small side, but are prettily done out in flowery provençal fabrics, carefully co-ordinated with stencilled headboards and fancy sconces. The salon is in similar style, with rustic-style painted chairs and dried corn bundles, as well as plenty of magazines.

OPEN All year exc. 3 weeks early Feb ROOMS 12 (all with bath or shower)

LES ARCS-SUR-ARGENS

Logis du Guetteur

place du Château
83460 Var
TEL 94 73 30 82; FAX 94 73 39 95

The Logis du Guetteur offers an affordable chance to stay in an 11th-century castle. A classic square tower surmounts the courtyard and medieval village. Comfortable bedrooms have been so heavily converted that they are rather unexciting, but views over the rooftops, cooing pigeons and tolling bells provide atmosphere. Vaulted stone-walled cellars have become the restaurant, opening on a terrace over a pool. Food is ambitious and generally more than competent (the no-choice half-board menu offers good value). Your welcome may be a little bland.

OPEN All year exc. mid-Jan to mid-Feb ROOMS 10 (all with bath or shower) FACILITIES Outdoor pool

ARLES

Hôtel d'Arlatan

26 rue du Sauvage
13631 Bouches-du-Rhône
TEL 90 93 56 66; FAX 90 49 68 45

Hôtel d'Arlatan is a fine, secluded, grey-stone mansion in the city centre, just off the place Forum, with a terrace and pretty walled garden. Some bedrooms are spacious, others fairly small; all are well furnished in traditional style, with pretty bathrooms. The beamed and tiled salon is elegant, with a tall open fireplace and rough-stone walls. There's a separate TV room, a courtyard patio for drinks, and a garage. Courtyard-facing bedrooms are quiet, street-facing rooms are noisy. No restaurant.

OPEN All year exc. 2 weeks Jan ROOMS 41 (all with bath or shower)

ARPAILLARGUES

Hôtel Marie d'Agoult

(at the Château d'Arpaillargues)
Uzès
30700 Gard
TEL 66 22 14 48; FAX 66 22 56 10

This is a dignified 18th-century château in extensive grounds three km from Uzès; there are lawns, trees and terraces near the house, pool and tennis courts across the way. Inside there's a blend of antique and well-chosen modern style – and the atmosphere is one of casualness and understated elegance. The more expensive bedrooms are beautiful and opulent, the cheapest much smaller but tastefully decorated. The food is neither very cheap nor highly imaginative, but dishes are well prepared.

OPEN Mid-Mar to mid-Oct ROOMS 25 (all with bath) FACILITIES Outdoor pool, tennis

LE BARROUX

Les Géraniums

place de la Croix
84330 Vaucluse
TEL 90 62 41 08; FAX 90 62 56 48

In a medieval hill village not far from Mont Ventoux, Les Géraniums is a popular family-run hotel in a simple stone building brightened with tubs of the eponymous flowers, with views of the plain and orchards below. The airy restaurant has exposed beams and rafters and cheerful pink cloths; for summer dining there's also plenty of terrace space. Food is unpretentious and hearty – perhaps *terrine de chasseurs* with onion confit, braised rabbit and lemon meringue pie. Neat, clean bedrooms are located either beneath the restaurant (there may be some noise from chairs scraping on the floor above) or in a separate annexe. Colour schemes are unadventurous (lots of brown and beige).

OPEN Early Feb to early Jan ROOMS 22 (all with bath or shower)

BARCELONNETTE

Azteca

3 rue François Arnaud
04400 Alpes-de-Haute-Provence
TEL 92 81 46 36; FAX 92 81 43 92

The Mexican influence on this modern hotel comes from the history of local villagers who emigrated to Central America in the 19th century, made their fortune in sheep farming, then returned to France to build themselves grand houses with their wealth. This mountain village is a popular little ski resort in the winter, and the hotel stands a short distance from the central square, with views of snowy peaks. The décor is bright and cheerful – yellow bedrooms, fancy candelabra of coloured metal and glass – with a liberal scattering of Mexican pictures and carvings.

OPEN All year ROOMS 27 (all with bath or shower)

LES-BAUX-DE-PROVENCE

Auberge de la Benvengudo

vallon de l'Arcoule
13520 Bouches-du-Rhône
TEL 90 54 32 54; FAX 90 54 42 58

This family affair with requisite dog and aproned chef/patron – Corsican Monsieur Rossi – is more welcoming (and cheaper) than its famous neighbours. Ivy hides the fact that the provençal-style building is only a couple of decades old. Four-course meals are served in the rustic-style dining-room that looks on to the large pool and big garden with olive trees and stone picnic tables. Bedrooms upstairs, though smaller and more gloomy than the annexe rooms, are more characterful: unwaveringly old-fashioned with furry wallpaper and jolly bathrooms containing 'telephone box' toilets. The hotel is found by the D78F a couple of kilometres south of the old village.

OPEN Early Feb to mid-Nov ROOMS 17 (all with bath) FACILITIES Outdoor pool, tennis

Le Mas d'Aigret

13520 Bouches-du-Rhône
TEL 90 54 33 54; FAX 90 54 41 37

This old, stone farmhouse is run by an enthusiastic English and French family as a sophisticated little hotel. It tucks into the rocks a short descent from Les Baux old village. It's a fascinating building, with a vaulted sitting-room, a dining-room hewn out of the rock, and bare slabs sloping through two 'troglodyte' bedrooms. Most bedrooms, in white and floral fabrics, have a balcony or terrace and command great valley views. There are English and French books and rubber ducks for the bath. The food has received plaudits; half-board lets you choose what you wish from the *à la carte* menu.

OPEN End Feb to early Jan ROOMS 15 FACILITIES Outdoor pool

BEAURECUEIL

Relais Ste-Victoire

13100 Bouches-du-Rhône
TEL 42 66 94 98; FAX 42 66 85 96

At the edge of a small village and surrounded by open fields, this restaurant-with-rooms has fine views up to the imposing crags of Mont Ste-Victoire – recorded so colourfully by Cézanne. Well-equipped bedrooms are excellent value, the best with their own terraces and decked out in imaginative fabrics. The main feature of the place is the two dining rooms – pretty and colourful, with large windows overlooking fields. The cooking is excellent, including inventive dishes and regional specialities. There are several very good-value fixed-price menus to choose from, the most expensive featuring foie gras and truffles.

OPEN All year exc. 2 weeks early Jan and 1st week Nov ROOMS 9 (all with bath) FACILITIES Outdoor pool

BIOT

Galerie des Arcades

16 place des Arcades
06410 Alpes Maritimes
TEL 93 65 01 04; FAX 93 65 01 05

An enormously atmospheric 15th-century inn, where tables are set under the arcades of Biot's most picturesque narrow square. The building is full of modern art: a cellar contains a gallery of Vasarély works. Pretty beamed bedrooms are full of splendid antiques, more paintings and wacky bathrooms: rooms 10, 11 and 12 are the grandest, others have terraces with lovely rooftop views. The cooking is simple: a short *carte* and a daily set menu with classic local specialities such as *soupe au pistou* or *ratatouille*. It's run with *joie de vivre*, and the bar is a cheerful local haunt. Great value – if you can get in.

OPEN All year ROOMS 12 (all with bath or shower)

LA CADIERE D'AZUR

Hostellerie Bérard

rue Gabrielle-Péri
83740 Var
TEL 94 90 11 43; FAX 94 90 01 94

At the top of the high street of a lovely, largely unvisited village up above the Bandol vineyards, ancient walls hide a sophisticated retreat. The oldest of its four buildings was a medieval convent. All contain a panoply of very individual and stylish bedrooms, some modern, some antique, others dowdy and old-fashioned. Many have panoramic countryside views, as does the elegant and upmarket restaurant, where Monsieur Bérard prepares well-thought-out, but pricey, menus, naturally accompanied by an exemplary selection of Bandol wines. Madame Bérard's welcome can't be bettered.

OPEN End Feb to early Jan ROOMS 40 (all with bath or shower) FACILITIES Heated outdoor pool

CALLIAN

Auberge du Puits Jaubert

route du Lac de Fondurane
83440 Var
TEL 94 76 44 48

This isolated restaurant-with-rooms next to the lake of St-Cassien was an old farmstead. The restaurant is appropriately rustic, with flagstone floor, old wooden beams and large central open fire. There's no separate lounge, but in summer you can sit out under the trees. The rooms are fairly basic but spacious, with wicker-style furniture and bold geometric-print bedcovers. In winter there may be a shortage of hot water. Food is good and service friendly.

OPEN Mid-Dec to mid-Nov ROOMS 8 (all with bath or shower)

CANNES

Hôtel de Paris

34 boulevard d'Alsace
06400 Alpes-Maritimes
TEL 93 38 30 89; FAX 93 39 04 61

Unfortunately, this big 19th-century cream building stands right beside the dual carriageway that runs through the centre of Cannes. However, all bedrooms are air-conditioned and sound-proofed and it's a short walk to La Croisette or the shops and restaurants (there are none in the hotel). Madame Lazzari has heavily renovated the interior, with Gothic-style arches, and has converted the basement into atmospheric breakfast rooms, decorated with photos of film stars, and a smart piano bar. The engaging old-fashioned bedrooms are good value, and for a splurge, there are sumptuous suites. The palmy pool is fine for a dip, but too noisy for relaxed sunbathing.

OPEN All year exc. mid-Nov to mid-Dec ROOMS 50 (all with bath or shower) FACILITIES Outdoor pool

CASSIS

Le Clos des Arômes

10 rue Paul Mouton
13260 Bouches-du-Rhône
TEL 42 01 71 84; FAX 42 01 31 76

This intimate restaurant-with-rooms, just a brief walk from the port, has its faults. Some bedrooms are just too small (avoid number 1), and Madame Grinda may get waylaid at dinner chatting to her friends. But it has charm: a lovely courtyard with mature trees for summer dining; a cosy, pretty candlelit dining-room for other times; and simple, attractive little rooms in white and floral fabrics. Inexpensive dinner menus offer tasty traditional provençal dishes with affordable Cassis wines for accompaniment.

OPEN Mid-Jan to Nov ROOMS 8 (all with bath or shower)

COLLIOURE

Casa Païral

impasse de Palmiers
66190 Pyrénées-Orientales
TEL 68 82 05 81; FAX 68 82 52 10

This is a stylish and characterful hotel. The loveliest feature of the 19th-century house, with its wrought-iron balconies, is the central courtyard, so thick with foliage that it's more like a garden; it contains a perfectly positioned pool. The public rooms are aesthetically pleasing, with tiled floors, heavy wooden furniture and, in the breakfast room, a sloping beamed ceiling. Bedrooms, though immaculate, are simple by comparison. There's no restaurant, but the hotel is right in the centre of Collioure, tucked away quietly down a side street.

OPEN Early Apr to end Oct ROOMS 27 (all with bath or shower) FACILITIES Outdoor pool

COTIGNAC

Lou Calen

1 cours Gambetta
83570 Var
TEL 94 04 60 40; FAX 94 04 76 64

This very provençal hotel, entered from a corner of the village square, is immediately welcoming. Tiles and tapestries, plants and paintings, flowers and bric-a-brac surround you with unpretentious rustic charm. There's a small lounge which serves as a breakfast room; log fires blaze cheerfully whenever the weather is dubious. Interesting old bedrooms and bathrooms continue the home-like feeling; there is much attractive detail, and the occasional signs of wear are made up for in the atmosphere. There's also a long tiled and raftered dining-room; tables on the terrace overlook a luxuriant garden with a swimming-pool (unheated) among the trees. Food comes in big portions – perhaps warm cheese salad, lamb cutlets with potato gratin and braised chicory or pavé normand.

OPEN Mid-Mar to early Jan ROOMS 16 (all with bath or shower) FACILITIES Outdoor pool

FOX-AMPHOUX

Auberge du Vieux Fox

place de l'Eglise
83670 Var
TEL 94 80 71 69; FAX 94 90 78 38

In a small and idyllic old hill village in the heart of the Provençal countryside, this charming auberge was once the presbytery of the Romanesque church which still adjoins it. It offers simple and cosy accommodation – a rustic dining-room with log fire and homely atmosphere; a smaller terrace dining-room (leading out onto a shady terrace with a fine fig tree) with good views; a small lounge with piano, squashy chairs and magazines; and small, cheerfully furnished bedrooms. The cooking is not sophisticated, but portions are large and all is fresh and good quality.

OPEN Feb to end Dec ROOMS 8 (all with bath or shower)

GIGONDAS

Les Florets

route des Dentelles
84190 Vaucluse
TEL 90 65 85 01; FAX 90 65 83 80

At the foot of the jagged Dentelles de Montmirail, Les Florets would make a good base for those wanting to explore the vineyards of the area or do some walking. Lacy metal chairs are set out around a fountain beneath shady chestnuts outside. The interior is slightly old-fashioned in that French kind of way – large-patterned wallpaper, lacy cloths, lots of pewter and china. Bedrooms are spotless, with modern bathrooms – in addition to the 11 rooms in the main building, there are four 'bungalows' behind the main building.

OPEN Mar to Dec ROOMS 13 (all with bath or shower)

GRIMAUD

Hostellerie du Coteau Fleuri

place des Pénitents
Grimaud-Village
83360 Var
TEL 94 43 20 17; FAX 94 43 33 42

This very peaceful little grey-stone hotel is built into the hillside in a corner of its high village, nearly 5km from the sea. White walls, an open hearth and traditional furniture give an impression of welcoming simplicity; there's a piano for guests to use. The lounge and bar lead to a pretty garden terrace. Bedrooms are small and simple, with good bathrooms. The modern provençal cooking is above average and interesting, with good-value fixed-price menus.

OPEN Feb to Dec ROOMS 14 (all with bath or shower)

JUAN-LES-PINS

Auberge de L'Esterel

21 chemin des Iles
06160 Alpes Maritimes
TEL 93 61 86 55; FAX 93 61 08 67

This modest hotel is a plain orange-coloured building in a quiet residential quarter a few minutes from the sea. There's no great charm indoors – a TV-dominated lounge, small, basic bedrooms (take one at the back – they have balconies) and a rustic-style dining-room. But in summer you can eat under the trees in the pretty rear garden, and the food is excellent: sophisticated and reasonable value for the Riviera, cheerfully served in an informal atmosphere.

OPEN End Mar to mid-Oct ROOMS 15 (all with shower)

Des Mimosas

rue Pauline
06160 Alpes Maritimes
TEL 93 61 04 16

A hotel since Napoleon III's time, this white-painted building with shutters and balconies stands in very pleasant palm-shaded gardens in a quiet residential area about five minutes' walk from the beach. There's no restaurant, but you can have breakfast on your balcony or in the garden. The reception/bar could be called 'experimental modern', with white sofas, primary-coloured panels and exposed brick. Bedrooms vary from the modern style to the more traditional; the more expensive front-facing rooms have big balconies. In the palm-shaded garden there's a swimming-pool (unheated). An attractive and friendly place.

OPEN Mar to end Sept ROOMS 34 (all with bath or shower) FACILITIES Outdoor pool

LE LAVANDOU

Auberge de la Calanque

62 avenue du Général de Gaulle
83980 Var
TEL 94 71 05 96; FAX 94 71 20 12

The imposing white building above the marina has evolved over the last half-century and now provides much comfort and a certain elegance. Ample, inter-linked public rooms – sitting-room, bar, and a commended restaurant – successfully mix old and modern furnishings. Through pillared arches, the dining-room terrace looks out to sea over a peaceful garden with pool, as do all the bedrooms, each with a terrace and stylish modern furnishings. Excellent value.

OPEN Mid-Mar to early Nov ROOMS 37 (all with bath or shower) FACILITIES Outdoor pool

LE LUC

La Grillade au Feu de Bois

Flassans-sur-Isole
83340 Var
TEL 94 69 71 20; FAX 94 59 66 11

Madame Babb has been here for 35 years: 'Take me as you find me,' says her shrug of the shoulders. Everything you find is wonderful: a lovely coarse stone farmhouse in the woods, with a super pool, a splendid terrace under an ancient mulberry tree, a barrel-vaulted dining-room, always with a display of local art, and a sitting-room full of fine furniture doubling as an antique shop. The four-course menu offers rustic terrines, grills and cheeses. Spacious and stylish bedrooms, some in the main building, some in a converted wine store, give fantastic quality for the price.

OPEN All year ROOMS 16 (all with bath or shower) FACILITIES Heated outdoor pool

MARSEILLE

New Hôtel Bompard

2 rue des Flots-Bleus
13007 Bouches-du-Rhône
TEL 91 52 10 93; FAX 91 31 02 14

This good-value pit stop lies in a residential neighbourhood a couple of kilo-metres from the bustle of Marseille's old port. It's a professionally run place, part of a small chain. The buildings, one turn of the century, others modern, are arranged around an arboreal courtyard with a breakfast terrace. Well-equipped rooms are modern in strong primary colours, some have kitchenettes, others have balconies.

OPEN All year ROOMS 47 (all with bath)

MONTE CARLO

Hôtel Balmoral

12 avenue de la Costa
98000 Alpes-Maritimes
TEL 93 50 62 37; FAX 93 15 08 69

The Madagascan consul occupies a room in this friendly and rather faded hotel, which is a short walk from the casino. It's by no means a great hotel, but comfortable enough and inexpensive by Monte Carlo standards (save your francs for the gaming tables). Many bedrooms in the turn-of-the-century building have fine views over the port, across to old Monaco. The décor verges on the garish, but the big, old-fashioned bathrooms have character. The breakfast room is unappealing: have a coffee in the Café de Paris in Place Casino.

OPEN All year ROOMS 77 (all with bath or shower)

MOUGINS

Le Manoir de l'Etang

Les Bois de Font Merle
66 allée du Manoir
06250 Alpes-Maritimes
TEL 93 90 01 07; FAX 92 92 20 70

This lovely white-shuttered 19th-century stone country house stands awash with flowers in a rural spot on the edge of Mougins suburbs, looking across a valley of cypresses and olives. It used to be the home of an architect who embellished it with painted ceilings and elaborately tiled bathrooms. For the last few years his daughter has run it as a smart but not overly formal hotel: bedrooms are full of quality antiques; the dining–room, opening on to a large poolside terrace, is thoroughly tasteful. The set four-course dinner is very affordable by the standards of epicurean Mougins.

OPEN Mar to mid-Nov, mid-Dec to end Jan ROOMS 15 (all with bath or shower) FACILITIES Outdoor pool

NICE

La Pérouse

11 quai Rauba-Capéu
06300 Alpes Maritimes
TEL 93 62 34 63; FAX 93 62 59 41

The hotel has arguably the best position in Nice, on the side of the château hill set back from the noisy seafront, just metres from the old town and from the beach. There's plenty of outdoor space: a sea-facing terrace for more expensive rooms, one on the roof and one which is an extension of the bar/restaurant (dinner in summer only), with lemon trees and a pool nestling under a rock.

Most rooms are well furnished, but a cheaper one may disappoint and you may find the welcome somewhat impersonal.

OPEN All year ROOMS 65 (all with bath) FACILITIES Outdoor pool, sauna

Hôtel Windsor

11 rue Dalpozzo
06000 Alpes Maritimes
TEL 93 88 59 35; FAX 93 88 94 57

This welcoming family-run hotel in the heart of the new town a few blocks from the Masséna Museum and the Négresco hotel has interesting quirks. Half the bedrooms have modern murals, Tintin posters adorn the stairs, and an attic room has a basic gym and hammam bath. The palmed courtyard garden offers a little pool and breakfast terrace (there's also a pleasant breakfast room/bar for inclement days). Quieter bedrooms overlooking the garden, some with french windows and balconies, are more expensive. None could be said to be elaborately furnished.

OPEN All year ROOMS 60 (all with bath or shower) FACILITIES Outdoor pool, exercise room, Turkish bath

PEILLON

Auberge de la Madone

Peillon Village
06440 Alpes Maritimes
TEL 93 79 91 17; FAX 93 79 99 36

In the middle of nowhere on the edge of a tiny, extraordinarily perched village with views down the valley and walks in the hills, this simple modern *auberge* among the trees blends into its setting. It has been in the Millo family for two generations. There's a sunny terrace and an attractive rustic-style restaurant. The cooking is homely, good value and prides itself on its local specialities. Bedrooms are peaceful and pleasing, with good bathrooms and balconies at the front. An idyllic place to escape from the clamour of the coast (though you might be woken by sheep bells).

OPEN End Dec to end Oct ROOMS 19 (all with bath or shower) FACILITIES Tennis

PLAN-DE-LA-TOUR

Le Mas des Brugassières

route de Grimaud
83120 Var
TEL 94 43 72 42; FAX 94 43 00 20

Just outside the quiet village of Plan-de-la-Tour in the hills behind the tourist frenzy of the Côte d'Azur, Le Mas des Brugassières makes a peaceful retreat.

Bedrooms here are simple with clean, well-equipped bathrooms, but don't expect luxury. Staff can be brusque, but at the same time generous, and the bar, which is open all day, is a help-yourself affair. There is no restaurant, and breakfast is served on the terrace around the pool where light lunches are available on request.

OPEN Easter to Oct and Christmas ROOMS 14 (all with bath or shower) FACILITIES Outdoor pool, tennis

POINT-SUBLIME

Auberge du Point-Sublime ◆

(nr Rougon)
04120 Alpes-de-Haute-Provence
TEL 92 83 60 35; FAX 92 83 74 31

The location – above the Verdon Gorge in wild surroundings, on the D952 – is superb: the large car park attests to the restaurant's popularity as a summer lunch stop. The modern conservatory extension is smothered in creepers outside; inside, the tables are covered in jolly red cloths, with café curtains hung from the top half of the windows so as not to obscure the view. The adjoining bar is the basic French model, largely in formica; the residents' lounge upstairs is far more comfortable, and the additional attraction of floor-to-ceiling windows makes the most of the views. Bedrooms are very simple – candlewick covers and rugs on tiled floors. Some have separate sunlit bathrooms, others a basin and shower behind a curtain in the room.

OPEN Early Apr to early Nov ROOMS 14 (all with bath or shower)

RAMATUELLE

La Figuière

route de Tahiti
83350 Var
TEL 94 97 18 21; FAX 94 97 68 48

You pay a premium to stay within walking distance of some of France's most fashionable beaches near St Tropez: this complex of provençal-style buildings, 500 metres from Tahiti beach, is better value than most. Figs, lavender, wistaria and roses are in abundance. A big pool and rustic dining-room serving simple grills and breakfast acts as the focal point. Bedrooms are spread around the old farm building and four bungalow annexes, one with terraces opening directly on to vineyards. All offer plenty of comfort, with chunky wooden furniture and first-rate bathrooms.

OPEN Early Apr to early Oct ROOMS 45 (all with bath or shower) FACILITIES Outdoor pool, tennis

REILLANNE

Auberge de Reillanne

04110 Alpes-de-Haute-Provence
TEL 92 76 45 95

Just south of the village of Reillanne (perched and pretty) on the D214, surrounded by open fields with views towards the edge of the Lubéron *massif*, this is a lovely 18th-century mellow stone farmhouse, well weathered and very inviting. It is a peaceful little hotel; the décor is simple but undeniably stylish – large stone-walled and beamed bedrooms, with complementary wood furnishings, modern prints and books (some in English) and spacious well-equipped bathroèoms. Home cooking on simple menus offers provençal dishes such as *gigot d'agneau* and *canard aux olives*.

OPEN All year ROOMS 7 (all with bath)

ROQUEBRUNE-SUR-ARGENS

La Maurette

83520 Var
TEL 94 45 46 81

This *maison d'hôte* (guest house) is wonderfully isolated on the top of a hill, with impeccable views of the wooded slopes of the Massif des Maures. Built in ruddy rock from the surrounding land, it comprises a splendid split-level dining-room-cum-sitting-room, with big sofas, a fire, plenty of books and nine bungalow bedrooms. These are smart and decorative, with old pots and paintings; some have a kitchenette. Each has its own terrace and there's a superbly sited pool. You might persuade the owners to provide dinner – featuring local specialities such as *bouillabaisse*.

OPEN Easter to mid-Oct ROOMS 9 (all with bath or shower) FACILITIES Outdoor pool

ROQUEBRUNE VILLAGE

Les Deux Frères

06190 Alpes-Maritimes
TEL 93 28 99 00; FAX 93 28 99 10

Named after the rocks on the square of this hill village encased in old castle walls, this smart restaurant with simple rooms has unbeatable panoramic coastal views (once a school, evidently too many pupils sat gazing out of the window). The restaurant is pricey; there's no obligation to eat, but the menus and lofty beamed dining-room that spills on to the square are very alluring. The ten cottagey bedrooms upstairs – small, white-walled, with pine and wicker furniture and gleaming bathrooms – all have good views, a couple out to sea, others over the square or across to the mountains.

OPEN End Dec to mid-Nov ROOMS 10 (all with bath)

SAIGNON

Auberge du Presbytère

place de la Fontaine
84400 Vaucluse
TEL 90 74 11 50; FAX 90 04 68 51

Three crumbly interjoined buildings overlook the fountain square of this off-the-beaten-track hilltop Lubéron village. Only half of the white and terracotta-tiled bedrooms are *en suite* but all are fantastic value. The best are Rouge and Bleu, with rooftop terraces and superb views, and l'Evêque, a *fin de siècle* timepiece. Downstairs, there's the village bar, a cosy sitting-room, a rustic dining-room and a terrace under a maple tree where the Bernardis serve honest-to-goodness provençal dishes from a short set menu.

OPEN All year exc. 2 weeks end Nov and 2 weeks Jan ROOMS 10 (5 with bath)

ST-JEAN-CAP-FERRAT

Clair Logis

12 avenue Centrale
06230 Alpes-Maritimes
TEL 93 76 04 57; FAX 93 76 11 85

Up one of the little inner roads of the wooded Cap, this is a 19th-century villa set in its own well-kept garden of tall trees and fragrant flowering shrubs. Indoor public space is limited to a small TV lounge and the simple high-ceilinged breakfast room. Bedrooms in the main house are attractively old-fashioned and spacious; there are two annexes, where modern-styled rooms vary in quality and size (some are small). Bath and shower rooms are adequate. The setting is lovely, the atmosphere relaxed and friendly, and prices low for so exclusive an area. No restaurant.

OPEN Mid-Dec to mid-Nov ROOMS 18 (all with bath or shower)

ST-PAUL-DE-VENCE

Auberge le Hameau

528 route de la Colle
06570 Alpes-Maritimes
TEL 93 32 80 24; FAX 93 32 55 75

Le Hameau consists of adjoining villas in the provençal style, just off the main road a few minutes' walk from the old village. It's set in groves of orange, lemon and apricot trees – home-made products appear at breakfast, on the pretty terrace if it's fine. There's no restaurant or bar, but the bedrooms have a mini-bar. Bedrooms vary in size and some (cheaper) are near enough to the road to suffer traffic noise; all, however, have charm and character. Informal and particularly friendly, this is an unusual and delightful hotel, and there's a smart swimming-pool for guests to use.

OPEN Mid-Feb to mid-Nov, end Dec to early Jan ROOMS 17 (all with bath) FACILITIES Outdoor pool

Les Orangers

chemin des Fumerates
06570 Alpes-Maritimes
TEL 93 32 80 95; FAX 93 32 00 32

In a similar situation to Le Hameau (a slightly longer walk to the village), a fine provençal house set among orange groves, with a pretty south-facing terrace with lovely valley views. There's a large, comfortable salon and traditional bedrooms with tiled floors and antiques, and good bathrooms. Some rooms have their own terrace. It's run by Englishman Thomas Franklin. No restaurant.

OPEN End Dec to end Nov ROOMS 4 (all with bath)

ST-REMY-DE-PROVENCE

Château de Roussan

13210 Bouches-du-Rhône
TEL 90 92 11 63; FAX 90 92 37 32

Two kilometres from St-Rémy on the Tarascon road, this is a lovely 18th-century house approached by a long avenue of venerable trees. It is set in beautiful grounds, sufficiently unkempt to accord with the untouched building. A faded elegance pervades the château, which has a grand old sitting-room and cosier places to breakfast and dine. Bedrooms range from the expensive and grand to much smaller and cheaper versions, though high ceilings and antiques are found throughout. The hotel has changed hands recently and is now run by an English couple.

OPEN Times vary – phone to check ROOMS 20 (all with bath or shower)

Le Mas des Carassins

1 chemin Gaulois
13210 Bouches-du-Rhône
TEL 90 92 15 48

Just on the edge of St-Rémy off the road to Les Baux, this pretty old house among fields and vineyards is utterly peaceful (apart from night-croaking frogs). The large attractive bedrooms – all in mint condition – are comfortable and imaginatively renovated, with excellent bathrooms; downstairs the tiny salon has a collection of books, and the breakfast-room is beamed and rustic.

Better still in summer is a table on the patio, enjoying the garden and the view. Simple snacks are available in the evening – *charcuterie*, cheese, fruit and cakes.

OPEN Mid-Mar to mid-Nov ROOMS 10 (all with bath)

ST-TROPEZ

Lou Cagnard

avenue Paul-Roussel
83970 Var
TEL 94 97 04 24

A night or two in this simple orange building, a five-minute walk from the port, is an effective, cost-cutting exercise for those wanting a decent bed in town. Book well in advance in summer: many know of those cosy little rooms with tiled floors, stencilled furniture and cheerful prints that Madame Rul has carefully fashioned over the last four decades. Most face a pleasant, flowery gravel courtyard (used as a car park and for breakfast), from either the main building or in bungalow extensions. Some have terraces or balconies.

OPEN Feb to mid-Nov ROOMS 19 (all with bath or shower) (Credit cards not accepted)

SEILLANS

Les Deux Rocs

place Font d'Amont
83440 Var
TEL 94 76 87 32; FAX 94 76 88 08

On one of perched Seillan's tiny squares, with outdoor tables round a fountain, this 18th-century house has been renovated with flair and charm by its *patronne*, Mme Hirsch. Downstairs, an intimate little area of deep-cushioned sofas leads to a peaceful dining-room with rough white walls and pretty tables; dinner is more memorable for the romantic setting, cheerful staff and relaxed atmosphere than for the imaginativeness of the food which, none the less, is good quality and well presented. Bedrooms are individual compositions of style and gaiety – unusual fabrics, shapely furniture – and bathrooms are modern. A delightful, simple hotel, civilised and personally welcoming.

OPEN End Mar to mid-Oct ROOMS 15 (all with bath or shower)

UZES

Hôtel d'Entraigues

8 rue de la Calade
30700 Gard
TEL 66 22 32 68; FAX 66 22 56 10

Opposite the cathedral and episcopal palace stand two superb 15th- and 17th-century buildings. Exposed stone abounds in walls, arches, steps, floors and secluded nooks and crannies. One building has a *crêperie*; upstairs on the first-floor terrace are a stylish little pool and comfortable rustic bedrooms, some with rooftop views. A boldly designed restaurant with pillars and murals has recently opened in the other building, on top of which is a stylish dining terrace; here too are some amazing apartments with lofty ceilings and many antiques. Under the same ownership as the Hôtel Marie d'Agoult, it feels professionally run, but may lack a warm, personal welcome.

OPEN All year ROOMS 36 (all with bath) FACILITIES Outdoor pool

VAISON-LA-ROMAINE

Le Beffroi

rue de l'Evêché
Ville Médievale
84110 Vaucluse
TEL 90 36 04 71; FAX 90 36 74 78

This delightful 16th-century town house (with a similar 'annexe' house), in the heart of the medieval *cité*, has a shady terrace and an elegant, formal salon. Furnishings such as antique wooden furniture, oil paintings and Persian rugs set off the high beamed ceilings and wooden floors. The bedrooms are not luxurious, but are large and beautifully furnished, with period charm; they are not always modern, but fit in well with the style.

OPEN Mid-Mar to mid-Nov ROOMS 22 (all with bath or shower)

VENCE

Auberge des Seigneurs

place du Frêne
06140 Alpes-Maritimes
TEL 93 58 04 24; FAX 93 24 08 01

A tall narrow building on a little square near the oldest part of Vence, this restaurant-with-rooms is full of character – ornate old fireplaces, quarry-tiled floors, ceiling beams and period furniture. The bedrooms have similar appeal; shuttered and quiet, they have ample space for solid beds and massive old wardrobes; each has a large modernised shower room. The *auberge* is famous for its dinners. In a dining-room of ancient panelling and coarse wooden tables, the waiter, Madame and Tim the Dog lay on a zestful performance as the many courses of down-to-earth provençal dishes on long set menus are served. The flavours are wonderfully direct and unembellished and the whole occasion is a splendid adventure. Dinner isn't cheap, but the rooms are good value.

OPEN All year ROOMS 8 (all with shower)

VILLEFRANCHE-SUR-MER

Hôtel Welcome

1 quai Courbet
06230 Alpes-Maritimes
TEL 93 76 76 93; FAX 93 01 88 81

Right by the old port and across from the Cocteau chapel, this singularly narrow peach building couldn't be better placed. It's been a hotel for well over a century (photos show a floor being added in Victorian times), and the Galbois family has been ensuring it lives up to its name for half that time. Most bedrooms are small but well equipped, and all but one floor have seaside balconies. Top floor attic rooms have been decorated as ship's cabins. A smart fish restaurant opens on to the quay, above which is a little breakfast terrace.

OPEN End Dec to mid-Nov ROOMS 32 (all with bath or shower)

VILLENEUVE-LES-AVIGNON

L'Atelier

5 rue de la Foire
30400 Gard
TEL 90 25 01 84; FAX 90 25 80 06

This inconspicuous 16th-century terraced house in the centre of town, once a residence for cardinals and fabric workshops, is now a very friendly, modest hotel. A sweeping staircase round what used to be the courtyard leads to lovely bedrooms decked out in extrovert wallpaper and old furniture, and bathrooms with decorative brass fittings. Croissants and coffee are served in a fresh little breakfast room and in the secluded shaded yard at the back. Though there's no restaurant, sample menus are provided to size up dining options in town.

OPEN Mid-Mar to early Nov ROOMS 19 (all with bath or shower)

(For more hotels near the Languedoc-Roussillon coast see also the Pyrenees Hotels on pages 282–6.)

Le Pont d'Arc on the Ardèche

To climb the trackless mountain all unseen,
With the wild flock that never needs a fold;
Alone o'er steeps and foaming falls to lean;
This is not solitude; 'tis but to hold
Converse with Nature's charms

[Byron]

THE MASSIF CENTRAL

The most major of France's minor mountain ranges is in fact no single range but a huge mountainous region covering one sixth of the country, separated from the Alps only by the Rhône valley, from the Mediterranean only by a narrow coastal plain, and from the Pyrenees by the vineyard carpets around the Aude. In such a large area it is the diversity and the unspoilt nature of the landscape that accounts for nearly all the appeal to tourists. There are curious volcanic cones, deep limestone canyons, caves with spectacular formations of natural architecture, eerily desolate windswept plateaux. There is also rural French life at its most attractively primitive. The Massif Central – at least in part – is the area for escaping from civilisation. You can walk for days across the Cévennes and come across isolated villages offering a few roofs and simple fare, just as Robert Louis Stevenson did when he travelled with his donkey Modestine just over a century ago. Since that time the region has become progressively more and more deserted as its population has moved to greener economic pastures elsewhere in France, and it is only just beginning to be discovered by French holiday-cottage buyers.

The southern part of the Massif Central is the best for escapism. The landscape of recently re-forested mountains and empty windswept plateaux pitted by deep grottoes and split by river canyons has a climate of extremes and has only proved suitable for summer sheep (which produce Roquefort, one of the most notoriously potent of French cheeses) and military manoeuvres (the Larzac Causse has one of the largest military camps in the country). There are isolated communities of dry stone farms with rough stone roofs which do little to soften the bleak impression made by the rocky landscape. Resorts have grown up only in the immediate vicinity of that most impressive natural curiosity, the Tarn Gorges, one of a series of such canyons in

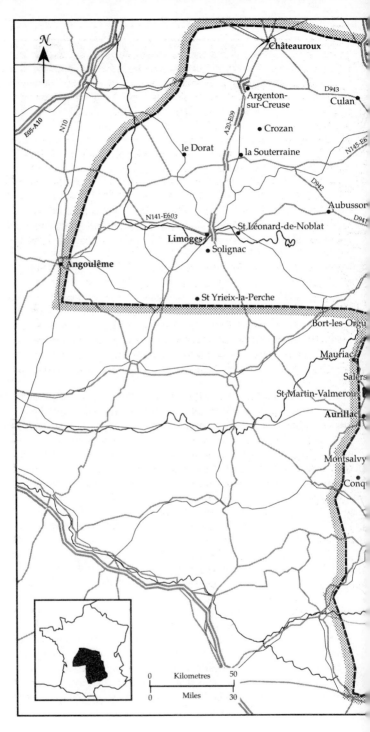

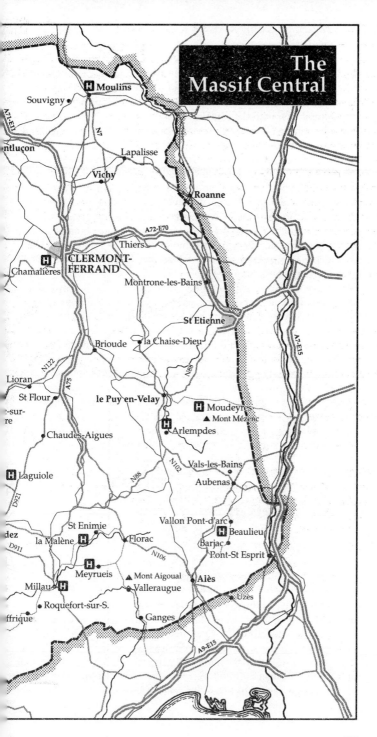

The Massif Central

Souvigny •
H Moulins
Lapalisse
Vichy
Roanne
A72-E70
Thiers
CLERMONT-FERRAND H
Chamalières
Montrone-les-Bains •
St Etienne
Brioude • la Chaise-Dieu
Lioran •
St Flour •
le Puy en-Velay
H Moudeyres
▲ Mont Mézenc
Chaudes-Aigues
H Arlempdes
H Laguiole
Vals-les-Bains •
Aubenas •
St Enimie
dez
la Malène H
Florac
Vallon Pont-d'arc •
H Beaulieu
Barjac •
Pont-St Esprit •
H
Meyrueis
▲ Mont Aigoual
Alès •
Millau H
Valleraugue
Uzès •
Roquefort-sur-S. •
ffrique
Ganges

the region. The Tarn is easy to fit into a drive towards the western Mediterranean, just as the spectacular Ardèche canyon (one of the classic canoe adventures in the country) is only a short diversion from the way south to Provence.

By comparison with the southern regions, Auvergne in the northern Massif Central is almost populous; its landscape is strangely volcanic but not wild, many of its towns and villages built from black volcanic basalt. The most attractive part is the Cantal, where the mountain scenery is beautiful and where the mountain pastures and long-horned dairy cows live up to Auvergne's rustic image. The rest of Auvergne has long been discovered: the volcanic waters of the numerous spa resorts have brought their own kind of tourism and Auvergne has become an outdoor holiday area for the budget holidaymaker. Accommodation is characterised more by value for money than refinement, and gastronomic specialities are limited to dark bread, mountain ham and mountain cheese.

It is easy to dismiss Auvergne as a holiday area – as many French people do, drawing unfavourable comparisons with the Alps and the Pyrenees. But there are a number of points in its favour. Precisely because it is not fashionable, its towns are quiet, unpretentious and inexpensive. The landscape is beautiful and unlike any other in France, thanks to its very obvious volcanic origins. Because the mountains are only moderately high (under 2,000 metres at their highest points) nearly all the peaks are easily conquered without equipment or experience. Auvergne also has much more man-made sightseeing interest than the deserted southern Massif; there are ruined fortresses perched on volcanic outcrops, and an inventive local style of Romanesque church architecture, which uses the volcanic stone to exceptionally colourful and decorative effect.

The Limousin

On its way down from Orléans through the Sologne and Berry, the A71 autoroute is without interest until the mountains of Auvergne come into sight. Travellers with more inclination to visit as they go may head south from the Loire to Loches and then join the Creuse valley to pursue the course of this very attractive river up some of the way to its source in the high Millevaches Plateau, east of Limoges.

West of Châteauroux lies the marshy **Brenne** region which is considered a hunter's paradise. Apart from game on the wing there isn't much to see, but on the north-western perimeter of the Brenne you can visit the **Château d'Azay-le-Ferron**, whose fortified tower dominating the village dates from the 15th century but most of which is the work of later periods in a more gracious style; it contains an opulent collection of 19th-century Empire furniture and varied *objets d'art*.

The Creuse valley is at its handsome best near Fontgombault, with cliffs of white stone to match the *tufa* along the banks of the Loire. The Benedictine **Abbaye de Fontgombault** was founded here on the river's left bank near the hermit Gombault's fountain. Although heavily restored, the originally 11th- and 12th-century abbey church is a splendid building with a majestic tall choir of great harmony and purity of line. After a long period of disuse the monastery was inhabited in the 19th century by Trappists who rebuilt the nave, and more recently by some Benedictines. You can go to services in the church and buy fresh local goat's cheese from the farms which occupy some of the old abbey buildings.

Argenton-sur-Creuse is pierced by the N20, which gives the town something of a roadside quality; there are however some old houses attractively lining the banks of the Creuse. Upstream of Argenton the Creuse runs down through a landscape of green pastures and lanes overhung with walnuts and vines. The area was a particular favourite of the novelist George Sand, who came here with her friends, many of them artists, and wrote in her book *Promenade Autour d'un Village* that from the attractive town of Gargilesse there is an *'embarras de choix pour les promenades intéressantes et délicieuses'*.

The ruins of the medieval fortress at **Crozant** are some of the most impressively situated in all France, high above the cliffs of a promontory at the meeting of the rivers Creuse and Sédelle. The Creuse has been dammed downstream from Crozant and you can take boat trips on the reservoir. From Crozant the tourist with a preference for mountainous scenery, perhaps on the way to the Massif Central, will follow the Creuse up towards its source, passing the former abbey church at **Moutier d'Ahun**, which dates mostly from the 12th century and has marvellous 17th-century wood carvings in the chancel.

The small town of **Aubusson** is tightly enclosed along the river between steep hills. Its weavers grew famous in the late Middle Ages, and Henry IV exempted Aubusson tapestries from customs duties. A further boost to the business was given by Colbert's designation of the town as *manufacture royale*, but in 1685 – on the revocation of the Edict of Nantes – many of the Protestant workers upped and left for safer lands elsewhere in Europe. The tapestry business still exists and has become known for the marvellous tapestries done after the designs of Jean Lurçat – you can see many of his works in the Tapestry Museum. There are also tapestry-weaving demonstrations and exhibitions in the town hall and several workshops which you can visit. Although Aubusson's high Protestant population attracted wreckers during the religious wars and Richelieu's destruction of the château in 1623, there are still some charming old narrow shopping streets.

Charm is not the conspicuous quality of the granite **Millevaches**

Plateau, named not after its cow population but because of the number of springs, of which the Creuse is one. It is a flat and bleak high plateau where winter temperatures descend below −20°C for long periods and where fewer and fewer people choose to spend their lives. It has been extensively reforested and many panoramas are now blocked by trees. For the tourist it is a good area for picnics – but for little else.

If you follow the course of the N20 from Crozant, you will not have to divert far to **La Souterraine** or **Le Dorat**, which both have large and severely impressive granite churches, many of whose features – especially the west façade with its little flanking bell towers and oriental-looking doorways – are characteristic of the Limousin style. Of the two, Le Dorat, which is named after the golden angel on top of the spire, is the more impressive church and also the more attractive, partly medieval, town. Its church was built in the 12th century and hardly seems to have weathered at all (it has been extensively restored). The overall view of the interior from the steps just inside the west door beneath one of the church's two domes is particularly striking.

The drive down through the Limousin is not an especially beautiful one, but it is green and hilly and full of the sweet chestnut trees which

have for many centuries played the key role in the local economy. The area is also particularly popular for fishing. In this featureless and unmemorable rural environment it is a surprise to come across the small village of **Oradour-sur-Glane**, which keeps alive the memory of a particularly unpleasant episode in the Second World War, when a division of SS troops swept through south-western France on their way up to Normandy just after D-Day with a brief to exact retribution for the response of the French Resistance to the news of the Allied Invasion. On 10 June 1944 all the inhabitants of Oradour-sur-Glane were rounded up and, with very few exceptions, killed. Before leaving, the SS burnt the village, whose ruins have been left just as they were, as a memorial.

The **Abbaye de St-Junien** was founded around the memory and the tomb of a 6th-century hermit. Only the church remains, very much in the style of Le Dorat and La Souterraine with the additional very great distinction of the tomb of Saint Junien – a masterpiece of early 12th-century carving.

Not far upstream from St-Junien, **Limoges** straddles the Vienne. It is one of the big cities of Central France and does not enjoy a reputation for great beauty or liveliness; like our Coventry, Limoges is where people are sent – in this case when they are sacked from high office. Limoges was the most famous centre for the making of enamels during the Renaissance and later for porcelain, the clay for which was discovered just south of Limoges in the 18th century. This industry has been responsible for the town's considerable modern expansion.

Sights in Limoges

• **Cathedral** Of the old Romanesque building only a small part of the entrance tower and porch beneath it remain. The rest is a construction of the Gothic period, so similar to the cathedrals of Narbonne and Clermont-Ferrand that they have been attributed to the same architect. The effect is one of great height and lightness and the interior is notable for the delicately carved screen which has been moved to the inside of the west end of the church. The north doorway has a wealth of delicate carving from the early 16th century.
• **Municipal Museum** An elegant setting of 18th-century archbishop's palace and gardens, distinguished by a superb collection of Limousin enamels.
• **Adrien-Dubouché Museum** Very fine collections of porcelain illustrating the development of the industry not only in Limoges but all over the world.

To the east of Limoges, **St-Léonard-de-Noblat** is an attractive small town with a Romanesque church whose octagonal belfry is one of the most famous and beautiful examples of the Limousin style. There are some amusing carvings on the capitals in the porch and especially on the wooden choir stalls in a distinctly satirical vein. The area around the church is full of old houses of interest, some of them dating from the 13th century.

To the south of Limoges, on the banks of the Briance just off the N20, **Solignac** has a beautiful 12th-century church with elegant arcading around the exterior of the apse and a single aisleless domed nave. **Chalusset** has some very picturesque and romantic old ruins of two fortresses, partly 12th-century, on a promontory at the meeting place of two rivers. It is a steep walk up from the river bank.

The great feature of the drive down to the fruit- and vegetable-growing basin of Brive-la-Gaillarde is the small town of **Uzerche**, splendidly situated on a promontory in a meander of the Vézère. The town houses are so well provided with turrets that they are referred to as Limousin châteaux. The N20 goes through the middle of town but it's worth getting out of the car for a short wander through the old streets, from the Place Marie-Colein up through the only surviving 14th-century gate to the 12th-century church of St-Pierre, whose typically Limousin belltower (square lower registers and an octagonal top) completes the picturesque scene. Instead of going on down to Brive you can head west from Uzerche to **Pompadour** – not much of a château (given by Louis XV to his most famous mistress), but a famous stud farm established by Louis in 1761, which specialises in Anglo-Arab horses (closed to visitors from mid-February to early July).

St-Yrieix-la-Perche lies at the heart of good fishing country and is the origin of the kaolin or clay for hard-paste porcelain, which was discovered in the 18th century. Like so many other places around here St-Yrieix possesses a splendid 12th-century church with porch and octagonal belfry. The nearby **Château de Jumilhac** is notable for its astonishing spiky roofscape of machicolations, pepperpot towers and lead statuette weather-vanes.

The Bourbonnais

The Bourbonnais is a fringe area, in appearance less closely related to the Massif Central than to Berry and Burgundy. At the end of the Middle Ages the dukes of Bourbon were among the most powerful princes in the land and **Moulins** their brilliant capital; the countryside around is fertile, with gently undulating hillsides and chubby cows – scarcely a part of France to go out of your way to discover, but rewarding enough for a short immersion. Long after its 16th-century heyday Moulins remained an important market town and staging post, and a notorious snarl-up on the main Paris–Lyon road. But thanks to the motorway, it is now a quiet and pleasant provincial town without much industry. A particular feature is the black stone lozenge patterning in the red brick of the old half-timbered houses.

Sights in Moulins

• **Cathedral** The late Gothic flat-ended choir has interesting windows, and the treasury has what is without exaggeration one of the greatest treasures of medieval French art – a triptych of the Virgin in Glory (as recorded in Revelations, clothed with the sun and crowned with a dozen stars), painted for Pierre and Anne de Beaujeu in about 1500 by the artist who is identified only as the Maître de Moulins.

• **Jacquemart** A frequently restored pink stone belfry and clocktower, named after the model family of Jacques (peasants) who hammer the chimes.

• **Lycée Banville** The chapel of this former convent contains the magnificent 17th-century marble tomb of the Duc de Montmorency (to visit, enquire at the tourist office).

To the south of Moulins lies **Vichy**, queen of watering places. It has cinemas, concerts, a casino, plenty of sports facilities, extensive bus tours (they have to be extensive to be interesting), good shopping and dozens of hotels, many of them rather institutional. This advanced infrastructure earned the town its selection in 1940 as the seat of the government of non-occupied France – a spa resort for the sick nation. Vichy's popularity is attributable to the allegedly beneficial effect on the digestive system of its highly carbonated waters, appreciated since Roman times. In the late 17th century Madame de Sévigné wrote that she sweated out over 20 pints a week and expected to be safe from rheumatism for life, but considered that the most effective part of her stay was a warm bed and the delights of the surrounding countryside with its river, sheep, goats and peasant girls dancing the *bourrée*. Two centuries later, Augustus Hare wrote that Vichy had no attraction but health to offer. Those in pursuit of health do so in an agreeable setting of neo-Muslim or post-modern thermal establishments, Second Empire casino, and parks and walks beside the Allier. The Parc des Sources itself is the focus of animation with a little crystal palace among the trees and promenades where *curistes* cluster round the troughs, filling their thermos flasks with waters from three separate springs (there's a small charge). The atmosphere falls somewhere between campside wash room, Champs-Elysées street café and pilgrimage basilica.

Excursions from Moulins and Vichy

• **Bourbon l'Archambault** (west of Moulins) A dull spa, despite having been an earlier medieval capital of the dukes of Bourbon. A few fragments remain of the old 14th-century castle destroyed by Revolutionaries.

• **St-Menoux** (west of Moulins) Romanesque church with a choir of splendid proportions and a miraculous tomb with a hole in the side for the mentally afflicted to put their 'soft' heads in and be cured.

• **Souvigny** Attractive small town with the most notable church in the Bourbonnais, built in the late 11th century when it was an important monastery and pilgrimage centre but much altered in the mid-15th century when the dukes of Bourbon made it their necropolis. Despite an extensive restoration programme, the church is more interesting than beautiful.

• **Besbre Valley** (south-east of Moulins) Very green and pleasant and full of little châteaux, some of them open to tourists. The **Château de Lapalisse**, though not the most beautiful, is the largest and most impressive, set high above the river, dominating the town and its important road junction. Inside, there are beautiful tapestries and a deeply coffered gilt ceiling in the Salon Doré. The **Château de Thoury** is much more endearing, a delicious little pink sandstone fortress, still inhabited, and well guided by the proprietor.

• **Château d'Effiat** (south-west of Vichy) A handsome ensemble of farming village and severe 17th-century château at the end of a splendid avenue of limes. Guided tours; beautiful furniture and decoration in period.

The Monts Dômes, the Monts Dore and the Cantal

South-west of Vichy lie the Monts Dômes volcanoes and the fertile lowlands of the Limagne. Rural life on the plain is more populated and less picturesque, but at Gannat (west of Vichy) there is a notable folk festival each July, maintaining the traditional *bourrée* dance and *cabrette* music (a form of bagpipes). The old market towns have considerable charm – for example, garlic-growing Billom, to the south of Thiers and Clermont.

At the foot of the chain of volcanic cones and dominated by the bulbous Puy de Dôme, **Clermont-Ferrand**, the big city of the Massif – and indeed of central France – is a merger of the old river cities Clermont and Montferrand. The city gave birth to the rubber industry in the 19th century, and the motor age brought lots of business. It is not a very endearing place, mainly because of the dark grey volcanic stone of its construction. The centre is a maze of old lanes in which the exemplar of the local Romanesque school, the church of Notre-Dame-du-Port (see page 236) is almost hidden. In contrast, the black Gothic cathedral stands out supreme, a lonely medieval skyscraper on the 45-metre mound on which the old city stands. The view of it from Royat is magnificent, thanks to Viollet-le-Duc who built the twin spires in the 19th century. The interior of the cathedral is as bright as can be expected given the employment of black lava, thanks in part to the strength of the stone which enabled such slender pillars to be used.

Royat was just a picturesque village grouped around its curious fortified Romanesque church until it was rediscovered in the 19th century and became one of the most fashionable of Second Empire spas, sprouting a sudden crop of hotels and other resort establishments. It still has its baths and its hotels beside the steep river gulley which runs down to Clermont from the volcanoes, but is now merely a moderately stylish suburb of Clermont. You can visit the Grotte du Chien, carpeted (to dog height) with carbonic acid gas which snuffs out candles and anything that inhales it.

Riom grew up like a *bastide* on a regular pattern within circular ramparts, now replaced by tree-lined boulevards. It was for a period the regional capital and has a number of old houses built in dark volcanic stone, a very good local ethnographic and folklore museum and a beautiful Virgin in the church of Notre-Dame-du-Marthuret.

Suburban Riom is not worthy of the once important old abbey church of **Mozac** (see page 236). Another nearby church at **Marsat** has a very splendid and much venerated 12th-century black Virgin, a severely iconic contrast to the sweet human vision of the Virgin in the late Middle Ages as exemplified in Riom. On a wooded spur high above Riom the ruined 13th-century fortress of **Tournoël** with its crumbling overgrown round tower and empty windows is splendidly romantic – as a local writer has described it: 'a ruin placed in majesty by a very expert ruin builder on this hillock so obviously destined to receive a ruin'. At the southern end of the Monts Dômes, the **Lac d'Aydat** is popular for weekend watersports and there are campsites among the trees.

Further south, the older and more eroded volcanic cones of the Monts Dore look more conventionally mountainous than the Monts Dômes; the area has a thriving spa and ski business within easy reach of Clermont.

Le Mont-Dore is the big resort, a spa and more recently ski centre, set in a superb amphitheatre of mountains with the Puy de Sancy at its head, easily reached by cable car. The resort is solid and somewhat dour, with a grandly theatrical thermal temple which you can visit. The chalets which have grown up along the valley nearer the winter pistes do not embellish its setting but there are sports facilities and good walking country all round and seasonal evening life. Here the Dordogne springs, and flows in its infancy down through **La Bourboule**, spa for infants and adolescents, whose waters have the highest arsenic content of any in Europe. There are fine driving excursions from Le Mont-Dore, including beautiful roads to Lake Chambon and Besse. **Orcival** is a deliberately charming little village of cafés and souvenir shops and a couple of hotels clustered in an intimate valley around its noteworthy Romanesque church (see page 236). Nearby you can visit the beautifully restored fortified manor of **Cordès**. **Lake Chambon** is one of the largest and shallowest of Auvergne lakes, with not so much a community as a functional straggle of buildings along the water, as well as campsites, beaches and water sports facilities. Nearby **Murol** is more of a little resort, with a few hotels tucked beneath the imposing ruins of a medieval fortress.

Lake Chambon is fed by waters which run down from the Puy Ferrand beside the Sancy through the steep-sided wooded and (above the woods) impressively rocky **Chaudefour Valley** – one of the best places hereabouts for walking, botanising and even climbing. Beyond Murol, **St-Nectaire** is well worth a visit to admire one of the finest

Orcival

examples of the local Romanesque style of church (see page 236), although the lower town and spa is dark and gloomy.

The most attractive of all the resorts in the Monts Dore is **Besse-en-Chandesse**, harmoniously or at least uniformly grey and medieval. Besse has a number of hotels and lots of animation, especially on market days when the whole village becomes a bazaar. There are lots of walking trails and organised excursions. The nearby **Lake Pavin** is one of the most typical of the crater lakes, small, deep and perfectly circular, surrounded by woods and, usually, by people.

South again, pastoral Cantal is comparatively unfrequented by tourists and increasingly depopulated as the ageing farming population dies out. Of the rest, many leave for good. The mountains are green and beautiful and with their grey villages are reminiscent of North Wales or Perthshire. Of the few resorts **Salers** is the most attractive; like Besse it is a medieval village with fortifications and a picturesque old charcoal-coloured market square with beautiful medieval and Renaissance turreted houses. There are excellent views from the ramparts. The nearby village of Fontanges is pretty enough to belong to the Dordogne rather than Auvergne. Between Salers and the avoidable town of Aurillac lies Tournemire, with a few convenient auberges, at the foot of the tall and substantially intact 15th-century fortress of **Anjony**. More comfortable living quarters were added later to the round-cornered keep. Inside château and chapel there are some splendid 16th-century wall paintings, including Anjony portraits.

The main (summer) excursion from Salers is the drive up into the heart of the ancient Cantal volcano via the **Puy Mary** (1,787 metres). The scenery around here is the most pleasing in Auvergne – you can walk without too much difficulty from the souvenir shops at the Pass de Peyrol up to the Puy Mary itself, and by walking a bit further on escape other people. Motorists should try the Route des Crêtes between Aurillac and Salers.

For those who want to do the Cantal on foot, the best places to stay are **Super-Lioran** (largely a modern ski resort), **Vic-sur-Cère**, which is large enough to have some animation, or **Salers** itself. From Super-Lioran you can reach all the peaks that are the remains of the original crater; the highest, **Plomb du Cantal** (1,855 metres), is served by a cable car. The Cère valley which runs down to Aurillac is one of the most verdant and charming of the lava paths that radiate from the old crater but spoilt by heavy lorries on a slow road. The valleys of the Bertrande (by St-Projet-de-Salers) or of the Aspre are more tranquil.

On the southern edge of the Cantal, the **Truyère** runs down through empty wooded countryside and impressive gorges whose appeal to tourists has been increased by the damming of the river in several places, making reservoirs popular for fishing and water sports. The best place to find out about facilities is at **St-Flour**, a not very charming grey town which enjoys a fine setting on volcanic cliffs (→ page 240)

Romanesque churches of Auvergne

Auvergne has a concentration of colourful Romanesque churches of great beauty and a character all of their own. The most attractive characteristic of the style is the varied geometric patterning of the exterior stonework exploiting the natural colours of the local volcanic and granite stone (red, black, white and yellow) which in some cases turns the walls into mosaics. Another feature is the raised central section of the transept which supports an octagonal lantern tower. Within many of the churches there are venerated Romanesque statues of the Virgin and Child, awe-inspiring in their stiff majesty, and richly jewelled caskets or reliquaries.

Clermont-Ferrand, Notre-Dame-du-Port One of the most perfect and delightful Romanesque churches in France, in the dark narrow heart of old Clermont. Decorative stonework inside and out, beautifully carved capitals; reproduction black pilgrimage Virgin in the crypt.

Royat, St-Léger A 12th-century church not very typical of the region, fortified in the 13th century and endowed with an octagonal belfry in the 19th. Set beautifully, high above the city of Clermont-Ferrand.

Mozac Once very important, now rather dilapidated abbey church with magnificent carved capitals and very precious reliquaries.

Ennezat The oldest surviving of the Auvergnat Romanesque churches (late 11th-century) curiously divided into two ill-fitting parts – Romanesque porch, nave and transept, much larger-scale Gothic choir with vivid 15th-century wall paintings.

Chauriat A typical local church with very colourful stonework.

Orcival, Notre-Dame A grey but charming church with pure and harmonious lines. Prisoners' shackles hang on the walls, given *ex voto* to the beautiful stylised pilgrimage Virgin enthroned against a pillar.

St-Nectaire One of the most attractive and beautifully situated of all the churches of this school, with an elegant and colourful east end, a harmonious interior rich in amusingly carved capitals and two magnificent 12th-century statues of Saint Baudime and the Virgin.

Issoire, St-Austremoine Beautiful east end, with geometric patterning and carved signs of the zodiac; splendid interior despite lurid 19th-century repainting, with beautiful capitals including one of the Last Supper with a tablecloth running all the way round the pillar, a crypt and a 15th-century painting of the Last Judgement in the porch.

Brioude, St-Julien Larger even than Issoire, and magnificent, thanks to the design and colourful decoration of the east end and the coloured stone of the interior and cobbled floor. Many beautiful works of art including frescoes. Statuary includes a disturbing 14th-century leprous Christ and a smiling Virgin.

Lavaudieu A vivid pink church in a particularly delightful village. Interior with frescoes under restoration; charming cloister.

Le Puy, St-Michel-l'Aiguille Extraordinarily situated atop a vertiginous 75 metre volcanic needle, and a long staircase. Beautiful carvings and coloured stone mosaics around the oriental-looking doorway, and some frescoes within. The even stranger **Cathedral** is one of the great pilgrimage churches of medieval France, built with as much virtuosity as Mont-St-Michel, into the air in projection from the side of the steep hill. Dazzlingly coloured stone exterior, domes, frescoes and a rich treasury within. Long-winded and expensive guided tour around beautiful cloister, and a fascinating maze of vaulted passages.

Le Puy Cathedral

Volcanoes and hot springs

Three of the four volcanic massifs in Auvergne have been cordoned off from random developments and declared the Regional Nature Park of Auvergne Volcanoes (between Clermont-Ferrand and Aurillac). The fourth volcanic area around the source of the Loire south and east of Le Puy is still so unfrequented that it needs no protection, for the moment at least. In the north the **Monts Dômes** are the youngest volcanoes and the most curious to look at, like boils spoiling the complexion of the landscape; over a hundred little isolated cones burst a few hundred metres above the high plateau in the most populous area of the Massif Central. While Magdalenian man painted caves in the Dordogne, the area was still erupting, some volcanoes throwing up solids which stayed in place leaving a domed mountain, others sending tons of molten lava spilling down their flanks and still shaped just as they were after eruption, with craters. The cones are not inhabited, nor even cultivated; they are simply strange phenomena to look at, best seen from the air or from the top of the highest one – the **Puy de Dôme** (1,465 metres) near Clermont, accessible via a toll road which spirals round it, giving marvellous views of the whole chain. On top of the dome, there are remains of a Roman temple, a modern observatory, a Volcano Park Information Centre, a bar/souvenir shop/hotel and week-end para-gliders. Not many people bother to explore any of the other *puys*. One of the most splendid is the **Puy de Pariou**, with concentric craters – the main one 100 metres deep and a kilometre round. It is a military training zone, and on certain days is closed to visitors. More reliably accessible to walkers is the **Puy de la Vache** which split its side when erupting.

The **Monts Dore** and the **Cantal** are two much larger and older volcanic areas. The enormous Cantal volcano, some 80km across, stood over 3km high. Dormant for several million years, the Monts Dore and the Cantal have been eroded by glaciers and the passage of time; both now culminate at a similar height – between 1,850 and 1,900 metres – and both consist largely of high pastures with alpine flowers, famous cheeses and moderate winter sports facilities. In some places the volcanic origins of the landscape are obvious – the **Roches Tuilière** and **Sanadoire** between Orcival and Le Mont-Dore are striking remains of an old crater. There are splendid jagged spikes on the Le Mont-Dore side of the **Puy de Sancy** (summit of central France at 1,885 metres) and in the **Chaudefour Valley**, just off the Besse/Mont-Dore road. There are a number of volcanic lakes, some filling old craters, others formed by eruptions closing valleys. The easily accessible **Puy Mary** gives wonderful views along the ruined ramparts of the old volcanic walls, with its lava paths radiating in all directions. St-Flour and Salers are set on fertile lava-based plateaux called *planèzes* which are a feature of all the perimeter of the Cantal volcano.

The Velay, the area around Le Puy, is also manifestly volcanic in origin – as Arthur Young noted, 'all in its form tempestuous as the billowy ocean'. The city of Le Puy itself is extraordinarily situated in a basin like a crater marked by three steep volcanic outcrops of which one is just wide enough at the top to support a small chapel. The volcanic massifs between Le Puy and Vals-les-Bains are among the most remote parts of the Massif Central, between the Rhône and the young Loire which has its source at the volcanic rocky cone which is the **Gerbier de Jonc**. The top of the region and the most celebrated viewpoint is the easily climbed **Mont Mézenc**. The region is one of severe and bleak beauty, without any developed resorts. The volcanic **Lac d'Issarlès** has been separated from the Loire by an eruption.

All this faulty earth and volcanic activity is not surprisingly accompanied by an abundance of hot springs and mineral-rich cold ones. At **Chaudes-Aigues**, south of St-Flour, the waters emerge nearly boiling at 82°C and have been used since Roman times for central heating. In other places the main use of the waters has been curative. **Vichy** has some 200 springs, of which 12 belong to the state. Most of the largest spas in the Massif were known to the Romans, but were not much exploited until the 18th and 19th centuries. The great spring named Eugénie in **Royat**, just outside Clermont, which produces over a quarter of a million gallons a day, was unleashed when the site of the Roman baths was being excavated in the 19th century.

high above a river. It has a grey Gothic cathedral of uncompromising harshness and is a busy tourist centre, although hardly a place to stay for long. The drive down the Truyère to Entraygues, which is long and extremely fiddly but in places quite magnificent, begins just south of St-Flour where Gustave Eiffel spanned the river with a prodigious cast-iron bridge. The Grandval reservoir has enhanced the wild setting of the ruined fortress of **Alleuze**, which is now surrounded by water, and looks altogether Scottish. A little further downstream the Truyère passes near **Chaudes-Aigues** of the hot waters (see page 239). If driving round the labyrinthine network of tributary gorges becomes tedious, the high deserted country of Aubrac round Laguiole will make a pleasant alternative. For many tourists the main reason for taking these routes out of Auvergne towards the Lot valley will be to join the medieval pilgrimage route from Le Puy to Moissac at **Conques**, an exceedingly picturesque and consequently tourist-ridden old village on a hillside above the river Dourdou, grouped around its magnificent Romanesque pilgrimage church of Ste-Foy, one of the most important in France. The grey-gold village has some accommodation and abundant craft and souvenir shops. The 11th-century church has been restored to its full splendour, of which the highlight is the vigorously animated representation of the Last Judgement over the main doorway. The treasury, arranged in two small museums beside the church, contains the gold reliquary statue of Saint Foy, mostly dating from the 10th century, but with later encrustations of jewellery. There are many other treasures of medieval goldsmithery and beautiful tapestries, all very well displayed, so you should not flinch at the relatively heavy entrance charge.

South of Conques, the great pull is the Tarn Gorges (see page 246), on the way to which lies the sleepy market town of the Aveyron, **Rodez**. Its cathedral is imposingly fortified, mostly Gothic but with a curious classical topping on the formidable west end, and a very elegant and delicate 16th-century belfry. North-east of Rodez, **Entraygues**, **Espalion** and **Estaing** are pleasant old villages beside the Lot, while **Bozouls** is famous for its 'hole' (a vertiginous cirque on top of which the village is built). All around this area, the rural domestic architecture is very attractive, with outside staircases, and vast, steeply pitched, rough-stone roofs.

The East

The area south of the Bourbonnais around and between the Allier and Loire is one of heavily forested hills, the Monts du Forez. There are few towns of any importance, except along the main rivers, and little of outstanding historical, architectural or scenic distinction. In fact, this is one of the most boring parts of France, only the villages on the eastern slopes of the Monts du Forez having any charm, and the landscape of the upper Loire having any beauty. Le Puy is the only place worth a special expedition.

Thiers, whose importance as a centre for cutlery manufacture dates from the Middle Ages, stands on a promontory above the river Durolle and has many well-preserved, substantial old 15th- and 16th-century houses with elaborately patterned and carved timbers. There is a small cutlery and other local crafts/traditions museum. The mountains of the Forez and Livradois are thickly wooded and thinly populated, with as many woodcutters as farmers. On the Clermont to Lyon road west of Feurs, the **Château de la Bastie d'Urfé** is well worth a visit. Originally built in the 13th century, it was completely reworked in a very Italian style in the 16th century, with loggias over the courtyard, a curious grotto of shells, and much of its original furniture.

High in the hills, at over 1,000 metres, the imposing village of **La Chaise-Dieu** stands on a crest in a clearing among the forests. It is a modest resort for cross-country skiers in the winter, and a reasonable place to break a journey in the summer in the hope of catching one of the occasional musical evenings in the abbey which towers over the village. The Gothic church of magnificent proportions and sobriety was built in the 14th century to the order of Pope Clement VI, an old boy of the abbey. To accommodate all the monks, the church has a larger choir than nave, and the two are separated by an elegant screen. You have to pay to penetrate, and should do so. There are very beautiful works of art within, including Clement's gleaming marble tomb surrounded by a series of marvellous 16th-century tapestries. There are also richly carved choir-stalls and a Dance of Death fresco.

South of **Brioude** the course of the **Allier** is an impressive one, through rocky gorges followed more closely by the railway than by the road. The Allier is favoured by campers and canoeists. One of the most perfectly shaped of all volcanic lakes of the Massif Central is the **Lac du Bouchet**, which fills a crater.

Le Puy is a big commercial and even industrial town, which sprawls between the old *cité* and the Loire. The extraordinary thing about the town is its setting. Three volcanic rocks tower above the agglomeration. The most spindly of them (the chimney of the old volcano), is crowned by a small Romanesque chapel (well worth the climb); the largest part of the cone supports a complete medieval pilgrimage city, beneath a massive 110-tonne, bright red 19th-century Virgin. The Holy City, as medieval Le Puy (cathedral and precinct) is called, is best attempted on foot – up the wide staircase street which extends the Rue des Tables, to the dazzlingly colourful west end of the cathedral (see page 237). Down in the modern town by the main road, the Musée Crozatier has among other things a good collection of local lace from different periods. Just north of Le Puy, the **Château de Polignac** – medieval home of the notoriously predatory noble family – stands superbly situated on an isolated volcanic rock.

The area south and east of Le Puy is bleak, unspoilt and beautiful in fine weather. The young Loire cuts through splendid gorges after it passes Le Puy, and before it passes St-Etienne (you should follow its example and bypass this town of football mania). Further upstream, it runs beneath the ruins of the **Château d'Arlempdes**, and past the beautifully situated Lac d'Issarlès. Around its source among the rocky volcanic cones, the countryside is wild, with thatched and rough stone farm buildings of great solidity, fields carpeted with narcissus in spring and volcanic hills. There are a few simple places to stay. **Vals-les-Bains** is a long and straggling spa of no particular character or charm, but is one of the few touring bases on the fringes of the hills, within easy range of the Cévennes and the Ardèche canyon.

The Cévennes and the Grand Causses

The Cévennes and the limestone plateaux of the Grands Causses offer some of the wildest, emptiest and most grandiose scenery in France. The most extraordinary landscapes, which make the area well worth visiting as part of a sightseeing tour, are those of the Causses: the desolate monotony of the high plateaux is interrupted by deep canyons, slashed like open wounds – the most famous being the Tarn Gorges between Florac and Millau. The riverbanks beneath the towering cliffs are green and friendly, and well provided with attractive accommodation, making the Tarn one of the best places to stay in the area, for those who want some comfort.

Many visitors come here for the opposite reason: to escape comforts, and all the trappings of civilised existence. For this purpose it is certainly the best area in France. There is very little in the region in terms of people, buildings, farming, even folklore, but plenty of imposing scenery and enough heat in summer to remind you that the Mediterranean is close at hand. The pull of these wild regions attracted the young Robert Louis Stevenson in 1877 to make the journey from Le

Monastier, a small town near Le Puy, over the high granite mass of Mont Lozère, across the Tarn and down to Alès. The Scottish novelist set off with a six-foot square sack ('luxurious turning room for one'), a fur cap with hood to fold down over his ears, and in case of heavy rain – the area is subject to the heaviest storms in France – a tentlet (waterproof coat, three stones, and a bent branch); for more immediate needs he had a leg of cold mutton and a bottle of Beaujolais. To carry him and his gear he took a donkey which he named Modestine, and which he only persuaded to accelerate beyond the most agonising funeral march when given a sharp needle by a wily peasant.

Stevenson may also have been attracted to the Cévennes by its history as a stronghold of Catholic repression and Protestant resistance. After nearly a century of peaceful co-existence, Louis XIV decided to encourage religious uniformity by ordering dragoons in the area to billet with Protestant families and behave as if they were in conquered territory, that is to say badly. Insincere conversions and inaccurate intelligence having persuaded the king that only handfuls of Protestants remained in his realm, he revoked the Edict of Nantes in 1685. Protestants, no longer guaranteed tolerance and political status, became outlaws. In the Cévennes the de-institutionalised church took to the empty countryside or *désert*. Eventually repressive action provoked guerilla resistance and war (1702–1704); the Protestants took the name of Camisards, after the white shirts they wore to identify each other during night attacks. In two years of war the Camisards burnt 240 churches, and the royal forces destroyed 41 villages, executed 147 desert pastors, and sent over 7,000 Protestants to the galleys. When one of the guerilla leaders was lured away to fight for the king abroad (he eventually became governor of Jersey) and the other was killed, the war ended; but the desert church continued to exist until the Revolution ensured its freedom.

There is a Camisard memorial museum at **Mas Soubeyran** near St-Jean-du-Gard, at the house of the chief who died – with a Protestant pilgrimage every September. Another reminder is the superb Corniche des Cévennes road, built from Florac to St-Jean-du-Gard by the royal intendant Barville, to dominate the guerilla territory.

Robert Louis Stevenson describes the landscape (specifically the Gévaudan north of the Mont Lozère) as 'like the worst of the Scottish Highlands, only worse – cold, naked and ignoble, scant of wood, scant of heather, scant of life'. This description conveys something of the bleakness of the Causses, but most of the landscape imprinted by Modestine's hoofs has been thoroughly reforested over the last hundred years, because the increasing nakedness of the mountains, stripped of their vegetation by man and sheep, brought major flood problems to the Cévennes valleys. Now the thickly wooded region has been turned into the huge **Cévennes National Park**, its main area scarcely inhabited by man. Its periphery (which includes the area of the Tarn

Gorges) is increasingly well organised for excursions on foot or horse-back (or in winter on cross-country skis) into the National Park itself, to enjoy its peace and space, and perhaps catch a glimpse of a soaring eagle. The best equipped of these bases on the edge of the Park are **Meyrueis, Florac, Le Pont de Montvert** and **Valleraugue**. For drivers the best way to get a fleeting appreciation of the Cévennes is to follow the **Corniche des Cévennes** road above the two Gardon valleys, getting superb views and passing an old medieval hostelry village (L'Hospi-talet) for pilgrims and travellers through this wild region. The smaller road, which closely follows the Gardon de St-Jean to the south, is equally attractive. Among the chaos of rocks beside **L'Hospitalet**, there is a plaque in memory of a desert assembly of 1689. You can also drive up to the summit (1,567 metres) of **Mont Aigoual**, which means wet. Here, Atlantic and Mediterranean air currents meet over the crest, and more than two metres of rain falls every year, most of it in the autumn. In all directions there are trails for walkers and skiers and old sheep paths, rarely used now by the flocks which once made their spring and autumn journeys up and down the mountain on well-worn *drailles*. Now the sheep are shunted around in lorries, and the transhumance paths have been taken over by transient humans.

On the Mediterranean side of the Cévennes, the Gardon rivers drop steeply down to Alès, and the scrub hillsides (*garrigues*) that lie between Montpellier and the mountains. The river Hérault runs south from the Aigoual through the *garrigues*, watering some of the most productive Languedoc vineyards before it flows into the Mediterra-nean. It drops quickly to Valleraugue, and afterwards has carved gorges in the rock around **Ganges**, a town famous in the past for silk. Silk-worms were a Cévennes speciality from the 17th to 19th centuries – much to the disapproval of the royal minister Sully, who thought that silk would be morally contaminating. Not far downstream from Ganges is the magnificent **Grotte des Demoiselles**, its great underground chamber full of natural pillars and known, inevitably, as the cathedral. It was a hiding place for Camisards and for priests during the Revolution, and is still the setting for a Christmas midnight mass. At the end of another stretch of stark rocky gorges, the **Grotte de Clamouse** was explored for the first time in 1945; it too is very well provided with strange and beautiful rock formations. **St-Guilhem-le-Désert** sounds as if it might be a place of Camisard memory, but in fact it goes back much earlier as a religious refuge: it was to this veritable wilderness that Charlemagne's brother-in-arms William of Orange retired from fighting after a heroic career to take up prayer and fasting, from which he soon died. St-Guilhem is hardly more than a hamlet of very old houses and an inn, grouped around a square with plane tree and fountain, in front of the Romanesque abbey church founded by William in 804 but in its present form dating mostly from the 11th century. The church itself has a particularly beautiful apse, and used to have a beautiful cloister until it was transported to a museum in New York.

Grottoes, underground rivers and gorges are particular features of the limestone area which makes up most of the southern Massif Central; they are more impressive than those around the Dordogne valley, though without the prehistoric treasures. Another feature is the bizarre rocky chaos, technically known as dolomitic, which looks like ruins. One of the most impressive and enormous of these, with a real village built curiously among the rocks, is the **Cirque de Mourèze** near Clermont-l'Herault. The **Grands Causses**, as the plateaux are called, extend to the Atlantic flank of the Cévennes, and are not much lower than the mountains themselves. There are four of these great *causses*, separated by river gorges; starting at the south near St-Guilhem–le-Désert, the **Causse du Larzac** is the largest and the best known. It was a *cause célèbre* of the '70s, when radical youth and local farmers united to save it from assimilation into a huge military zone between Millau and Nant. One excellent reason to save the Larzac is that its pastures nourish innumerable flocks of summer sheep whose milk is made into cheese and sent to the natural cellars (in this sense the French word *caves* is the right one) of **Roquefort-sur-Soulzon**, just south-west of Millau, to evolve into the eponymous cheese known to Pliny and Charlemagne, its structure as labyrinthine as the limestone underground, and its taste as sharp as a winter wind on the *causse*. Like champagne, Roquefort owes its quality to the surroundings of its maturing – a constant temperature of 5°C–7°C with damp draughts issuing from faults in the rock. You can visit the vaults, which smell less frightful than you might expect from a taste of the end product.

From the south the most impressive way to approach the Larzac (or to leave it if you are travelling south) is from **Lodève** and the green and pleasant Largue Valley with its vines and olives, by means of the Pas de L'Escalette, a hairpin cliff road which has been built to replace ladders attached to the 300 metres of rock face – until a century ago the only way up or down. A new tunnel has now taken away much of the drama. The Pas de l'Escalette road is the old one across the Causse du Larzac, used not only by sheep (which had to be carried down the ladders) but also by pilgrims on their way to St-Guilhem-le-Désert and Compostela. The passage of pilgrims was the *raison d'être* of the fortified village of **La Couvertoirade**, built by the Knights Templar in the late Middle Ages. It never outgrew its fortifications, and in this century lost all of its original population, becoming a craft village instead, and well worth the short detour from the main road.

To the east of La Couvertoirade the Vis runs down from the Cévennes between two minor *causses* before it joins the Hérault at Ganges. Its course is often dry and severely rocky as far as the beautiful Source de Lafoux, which is accessible on foot from the Cirque de Navacelles. There the Vis, no longer dry, has broken through an isthmus of rock which once overlooked a deep meander, leaving a rounded theatre of scrub-covered rock with a green forsaken river-bed and the small village of **Navacelles** itself. The Cirque is one of the most impressive in the *causses*, both sides negotiable by a hairpin road.

The river Dourbie separates the Causse du Larzac from the **Causse Noir**, the smallest of the Grands Causses, with the most curious formations of dolomitic rock. To the north it in turn is split from the **Causse Méjean** (the highest and bleakest with an average height of over 1,000 metres) by the river Jonte. These two rivers are tributaries of the Tarn, and their impressive gorges are subsidiary in grandeur only to those of the Tarn.

Not only are the **Tarn Gorges** the outstanding sight in a region of outstanding natural phenomena, the valley also has a number of attractive places to stay, which makes it a good base for exploring the surrounding area, provided you are prepared for some tiring and sometimes hair-raising driving. The Tarn Gorges are some 80km long, as the river flows, between Florac and Millau. In places the *causse* walls either side are over 500 metres high, and the width of the canyon at the top varies from just over one kilometre to about two. In stretches the bottom of the gorge is very narrow and dark, in others wide and fertile with cultivations and communities alongside the river. One of the most attractive is the old village of **Ste-Enimie**. All along there is the striking contrast between fertility at the riverside and the barrenness of the *causse* above. The rock walls are beautifully formed and coloured where they are not covered with scrub, and there are a number of very picturesque châteaux, half-hidden among the trees. The prettiest of them, the **Château de la Caze**, has been turned into a hotel of some distinction. The gorges can be seen very well by car, for a road follows the river, except at its narrowest parts, and in a number of places roads have been engineered from the *causse* in hairpins down the canyon walls. But the drive cannot compare with a boat along the river. The

Château de la Caze

classic excursion is to hire a canoe from **La Malène**, and sit back beneath the towering walls of the canyon as you drift for about an hour down the river, passing some of the narrowest and most impressive parts of the gorge, most not easily viewed from the road. The light is best early in the morning. For canoeists the Tarn is very popular and much less dangerous than Ardèche. Even so, the current can take you by surprise if you try to swim. By car or by boat, it is best to do the gorges in the same direction as the river flows. For those without a car there are bus excursions from **Millau**, **Mende** and **Meyrueis**, all busy little towns with plentiful accommodation. Meyrueis has by far the most charm.

Excursions from the Tarn

● **Le Rozier** From this beautifully situated village – between the junction of the Tarn and Jonte – there are some long, spectacular and, in a few cases, vertiginous walks, high up on the cliffs above the two rivers. Information should be sought before setting off.

● **Gorges de la Jonte** The course of the Jonte, which runs from the **Aigoual** through **Meyrueis** to the Tarn, is only marginally less impressive than that of the Tarn itself and can also be followed by road.

● **Grotte de Dargilan** The best of the many caves on or close to the river, with splendid natural rock forms.

● **Aven Armand** The most exciting and unworldly grotto yet discovered in France, with a petrified forest of 400 of the biggest and best stalagmites. A funicular railway takes you into the depths.

● **Montpellier-le-Vieux** Named because of its resemblance to a ruined city, an enormous and desolate chaos of weird dolomitic rock forms.

247

The Ardèche gorges north-east of the Cévennes rival those of the Tarn in popularity and in outstanding scenery. The section of the Ardèche Valley which must be seen is between **Vallon-Pont-d'Arc** and **St-Martin-d'Ardèche** where the river runs for some 32km at the foot of a superb canyon, in places nearly 300 metres deep. Until recently the only way to see the gorge was to take a canoe and brave the white waters of one of the fastest flowing of France's rivers. Now there is a corniche road along the empty scrub-covered hilltops on the north side of the river which does not follow the gorge bend by bend, but gives a number of magnificent views down into it. There being no communities and no road down by the river, the Ardèche presents a less varied sight than the Tarn which has fertile cultivations and villages at the foot of the cliffs; but in many ways the Ardèche is grander. It is also much more exciting for canoeists, with the attraction of escapism as well as the challenge of the rapids. You can hire canoes from a number of resorts between Vallon-Pont-d'Arc and Pont-d'Arc itself, which is a splendid natural limestone arch over the river. After a day's canoeing you will be picked up at St-Martin and brought back by car. It is not a canoeing trip for beginners; in autumn, the Ardèche becomes a river of violence and dangers, its waters capable of rising by over six metres in a matter of hours, and accelerating like tidal waves. May and June are the best times for a canoe trip. Along the river, rapids and gentle sweeps of water alternate; there are grottoes, and waterside rocks which make perfect picnic tables. The unspoilt natural beauty of the canyon is usually complemented by unclothed campers and there is a naturists' campsite nearby.

HOTELS

Key: ◆ = 0–250FF, ◆◆ = 251–450FF, ◆◆◆ = over 451FF; prices are per double room without breakfast, which costs around 35–60FF extra. Some hotels may insist on half-board during high season, some hotels or restaurants may close at specific times during the week – it is always worth checking. Most hotels accept the major credit cards; we have indicated where a hotel takes no credit cards.

ARLEMPDES

Du Manoir ◆

43490 Haute-Loire
TEL 71 57 17 14

Tucked under a vertiginous slab of rock crowned by a ruined castle, this is a modest village inn in an area lacking plush accommodation. The location, above the young Loire, is excellent, and while there is absolutely nothing fancy or luxurious about the place, you will find clean paintwork, showers which work properly and a friendly welcome. There's only the bar or the outside terrace to sit in, but these, along with the restaurant, attract such life as there is among the scattered houses of the village. Food is simple and filling, and the wine list good value.

OPEN Early Mar to Nov ROOMS 16 (all with shower) (Credit cards not accepted)

BEAULIEU

La Santoline

07460 Ardèche
TEL 75 39 01 91; FAX 75 39 38 79

Close to both the Ardèche gorges and to the Cévennes, but out in the middle of nowhere in an area of hot and rocky scrubland, this old farmhouse has been converted by its owners into a simple, most pleasing hotel. The conversion has been done without the building losing character – the cool hallway and the rough-stone barrel-vaulted cellar restaurant are both charming spots, while the bedrooms are prettily and sparsely furnished in very good taste. The two under the roof have air-conditioning units. Shower rooms are small but adequate. The menus proclaim simple regional cooking. There's also a small swimming-pool.

OPEN End Mar to early Nov ROOMS 6 (all with bath) FACILITIES Outdoor pool, horse-riding

CHAMALIERES (nr Royat)

Radio

43 avenue Pierre Curie
63400 Puy-de-Dôme
TEL 73 30 87 83; FAX 73 36 42 44

On a hillside in a quiet corner of Clermont-Ferrand's spa suburbs, the art deco building of the Hotel Radio is instantly distinctive in its ocean-liner outline. The interior is faithful to the period, although not all of it is original. However, there are enough geometric dados and effects created from ground glass screens to satisfy most enthusiasts – especially in the salon, where it is particularly harmonious. Bedrooms are less obviously art deco, but are pleasing, fairly standard town-hotel rooms. The food here continues to be an excellent reason to visit, and quite compensates for the fact that the hotel is on the wrong side of town for a quick getaway on the autoroute.

OPEN Feb to Dec ROOMS 26 (all with bath or shower)

LAGUIOLE

Michel Bras

route d'Aubrac
12210 Aveyron
TEL 65 44 32 24; FAX 65 48 47 02

High in the bare pasturelands of the Aubrac, south of the Cantal mountains, Michel Bras' new hotel and restaurant is placed on the hillside like a modern-day ark. Something of the same dedication and mildly batty single-mindedness which made Noah seem an oddball to his neighbours infects this place too – both architecture and the cooking are explained in mystical terms, and the sous-chefs may seem more like disciples. But throw off Anglo-Saxon cynicism, and this is a place well worth splashing out on, even though it is far more expensive than any other in this chapter. The building is both graceful and tasteful – at times like a sailing ship held together by glass and wire, at other times like the local farmhouses it intends to pay homage to. The food draws maximum praise from those connoisseurs who venture into this traditionally no-hope area of France, and you can be assured that your meal will be garnished with herbs drawn straight from the local mountainsides. A wonderful salon, with views reaching into the blue haze, and bedrooms which are luxurious, if not over-spacious for the price, are the chief advantages of staying here. Even in the mist this is a place which reeks of class.

OPEN Early Apr to end Oct ROOMS 15 (all with bath or shower)

LA MALENE

Manoir de Montesquiou

48210 Lozère
TEL 66 48 51 12; FAX 66 48 50 47

Buried at the very bottom of one of the most impressive sections of the Tarn gorges, this 16th-century manor house seems to grow out of the cliff face, an impression heightened by the creepers, the tower and the warm local stone. The inside of the house is attractive too, notably because of a creditable attempt to stay in period wherever possible, which has resulted in some very beautiful and ancient pieces of furniture. One of the suites has a huge four-poster with Satan carved into the footboard and the local saint at the head, and even the smallest bedroom has something of interest. The public rooms consist of a large restaurant and a small TV room. Food is reasonably priced and the menus remarkably comprehensive considering the route the ingredients must travel.

OPEN Early Apr to mid-Oct ROOMS 12 (all with bath or shower)

MEYRUEIS

La Renaissance et St-Sauveur

rue de la Ville
48150 Lozère
TEL 66 45 60 19; FAX 66 45 65 94

In the middle of this busy village at the head of the Jonte gorges, the genial Bourguets run a pair of hotels to suit most tastes. The St-Sauveur is a bland but big town house with shady plane tree outside; the Renaissance is old, decorated with some fine stone carving and blessed with wooden floors and antique furniture. Bedrooms in the St-Sauveur are extremely simple with basic furniture and pretty old-fashioned bathrooms. La Renaissance rooms have more class but are pricier, and there is a very attractive salon for relaxation. The two big rooms which make up the hotels' restaurant are at the St-Sauveur, and competent regional fare is the order of the day.

OPEN Early Apr to mid-Nov ROOMS 35 (all with bath or shower)

Château d'Ayres

48150 Lozère
TEL 66 45 60 10; FAX 66 45 62 26

Just outside the village, this conglomeration of a building (12th-century at its core) is given some feeling of unity by the creepers which cover it. It is a château-hotel which is doing its utmost to provide a country-house style for its English guests while valiantly combating the inherent defects of a large house which was never designed to be a hotel. Public rooms, especially the hall and the two salons, are very comfortable, although one of the dining-rooms is rather airless. Bedrooms are not large at the cheaper end, and the furnishings are fairly basic for the price. To compensate, there is a good, friendly atmosphere and a genuine welcome.

OPEN End Mar to mid-Nov ROOMS 26 (All with bath or shower) FACILITIES Heated outdoor pool, tennis

MILLAU

Château de Creissels

route de St-Affrique
12100 Aveyron
TEL 65 60 16 59; FAX 65 61 24 63

This amiable and well-placed hotel is no great beauty – the old château is a maze of corridors and large bedrooms and is crumbling to bits in some places. In some ways more like a convent or boarding-school than hotel, but eminently good value and with bags of character, it is a popular stop-off point for a cosmopolitan crowd, many of them with young families. No one is ever going to write home about the food, served in the cool, barrel-vaulted cellars, but it is filling and satisfactory. Upstairs, leather-bound books stand in rank in the old library overlooking a billiard table, and there is a quiet salon full of creaky formal chairs. You get what you pay for in the bedrooms – perhaps a bathroom a hundred metres down the corridors at the cheaper end, rather more conventional facilities elsewhere.

OPEN Mar to Dec ROOMS 33 (all with bath or shower)

MONTSALVY

Auberge Fleurie ◆

place du Barry
15120 Cantal
TEL 71 49 20 02

It is not so much flowers as a rampant Russian vine that covers the outside of this inn – a small hostelry just outside the medieval gateway of a very attractive village off the main road south of Aurillac. The Auberge is cheap, full of local trade and gossip, and is absolutely made for those who desire nothing better than to plunge into the thick of provincial life. The huge restaurant, furnished with copper pans and fresh flowers, is just what you expect a good village eating place to be. The bedrooms are small, spotless and old-fashioned, with floral wallpaper, bouncy beds and chocolate-coloured tiles in the shower rooms (though the showers are up to date). Best of all, the welcome is friendly and you are just expected to mix in.

OPEN Mid-Feb to mid-Jan ROOMS 11 (8 with bath or shower)

MOUDEYRES

Le Pré Bossu ◆◆

43150 Haute-Loire
TEL 71 05 10 70; FAX 71 05 10 21

In the high, lonely countryside close to the source of the Loire, this dark stone farmhouse stands just outside a small, battered village. Beautifully restored by its Flemish owners, Le Pré Bossu is a place of much character. The old farm kitchen with its flagstone floor and ancient dresser makes a good salon, while the restaurant, long and low with rough stone walls and gently spotlit tables, is a classy place. Bedrooms, all on the first floor, are fractionally small for the price, but are well co-ordinated with pleasing country furniture and fresh décor. The atmosphere and many of the guests belong to the Low Countries rather than to the wilds of France, but the location and the comfort of this hotel makes it a good place to retreat to.

OPEN Easter to Nov ROOMS 10 (All with bath or shower)

MOULINS

Paris-Jacquemart

21 rue de Paris
03000 Allier
TEL 70 44 00 58; FAX 70 34 05 39

This is a solid and satisfying hotel close to Moulins' attractive centre. Its chief virtue is impeccable service, but there are other advantages too, notably the distinctly above-average food (the fruit tartlets are mouth-watering) and the tiny but relaxing terrace and swimming-pool. Bedrooms are bland, without much personality, but have been well refurbished and have good lighting. The restaurant is the star among the public rooms – a dignified, even grand, old lady of a room – and there is a bar and salon as well.

OPEN All year exc. 3 weeks Jan, 2 weeks May ROOMS 27 (all with bath or shower) FACILITIES Heated outdoor pool

SAINT MARTIN VALMEROUX

Hostellerie de la Maronne

Le Theil
15140 Cantal
TEL 71 69 20 33; FAX 71 69 28 22

This smartly converted Auvergnat farmhouse makes an excellent base on the western side of the Cantal mountains. It is close to Salers, built on the side of one of the most attractive of the long valleys which stretch towards the core of the old volcano. The exterior is characteristic of the region – 'lauze' roof, dormer windows, black basalt stone – but the interior is that of a modern and comfortable hotel, with ample space to sit. The restaurant, built into the slope beneath the main building and reached through a tunnel, is L-shaped and pretty; the food (modern cooking) is beautifully flavoured and presented. The crème caramel may be the best in France. Bedrooms are well fitted out with waxed wood furnishings, spotlights and excellent bathrooms, and there are sizes and positions to suit most tastes and pockets. For a comfortable and well-run modern hotel, the prices are not too steep. Much the best option in the area.

OPEN End Mar to early Nov ROOMS 25 (all with bath or shower) FACILITIES Heated outdoor pool, tennis

Roquefixade

A castle girt above and bound
With sorrow, like a spell

[Swinburne]

THE PYRENEES

Rising gently from the Atlantic and falling steeply to the Mediterranean, the Pyrenees form a wall between France and Spain which soars abruptly to peaks of over 3,000 metres from the plains of Gascony in the north and Aragon in the south. Easily crossed at both ends, the wall's height is almost unbroken in the central section, where narrow passes are only a few hundred metres below the summits. Although the Pyrenees are significantly lower than the Alps, and no rival for them for the tourist seeking a picturesque contrast of pastures against summer snows and glaciers – they have only a few square kilometres of glacier compared with several hundred in the Alps – and although they are much less developed for winter and summer sports, the Pyrenees are much more than just a poor substitute for the higher range.

While there are climbs which demand the highest degree of expertise, it is possible for a tourist who is no more than energetic to make the ascent of one of the most majestic of all Pyrenean peaks, the Canigou, which towers over Catalonia from around 3,000 metres. Alternatively you can follow part at least of hiking trail No. 10 of the *Grandes Randonnées*, which joins the Atlantic to the Mediterranean, traversing the foot and at times the shoulders of the Pyrenean wall. For much of its course it's a magnificent mountain path within the bounds of the Pyrenean National Park, punctuated by inexpensive (and usually very simple) mountain refuges, bases for hikers and climbers alike.

The Pyrenees' relative lack of development adds to their attraction for tourists who want no more than a bed and a roof, or just a campsite and a cheap wholesome meal. The high mountain areas are unspoilt, and in most cases unscarred by the cable-car pylons that go with Alpine development. There are very few high resort villages; though this means that in many places walkers have to climb through wooded hillsides rather than from a cable-car or hotel above the tree line, it does not mean that the mountain range is remote and inhospitable.

Right across their breadth the Pyrenees are characterised by low valleys that cut deep into their heart. The arrangement of parallel steep-sided valleys running north/south from the peaks to the plain

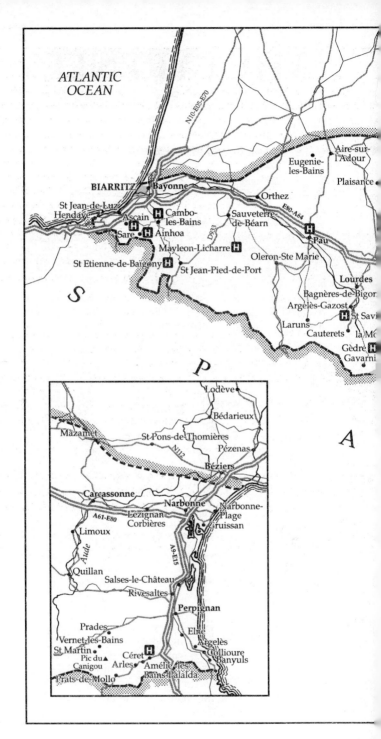

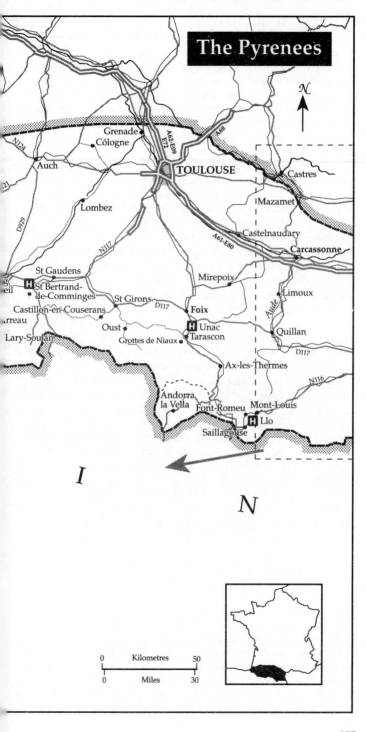

The Pyrenees

N

N124
Auch
Grenade
Cólogne
A62-E09 E72
A68
TOULOUSE
Castres
Mazamet
Lombez
Castelnaudary
A61-E80
Carcassonne
N117
St Gaudens
Mirepoix
Limoux
H St Bertrand-de-Comminges
St Girons
D117
Foix
Aude
Castillon-en-Couserans
Oust
H Unac
Tarascon
Quillan
Lary-Soulan
Grottes de Niaux
D117
Ax-les-Thermes
N116
Andorra la Vella
Font-Romeu
Mont-Louis
H Llo
Saillagouse
D229
N124

I

N

Kilometres
0   50
Miles
0   30

makes communication from east to west time-consuming. Where there are roads running laterally, as it were, to link valleys, they are usually slow and narrow, and by comparison with the Alps do not present many dramatic views. The Pyrenees are not ideal mountain territory for those who wish to get their enjoyment from a car or from a cable-car.

The valleys are well watered and fertile, except at the eastern end of the range. They have always sheltered pastoral communities, which have existed often without much communication from valley to valley, but with more links across the range with the Spanish side. Many of the valley folk lived for centuries unaffected by national politics, and for practical reasons they were granted the right to look after themselves in accordance with their own local laws, and remained exempt from national taxes. They settled territorial disputes amicably with their neighbours, agreed rights and routes for their migrating flocks, which spent the winters in the plains, and generally appear to have lived a rustic idyll until the age of asphalt brought the benefits of civilisation. Andorra survives, at least administratively, as the last of these independent high mountain areas, with its jealously guarded local laws and its effective autonomy vis-à-vis the two theoretical overlords, Spanish and French. But such has been its success in exploiting its special tax-free status that its character has changed infinitely more than the other valleys, long gobbled up by France.

The relative isolation of all the valleys and the traditions of local independence have led to the development of very pronounced regional differences from valley to valley. The Pyrenees attract lovers of folklore, above all to the two separatist and non-French speaking regions which span the Franco-Spanish border at both Mediterranean and Atlantic ends of the range: the Basque country and Catalonia. Both regions are outstandingly interesting for domestic (Basque) and church (Catalan) architecture, and for language, local dances, sports and food. Like the Pyrenees themselves, both areas occupy more space in Spain and are more concentrated in human, economic and politically activist terms in Spain than they are in France, where Catalans and Basques are just a proud picturesque tourist-drawing fringe.

Regions of the Pyrenees are also sharply differentiated by the effects of the weather. Again, the Basque country – well watered to a fault – and the harsh dry mountain plateaux of Catalonia are the extremes. The Atlantic, which brings all the rain, extends its lush influence more than halfway across the range; the eastern area is the driest and sunniest corner of France. The high modern resort of Font-Romeu, with 3,000 sun hours a year, has a solar oven.

Although the pastoral Pyreneans have always kept up contact and trade with the valley inhabitants on the Spanish side of the range, there is a great geographical and human contrast between French north and Spanish south. A recent guide to the Pyrenees, Henry Myhill, described the impression left on him by a drive up from the scorched stubble of Upper Aragon around Jaca, over the Col du Somport and down into the green and damp foothills of Béarn: 'in less than fifty miles, I seemed to have travelled most of the way from Africa to Scotland'. Less hospitable and populated than the French Pyrenees, the Spanish ones have the highest peaks and areas of supreme natural beauty. The keen hiker can ignore the frontier, and in the steps of locals and pilgrims climb through the high *ports* that are the only breaches in the wall and down from the French National Park into the Spanish one. The driver too will find that the journeys east to west can sometimes be most quickly accomplished by crossing into Spain, and back by another pass.

Although the mountains are very snowy in winter, the development of winter sports in the Pyrenees has not taken place on the same scale as in the Alps. It remains mostly a local phenomenon, and cheap, and has done little to spoil the essentially quiet pastoral nature of the region which accounts for so much of its charm. But development has come to the area of Catholicism's most frequented pilgrimage resort, Lourdes, which attracts millions of *curistes* and pilgrims to the place where a simple peasant girl of the mid-19th century saw a vision of the Immaculate Conception 18 times, and where a miraculous spring appeared. Whatever you may feel about Lourdes – and there are not a few who consider it to be offensive commercialised exploitation of human weakness – there is no denying its influence over the central Pyrenees, for many of the pilgrims come to sightsee as well as to make their requests of Saint Bernadette.

Lourdes is a recent phenomenon, but to resort to the Pyrenees for cures is not new. The range is full of sulphurous and salty spas, many of which date back to Roman times. Most of these places are cheap and some of them are nasty. But until the development recently of a few modern sports resorts (Font-Romeu, Gourette, La Mongie) they have been the only places to stay in any comfort. Some of the spas are set deep in the mountain valleys and have developed into ski resorts as well; of these the most stylish by far is Luchon. The alternatives to spas or modern resorts are campsites, mountain refuges, and simple mountain villages which put up with tourists, but hardly put themselves out. Pyrenean villages have no more gaily colourful chocolate-box charm than the French Alps. They are simple, often basic, rough-stone communities – except in the Basque country, where the house-proud inhabitants whitewash their walls, and fill their window boxes almost as decoratively as the Tyroleans.

Tourist development is probably too recent to be blamed for the fact that the rare species of Pyrenean wildlife have become so rare that they cannot fairly be claimed as an important reason for the amateur to visit the Pyrenees. There are a lot of izards, the Pyrenean version of the chamois, and there are still large numbers of vultures. But the lynx prefers Spain, and there remain only a few dozen bears and eagles. It is not surprising that the bear has taken to the darkest forests and adopted nocturnal habits. More even than the wolf, it is the great scourge of the shepherd; bears still kill dozens of farm animals every year, and the National Park has to compensate the farmer.

The National Park, which runs in a strip along the high mountains of the border country in the centre of the Pyrenean range, is more reliably rewarding for the botanist, who can climb beyond the woods and cultivations to find gentians, saxifrage and edelweiss; and – more surprisingly perhaps – for the fisherman, who can pursue the sport in nearly all the many hundreds of Pyrenean mountain tarns under no more control than elsewhere in France.

As well as being such a naturally attractive holiday area, the Pyrenees have (for a mountain range) a unique wealth of historical and cultural interest. Prehistoric man painted the limestone caves of the Ariège. In the Middle Ages, Arab domination of much of Spain meant that the Pyrenees were the natural border between Europe and Africa, between Christian and Infidel. The first glorious chapter of the crusading epic of the Middle Ages was written on the basis of what was actually an insignificant ambush of Charlemagne's rear-guard by Basque marauders in the Pyrenean valley of Roncevaux in 778. In epic poetry this became a heroic victory for chivalrous Christian prowess and sacrifice over the Saracens, achieved by Charlemagne's legendary nephew Roland. An angel had provided Roland's magic sword Durandal, and with it he had conquered Anjou, Brittany, Poitou, Maine, Normandy, Provence, Aquitaine, Lombardy, Romania, Bavaria, Flanders, Burgundy, Poland, Constantinople, Saxony, Scotland and England. Having resisted the Saracen attack at Roncevaux the invincible Roland split his temples blowing his own trumpet to summon Charlemagne, and to prevent Durandal getting into Infidel hands, he tried to break the sword before he expired, smashing Durandal repeatedly against a rock. He only managed to break the rock – which is why many a cleft in the mountains is called Roland's Breach, however remote from Roncevaux (there is even one in the Massif Central). Throughout the Middle Ages, pilgrims flocked across to Roncevaux, planting crosses on the hill where Charlemagne had done so. The pilgrims were on their way from all over Europe to Santiago (St James) de Compostela in north-west Spain, and the routes converged in the Pyrenees. From all this transit traffic, there is still a wealth of beautiful pilgrimage churches great and small (the most notable are St-Sernin in Toulouse and St-Bertrand-de-Comminges).

The Mediterranean Pyrenees, Spanish and French, are also an exceptional hunting ground for the admirer of Romanesque churches. Even without pilgrims Romanesque art would have flourished in the area, for in the 11th and 12th centuries Toulouse was the capital of a civilisation of great refinement and cultural brilliance, where influences from east and south mingled to fascinating and fruitful effect in poetry and sculpture. Under the influence of the Arabs there was none of the passionate bigotry common in medieval Europe – women had rights of property, the feudal hierarchy was very loose, and many towns governed themselves. The Count of Toulouse welcomed Jews and Arabs and, to their ruin, those Christians whose beliefs deviated from Roman orthodoxy but who were well suited to the social fabric and temperament of the south-west. The beliefs of these Cathars, or Albigensians as they came to be called, implied such fundamental criticism of the church establishment and gained such widespread acceptance in all layers of the Languedoc society (as they did not in other areas of France) that Rome had to launch a crusade to crush the heretics and bring south-western France into the doubly fortified fold of Roman church and French monarchy. Facing the organised might and greed of feudal France, the pacific sophisticates of Toulouse could not defend themselves; the Cathars retreated to remote rocky strongholds, which today stand ruined and impressive, many of them not easily conquered by the tourist even without defenders. They are evocative tributes to no less than three-quarters of a million inhabitants of south-western France massacred indiscriminately by their compatriots in the name of God. The crusade eventually crushed the heretics and, thanks to the opportunity it provided, the French monarchy took control of most of south-western France as early as the 13th century.

The Pays Basque and Lower Béarn

The Basque country is one of the most colourful, attractive and fascinating of all France's fringe areas. It is an intimate small-scale landscape, characterised by low-rise Pyrenees which near the coast are hardly more than grassy hills, very green and well watered by the winds that blow in from the Atlantic. The countryside is enhanced by the sparkling whitewash and the rust-red painted timbers and shutters of the solid squat Basque houses, which give the countryside a neatness more characteristic of Switzerland than France or Spain. Like the Pyrenees, most of the Basque country is in Spain. The French part consists of three of the seven provinces: the Labourd, prettiest and most typically Basque; the Basse Navarre; and the Soule. The Basque mountains in the Basse Navarre and the Soule are densely forested and relatively deserted. The coastal area is full of small farms and villages, but unlike the Spanish Basque country neither industrialised nor an active political volcano.

Compared with some half-million Spanish Bascophones, there are only about 50,000 in France who speak one of the least comprehensible and least understood languages in the world, one full of recurring combinations of unlikely consonants and of which, it is said, the Devil only mastered three words after seven years' study.

Like so many other proud fringe ethnic groups the Basques are fiercely religious, family orientated and traditionalist, and their ritual of local folklore, arts and crafts is carefully maintained. They have a particular cult of the dead, whom they commemorate with curious little round gravestones, carved with a Basque cross thought to be a Hindu motif. They have their own dances, masquerades, left-over medieval mystery plays or *pastorales*, their own musical instruments (a three-hole flute and a little drum called a *ttun-ttun*), their own costume – the Basque beret and the *espadrille* have spread far beyond the confines of the Basque country in popularity – and their own sport. The famous pelota is not one game, but many different varieties based on the old *jeu de paume*, sometimes played against the characteristic round-topped *fronton* wall which stands next to the church at the heart of so many Basque villages. When played at high standard, it is a marvellous game to watch, even if the subtleties of the rules escape you.

The Béarn isn't such a conspicuously individual area nowadays, but was an important political unit in the Middle Ages, maintaining its independence of the French and Spanish crowns until Henri, king of Navarre and lord of Béarn, became king of France in 1589. He brought as he said France to Béarn, rather than Béarn to France, a distinction which was maintained in law until 1620. Henri turned out to be a far-sighted statesman, and the most beloved of all French kings. On religious

Pelota, played against a *fronton*

issues which had torn the country apart for decades, he was an example of good sense and compromise when all around was intransigence. His Edict of Nantes confirmed the right of the Protestants to freedom of religious practice but could not itself solve the question of religious conflict. In a Paris street in May 1610, Henri IV was stabbed to death by a fanatic. Paris was grief-stricken.

The best place to start a visit to the Basque's south-western corner of France is **Bayonne**, a large town at the meeting of the rivers Nive and Adour. In the Middle Ages it was a port much used by the British for the export of wine, and is still very active – especially at carnival time (first week of August) when there are bull-fights, dancing and displays. The quais and bridges across the Nive are attractive, and so is the animated and arcaded shopping street, the Rue du Pont Neuf, which leads up from the river towards the cathedral.

Sights in Bayonne

• **Cathedral** A handsome building of the 14th and 15th centuries with twin spires added in the 19th. The arms of England are on some of the keys of the vault, and there are some fine Renaissance stained-glass windows. There's an attractive 13th-century cloister, and behind the cathedral some of Vauban's ramparts survive among gardens and trees.

• **Musée Basque** One of the most fascinating and best-presented regional museums in France, a reason by itself for coming to Bayonne. Varied collections illustrating Basque styles of furniture and interior decoration; local crafts, history and witch-hunts; and a section on pelota with many beautiful old *chisteras* (basketwork rackets).

• **Musée Bonnat** Like Granet in Aix-en-Provence, Bonnat was an unexceptional artist, but an exceptional collector who left his extremely high-quality collections of paintings, and especially drawings, to his home town. Drawings by Dürer, Raphael, and Leonardo, paintings by Botticelli, Rubens, El Greco, Rembrandt and Goya. Also some of Bonnat's own works – and those of his more distinguished contemporaries, including Géricault and Delacroix.

The main attraction of the interior of the Labourd is the green and peaceful countryside, and the pretty little typical Basque villages. None is prettier, more typical, nor more pleasant a place to stay than **Sare**, which has a 17th-century arcaded *mairie*, a *fronton*, and, in the church, wooden galleries for men (a typical Basque feature). Other places with a variety of accommodation are **Aïnhoa**, **Espelette** and **Ascain**. Between Ascain and Sare there is a rack railway up to the top of the main peak of this bumpy landscape, the 900-metre **Rhune**. **Cambo-les-Bains** is an attractive, very flowery spa resort.

East of Cambo you can visit the caves of **Oxocelhaya** and **Isturits**, interesting by the standards of the Pyrenees, if not those of the Dordogne and the Grand Causses. The upper cave (Isturits) consists of excavations and evidence of the presence of early man, the lower cave is full of concretions and becomes very crowded with visitors.

St-Jean-Pied-de-Port was one of the important through-towns of medieval Europe, the place where several different pilgrimage routes to Santiago de Compostela converged on their way through the narrow low pass to Roncevaux and Spain. The road which goes through now is not the one which Roland and the rear-guard used to go across to Spain, and through which Roland never returned – this was the Ports de Cize route, now open only to walkers. Churches of the area around St-Jean still show the characteristic shell motif which was the emblem of the Compostela pilgrimage (and which gave its name to *coquilles St-Jacques*). St-Jean is an attractive little town beside the Nive, with a citadel and some 15th-century ramparts. It is a busy base for travellers and an attractive place to stay, though many of the hotels line the busy main road. To the south-east is the dense **Iraty Forest** which has some of the finest beeches in the country, but no longer eagles and bears.

St-Etienne-de-Baïgorry is a village of pinkish-stone houses, several with inscribed door lintels. **Sauveterre-de-Béarn** is more substantial and beautifully set high above the right bank of the Gave d'Oloron. There is a ruined castle, and a 12th- and 14th-century church with a Roman-esque door and carved tympanum. Below the village there are remains of a fortified bridge. The nearby spa of **Salies-de-Béarn** is famous for the salt content of its waters, nearly ten times greater than the sea.

Orthez, the capital of Béarn up to the 15th century, is a town of grey houses and brown-tiled roofs. It too has an old fortified bridge with four Gothic arches and a single defence tower. In the busy through-town of **Oloron-Ste-Marie** are two churches of distinction: Ste-Marie has a marvellous Romanesque doorway within the porch, and a marble carving of the Descent from the Cross surrounded by delightful scenes from everyday life; St-Croix has a fortified tower, and a dome over the crossing which is supported by Compostela shell forms.

To the south and south-west of Oloron, the mountainous **Haute Soule** (also accessible from St-Jean-Pied-de-Port and the Vallée d'Aspe) offers attractive excursions. Much of the area is densely forested. The small village of **Gotein** has a charming church typical of the region with its three-pronged belfry. Up the Saison valley, the great curiosity is the **Kakouetta Gorges**, a narrow ravine overhung with mosses and lichens. Floods washed away paths and parts of the road here in 1992 and the gorge was still officially closed as we went to press (to check whether it is open again phone 59 28 60 83).

The **Vallée d'Aspe** is long and narrow, wooded and green, and unfrequented despite the old pilgrimage route through to Spain over the Somport pass. A few kilometres off the road, the dead-end village of **Lescun** is an attractively rough high village in a beautiful setting of jagged mountains above the pastures. There is some simple accommodation and it is a good base for walks; there are guides for the more severe climbs, and a refuge near the village accessible by car. Those not on foot can go over the **Col du Somport** down into Spain and round back over the **Col du Portalet** into the Vallée d'Ossau – a splendid round trip.

Standing high above the *gave* (the Pyrenean for river) that bears its name, **Pau**, historical capital of Béarn, is a large and handsome town whose charms and those of its surrounding region seduced many of the returning campaigners from the Spanish wars of the early 19th century, who never made it back to England. Pau became a very popular British resort from the 1820s onwards, had the first golf course on the Continent (1856) and lots of other British horsey events and sports – there is still a fox hunt.

Winter is the best time to go to Pau to see its famous view of the Pyrenees, whose snowy peaks are strung out in a chain like a theatrical backdrop, some 48km due south of the Place Royale – such a privileged viewpoint that Dornford Yates, the popular novelist of the '20s and '30s who loved the area, termed it the Royal Box of the Pyrenees. The old part of Pau is dominated by its château, partly built in the 14th century, added to and redecorated in the 16th, and restored with rather too much imagination in the 19th. There is a guided tour round the interior, which reveals many splendid 17th- and 18th-century tapestries, and a lot of documentary and anecdotal information about Henri IV. Also in the château (a separate visit) is the local Béarn museum.

To the west of Pau, the suburb of **Lescar** also has splendid views of the Pyrenees from beside its old Romanesque cathedral, which has 12th-century mosaics in the chancel and beautifully carved Renaissance stalls.

The High Pyrenees

The most mountainous part of the Béarn and the Bigorre is the highest and most impressive part of the French Pyrenees. In the Alps the main massifs rise up in blocks; here there is a wall of almost unbroken altitude running along the Franco–Spanish border, with a few passes or *ports*, formerly important trading communications but none now crossed by roads. Most of the highest peaks of the Pyrenees are behind this wall of frontier mountains on the Spanish side and can only be seen by climbers and walkers. This is the area for spectacular rocky amphitheatres – of which Gavarnie is the most celebrated.

The **Pyrenean National Park**, a strip of land along nearly 100km of national border between the Vallée d'Aspe and the Vallée d'Aure, is an area of supreme natural beauty, with hundreds of small high mountain lakes reflecting the granite peaks and the few small glaciers clinging to their sides. There are four main gateways with information centres, guides and walking trails; the most important is at Cauterets. The others are in the Vallée d'Aspe, the Vallée d'Ossau (Gabas), and the Vallée d'Aure (St-Lary). Within the park there are a number of mountain refuges, some easily accessible, others more remote and mainly used by climbers. One of the obvious attractions of the park is the very special wildlife – animals, birds and flowers. You will almost certainly see the izard, and marmots, which have been reintroduced and flourish. Other interesting species survive in the Pyrenees not because this is their ideal terrain, but because they are simply in retreat; you are most unlikely to see a bear, civet, or lynx, but you may catch a glimpse of one of the few dozen eagles which nest in the Atlantic Pyrenees.

The Béarn's most spectacular valley, the **Vallée d'Ossau**, plunges due south from Pau into the heart of the mountains, where the Pic du Midi d'Ossau rears twin peaks like a mitre to a height of 2,885 metres – one of the most splendid components of the view from Pau. At the head of the valley, the **Col du Pourtalet** leads over into Spain, making it possible to do a magnificent round drive down to Jaca and back up into the Vallée d'Aspe via the **Col du Somport**. The Vallée d'Ossau doesn't start to climb or narrow until after **Laruns**, a busy market village, from which roads branch left over the **Col d'Aubisque** into the Bigorre.

There are good walking excursions in the wooded hills around, and simple accommodation in the small spas and villages, but the tourist should press on up the valley to **Gabas**, a simple base for excursions on foot into the National Park where the narrow valley opens out into green pastures around the *gave*. At the foot of the great granite colossus of the Pic du Midi there is a reservoir and a number of natural lakes, a mountain refuge and a campsite. From the skiing station of **Artouste** you can take a small cable-car excursion to the **Pic de la Sagette**, and from there a train ride to the **Lac d'Artouste**. From here, an hour's walk through wild and grandiose scenery takes you to a mountain refuge; sensibly equipped, you can continue for another hour or two and gain the highest Pyrenean ridge accessible to walkers.

The **Col du Pourtalet** itself crosses the border and the mountain range at 1,792 metres and descends to Jaca via Biescas, which gives access to the magnificent **Ordesa National Park**, whose red marble canyon of Arrazas forms the back of the Cirque de Gavarnie. Unusually for the Pyrenees, a road joins the Vallée d'Assau to the Bigorre.

The **Route du Col d'Aubisque**, up past the ski resort of Gourette, which has some summer activity, is a fine one. The Col – high by French Pyrenean standards (1,710 metres) – is impressively engineered to the east; the Tour de France passes here, and even when it doesn't the road is always full of toiling cyclists pushing themselves through

the pain barrier. The road descends to the active valley, resort and spa of **Argelès-Gazoste**, which has a lot of accommodation. Just south of Argelès, **St-Savin** has an interesting fortified early Romanesque church. Beyond lie the high mountains of the seven valleys of the **Lavedan**.

To the north lies **Lourdes**, for many centuries a strategic stronghold on the Gave de Pau, with one of the most powerful fortresses in the Pyrenees, which still stands, restored and impressive and housing an interesting regional Pyrenean museum. But there aren't many other old buildings, for Lourdes' fame dates only from the 19th century. Now five million pilgrims and tourists come to Lourdes every year. There are hundreds of hotels and dozens of campsites. Its underground basilica is capable of holding over 20,000 people, the whole permanent population of Lourdes. These facts alone, plus the crass commercialism, will suffice to put most non-pilgrims off a casual visit. But whatever one may feel about shops full of plastic Virgins, miraculous water sold by the fluid ounce, and lines of people in wheelchairs waiting by the spring, there is no denying that Lourdes is a remarkable phenomenon.

The healing powers of the waters of Lourdes had such a profound impact on the humanity of France that it inspired the great observer and analyst of human behaviour Emile Zola to go there in 1892 to investigate the phenomenon for himself for a novel called *Lourdes*. He found hard facts about miracles difficult to come by, but he acknowledged that it would be a crime of *lèse-humanité* not to recognise the ray of hope that Lourdes gives to so many unfortunates: 'I do not believe in miracles, but I believe in their necessity for mankind'. Then as now Lourdes was a great commercial phenomenon; today it is no longer so conspicuously one enormous hospital ward, but an animated resort.

The nearby **Grottes de Bétharram** are extremely busy; chambers with concretions are visited by train and boat.

Long before Lourdes became popular, the Bigorre had been attracting visitors to the spas at the foot of the highest peaks of the Pyrenees; like Aix-les-Bains in the Alps they rose to fame and high fashion in the early 19th century, when curative travel became chic. **Cauterets**, whose popularity dates back to the 16th century, is the biggest and busiest of the centres. It doesn't seem to have much that is very old now, not even the average age of the visitors, for it is a lively and growing resort on the edge of the National Park, within striking range of the very high peaks and beautiful mountain lakes. In winter it is a busy ski resort.

Beside the road leading south from Cauterets, there are a number of waterfalls, particularly splendid at **Pont d'Espagne**. From here there's a choice of walks and climbs, notably up to the superb Lac de Gaube, beneath the towering Vignemale (3,298 metres) with its glaciers. You can take the puff out of the walk by going up on a chairlift most of the way to the lake. Another route takes you up the charming **Vallée du Marcadau** to a refuge, and to the lakes above. You can continue beyond the Lac de Gaube on the GR 10, which leads to more refuges, mountain lakes and eventually, via a tough mountain route, to Gavarnie.

Luz-St-Sauveur is a combined spa resort and old village. It is smaller than Cauterets and altogether more attractive in atmosphere and setting. It stands in a beautiful isolated high mountain valley, which was for centuries a self-administering republic of communes with its own representative government and its own diplomatic relations with the high mountain valleys of Spain. The old village of Luz is animated without being hectic or spoilt, and well-kept, with whitewashed houses with slate roofs and wrought-iron balconies and a number of spruce little hotels. There is a curious 13th-century church, founded by the Knights Hospitaller, with a crenellated curtain wall, and a fine carved doorway.

South of Luz, the **Vallée de Gavarnie** ascends through a famous wilderness of chaotic boulders, described by George Sand as hell. Beyond the chaos is the most celebrated and most visited beauty spot in the Pyrenees, the enormous **Cirque de Gavarnie**, a deep majestic amphitheatre of mountain wall, towering above the valley floor. Waterfalls crash down from the north-facing snows in greater or lesser abundance depending on the season (spring is the most impressive). The five-kilometre donkey ride along the pebble track from the village of Gavarnie up into the pit of the amphitheatre is one of the classic

Pyrenean excursions; thanks to the coachloads from Lourdes, the strings of animal transport do very good business. At the end of the track it is well worth walking up to the base of the great waterfall, which at peak periods drops over 420 metres without touching rock, and often brings ice and snow down with it. The cirque faces north and is best admired in the light of the end of the day. If the crowds along the track have put you off, you can return from the cirque by the stunning – but easy – high-level track which starts just behind the hotel. You can also get a marvellous view of the top of the cirque by driving up from Gavarnie towards the Port de Gavarnie – formerly a pilgrimage crossing over into Spain, but now the end of the road – and scrambling up the grassy but steep Pic de Tantes.

The **Cirque de Troumouse** is a more spacious amphitheatre than Gavarnie, and if somewhat less grandiose, it has the attraction of being much less frequented and accessible by car (toll road). From the end of the road there are walks and climbs for all categories of explorer.

East of Luz the **Route du Tourmalet** – one of the most famous sections of the Tour de France – passes through the steeply enclosed old spa and new ski resort of **Barèges**, whose waters are said to be particularly beneficial for bone problems. There are several long and relatively easy walks, including the Montagne Fleurie, which as the name implies is good for botanists.

The **Col du Tourmalet** at 2,114 metres is very high by French Pyrenean standards, and is empty and bare. From it there are hikes south to the Col d'Aubert and the Massif de Néouvielle (the GR 10 again, which goes on through the lakes down to St-Lary-Soulan) and to the north a rough toll road which leads most of the way up the superb **Pic du Midi de Bigorre**. The panorama from the top (2,865 metres) is magnificent: they say you can see one per cent of the circumference of the earth (400 kilometres).

Beyond the Tourmalet the greener but still wide open and treeless landscape is marred by the ugly modern resort of **La Mongie**, at 1,800 metres the highest of the Pyrenean ski resorts. Things improve below La Mongie, though: the **Vallée de Campan** is wide and lush and full of farmhouses attractively roofed with thatch and stepped stones.

Turning north to Bagnères-de-Bigorre and Lourdes has nothing outstanding to commend it, except the **Grotte de Médous** (exceptional concretions and a boat trip on an underground section of the Adour, within the park of the Château de Médous) near the large old spa and industrial townlet of **Bagnères-de-Bigorre**. **Tarbes** is larger still, and similarly avoidable for tourist purposes.

In contrast with the Tourmalet, the **Route du Col d'Aspin** is pretty and gentle, running between wooded hills, with magnificent views of the higher peaks behind. The **Vallée d'Aure** is rural and productive with substantial farms, fruit and maize. The villages are handsome, old and prosperous too, especially Arreau. **St-Lary-Soulan** (*soulan* means a slope exposed to the sun) is the main resort whose recent skiing development hasn't really spoilt the attractive old part and has added much activity, winter and summer. Roads continue past the resort to some magnificent walking territory at the end of the **Vallée du Riou-majou**, and especially up in the Massif de Néouvielle, where a series of 3,000-metre peaks are clustered more like an Alpine massif than the customary Pyrenean wall along the border. The road goes up to a splendid reservoir (**Cap-de-Long**) beneath the Pic de Néouvielle. There are lots of other natural lakes, but fishing is not allowed. Beyond **Fabian** a road tunnel has been cut through the mountains to Bielsa and Spain which gives access to the superb Cirque de Barosa, which forms the back of the Cirque de Troumouse. On the GR 10, there are interesting churches at Vieil Aure, and at Bourispe.

From Arreau a pleasant though unspectacular road leads over the **Col de Peyresourde**, past some attractive 11th- and 12th-century churches at St-Pé, Cazeaux and St-Aventin. The last is particularly beautiful, with twin towers, a carved marble doorway and 12th-century ironwork choir screen.

Luchon is the most lively and fashionable of Pyrenean spas, much the most attractive as a base for excursions and well situated exactly halfway across the range. It is set in a wide flat bowl, surrounded by mountains. Its waters, the most radioactive in France, were well known to the Romans, who considered Ilixo, as it was, second in curative quality to Naples. Luchon was never forgotten, but it was not really launched as a fashionable spa until the early 19th century. When Arthur Young went in 1787 he wrote: 'the present baths are horrible holes, the patients lie up to their chin in hot sulphurous water which with the beastly dens they are placed in one would think sufficient to cause as many distempers as they cure. They are resorted to for cutaneous eruptions'.

Nowadays Luchon is a spacious and almost stylish resort, with lively cafés, elegant shops and hotels leading up to the thermal establishment and gardens.

Excursions from Luchon

● **Superbagnères** A ski resort on a high grassy plateau. Superbagnères is hardly more than one huge Edwardian hotel, but commands magnificent views over to the highest Pyrenean peaks on the Spanish side of the border, and is very popular for hang-gliding. Well worth visiting just for the drive, a steep and beautiful climb.

● **Vallée du Lys** Beautiful mountain views from a flat and pretty valley. From the end, long walks up to wooded cirques with waterfalls. Worth the drive even if you don't walk.

● **Hospice de France** The classic Luchon excursion, an old pilgrimage route up to an old hostelry among pastures, woods and waterfalls, whence a long walk up a mule track past mountain lakes takes you to the frontier **Port de Vénasque** (at 2,448 metres the lowest point of the frontier around here). From the Port, there are sublime views of the Spanish Pyrenees. The road up to the Hospice de France is not open all the way and only worth covering if you are going on a long walk.

• **Lacs d'Oô and d'Espingo** Walk up with many other tourists to the splendid mountain lake of Oô (about $1\frac{1}{2}$ hours from the car park); to escape the crowds continue for another $1\frac{1}{2}$ hours up to the refuge near the Lac d'Espingo, whence paths go on round to Superbagnères. Not an excursion for the car-bound.

The Comminges, the Couserans and the Pays de Foix

North of Luchon the Pique runs into the Garonne, the great river of south-west France, whose upper valley is the centre of the region of **Comminges**. Its most important settlement in the Roman era and in the Middle Ages was the isolated hill dominating the wide green valley where the Romans built a city called Lugdunum Convenarum, and where a 12th-century bishop of Comminges, soon to be St-Bertrand, built a magnificent cathedral which became a port-of-call for pilgrims on their way to Spain. Much of the church of **St-Bertrand-de-Comminges** was rebuilt in the late 13th and early 14th century. Of the Romanesque cathedral, the westernmost part (belfry and carved west doorway) survives, as well as three sides of the cloister, full of relief sculptures and carved capitals of exceptional beauty, and with its south gallery open to the wooded hillsides. The rest of the church (guided tour – well worthwhile) is Gothic and later, and contains a wealth of beautiful works of art: Renaissance stained glass, 16th-century wooden choir stalls whose carving is full of life and fun, and an organ which sounds as good as it looks (there is an organ festival every July).

The *cité* is picturesquely huddled within old walls around the feet of the great church which dominates miles of the surrounding landscape. At the foot of the hill, the archaeological site of the Roman city has been excavated; beyond it, the Romanesque church of **Valcabrère**, with its golden stone and red-tiled roofs, its square belfry standing above the cypress trees, in a landscape of almost Umbrian tranquillity, forms a delightful contrast to the majestic pilgrimage church on the hill.

To the east of the Comminges, the 18 valleys of the **Couserans** seem relatively gentle, wooded, unfrequented and pretty. Until quite recently, the different valleys were all very isolated and maintained

Valcabrère

their local traditions, dialects and costumes (including clogs). The most attractive villages are south of Castillon-en-Couserans, in the **Vallée de Biros** and the **Vallée de Bethmale. St-Girons** is the main market town of the Couserans, and nearby run-down **St-Lizier** its traditional religious centre, with a 12th-century former cathedral in the shadow of an ugly and dominant bishop's palace. The church has an octagonal belfry in the style of Toulouse, frescoes and two-storey cloisters of simple beauty.

The most attractive route eastward, unless you are in a hurry, is the Massat road to Biert, then the D18 over the **Col de la Crouzette** and the **Col de Péguère**. From here a short walk takes you to the **Sommet de Portel**, which despite its modest altitude gives marvellous views of the mountains to the south and the seemingly infinite plains extending northwards.

The limestone hills of the Ariège, as the old **Pays de Foix** is now called, are rich in caves and in minerals. The Vicdessos valley was a centre of iron production and because of the industry lost most of its forests for burning. The area has a harsh history – its rocky spurs still bear the ruins of fortresses – like broken crowns – that were the last refuges of the Cathar heretics in the 13th century. **Foix** is the main town, overlooked by the three towers of its castle standing on a rock above the town (to be admired rather than visited). Foix is not an especially attractive place, busy with traffic on the way south to Andorra; but to its south and east lie some of the area's finest caves and Cathar fortresses.

Excursions from Foix

• **Grottes de Niaux** (near Tarascon-sur-Ariège) One of the three great painted caves in Europe (the others are Lascaux in the Dordogne and Altamira in Spain). Unlike Lascaux, Niaux is open to visitors, but numbers are strictly limited and you may have to reserve a place several days in advance (for information and booking phone 61 05 88 37). You scramble along nearly a kilometre of galleries to the huge *salon noir*, a sanctuary whose rounded apse is decorated with a marvellous array of beasts – bison (one known as the Mona Lisa, because his eye follows you everywhere), deer, ibex, horses. Mostly drawn in dark outline with occasional ochre-red highlights, they are not as brilliantly colourful as Lascaux, but viewed by the single light held by the guide, the magical beauty and above all the vitality of the paintings (about 15,000 years old) is irresistible.

• **Lombrives** (Tarascon-sur-Ariège) Grottoes connecting with Niaux, but accessible from the spa of Ussat, where information about visiting should be sought. A train takes you through long and often treacherously slippery galleries and chambers, with concretions, including one astonishing mammoth-like mass of stalactites and a chamber called the cathedral, covered in graffiti.

• **Underground river of Labouiche** (north-west of Foix) A magnificent underground boat trip (over an hour) past splendid well-lit concretions.

• **Mas d'Azil** Speleology for the motorist. The Arize has carved an enormous tunnel through it, and the N119 (from St-Girons to Pamiers) follows the river. You can get out of the car to visit an audio-guided maze of galleries and chambers in which man sought refuge from pre-Magdalenian times to the religious wars. The wall paintings are not on display, but many of the finds from the galleries are, including 21 bear skulls.

South of **Vicdessos**, there are a few narrow roads, and climbs south into a very mild and unfrequented mountain area, the desolate valley of Montcalm.

After Foix, the main staging post on the road south to Andorra is **Ax-les-Thermes**, a spa known to the Romans (Ax like Aix being a corruption of Aquae) and also a modest ski resort.

The small feudal relic of **Andorra** is historically interesting as a phenomenon, and its landscape has a severe beauty, away from the main road – the average height of Andorra is over 1,800 metres and

Cathar fortresses

The Albigensian crusade, when northern French Christians slaughtered southern French Christians, is one of the more bloody and dramatic episodes of medieval history. The Cathars (the word, like catharsis, comes from the Greek for pure), or Albigensians as they came to be called, held Christian beliefs irreconcilable with Roman orthodoxy. They rejected the value of the sacraments of baptism and marriage, and did not believe in the concept of grace being dispensed or sold by a chosen priesthood but rather in salvation being earned through a series of reincarnations. The Cathar *parfaits* – priest or 'perfect man' as the minority of mystical and ascetic initiates were known – set a shining example of goodness without making excessive demands on the mass of simple believers. By emphasising that life on earth was life in the kingdom of the Devil – in fact, Hell – they removed the fear of punishment in an unknown afterlife.

Cathars were hardworking and did not forbid the lending of money for interest, so the beliefs were well received among the merchant classes. They were also welcomed by the nobility of the traditionally tolerant south-western France, where people of all creeds and nationalities, including Jews and Arabs, lived harmoniously together, and where women enjoyed a remarkable degree of emancipation by comparison with France of later centuries. There were *parfaites*, many of them noblewomen. By the end of the 12th century there were four Cathar bishops, at Albi, Toulouse, Agen and Carcassonne.

The beliefs of the Cathars implied such fundamental criticism of the church establishment (effectively denying it any role in human salvation) that Rome decided on a crusade to crush the heretics. The crusade became an excuse for the King of France and the nobility of northern France to go land-grabbing in the south. In exchange for 40 days' service, the crusaders were promised the cancellation of all their debts, and the remission of all their sins past and future. On 22 July 1209 they descended on Béziers to make an example of the city, and when someone asked the abbot of Cîteaux whom to kill, he replied in a celebrated formula, 'kill them all, God will know His own'. The indiscriminate massacre of Béziers persuaded most of the nobility of Languedoc not to resist. The formidable fortress of Carcassonne barely lasted a month of siege, affected by a lack of water and by disease. When the 40 days were up many of the crusaders went home; but the job was not done, for the hard-core Cathars refused to abjure their faith.

Pope Innocent III gave Béziers, Carcassonne and charge of the crusade to Simon de Montfort, father of the early British parliamentarian. In one place Simon de Montfort rounded up a hundred inhabitants, cut off their noses and upper lips, and marched them around as propaganda. At Minerve, 140 Cathars walked into the flames rather than recant. At Lavaur, 80 knights were slaughtered, the lady of the place was thrown down a well and buried under stones, and 400 people were burnt. All in all, it is estimated that as many as 400 villages were wiped off the map. In the face of blatant territorial acquisitiveness, the Count of Toulouse could not but make some resistance: together with the King of Aragon, he mustered an impressive force, but they couldn't agree on tactics and were slaughtered by de Montfort at the battle of Muret in 1213. Resistance continued though, and Simon de Montfort was eventually killed outside Toulouse. In 1224 there was peace, then a second crusade in 1226, and in 1229 the King of France got what he wanted – recognition of his overlordship in Languedoc. In 1233 the Inquisition was sent in for more bonfires. Over the whole period of the first half of the 13th century only one *parfait* is recorded as having abjured his faith. Then in 1242 came an episode of murdered inquisitors, and a nine-month siege of the Cathar capital of Montségur, which ended with 200 burnt martyrs. In 1271 Toulouse and Languedoc came under direct royal control in the absence of a male heir, and one of the most brilliant and refined civilisations that Europe had seen was extinguished.

East of Foix, you are in the heart of Cathar country. Because of the nature of the crusades, few of the Cathar castles remain intact for the curious student of military architecture, but they are evocative ruins usually in impressively inaccessible situations. At **Montségur**, more than anywhere else, the steep and apparently impregnable rocky hill hardly needed fortifications, and all that was built was a single keep and a walled triangular courtyard, which it is hard to imagine as having been the main centre for Cathars from the late 1230s. Even on its easiest side it's a steep half-hour climb to the citadel. There are other beautifully situated fragmentary fortresses at **Roquefixade** and **Usson** (reputed destination of the lost Cathar treasure) and more substantial remains at the former troubadour court of **Puivert**, in a wild romantic landscape.

Montségur

there are few trees. But it is no longer a remote place since the road was built over the mountains from France in 1931, and more than anything else Andorra is a duty-free-for-all, its capital lined with modern super-markets. The road up from France is a four-lane highway, flanked with pylons and busy with tankers and lorries taking petrol and drink to Andorra, and cars going to bring it back. The French make regular journeys from as far as Toulouse to stock up and risk the spot-checks on the N20. In 1278 the Spanish bishop of Urgel and the French count of Foix came to a sharing or *pariage* agreement to share the overlord-ship of these remote mountain valleys, and to respect their local laws and customs. Every alternate year Andorra pays a tribute of 1,920 francs to France and 450 pesetas to Spain, in addition to 12 cheeses, 12 capons, 12 partridges and 6 hams. Andorra has laws based on no written code (capital punishment consisted of being pushed off a cliff on the Spanish side).

If you do choose to spend any time in Andorra, there are hikes up into the bare mountains, and some rough and charming Romanesque churches. In winter, it is a popular ski area for the budget-conscious and thirsty.

The Cerdagne and the Roussillon

French Catalonia is a transitional land, neither French nor Spanish, neither wholly Mediterranean nor wholly Pyrenean. It is in the mixture of influences that the charm of the region lies. The Canigou towers white-headed above the Roussillon, long into the heat of the early summer, in this the driest and sunniest part of France, where cherries ripen before the end of April. The very numerous and very beautiful Romanesque churches reveal all sorts of fascinating influences from Moslem south and Lombard east (the Catalans were great sailors).

The Cathar castle of **Usson** stands high above the river Aude, which runs down from the high plateau of the Cerdagne to water the vine-yards and fertile plains of the Languedoc. Before dropping down through forests and gorges the Aude crosses two high plateaux: the **Capcir**, sparsely populated and often bleak on the north side of the mountains, and the **Cerdagne**, a great suntrap on the south face or *soulan*. The Cerdagne is artificially (and not at all neatly) split by the national frontier which was established by the Pyrenean Treaty of 1659. The 33 villages of the Cerdagne were ceded to France but the largest, Llivia, considered itself more than a village and remains a little Spanish enclave a few miles north of the border.

The Cerdagne has become a popular summer and winter sports area thanks to the creation of the modern resort of **Font-Romeu** on the site of an old pilgrimage sanctuary. Around pilgrimage times the statue of the Black Virgin is housed in a beautiful chapel in the hermitage. The rest of Font-Romeu is new and less than beautiful, but lively and by Pyrenean standards very well provided with sports facilities. It was selected as the place for acclimatisation training before the Mexico Olympics, thanks to its altitude and climate – 3,000 hours of sun a year. Near Odeillo, a hillside covered with gleaming rotatable mirrors could be mistaken as the set for a Bond movie but is in fact part of an alternative energy research project. There is an exhibition deciphering the scientists' high-temperature, solar-powered fan.

There are plenty of good walking areas surrounding the plateau – around the **Lac des Bouillouses** and south of the attractive old village of **Llo**; and from the international railway terminus of **Latour-de-Carol** you can catch the narrow-gauge *Petit Train Jaune* which runs through the Cerdagne and steeply down to Vernet-les-Bains in the Conflent.

There is no more striking way of appreciating the height of the Cerdagne than to drive down from **Mont-Louis** to **Villefranche-de-Conflent**, a serpentine descent which demands concentration and patience. Villefranche is the key to the Têt valley, a strategic stronghold since the early Middle Ages. It has kept the walls that the great 17th-century fortifier Vauban gave it, and the towers, barbicans and fortress on a rock some 150 metres above the town, reached from it by an underground staircase of 750 steps. Nearby **Corneilla-de-Conflent** has a Romanesque church with a curved white marble façade, and crenellations between a fortress-like belfry. Inside there are several Romanesque wooden Virgins.

Vernet-les-Bains is a characterless spa with a little old quarter which became very popular with the British in the late 19th century. Its main attraction is as a base for visits to the magnificently situated **Abbaye de St-Martin-du-Canigou**, whose typically Catalan square and decorated crenellated belfry so impressively crowns a rocky spur that later Cathar fortress builders must have been jealous. The abbey was founded in the 10th century and after many centuries of dilapidation functions once again as a retreat. The abbey church has been restored to its beautiful rough-stone pre-Romanesque simplicity. The cloister too has been substantially and obviously restored and contains many beautiful carvings. To visit St-Martin, you can catch a jeep up the road from Vernet-les-Bains, but for anyone capable of a moderately stiff half-hour climb it is much more satisfying to drive as far as you can (Casteil) and then walk up. A further ten minutes' walk is repaid by a splendid view over the abbey. Going in the morning means fewer crowds at the monastery, and a timely return for lunch in one of the several inviting little cafés in Casteil.

Towering above the rocks and woods of St-Martin is the **Canigou**, eastern bastion of the Pyrenees (2,784 metres) and to many eyes the most majestic peak of the range. Rudyard Kipling thought that the area, with its densely vegetated valleys overlooked by the snowy peak, was like the high valleys of Hindustan. The Canigou is now easily climbed, especially with the help of the Vernet jeeps which take you up along a forest road (suitable for cars in dry weather, but steep, narrow and rutted) to the Chalet Hôtel which is about two hours below the summit. If you sleep there you can see the sun rise from the waters of the Mediterranean.

The Têt valley or Conflent is a particularly rich region for Romanesque churches, thanks in part to Villefranche marble, often veined with pink, but thanks also to the influence of the important **Abbaye de St-Michel-de-Cuxa**, founded in the 9th century, not far from **Prades** (an alternative departure point for the ascent of the Canigou and the site of an annual Pablo Casals festival). The abbey church dates in part from the late 10th century and has many fascinating features: horseshoe arches, a pillar like a palm tree supporting the crypt, a tall and beautiful belfry and attractive roofs with red tiles. If you go in be prepared for a lengthy guided tour around what remains of the cloister (much of it is in a museum in New York), which has columns of pink marble and capitals decorated with fantastic rather than religious subjects – an example of Arabic influence. On the sunny side of the Têt the handsome village of **Eus** basks on the hillside beneath a powerfully imposing church.

To the south of the great monolithic massif, the Tech valley or **Vallespir** runs parallel to the Conflent into the fertile Roussillon vineyards. In the severe scrub-covered hills beneath the two valleys stands the lonely, grey, windowless priory of **Serrabonne** (which means good mountain). The contrast between this forbidding exterior and the richly carved pink marble tribune inside is a wonderful, calculated surprise.

St-Michel-de-Cuxa

The Vallespir is even drier and sunnier than the Cerdagne. It is full of orange groves and torrential gorges, and like the French Riviera it was patronised at the beginning of this century by artists including Picasso and Braque who divided their time for a while between Collioure and Céret. **Céret** is an attractive town with some accommodation, a modern art museum, magnificent plane trees, and all around an abundance of orchards – mainly cherries, the first to ripen in France. On the edge of town, a restored 14th-century bridge soars in a single span high above the Tech.

Until recently, the Vallespir was a relatively quiet dead-end, but a road now gives a passage over the **Col d'Ares** down into Spain, making it possible to do a round trip from Céret or from Argelès-sur-Mer up the Tech into Spain, to see the superb religious monastery of Ripoll – heavily restored like St-Martin-du-Canigou – and back into the Cerdagne and down the Têt. This is one of the most beautiful church crawls imaginable for admirers of the wholly admirable Catalan Romanesque. Apart from the churches already mentioned, the enthusiast should also include **St-Martin-de-Fenollar** in the roar of the Costa's motorway, with brilliant and beautiful frescoes, and **St-Genis-des-Fontaines**, whose decorative, lively and very Arabic carved lintel with Christ and the Apostles, inscriptions and horseshoe arches, is France's earliest dated sculpture (1020). Both lie close to the main Céret/Argelès-sur-Mer road. It is also well worth visiting the abbey church at **Arles-sur-Tech**, which faces west – evidence of great age – and has a 9th-century façade, a charming 13th-century Gothic cloister, and a 4th-century sarcophagus, always inexplicably full of pure water. When the Roussillon became French, the old town of **Prats-de-Mollo** (pronounced Moyo) was fortified by Vauban, and the church, which retains its Romanesque belfry, was rebuilt in a curious semi-fortified Gothic style. For a break from churches, you can go for a walk of an hour or so through the impressively narrow and steep **Gorges de la Fou** near Arles-sur-Tech.

North of the Pyrenees

The slopes of the **Corbières** produce large volumes of wine and continue the chain of hilltop fortresses, which mark the heights like beacons eastwards from Foix to the Mediterranean. **Puilaurens, Peyrepertuse** and **Quéribus** are the most dizzily impressive of these, and like the ones in the Foix are closely associated with Cathar refuge from the 13th-century crusade – Quéribus was the last Cathar stronghold to fall, in 1255. These fortresses were not originally set up on their soaring perches to shelter heretics but as defences along a traditional frontier land.

The key point in the system and the mother of all these fortresses was **Carcassonne**, the biggest fortress in Europe, defending the invasion route to Toulouse from the sea. Carcassonne was surely a fortress for the Romans, and certainly one for the Visigoths, part of whose walls can still be seen. The fortified city put up a poor showing against the Albigensian crusade, lasting only a month. The fortifications of the upper town or *cité* were rebuilt and when the Black Prince came by and sacked the lower town he gave the *cité* a respectfully wide berth. In the wars of religion, too, the *cité* of Carcassonne, unlike the lower town, remained true to France and resisted all Protestant advances.

Like the other fortresses, Carcassonne's strategic role was played out by the 17th century, and it was used as a quarry until Prosper Merimée sounded the antiquarians' alarm in 1835. Some 15 years later, Viollet-le-Duc started rebuilding; the task continued long after his death. The great restorer himself said of Carcassonne: 'I do not know if there exists anywhere in Europe so complete and so formidable a collection of defences from the 5th, 12th and 13th centuries.' Thanks to his efforts, Carcassonne, the fortified acropolis, stands again complete as an unrivalled example of medieval fortifications, pointing its multiple warhead turrets skywards from the crenellations of its double system of walls; standing high above the large modern town it presents a tremendous silhouette from afar. For academic visitors, there is the interest of sorting out the works of different periods and the styles of defence which evolved to respond to different styles of attack. For all, there is the enchantment of wandering down the grassy areas which separate the inner and outer walls and feeling the effect of the time machine. Inside the walls, the old town buzzes with tourist life, with a few attractive leafy squares and restaurants for those who tire of wandering around. The part-Romanesque, part-Gothic former cathedral of St-Nazaire has some marvellous stained glass and statues in the 13th-century choir; in its composite form and general impression the church is comparable with the Merveille of Mont-St-Michel. The guided tour inside the old viscount's castle – the keep of the whole fortress – is of relatively minor interest, but it does get you up on to the walls for splendid views.

The great red-brick city of **Toulouse** stands on a natural crossroads for pilgrims, merchants and waterways half-way between the Mediterranean and the Atlantic. In the early Middle Ages, Toulouse was the brilliant centre of civilisation of scholarship and lyric poetry, which was crushed under the steamroller of the northern French crusaders. Toulouse is still one of France's big cities, at the centre of spacious, fertile and not particularly interesting plains. It is an exhausting place, horrific to drive around or park in, and lacking a particularly picturesque old town centre. But for the admirer of medieval religious art, Toulouse is not to be missed.

Sights in Toulouse

- **St-Sernin** The biggest and most splendid Romanesque church in Christendom and one of its greatest pilgrimage churches, containing relics of over a hundred saints and six apostles. The crossing supports a five-storey octagonal tower, there is a beautiful splay of little round chapels all around the apse and transepts, and marvellous sculpture decorating the doorways on the south side of the church. When Viollet-le-Duc restored St-Sernin, he took down much of the woodwork which framed all the reliquaries in the chapels around the choir and, as was his wont, painted the vaults. The effects of restoration have recently been removed, and the marvellous carved and gilt 17th-century woodwork put back in its place. The church is lit up to magnificent effect at night.
- **Eglise des Jacobins** An unusual Gothic hall church, externally severe, but bright and colourful inside with brick vaults of great complexity, supported by palm-tree pillars; a simple Gothic cloister and octagonal belfry.
- **Musée des Augustins** Superlative collections of medieval sculptures, mostly from Toulouse churches, in the words of the museum's guide: 'witness of a disaster, the fruit of systematic destruction of an inestimable patrimony'. This included St-Sernin, whose cloister was destroyed in the 19th century, and the totally demolished church of La Daurade, the headquarters of the south-western school of Romanesque sculpture. Also very fine collections of Gothic religious sculpture and painting.
- **Musée St-Raymond** Exceptional collection of Roman statues, relief sculptures and mosaics.
- **Post-Renaissance Toulouse** Inheritor of Roman traditions, Toulouse was ruled until the Revolution by elected consuls or *capitouls*. The town hall or Capitol is a grand pink-and-white 18th-century building, looking over the busy central market square. To the south are many splendid *hôtels*: the 16th-century Hôtel d'Assézat on the Rue de Metz is the most palatially impressive.

Like the Quercy, the plains of the **Armagnac** to the west of Toulouse lie on the borders between the medieval lands of the kings of England and the kings of France. These green and fertile but not populous areas are characterised by large numbers of *bastides* or planned medieval villages, built by local churchmen, petty nobles or more important distant overlords to establish power bases and potential fortresses in these disputed and strategic regions. After the Albigensian crusade in the early 13th century the Count of Toulouse built *bastides* all over his not very extensive remaining lands, and later in the century Alphonse of Poitiers started the arms race with the kings of England which built up to the Hundred Years' War. In 1200, Gascony had about 100 fortresses;

by the early 14th century it is thought to have had about 1,000. Of all the *bastides*, one of the most curious and attractive is **Fourcès**, built exceptionally on a circular plan, its low houses with timbers and red-tiled roofs and arcades surrounding a central shady copse. Some of the *bastide* names were merely expressive – Ville Nouvelle or Montréal – others exotically enticing for prospective settlers – Grenade, Valence, Cologne, Plaisance. Many have uncompromisingly fortified churches; there are two fine examples south-east of Auch at **Lombez**, and at **Simorre**, which has stalls and windows in the style, if not the brilliant profusion, of Auch, and owes part of its military appearance to the enthusiasm of Viollet-le-Duc.

Auch is the Gascon capital, standing on a hill beside the river Gers, and is the centre of production of Armagnac, France's oldest eau-de-vie, which became an export business when Americans boycotted Scotch during the War of Independence. A monumental staircase climbs up from the river to the central squares around the large pale yellow cathedral, which was built in the Gothic style from the 15th to the 17th centuries. The choir stalls are a masterpiece of oak carving which took over 50 years to complete; and there is a very fine series of Renaissance windows.

HOTELS

Key: ◆ = 0–250FF, ◆◆ = 251–450FF, ◆◆◆ = over 451FF; prices are per double room without breakfast, which costs around 35–60FF extra. Some hotels may insist on half-board during high season, some hotels or restaurants may close at specific times during the week – it is always worth checking. Most hotels accept the major credit cards; we have indicated where a hotel takes no credit cards.

AINHOA

Ithurria

64250 Pyrénées-Atlantiques
TEL 59 29 92 11; FAX 59 29 81 28

A spruce and typical Basque house – a former pilgrim's halt on the Santiago de Compostela route – Ithurria is set at the edge of a Basque village, all red and green shutters, with a fronton by the church, set in lush, green, well-watered fields and low hills. There's an attractive garden, a few small civilised seating areas, and a large and dignified rustic dining-room. Bedrooms are pretty, reasonably spacious, and also in rustic style – but modern, not ancient. The food is good, with plenty of local dishes, but also many inventive ones.

OPEN End Mar to mid-Nov ROOMS 27 (all with bath or shower) FACILITIES Outdoor pool, sauna

BOURG D'OUEIL

Le Sapin Fleuri

Luchon
31110 Haute-Garonne
TEL 61 79 21 90

The setting – at the head of a valley, and surrounded by wooded mountain-sides – is the main attraction of this hotel. Inside, the rustic dining-room is the best feature, with its huge open fireplace, wood-lined walls and grandfather clock. The bedrooms, named after flowers, are good value, though some are cramped and have rudimentary facilities. The family which runs the hotel is extremely hospitable.

OPEN End Dec to end Sept ROOMS 22 (all with shower) (Credit cards not accepted)

CAMBO-LES-BAINS

Errobia

avenue Champs d'Eclair
64250 Pyrénées-Atlantiques
TEL 59 29 71 26; FAX 59 29 96 36

This traditional Basque house is beautifully set in its own grounds (fine old trees, rhododendrons and a swimming-pool) well away from the town centre. There's no restaurant; breakfast is a pleasure, taken in the garden with its pretty view. The small lounge has a panelled library with armchairs round its marble fireplace; upstairs, the bedrooms are light and peaceful, their elegance rather faded but their old-fashioned style very comfortable. A relaxing place to stay.

OPEN Easter to end Oct ROOMS 14 (most with bath or shower) FACILITIES Outdoor pool

CERET

La Terrasse au Soleil

route de Fontfrède
66400 Pyrénées-Orientales
TEL 68 87 01 94; FAX 68 87 39 24

Set in the wooded Pyrenean foothills a couple of kilometres out of Céret, this heavily restored farmhouse is surrounded by a pleasant garden with a good swimming-pool and has views of the Canigou. The smart, fresh décor shows a Catalan influence with colourful tiled walls. The restaurant, spilling on to a terrace, takes itself seriously, presenting accomplished nouvelle cuisine. Bedrooms are interesting and pleasant without being luxurious; many have a terrace. The overall atmosphere is friendly and relaxed.

OPEN Early Mar to early Jan ROOMS 27 (all with bath or shower) FACILITIES Heated outdoor pool, tennis

GEDRE

A la Brèche de Roland

65120 Hautes-Pyrénées
TEL 62 92 48 54; FAX 62 92 48 05

The location of this hotel is useful for walkers and mere sightseers whose tastes are simple – near, but not in, Gavarnie, and within easy reach of the Cirque de Troumouse. It's in the centre of Gèdre village, set back from the main road, with fine scenery all round. There's a comfortable bar/sitting area and a large dining-room; bedrooms are pleasantly decorated. The *patron* is prepared to organise games in the TV salon in wet weather. The food is simple – a cheap fixed-price menu with little choice.

OPEN End Dec to early Oct ROOMS 28 (all with bath or shower)

LLO

Auberge Atalaya

66800 Pyrénées-Orientales
TEL 68 04 70 04; FAX 68 04 01 29

On the edge of one of the prettiest villages in the area, this is a beautiful, creeper-covered stone auberge converted from an almost derelict mas, decorated with real flair by the engaging owners. The lovely dining-room, with stone walls and beams, is the best of the public rooms, and you can eat on the flowery terrace in summer. The more characterful bedrooms, with floral themes, lie in the main building; those in the new annexe, though equally comfortable, have a more contrived style. All face south over the valley and village.

OPEN End Dec to early Nov ROOMS 13 (all with bath or shower) FACILITIES Outdoor pool

MAULEON-LICHARRE

Hôtel Bidegain

13 rue de la Navarre
64130 Pyrénées-Atlantiques
TEL 59 28 16 05; FAX 59 28 09 96

This old coaching inn, with a cobbled passage leading through to a pretty terrace and garden, has probably not changed in decades. Its old-fashioned charm is particularly appealing in the dining-room, which opens on to the garden; there are cabinets full of bric-a-brac and flowery wallpaper. Bedrooms are spacious and clean, but not very bright. Old-fashioned amenities are fitted into a selection of partitioned cubicles in a way that is adequate if a little quaint, but some rooms have new bathrooms. The cooking is reasonable and the owners friendly.

OPEN All year exc. mid-Dec to mid-Jan ROOMS 30 (20 with bath or shower)

PAU

Hôtel Roncevaux

25 rue Louis Barthou
64000 Pyrénées-Atlantiques
TEL 59 27 08 44; FAX 59 82 92 79

Five minutes' walk from Pau castle, the Roncevaux is a smart hotel right in the centre of town, with modern décor and good facilities. Bedrooms at the front can be noisy due to the main road, while those at the back overlook a small courtyard. All are comfortable and well equipped. Safe parking adds to the hotel's attraction as a stop-over for people touring the area. There is no restaurant.

OPEN All year ROOMS 40 (all with bath or shower)

ST-BERTRAND-DE-COMMINGES

L'Oppidum

rue de la Poste
31510 Haute-Garonne
TEL 61 88 33 50; FAX 61 95 94 04

Right in the old and beautiful hilltop town, this is a modern converted building with a maze of corridors leading to smart bedrooms. Like the bedrooms, the ground-floor tea-rooms are immaculately kept and run by a friendly team which manages to keep the prices low. Excellent value for money.

OPEN End Dec to end Nov ROOMS 15 (all with bath or shower)

ST-ETIENNE-DE-BAIGORRY

Arcé

64430 Pyrénées-Atlantiques
TEL 59 37 40 14; FAX 59 37 40 27

Good value, though not cheap, this hotel is in a picturesque spot right next to the River Nive and backed by hills. Service is attentive and the food good; bedrooms are comfortably old-fashioned, varying from small with a shower to a full suite. In summer the restaurant spills onto a riverside terrace under plane trees.

OPEN Mid-Mar to mid-Nov ROOMS 27 (all with bath or shower) FACILITIES Heated outdoor pool, tennis, billiards

THE PYRENEES

ST-SAVIN

Le Viscos

65400 Hautes-Pyrénées
TEL 62 97 02 28; FAX 62 97 04 95

At the centre of a lovely mountain village in the heart of the Pyrenees, Le Viscos is an informal hotel with very friendly hosts and excellent food, which more than compensate for its dated décor and plain rooms. The smell of fresh coffee, an open fire, and the resident dog make a homely hotel reception, where you're likely to be joined by the locals popping in for a drink and a chat.

OPEN All year exc. 3 weeks Dec ROOMS 16 (all with bath or shower)

SARE

Arraya

place du Fronton
64310 Pyrénées-Atlantiques
TEL 59 54 20 46; FAX 59 54 27 04

This lovely old inn is in a very pretty village, with a covered pavement terrace near the square and its fronton, and a secluded grassy garden at the back. The rooms have dark wooden beams and solid shapely old furniture; everything gleams with polish and care. In the relaxed and rustic dining-room you can order until an agreeably late hour. The cooking is very good: innovative, using local produce, game and wine.

OPEN May to mid-Nov ROOMS 21 (all with bath or shower)

UNAC

L'Oustal

Luzenac
09250 Ariège
TEL 61 64 48 44

There are just six rooms in this ancient auberge at the top of the village with views over wooded hillsides. While the mainstay of the business is the excellent and very popular (though pricey) restaurant, guests staying overnight are by no means neglected. You can expect a good-sized bedroom with cottagey fabrics and luxury bath towels, and a friendly reception from the Descat family.

OPEN All year exc. last 2 weeks Nov ROOMS 6 (all with bath or shower)

Castelnaud

Meadows trim with daisies pied,
Shallow brooks and rivers wide.
Towers and battlements it sees,
Bosom'd high in tufted trees

[Milton]

THE DORDOGNE

Sandwiched between the plains of the Atlantic seaboard and the mountains of the Massif Central, a long slice of territory (the Massif's doorstep) is crossed by dozens of rivers – some large, many small – bearing the waters down from the mountains to the ocean. The only north/south communication which unites the area is the N20 from Orléans to Toulouse, one of France's most notorious trunkroads which winds tortuously through the hills of the Limousin and the Périgord and delays impatient travellers drawn southwards in the magnetic field of the Spanish sun. The greatest and most beautiful of the rivers crossed by the N20 is the Dordogne, which rises at Le Mont-Dore and runs into the Gironde near Bordeaux.

The Dordogne is a name often taken in vain; as well as the name of the river, it is a *département*, and it is the name given by British holidaymakers to a vaguely defined rural area around the river valley. The area covered by this chapter is greater than the term Dordogne should cover and extends from the Périgord to the river Garonne and the town of Albi in the south.

A traveller, however, will be tempted to tarry for the longest while on the banks of the Dordogne itself, to admire the beauty of France's best-loved river; but he or she should not underestimate the dangers of so doing. Sixty years ago a British man of the soil, Philip Oyler, set off southwards from Paris, not knowing exactly where he was going, following the sun. When he came over a hill and looked down over the wide Dordogne valley, suddenly 'the desire to go south, farther south, was no longer there. I have seen the Midi and Mediterranean seaboard – its sunshine and its aridity, its lack of comforting greenery in the summer months – it compared ill with the panorama before me. I felt at peace, more than that, I felt at home. All was bounty and beauty, God-given, and man had not desecrated it. He had substituted his crops and his fruit trees for wild flowers and bushes; he had utilised the river to drive his water mills; he had felled trees from time immemorial as he needed them and filled up the gaps with seedlings. He had been wise enough to make return for aught he had taken. If anyone should desire earnestly to know how this earth of ours can be used to serve all the needs of man without being spoilt, he can go and see for himself.'

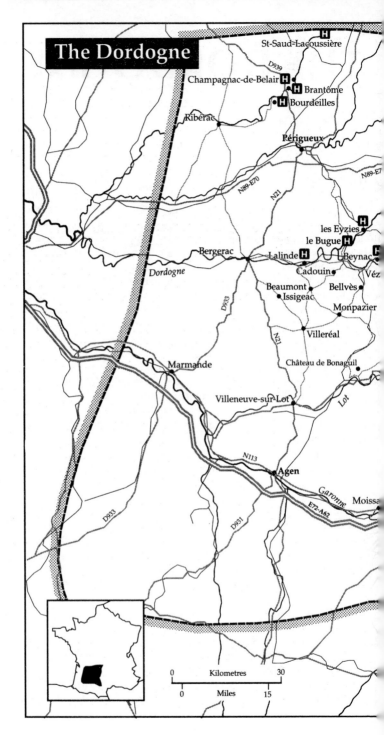

The Dordogne

St-Saud-Lacoussière

D939
Champagnac-de-Belair
Brantôme
Bourdeilles

Ribérac

Périgueux

N89-E7

N89-E70

N21

les Eyzies
le Bugue
Bergerac
Lalinde
Beynac
Cadouin
Véz
Beaumont
Bellvès
Issigeac
Monpazier

D933

Villeréal

N21

Marmande

Château de Bonaguil

Villeneuve-sur-Lot

Lot

N113

Agen

Garonne
Moissa

E72-A62

D933

D931

Dordogne

0   Kilometres   30

0   Miles   15

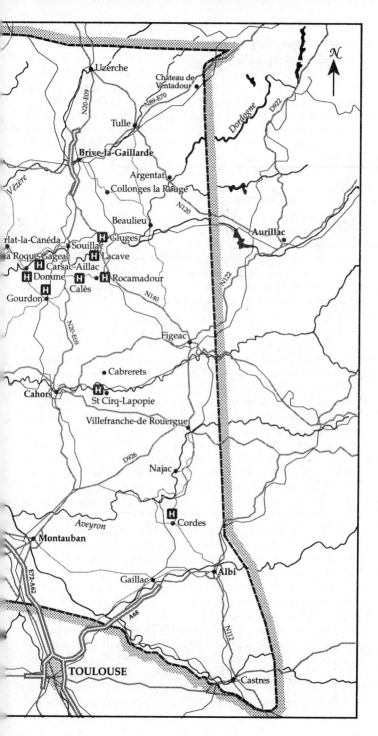

THE DORDOGNE

The title of Philip Oyler's book about the Dordogne, *The Generous Earth*, captures the appeal of an area which has won a large and faithful following of British visitors and *emigrés* in the decades which have followed his writing so fervently. It is not an area where nature impresses itself with breath-taking spectaculars, as in the Alps or in the gorges of the Massif Central; nor has man forced nature to bow to his designs, as at Versailles; here man and nature have achieved an enviable relationship of mutual advantage. In few areas has man contributed so much to the beauty of the landscape. It is not just the warm golden stone and russet tiles of the old villages whose reflections sway on the languid waters of the river, which itself adopts the deep green of the surrounding hills; nor is it the abundance of old fortresses standing high above the river's course in memory of a far-off time when the Dordogne stood on the disputed edge of two kingdoms and when the fruits of its earth were easy pickings for under-employed soldiery. There is also beauty in the cultivation of the land which is of great variety; the small parcels of mixed vegetation give the landscape intimacy and the decorative charm of a patchwork.

The secret of success of the Dordogne rural economy, at least in the eyes of Philip Oyler, was that the peasants who have so much in their own back gardens have never tried to maximise their yield by concentrating on one crop, but have preferred the wealth and satisfaction of self-sufficiency to financial gain. The fertile valleys of the Périgord and the Quercy to its south produce great quantities of fruit, vegetables, cereals and nuts. Pigs are fed on sweet chestnuts which cloak the hills, geese are fattened to yield lusciously rich livers and the fat which, along with walnut oil, forms the basis of Périgord cuisine. There are vines all along the river, mostly for home consumption. Around Bergerac, where the Dordogne approaches Bordeaux country, the vine gains the ascendant and yields a noble red wine and the famous dessert white of Monbazillac. Bergerac is also the centre of French tobacco production and every Dordogne farmer grows and rolls his own. The self-sufficiency and independence of the Dordogne farmer extends even beyond the provision of his daily needs; produce is often sold not by an entrepreneurial shopkeeper, but directly by the producer who takes the cash home and stores it under a mattress.

There are similarities between the landscape of the Dordogne and some of the most greenly attractive places in rural England. Philip Oyler remarked that the visitor 'will look upon faces nearly all of which could be English; he will look upon a landscape that might remind him of the Wye valley around Tintern; he will also see all his familiar trees and also a few added, and he will find a similar temperament'. He wrote of a time a few decades ago when the Dordogne peasantry was riddled with English surnames and Christian names, and when English words like cat, dog and country cropped up in the local patois. The French were 'they' who collaborated in the War and who tried to make 'us' pay to fish in our own rivers and to shoot on our land (and very often tasted the river or felt the buckshot if they came to try to enforce the law); the English were the old ancestors from the 13th and 14th centuries, and the people who flew in help for the wartime resistance which was at its most vigorous, and most vigorously punished, in the Dordogne. The people of the Dordogne were British, down to their very un-French habits of getting drunk on Saturday nights and telling dirty jokes and neglecting the formalities of Gallic social life. Whatever the truth of these ethnological observations it is indisputable that English people have felt themselves, as Oyler predicted, at home in this area as nowhere else in France, and whereas for the French the Périgord is a region to enjoy for its many domed churches, its prehistoric cave paintings and its foie gras, for the English it is a place to inhabit, if only for a few weeks a year.

The Dordogne has, of course, been changed by its sudden use as a tourist and second home area. Houses and whole villages are being carefully restored and property prices have shot up. Crafts have flourished, both those which are associated with renovation of houses and furniture, and others such as pottery and carved wood, examples of which are sold directly (along with farm produce) from the stalls by the roadside. You see large numbers of clearly British cyclists, pottering along through the orchards on their heavy three-speed machines, skirts billowing in the breeze; the area is nowhere near steep enough for the serious-minded French who take their many-geared racing cycles, their drip-feed water bottles, their salt tablets and their Peugeot T-shirts to more challenging regions.

Because of its charm the area around the river valley is relatively frequented, but not unduly so even in July and August, for the French do not come here *en masse*. In general the impact of tourism on the area is less profound than the density of GB and NL stickers in July (at Les-Eyzies or Domme for example) would suggest, for Dordogne tourism is not of the sun, sand and sea variety; rather it is the tourism of those who follow in the footsteps of Philip Oyler, seeking spiritual nourishment from the atmosphere of the Dordogne.

Because of its pulling power the name is often applied to places which are a long way from the river valley, where you may well have a relaxing and satisfactory holiday in a country cottage – as you may almost anywhere in rural France – but where you will not, without a long commute, see what the Dordogne has to offer.

For the sightseer the Dordogne has more to offer than its picturesque crop of fortresses, built in most cases for defence rather than gracious living and adequately admired from without. Much rarer is the abundant evidence that early man appreciated these eminently hospitable river valleys, especially the Vézère, whose limestone cliffs are full of caves which offered shelter from the weather, the bears and the mammoths. Since the famous and momentous discovery of the skeletons of Cro-Magnon man in a rock shelter at Les Eyzies in 1868, sepulchres, stone tools and ornaments have been found in dozens of sites and have yielded many, yet relatively few, of the secrets of early man's progress. The importance of the area is such that Dordogne excavations, like La Madeleine and Le Moustier, have given their names to different prehistoric eras. There are good prehistoric museums in Les Eyzies and Périgueux to illuminate the darkness of most of our ignorance of Magdalenian or Aurignacian man of the Upper Palaeolithic (Old Stone) Age, about 40,000 to 10,000 BC. But probably of more interest are the cave paintings, drawings and engravings that have survived from this extraordinary period, when man did not merely refine his standard of living by making better tools to defend and clothe himself but also left evidence of a developed spiritual and artistic sense. Cro-Magnon man crawled into the remotest networks of underground grottoes and by the light of a primitive oil lamp decorated nature's sanctuaries with images of the animals which threatened his life but on whose healthy abundant survival he depended as a hunting carnivore. The survival of these works of art is one marvel – thanks to a stability of natural conditions underground, which is so fragile that in many cases only a few tourists (and in one case none at all) can be allowed in to pollute the air; the other marvel is the quality of the paintings and engravings. It is easy to be sceptical of what in some caves looks at first glance like a mass of scribbles – successive artists often went over the same piece of wall several times – but when your eye becomes accustomed to the handwriting and the tricks of exploiting natural forms, you will be more amazed by the subtlety and life of the art than by its antiquity. The greatest find and the most regrettably inaccessible is Lascaux, discovered by some local lads who followed their dogs down a hole in September 1940 and found not a rabbit but herds of bison, bulls, ibex, deer and horses in a multitude of brilliant colours. When they led the great prehistorian Abbé Breuil to the place a few days later, he could only gasp in astonishment: 'It's the Sistine Chapel of prehistory'. In less than 20 years the paintings which had survived in all their vividness for over 30,000 years showed such signs of irrecoverable decay that the cave was closed.

The sanctuaries which later man built for himself have not the power to surprise that the cave paintings have, but they are none the less fascinating. The Romanesque schools of architecture and sculpture of south-west France are the finest in Europe. Different regions of France have their own very distinctive variations of the Romanesque, and regional influences are swapped. The Auvergne, Poitou and Limousin variations come outside the boundaries of this chapter. The Dordogne churches are as good as anywhere in France – many have emphatically carved Last Judgements over their doorways, ranging from the terrifying to the uplifting. Sculptors seemed to have travelled more widely than architects, and supremely decorative, stylised and similar carvings crop up all over the place, from Moissac in the south to Souillac on the

Dordogne. The great speciality of the Périgord is churches with domes, not just over the main crossing but over every bay of the nave. Of some 60 of these churches which survive from the Romanesque age fully a half are in the Périgord.

Another curiosity of the region is the number of *bastide* towns between the rivers Dordogne and Lot, in the border country between the lands of the late 13th- and 14th-century French and English kings. Where the countryside to be defended was empty of fortresses or of villages on whose loyalty the kings could rely, Edward III and Philip the Bold built village fortresses on strictly geometric lines, not usually characteristic of towns surviving from this period. At the centre of the grid is an arcaded square and nearby a fortified church which served as the keep of the fortress. To encourage their loyalty the new settlers in the *bastides* were given enviable privileges and freedom – Villefranche is a typical name. Some of the most important *bastides* (such as Libourne) have had their particular character dwarfed by the later growth of towns, others have hardly grown at all (Monpazier, Domme). *Bastides* are not a phenomenon unique to this region – Saint Louis's port of Aigues-Mortes in the Camargue was founded for much the same reasons and has the same unspoilt geometric medieval plan – but the scale of the dispute in south-west France which gave rise to the Hundred Years' War and the lack of natural fortresses along the border lands means that *bastides* are here in greater number than anywhere else.

Of all the delights of the Périgordian table the mysterious truffle is king. Not so much a crop as a precious treasure which is mined, the truffle is an edible fungus which enjoys a symbiotic relationship not far below the surface of the soil with the roots of oak trees. The conditions for its healthy growth are not really known for sure, or if they are the wily Périgordians do not publicise them. Truffles are sniffed out by discriminating pigs and dogs (who are less inclined to devour what they unearth), weaned on truffles from birth. Occasionally, gnats with a gourmet's appreciation for good smells can be seen hovering in thin columns above the location of a truffle, thereby helping a keen-eyed farmer to find it – an economical but unreliable method. Once unearthed, the truffles, like garlic, are, or should be, less noticeable when they are present than when they are not. Not a few visitors decide that the truffle is no better than a cunning peasant's trap for the gullible consumer eager to praise everything that is expensive for that reason alone – something of a Périgordian ginseng. But truffles are not cracked up to do you good, merely to delight your palate, and you will not find anyone who knows his or her food casting irreverent aspersions.

To the south of the Dordogne, the Quercy has caves, cave paintings, most of the region's *bastides*, and most of the truffles. At Cahors, there is what is considered to be the prototype for the domed churches of Périgord; at Moissac one of the most beautiful Romanesque churches in France; and at Bonaguil a medieval fortress finer than any of the ones that smile down like Narcissus into the Dordogne. But however impressive the list of points in its favour, the Quercy simply does not have the atmosphere of the Dordogne. In the south of the Quercy, between the rivers Lot and Garonne, the fruits of the earth are the best fruit in France, but the countryside is rather uninteresting. In the north the landscape is harsher: the limestone plateaux are in places barely covered by soil, and announce the bleak Grands Causses of the southern Massif Central where the porous rock is carved into enormous subterranean caverns. Even the river valleys are steeper and darker, less of a pastoral delight. The balance between man and nature is tilted just a little against man.

North and West Périgord

In the north of *Périgord blanc* – called white because it was once less forested than *Périgord noir* to the south-east – lies **Brantôme**, a lovely place to stay, and peaceful outside high season, with some good hotels and restaurants. Its surrounding area (with the village of Ribérac at its heart) is very popular for the country cottage holidays with which the Dordogne has become synonymous. It is not however convenient for exploration of the Dordogne valley itself. The river Dronne flows through the town beneath weeping willows and limes and elegant 18th-century abbey buildings. Behind the abbey is a beautiful Romanesque belfry which stands apart from the church. An elbow bridge crosses the Dronne by a noisy weir and millwheel; and in the evening fishermen wade out in their thigh boots into the gathering gloom and stand like herons in mid-stream casting for trout until it is completely dark.

Brantôme

Excursions from Brantôme

● **Bourdeilles** Only a few kilometres downstream from Brantôme, Bourdeilles' situation is no less attractive, with a handsome mill beside the river and a château above. The sister-in-law of the indiscreet chronicler Brantôme designed the château in a hurry to receive Catherine de' Medici. When she didn't arrive the building was left unfinished; it gives a perhaps unfair impression that the lady of the house would have done well to seek professional architectural advice. A guided tour round the interior of the château is very rewarding, for Bourdeilles was owned not long ago by a couple of Burgundian art collectors who had selected it as the ideal place for the display of their beautiful and varied collections of furniture, paintings and tapestries. Many of the finest items are Spanish.

● **Chancelade and Merlande** Near Périgueux, there are monastic ruins at Chancelade and an abbey church at Merlande which has been damaged greatly over the centuries but still displays some splendid carving on the capitals around the arcades of the apse.

● **St-Jean-de-Côle** A delightful village which has won a national 'best roof award' in its time and which clusters around an ensemble of market buildings, château and 11th-century church. The nearby **Villars** caves are not by any means the Périgord's most important subterranean tourist attraction, but the narrow corridors take you to some splendid concretions and a few paintings (very old even by the standards of the Périgord) which are thought to date back to the early days of the Upper Palaeolithic Period.

● **Château de Hautefort** The small town and the countryside for miles around are dominated by this magnificent 16th- and 17th-century château whose round towers are crowned by elegant domes and lanterns. All around the castle there are immaculately kept gardens and you can go on a guided tour of the interior; but since a devastating fire in 1968 only a few rooms have been restored for the visitor. Hautefort was the home of one of the most celebrated 12th-century troubadour poets, Bertrand de Born, whose political machinations earned him a place in Dante's *Inferno*. Only the foundations of the château date from Bertrand's time.

Périgueux is the big market town of the whole Dordogne region. It is not a particularly enticing base for a holiday, but well worth visiting in passing because of the great curiosity value of its cathedral and because it is a very good place to shop for all the fruits of the earth that have made Périgord a gourmet's paradise and – unless he or she has an iron constitution – a glutton's purgatory. In the Middle Ages the once-important Roman city languished while an independent commercial town prospered around the tomb of Saint Front. The two towns merged but have kept their separate characters, with the area around the cathedral old and attractive and commercial; the rest is rather dull despite the survival of some fragmentary Roman ruins.

Sights in Périgueux

- **Cathedral** Seen from afar and at its best from across the river, St-Front with its roofscape of lanterns and domes beneath a tall belfry rising some 60 metres above the market square cannot fail to make you think of the Orient. The plan of the church – that of a Greek cross – is in fact very close to St Mark's in Venice and the church of the Apostles in Constantinople, and its building clearly has something to do with the experience of crusaders. Part of the 11th-century church remains (the austere west façade and fragments inside it) but the rest of the church was restored in the 19th century and in the words of Augustus Hare, 'under the name of restoration one of the most remarkable churches in France has been entirely destroyed ... white and unsympathetic, the modern church is utterly without beauty and has nothing of interest but its architectural features'. Thanks to all the domes the interior is impressively spacious but cold, grey and soulless.
- **St-Etienne-de-la-Cité** The old cathedral is very mutilated but still has two of its 12th-century domes and a finely wrought 17th-century wooden altarpiece.
- **Périgord Museum** Prehistoric collections from the surrounding area, in many ways more interesting than the museum at Les-Eyzies. There is a complete skeleton of Chancelade man, a mammoth's tusk and fragments from the Gallo-Roman settlement, including mosaics.
- **Roman remains** A 24-metre high round tower (the Tour de Vésone) is all that remains of a Roman temple. Near St-Etienne-de-la-Cité there are some fragments of the old amphitheatre.

The road south-west from Périgueux meets the Dordogne river itself at **Bergerac**, the area's second town in importance and approximately the western limit of the part of the Dordogne river which is in the Dordogne *département*. Bergerac has many affinities with the Bordeaux region in that it is more of a wine town than anything else, except perhaps tobacco – of which it is the French capital, thanks to the favourable combination of very fertile soil and summer warmth. Bergerac, like Aubusson, was a centre of Protestantism, and not much of the old town survives except a small area by the river which has been restored. There is a tobacco museum which is fascinating whatever you think of the habit, which reached France in 1560 when an ambassador sent some tobacco from Lisbon as a cure for Catherine de' Medici's migraines. In the 17th century Louis XIII outlawed the use of tobacco. Pope Urban XVIII excommunicated smokers; but soon the authorities realised that what they couldn't defeat they could exploit. The museum is full of details of the industry and a splendid collection of old smoking-related items from pipes to snuff boxes and 19th-century cartoons making fun of the shocking adoption of the smoking habit by women. The Maison du Vin is nearby and has details of the

Monpazier

local wine-producing châteaux which receive tourists. The most hand-some and the most famous is the 16th-century **Château de Monbazillac** which contains a museum which has less to do with the luscious wine than with the very bloody religious history of the region.

The western stretch of the Dordogne valley, between Bergerac and the Vézère river, is not its most attractive, apart from the wide *cingle* or loop of **Trémolat**, of which there are fine views from the road on the north bank. Trémolat itself is a small town that will interest those who remember Claude Chabrol's film *Le Boucher*, where the lush rural atmosphere of the area is brilliantly evoked to contrast with the less than idyllic events making up the plot. The church in Trémolat is an almost windowless, decaying fortress of a building. On the sluggish loop of the river there is a water sports centre.

The **Vézère** is an attractive river with many of the qualities of the Dordogne in its lower reaches. Its overwhelming attraction is not its landscape, but its status as the capital of prehistory. The centre of modern tourist congregation – as it was the centre of habitation by Upper Palaeolithic man – is **Les Eyzies-de-Tayac**, not an attractive little town and very commercialised, but a reasonable place to stay while exploring the area, with plenty of accommodation. The museum of prehistory in the old château tells the story of excavation, which was something of a gold rush at the turn of the century. There is a display of fascinating artefacts, such as red-clay bison and the grave and skeleton of a 20-year-old Magdalenian woman. The museum is clearly labelled, with a good guidebook for sale in English. It is a good preparation for visits to the caves in the surrounding area (see next page).

Of the few places of later than prehistoric interest around the valley, the most attractive is **St-Amand-de-Coly**, a small village of houses with rough stone (*lauze*) roofs, clustered around a beautiful fortified Romanesque church.

Excursions from the western Dordogne

● **Bastide towns** A good selection of the many *bastides* in the area between the Dordogne and the Lot – not the most important necessarily but some of the least affected by subsequent urban development – can be incorporated in a round trip south of Bergerac and back up to the Abbaye de Cadouin. Some are French (in the south), others nearer the Dordogne river are English; there is no noticeable difference in style of construction. At **Beaumont** there is a good example of the fortified church which served as a keep. **Castillonès** is another typical *bastide* with a central arcaded square; **Villeréal** has market buildings on the square; **Monflanquin** is an attractive hilltop *bastide*; and **Montpazier** is the most complete of them all, with much of its ramparts and very beautiful low pointed-arch arcading around the square.

● **Château de Biron** This is a superb mostly 15th-century fortress in a dominant position surveying vast tracts of open countryside, and larger than the small village that kneels at its feet. The most curious feature is the chapel with two storeys, one opening on the courtyard of the château, the lower serving as the parish church for the village which knows its place.

● **Abbaye de Cadouin** An old abbey which for many centuries flourished on pilgrimage business, thanks to its bogus holy shroud which was finally discredited in 1934 when it was discovered to be an extremely precious oriental fabric dating from not much earlier than the time it was brought back from crusade. Cadouin's main distinction is the Flamboyant Gothic cloisters, full of intricate carving of great beauty. A typed sheet in English guides you round and explains all the carvings.

Visiting caves

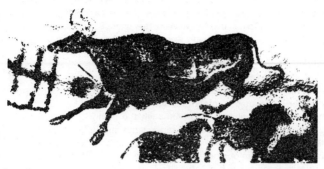

Lascaux

The porous limestone plateaux of the Périgord and Quercy have been hollowed out by the drainage of rain water into vast networks of underground caverns, lakes and rivers. You can visit a large number of these and admire the natural curiosities therein – not just waterways, but also concretions (stalagmites which grow up and stalactites which grow down) formed by the dripping of mineral-rich water from ceiling to floor, leaving deposits whither and whence it falls. Eventually mites and tites, which grow at a rate of between one and two centimetres a century, meet to form pillars. The action of the rivers has also produced an astonishing variety of different forms, including perfect spheres like ballbearings, and rounded discs which look as if they have been carefully formed on a potter's wheel. Caves, for obvious reasons, are visited with guided tours and in many cases numbers and cramped space make it difficult to hear what the guides are saying and difficult to see what they're saying it about, unless you push. Most of the time the guides help you to play the great grotto game, which consists of identifying familiar shapes among the natural forms, which are mostly illuminating about the preoccupations of the French mind – mushrooms everywhere, oven-ready trussed chickens, bunches of carrots and, to quote several guides, 'the classical natural form which imitates the statue of the Virgin and Child'.

Of all the grottoes in the region, few can rival for splendour those in the Massif Central; those in the Dordogne are much more crowded and you may have to queue for a long time to get in. What you cannot see better in any other area are the caves decorated with wall paintings, nearly always of animals. There are other painted caves in Europe, notably in the Pyrenees and in north-western Spain, but nowhere was there such a concentration of activity as around the Dordogne – and especially around the Vézère, near Les Eyzies. Cave art flourished during the relatively restricted period of 15–8,000 BC with the peak of achievement and artistic refinement coming in the period known as the Magdalenian era. The beginning of the period marks the end of the last

THE DORDOGNE

Ice Age, when most of the European landscape was bare tundra, full of wildlife but not hospitable to man who clustered during the winters in a few sheltered valleys like the Dordogne, returning again and again to the same caves to paint animal images. Only occasionally are human forms represented – usually women, as symbols of fertility. As the millennia went by the climate warmed up, more and more of Europe became forest, the mammoths and bison and reindeer all went north and their hunters followed them.

In a few caves the two sorts of interest, natural and artistic, are combined; but in many cases man chose extremely remote or narrow corridors to decorate – some were only a few feet high and have had to be enlarged to admit visitors. Although the paintings have in many places been preserved in astonishing clarity and brilliance of colour, thanks to their being fixed in the rock face (rather like the drying of a fresco), the advent of modern man in large numbers after the discovery of the cave paintings has had severely damaging effects. The greatest paintings of all, at Lascaux, had to be closed after only 20 years (120,000 people breathed carbon dioxide at the bestiary in 1962). Elsewhere, numbers of visitors are strictly limited and the air in the cave periodically flushed. The colours of Lascaux, obtained by the use of red ochre, are not to be found in many caves – black outline often reinforced by engraving is more frequent. Artists repeatedly came back to reuse the same pieces of wall and did not hesitate to draw and engrave over existing drawings and paintings, often reusing the forms to depict different images. The result can be that the maze of lines is difficult to untangle for the uninitiated eye. Before going to look at the cave paintings it is well worth visiting the prehistorical museum in Les Eyzies to find out about the men who produced the works of art. The following lists of caves, painted and unpainted, is not exhaustive.

Lascaux (Near Montignac) The most important group of cave paintings known to man cannot now be visited, but a realistic facsimile has been opened near the site. Well worth visiting. Tickets are on sale at Montignac tourist office – aim to get there by 8.30 am in high season. Included is entry to the museum at nearby Le Thot, where you can compare living bison, deer and small horses to the Lascaux paintings.

Rouffignac An electric train ride through extensive caves which have been known to modern man for centuries, but whose Magdalenian paintings were only recently discovered among fakes and multitudes of graffiti. There are over a hundred mammoths, dozens of rhinoceroses and bison, horses, ibex and even a few humanoids.

Abri du Cap-Blanc Subtly signed, a short walk down through the woods from the road above the river Beune, a small rock shelter rather than a grotto with a single superb relief sculpture of 15,000-year-old horses and a copy of a skeleton of what is said to be a 23-year-old female.

Combarelles Two long passages originally only a few feet high, and a wealth of engravings and outlines in many places difficult to decipher but very well explained. In high season, tickets have to be reserved days in advance – telephone the Font-de-Gaume ticket office.

Font-de-Gaume The most beautiful decorated cave you can visit around Les Eyzies, with some coloured as well as outlined beasts, including a magnificent frieze of bison, and some concretions. It sells out weeks in advance in high season – you can telephone from Britain (53 06 90 80) to reserve tickets.

Grand-Roc Colourfully lit and colourfully guided concretions in a grotto high above the river beside Les Eyzies. Interesting formations, but extremely popular and can be claustrophobic inside; frequent queues outside.

La Roque-St-Christophe A series of galleries in the cliffs over the Vézère, where troglodyte man lived from prehistoric times until the 18th century. Heavily marketed in Les Eyzies and much frequented but not particularly exciting. Some elements of defences remain and a laughable model of an ape man fighting a bear.

Proumeyssac Man-made tunnel into a large domed chasm with river and fine concretions.

Le Thot (near Montignac) An interesting alternative to the prehistory museum with an audio-visual presentation of generalities about cave painting in its historical context. In the neighbouring park there are prehistoric-style animals including bison.

Cougnac (near Gourdon) An interesting mixture of delicate concretions and animal paintings. Not usually crowded.

Lafage (near Turenne) Colourful concretions.

Lacave (near Souillac) Concretions and underground waters. Long queues.

Padirac (near Rocamadour) The great natural curiosity of the region seems to attract more tourists than you would imagine fitted in the whole of the Dordogne valley and the overall experience is not dissimilar to visiting London's underground. The gaping hole in the ground was for centuries thought to be one of the gates of Hell, but late 19th-century exploration revealed marvellous underground rivers and lakes and huge caverns, one nearly 90 metres high. You visit partly by boat and partly by foot.

Pech-Merle (near Cabrerets) An enormous and magnificent grotto, decorated with paintings and second in splendour only to inaccessible Lascaux. If you only want to visit one grotto in the area this is the one to choose. In addition there is a good audio-visual presentation in the museum at the entrance. As well as the splendid animal paintings there are signatures with hands outlined by ochre blown on to the rock through blow pipes, and fossilised footprints of a prehistoric man and child. The allocation of tickets for the day (700) often sells out at opening time in high season.

Villars (north-east of Brantôme) A few paintings and some fine concretions.

The Central Dordogne Valley

The Dordogne between the Vézère and Souillac is at its most beautiful. It winds between cliffs of gold, overlooked by the turreted crowns of fortresses and châteaux which coyly hide themselves in the vegetation of the hillsides. The valley is a succession of beauty spots, and they are enjoyed by large numbers of tourists – campers, cyclists and canoeists among them. One of the prettiest places (which does not neglect to exploit its attractions) is the village of **Beynac-et-Cazenac**, with old houses along the riverside beneath a 135-metre cliff, and others on top of it beside the truly dominant 13th- to 15th-century fortress, one of the greatest Périgord strongholds in the Middle Ages. It is now restored inside and informatively guided, but there is not much furniture. From the ramparts there is a splendid view up and down the river and across to the rival fortress of **Castelnaud**, hardly less impressively set. For much of the Hundred Years' War, Castelnaud was in the hands of the English, Beynac was French. Castelnaud has recently been restored and its interior turned into an instructive museum of medieval warfare. Huge siege weapons and Heath Robinson-style catapults are displayed around the castle's fortification and a video shows how they were used in great, and sometimes lurid, detail.

La Roque-Gageac is the other archetypal reflected village, squashed between a golden cliff and the river, many of its houses carved out of the rock. To accentuate the stage-set atmosphere there is a mock 15th-century château built a century or so ago. Unlike Beynac or La Roque-Gageac, the nearby village of **Domme** stands high above the river on a cliff. It can only be reached (or so it was thought, until some Protestants climbed the cliffs in 1588) from the gentler hills behind – on which side Domme is defended by some splendid fortified gateways and ramparts. Once inside the walls the martial frown of Domme changes to a charmingly inviting smile. Its houses are of gold-coloured stone and beautifully restored, decorated with geraniums and roses and vines – as if the streets needed prettifying. At the top of the *bastide*, there is an old market hall which gives access to some caves with concretions, and a shady esplanade offering a superlative view over the valley. Domme is one of the most picturesque places of the Dordogne and one of the most popular. There are scores of restaurants and shops selling pâté, potted goose, and other local delicacies. During the day it teems with campers who come up from the riverside in nothing but their bathing shorts. But it quietens down in the evening, and is a very pleasant place to stay.

Sarlat, the market town of this arcadian stretch of the river, is appropriately handsome apart from the very busy main shopping street. The area to the east of the main street has a number of beautiful and well-restored medieval houses – the Place du Peyrou is a particularly fine ensemble. Sarlat's cathedral was rebuilt during the 16th and 17th centuries with the exception of its 12th-century belfry and porch. In the gardens behind there is a curious round, conically-roofed Romanesque funerary chapel, the Lanterne des Morts. Sarlat is the most animated town of the region, with pavement entertainers; there is an open-air drama festival at the end of July and the beginning of August.

Souillac is the through-town where the mighty N20 crosses the Dordogne. It is full of amenities for the traveller – shops and banks and

Goosefair at Sarlat

305

hotels and restaurants – but in general it is pretty ordinary apart from its one glorious redeeming feature, a domed church, the beautiful rounded forms of whose east end are admirably disencumbered (by a car park) for your admiration. The interior is a warm and spacious harmony of rounded forms as well, without much decoration except for the astonishingly rich carving on the old west doorway which has been re-installed inside the church. Beneath a three-tier relief illustration of the legend of Theophilus – who like Faust made a pact with the devil but unlike him earned forgiveness – the pillars are carved with a densely decorative tangle of weird beasts of fantasy, and the dancing figure of the prophet Isaiah.

Upstream from Souillac the beauty spots along the river are fewer and further between, but the river itself winds beautifully on, flanked by yet more fortresses. There are caves to visit at **Lacave**, with well-lit concretions, but being by the river they attract more crowds than they deserve. The medieval town of **Martel** stands some distance north of the river and is little affected by tourists. It was named after an abbey founded by Charles Martel to commemorate his victory over the Infidel in the 8th century. It has many beautiful houses, some dating from the 15th century, as does the massive church, built more like a castle than a place of worship, except for the splendid carving of the Last Judgement over the main doorway. Martel also has an attractive old covered market, and is an important centre for the truffle business.

Carennac, where François de Salignac de La Mothe-Fénelon was prior for many years and where he is said to have written *Télémaque* – the romantic moral tale of the adventures of the son of Ulysses, which was the most popular work of the French 18th century – is a delightful and peaceful village which slumbers changeless near the waters of the Dordogne. Its church has a very beautiful 12th-century doorway whose tympanum with Christ in Majesty in a mandorla (almond frame) is closely related to that at Beaulieu among others. Inside there is a moving group sculpture of the Entombment. The partially Romanesque cloister is often used for the sale of local craft and food produce.

Just north of Carennac, the large plateau of **Puy d'Issolud** may be the site of the battle of Uxellodunum. The Gauls finally yielded before the might and cunning of Caesar, who triumphed by diverting their water supply – the battle has been described as the death-rattle of Gallic freedom. There is more to see from the high plateau than on it.

Perhaps the most impressive château of the whole valley is the **Château de Castelnau-Bretenoux**, which surveys the confluence of the Dordogne and Céré from the isolated rocky end of a promontory between the river valleys. Its outer walls could enclose a town, so great is the area they surround. The buildings within are magnificent, and despite having been burnt down in the last century – arson for insurance it is said – the interior was restored by a tasteful tenor who left his varied art collection and the château to the nation on his death. The guided tour is more interesting than most, and from the fortifications of this red-stone stronghold (described by Pierre Loti as a blood-red cockscomb) there are magnificent views.

Beaulieu-sur-Dordogne is a small township beside the river, where the Dordogne ceases to be a river of the hills, and starts out on its most beautiful middle section. Beaulieu is a pleasant place with its busy market and plenty of facilities by the river for camping, swimming and hiring canoes. Its fame rests not on any of these, but on the deeply recessed south portal of its former abbey church. This is a magnificent work of Romanesque carving, very much in the style of Moissac as are the less monumental doorways at Carennac, Martel, Collonges and others. Above the door the Last Judgement is represented with great vigour around the central figure of Christ. On the pillars below there are some wonderful demonic figures given an unintended gruesome aspect by the weathering of the stone. The scenes represented in these nether regions are the Temptation of Christ, Daniel with lions and some figures symbolising the punishment of avarice and luxury.

Upstream, the small town of **Argentat** enjoys a picturesque setting, its steep grey *lauze*-roofed houses mirrored in the river. Above Argentat the Dordogne descends through the wooded gorges – or used to until it was dammed in no less than five places between Argentat and Bort-les-Orgues, making a succession of long-stepped narrow reservoirs flanked by hills. This landscape has its beauty although it lacks the variety and colours of the valley lower down. For most of the way you can drive along the side of the river and reservoirs and there are a number of good viewpoints, especially from the hills behind **Bort-les-Orgues**, a small industrial town named after the basalt pillars which stand in a row like organ pipes – in some places 60 metres high. The damming of the Dordogne has improved the setting of the delightful **Château de Val**, whose round towers are now lapped by the waters of the reservoir.

Excursions from the eastern Dordogne

● **Rocamadour** One of the most important pilgrimage destinations in Europe in the early Middle Ages. The origin of the pilgrimage was the discovery in the 12th century of an uncorrupted body, that of the hermit Amadour, identified as none other than the Zacchaeus of the New Testament. The incorruptible Amadour was chopped to pieces by the Huguenots and cannot be carbon-dated. Everyone who was anyone in medieval Christendom came to Rocamadour (Henry II came twice) but it was sacked repeatedly and fell into decline before being revived in the 19th century as a tourist attraction and a pilgrimage destination. Today it is still both, but predominantly a place for tourists (with its fair share of tackiness) thanks to its remarkable setting.

The village is built along a couple of very narrow ledges on an apparently sheer cliff-face which is one side of the almost empty Alzou canyon – a cleft in the stony arid *causse*. The main street is very trippery but has a number of restored medieval gateways and houses. From it a staircase of over 200 steps – penitent pilgrims used originally to go up on hands and knees with chains around their neck and limbs – climbs the rock face to a number of restored sanctuaries built into the rock, to an also restored château on the top of the cliff. The ascent can also be made by lift. Although the extensive restoration and rebuilding of Rocamadour gives it a less than authentic look, the overall atmosphere is probably not very different from what it was 700 years ago. The sanctuaries themselves are of no particular distinction as buildings, but the famous Black Virgin is spindly and mysterious, and for once not clothed in the usual lace and jewellery. Rocamadour being what it is, many people will find the best thing to do is to appreciate the overall view of the setting – from the road down from L'Hospitalet – and go no further.

- **Causse de Gramat** The road between L'Hospitalet and Calès is a good one to take to see some of the bleak but beautiful rocky scenery of the limestone plateau, with its dry-stone walls and shepherd's huts.
- **Around Autoire** Above the beautiful village of **Autoire** there is an impressive amphitheatre of rocks and waterfalls. The **Château de Montal** is a small Renaissance château whose exquisite grace is tinged with sadness. The three-sided courtyard is decorated with a marvellous series of portrait busts depicting among others the château's creator, Jeanne de Balzac, who intended Montal for her son Robert de Montal, also represented. When he died young in battle, she inscribed the sombre message 'Plus d'espoir' (no more hope) around the beautiful gabled windows of the château. Only a few rooms are on show, but there are some splendid works of art, including a tapestry depicting a Renaissance game of croquet; the staircase is a masterpiece of 16th-

Dry-stone shepherds' huts

century decoration. Montal is a tribute to the energy and devotion of the man who bought it at the beginning of this century, after its contents and the decorative elements of its exterior had been dispersed for easy money at the end of the last century. The new owner bought back all the pieces he could from the museums and private collectors who had snapped them up and there is nothing in the interior which is not in period.

• **St-Céré** A small market town with considerable charm but not much specific interest except the brilliantly colourful Aubusson tapestries on display in the old casino. Their designer was the modern artist Jean Lurçat who lived at St-Céré and whose beautiful house and studio on the hilltop above the town can be visited in July and August.

• **Collonges-la-Rouge and Aubazines** Well-named **Collonges-la-Rouge** is an enchanting village of extraordinary deep purple-red sandstone; like Pérouges near Lyon and Cordes near Albi it has been saved, restored and preserved from change thanks to a society of friends who got together at the beginning of the century. It is bypassed by the modest D38 though not by the crowds of visitors. The large red Romanesque church has a handsome Limousin belfry – one of the oldest of the genre – and a beautifully carved west doorway. Some of the fortifications which were added to the church in the 15th century are still visible. The small village of **Aubazines** near the Corrèze upstream from Brive was the site of a Cistercian abbey in the 12th century, and its church is typical of that order in the sobriety of its style. It is a building with a typical Limousin belfry, but with the unusual feature that the bays of the nave climb in steps towards the choir. Contents of particular interest include amusing carved choir stalls, a very old oak cupboard in the south transept, and a masterpiece of delicate Gothic stone tracery enclosing the recumbent statue of Saint Stephen.

• **Turenne** This village lacks the glorious technicolour appeal of nearby Collonges, but is an attractive old village all the same, and far less crowded, built at the foot of two impressive windowless towers – one round, one square – which are all that remain on the top of a hill of a fortress which was the power base of a mighty lordship, independent of the crown until 1738. The most famous of its rulers was the great Turenne himself, the 17th-century general whom Napoleon rated more highly as a soldier than any other, except perhaps one.

• **Tulle, Gimel and Ventadour** The large town of Tulle is enclosed by hills and has had to grow for a long way along the banks of the fast-flowing Corrèze. It has given its name to a kind of lace work, which has long deserted the town and since the last century has been established mainly in Calais. The cathedral has an elegant belfry; there are 13th-century cloisters which contain a local museum and some old houses nearby. The small village of **Gimel** enjoys a wild setting beside a series of waterfalls whose total drop is nearly 150 metres, and at the foot of which the waters run through gorges called The Inferno. To get to the best viewpoint to admire all this you have to pay. The glory of the treasury in Gimel church is a 12th-century reliquary of Saint Stephen (the same one as at Aubazines), decorated with jewel-studded enamels. Above the gorges of the Luzège, north-east of Gimel, are the impressive ruins of **Ventadour** castle, best seen from the narrow approach roads from Moustier-Ventadour.

● **Tours de Merle** Ruined feudal fortress which comprised seven individual castles, vulnerably situated surrounded by hills.

The Lot Valley

The Lot charts an unbelievably tortuous course of endless meanders through the *département* that bears its name. One of the most tedious loops, at Luzech – where the river travels for more than five kilometres to cover less than 200 metres of ground – was canalised; but it has since been filled in and nowadays those who canoe or boat down the Lot (and it is one of the safest and most beautiful waterways in France for this purpose) will have to do the full course. Not unlike the Dordogne in many ways, this part of the Lot Valley is flanked by the limestone cliffs of the Causse. High on the rocks there are a few splendidly perched villages and a few fortresses; down below, small cultivations of tobacco, maize and rows of poplars.

The swift Célé is hardly less attractive, as it runs down through narrow limestone gorges with old mills and little waterfalls from **Figeac** – a town with many old houses of character but no individual monuments of great distinction – to Conduché where its waters are absorbed by the Lot. Between Figeac and Cahors there are lots of beaches where enterprising souls have set up cabin-style chips and beer stops; the river is shallow and bendy here so ideal for first-time canoeists.

Apart from the look of the Lot Valley the main reason to follow its course is to visit the **Pech-Merle Cave** near Cabrerets – the most interesting of all the prehistoric painted caves currently open to the public, and beautiful as a grotto as well (see page 303). **St-Cirq-Lapopie** is a carefully restored old village of beautiful houses which would be worth visiting anywhere and which has the added attraction of a truly magnificent setting on a spur high above the left bank of the Lot. The narrow streets climb up towards a ruined château and a Gothic church – if you wander around the back the view is positively dizzy. In the past St-Cirq has been a traditional centre for wood craftsmen and today it is still very much a place for arts and crafts. The powers that be, it would seem, not only prevent the inhabitants of the village from replacing their impractical but picturesque old roofs, but also make sure that the tourist shops are *de style*.

Cahors is the capital of the Quercy which in the Middle Ages produced the greatest if not the most likeable of French popes (John XXII), and a blood-red wine which enjoyed a greater reputation then, in the days before phylloxera, than it does today. John XXII may have had something to do with the tradition that the popes had the robust Cahors wine for communion; he also founded a university in his native town and had the bishop of Cahors flayed and torn apart by wild horses for alleged sorcery. The town, which still shows some remnants of the old fortifications, stands on a peninsula in the Lot – whose neck is only half a mile wide, but whose meandering river moat is more than four miles around. Until as recently as 1850 there were three magnificent fortified bridges; only one survives today but it is enough to ensure Cahors an illustrated place in most guide books. Strangely the old town did not fill the peninsula; today the N20, which goes straight through the middle of town, divides the old town on the east from the new and anonymous one to the west.

Sights in Cahors

• **Cathedral** The two enormous rough domes of the nave are some of the earliest of the style which was to spread all over the Périgord. The effect of the interior is warm and imposing. Some 14th-century paintings on one of the domes have survived and depict the stoning of Saint Stephen, to whom the church is dedicated. The glory of the cathedral is its north doorway – a work of the same period and style as Moissac and others. Unfortunately the portal at Cahors is not really shown off to advantage, and standing on the narrow street in front of it involves considerable risk from passing traffic. It is worth braving most dangers to see it though, for the central figure of Christ in the mandorla – less awesome than Moissac, but more human – is one of the noblest creations of Romanesque sculpture.
• **Pont Valentré** France's most beautiful bridge (early 14th century) spans the western side of the loop of the Lot, and was not originally part of the town and its defences but an isolated self-sufficient fortress. Three 42 metre towers dominate the bridge of six pointed Gothic arches, with gates at either end, and protruding machicolations which enabled the inmates to drop unpleasant missiles on anybody who dared approach. The English, who spent a long time outside Cahors in the Hundred Years' War, never even tried.

The fortress of **Bonaguil** is one of the finest survivals of late medieval military architecture, set somewhat eccentrically: not commanding the Lot or a vast expanse of fertile countryside, but in a remote and unproductive glen a few kilometres north of Fumel. Curiously, much of what remains was built in the early 16th century when most other

Pont Valentré, Cahors

people were erecting pleasure palaces. The fierce and reactionary lord
Bérenger de Roquefeuil preferred the style of an earlier, more warlike
age, and rebuilt the fortress at Bonaguil to repel the most determined
attackers who in the event never came. The defensive buildings of the
previous century were adapted to cope with new advances in artillery,
and the long and learned guided tour around the impressive but empty
buildings concentrates on these weighty technicalities of military architecture. In midsummer some musical evenings are held at Bonaguil.

South of the river Lot the countryside is increasingly fertile as it
approaches the Garonne, but it has no great variety or beauty. **Agen** is
the centre of a great fruit-growing area famous for prunes, plums and
fruit liqueurs. Its art museum has Spanish works of art collected by a
French ambassador, with a number of works by Goya.

Moissac is another unprepossessing town in the fruit belt which
suffered much from a great flood in 1930, none of which dims the
beauty of the cloister and main doorway of its great abbey church.
Together they make Moissac a high point of 12th-century artistic

achievement. The church itself, changed in the 15th-century, is not spectacularly beautiful. Below the solid squat belfry tower the south doorway is deeply recessed, which may have helped to preserve from weathering the majestic and awe-inspiring carving on the tympanum which represents the Last Vision of the Apocalypse, as seen and written by Saint John the Divine. The surrounding bands of ornamental sculpture are wonderfully decorative, and on the central pillar supporting the whole edifice the figures of Jeremiah and Saint Paul flank a pride of interlaced lions. The carvings around the doorway are more damaged – on the left various sins of avarice and luxury are punished and on the right a number of scenes from the New Testament are depicted. The large cloister is architecturally uncomplicated, the vault of each gallery being simply pitched and supported by wooden beams, so there is nothing to distract the eye from the endlessly fascinating wealth of carving on the capitals which support alternately twinned and single columns all around the cloister, earning its reputation as the most beautiful in France. Some of the capitals are ornamental and reveal classical influence; others depict imaginary monsters of oriental inspiration; others detail biblical and apochryphal scenes. To do these carvings justice, a detailed guide is essential.

Montauban is yet another large unattractive town, whose suburbs spread far and wide across the plains. It was a Protestant stronghold and most of its medieval buildings have been destroyed. The only compelling reason to go to Montauban is to see the museum named after and mainly devoted to Montauban's greatest son, the painter Ingres, born here in 1780. The museum has a superb collection of works of the artist, who set himself up as the champion of classical orthodoxy at a time when France was troubled by romantic (in the form of Delacroix) as well as political subversion.

East of Montauban, the Aveyron, which carves almost as intricate a path as the Lot, has a few places that are worth seeing. The old village of **Penne** and its ruined fortress are set dizzily on a promontory above the river. **Bruniquel**, named because this is where the Visigoth princess Brunhilda is thought to have built a castle, has links with Penne in being an old fortified town with a fortress standing on its perpendicular precipice above the river, and also in the frustrated inscription which can be seen in the Château, *'Rien sans peine'*, a pun on the name of the neighbouring fortress which the lords of Bruniquel wished to possess but never did.

Of all the ruined medieval fortresses in France, **Najac** perhaps enjoys the most romantic setting, and conforms best to our ideal. It stands on a conical rocky promontory which plummets 135 metres down to a meander of the river Aveyron. As you walk down its single street of picturesque grey medieval houses which leads along the narrow promontory up to the fortress, the massive cylindrical keep of the great castle looms majestically to monopolise your field of vision. The fortress is mostly the work of the great local fortifier Alphonse de

Najac

Poitiers, brother of Saint Louis, who as a royal representative in the days following the Albigensian crusade had reason to fortify himself. The church was also built in his time by the local inhabitants, who thereby earned absolution for their heretical leanings.

Villefranche-de-Rouergue is a 13th-century *bastide* which has outgrown its old grid; its central square is a splendid example of the style and unusually has an impressively massive church tower built into the square.

South of Najac, the beautiful medieval village of **Cordes** sits on top of an isolated symmetrical hill and, thanks to the Society of Friends of Cordes, has been admirably preserved and restored. Some of the old fortifications remain – it was built in the 13th century as a *bastide* by the Count of Toulouse – but its great distinction is the number of large and handsome Gothic houses with arched windows which line the main street through the town. Cordes was in the 14th century a prosperous centre for weaving and leather working. Recently artists and craftsmen have returned to the town, adding to its prosperity.

The large red town of **Albi** is not as a whole a place of beauty. After the murderous crusade against the Cathar (Albigensian) heresy, the 14th-century bishops still had to face popular uprisings; their awe-inspiring red-brick warship of a cathedral and adjacent bishop's palace were fortresses from a time when faith meant war and bloodshed rather than contemplation and joy. The cathedral's dedication to the Saint Cecilia – patroness of music – who smiles so sweetly from Renaissance paintings is not inappropriate: this early Christian martyr took three days to die in agony after three blows of the axe on her neck.

Sights in Albi

● **Cathedral** For all its severity, this is a magnificent building with a huge keep of a tower and a single vessel of a nave without choir or transept; its buttresses are like round towers, its windows like arrow slits. Within these forbidding walls there is a wealth of decorative interest. The early 16th-century porch on the south side of the church contrasts with the rest of the exterior, in colour and in its dense sculptural richness. Dating from much the same period is the enclosure built inside to make up for the lack of a choir in the architectural scheme of the building. This stone screen invites comparison with lacework and was described by Viollet-le-Duc as the last limits of delicacy and complication of Gothic forms. Amid the delicate tracery there is a very fine series of statues of apostles and sibyls, coloured and depicted with the realism of a portrait and in many cases with a sensuous materialism typical of decadent late Gothic art. The inside of the west end of the cathedral is decorated with an enormous fresco of the Last Judgement where the damned in their punishment are depicted with relish. The middle of the fresco, where Christ in Judgement used to be, was spoilt by the later piercing of a doorway. In the early 16th century the entire vault was painted by Italian artists with scenes of apostles and angels.
● **Palais de la Berbie** Inside the old bishop's palace there is a varied museum, of which the highlight is the unique collection of works by the artist Toulouse-Lautrec, who was born of noble parentage in 1864 in Albi, was crippled as a youth and grew up the obsessional and merciless observer of seedy and theatrical Montmartre life.

The large town of **Castres**, between Albi and Carcassonne, is well worth a visit. In the former bishop's palace there is a Musée Goya which contains some of the Spanish painter's works including a complete series of his etchings.

HOTELS

> Key: ◆ = 0–250FF, ◆◆ = 251–450FF, ◆◆◆ = over 451FF; prices are per double room without breakfast, which costs around 35–60FF extra. Some hotels may insist on half-board during high season, some hotels or restaurants may close at specific times during the week – it is always worth checking. Most hotels accept the major credit cards; we have indicated where a hotel takes no credit cards.

BEYNAC-ET-CAZENAC

Le Bonnet

24220 Dordogne
TEL 53 29 50 01; FAX 53 29 83 74

On a bend in the River Dordogne, at the foot of the medieval *bastide* town of Beynac, Le Bonnet's position is marred only by the busy main road that squeezes between the river and the gorge walls. Once inside the hotel, there's no real disturbance from the traffic noise and the first-floor terrace makes a popular spot for lunch. The Bonnet family runs a friendly household and the atmosphere in the rustic restaurant is informal and chatty. Bedrooms are old-fashioned and some have suspect plumbing, but if a clean, good-value room is what you're looking for, Le Bonnet is a good bet.

OPEN Early Apr to mid-Oct ROOMS 21 (all with bath or shower)

BOURDEILLES

Hostellerie Les Griffons

Brantôme
24310 Dordogne
TEL 53 03 75 61; FAX 53 04 64 45

The location, on the willow-lined bank of the River Dronne under the battlements of Bourdeilles' castle, is hard to beat. To make the most of the river, the restaurant extends on to a small terrace which catches the sunset beautifully. Most of the bedrooms also face the water, with windows opening on to the village's hump-backed stone bridge, though there's little traffic to disturb sleep. Inside, the décor is plush rustic: tapestry-covered chairs, animal skins and a grand ornamental staircase. Bedrooms have huge carved chalk fireplaces and beamed ceilings.

OPEN Mid-Apr to early Oct ROOMS 10 (all with bath)

BRANTOME

Le Châtenet

24310 Dordogne
TEL 53 05 81 08; FAX 53 05 85 52

Two km south-west of Brantôme on a quiet lane off the D78, Le Châtenet is a characterful old farmhouse. On one side of the courtyard, sweeping steps lead up to a 17th-century verandah and the main entrance, through which you reach eight large comfortable bedrooms; some are on a grand scale, with a mix of old-fashioned furniture and antiques. Across the courtyard a converted stable-block houses a rustic sitting-room with plenty of books and games. For sunny days there's a pool, better for plunging than swimming, and a full-size tennis court. Le Châtenet has no restaurant but there are plenty nearby.

OPEN All year, but call between Nov and April ROOMS 10 (8 with bath or shower) FACILITIES Heated outdoor pool, tennis

LE BUGUE

L'Auberge du Noyer

Le Reclaud de Bouny Bas
24260 Dordogne
TEL 53 07 11 73; FAX 53 54 57 44

It took five years for English couple Jenny and Paul Dyer to make a hotel out of their 18th-century farmhouse in peaceful green countryside 5km west of Le Bugue. Beautifully renovated, Auberge du Noyer has good-sized rustic bedrooms, with beams and exposed stone walls or pretty flowery wallpaper, and well-equipped bathrooms. Paul prides himself on a simple menu which changes daily and is made up of fresh local produce. The auberge makes a tranquil base for exploring the region.

OPEN End Mar to early Nov ROOMS 10 (all with bath) FACILITIES Outdoor pool

CALES

Le Pagès

Payrac
46350 Lot
TEL 65 37 95 87

Le Pagès makes a comfortable, good-value overnight stop in a quiet village of mellow stone buildings convenient for exploring the eastern Dordogne. Until recently the hotel was a no-frills family-run business, but since refurbishment it has become rather more luxurious while retaining its friendly atmosphere and inexpensive menus in the café-style restaurant. Rooms in a new block are large and characterful with spotless well-equipped bathrooms, and some overlook the large wild garden.

OPEN All year exc. 2 weeks end Oct ROOMS 20 (all with bath or shower)

THE DORDOGNE

CARSAC-AILLAC

Le Relais de Touron ◆◆

Le Touron
24200 Dordogne
TEL 53 28 16 70

The main attraction of this hotel is its large and lovely garden which has a good size swimming-pool as well as lawns and shady trees and a little river flowing through. Most bedrooms (simple but comfortable) are situated in a modern annexe and overlook the garden and pool, and so does the restaurant terrace. The food is local, homely and tasty. Le Touron stands on its own, half a kilometre outside the village of Carsac on the D704 road to Sarlat.

OPEN Early Apr to mid-Nov ROOMS 12 (all with bath or shower) FACILITIES Outdoor pool

CHAMPAGNAC-DE-BELAIR

Moulin du Roc ◆◆–◆◆◆

24530 Dordogne
TEL 53 54 80 36; FAX 53 54 21 31

The old walnut mill on the Dronne was converted in the late 1960s; you can still see the ancient grinding stone and the press incorporated into the lush (there is no other word for it) décor of the sitting-room – low-beamed ceiling, flowery chairs, carved oak doors, chests and columns, flowers, elaborate table lamps. The same baroque effect is achieved throughout the rest of the hotel, including the bedrooms, where several of the beds have canopies or are four-posters. To complete the idyllic never-never world picture, a bower stands by the river and a narrow curved wooden bridge crosses to more tree-shaded gardens and a secluded swimming-pool, which is covered in winter. Gourmet menus are excellent, though not cheap, and breakfast is a cut above average.

OPEN Mid-Feb to mid-Nov, mid-Dec to mid-Jan ROOMS 14 (all with bath) FACILITIES Heated indoor pool, tennis

CORDES

Le Grand Ecuyer ◆◆◆

rue Voltaire
81170 Tarn
TEL 63 56 01 03; FAX 63 56 18 83

This is an expensive hotel, but worth it for the glory of the building (a 13th-century stone Gothic house on the main street of this ancient, rich medieval town) and for the beauty of the furniture. Massive, simple cupboards, gilded mirrors and enormous stone fireplaces are everywhere. Every room has something wonderful to look at, and a very clever choice of fabrics means that every piece is shown off to best advantage. There is a sequence of sitting-rooms, some little more than comfortable corners, others with beams and deep sofas. The dining-room is cool and superbly elegant and the menus are surprisingly reasonable. For once, the suite is almost worth the extravagant cost – huge bathroom and luxurious furnishing, while the cheaper bedrooms are also worth the money. Some rooms have air-conditioning. This is a fine place to splash out in.

OPEN End Mar to mid-Oct ROOMS 13 (all with bath or shower)

DOMME

L'Esplanade

24250 Dordogne
TEL 53 28 31 41; FAX 53 28 49 92

L'Esplanade is at the top of the *bastide* town of Domme, with a brilliant view of the river gorge. People flock here for the sunset as much as for the food. The large restaurant is the focus of the hotel – a beautiful room with beams, potted plants and bright sunny yellow tablecloths, where a team of professional staff serves regional dishes including *cèpes* in various guises and their famous fillet of lamb in brioche. The bedrooms appear rather plain after the public rooms, but are well kept with good bathrooms. Late-comers find themselves rather cut off in the annexe down the road, so it's worth booking ahead and asking for a room overlooking the river.

OPEN Mid-Feb to mid-Nov ROOMS 25 (all with bath or shower)

LES EYZIES-DE-TAYAC

Les Glycines

route de Perigueux
24620 Dordogne
TEL 53 06 97 07; FAX 53 06 92 19

Les Glycines' friendly, informal atmosphere combined with its high standard of service make it very good value. At the quiet western end of the tourist centre of Les Eyzies, this hotel makes a good base for visiting the caves of the Vézère valley; the beautiful gardens and pool area mean you could happily spend a rest day here, too. Well-kept bedrooms, clean and comfortable rather than stylish, overlook either the road, the river or the garden where you can have breakfast and lunch. The smart restaurant serves regional dishes using fresh produce from its own riverside plot.

OPEN Late Apr to end Oct ROOMS 25 (all with bath or shower) FACILITIES Outdoor pool

THE DORDOGNE

Le Centenaire

Rocher de la Penne
24620 Dordogne
TEL 53 06 97 18; FAX 53 06 92 41

Treat yourself to dinner at Le Centenaire even if you choose not to stay here. On a road junction at the southern end of the village, the hotel's location is not its main attraction – though the pool area is prettily laid out. People come here chiefly for Le Centenaire's reputation for food. None of the menus is cheap, though the middle-priced set menu is good value. In the expertly run but unstuffy restaurant, uniformed staff serve regional favourites such as foie gras, truffles and lamb as well as caramelised fish, pigs' trotters and a dazzling range of puddings. Bedrooms are modern and well equipped, though not cheap.

OPEN Early Apr to early Nov ROOMS 24 (all with bath) FACILITIES Heated outdoor pool

GLUGES

Hôtel Les Falaises

Martel
46600 Lot
TEL 65 37 33 59; FAX 65 37 34 19

Backed by sheer limestone cliffs on the banks of the river, Gluges is a tiny medieval village some distance from the tourist bustle of western Dordogne, but within striking distance of the main routes heading north. On the edge of the village, Les Falaises is in a quiet spot and has a pretty vine-covered terrace. Service in the conservatory-style restaurant can be slow but the food is worth waiting for – regional dishes include trout, which was particularly good when we visited. Bedrooms are clean, simple and well decorated, though those on the second floor have very thin walls. Larger rooms are better value.

OPEN Early Mar to end Nov ROOMS 15 (all with bath or shower)

GOURDON

Hostellerie de la Bouriane

place du Foirail
46300 Lot
TEL 65 41 16 37; FAX 65 41 04 92

Staying at La Bouriane will not put you in Gourdon's medieval centre, but you'll be just a short walk away down the hill, in a quiet leafy suburb. A spruce white façade and a courteous greeting welcome guests. Attentive service extends to the bright, air-conditioned restaurant, where flowers and crisp pink clothes decorate the tables against the backdrop of a huge stone fireplace. Food is good value and beautifully presented, although it can be a little bland. There's also a summery residents' lounge and a sunken front patio shaded by chestnut trees. Bedrooms are very well maintained, with gleaming white bathrooms, though the décor is rather plain and unimaginative.

OPEN Mar to mid-Jan ROOMS 20 (all with bath or shower)

LACAVE

Le Pont de l'Ouysse

46220 Lot
TEL 65 37 87 04; FAX 65 32 77 47

At the end of a quiet road overlooking the Ouysse – a tributary of the River Dordogne – this hotel has a popular leafy terrace restaurant, a landscaped swimming-pool area and access to a small beach on the river. Combined with prettily furnished rooms, friendly professional service and good food, the hotel scores highly on all fronts. The restaurant has a particularly good reputation, and includes eel and crayfish for variety, in addition to the usual regional specialities like foie gras. Though still not cheap, the smaller rooms are good value for money.

OPEN Mar to Dec ROOMS 13 (all with bath) FACILITIES Heated outdoor pool

LALINDE

Hôtel du Château

rue de Verdun
24150 Dordogne
TEL 53 61 01 82; FAX 53 24 74 60

If lingering for a day or two in the western Dordogne, near Bergerac, you could do worse than base yourself at the little castle right on the banks of the river in Lalinde, complete with winding staircase and witch-hat turrets. It's part of the Logis chain, family-run and very easy going and friendly, with good regional cooking and newly smartened up bedrooms – all tastefully decorated in pastels with matching drapery. There are good showers or bathrooms – one, in room number 7, is positively palatial. For hot days there's a terrace above the river and even a little swimming-pool at the back.

OPEN Apr to Dec ROOMS 7 (all with bath or shower) FACILITIES Outdoor pool

---

Key: ◆ = 0–250FF, ◆◆ = 251–450FF, ◆◆◆ = over 451FF; prices are per double room without breakfast, which costs around 35–60FF extra. Some hotels may insist on half-board during high season, some hotels or restaurants may close at specific times during the week – it is always worth checking. Most hotels accept the major credit cards; we have indicated where a hotel takes no credit cards.

ROCAMADOUR

Les Vieilles Tours

Gramat
46500 Lot
TEL 65 33 68 01; FAX 65 33 68 59

In open countryside on a hill with vast views of the Alzou and Ouysse valleys, Les Vieilles Tours is a peaceful alternative to staying amongst the tourist frenzy of Rocamadour, 4km to the east. Dating from the 13th century, the hotel is a motley collection of former barns and outhouses with good-value rooms which vary in size and luxury, most leaning towards simplicity. Mealtimes are flexible – an encouraging sign of hospitality – and include late breakfasts around the pool, from where the views are best. Booking ahead is advisable.

OPEN Early Jan to end Oct ROOMS 18 (all with bath or shower) FACILITIES Outdoor pool

LA ROQUE-GAGEAC

La Plume d'Oie

24250 Dordogne
TEL 53 29 57 05; FAX 53 31 04 81

This auberge fronts the riverside road below the sheer rocks in the pretty though touristy village of La Roque-Gageac. The instant impression is one of space, neatness and light, with much use of tiles, stone and pale wood. The main attraction here is the food, with excellent use of local ingredients in a nouvelle cuisine-style presentation. Even the breakfast is mouthwateringly presented, and includes an artistically arranged fruit bowl. The creator of all these gastronomic delights is English (Marc-Pierre Walker); his Dutch wife, Hiddy, performs her front-of-house duties with friendliness and gusto.

OPEN Mar to mid-Nov, mid-Dec to end Jan ROOMS 4 (all with bath or shower)

ST-CIRQ-LAPOPIE

Hôtel de la Pélissaria

46330 Lot
TEL 65 31 25 14; FAX 65 30 25 52

The main attraction of this hotel is its location near the centre of St-Cirq-Lapopie, which clings dramatically to a cliff above the River Lot. The hotel is built into a steep slope so that many of the well-equipped rustic rooms have their own terrace with parasol and loungers, from which there's an uninterrupted view of the gardens and the gorge. The hotel has only seven rooms and a small restaurant, so you'll need to feel sociable; you are required to order dinner an hour in advance. Home-made fresh pasta dishes, smoked trout, delicious lamb with strong flavoured *cèpes*, and local cheeses make up a typical meal, and the male voice in the background music is a recording of your host.

OPEN Early Apr to mid-Nov ROOMS 10 (all with bath or shower)

ST-SAUD-LACOUSSIERE

Hostellerie St-Jacques

24470 Dordogne
TEL 53 56 97 21; FAX 53 56 91 33

In the centre of a small village in the northern part of Périgord, Hostellerie St-Jacques is an old ivy-covered coaching inn run by the friendly Babayou family. Recently refurbished in parts, the hotel has a mix of atmospheres – the sitting-room, with its grandfather clock and books, has an old-fashioned rustic feel, while the sunny restaurant, with its yellow tablecloths and windows open on to the garden, is more cheerful. Bedrooms are well equipped and comfortable, with simple furnishings and generally lots of space. Those overlooking the pretty garden and pool area are the most peaceful and the best value.

OPEN Apr to end Sept ROOMS 15 (all with bath or shower) FACILITIES Tennis, heated outdoor pool

VEZAC

Manoir de Rochecourbe

24200 Dordogne
TEL 53 29 50 79

As a bed-and-breakfast base from which to explore the Dordogne, Manoir de Rochecourbe is hard to beat. Its location 7km west of Sarlat, along with its 16th-century turrets and creeper-clad mellow stone walls, gives it bonus points for both location and romance, while the rest is down to the hospitality of the Rogers. The five bedrooms are named after wild flowers and are individually decorated with comfortable solid furniture, while the bathrooms are modern and good-sized. The sitting-room, with its heavy antiques, huge stone fireplace and beamed ceiling, has a baronial feel, while the breakfast room is warm and pretty, with deep orange walls and fresh flowers on every table. Madame Rogers' breakfasts are a cut above elsewhere too.

OPEN Mid-Jun to mid-Oct ROOMS 6 (all with bath)

Talmont

Give me my scallop-shell of quiet...
And thus I'll take my pilgrimage
[Walter Raleigh]

THE ATLANTIC COAST

If the Côte d'Azur sounds or has proved too expensive, too polluted, too noisy, too hot, too built up, too *mondain*; if its beaches are too few, too stony, too small, and too crowded; if, in short, your taste in beach holidays is for tides and waves, sands and dunes, not too many people and not too many trappings of sophistication, then the Atlantic coast of France, from the mouth of the Loire to the Spanish border, may be more to your liking. On the Côte d'Argent (south of the Gironde), a silver tongue of incoming and outgoing waves constantly refines the sands of exactly 288 kilometres of arrow-straight beach, interrupted only once by the oyster-rich bay of Arcachon. There are few resorts of any size, and nowhere is it so easy to have stretches of beach to yourself.

There is so much sand that before the dunes were stabilised by the planting of pine forests, villages near the sea were buried and it was feared that the mighty mercantile port of Bordeaux would in its turn disappear beneath hundreds of metres of shifting dune. So dangerous are the currents in the ocean that many of the modest bathing resorts have grown up inland, on the lakes that have formed in a row behind the dunes which deny marshy streams access to the sea. Because the area was a wilderness until the last century, the coast has no ports or towns of any age or picturesque charm. Where resorts have grown up, shanty villages are squashed between an infinity of pines and huge dunes which block all sea views. The beachscape is abstract – no crescent sands, no background hills, no rocks, no offshore islands, no promenades, no wedding-cake casinos – just Second World War blockhouses and litter not washed away by the tides but piled up at the high water mark beneath the dunes. Yet the peace and quiet and the pine forests behind the Landes coast do have their appeal, and the Bordeaux bourgeoisie has had its villas at Arcachon since the 19th century. Children love the sand, and most of the small resorts – particularly those on the lakesides – are family orientated. Recently the emptiness has attracted large numbers of impecunious travellers, who settle among the pines and live out their

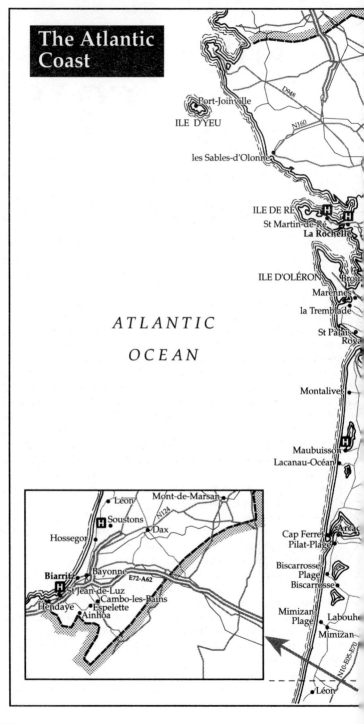

The Atlantic Coast

Port-Joinville
ILE D'YEU

les Sables-d'Olonne

ILE DE RÉ
St Martin-de-Ré
La Rochelle

ILE D'OLÉRON
Brou
Marennes
la Tremblade
St Palais
Roya

ATLANTIC

OCEAN

Montalivet

Maubuisson
Lacanau-Océan

Léon
Mont-de-Marsan
Soustons
Dax
Hossegor
Arcac
Cap Ferret
Pilat-Plage
Biarritz
Bayonne
Biscarrosse-
Plage
St Jean-de-Luz
Biscarrosse
Cambo-les-Bains
Hendaye
Espelette
Ainhoa
Mimizan-
Plage
Labouhe
Mimizan

Léon

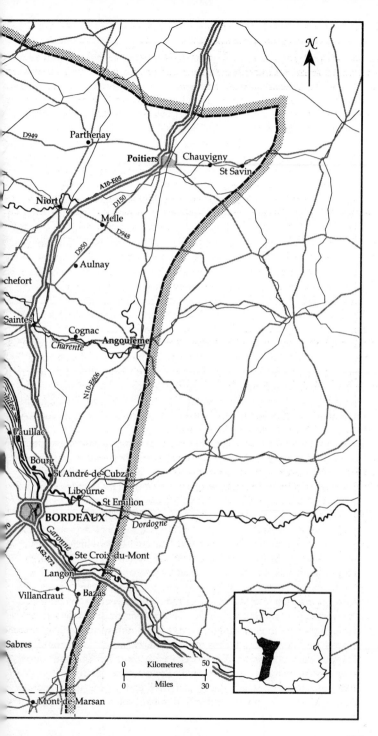

ideal of noble savagery, ignoring families and resorts. The comparatively recent development of modern complexes along much of the Landes coast (*Mission Aquitaine*), a similar project in a similar style to the development of the Languedoc coast, has resulted in resorts designed for convenience, with multiple facilities – campsites, self-catering flats, supermarkets, beach clubs and sports – but few hotels.

The interior of the Landes is the biggest pine forest in western Europe. One hundred and fifty years ago it was a desolate region of extreme summer aridity and winter floods. Its immense plains – as Dumas wrote, 'mottled with wild heather, like the skin of a huge tiger' – were the realm of skylarks, partridges, quails, bees and flocks of sheep led by shepherds walking on stilts through the mosquito-ridden marshland. Irrigation dried out the Landes, making it healthier; and the planting of pine trees started a resin industry. Now the area is becoming increasingly prosperous from tourism and the discovery of oil. But the landscape of the Landes today, its endless pines never changing in colour and never shedding their leaves, has an oppressive monotony all its own, with the piercing smell of pine and insistent grating of the strident cicada.

To the south of the Landes, the brief stretch of Basque coast is much more attractively varied; grassy Pyrenean foothills, adorned with colourful Basque villages, roll down to splendid beaches between rocky headlands where surfers enjoy the best waves in France. Biarritz had class and style once, and still has a little. St-Jean-de-Luz pulls in amateur artists and has an excellent, safe beach. The Basque resorts have more to offer than just the seaside; there are excursions into the mountains and to Spain, and there is the fascinating Basque country itself (see the chapter on the Pyrenees).

North of the Gironde, the Charentes and Vendée coast is less desolate and less straight than the Côte d'Argent, but almost as flat and almost as sandy. Resorts such as Royan and Les Sables-d'Olonne have a firm bucket-and-spade emphasis and not much chic. So gently do the beaches of much of this part of the coast shelve that reaching the sea at low tide means walking for miles across mud flats. It is oyster and mussel and salt-pan territory, and these traditional aspects of the maritime economy add some interest to a landscape which the writer and painter Fromentin described as 'a doubly flat horizon of land and waters, which takes on striking grandeur because of its emptiness'.

Like the coast, the inland region of Poitou and Charentes is flat, its horizons are huge and it has few of the obvious visual attractions and the variegated prettiness of rural France. For most tourists it is a through route with very straight roads to the south-west and Spain – as it was for medieval pilgrims on their way from Ile-de-France to Compostela. There is at least no chance of boredom for the tourist interested in medieval (and especially Romanesque) churches, frescoes and sculpture, with which Poitou is as well endowed as any region in France. Most of the towns in this traditional Protestant region present an austere, grey face to the passing visitor. Two exceptions are the ports of La Rochelle, a very attractive yachting and fishing port, and Bordeaux, an elegant, somewhat formal city of 18th-century bourgeois wealth, a mixture, in Victor Hugo's words, of Versailles and Antwerp.

The wealth of Bordeaux, without equal in 18th-century provincial France, came from trade, primarily in wine. The surrounding region – the two banks of the Gironde, and the four banks of the Garonne and Dordogne which flow into it – is the largest area of quality vineyards in the world; over a hundred million bottles of Bordeaux are exported every year to over a hundred countries. It is the area of Rothschilds (Lafite and Mouton), of Margaux, Latour and Yquem, of the *grands crus classés*, and of the noble rot which concentrates the sweetness of a very few Sauternes grapes to produce the greatest sweet white wines.

The wine trade has traditionally been dominated by the British, who adopted the Old French word *clairet* for Bordeaux red wine. The English controlled Bordeaux and Aquitaine for three centuries after 1154, when Henry Plantagenet (just married to Eleanor of Aquitaine) came to the throne of England. They developed a taste for claret, and gave Bordeaux privileged status which it was reluctant to sacrifice even when the English cause was lost. After the English departure, the claret connection remained; when the philosophical writer Montesquieu, proprietor of a château near Bordeaux, learnt that his books were selling well in London, his greatest joy was that it might help the marketing of his wine there. Wine labels still tell of the British involvement – Palmer, Talbot, Barton, Lynch; you may hear buyers and proprietors business-lunching in English.

Wine buffs will need no encouragement to visit the Bordelais, especially the Médoc region on the south bank of the Gironde, which comes close to the ideal of grand châteaux surrounded by vineyards with wines maturing in the cask in secular cellars beneath sumptuous reception rooms. Although the châteaux are well worth admiring, and in many cases visiting, it is not a place for the amateur to interrupt a seaside holiday for the odd free tasting – you may not be offered any.

When you are eating in an Atlantic coast restaurant, and the sea breeze turns your appetite to oysters or a *mouclade* (mussels in a white wine sauce), you may wonder why a region of seafood should be blessed with such distinguished red wines, which always heavily outweigh the few humbler whites on the local wine lists. Practical Bordelais will tell you that you can drink claret with fish, and if you are not open to this kind of *nouvelle dégustation*, there is always the magnificent game from the Landes to do justice to the finest of clarets. Your gastronomic experience of the Bordelais may be preceded and crowned by yet more alcoholic specialities: the local aperitif, *Pineau des Charentes*, a mixture of cognac and grape juice, and cognac itself. The publicity-conscious brandy firms (many of them also British in origin) are pleased to show tourists around their production lines.

The Vendée and Charentes Coast

The Vendée is a land of granite rocky hills south of the Loire estuary. Its only claim to historical fame is the war of repression which followed a royalist peasants' revolt a few weeks after the execution of Louis XVI. On 13 March 1793 news of national conscription reached the well-respected 'Saint of Anjou', Chatelineau, who put down the dough he was kneading and marched off with a few peasants wielding pitch forks. A couple of days later they took the town of Cholet, and by June were in charge of Saumur. Here Chatelineau was formally sworn in as *Généralissime* of the Royal and Catholic Army, in the first year of the reign of Louis XVII. Not long afterwards he met his death, but brutal repression and resistance went on for years in the unruly *bocage* of hedgerows and low trees and 14 rivers, not one navigable.

On the coast, the main resort is **Les Sables-d'Olonne**, a simple family resort, large and busy with an excellent beach. **Pornic**, to the north, is a pretty fishing port and rocky creek, without any good beaches.

A short way north of Les Sables lies the **Ile de Noirmoutier**; it is not always an island – there is a road across the mud at low tide, which is much more fun than the modern toll bridge from Fromentine, but only practicable for a few hours a day. If your car breaks down, or if you set out when the tide is coming in fast, you may have to climb one of the refuge poles, and watch the development of a major rust problem. The only village on the island is old and attractive, with a fortress, and a fishing port linked by canal to the sea. Nearby, there are woods and some very good beaches, but most of the island is wide open with salt-pans and oyster beds, and fertile farmland. Though by no means empty in summer, Noirmoutier is quiet.

From Fromentine, there are boats to the smaller, impressively rocky **Ile d'Yeu**, which is thoroughly Breton in character, with its rocky Côte Sauvage and its small sandy beaches on the sheltered north around **Port-Joinville**. From 1946 until his death in 1951, Marshal Pétain, premier of Vichy France, was imprisoned at Port-Joinville.

Between **Niort** and the sea, the Sèvre Niortaise is flanked by the **Marais Poitevin**, a network of waterways, mostly the work of medieval monks. The area is at its most picturesque inland; lush woodlands surround and overhang the mossy waters, and locals travel in large punts, if need be taking their cattle with them. The best (indeed the only) way to sample the beauty of this enchanted world is to take a boat trip, most easily done from **Coulon**, where there is also a small museum.

In the Renaissance age, **La Rochelle** was one of the greatest maritime powers in France, and the most proudly Protestant. It starved for 15 months waiting for English relief from Cardinal Richelieu's blockade. When Mayor Guiton opened the gates on 28 October 1628 there were only 64 French and 90 English soldiers left in the town, and they were too weak to lift their weapons. During the siege, the population of La Rochelle had declined from 28,000 to 5,000, and of those, 1,000 died almost immediately afterwards. When asked by Richelieu about his loyalties, Guiton remarked that he preferred to deal with a king who had conquered La Rochelle than with one who failed to defend it. Most of the defences of the town were pulled down, but the old port today is still guarded by three medieval towers. It is reserved for yachts and fishing boats; there are artists, smart quayside cafés, and severely handsome buildings around the domed clock-tower and archway. There are more sleepily charming ports in France, but none which has a more appealing combination of beauty and vitality. The main streets are full of attractively decorated and individually arcaded Renaissance houses, and offer good shopping. There are spacious gardens but only a small town beach. Of the several museums the most unusual is the Musée Lafaille, devoted to 18th-century oceanography, with many beautiful and interesting old exhibits. The coast around La Rochelle is particularly popular with the sailing fraternity, which contributes to the well-to-do, cheerful atmosphere. There are boat trips from the old port, and if you want to take your car across the water to the Ile de Ré, you can drive across the new toll bridge.

Just as La Rochelle stands out in terms of charm and style from other towns on the west coast, so wasp-waisted **Ile de Ré** stands out among the islands. Like the others, it is flat, and has an attractively mixed economy of salt, oysters and mussels, a little fishing, but also wine and farming. Compared with the other islands, its villages seem more brightly whitewashed, their shutters more brightly painted; and the Ile de Ré has history. In centuries past it had its own militia and fleet, and being exempt from national customs duties it became an important trading port. The old houses of its miniature but proud capital, the fortified port of **St-Martin-de-Ré**, tell of past prosperity. **La Flotte** is another attractive little port, and there are good long sands on the other side of the small island. In season, Ré is attractively and colourfully lively, and you can take boat trips and learn the local fishing techniques. Out of season, it is no less charming in a very different way – fishermen mind their tackle and their own business, and discuss life over a *Pineau* in cafés around the port. All year round, wealthy villa owners come to enjoy weekend seclusion among the pines.

The larger **Ile d'Oléron** has no ports of any age, but its sandy coast between La Cotinière and St-Trojan has very good beaches and is popular with campers. There is a toll bridge joining it to the mainland.

The east coast of Oléron is muddy and full of oyster beds; so too is the mainland coast between the two islands, although the resort of **Fouras** does have some sandy and sheltered beaches. **Rochefort** is a large and architecturally severe 17th-century military port, some way inland from the Charente estuary. There is little here for the tourist, except the house of novelist Pierre Loti, its interior a strange world of exotic oriental fantasy. Nearby **Brouage** is a lonely spot of melancholy beauty. Its compact 17th-century fortifications, intact but overgrown, look out over expanses of flat country which was ocean when Brouage was the busiest salt port in Europe, and the rival of La Rochelle. Now there are not enough houses to fill the walls and many are empty.

Many of the salt pans of the muddy half-land of this part of the coast have been turned to oyster farming. **Marennes** and **La Tremblade** (joined by a toll bridge) are the local capitals, with the characteristic oyster farmer's huts built on stilts in the mud. The coast between La Tremblade and Royan, at the mouth of the Gironde, is one of the major tourist areas of the Atlantic coast. The big resort of **Royan** was totally reconstructed after two short air raids in 1945 reduced it to rubble; it has a variety of very good beaches, and in season is very lively. Ferries cross the Gironde to the **Pointe de Grave** at the top of the Côte d'Argent. Among the trees on the edge of Royan, the sedate villa resort of **St-Palais** escaped the bombs. To the north, where the Gironde becomes the Atlantic, the coast becomes grandiose, with rocks and spray; at **La Grande Côte**, bathing is dangerous even in calm weather. Around the cape, where you can visit the lighthouse of La Coubre, there are enormous beaches with very few tourists (they have to walk some distance from the forest road). At **Ronce-les-Bains**, a popular resort for families camping, beaches are muddier but more sheltered.

Poitou and Inland Charentes

Although the landscape is no great enticement to venture inland from the coast, there are plenty of sightseeing opportunities for a rainy day, particularly attractive to those with a taste for Romanesque architecture. **Poitiers**, not as a whole a town of conspicuous charm, has a number of very interesting churches, and is at the centre of a region which produces France's best goat's cheese; it is also an important town in the history of France. In 732, Charles Martel reversed the tide of Saracen invasion near Poitiers; in 1356, the Black Prince routed the flower of French chivalry in a few hours before lunch, taking twice as many prisoners as he had English troops.

Sights in Poitiers

• **Baptistery** Isolated on a main street roundabout, this is one of the oldest Christian buildings in France, dating partly from the 4th century. Despite alterations in later centuries, there are many classical elements in the architecture and beautiful medieval frescoes inside.

• **Notre-Dame-la-Grande** On the market square, one of the most famous churches in France, thanks to the blackened and damaged but richly decorated façade – the finest example of the great feature of Poitevin Romanesque. A rather gloomy interior, with 19th-century repainting, but a beautiful choir and vault fresco.

• **St-Hilaire-le-Grand** Surprising, eccentrically planned Romanesque church with a row of domes, seven aisles and some delightfully carved capitals.

• **Cathedral** Bright, spacious Gothic cathedral, which seems conventional by comparison with the other churches; 13th-century choir stalls.

• **Palais de Justice** 19th-century buildings enclose a medieval tower of the Ducal Palace, and the magnificent 13th-century Gothic Salle des Pas Perdus. It was here that Joan of Arc was grilled for hours by the learned doctors of the University of Paris, who could find no fault with her.

• **Futuroscope** A jazzy modern theme-park of the cinema, with glass buildings and many special effects.

Within a 48-kilometre radius of Poitiers, there is a high concentration of very old and beautiful churches, of which the following selection is not exhaustive. To the north-west, **St-Jouin-de-Marnes** is outstanding; others are at **Parthenay-le-Vieux** (just outside the attractively situated small market town of Parthenay), and the exceptionally well-preserved pre-Romanesque church of **St-Généroux**. To the east of Poitiers, **Chauvigny** on the Vienne has an impressive fortress and church grouped on a hilltop above the town – the church is excruciatingly restored, but has marvellous capitals around the choir; quietly set beside the river on the southern edge of town, the church of **St-Pierre-les-Eglises** has 9th-century frescoes. Of all the Romanesque churches in the region, **St-Savin-sur-Gartempe** (east of Chauvigny) is the one whose beauty will most surely endure in the memory; it is a large and graceful old abbey church with tall belfry, between the river and a wide market square. The narthex is decorated with vivid frescoes of the Apocalypse, a foretaste of the magnificent series of paintings all along the high barrel vault, which have earned St-Savin its title 'the Sistine chapel of medieval France'. There are binoculars for rent outside, and detailed explanatory leaflets, both advisable for appreciation of the Old Testament scenes, depicted in harmonious tones of red and yellow ochre and green. The crypt also has marvellous frescoes, much closer to the eye.

On the pilgrimage route south of Poitiers, **Melle** has three Romanesque churches worth admiring, but not one to compare with **Aulnay**, which stands in isolation beside the road among cypresses. It is the very image of a pilgrimage-road church, and has one of the most beautiful of all Poitevin doorways, with decorated arches.

Saintes does not make much of its interesting monuments, apart from a Roman archway which used to stand on a bridge across the Charente, but now graces one of its banks. The town has long tree-lined avenues, and whitewashed houses giving a foretaste of the coastal style. River cruises up and down the indolently meandering Charente can be taken from Saintes and Cognac.

Sights in Saintes

- **St-Eutrope** Once an important pilgrimage church, with a very beautiful Romanesque underground sanctuary.
- **Roman amphitheatre** Well preserved, and attractively set near St-Eutrope.
- **Abbaye aux Dames** One of the many abbeys famous for the education of noble females under the *Ancien Régime*, subsequently used as a barracks. The Romanesque church has been restored, and houses a photographic display illustrating local architectural features.

Perched photogenically on a rock above the waters of the Gironde south-west of Saintes, the church of **Talmont** is one of the most charming examples of Saintonge Romanesque.

Saintes is on the edge of the region with the highest quality cognac production, to the south of the Charente around Cognac itself. The *appellation* of Cognac covers a large area, including the Charentes coast and islands. The white grape vines of the region are not in themselves

Amphitheatre, Saintes

especially distinguished, and the hierarchy from modern Bois Ordinaire to Grande Champagne has less to do with the grapes than the alchemy of the distillation process and the ageing of the spirit in the wood (split, not sawn) of Limousin or Berrichon oaks, which give different brandies their particular characteristics. The history of cognac goes back to the Renaissance, when Dutch wine shippers (who had moved in to take the place of the expelled English) thought of distilling the wine to reduce its volume and ensure its long conservation. They called it *brandewijn* (burnt wine), whence brandy. In the 17th century, as Bordeaux produced better and better wines, it became clear to the Charentais that their wine was only good for distilling. Like champagne, the cognac business is dominated by big firms (mostly concentrated in Cognac). They blend their brews to ensure that the taste is always the same, and produce a range of brandies which differ in quality according to the age of the various ingredients of each blend, from three star to VSOP. Cognac can mature for up to 50 years in the cask; once in the bottle it does not improve.

The town of **Cognac**, blackened by microscopic mushrooms which thrive on the alcoholic atmosphere, has little sightseeing apart from the cognac houses. The tourist office has information about visits, which reveal the blending and production lines, but not the distilling: this is carried out by thousands of *vignerons* throughout the region.

At the eastern edge of cognac country, **Angoulême** is a thriving large town whose commercial centre is situated high above the Charente. Stop here to shop or look at the domed cathedral, restored by Abadie in the 19th century almost as hideously as St-Front at Périgueux; the future architect of the Sacré-Coeur in Paris added to the exotic silhouette, but could not spoil the marvellous carvings all over the main façade, which include splendid battle scenes. Much restoration work has taken place in Angoulême in recent years, as well as new and innovative building projects, including the new comic museum.

Bordeaux and its wine area

Of all the great wine-growing areas of the world, few can match the Bordelais for quality and none for quantity of quality. **Bordeaux** is an ideal base for the viticulture vulture. There are small hotels in the centre, or, if you prefer, large modern business hotels on the edge of town; there are plenty of good restaurants, and in the centre of town, the Vinothèque is an excellent wine shop to fill your picnic hampers with the clarets you cannot afford in restaurants. Central Bordeaux is a splendid mixture; there is grand 18th-century monumental architecture, appropriately in this trading port at its finest along the *quais* around the magnificent Place de la Bourse (commercial exchange).

Later in the century, the prosperous bourgeoisie demanded entertainment; the Grand Théâtre is classically restrained outside, sumptuously decorated inside – its domed staircase was the inspiration for the Paris Opéra a century later.

Sights in Bordeaux

- **Old town** Between the theatre and the cathedral, elegant pedestrian shopping areas and narrow old streets and squares. Lively restaurants and bars, many open late. Medieval fortress gateway (Porte Cailhau), turned into a triumphal arch; and a 15th-century belfry (Grosse Cloche).
- **Cathedral** Large and imposing 11th- to 15th-century mostly Gothic church, with very beautiful carvings on the exterior doorways.
- **Musée des Beaux-Arts** A well-endowed and varied museum of paintings (including Titian, Van Dyck and Delacroix), etchings (Goya) and sculpture, in part of the 18th-century Archbishop's Palace.
- **Musée des Arts Décoratifs** Excellent silver, porcelain, locks and regional furniture
- **Musée de Chartrons** Collections of wine labels, aged bottles and other wine-related exhibits.

In general, the Bordeaux vineyards lack the charming country villages, simple accommodation and even the restaurants that are such an attractive component of wine touring elsewhere in France. The notable exception is **St-Emilion**, a beautifully situated small town, old and confined within well-preserved ramparts on a horseshoe hill surveying its own subsection of the Bordeaux vineyards. St-Emilion has a good range of accommodation, a monolithic church carved out of the hillside, a medieval fortress, and beautiful houses of golden stone.

Most of the vineyard country is flat and dull, none more so than the **Médoc**, but this is the area of the greatest wines (with a few honourable exceptions) and the most impressive châteaux, which makes it worthwhile driving through even if you have no intention of paying any visits. Some of the finest châteaux to be seen from the road are Issan, Margaux, Palmer and Cos d'Estournel. On the banks of the Gironde stands Vauban's eerily desolate **Fort-Médoc** citadel, which defended the Gironde with the help of the fortified port of **Blaye** opposite. Blaye's citadel is not empty but encloses a campsite and hotel. Inland vineyards are more attractively hilly and rural, especially the **Sauternes** between the Garonne and the Landes. Even if, as is to be feared, you are denied access to Château d'Yquem, home of the world's finest sweet white wine, the medieval château is worth admiring and you can contemplate the vines, each of which produces just a single glass of wine a year. Across the river, attractive **Ste-Croix-du-Mont** has a picturesque group of church and château on a cliff-top terrace.

Visiting Bordeaux vineyards

If you want to do more than admire châteaux from the outside, advance organisation is necessary for the majority of Bordeaux vineyards. Either make an appointment through a wine merchant at home, or contact one of the wine information bureaux below for details of châteaux which receive visitors and offer tastings.

In Bordeaux, the Office de Tourisme arranges vineyard coach tours daily from May to October and twice weekly in winter. The Maison du Vin, 1 cours du 30 Juillet, Bordeaux, 33000, tel: 56 00 22 66 can give information on vineyards all around the Bordeaux area and has touring maps showing the châteaux. Centres in the individual wine-producing areas have their own *maisons du vin* which offer more detailed local information, and some sell wines; these include the Maison du Vin de Pauillac, 33250 Pauillac; Maison du Vin de Margaux, 33460 Margaux; Maison du Vin de St-Estèphe, 33250 Pauillac; and the Maison du Vin de St-Emilion, 33330 St-Emilion. For information about the *crus bourgeois*, contact the Syndicat des Crus Bourgeois du Médoc, 24 cours de Verdun, 33000 Bordeaux, tel: 56 44 90 84.

Instead of, or in addition to, *maisons du vin*, some areas (including Pomerol, Barsac, Ste-Croix-du-Mont, Côtes de Bourg) have informative *syndicats viticoles*. There are also many local co-operatives producing good-value blended wines; at most of them you are able to taste and buy (including a particularly good one in St-Emilion which sells a large range of vintage wines).

Ask at any of the *maisons du vin* for information on visiting the châteaux or get leaflets, such as Médoc *Découverte*, which have full details. Note that many châteaux are closed to visitors in August.

The Landes and the Basque Coast

Judged from the N10, which streaks through the Landes from Bordeaux to Biarritz, the pine forests which have replaced the sandy wilderness are not much of an improvement: Pyrenean views have been obscured, sheep and shepherds have disappeared. But the forest is not all pine, and in clearings among the trees – like pioneers' impressions on a new world – there are small rural communities with low farmhouses of painted timbers and patterned bricks, surrounded by fields of maize and tobacco and gaggles of geese. The most convenient way to find out about traditional life in the Landes is to take the small train from **Sabres** in the heart of the **Landes Regional Park** to the **Marquèze Ecomuseum**, which is indeed a preserved and reconstituted total ecosystem. There are explanatory displays about the sheep and

the bees which formed the basis of the Landes economy, and beautiful old farmhouses traditionally furnished.

In the Landes the great sports are rugby, *pelote*, and the *course landaise*, a bull-fight where, as in Provence, the bulls are not in danger: the *écartant* thrills the assembled crowd with virtuoso leaps at the very last second to avoid the bull's charge. Spanish-style *corridas* are also staged, notably at **Mont-de-Marsan**.

To the north of the forest, **Bazas** has a very attractive town centre, with old arcaded houses beside the cathedral looking down over an expanse of cobbles; nearby **Uzeste** has a surprisingly large and impressive Gothic church. The medieval **Château de Roquetaillade**, in a fine setting, is an entertaining example of 19th-century Gothic restoration, and the beautiful moated **Châteaux de Labrède** preserves the enormous library of the 18th-century philosopher Montesquieu. To the south, sedate **Dax** is a famous hot-water spa, with a hot spring right in the middle of town.

Along the Landes coast the beaches vary little, except within the large **Bassin d'Arcachon**, emptied almost completely twice a day by the tide. If you stay around the basin, expect at best muddy bathing. It is an area of oyster farms, and stalls by the road sell oysters very cheaply. There is also a bird reserve, **Le Teich**, open to visitors (signposted walk and explanations). **Arcachon** is large, and by the standards of the Atlantic coast lively and smart; there is a promenade, shaded with small pines, and a spanking white casino, looking out over the pier to Bird Island. Arcachon's beaches are less good than the ones to the south, around the peaceful and prosperous resort suburbs of **Pyla-sur-Mer**, and **Pilat-Plage** which nestles among the pines beneath the elephantine bulk of Europe's biggest dune (114 metres). You can climb the sand at the expense of considerable energy, or use a staircase. From the top there are magnificent views across the mouth of the basin to Cap-Ferret, its waters usually flecked with sails, and over the pine forests behind.

Cap-Ferret, set on the sheltered side of the point which almost encloses the Arcachon basin, is a quiet, small but sprawling resort, whose beaches – on the Atlantic and Arcachon sides – are linked by a miniature train service. An old rig fenced off from the curiosity of tourists nods up and down in perpetual motion in the middle of the sands.

North of Arcachon, the **Côte d'Argent** is within afternoon sunbathing range of Bordeaux. The main resorts, old (turn of the century) and new, are situated around the two large lakes of Carcans and Lacanau, and on the ocean beyond the dunes. The most attractive village resort is **Le Montant/Maubuisson**, a quiet leafy little lake port with a large beach. At **Bombannes** there is a new forest and lake recreation centre for campers, sailors and self-caterers. Further north, **Montalivet-les-Bains** is one of the oldest and most traditional of the Landes coast resorts, with a large naturist centre in the forest nearby. At **Soulac-sur-Mer** a Romanesque pilgrimage basilica (Notre-Dame-de-la-Fin-des-Terres), which disappeared under the accumulating sand dunes in the 18th century, has been partly disinterred.

To the south of Arcachon are more lakes between forests and dunes, with water-sports and camping; the **Lac de Parentis** is distinguished by oil rigs and a military zone. **Port de Maguide** is the most lively tourist complex, **Gastes** is more of a real village resort. The towns of **Biscarosse** and **Mimizan** are useful service areas for campers, and both have their substantial seaside resorts nearby. South of Mimizan, the Landes coast is at its emptiest, with an occasional track from the forest road down to a few shacks beneath the dunes. At **Léon**, there is a small lake with some amenities, including a naturist colony; you can take a boat trip down the **Courant d'Huchet**, which has almost sub-tropical vegetation, and a wealth of noisy birdlife. At the southern end of the Côte d'Argent there is a concentration of resorts of which the most important is **Hossegor**, with a canal linking lake and beach. Lakeside Hossegor has the more style, a safer beach, and an attractive Basque influence.

The **Basque coast** combines long sweeping curves of sandy beach with the beauty of cliffs and rocks which, with the Biscay gales, make surf. To veterans of the Riviera, the Basque Corniche road is a disappointment, the summer weather is less reliable, and the pace of life in the resorts strung from Biarritz to the Spanish border is also considerably less hot. **Biarritz**, queen of the coast, has a beautiful setting on tamarisk-covered rocky headlands, three beaches (the surfing one should be treated with respect) and two casinos. But it has kept little of its style, except Empress Eugénie's villa – now the sumptuous Hôtel Palais, which stands above the ocean, imperially aloof from the march of time; the old villas and the Russian Orthodox church are peeling, and summer visitors are an ill-assorted mixture of self-sufficient self-caterers, surfers and a nostalgic older generation. There is a lack of middle-range and inexpensive accommodation and restaurants.

Although Biarritz does not look Basque, it is, and its sea-faring inhabitants used to be whalers when whales abounded in Biscay Bay; now there is only a token fishing port beneath the rocks. **St-Jean-de-Luz** has maintained its traditional fishing activity, and remains an important and colourful tunny port. It is an exceptionally attractive resort – old, picturesque of setting and architectural style (painted Basque timbers), smart and lively. Artists, art galleries and cafés surround the port, and the beach (exceptionally for this part of the coast) is as safe as it is sandy, for St-Jean-de-Luz is on a deep and sheltered bay. You can visit the old house beside the port where Louis XIV waited a month in 1660 for his Infanta to be delivered; the marriage took place in the church of St-Jean-Baptiste, which is a splendid example of the Basque style, with a massive gilt altar-piece covering the east end, wooden galleries around the walls, and a painted wooden vault. The adjacent fishing village of **Ciboure**, with its handsome Basque houses reflected in the water, is unaffected by tourists.

Hendaye, railway station border town beside the Bidassoa, on whose bridge many historic encounters between French and Spanish rulers took place, has two parts. The town, set back from the ocean, is bustling but without particular appeal; the resort – which sprawls along the whole length of an enormous sand beach – is well kept, pleasantly old-fashioned and spacious, but suffers from a lack of focus for its seasonal animation.

HOTELS

Key: ◆ = 0–250FF, ◆◆ = 251–450FF, ◆◆◆ = over 451FF; prices are per double room without breakfast, which costs around 35–60FF extra. Some hotels may insist on half-board during high season, some hotels or restaurants may close at specific times during the week – it is always worth checking. Most hotels accept the major credit cards; we have indicated where a hotel takes no credit cards.

MAUBUISSON

Hôtel du Lac

33121 Gironde
TEL 56 03 30 03

Maubuisson is one of the most attractive lakeside village resorts on the Côte d'Argent, and this hotel is right in its centre. It is a seafood restaurant with rooms, with emphasis on the former – a large open room filled with plants and with tables spilling on to an outside terrace. The bedrooms are plain and clean – half of them are located in an annexe.

OPEN Apr to end Sept ROOMS 40 (20 in annexe, all with shower or basin/bidet)

LA ROCHELLE

Hôtel François 1er

13–15 rue Bazoges
17000 Charente-Maritime
TEL 46 41 28 46; FAX 46 41 35 01

A mellow stone neo-classical gateway leads into a small cobbled courtyard and the entrance of the hotel; it's a very peaceful spot in the heart of the old town, with everything La Rochelle has to offer within walking distance. The style of the décor throughout is formal and pleasant. There is a neat breakfast room, but no restaurant – plenty can be found nearby. The private parking comes in handy, as spaces are limited in the old town.

OPEN All year ROOMS 38 (all with bath or shower)

ST-JEAN-DE-LUZ

La Devinière

5 rue Loquin
64500 Pyrénées-Atlantiques
TEL 59 26 05 51

This precious little hotel is located on a pedestrianised street in the centre of the resort. It has high-quality antiques and small, but luxurious, bedrooms. You can have breakfast in your room, at a large oak table in the ante-room of the lounge or in the tiny garden.

OPEN All year ROOMS 8 (all with bath)

La Fayette

20 rue République
64500 Pyrénées-Atlantiques
TEL 59 26 17 74; FAX 59 51 11 78

One of several little hotels in the heart of St-Jean's main restaurant street, La Fayette is just moments from the beach and not much further from the port. Bedrooms are fairly small, but comfortable; the restaurant is large and lively, with a terrace on the street. Food is plentiful and good value, with the emphasis on Basque specialities and fish. The whole place has a busy atmosphere, very much in keeping with St-Jean itself.

OPEN All year exc. mid- to end Jan ROOMS 18 (all with bath or shower)

ST-MARTIN-DE-RE

Le Galion

allée de la Guyane
17410 Charente-Maritime
TEL 46 09 03 19; FAX 46 09 13 26

On Ré, this bed and breakfast establishment is a good base for exploring the island and enjoying the lovely little capital port. The building is modern and purpose-built, all in good condition and decorated in a pleasant, light, if a little bland, style.

OPEN All year ROOMS 31 (all with bath)

SOUSTONS

La Bergerie

avenue du Lac
40140 Landes
TEL 58 41 11 43

Soustons is one of a concentration of resorts at the southern end of the Côte-d'Argent, by the lake between forest and dunes. It is a friendly family-run place, in spacious and neat-lawned gardens. The sitting-room is formal and laden with antiques; bedrooms are old-fashioned in a pleasing way, with some large bathrooms.

OPEN Mid-Mar to mid-Nov ROOMS 12 (all with bath)

(For more hotels near the Atlantic Coast see also the Pyrenees Hotels on pages 282-6.)

Château de Montsoreau

I love thin slate more than hard marble, my Gallic Loire more than the Latin Tiber . . . and more than the sea air the sweetness of Anjou
[Du Bellay]

THE LOIRE VALLEY

The Loire is France's longest river, running more than 960km from its high volcanic source in the south-east of the Massif Central to the Atlantic coast. But the area called the Loire Valley or *Val de Loire* is only a part of the course of this great river, which changes character many times as it descends, slows down and widens. It is a section of the Loire in its maturity, after the definitive change of direction westwards (the Orléans loop) and before the seaward stretch, and it is also the area of tributary river valleys north and south.

The *départements* making up the Loire Valley are many, and significantly all named after rivers – such as Cher, Eure-et-Loir, Indre-et-Loire and Loir-et-Cher, but not 'Loire' which is in the Massif Central, a long way upstream. These divisions mean less than the provinces familiar from all our history books: Anjou, land of mighty medieval warlords and home of the Plantagenet kings of England; Touraine, bountiful heart of Loire châteaux country, so-called garden of France and the only French region that has never borne the yoke of a foreigner; the Orléanais, where the tide of the Hundred Years' War was dramatically turned; and the wooded and agricultural Berry, rich in treasures from the Middle Ages and Renaissance.

This part of the Loire Valley is one of the most popular tourist areas of France, the simple reason being its unique endowment of Renaissance châteaux. Without them the area's historical associations, its convenience to Paris and even England for weekend visits, its good wine and food and its pleasantly fertile landscapes would attract no more visitors than other areas. The Loire's peculiar richness in châteaux is not just luck: from the time of the Hundred Years' War (when the English and Burgundians kicked the kings of France out of Paris and the north), until the end of the 16th century (when Paris and the

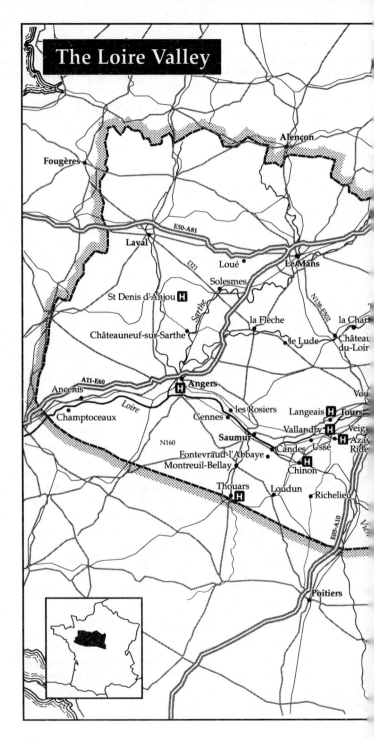

The Loire Valley

Fougères

Alençon

Laval

E50-A81

Loué

Le Mans

D21

Solesmes

St Denis d'Anjou Ⓗ

la Flèche

la Chart

Sarthe

Châteauneuf-sur-Sarthe

le Lude

Châtea
du-Loir

N138-E502

A11-E60

Ancenis

Loire

Angers Ⓗ

Vou

les Rosiers

Langeais Ⓗ Tours

Champtoceaux

Gennes

Vallandry Ⓗ

Veig

Saumur

Candes

Ussé

Ⓗ Azay
Ride

N160

Fontevraud-l'Abbaye

Montreuil-Bellay

Chinon Ⓗ

Thouars Ⓗ

Loudun

Richelieu

E05-A10

Vie

Poitiers

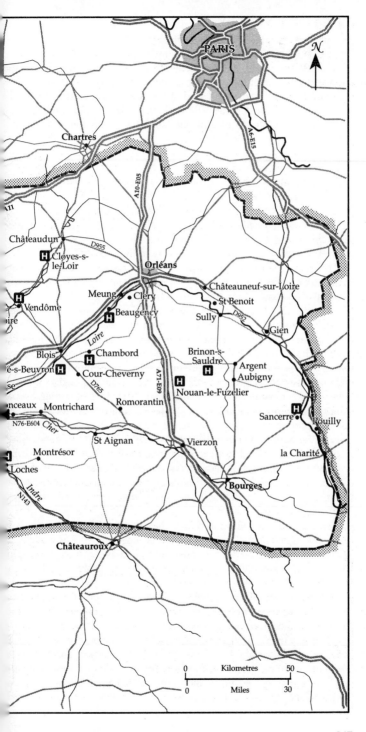

Ile-de-France became an irresistibly powerful magnet for the court), the monarchs and their retinue spent more time in the Loire than anywhere else – hunting, playing, and building châteaux.

At first the royal court reflected, in its lack of splendour, straitened royal circumstances. Charles VII, mockingly referred to by his enemies as the king of Bourges because his home town was the only one in France on whose loyalty he could depend, held court at Chinon – a fortress lacking in luxuriousness even before it fell into ruin. Joan of Arc found him here in 1429, despite his attempts at disguise, and stirred him into action with the result of the almost immediate relief of Orléans and the expulsion of the English from nearly all of France within 25 years. The end of this morally and financially sapping conflict coincided with developments both in the art of war and in the extent of royal power which made the fortification of houses and castles redundant. The fortress gave way to the château.

The end of the 15th century was a period of transition: the château at Langeais, built as a stronghold by Charles' son and successor Louis XI, looks like a medieval fortress on one side with its great barbican and drawbridge, but like a Renaissance dwelling on the garden side. Louis himself was a calculating political operator who had little time or taste for gracious living and preferred to spend his time in the modest château he had built at Plessis-lès-Tours (near Tours). His son Charles, whom Louis had installed with his mother at Amboise, was quite different, and his reign (1483–98) marks the beginning of the glorious century of courtly magnificence and gracious châteaux-building in the Loire. The spirit of the area seems to have changed very suddenly. A very important reason was the French awakening to Renaissance Italy brought about by Charles VIII's otherwise fruitless military campaigns there. The French fell not for Brunelleschi's Florence but the extravagant ornamentation of decadent Gothic buildings around Milan (the Certosa at Pavia is the accepted model for the architectural style of the Loire) and set about building their own Italianate Renaissance châteaux in the Loire Valley.

The typical Loire château is not, as châteaux in other areas are, a vast palace designed and situated to impress a sense of awe, but is rather a private dwelling for gracious and comfortable living, built by people bursting with new ideas and enthusiasm for embellishing rather than dominating the landscape. Loire châteaux seem to express not variations on a theme but personalities; Chenonceau's proprietor Thomas Bohier had as his motto, *'s'il vient à point me souviendra'* – roughly, 'if it (the planned château) is achieved they will remember me'.

Scenically the Loire Valley disappoints many visitors. The river itself, at least in this section, is not one of France's prettiest, and does not compare with the Dordogne, the Tarn, the Doubs or even the rivers of the Ile-de-France – so much more appreciated by painters. Between Orléans and Tours the Loire is wide and shallow, very often with unsightly mud banks divided only by a few thin streams of water. This makes the river unsuitable for the activities which attract active tourists – canoeing, boat trips, swimming. Its wide bed cuts little into the landscape: there are no steep riverbanks, and in many places the road along the Loire offers views across spacious fields on one side, while on the other an anti-flood bank obscures the river itself from view. So the Loire is a difficult river to admire, especially from any height. Its secretive tributaries are even more so, having made equally little impression on the soil and being flanked more often by woods than roads. The traveller arrives, having seen French Railway posters of Loire châteaux, and assumes that everything about the region will have the same picturesque qualities – Mosel-like vineyard-covered river-banks, Dordogne-like golden villages reflected in the sluggish water. To his dismay he finds that the Loire proclaims itself, *'Fleuve Nucléaire'*, and that great power stations loom over the landscape beside the historic ruins of Chinon castle and the elegantly prominent belfry of St-Benoît-sur-Loire. Many of the villages seem disappointingly grey and anonymous, and many of the finest châteaux do not make majestic river compositions, but are hidden away in the woods beyond.

Disappointment has a good pedigree; the traveller Arthur Young wrote of his impressions from a visit in 1787: 'The Loire for so considerable a river and for being boasted the most beautiful in Europe, exhibits such a breadth of shoals and sands as to be almost subversive of beauty'. Between Tours and Amboise he found the country 'more uninteresting than I could have thought possible for the vicinity of a great river'. But Young was intrigued by the cliff dwellings beside the river, inhabited then as now: 'Where the chalk hills advance perpendicularly towards the river they present a most singular spectacle of human habitations; for a great number of houses are cut out of the rock, fronted with masonry, and holes cut above the chimneys, so you sometimes know not where the house is from which the smoke is issuing. The people seem satisfied . . . a proof of the dryness of the climate. In England the rheumatism would be the chief inhabitant'.

These reservations are not the whole truth, and if you have time and inclination to explore minor roads along the river you may acquire a taste for the subtle beauty of parts of the valley. They will not quench a thirst for the spectacular, but if the time, the weather and the light are right as you drive along the grassy south bank of the Loire downstream and across from Langeais, the farmworkers will be pedalling idly home, the poplars swaying melodically and shimmering like olive trees, the swallows skimming along the surface of the silvery water, and you will never again say without qualification that the Loire is scenically dull.

Considering the amount of tourism and the importance of the river it is surprising that the area isn't more commercial and industrial. One reason has been the river's impracticability, over the last two centuries, for heavy traffic. Another has to do with the quality of the tourism: people come to visit châteaux and to eat and drink well, not to pass the time of day in bars and tourist shops, and the time of night in discos. Relatively few local people seem to be involved in or affected by tourism.

One aspect of tourism which does thrive is the hotel business. The people of the Loire, and of Touraine in particular, have long enjoyed other people's enjoyment of it. Elizabeth Strutt wrote of her stay at the Hôtel du Faisan in Tours in 1832: '. . . we sat down to a *table d'hôte* served with all the variety and profusion which renders travelling on the direct roads in France a luxury rather than a privation to those who may make a gratification of their appetite a primary consideration: sixteen or eighteen dishes including soup, fish, ragout, roast meats and winged fowl of all descriptions, with creams, fruits and dessert was the bill of fare, for 2 francs and a half, including excellent wine and the attendance of the best humoured and most civil servants I ever saw'. The coachloads of affluent culture-cravers spending two days of their French week in the Loire have of course had their effect on prices and quality in some establishments, but these are usually easily identified (if only by the coaches) and avoided.

The Loire from Sancerre to Orléans

This region, bounded to the north and east by the Loire as it describes its slow westward bend, is not châteaux country, nor scenically typical. Extremely attractive exceptions to the general flatness of the lower Loire valley are the hills of the Sancerrois, which give extensive and beautiful views and which produce the most prestigious and delicate of Loire white wines. **Sancerre** and **Pouilly-sur-Loire** (centre of Pouilly-Fumé production) are the best places to taste and buy, with lots of direct growers' outlets in the two villages. Sancerre is the more attractive of the two, finely situated on a round hill topped by a 14th-century round tower with views over the river and the vineyards; it is a pleasant place to stay or pause for a wander around the old streets. To admire the remarkable setting of Sancerre at its best, take the little road through the hills to Vailly (towards Bourges), and look back.

Gien is a much larger town on the water's edge, carefully restored after heavy war damage. The view across the river is imposing: the vast château with its turrets and patterned red brick walls (more like nearby Burgundy than the Loire in this respect) looks down over the town and its very handsome, squatly buttressed old bridge. The main road along the river is the most animated focus of town life.

Sights in Gien

• **Château** The 15th-century building houses an impressive hunting museum, which justifies its adopted title of 'international' by having a lion's head as well as fauna more plausibly of local provenance. There are boars, bears, antlers, fine hunting paintings, prints and tapestries, weapons, horns and falconry-related items, all very well displayed.

• **Ste-Jeanne-d'Arc** Next door to the château and fitting well into its setting, this modern church is remarkable for having attracted nothing but praise. It may seem an unadventurous attempt to re-create a Romanesque church, with the added height and slenderness of pillar that modern techniques allow, but undoubtedly leaves a warm and harmonious impression. Terracotta capitals tell the story of Joan's life.

Sully-sur-Loire is a large riverside village dominated by the splendid, mostly 14th-century **Château de Sully**, which since the 17th century has been surrounded by its own moat separated from the river by an embankment and more recently a large campsite. It is one of those châteaux which looks magnificent and is rich in historical associations, but, like most of the Loire châteaux, has little inside. Swans glide along the still waters at the feet of massive round corner towers topped by swelling crenellations and conical roofs. Inside you are shown chilly medieval halls where Charles VII had two of his interviews with Joan of Arc, and where the young Voltaire, an exile from Paris, entertained with his plays the broad-minded Duke of Sully of the time. A modern (17th-century) wing was added by Sully's most distinguished duke, Maximilien de Béthune, one of France's most energetic and omni-competent servants, about whose working habits and financial acumen the guide will tell you much. The tour would be of minority interest were it not for a remarkable chestnut vault spanning the upper hall. The trees had their tops tied together as saplings so they grew to the required shape, and the beams arch unbroken from the floor to meet nine metres above like an inverted boat hull and have done so without restoration for over 600 years.

The unspectacular course of the Loire from Sully to Orléans is made memorable by two of the most interesting churches of the whole region. The **Abbaye de St-Benoît-sur-Loire** was a Benedictine abbey called Fleury until its monks rescued their founding father's remains from pillaged Monte Cassino at the end of the 7th century and earned St-Benoît its rechristening. The saint's relics made St-Benoît an impor-tant shrine, and by the 11th century the abbey could afford to erect the magnificent Romanesque church which still stands, with the relics still in the crypt. The most remarkable feature of the building is the vaulted porch supporting the belfry at the west end. One of the richly deco-rated capitals is signed by a justifiably proud Umbertus. Inside, the nave is tall and light; you can admire a sweetly sentimental alabaster

Virgin, but not go into the elegant chancel without a guide, for whom you apply to the bookshop next to the church where monks sell souvenirs and home-made sweets. Daily services in the basilica, with Gregorian chant, are open to the public.

At the end of the 8th century the abbot of St-Benoît and bishop of Orléans found his abbey too noisy for fruitful contemplation, and built himself a country place with its own small church a few kilometres downstream at **Germigny-des-Prés**. The church still stands in the centre of a small village, with a nave added later to the original Greek cross plan. The whole was restored so thoroughly in the last century that it is hard to believe it is one of France's oldest churches, but it contains a fine Byzantine mosaic which was executed, along with many others now disappeared, by a 9th-century artist from Ravenna.

Châteauneuf-sur-Loire promises much but yields little. What's left of the 17th-century château is the town hall, with a little museum devoted to the maritime history of the Loire and its tributaries.

Orléans is a large town spreading over both sides of the Loire at its northernmost point. The town centre is on the north bank, severe, grey and treeless. There are some good shopping streets with attractive arcades, but the general impression is of a stark, unadorned place, although not without things of some interest to see.

Sights in Orléans

• **Cathedral** The most curious thing about this building is that it represents an attempt (rare before the end of the 19th century) at restoration in the Gothic style of the original cathedral, partially destroyed in the 16th century. The attempt worked well enough for the architecture, but the sculptors working on the façade were clearly unable or unwilling to do their bit in the old-fashioned way. Inside, beautiful 18th-century carved panels surround the choir, open with the crypt and treasury to those prepared to undertake a guided tour.

• **Museums** Two of Orléans finest medieval *hôtels* house the fine arts and local history museums. A small museum in the so-called Maison de Jeanne d'Arc is devoted to the exploits of the Maid of Orléans, with documents and model battles.

• **Olivet** An attractive garden suburb of Orléans on the banks of the Loiret, with restaurants, and boat hire; popular at weekends.

• **Orléans-la-Source** A very fine array of labelled flowers, shrubs and trees in the park surrounding the bubbling spring which is the source of the Loiret, a resurgence of Loire water which takes an underwater shortcut from near St-Benoît, and runs only a few kilometres above ground before it rejoins the main river.

The Sologne and the Berry

The large area between Orléans and Bourges is quite different from other parts of the Loire valley – an infertile wilderness of marsh, meres and forest. Until it became the beneficiary of improvement schemes, the **Sologne** was suitable for neither healthy habitation nor profitable cultivation, so it has a small population and few buildings of note. Important exceptions are the châteaux of Chambord and Cheverny on its northern fringe (see pages 372 and 373).

The Sologne landscape has a somewhat desolate beauty, with isolated low red-brick and timber-framed buildings, and thatched hides and boathouses beside the ponds; the area is excellent for fishing and shooting (and popular with the Parisian weekend cottage set). The signed tourist route between Romorantin and La Ferté takes you through some of the most characteristic Solognescapes, but almost any by-road will do, even if it is only for a short detour from the road between Chambord and Cheverny. Anyone who has succumbed to the charm of Alain-Fournier's supremely atmospheric novel *Le Grand Meaulnes*, set in the southern Sologne, will see the area through his eyes as a melancholy, misty and mysterious land; but nobody seems to feel that way about the Brenne, a very similar region south-west of Bourges.

The main town in the Sologne is **Romorantin-Lanthenay**, childhood home of the future François I. The old centre of town seems to have changed little since his day – a few streets of picturesque brick-and-timber houses with a wealth of interesting carving on their pillars and beams. There are also attractive gardens beside the Sauldre, and an interesting local museum.

Other places of interest in the region include the charming miniature **Château du Moulin**, beautifully furnished in Renaissance style; and **Aubigny-sur-Nère**, an attractive small town with old gabled houses, which became associated with the Stuart clan after Charles VII made one member a gift of the town in 1423. Nearby is the very pretty **Château de la Verrerie**, where you can go on a guided tour to see an elegant Renaissance gallery and 16th-century frescoes in the chapel. Near **Argent-sur-Sauldre**, the Etang du Puits is a large lake with lots of facilities for water sports, fishing and swimming.

Stendhal's description of the prosperous, rolling agricultural region of the **Berry** as one of 'bitterly ugly plains' is unkind and inaccurate, but all the same there would be little to attract the Loire Valley tourist south through the Sologne were it not for the Berry's fascinating old capital, Bourges.

Bourges is a large town with unsightly industrial outskirts, but an unspoilt historic heart, to borrow the favourite pun of Bourges's most famous bourgeois son Jacques Cœur; he was a wizard trader who amassed vast fortunes from the East, and financed the French recovery in the Hundred Years' War single-handed, to be rewarded with jealousy, disgrace and exile before he could enjoy the palace he had built for himself in his home town.

Sights in Bourges

- **Jacques Cœur's Palace** This is one of the finest secular Gothic buildings to come down to us intact, albeit cold and unfurnished. Over the entrance, carved figures lean out of *trompe l'oeil* windows to greet you, setting a tone of witty decorative exuberance which is sustained inside on the carved fireplaces and in details all over the palace including Jacques Cœur's ubiquitous motto, 'nothing impossible to valiant heart'. There are also very fine wooden vaults, and a beautifully preserved ceiling painted by Fouquet in the chapel.
- **Cathedral** This mostly 12th- and 13th-century building, which dominates the town and the 'bitterly ugly plains', is one of France's great cathedrals, with marvellous Gothic and Romanesque carvings outside and beautiful, easily decipherable stained glass. The tall five-aisled interior is of grand proportions, and in the crypt lies the recumbent statue of Jean duc de Berry who commissioned the famous book of *Très Riches Heures*, now at Chantilly.
- **Museums** Two fine Renaissance town houses are the Hôtel Lallemant (history of decorative art) and the Hôtel Cujas (Berry Museum: local history, archaeology, folklore).

Excursions from Bourges

Three interesting châteaux lie due south of Bourges on the so-called Route Jacques Cœur.

Jacques Cœur's Palace

- **Château de Meillant** This is the finest of them, an early Renaissance château completed, like Chaumont, by the ex-Governor of Milan, Charles II of Amboise. Its exterior decoration rivals the exuberance of the Loire châteaux, and it has the added attraction of being inhabited and beautifully furnished.
- **Château d'Ainay-le-Vieil** A charming and surprising mixture of medieval fortress and Renaissance dwelling.
- **Château de Culan** A mighty medieval stronghold dominating the river Arnan, well-furnished with chests and precious tapestries, although not in period.
- **Abbaye de Noirlac** An old abbey on the banks of the Cher between Meillant and Ainay-le-Vieil, this is a typical and well-restored example of the simple Cistercian style of building; some of the monk's quarters are furnished.
- **George Sand country** For literary tourists. The area around **La Châtre** is the thickly wooded 'Black Valley' where Aurore Dupin de Francueil, later George Sand, grew up. She herself was much more interesting than her output, and her château at **Nohant** is full of souvenirs of her and her circle, the intellectual and artistic élite of mid-19th-century France. The château of La Châtre also contains a museum devoted to the 'good woman of Nohant'.

The Loire from Orléans to Tours

This stretch of the river is the heart of châteaux country, the royal Loire of the Renaissance kings. On the left or south bank the first place of interest west of Orléans is **Cléry-St-André**, distinguished only by its basilica – pilgrimage destination and burial place of one of its most devoted pilgrims, Louis XI. Inside the unadorned church, a 17th-century statue of the monarch kneels facing the miracle-working Virgin, as Young supposed 'praying forgiveness, which doubtless was promised him by his priests, for his baseness and his murders'. If you find the right house behind the church you can visit the vault where Louis's and other bones lie, and a beautifully ornate chapel with Renaissance decoration.

Meung-sur-Loire is a small town of medieval literary associations: Jean de Meung was the author of the greater if not better part of that allegorical compendium of medieval thought, the *Roman de la Rose*, and the more accessible poet Villon was imprisoned in the château. Church and château make a handsome picture at the centre of the well-preserved old town. One of the most important bridgeheads on the river, much fought over and still maintaining its military aspects and a fine, mostly old bridge, is **Beaugency**. The centre of town is dominated by a romantically ruined 11th-century keep, complete with circling rooks; it adjoins a later castle, now housing a regional museum. Old streets run down to the river from the central square; an isolated church tower stands, like a Californian redwood, with a road going through its trunk. In the Renaissance town hall you can admire a series of beautiful 17th-century embroidered panels.

Downstream it's no great wrench to tear yourself away from the Loire, disfigured as it is by the nuclear power station of St-Laurent-des-Eaux. A few kilometres north of Mer is the charming **Château de Talcy**, flatly situated on the southern edge of the Beauce plain. A fortified medieval keep hides a beautifully furnished Renaissance dwelling where Ronsard was fruitfully entranced by the owner's daughter, the Cassandra of his poems which allude to the large dovecot which is still there, but not to the even older wine press.

On the wooded fringe of the Sologne south of the Loire, François I chose to transform a hunting lodge of the counts of Blois into the enormous **Château de Chambord** (see page 372). Its fanciful roofscape of lanterns, chimneys, dormers and turrets looks out over a large area of forest, mostly a hunting reserve closed to the public, but crossed by magnificent straight avenues leading up to the château. There can be few more exciting drives in France than this, as the château, at first all but hidden behind the trees, slowly unveils the full majesty of its façade to your advances.

Further south still are the two villages of **Cheverny**, one (Cour-Cheverny) a popular place to stay, the other (Cheverny) famous for the most beautiful classical château in the Loire (see page 373). If you are deterred by the crowds, or even if you are not, the nearby **Château de Beauregard** is almost sure to be unfrequented. It is another of François's hunting lodges, but unlike Chambord is still inhabited, and full of character. You tug on a bell rope on the side of the house to summon a guide who shows a surprising and varied collection of things – caricature portraits in medallions over the porch, a gallery of fame with 363 portraits and a Delft tile floor, a small but choice art collection, and an exquisite little room decorated in the densely allegorical style of the 16th-century Fontainebleau School.

The road north takes you back to the river, the beaten track, and **Blois**, capital of the Renaissance Loire Valley. The lively and touristy town is impressively dominated by its great royal château (see page 371) on the flat top of a cliff, set back from the north bank of the river. It's an interesting (but hilly) place to explore, with pedestrian shopping streets and more picturesque old quarters down by the river.

Downstream, the **Château de Chaumont** (see page 372) enjoys one of the most perfect settings of all, its round towers half hidden among the trees of a gracious park on a hill above the river, giving splendid views. Not far south-east of Chaumont the **Château de Fougères** is almost contemporary but looks like something from a different age. It stands at the heart of a small village and shows no sign of the passing of the Middle Ages. It is none the less impressive for that and must have been even more so before the moat was filled in, the drawbridge thrown away, and windows installed in the thick curtain walls.

Back on the Loire's south bank, **Amboise** bears comparison with Blois, in most ways favourably; the town is smaller and prettier, the situation of the château (best admired from across the river) more picturesque and a tour around it of more varied interest (see page 371). There are other things to see too – a museum devoted to the postal service, and an attractive manor house (Le Clos-Lucé) where Leonardo da Vinci lived and died, and in which are displayed working models constructed from his mechanical drawings. Just over 3km south of the town an isolated pagoda stands on a hill, all that remains of the magnificent 18th-century **Château de Chanteloup**. You can climb up inside for an extensive panorama.

The road along the north bank to Tours passes the village of **Vouvray**, home of both still and sparkling white wines (with lots of buying and tasting opportunities), and numerous cave-dwellers.

Tours is today's large and thriving capital of the châteaux country, conveniently situated for exploration of the region, but with too much traffic on its long suburban arteries to make a good base, unless you have no car (there are lots of coach excursions from here). Dominant features of the town plan are two long straight boulevards which intersect at right angles near the station and tourist office and the pedestrianised old town in the north-western quarter. The main shopping street (Rue Nationale) had just been built when Arthur Young arrived, and duly impressed him: 'The entrance of Tours is truly magnificent, by a new street of large houses built of hewn white stone with regular fronts. This fine street which is wide and with foot pavements on each side is cut in straight line through the whole city from the new bridge of fifteen flat arches each of 75-foot span. Altogether a noble exertion for the decoration of a provincial town'. Fortunately Tours wasn't completely redecorated in the eighteenth century.

Sights in Tours

• **Old Town** The very picturesque medieval quarter around the Place Plumereau has been restored after heavy war damage. The narrow streets are full of interesting old houses, new shops and lively bars and restaurants (Tours teems with students, French and foreign). There are two museums, one with archaeological finds and medieval art, the other devoted to modern stained glass (*gemmail*). Two isolated towers are about all that remain of an enormous Romanesque pilgrimage basilica.
• **St-Julien** In the cloisters beside the imposing Romanesque tower a local wine museum has been installed in the old wine cellar.

- **Cathedral** Remarkably ornate façade crowned by twin Renaissance lanterns. Extensive view from tower. Earlier and conventionally Gothic interior.
- **Fine Arts Museum** Housed in the elegant Archbishop's Palace and full of treasures, mainly thanks to appropriation from demolished châteaux.

The Indre, Cher and Indrois

The Loire's prolific man of letters, Honoré de Balzac, was a more distinguished observer of man than nature but did leave some word paintings of the Touraine he loved best – the Indre Valley around his residence at Saché. The Indre is considered the most beautiful of the southern tributaries, meandering through woods and chalky escarpments; the Cher is bigger, but, like the Indre, lined with interesting châteaux. By far the most interesting of the châteaux is Chenonceau (see page 373), one of the highlights of any visit to the Loire. The village, curiously spelt **Chenonceaux**, does no more and no less than cater, very well, for tourists. One of the joys of staying there is being able to wander down to the château first thing to see it before the crowds arrive. The château that sits weightless on the Cher like a mirage is familiar from photographs, but somehow never fails to delight the eye when seen afresh.

Montrichard is a lively little market town beside the river, with its own beach and an old bridge that gives a fine view of the old houses overlooked by ruined keep and ramparts. The hillsides on the edge of town house troglodytes, and wine cellars where you can sample sparkling Vouvray.

Quietly hidden away at the end of an enclosed valley, the **Château du Gué-Péan** is a splendid late Renaissance building, tumbledown but being done up by the energetic owners, who also take paying guests. The guided tour is most informative about the scale of the task they have taken on, and the rooms shown contain a remarkable mixture of antique jumble – from Sicilian puppets to Talleyrand's gigantic waistcoat and photocopies of de Gaulle's will. More attractive than all this is the friendly, rather chaotic family atmosphere. There's a riding school in the outbuildings.

St-Aignan is another small town attractively situated by the river, climbing up wooded slopes at the foot of a Renaissance château. The solid late 11th-century church is more interesting, with lively capitals in the chancel and frescoes in the crypt.

Valençay is quite a drive from the normal Loire Valley tourist area, but worth the trouble. The village is well provided with accommodation and the château a magnificent example of the classical Renaissance, its great round towers domed and decorated with classical pilasters. Valençay's associations are mostly with the 19th century when it came into the possession of one of history's greatest diplomats, manipulators and political survivors, Charles Maurice de Talleyrand. The furnishings are luxurious, mostly in Louis XVI and Empire styles, and there are many beautiful *objets d'art*. Peacocks, cranes, black swans, sheep and deer wander around the surrounding park and gardens.

Montrésor is impressively situated beside the little Indrois. Its château was one of the many built in Anjou and Touraine in the late 10th century by the mighty count of Anjou, Fulk Nerra; within the well-preserved medieval walls is a late 15th-century manor, beautifully restored and furnished by its Polish owners. Originally the castle was built for the Basternay family who are commemorated by a splendid tomb in the elegant Renaissance church. The road on to Loches passes fragmentary remains of the Carthusian monastery of **Le Liget**, founded by Henry II in expiation for the murder of Thomas à Becket. The most interesting fragment is the round chapel with remarkable frescoes – ring the bell of the main building if you want to visit.

The fortified medieval city of **Loches** is preserved intact on a rocky hill high above the modern town and the Indre. You walk up through a fascinating Renaissance quarter of ornately decorated houses with a fine gateway and belfry beside the town hall, to the old city, entered by the 13th-century Porte Royale. Inside there are some elegant private houses and a number of historical monuments.

Sights in Loches

● **St-Ours** Romanesque church with a domed nave – unusual so far North. The outside, with octagonal pyramids covering the domes, is even more unusual.
● **Château and keep** Separate buildings at either end of the city walls, full of history, but little else. Agnès Sorel, first public royal mistress (of Charles VII) lived here; Joan of Arc came to see Charles VII here; Louis XI kept prisoners in cages here, and Loches remained one of France's fearsome prisons for long afterwards. A walk around all or part of the walls may be more rewarding than the guided tours which demand good French and an interest in history and architecture.

The road back to the Loire along the Indre is a pretty one, but without imperative stops until you reach **Azay-le-Rideau**, a pleasant village full of tourists on their way to and from the most seductive of all the châteaux (see page 373). Literary tourists may choose to pay their respects to Balzac, whose rooms at **Saché** have been arranged as a museum. At nearby **Villaines-les-Rochers**, wickerwork is a cottage industry (see illustration overleaf); you can watch the industrialists at work and buy their produce from co-operatives.

The Loire from Tours to Saumur, and the Vienne

The road downstream along the north bank of the Loire misses **Luynes** but offers a fine view of its severe medieval fortresses. The château isn't open to the public but the village is old and pretty enough to justify a diversion. A few kilometres further on, two medieval towers survive from the old château of **Cinq-Mars-la-Pile** (and are open to the public); on top of the hill is the mysterious monument which has earned the village its name – a solid tower nearly 30 metres tall, built to what end and by whom nobody knows.

Langeais is an unprepossessing, noisy town on the main road but it has a remarkably well preserved and furnished fortress (see page 373). A suspension bridge crosses to the south bank of the Loire where beautifully peaceful countryside stretches up and downstream, with a tiny road along the river which contrasts pleasantly with the north-bank highway. On the way back to Tours, **Savonnières** has some large caves with concretions, rivers and waterfalls. A more typical Loire attraction is the nearby **Château de Villandry**, a fine, classical-looking building added on to the old keep at the end of the 16th century. Villandry's great pride is its Renaissance garden (flowers and vegetables), faithfully reconstructed from old drawings, with a complex symbolic design and a wealth of colour at the right time of year (midsummer). You pay only a few francs extra to do the guided tour of the château interior as well, and although there isn't much of interest

360

Villandry

(mostly Spanish paintings and furniture, and a mosque ceiling transported intact for the Spanish owners) you do get a good view and an explanation of some of the garden layout – hedges shaped into billets-doux or hearts swollen with illicit passion or starved by rejection.

Following the south bank downstream to the junction of Loire and Indre brings you to **Rigny-Ussé** where the creamy 15th-century **Château d'Ussé**, bristling with dormers, turrets and chimneys, peers out from a wooded hillside over the fertile farmland. This really looks like a fairy-tale castle, and in a sense it is – Perrault is said to have used Ussé as the setting for his 'Sleeping Beauty'. To appreciate the château's superb setting, look back from the little bridge over the river or even further towards the Loire. The privately owned château isn't as special inside as out, but is not without interest. The delightful Renaissance chapel has lost its fine tapestries, but not its della Robbia terracotta. Inside the main building the *chambre du roi* retains its unrestored 18th-century furniture; and you can do a partial tour of the sentry-walk.

The wooded slopes from which Ussé surveys the valley form the northern edge of the splendid oak forest of Chinon which joins up with the forest of Villandry and stretches all the way from Chinon to Tours. The main road between the two cuts impressively through it, straight as an arrow but up and down like a big dipper. The riverside road passes **Avoine-Chinon** nuclear power station, gilt-domed like a cathedral. Though the countryside between Loire and Vienne is fertile it is not strikingly beautiful, but the confluence of the two rivers is grand – so open and spacious that you suddenly think of the approaching Atlantic; it marks the divide between Touraine and Anjou. The scene is made by the setting of **Candes** on the Angevin side of the junction. Appropriately enough the impressive fortified church (St-Martin) at the centre of the village is an exemplary place to study the Angevin style of Gothic vaulting (the keys of the main ogive arches are higher than those of the other arches). The village is rather spoilt by main road traffic in the narrow high street, but you can escape by climbing up the hill behind the church for a splendid view.

The Anjou Loire, fed by the Vienne, at last seems to have enough water to fill its bed and becomes a river of stature. At **Montsoreau** a tall white 15th-century château rises powerfully from the river bank. The interior has been restored to its original style and houses a museum devoted to Goums (Moroccan Cavalry). From Montsoreau the road south leads to the **Abbaye de Fontevraud**, founded by an itinerant 11th-century preacher to cater for all elements of his substantial following – male, female, sick and sinful. The Fontevraud order enjoyed great success and social cachet – Louis XIV's daughters were educated there and the list of abbesses (a female always presided) reads like a who-was-who of the French nobility. The abbey was turned into a prison in 1804 but has been extensively restored by forced labour and offers a great deal of beauty and interest to the guided tourist – especially the British since the abbey is something of a Plantagenet necropolis. The most remarkable feature is the Romanesque kitchen, an almost free-standing building where a style usually associated with churches is ingeniously applied to domestic purposes, with a rare and very successful concern for architectural beauty. Round the central space fireplaces are set in towers like apsidal chapels with a complex arrangement of little domes, arches and chimneys. The abbey church, stripped bare, can be admired in its architectural purity; recumbent figures of Henry II, the formidable Eleanor of Aquitaine, Richard Coeur de Lion and his sister-in-law Isabelle of Angoulême lie in the south transept. The elegant Gothic chapter house has lively 16th-century murals full of costume and portrait interest, and vaulting which fans out like palm leaves from slender columns.

South of Candes the Chinon road starts off following a particularly handsome stretch of the Vienne bordered by massive shady plane trees, which make you realise what the Loire lacks. You can turn off for a pilgrimage to the manor (La Devinière) where the 16th-century humanist writer Rabelais was born; the area around Chinon and the Vienne was the setting for much of his work. **Chinon** itself is a fine old town attractively situated on the banks of the river and crowned by the imposing ruins of its medieval castle, of interest to imaginative students of military architecture and for its wealth of historical associations. But many tourists will find a guided tour less rewarding than a walk around the streets of old Chinon, especially around the one-time focus of Chinon life, the Grand Carroi. It isn't hard to imagine the town teeming with Rabelaisian life; the author lived in the Rue Jean-Jacques Rousseau.

For church lovers the small village of **Tavant** on the south bank of the Vienne has a treat in store: the little Romanesque church is a building of great charm with remarkable frescoes in its low crypt (you must ask around for a key, inseparable from an admirably explanatory guide). The four aisles of the crypt are no more than head high and well lit, so you can see perfectly the lively biblical and symbolic figures decorating the vault.

South of Chinon on the way to Richelieu, **Champigny-sur-Veude** is a shadow of its former self, but a fine one. Its palatial Renaissance château excited the jealousy of Cardinal Richelieu who did not want to be outshone so close to home and had it demolished, except for a few outbuildings (now beautifully restored as a private home) and the chapel, a marvel of Renaissance ornament clothing a skeleton of Gothic architecture. The interior, empty except for the kneeling figure of Henri de Bourbon de Montpensier, rejoices in a superb series of stained glass windows; there are family portraits and scenes from the life and death of the crusading Louis IX (Saint Louis).

Appropriately enough Richelieu's own palace suffered at the hands of the Revolutionaries much the same fate as Champigny – but they did a more thorough job. All that remains is a large park and a few domed pavilions on the edge of town. But **Richelieu** is still worth a visit as a remarkably unspoilt (although sadly ill-maintained) example of a classically planned town, walled and gated, with geometrically straight streets of noble town houses. There is a Richelieu museum in the town hall which gives some idea through old prints of the splendour of the place in the 17th century. On summer weekends a steam train runs between Richelieu and Chinon.

Westwards, the spacious Poitou plains are interrupted by the abrupt hill town of **Loudun**, famous for the 17th-century witch-hunt which enabled Richelieu to get rid of the subversive priest Urbain Grandier. At the time, Loudun was commercially as well as intellectually a vigorous town of over 20,000 inhabitants. Today's Loudun (twinned with Ouagadougou in Burkina Faso) is less than half as populous – which accounts for a somewhat depressing atmosphere of urban neglect. The town is topped by a tall windowless square keep which is admirably expressive of the modest aesthetic aspirations and attainments of its builder, the rugged Fulk Nerra. The return to the Loire can embrace the impressively situated château and subsidiary village of **Montreuil-Bellay**. Beneath the old walls the river Thouet lingers in a wide pool, before running on northwards to the Loire. Inside the mostly 15th-century château you can see some heavy furniture, tapestries, and a fine old kitchen.

Saumur is a busy town spreading along both banks of the Loire and across an island in midstream. For many kilometres around you can distinguish the pinnacles of its massive castle, which stands alone on a rocky hill above the town. Saumur is the home of the celebrated Cadre Noir crack cavalry squad, 2,200 of whose cadets staged a heroic three-day defence of the town against 25,000 Germans in 1940, and which gives an annual display of cavalier virtuosity in July. At other times they can be seen practising (information from the local tourist office). Saumur is also the centre for the production of sparkling wine made by the champagne method, and over half of France's total output of mushrooms which flourish in the local tufa caves. But, apart from the small old town area below the château and the ornately decorated town hall by the river, modern Saumur lacks charm.

Sights in Saumur

● **Château** Since the time the Brothers Limbourg portrayed it looking gaily down on the labourers in the vineyards, for the Duc de Berry's book of *Très Riches Heures*, the 14th-century fortress has been much altered; but it is still an impressively fortified square-looking building with octagonal corner towers pointing skywards like rockets. Inside there are two museums, one devoted to the decorative arts with a particularly fine porcelain collection, the other to horses, with skeletons, harnesses, spurs, engravings and historical documentation. There are fine views from the watch-tower.

● **Notre-Dame-de-Nantilly** A grey, mostly Romanesque church near the château with a very fine collection of 15th- to 17th-century tapestries.

● **Dolmen de Bagneux** Anjou's most important megalithic monument is somewhat out of context in the thick of modern suburban sprawl. Stones form a long, covered burial chamber.

● **Wine tasting** A number of wine houses open their doors to the public in Saumur and in the suburb of St-Hilaire-St-Florent. Ackerman-Laurence is the best-known house for Saumur sparkling wines.

The Loire from Saumur to Angers

As is the case for most of the Loire Valley, the road along the south or left bank is less frequented and prettier than the northern route. But it is worth making the excursion a few kilometres north from Saumur to the **Château de Boumois**. Built at the end of the 15th century it looks – with its solid round towers and machicolations – like a defensive castle, but hides like so many of the architectural hedgehogs of the same period a delicate Renaissance courtyard façade and interior.

The south bank road passes through **Chênehutte-les-Tuffeaux**, an attractive village in the heart of troglodyte and mushroom country. **Cunault's** greatest distinction is one of France's noblest Romanesque churches – tall, white and slim (there is no transept). The view as you pass through the fortified west end to the head of a tall stairway down to the floor of the nave is one of great beauty, the sort they often have on postcards but which you usually can't enjoy without a ladder. The carving on the capitals is marvellous but they are hard to appreciate without binoculars and a stiff neck.

At **Gennes** you face the choice of taking the suspension bridge across the Loire to Les Rosiers (of primarily gastronomic interest) and going to Angers via Montgeoffroy, or staying south for the **Château de Brissac** and the wine villages of the Layon Valley. Brissac is a château of contrasts: 15th-century round towers which no one could pull down flank a mostly restored 17th-century building which is sumptuously decorated inside and out. As time and building went on and the flow of funds slowed to a trickle, the decorative exuberance of the Renaissance gave way to the sobriety of the Louis XIII style. Inside there is a gallery of family portraits (the Cossé-Brissac family have been here since 1502), rich tapestries and carved and gilt ceiling beams. To the considerable interest of the visit is added the pleasure of sampling the proprietary wines brought up from the château's 11th-century cellars.

The **Layon Valley** which runs north into the Loire just downstream from Angers is attractive and its slopes produce fine dessert wines. **Beaulieu-sur-Layon** is a good place to get a flavour of the scenery and its produce. There is a small wine museum and wine tasting, and there are fine views. The road back up to Angers crosses the Loire at **Béhuard**, a very picturesque old village on an island with an interesting church built in the rock to the order of the timorous Louis XI who nearly drowned there.

Accessible from the northern route to Angers, the **Château de Montgeoffroy** is a severely handsome, harmonious 18th-century building, which was only just completed before the Revolution. You are shown a small but beautiful series of rooms remarkable for the unrestored original Louis XVI furniture. One wing houses some splendid old carriages and an interesting saddle room.

Angers is a big and busy town on the banks of the short-lived Maine, in the land of black schist stone which contrasts grimly with soft white Touraine tufa. The old town centre around the cathedral has some admirable houses, none finer than the richly carved, seven-storey Maison d'Adam on the Place Ste-Croix.

Sights in Angers

• **Château** The massive 13th-century fortress walls are nearly a kilometre round and punctuated by seven 45-metre round towers. The fierce black stone exterior is brightened by decorative veins of white, and by the formal gardens which now occupy the deep moat. The 15th-century chapel and inner buildings would hardly pull in the crowds, but the collection of tapestries more than justifies a visit. Anger's great treasure, and one of the Middle Ages' most valuable legacies, is the incomplete series of 70 14th-century tapestries illustrating the Apocalypse of Saint John the Divine, originally woven for Angers cathedral and saved from dispersal by the bishop of Angers who bought them at auction for 300 francs in 1843. The tapestries provide a supremely decorative, lively, and graphically literal illustration of Saint John's writings, complete with plagues of locusts, horses with lions' heads and snakes' tails, rivers of blood, and whores of Babylon.

• **Cathedral** A fine church dating from the period of transition

Château d'Angers

between Gothic and Romanesque styles, with a splendid Christ in Majesty carved over the west door. The interior has fine stained glass, mainly high up and hard to decipher.

● **Former Hospital of St John** The late 12th-century triple-aisled hall is an excellent setting for display of Jean Lurçat's dazzling modern tapestries called the Song of the World, inspired by the Apocalypse.

● **Fine Arts Museum** In the Logis Barrault near the cathedral, a varied collection of paintings and sculptures, with a number of more interesting items than the complete works (mostly in cast) of the 19th-century sculptor David d'Angers.

Excursions from Angers

● **Château de Serrant** An imposing and very beautifully furnished Renaissance-style château. A magnificent staircase and tapestries, and Coysevox's very baroque tomb of the Marquis de Vaubrun.

● **Château du Plessis-Macé** A charming medieval fortified manor with moat and keep, updated for more gracious living in the 15th century. Little furniture.

● **Château du Plessis-Bourré** A moated 15th-century fortress built, like Langeais, by Louis XI's factotum Jean Bourré. The highlight of the interior is the ceiling of the guardroom painted with allegorical and comic figures.

The Northern Tributaries

The **Sarthe** runs from Le Mans to its junction with the Loire just north of Angers through a fertile valley of apple orchards, and piggeries which produce excellent potted pork (*rillettes*). On the way up to Le Mans there isn't a lot to see except the Benedictine **Abbaye de Solesmes**, less distinguished architecturally than chorally; you can attend mass to hear some of the finest singers of Gregorian plainchant. In the abbey church there are some beautiful 15th- and 16th-century sculptural groups. Not far away up the Vègre valley, **Asnières** enjoys an attractive setting and has several fine old buildings including a church with extensive wall paintings.

The old Gallo-Roman (and earlier) city of **Le Mans** is of great interest even if you aren't tempted to join the thousands of pilgrims who flock every June to witness the 24-hour race, when competing cars travel nearly 5,000km round a track (partly public roads) south of Le Mans. Near the track a large motor museum is open through the year. The city itself has an extremely attractive medieval centre surrounded by the partially surviving Gallo-Roman ramparts, and a number of interesting monuments both in the town and in the suburbs.

Sights in Le Mans

● **Cathedral** A bizarre building of discordant but beautiful parts: a long low Romanesque nave with a soaring Gothic transept. The beauty of Laurana's recumbent Charles of Anjou is hard to appreciate without a bit of climbing; on the other side of the chapel Guillaume du Bellay, dressed as a Roman soldier, reclines nonchalantly propped on one elbow, his hand draped elegantly around a sword. There are lively elongated sculptures round the Romanesque south door.
● **Eglise de la Coutoure** Interesting old abbey church with fine but damaged sculptures round the west door, elegant vaulting in the Angevin style, a squat Romanesque arcade round the choir, and a very sweet white marble Virgin and Child by Pilon (16th-century).
● **Ste-Jeanne-d'Arc** A hall church (originally a hospital) with three rows of slender pillars supporting fans of Angevin vaulting.
● **Tessé Museum** The old bishop's palace houses a rich collection of paintings, pre- and post-Renaissance.

• **Abbaye de Notre-Dame-de-l'Epau** An attractive Cistercian monastery founded by Richard Coeur de Lion's widow, Berengaria, shortly before her death here in 1230. Most of the standard features of the architectural style of the order can be admired in the remaining buildings which date from after the abbey was burnt down in 1365.

• **Museum of History and Ethnography** The setting – the elegant 15th-century *hôtel* near the cathedral anachronistically called the House of Queen Berengaria – is of as much interest as the contents: local pottery, old prints.

The **Loir Valley** is hardly shorter than the section of the Loire covered in this chapter; the confusingly named tributary runs over 300km from just south of Chartres to Angers. *Le* Loir cannot match *La* Loire for architectural magnificence; but there is no lack of sightseeing and the river itself is to most eyes more attractive than its bigger sister, meandering slowly through a green and fertile, lightly wooded landscape, with little bridges across the river at every village, and few tourists. It is at its most attractive, and most interesting from the sightseeing point of view, between Vendôme and Château-du-Loir, which was the homeland of the Renaissance poet Pierre de Ronsard, who delighted in the charms of his native surroundings. For much of its course the Loir runs parallel to the Loire within easy reach of any of the big towns on the main river – Saumur, Tours, Blois, Orléans. Particular features of the villages along its banks are churches with medieval wall paintings, and some of the most interesting examples of cave dwellings.

Châteaudun is a busy market town on the Paris/Chartres/Tours road; its massive château, rising dramatically from the banks of the Loir, deserves more than an admiring glance as you speed by. Joan of Arc's brother-in-arms Dunois had much to do with its building. There are two wings – one Renaissance, the other (the Dunois wing) Gothic – which have some fine architectural features but little furniture. The late Gothic Sainte-Chapelle contains 15 colourful and expressive statues of female saints and a portrait alleged to be of Dunois.

The drive south from Châteaudun is a pretty one provided you follow the minor roads along the Loir, not the N10. **Vendôme** is a fascinating and picturesque town built on islands in the river, with leafy waterside mills and weirs and gardens. On the wooded southern bank there stand enough remains of the old castle to look well, but not enough to make a very interesting visit.

The naturally moated centre of town is reached by the splendid bridge and richly decorated gateway of St-Georges. The busy market square (Place St-Martin) is graced by an elegant Renaissance bell and clock tower which lost its church long ago and now houses the tourist office. The Rue de l'Abbaye takes you into the precincts of the old abbey of La Trinité, once an important place of pilgrimage thanks to Geoffrey Martel's bringing back as an unlikely souvenir from the East the Holy Tear which Christ shed on the tomb of Lazarus. The handsome abbey buildings have been requisitioned for the army and local museum (which has an interesting section on local mural painting); their simplicity contrasts with the extravagance of the 16th-century west end of the church. The elaborate tracery of the window curls like flames and explains better than most places the use of the term *flamboyant*. The interior is relatively simple, tall and light with a gallery all round the triforium, some fine stained glass and 15th-century choir stalls.

On a particularly charming wooded stretch of the Loir, **Lavardin** is a small village of carefully restored old houses at the foot of romantic overgrown castle ruins. The castle has been closed, for safety reasons, since 1986, and shows no sign of opening again in any hurry. Lavardin's church (St-Genest) is no less in need of attention, damp and decaying inside, but has a variety of interesting wall paintings, with a particularly vivid representation of Hell in the gruesome taste of the late Middle Ages. Two and a half kilometres away, the bigger town of **Montoire**, where Hitler and Pétain negotiated in October 1940, has a less interesting ruined castle and more interesting frescoes, tucked away in the little chapel of St-Gilles where Ronsard was prior (the key is kept in one of the shops ('Art Antique') on the main street leading from the château to the bridge over the Loir, from which an alley leads to the chapel itself). The river is overhung with weeping willows and old houses, the chapel diminutive and cruciform, and the frescoes dazzling, especially the stylised red and white Christ (early 12th-century) over the main vault.

There are some more very fine frescoes in the small church of St-Jacques-des-Guérets which is attractively set beside a watermill across the Loir from the steep hill village of **Trôo**. There are scores of troglodyte houses in the hillside, a fine view from the top of the hill beside the mostly Romanesque church of St-Martin, and a cave which you can visit at the bottom of the hill to see stalactites and usually get soaked. A speaking well (*puits qui parle*) is advertised; it is no more supernatural than a deep well shaft with a remarkable echo.

La Possonnière is the Renaissance manor where Ronsard was born. You have to arrange an appointment in advance if you want to go inside; if not the house can be seen from the road, with its decorative windows surrounded by Latin and French inscriptions. Nearby **Poncé** has more to offer: a mostly wooden Romanesque church with very interesting wall paintings (12th-century) and a Renaissance château with an exceptionally richly decorated six-flight staircase, and a local history/folklore museum.

From Poncé or nearby Château-du-Loir you can head back to Tours and the Loire, or carry on down the Loir for the only moderately interesting towns of Le Lude and La Flèche. The Renaissance **Château du Lude** is externally impressive and set in a fine park (→ page 374)

Visiting châteaux

The great châteaux, built of the local tufa stone which whitens with age, live up to all expectations from the outside, but their interiors may come as a disappointment. Most of the châteaux, the most famous ones at least, have been uninhabited for centuries and lack furniture. Compared with a typical stately home in Britain you will, in almost all cases, find less in the way of beautiful *objets d'art* to admire, and none of the curiosity interest of seeing family photos and everyday clutter to prove that the house is lived in. Most châteaux force you to troop around with a guide (rarely English-speaking), even if notes in English are available. Occasionally this will enhance your enjoyment, but not often. Going around in groups exaggerates the serious problem of overcrowding, especially in small and popular châteaux like Azay-le-Rideau; even if you can understand the guide you probably won't be able to hear, and you almost certainly won't be able to see, what he's talking about. The guides are often bored, a problem which isn't new; when Arthur Young visited Blois nearly 200 years ago he wrote: 'the guide tells many horrible stories in the same tone (from having told them so often) in which the fellow in Westminster Abbey gives his monotonous history of the tombs . . . the character of the period and of the men that figured in it are alike disgusting. Bigotry and ambition equally dark, invidious and bloody allow no feelings of regret. The parties could hardly be better employed than in cutting each other's throats'.

A final warning hardly needs to be spelt out. Much of the interest of the Loire and its châteaux is historical – you stand in rooms where important things happened. If you are not familiar with or interested in learning about the history of France from 1420 to 1590 you will soon get bored in châteaux such as Blois, Amboise and Loches. If you do want to learn there can be no more fascinatingly illustrated way of doing so, but do not go unprepared. Unless you get your kings, queens and mistresses sorted out visits can be confusing and meaningless, and naturally French guides assume a greater knowledge of French history than most of us foreigners carry around as intellectual baggage. Unless you want a history lesson, an unspectacular private château like Beauregard may make a more amusing visit than a great showpiece like Blois. It will also be less crowded.

These magnificently beautiful, historically rich but empty châteaux are ideally suited to the *son et lumière* treatment – there are dozens of these spectacles throughout the summer, but very few in English. The tourist office near the station in Tours is one of the best places for information about them, and about organised coach tours.

Below we've listed the greatest of the Loire châteaux, by whose architects the valley's image in the railway stations and the travel agencies of the world has been fashioned. No tourist in the area should pass through without seeing the outside of all or most of them, and visiting at least one or two. To try to do more is to risk indigestion, boredom (at the historical repetition), and the muddling in the memory of buildings whose greatest quality is their individuality. Rather than try to sample everything on a long menu, choose a few of the *spécialités de la région*; to enhance your appreciation of them take your time and separate the courses with sorbet-like visits to smaller châteaux off the beaten track – with less of an onslaught of historical information and jostling crowds to satiate your appetite for château visiting.

The following comments on the eight greats are intended to help you choose, not to describe contents or historical associations extensively.

Château d'Amboise Fragmentary but still substantial remains of one of the great royal châteaux, with something of the empty magnificence associated with them. It has a superb setting above town and river, with excellent views from the terrace and roof. The visit is distinguished by the remarkable Tour des Minimes, within which a ramp spirals up 20 metres from river level to the châteaux and which was the main entrance for horses and carts. On the ramparts, the small chapel of St-Hubert has exceptionally beautiful stone carving over the entrance. The interior of the château is a curious mixture of medieval and 19th-century decoration and works of art, and Louis-Philippe's ocean-going-liner of a bed.

Château d'Azay-le-Rideau A perennial favourite, incomparably gracious and decorative and built on a scale that fits snugly into a camera frame, with the repertoire of military architecture irresistibly translated into the ornamental Renaissance language. Beautifully set among trees on the edge of a small village, moated by the Indre, Azay is hard to admire from outside the perimeter and deserves at least a wander around the gardens. The inside boasts a beautifully decorated and pioneering straight (as opposed to the previously conventional spiral) staircase, but apart from some very fine and very old tapestries and beds, little furniture of interest. Being a small and exceptionally popular place, it also gets extremely crowded. Stay in the village and go early.

Château de Blois A vast royal château, architecturally interesting for its great variety and the beauty of some of its parts – notably the spiral staircase, acknowledged masterpiece of the Renaissance Loire, and François I's loggia which looks out over the town. A guided tour of the interior (English text available) reveals richly painted ceilings and walls which owe as much to 19th-century restorers as to the original decorators. It is light on furniture, but heavy on history, of which the most famous episode

371

Visiting châteaux continued

was the bloody assassination in 1588 of the enormous Duc de Guise, who despite being carved up by eight daggers took as long to fall and die as a bull. There are *son et lumière* performances in English.

Château de Chambord Externally the most breathtaking of the châteaux, built on an enormous scale in the thick of an enormous forest following a fairly conventional ground plan (keep and outer wings in the corner towers round a courtyard) but with a dream topping of a Renaissance roofscape like a crown heavy with jewels. Chambord is the sort of château you might expect to find inhabiting a fanciful architect's portfolio of daydream designs, but not the French countryside. Inside (there's no guided tour) recent refurnishing efforts have done a little to fill the enormous vacuum (there are 440 rooms). A few rooms are devoted to the Comte de Chambord, a 19th-century pretender to the throne for whom Chambord was bought by public subscription; others have tapestries and paintings from earlier periods and a hunting museum. There are coffered and carved ceilings, and a remarkable double spiral staircase which gives access to the roof terrace, designed for hide-and-seek and hunt-observation. Access to much of the forested park, once again a hunting reserve, is strictly regulated, but there are enough waymarked rides to satisfy any craving for a stroll.

Château de Chaumont Often undeservedly missed out, but, for those who do persevere, all the more pleasant for that. Beautifully situated in a park high above the Loire, Chaumont presents an imposing fortified exterior, beautifully creamy and decorated with proprietary emblems. The guided tour of the interior gives an excellent flavour of a less-than-luxurious château lifestyle. There are very fine tapestries, a majolica floor and, near the château, superb stables.

Château de Chenonceau Thanks to the 60-metre gallery built across the Cher by one of Chenonceau's six great female inhabitants, Catherine de' Medici, this is everyone's choice for the top of the Loire pops, the chocolate-box château now appropriately owned by the Chocolat Menier family. A visit is essential for the view from formal gardens; there's no guided tour, but you receive a free explanatory leaflet. The interior contains very fine paintings, tapestries and some furniture, adequately explained by notes in each room. You can go on a train ride round the gardens in summer and visit an outbuilding containing an amusing if crudely executed wax museum with scenes from Chenonceau's distinguished past. Chenonceau gets very crowded so it is best to stay in the village and go early.

Château de Cheverny Like several of the great châteaux of the region, Cheverny was built by a lady proprietress. Untypical for the region though, it's a severe, symmetrical classical château, small, private, and unaltered since its original completion, a stately home still stylishly inhabited and sumptuously furnished with its original 17th-century décor. Unfortunately this is one of the very worst of the châteaux for crowds, with queues at the entrance to each room. But if you avoid rush-hour and high season, it's a richly rewarding visit – paintings, tapestries, furniture, leatherwork are all of rare quality. The château has a famous hunt; the kennels and trophy room are open to visitors.

Château de Langeais Apart from an unspectacular town-centre setting, a remarkably impressive late medieval fortress. And it is much more interesting than most to visit, thanks to the lack of subsequent alterations to the original disposition and decoration of the rooms, and the exceptionally rich collection of medieval furniture and works of art accumulated by Langeais's last private owner in the late 19th century. Escorted visit, but commentary broadcast by loudspeakers in each room. You may have to wait some time for the English recording to come round; if impatient you can go on the French, or any other, tour with an English translation in your hand, which has the advantage that you can study individual items out of sequence while the crowd is straining to look at something else.

where the most spectacular *son et lumière* show in the Loire region is performed by a huge cast on some summer evenings. The château consists of three wings from different periods (Louis XII, François I, Louis XVI) with massive round corner towers; the inside (guided tour) is very richly furnished and has Italian frescoes in the oratory of the François I wing. At **La Flèche** you can visit a famous military training school founded by Henri IV in 1604 and run by Jesuits until shortly before the Revolution. A few kilometres south of La Flèche is a large zoo (La Tertre Rouge), and to the east the gracious 15th-century **Château de Gallerande**, visible in beautiful gardens from the road, but not open to the public.

HOTELS

Key: ◆ = 0–250FF, ◆◆ = 251–450FF, ◆◆◆ = over 451FF; prices are per double room without breakfast, which costs around 35–60FF extra. Some hotels may insist on half-board during high season, some hotels or restaurants may close at specific times during the week – it is always worth checking. Most hotels accept the major credit cards; we have indicated where a hotel takes no credit cards.

ANGERS

Hôtel d'Anjou

1 boulevard Maréchal-Foch
49100 Maine-et-Loire
TEL 41 88 24 82; FAX 41 87 22 21

A town-centre hotel with style, the Hotel d'Anjou is the classiest act in Angers, and well worth the slightly inflated prices. Featureless from the outside, the building reveals its charm only once you enter the Venetian-style lobby, which is a riot of marble and badly painted ceiling cherubs and features an art deco lift door. You can admire it from the lounge bar, where clever use of mirrors helps to create the effect of space. The restaurant goes overboard in re-creating the style of François I, so there is a beamed ceiling, stained glass and a huge medallion of the king on one wall. The food is superb. After the extravagant beginning, the bedrooms are conventional, modern, town-centre hotel style, with even the largest being somewhat pushed for space. They are helped by having some fine antiques, good modern bathrooms and restful colour schemes. Ask for the cheaper rooms, as the difference in size is minimal compared to the difference in price.

OPEN All year ROOMS 53 (all with bath)

AZAY-LE-RIDEAU

Le Grand Monarque

3 place de la République
37190 Indre-et-Loire
TEL 47 45 40 08; FAX 47 45 46 25

A creeper-covered three-storey town house, Le Grand Monarque is bang in the centre of an extremely popular village – popular because of that most picturesque of châteaux which lies in the hollow beneath. To be able to walk to the château and avoid the horrendous parking problems is one good reason for staying here, but a better one is that it is a friendly, well-run hotel, both comfortable and comforting. Downstairs, the open-plan lounge, bar and reception area benefits from extensive use of sheet glass round the entrance. The restaurant is darker and more traditional, and chef Maxime Rochereau will serve you his 'Ballade en Touraine' – a sequence of excellent regional dishes – for a reasonable price. The bedrooms vary hugely in size, standard of furnishing and cost; the hotel's location means that most of them are a shade more expensive than they would be elsewhere.

OPEN Feb to mid-Dec ROOMS 27 (all with bath or shower)

BEAUGENCY

Hostellerie de l'Ecu de Bretagne

place du Martroi
45190 Loiret
TEL 38 44 67 60; FAX 38 44 68 07

Fronting the main square of this attractive old Loire town, the Ecu de Bretagne is an old inn which keeps up with the times, although it has nothing exceptional to offer by way of decoration or comfort. As a hotel, it is a good mid-range option, with rooms which are comfortable if characterless (those in the annexe are particularly deficient in interest), a convenient location and a useful amount of car-parking space. The main appeal of the place rests in its restaurant, and it is here that the considerable energies of the patron are brought to bear, with extremely good food at very reasonable cost being the result. The *roulade au chocolat* is not to be missed.

OPEN Mar to Jan ROOMS 25 (all with bath or shower)

La Sologne

6 place St-Firmin
45190 Loiret
TEL 38 44 50 27; FAX 38 44 90 19

Attractively situated on the edge of one of Beaugency's small squares, this is a good budget hotel. It is a mellow stone building on two storeys, most of which is taken up by the bedrooms, but there is also room for a small lounge by the reception desk and a verandah breakfast room (though no restaurant), which also makes a sunny place to sit. Bedrooms are all on the small side, but are brightly lit and have clean, light furnishings, although the décor – reflective floral wallpaper for example – is not modern. There are, however, plenty of extras, such as hair-dryers and dandruff removers, while headphones above every bed allow guests to watch Eurosport without disturbing others. The owner could hardly be more friendly.

OPEN Early Feb to end Dec ROOMS 16 (14 with bath or shower)

BRINON-SUR-SAULDRE

La Solognote

18410 Cher
TEL 48 58 50 29; FAX 48 58 56 00

In the heart of the Sologne and within easy reach of Paris, the popularity of this smart little hotel is assured. It is an ancient red building on the corner of a street with a small courtyard garden, alongside which the bedrooms are ranged. These are pretty rooms, modernised in country style, with spriggy wallpaper, old baskets or chests and excellent bathrooms. A short stroll from the bedroom wing brings you into the main building, most of which is taken up by the restaurant. This is a fairly formal place serving competent, very fresh food, but without any pretensions to haute cuisine. One of the best features of this hotel is its friendliness: the Girards are well used to British visitors and go out of their way to please.

OPEN Mid-Mar to mid-Feb exc. 8 days May and Sept ROOMS 13 (all with bath or shower)

CANDE SUR BEUVRON

La Caillère

36 route des Montils
41120 Loir-et-Cher
TEL 54 44 03 08; FAX 54 44 00 95

Jacky Guindon's well-reputed hotel and restaurant is now dominated by the successful modern extension which contains his new bedrooms and breakfast room. The older L-shaped cottage lies beyond; as well as the restaurant it has several bedrooms and is surrounded by a peaceful garden. The modern extension is chalet-style, with plenty of varnished pine, but interior decoration is tasteful and modern – bedrooms have parquet flooring, svelte modern shower-rooms complete with radio and restful blue colour schemes. The older rooms are simple, with solid oak furniture and elegant bathrooms. M. Guindon continues to draw awards for his cookery, which you sample in the low-beamed restaurant, brightened by orange-and-cream colour schemes and modern prints. The hotel is excellently located for châteaux visiting.

OPEN End Feb to Dec ROOMS 14 (all with shower)

CHAMBORD

Grand St-Michel

41250 Loir-et-Cher
TEL 54 20 31 31; FAX 54 20 36 40

Position is everything here, for this hotel stands adjacent to the magnificent fantasy which is the château of Chambord. For this reason alone it would doubtless be booked solid by tour operators if it were not for Mme Lemeur's insistence on running her hotel the way she wants – as a traditional, fairly formal institution for individuals, not groups, which makes up in atmosphere for what it may lack by way of style or comfort. The public rooms are spacious but not noticeably relaxing, while the restaurant is cavernous and echoing. There is no bar service once the tables on the terrace are packed away for the night. The appeal of staying here is to be alone with the château – although you really need to be in room 7 to be able to see it from your window. Other bedrooms have less of a view, but some on the second floor are pretty in their own right, with sloping ceilings and good decoration.

OPEN End Dec to mid-Nov ROOMS 39 (all with bath or shower)

CHENONCEAUX

Du Bon Laboureur et du Château

37150 Indre-et-Loire
TEL 47 23 90 02; FAX 47 23 82 01

This hotel becomes better and better. Our last edition punningly described it as workmanlike – it is now rather more than that. Mme Jeudi runs the place with immense verve, and it fairly hums. The hotel is a good deal larger than it appears at first, for a cluster of houses surrounds the main building, and in or among them you can find most things you might need, including a swimming-pool, a grill-restaurant, an extensive *jardin du plaisance* and an equally extensive *potager*. As you might expect, rooms vary enormously. Those recently re-done in the main building are superb – all in blue, with sparkling blue-tiled bathrooms; they are also the most expensive. Elsewhere pastel colours rule. The family suite has a huge bathroom. The restaurant – with one side open to warm summer days – promises well.

OPEN Mid-Mar to mid-Nov ROOMS 36 (all with bath or shower) FACILITIES Heated outdoor pool

---

Key: ◆ = 0–250FF, ◆◆ = 251–450FF, ◆◆◆ = over 451FF; prices are per double room without breakfast, which costs around 35–60FF extra. Some hotels may insist on half-board during high season, some hotels or restaurants may close at specific times during the week – it is always worth checking. Most hotels accept the major credit cards; we have indicated where a hotel takes no credit cards.

CHINON

Chris' Hôtel

12 place Jeanne d'Arc
37500 Indre-et-Loire
TEL 47 93 36 92; FAX 47 98 48 92

At the quieter end of Chinon's *quai*, just where it blends into the place Jeanne d'Arc, the Chris' lacks the dignified atmosphere of antiquity to be found at the Diderot, but has a garden by way of compensation and is, in some respects, a more genuinely French hotel. Taking its name from the owner's wife Christianne Girard and now run by her son, this is a hotel in three parts. To the right of the courtyard gate, enormous family rooms, very well decorated, take up most of one building. Behind the hotel, a more modern wing has chalet-style bedrooms which lack character and up-to-date décor, but which are reasonably sized with fair bathrooms. In the main building, the cheaper rooms need modernising, but are again of fair size. A busy lobby where hotel traffic and local gossips compete with the television, and a more peaceful breakfast room (though no restaurant) complete the picture. The welcome is friendly.

OPEN All year ROOMS 40 (all with bath or shower)

Diderot

4 rue Buffon
37500 Indre-et-Loire
TEL 47 93 18 87; FAX 47 93 37 10

An old friend to many British visitors, the Diderot continues unchanged in atmosphere, although M. Kazamias has built five new rooms in his courtyard. The appeal of the hotel lies in the building itself, which is a restrained and dignified 18th-century mansion at the quieter western end of Chinon. It has an open, sunny aspect, parking space in its gravel courtyard, and a notable range of home-made jams for breakfast. They key to staying here is to get one of the rooms at the front of the old building, where you will find polished wood flooring, lovely old country furniture and the sun pouring through the windows. At the back, rooms are smaller, darker and have less character, although they are comfortable enough. Light sleepers should note that noise travels easily in the old house. There's no restaurant in the hotel, but the centre of town is only five minutes' walk away, and l'Océanique restaurant is recommended.

OPEN Early Jan to mid-Dec ROOMS 28 (all with bath or shower)

Hostellerie Gargantua

73 rue Voltaire
37500 Indre-et-Loire
TEL 47 93 04 71

Good food and accommodation merge under one roof at this elegant hostellerie found in one of Chinon's oldest streets. Built in the 15th century, this former palace is furnished in suitably medieval style with baronial public rooms awash with antiques and drapes. There are only a handful of bedrooms, but all are stylish – some with four-posters and vast fireplaces. A pretty terrace shaded with umbrellas and edged with creepers overlooks Chinon's château and is used for lunches in good weather. Fish terrines and lamb stews are specialities and you won't find the wine cellar lacking in Loire wines.

OPEN Mid-Mar to mid-Nov ROOMS 6 (all with bath or shower)

CLOYES-SUR-LE-LOIR

Le Saint-Jacques

place du Marché aux Oeufs
28220 Eure-et-Loir
TEL 37 98 40 08; FAX 37 98 32 63

This old coaching inn at the heart of a small Loir town (pretty rather than historic) makes a good stopping point on the road south. Its chief attraction is its garden, extending away from the hotel to the banks of the Loir, where a small boat waits, ready for guests to use. Shady trees for hot summer days and plenty of wildlife make this an agreeable spot. Back in the hotel, which is well isolated from the street by a thick archway, the lounge and reception area is to be found in a species of conservatory, with the bar opening out of it. The restaurant seats 50 in fair comfort and is distinguished by its large carved fireplace. Menus, in comparison to the bedrooms, are a little pricey, partly because they include a lot of expensive fish. All of the bedrooms are well co-ordinated, with some lovely furniture – notably old chests and wardrobes. They are not zealously smart, but very well kept and clean. Those in the cottage annexe are the smallest.

OPEN End Feb to mid-Nov ROOMS 22 (all with bath or shower) (Credit cards not accepted)

LANGEAIS

Le Castel de Bray et Monts

Le Bourg
37130 Bréhémont
Indre-et-Loire
TEL 47 96 70 47; FAX 47 96 57 36

Perhaps the closest thing in the Loire valley to an English country-house hotel, this is an utterly charming place, although you pay for prettiness rather than luxury. It is tucked away on the edge of a very small village in one of the quietest and most attractive parts of the Loire. The house is a curious late 18th-century creation, fairly plain from the outside, but with a large and shady garden where ducks dabble and a half-buried summer-house waits to be discovered. From the reception area, a delicate double stair curves up to the bedrooms on the first floor. These are romantically furnished with floral curtains, bird-patterned wallpaper, patchwork hangings and heart-shaped mirrors. At the far end of the garden a converted chapel now forms a gothic suite. The restaurant is vaguely Georgian in tone, and concentrates on food, not frills.

OPEN Early Feb to Dec ROOMS 9 (all with bath) FACILITIES Tennis

Hostellerie du Château de Rochecotte

St-Patrice
37130 Indre-et-Loire
TEL 47 96 91 28; FAX 47 96 90 59

This is a well-placed hotel for visiting the châteaux of the central section of the Loire. It is an elegant château in its own right and was once Talleyrand's stamping ground. Severely classical in style, it fronts acres of rough lawn. Inside it is all modern and arty, hung with paintings from local galleries and scattered with strange glass tables, interesting statuettes and ceramics. There are also some very nasty green ceramic coffee tables. The two restaurants (one with spotlights balanced on isolated Corinthian pillars and a moulded frieze running round the ceiling) are separated by a library lined by ebony bookcases. Weird though it is in parts, the overall effect manages to be both successful and soothing. The bedrooms also soothe: they are sparsely, but extremely well furnished with bright bedspreads picked out with tulips or birds. Those on the first floor are expensive; on the second, equally good quality is to be had for less money. The cooking is fairly fancy, to go with the rest of the place. The welcome is down to earth and warm.

OPEN All year ROOMS 28 (all with bath or shower)

LOCHES

George Sand

39 rue Quintefol
37600 Indre-et-Loire
TEL 47 59 39 74; FAX 47 91 55 75

Under the walls of the medieval citadel, the George Sand fronts a street of run-down and grubby houses, but is much more pleasing at the rear, where the River Indre runs past its terrace. It is an older and more extensive building than it looks, with a stone spiral staircase leading up to the bedrooms. There is no lounge to speak of, but the restaurant spreads over two rooms. Very good plain French country cooking in ample portions is the order of the day. The bedrooms, opening off various landings and short corridors, are unexceptional but well kitted-out, while the bathrooms are modest rather than palatial. The George Sand is the best choice in Loches – a town that certainly should be visited.

OPEN End Dec to end Nov ROOMS 20 (all with bath or shower)

NOUAN-LE-FUZELIER

Moulin de Villiers

route de Chaon
41600 Loir-et-Cher
TEL 54 88 72 27

For a day or two in the half-hidden tranquillity of the Sologne, this is the place
to come. It is a very simple hotel, where bedrooms are sparsely furnished, but if
you don't mind this, it has bags of atmosphere. The long two-storey mill stands
all alone at the end of a private road, surrounded by oak and poplar forest and
with a small reedy lake, typical of the Sologne, a few steps away. M. Andrieux
has turned the best part of the building into the restaurant – a pretty room with
low beamed ceiling and light pouring through the windows. The basement
lounge is too dark to sit in for long, but there is another small sitting area on the
first floor landing. Weekday menus are short on choice but long on value. More
elaborate meals are served on Sundays and holidays.

OPEN End Mar to early Jan, closed 2 weeks Sept ROOMS 20 (16 with bath or shower)

ST-DENIS D'ANJOU

Auberge du Roi René

53290 Mayenne
TEL 43 70 52 30; FAX 43 70 58 75

In the heart of this pretty village, the Auberge du Roi René would suit travellers
looking for a leisurely overnight stop en route to the Dordogne or the Loire
area. Succumb to its rural charms and you could find yourself staying longer.
With only three rooms, it's more of a restaurant-with-rooms than a hotel but
you'll find just as much care has been lavished on the accommodation as on the
ground-floor dining rooms. With polished, honeycomb tiles, wobbly stone
staircases and a sunny terraced garden, the old 15th-century building blends
happily into the 18th-century addition. A good range of set menus is available
or a well-priced à la carte alternative.

OPEN All year ROOMS 3 (all with bath or shower)

SANCERRE

Du Rempart

18300 Cher
TEL 48 54 10 18; FAX 48 54 36 30

Sancerre, in the centre of the wine-growing area south-east of Orléans, is an
attractive hill-top town, and this hotel on the perimeter of the old ramparts is
the obvious place to stay if you are visiting the vineyards. It is a conventional
village inn without frills, consisting of a large restaurant with small alcove bar
and a little breakfast room. A shady car-parking area and scattered tables on the

381

street complete the picture. Bedrooms are being renovated by the enthusiastic young owner, and those that have been re-done are fresh and clean. Prices are moderate and the atmosphere appealing.

OPEN All year ROOMS 18 (all with bath or shower)

THOUARS

Hostellerie le Clos Saint Médard

14 place Saint-Médard
79100 Deux-Sèvres
TEL 49 66 66 00; FAX 49 96 15 01

Thouars is not a town to spend long in, but it does have a small medieval quarter where this hotel is located. As a stop-over on the way south or north, it is ideal. In the shadow of the church from which it takes its name, this is a very ancient town house (the stair is 13th-century) run as a restaurant-with-rooms by M. and Mme Aracil, both of whom are utterly charming. The restaurant (where the cooking is highly praised) has a tremendous view over the edge of the escarpment beneath, and is a smart room in charcoal and grey. The four bedrooms, reached by a steep staircase, are medium-sized with rattan headboards, bright modern prints on the walls and green or apricot colour schemes. Their price is modest.

OPEN All year exc. school hols in Feb ROOMS 4 (all with bath)

VEIGNE

Le Moulin Fleuri

route du Ripault
Montbazon
37250 Indre-et-Loire
TEL 47 26 01 12

For those wishing to be based near Tours, this wonderful, simple hotel comes as a welcome alternative to searching through the somewhat soulless accommodation of the city itself. It is not easy to find – a good map will be required – but once down the long entrance lane to the banks of the swirling Indre, it is difficult to believe you are actually sandwiched by main roads and autoroute. The mill is four-storey, rectangular and slate-roofed. Inside, its chief glory is the restaurant bar in the old machinery space – a long-beamed room with an ancient fireplace kitted out in country-restaurant style. The bedrooms, spread over the storeys above, are remarkably cheap considering their fair size, their good big simple country beds and the fact that several overlook the river. Shower rooms are small but adequate. Alain Chaplin's food, as you can tell from the rich aromas which perfume the restaurant, is to be taken seriously – menus are based heavily on regional produce.

OPEN Early Mar to early Feb ROOMS 12 (8 with shower)

VENDOME

Hôtel Vendôme

15 Faubourg Chartrain
41100 Loir-et-Cher
TEL 54 77 02 88; FAX 54 73 90 71

Although it is primarily a business hotel, this is the best place to stay in this attractive old Loir town. A distinguished-looking off-white three-storey town house of indeterminate age, the Vendôme has been thoroughly modernised inside, and done up in late-'80s style with pastel-coloured soft furnishing throughout. The restaurant, in pinks, apricots and whitewood, is overlooked by the small gallery lounge. A lift leads to the bedrooms, which are bright and clean if on the small side. Those under the roof are much the cheapest (apparently velux windows are not classy enough for the clientele) and just as nice as the rest. The menus are fairly cheap if unexciting.

OPEN All year ROOMS 35 (all with bath or shower)

VILLANDRY

Le Cheval Rouge

37510 Indre-et-Loire
TEL 47 50 02 07; FAX 47 50 08 77

Almost next door to the château and its famous gardens, this is an undistinguished-looking roadside hotel, but one where you will find an excellent welcome, a fair degree of comfort, and plenty to look at. Mme Rody, who has taken over the Cheval Rouge from her parents, has inherited a hotel which was decorated in the late 1960s with an astonishing lack of harmony. The huge open-plan lounge and bar is sprinkled with big black leatherette sofas, modern plain-coloured high-backed chairs and filigree steel baskets for bar stools, while further eye-opening effects are to be found in the bathrooms, where aquamarine baths flourish alongside avocado or sunflower sink units. The restaurant has as its focal point a horse etched on glass and surrounded by grey marble. Luckily the bedrooms are sober – plainly furnished with striped papering and old wooden tables – and on offer at a very reasonable price. While the décor may not be to everyone's taste (and may soon be modernised anyway), the advantages of convenience, friendliness and spaciousness should not be ignored. Food is simpler than it was under the previous ownership.

OPEN Mid-Mar to Dec ROOMS 20 (all with bath or shower)

The sea being smooth,
How many shallow bauble boats dare sail
Upon her patient breast

[Shakespeare]

BRITTANY

Brittany, meaning little Britain, is France's Celtic fringe – geologically, ethnographically and linguistically closer to Wales and Cornwall than to France. In many ways its holiday appeal is closer to these areas too. For the tourist, Brittany is first and foremost a coastline – in Breton the *Armor* or 'land of the sea'. From the Loire estuary to Mont-St-Michel it is so jagged and indented that estimates of its length vary from 1,100 to 3,000km (either way that is a lot of beach space). Brittany is France's most frequented holiday region after the Mediterranean coast; but it never gets crowded to the nightmarish degree of the Côte d'Azur in August. You can find seaside resorts that are still little more than quiet villages; you can drive a car along the coast roads; you can find a place to lie down on the beach, and if you go just a few kilometres inland into the *Argoat* – or 'land of the forest', no longer wholly appropriate – you lose people altogether. The south coast of Brittany has sheltered sandy coves and inlets and is a popular area for sailing holidays. The north coast has remarkable stretches of huge pink granite boulders and sections of impressively savage cliffs. But the best area for dramatic coastal scenery is the extreme west of Brittany, the bared teeth of France's transatlantic growl.

Like Wales, Brittany has the added attraction of its regional (Bretons would say national) individuality – distinctive local traditions, costumes, culture and language which all attract interest partly because of their tourist value, and partly because the Bretons have learnt that their provincial identity is something of which to be proud.

For many hundreds of years Brittany was a backwater isolated from the impact of political events and from economic and artistic developments elsewhere in the kingdom. It has its own dense and colourful tissue of history (medieval, and much earlier) and legend – often hard to disentangle from each other. Religious feeling runs deep and strong: even the smallest villages boast large and richly decorated churches, and Bretons persist in the veneration of obscure local saints – mostly early Celtic missionaries from Britain and Ireland, many struck off the official register long ago. All over Brittany tens of thousands of people

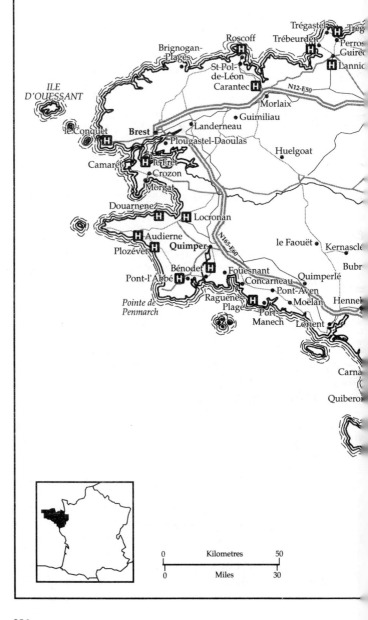

Brittany

ILE D'OUESSANT

Trégastel Trég
Roscoff Trébeurden Perros
Brignogan-Plages Guire
St-Pol-de-Léon Lannic
Carantec
N12-E50
Morlaix
le Conquet
Landerneau Guimiliau
Brest
Plougastel-Daoulas Huelgoat
Camaret le Fret
Crozon
Morgat
Douarnenez Locronan
N165-E60
Audierne **Quimper** le Faouët Kernascle
Plozévet Bubr
Bénodet Fouesnant Quimperlé
Pont-l'Abbé Concarneau
Pont-Aven
Pointe de Penmarch Raguenès-Plage Moëlan Hennel
Port-Manech Lorient
Carna
Quibero

| 0 | Kilometres | 50 |
| 0 | Miles | 30 |

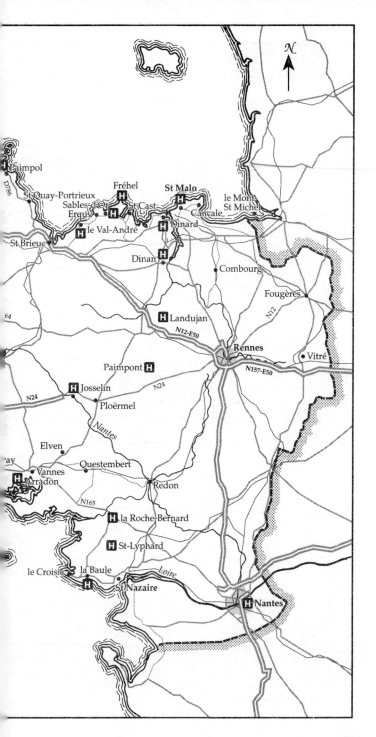

join in the picturesque local religious processions – called *pardons* – to the shrine of the local saint. Their popular religious fervour, as uncomplicated as it is strong, is reflected in Breton art (mainly the decoration and sculptural ornaments of churches).

Brittany is one of France's under-developed areas which at times in the past seemed to have so little going for it that total depopulation was once seriously proposed as the most sensible economic plan for the region. Its population is concentrated around the coast, in the big modern industrial ports of Brest and Lorient, or in fishing ports such as St-Malo, Douarnenez and Concarneau. The architecture of coastal villages is practical – once again the obvious comparison is with Wales – with small, unadorned whitewashed or plain grey cottages lying low in the open, wind-swept landscape. There are only a few villages where the severity of the grey stone is relieved by thatch. Inland Brittany, once the most densely forested of all French regions, is now one of the least so. Although uncultivated heath and waste land has taken its place in some areas (the Black Mountains, for example, originally named after their dark mantle of trees), there is plenty of productive farmland, too, with tasty lamb reared on the coastal salt pastures (*pré salé*) and vegetables of high repute. But the interior of Brittany, increasingly prosperous as it may be, has relatively little to offer the tourist. There are areas which retain the forest beauty of the old Argoat; there are a few impressive castles and some fine churches; and – particularly in Finistère – there are groups of religious monuments around the churches, called parish closes. But in general the countryside lacks the interest of noble country houses, or historic and attractive towns.

Eastern (Upper) Brittany, for all its attractions, is a disappointment to any tourist in search of specifically local colour. Western (Lower) Brittany, called Bretagne Bretonnante because of the survival there of the Breton language, is more rewarding. The language is not easy to understand but its close affinities with Welsh can be seen from any signpost – Aber Ildut, Landéda, Pont-Pol-Ty-Glas, Pen Lan. Local costume is now mostly reserved for special occasions, but in the south-west you can still see some of the many varieties of *coiffe* (head-dress).

Long before the Celts, the Romans and the Gauls, an unknown race specialised in raising megalithic monuments all over Brittany. The stones of these primitive open-air cathedrals and burial grounds whose religious significance, in the absence of any practical utility, is generally accepted (as is their connection with the sun and moon) are thought to have been erected some time between 4,000 and 1,800 BC.

Brittany was one of the theoretical destinations of the Holy Grail, and what remain of the dark forests of the Argoat are thick with the characters of Arthurian legend. The coast is no less rich in more-or-less mythical associations. The old city of Is, once-glorious capital of Cornouaille, was engulfed in the ocean in punishment for the licentious behaviour of the king's daughter who went with the city to the bottom of the ocean and stays there as an irresistible mermaid luring sailors to their doom. Other hazards to shipping were less romantic: islanders made a living out of drawing vessels onto the rocks and looting them. For centuries no merchantman in the Channel was safe from the infamous privateers of St-Malo who wrought havoc as licensed pirates.

The medieval history of Brittany is one of complicated power struggles between Breton nobles and rival claimants to the duchy. During the 14th and 15th centuries Brittany became a zone of proxy war between the French and English. This devastated the province but did produce Bertrand du Guesclin, the great hero of the French cause in the early stages of the Hundred Years' War. This swarthy little Breton was born in 1320 near Dinan, fought a celebrated single combat with an English knight there in 1359 and asked to be buried there. On his death, in 1380 in the South of France, his wishes were partially fulfilled: du Guesclin's last campaign, the funeral journey, swept through Le Puy (entrails buried), Montferrand (flesh buried), Le Mans (skeleton and heart split up), St-Denis (skeleton buried), and finally Dinan (heart buried in St-Sauveur). In spite of du Guesclin's efforts, the English-backed claimants won control, and the French crown's eventual success in appropriating Brittany was neither easily achieved nor total. Duchess Anne of Brittany first married Charles VIII and then his successor Louis XII, but was careful to retain separate control of her duchy. On Anne's early death, her daughter Claude was swiftly married off to her father's heir, the future François I, and was prevailed upon to permit the union of Brittany and France in the person of their son Henry II.

The Côtes-du-Nord and Ille-et-Vilaine

The Bay of Mont-St-Michel is gradually filling up with mud; west of the Couesnon, it has little to offer the traveller except views of the rock, oysters, mussels and tasty salt-marsh lambs. **Dol-de-Bretagne** used to be a bishopric, beside the sea, and important. It is now none of these things but still an attractive small town with the mainly 13th-century cathedral of St-Samson suitably big, strong and imposing. **Cancale** is an important seafood port, one of the most single-minded shellfish factories in Brittany. The Latin poet Ausone wrote favourably of Cancale's oysters, which were in his day harvested from natural banks in the bay. At low tide you can see the drained beds or parks and the stakes in the sands that mussels grow on, and you will understand why it's called farming not fishing; but the sheer scale of the enterprise is probably best appreciated from the air – in one of the small planes that take tourists around Mont-St-Michel.

North of Cancale the **Pointe de Grouin**, most easterly cape of Brittany's impressive rocky coastline, gives a splendid panorama of the bay and the distant Mont-St-Michel. The inhospitable coastline westward is interrupted by the deep inlet of **Rothéneuf**, where the calm waters are popular for watersports and the granite cliffs along the rocky shore have been remarkably decorated with sculptures and relief carvings by the Abbé Fouré, hermit of Rothéneuf.

A virtually uninterrupted built-up area extends round the corner of the Rance inlet from Paramé to St-Servan, and does not do justice to the splendid situation of the granite citadel of **St-Malo**, which is one of the most interesting and attractive of the Channel ports. The city (known as Intra Muros) is packed within medieval ramparts later strengthened by Vauban. It lies on a sandy island, once joined to the mainland only at low tide, flanked on one side by the docks, on the other by beach. The fortifications and stark grey uniformity of the tall houses of Intra Muros make it tremendously impressive as you approach from the sea. As you get closer and go into the town beneath the towers of its cheerless fortress (once a prison, now a waxwork and local history museum) it becomes clear that all, or nearly all, is new. St-Malo was very badly damaged in 1944, and has been rebuilt in a severe style which may approximate to the original but is not welcoming. The city is nevertheless busily commercial and touristy, the walk round the ramparts is very rewarding, and there are other interesting walks at low tide to Vauban's 17th-century fortress and the island of Grand Bé, the chosen tomb of St-Malo's own literary colossus, Châteaubriand. The port's neighbours – Paramé on the sea, and St-Servan on the rocks – are fairly busy resorts with good beaches (Paramé) and rocky cliff walks (St-Servan) but rather urban. From St-Malo there are boat excursions along the coast to the Cap Fréhel, up the Rance to Dinan, across it to Dinard, as well as boats to the Channel Islands.

The Rance, like so many Breton rivers, is insignificant by comparison with the size and splendour of its estuary, which stretches over 30km from Dinan to Dinard and St-Malo at its mouth on the sea. For the harnessing of tidal power the Rance has been dammed: you can visit the installation, the first and one of the most important of its kind, drive across it and sail through it via a lock.

Dinan is a beautifully situated, walled medieval town high above the river where there is a small port for excursion boats and a rebuilt Gothic bridge. At the south of the complete ramparts is the small castle which houses a local history and folklore museum. In the stylistically very mixed basilica of St-Sauveur is a memorial to Bertrand du Guesclin. More rewarding than any specific visit, though, is a wander around the maze of old streets at the heart of town, with their cobbles and overhanging timbered houses. Dinan had a sizeable expatriate

community in the 18th and 19th centuries, and still has its Jardin des Anglais on the east of the old town which gives splendid views out over the Rance. It's a busy and lively town, a very popular place to visit and a very good base for the coast and interior.

Facing St-Malo across the mouth of the Rance, **Dinard** is one of Brittany's two traditionally fashionable resorts (the other being La Baule). Dinard is the older, a British creation of the turn of the century, and shows its age: spacious neo-Gothic villas and a sedate atmosphere. There is plenty to do though – sports, boat excursions, cliff-top walks – and the beaches are sandy and sheltered. There are more good beaches at **St-Lunaire** and **St-Briac-sur-Mer**, a resort with one of France's oldest and best golf courses. **St-Cast-le-Guildo** is an altogether more popular family resort with a busy fishing and yachting harbour. From the Pointe de St-Cast, as from any number of rocky outcrops along this coast, there are splendid views; most impressive of all is the **Cap Fréhel**, whose 60 metre high grey and reddish cliffs are popular with tourists and no less so with nesting birds. Barely visible along the cliffs is the magnificently situated, mostly medieval **Fort la Latte** (with guided tours) complete with drawbridge access over clefts in the rocks. Beyond Cap Fréhel the Emerald Coast descends, less savagely rocky, to the big town of **St-Brieuc**, unremarkable except for its fortified 14th-century cathedral (St-Etienne). **Sables-d'Or-les-Pins** speaks for itself – the golden sand beach is enormous, and pines shade a spaciously regular grid of villas and mock-rustic hotels, but there is very little else. Trippery **Le Val-André** also has a long sandy beach. A pleasant contrast with both is **Erquy**, a proper little port well known for its scallops, where there are campsites, good wet sand beaches, and old plain Breton cottages, not the neo-Gothic of so much of this coast.

The west side of the deep V of St-Brieuc Bay has no shortage of sandy beaches but few resorts of any compelling charm. **St-Quay-Portrieux** (port and resort) is the biggest, and best equipped for land and water sports – there is a sailing school and casino. You can make a brief inland detour to two interesting churches. The small pilgrimage chapel of **Kermaria-an-Iskuit** has a remarkable mural of the Dance of Death, and typically Breton statues in the porch – sharply characterised to the point of caricature and vividly painted. **Lanleff** has an even more curious temple: a ruined round Romanesque church based on the Holy Sepulchre in Jerusalem. Back on the coast, there are some scanty remains of a Gothic abbey at Beauport just outside **Paimpol**, which was once an important fishing port – made famous by Pierre Loti's novel *Pêcheur d'Islande*, about cod fishing in the Arctic. Now its inhabitants are engaged in less arduous and more profitable oyster farming. North of the town the Pointe de l'Arcouest looks across pinkish rocks and little islands to the nearby **Ile de Bréhat** which is peaceful, lush, sunny and not neglected by tourists.

Tréguier is a small old cathedral and pilgrimage town lying at the heart of an inlet of oyster beds. The former cathedral, dedicated to the 6th-century Welsh missionary Tudwal, dates mostly from the 14th century but of its three towers, one – the Hastings Tower – is Romanesque. The 15th-century cloister is full of flowers and recumbent statues.

North of Tréguier, **Port-Blanc** is a particularly charming little fishing port and resort tucked into a sheltered bay in another inhospitable stretch of coast where isolated rocks and treacherous reefs are exposed at low tide. **St-Gonéry** has a curious little chapel with a crooked spire, painted wooden vaults, an outside pulpit, a Calvary, a very old yew tree, and a 16th-century mausoleum. The stretch of coast from Perros-Guirec to Trébeurden is known as the Corniche Bretonne or, more helpfully, as the Pink Granite Coast. All along the coast the granite, which really does have a dark warm pinkish tint, has been eroded into weird boulders as if fashioned and polished lovingly by an abstract artist. One of the by-products of granite erosion is fine sand, and among the boulders and headlands are some very good beaches and northern Brittany's most frequented family resorts – **Perros-Guirec** (the biggest), **Ploumanach**, **Trégastel-Plague** and **Trébeurden**, without much to choose between them. You can take a boat round the bird sanctuaries of the **Sept Iles**, but can only land on one – the Ile aux Moines, where Vauban built a fortress.

On the banks of the salmon-rich river Léguer, **Lannion** is an expanding modern town, with an unspoilt and very picturesque old centre. A little further upstream is **Kerfons** chapel, which boasts a remarkable carved wooden screen, and the ruins of the 13th-century Tonquédec castle.

Excursions from Dinan and the coast

The north-east interior of Brittany is the main region for fortifications and castles, built along its frontier with France.

● **Combourg** A small old town with an imposing but internally much altered feudal fortress which belonged to the du Guesclin and Châteaubriand families. It was haunted, according to Châteaubriand, by a black cat and a wooden-legged man; even if you aren't afraid of ghosts it is best admired from a distance. Not far from Combourg there are medieval castle remains at **Montmuran**, a church of interesting stained glass at **Les Iffs**, and a zoo in the park of the classical **Château de la Bourbansais**.

● **Fougères** A large frontier town, and traditional centre for the manufacture of shoes. Fougères attracts tourists in large numbers to admire its thoroughly admirable and massive 13th-century (and later) fortress which Victor Hugo described as the Carcassonne of the north. The castle is built somewhat eccentrically below the town, beside the river Nançon. However doubtful as defensive strategy this does mean that there are splendid views to be had of the castle as a whole from above (notably from the Place aux Arbres at the end of the town which forms an extension of the curtain wall of the castle). There are guided tours within and around the walls, for a closer and more detailed appreciation of the military architect's achievement. In the lower town outside the castle walls there are some attractive old houses and the interesting Gothic church of St-Sulpice.

● **Vitré** Like Fougères, Vitré is a powerful fortified frontier town on the River Vilaine, still enclosed on three sides by its old ramparts and the splendid towers and walls of its late-14th-century castle. The approach to the town, from the direction of Fougères or Rennes, is very picturesque, and the old streets with their carefully timbered and slate-fronted houses are no disappointment. Notre-Dame is an elegant Gothic church with an external pulpit for open-air religious debating, and the castle itself houses a museum of local antiquities and folklore. The nearby **Château des Rochers-Sévigné** is chiefly of interest for its memories of the late 17th-century letter-writing Marquise de Sévigné who spent most of her last 20 years here.

● **Rennes** Unless the weather is really terrible you're unlikely to be tempted to give much time to the commercially, industrially and administratively important capital of Brittany, most of whose medieval centre was burnt down in 1720. But like most provincial capitals, Rennes has museums of interest: two in the same building, one devoted to Breton history and folklore, the other to fine arts. You can also visit the impressive 17th-century law courts with their ornately decorated parliament chamber, and the cathedral which houses an exquisite carved wooden altar-piece in a chapel off the south aisle.

Finistère

The three peninsulas of France's end of the earth (Finis Terrae) may look on the map like the snapping jaws of a Celtic dragon breathing the fire of Breton defiance across the Atlantic, but on the spot it is very clear that here land is on the defensive. All the attacking is done by the sea which hurls crashing blows against the rocky capes in spectacular storms. Sometimes the low-lying island of Sein off the Pointe du Raz is totally submerged. In the days before the Entente Cordiale the French historian Michelet wrote: 'This whole coast is a cemetery. The sea is English by nature – she does not like France, she breaks our ships.' Some of the Finistère coastline – the far-western capes ravaged and scarred by the fight against the sea – is very dramatic. Other parts – the north-west and south-west – are just windswept and bleak. The rest, as it were sheltered behind the front lines of defence against the Atlantic assault, is Brittany at her most attractive and frequented. The sheltered coastline between the estuaries of Quimper and Quimperlé has become the favourite for camping and yachting holidays: its succession of sandy wooded coves and deeper inlets forms a marked contrast with the exposure of the harsher Finistère coastline. The grassy cliff-tops are sparsely scattered with low grey cottages and isolated granite chur-ches, and the villages turn on the charm, with crêperies and coiffed old ladies selling lace at every turn. It is in this part of Brittany that local costumes, customs and languages will be most obvious to the tourist greedy for a diet of folklore, though in other parts of Finistère (inland and in the extreme south-west) the same features of Breton life have a truer ring.

Finistère is not really one area, but two (at least): the north is Léon, unspectacular land of cauliflowers, artichokes and long, estuary-like *abers* left muddy and weedy at low tide, shallow and still weedy at high tide; the south is Cornouaille, the Brittany of medieval history and legend and modern picture-books.

Léon's north coast is rocky, indented and pinkish-grey. **Locquirec** is a very popular and lively little fishing and pleasure port (as the French call marinas), with a very attractive church and a profusion of sandy beaches. At the other end of the Armorique Corniche is the enormous Lieue de Grève beach, a league long and almost as wide when the tide is out.

Carantec is a more substantial beach resort at the end of the Morlaix River; hydrangeas and pine trees embellish the colonies of villas at Pen-al-Lann Point, and there are islands close inshore, one of which is accessible on foot at low tide.

Roscoff is the westernmost and most attractive of Channel ports, with many associations with Britain. Mary Stuart is thought to have landed here in 1548 on her way to meet the Dauphin, and the Young

Pretender nearly 200 years later in his flight from Culloden. The elegant Renaissance belfry above the church sports stone cannons to warn off the English, and inside has seven beautiful alabaster reliefs. There are attractive old streets decorated cheerfully with flowers, and boat trips to the nearby island of Batz (pronounced Baa). As this is a ferry terminal for Britain, shops are full of goodies to take back home. Roscoff itself does not have much of a beach, but there are good sandy ones a few kilometres to the west. Like all the Léon coast Roscoff specialises in the exploitation of seaweed – there are over 70 varieties here – for health and agricultural efficiency. Vegetable cultivation (artichokes, cauliflowers and onions) and privateering have brought the Roscovites prosperity for many centuries (though in the 1480s they went in for that least profitable of medieval activities, the financing of their sovereign's war against the French).

Just a few kilometres south, the vegetable market town of **St-Pol-de-Léon** is one of the seven original Breton bishoprics around the coast established by evangelising saintly invaders, in this case Saint Paul Aurelian. They made up the once famous pilgrimage, the Tro-Breiz, from Vannes to Dol-de-Bretagne, via Quimper, St-Pol, Tréguier, St-Brieuc and St-Malo. The popularity of the pilgrimage is no doubt attributable to the belief that if not achieved in life the journey had to be made after death, at a rate of a coffin's length every seven years, which would mean a wait of some 1 million years before even a very tall Breton, of which there are few, could expect to rest in peace. Arriving in the year 530 via the islands of Ouessant (or Ushant) and Batz, Saint Paul made his way to an oppidum surrounded by earthworks, which he penetrated to find a garrison of bees in a hollow tree, a bear, a wild bull, and a sow suckling its young. Expelling all but the last family group which he kept as pets, Saint Paul established himself in what became his see for 36 years until he went back to Batz where he died at the age of 104, so frail that his hands were translucent. St-Pol-de-Léon's former cathedral is a fine 13th- to 16th-century building of contrasting Caen limestone and granite, architecturally inspired, it is said, by Coutances. It may not surpass its model, but the nearby Kreisker chapel – its belfry is one of Brittany's most celebrated landmarks – did until its Norman prototype St-Pierre de Caen was destroyed in the War.

The amorphous resort of **Brignogan-Plages** straggles round a wide sandy bay littered with huge boulders. Beyond, the coastline wiggles round from Channel to Atlantic (a line from the rock on the right of the Aber-Ildut to the centre of Ushant theoretically divides one from the other), rocky and unremarkable save for the *abers* themselves; the northernmost and biggest of them, **Aber-Wrac'h**, is the best looking and best provided with tourist amenities. Further south the **Pointe de Corsen** is the true Finis Terrae, the westernmost point of mainland France – although most maps, being flat, will fool you into thinking that the Pointe du Raz sticks out further.

Where the coast turns abruptly back eastwards towards Brest, the **Pointe de St-Mathieu** commands splendid views southwards and indeed all round (especially from the top of the lighthouse) and has evocative medieval ruins of an old monastery founded in the 6th century.

Brest lies on one of the finest natural harbours in the world, with nearly 60 square miles of deep anchorage narrowly linked to the furious Atlantic. The great naval port was relentlessly bombed through the Second World War but has since grown up again big, clean, logical and uninteresting. The creation of the naval base and the shipbuilding colony of forced labourers (which was shifted to Devil's Island off French Guyana in the mid-19th century) is interestingly remembered in the Museum of Old Brest in the Tour Tanguy.

An impressive new bridge spans the Elorn and links Brest to the strawberry-growing Plougastel peninsula. Its main town, **Plougastel-Daoulas**, is not attractive, and the church there is very unpleasant, but the church's Calvary is one of the most elaborate and celebrated in Brittany. It was built shortly after a great plague in 1598; of its 180 figures the most vivid is poor Catell-Gollet, a Breton girl who refused her father's advice to get married because she liked dancing too much and ended up taking the Devil for a lover and giving him the body of Christ in the form of a communion wafer. Her punishment, as depicted here, was to be delivered on the Day of Judgement to the not altogether amorous treatment of the Devil and his ravenous fiends. Daoulas has a parish close (see page 398) which is not outstanding in Breton terms, and Romanesque abbey ruins, which are. Nearby **Dirinon's** low church is surprisingly crowned by an elegant Renaissance belfry with twin balconies below the spire.

Excursions from the coast

● **Huelgoat** A pleasant enough, though busy, woodland resort which makes a good base for pedestrian and motorised explorers. It's on the edge of the main chunk of the Armorican Regional Park, established to look after some of the most characteristic areas of islands, coastline and (as here) woodland or *argoat*. All round Huelgoat there are huge chaotic mossy boulders, and roaring underground rivers and grottos; and there are plenty of marked walks (maps are available at the tourist office in town).

● **Monts d'Arrée** Brittany's principal mountain range climbs wild and desolate or purple and gold according to the state of the heather and the gorse, to a peak of 384 metres, north of the once darkly wooded and increasingly reforested **Montagnes Noires**. Once these heights of Brittany stood over 4,000 metres tall, and when the Alps are as old – in some 300 million years time – they will be eroded to about this size, say the Bretons to those who scoff at their so-called mountains. Panoramic views are to be had from the **Roc'h Trévezel**, the **Montagne St-Michel** (both in the Monts d'Arrée), the **Roc'h de Toullaëron** in the Montagnes Noires, and most spectacularly of all from the isolated **Menez-Hom** at the base of the Crozon Peninsula.

Jutting out between Léon and Cornouaille, the **Crozon Peninsula** is blunted by the ocean into a hammerhead and shuts in the bays of Brest and, to a lesser extent, Douarnenez. At the foot of the Menez Hom the estuary of the Aulne River (rich in salmon) has been included in the Regional Park, as have sections of the rocky coastline at the end of the peninsula, the Pointe de Penhir and the Pointe des Espagnols. So these are officially typical Breton landscapes. Certainly the two capes are very fine examples of the wild grandeur of Finistère at its best, with dizzy views down on to crashing breakers and rough scrambles for the brave. There is also an alignment of menhirs near the lobster port and resort of **Camaret**, itself alluringly shabby. The Pointe des Espagnols, though less impressive than Penhir, does give excellent views towards Brest.

Morgat is the main resort on the peninsula, sheltered from the Atlantic in Douarnenez Bay, with a fine sandy beach and a number of grottoes to explore by boat or on foot.

Past the lonely chapel of **Ste-Anne-la-Palud** – distinguished by its *pardon*, its beach and its hotel, all among the finest of their kind in Brittany – a long empty sand and shingle beach curves round to **Douarnenez**. This was once the capital of Cornouaille and the sardine industry, but is no longer either, though it's still a large and busy fishing port. A new Port-Musée has opened here recently, encompassing almost every kind of marine attraction possible, including old sailing and fishing vessels.

Just a few kilometres inland, **Locronan** is an extremely picturesque village which once grew prosperous from cloth trading and which now stays so from tourism. There are craft shops (they still do a lot of weaving and sell jerseys), tea-shops, organic food shops, and antique shops. None of these should detract from the severe beauty of the monochrome main square with its Renaissance houses and church, all the same dark, damp grey which gives Locronan something of a Scottish look, reinforced by the open moorland hills behind. The church is full of interesting things, including an amusingly naïve carved and painted pulpit, telling the story, or several stories, of Saint Ronan, whose gleaming, black granite tomb lies nearby. When Saint Ronan died in the 5th century, the Bretons, uncertain as to where he should be buried, put his body in an ox-drawn cart to find its own resting place. The oxen did a circuit of his daily walk and had to squeeze between two rocks, where the passage of the cart left a mark. The steps of saint and oxen are retraced by pilgrims to the Locronan *pardons*. There are small ones in July every year and an extra special bonanza every six (1995).

Parish closes and pardons

The parish close, or enclosure, is a churchyard entered by a gateway which often takes the form of a triumphal arch, symbolic as it is of the entry into heaven. Within the enclosure are the graveyard and the church. In Brittany in the 16th and 17th centuries the graveyard became an elaborate work of art as it did nowhere else. One reason was the intensity of religious feeling and a particular preoccupation with death – the skeletal figure of Ankou, death itself, is one of the most important members of the dramatis personae of Breton religious art. Another important contributory factor to the development of the parish close was a fierce local rivalry that forced villages to try to outdo their neighbours by building bigger, better, and more elaborate closes. The parish close is a phenomenon not of the big towns but of the country villages. The art is popular art, and has unambiguous illustrations of the Scriptures for the majority who could not read. The medieval custom of passion plays lasted in Brittany, and the particular liveliness of the parish close sculptures clearly has much to do with this local dramatic tradition.

The church is typically charged with woodcarving, much of it brightly painted, all of it vigorous and expressive, but by no means always crude in its execution. A popular feature is a painted Glory Beam across the nave, usually with a Crucifix and often supported by carved pillars or a complete screen. Lively statues decorate the walls of the porch, the meeting place of the notables of the local parish councils. Outside, in the graveyard, the gateway becomes a triumphal arch, and a simple cross in front of the church becomes the Calvary – a complex freestanding monument in its own right with a Crucifixion scene on a base decorated with a wealth of relief carvings and statuettes telling the stories of the life of Christ and the Passion, with a few local moral tales thrown in for the edification of the masses (these Calvaries were often used as visual aids for sermons). Being carved in granite the Calvaries are mostly preserved in all their detail, if sometimes a little mossy,

Guimiliau

despite being out of doors; they have also been spared most of the depredations of the religious wars and the Revolution. Beside the church, simple charnel houses or ossuaries, built to house the bones exhumed to make room in the graveyard for the newly deceased, became as elaborately designed and decorated as the rest of the ensemble.

The extreme development of the parish close is to be seen in the neighbouring villages of **St-Thégonnec** and **Guimiliau**, south of the Landerneau/Morlaix road. St-Thégonnec is the later of the two and perhaps the more elegant as a whole; Guimiliau boasts Brittany's most crowded Calvary with over 200 figures, and has especially fine wood-carving in the church. There are many other less elaborate, but almost complete parish closes in Léon and northern Cornouaille (and one isolated one in the Morbihan at **Guéhenno** with a splendid Calvary), which may seem more attractive for being less showy. There are also a number of isolated Calvaries all over lower Brittany.

The following tour of religious monuments in the area, not all parish closes, proceeds anti-clockwise from Huelgoat, and does not include places mentioned elsewhere as part of the coastal tour. **St-Herbot**: very fine carved wooden screen in Gothic church; ossuary. **Notre-Dame-du-Crann**: a series of 16th-century stained-glass windows. **Pleyben**: parish close with magnificent Calvary and Renaissance church. **Brasparts**: interesting church and Calvary. **Sizun**: parish close with fine arch and ossuary. **Le Folgoët**: large pilgrimage church, much restored but with very fine granite screen and porch sculptures. **Berven**: parish close with fine arch outside and screen inside the Renaissance church. **Lampaul-Guimiliau**: parish close with exceptional painted carvings inside church. **Guimiliau** and **St-Thégonnec**: parish closes – see above.

Many Breton Calvaries form the object of regular pilgrimage processions called *pardons*, because of the absolution that is their motivation. Like the use of pre-Christian dolmens as crypts and the Christianisation of menhirs by carving a cross on them (the ancestor of the Calvary), Breton *pardons* exemplify the survival of pagan ritual in popular religious observance. The serious procession, like a pilgrimage, makes its way with due solemnity to the given Calvary or chapel, with participants in the costume of the region. Profane celebrations usually follow the ceremony, with drinking, dancing and trials of masculine strength – wrestling and stone-tossing.

The biggest *pardons* are at **Ste-Anne-d'Auray** all through the summer, but with the main event (Ste-Anne's day) on 26 July. There are other important ones at Pentecost and on 15 August.

Other particularly important *pardons* are: **Rumengol** (Trinity Sunday and 15 August); **Tréguier** (third Sunday in May); **Perros-Guirec** (15 August); **St-Jean-du-Doigt** (23/24 June); **Ste-Anne-la-Palud** (last Sunday in August; one of the most frequented and spectacular of all from the costume point of view); **Le Folgoët** (first Sunday in September). Several others take place in May, July and August.

From Douarnenez the **Cornouaille Peninsula** stretches out to Brittany's most famous cape, the **Pointe du Raz**, which would be impressively wild but for the complex of tourist shops and a car park where, here at the end of nowhere, you have to pay to park. Still, the popularity of the place is a measure of its natural grandeur. Beneath a strenuously emotive white statue of Our Lady of the Shipwrecks, a jagged rocky finger points westwards to the horizon, just broken by the almost flat island of Sein. When the spray leaps thundering around these rocks, under the bleak skies of winter storms, no question arises of nature's grand effect being spoilt. There is a path round the point (with a safety rope), which gives some dramatic views.

Between the Pointe du Raz and the less-crowded **Pointe du Van**, the gracefully curving **Baie des Trépassés** is rich in legend, inhabited by the spirits of the drowned, who are to be seen in the crests of the waves on All Souls' Day. The bay is also the conjectured site of the legendary city of Is, Brittany's Sodom, submerged in the 5th century in punishment for the licentious and murderous behaviour of King Gradlon's daughter Dahut.

There are more rocky points, mostly deserted and impressive, along the northern coast of the peninsula, and a bird reserve (Cap Sizun). Set in a deep estuary on the south coast, **Audierne** is a handsome old fishing port of some importance and considerable charm, with an unattractive beach resort nearby. There are boats from here to the Ile de Sein.

The low-lying **Penmarch Peninsula**, south of Audierne, is the best place in Brittany for the spotting of traditional costume and headgear: the local *coiffe* (the Bigoudène) is one of the most remarkable, perched like a menhir. Centuries ago the peninsula was very prosperous and populous, but the cod deserted its coasts and a rapacious Douarnenez bandit called La Fontenelle laid waste to it. Now the landscape is wide open and unlovely, dotted with little modern cottages. There remain for your admiration the fine late-Gothic church (St-Nonna) at Penmarch itself (still a sizeable town), and one of the earliest Calvaries of Brittany in a splendid windswept situation by the bleakly impressive coast at **Tronoën**. The spacious, unpretentious fishing port of **St-Guénolé** has a long beach, a tall lighthouse and a museum of prehistory. **Loctudy** is another spread-out, fishy, not very charming little resort, with one of Brittany's finest Romanesque churches. The nearby **Château de Kerazan** has a collection of works of art.

Pont-l'Abbé, the capital of Bigouden, isn't really a place to spend much time, but it does have an interesting local museum in the old castle, with lots of costumes.

The intimacy of the long, narrow, wooded estuary of the River Odet contrasts strikingly with the wide, windy openness of the west coast. This is the start of perhaps the most attractive and certainly the most popular stretch of the Breton coast – at least with the camping and yachting fraternity – which extends from Bénodet to Le Pouldu. **Bénodet**

Traditional costume and headgear can still be seen in the Bigouden,
around Pont l'Abbé

is one of the most popular and lively of all the resorts, more commercialised than other Breton resorts, but undeniably pretty. There's lots to
keep everyone amused – sports facilities, boat trips, and even a certain
amount of life after dark (not Brittany's speciality).

Quimper has been the capital of Cornouaille since King Gradlon
arrived there in flight from the tidal wave which engulfed Is. The old
king still rides on a steed of granite between the twin towers of the
cathedral. This is more of an inland than a seafaring town, spanning
the junction of the Rivers Odet and Steir where the two become an
estuary. In the centre, at least, it is a very attractive old market town,
with timber-framed houses, cobbled streets and plenty of shops selling
pottery and lace. There are bus and boat excursions, and a folklore
festival at the end of July.

Sights in Quimper

● **Cathedral** Twin slender spires of this interesting Gothic building
dominate the Quimper skyline. Its most striking feature is the
pronounced northward list of the choir; there is also some fine stained
glass and tomb sculpture. Extensive restoration work was in progress
in the choir and chancel when we visited in 1993.
● **Breton Museum** In the old Bishop's Palace, worth a visit in itself:
cloisters, ramparts and a spiral staircase. Interesting local costumes,
wood and stone carving, and pottery, well laid-out.
● **Fine Arts Museum** A collection well worth seeing, including Dutch
paintings and canvases by Boudin and Corot.

Excursions up the **Odet** river from Bénodet to Quimper (or vice versa) are very popular and a good way to see the thickly wooded and peaceful estuary – to see the Odet by any other means is difficult: this is one of its charms.

Beg-Meil is a much-frequented resort with beaches offering a variety of sand, dunes and rocks. **La Forêt-Fouesnant** is not much of a village but has a little modern marina at the head of an attractive wooded inlet much favoured by campers and sailors. Walks all round are very pleasant. A few kilometres inland, **Fouesnant** itself is known for the best Breton cider and the local headdress; it has an interesting 12th-century church.

The big tourist attraction, even trap, of this part of the coast is the old walled town which sits on an island in the waters of one of Brittany's most important fishing ports, **Concarneau**. The rest of Concarneau is of moderate interest, as busy ports are, and has a few rather scruffy beaches. The Ville Close, as the old town is called, is picturesque in the extreme, with ramparts giving good views over the port and town. The single long central street is lined with crêperies and souvenir shops selling costumed dolls; there is a comprehensive fishing museum with old boats and items illustrating local history. The Ville Close is linked to the mainland by a fortified bridge at one end and a little ferry at the other.

The next estuary along the coast is the famous Aven, less frequented for its seaside facilities than for the artistic associations of Pont-Aven upstream, where the estuary begins to open out. The inlet itself and surrounding countryside are very attractive: hedgerows, curving lanes, woods and rocky river banks. **Kerdruc** is a charming little port, and **Kerascoët** has several of the thatched farm cottages that remain in this area. **Raguenès-Plage** is a small village with several beaches and camp-sites; **Port-Manech** is a delightful little fishing cove and resort, with a sheltered beach.

Pont-Aven is intimately tucked below beech- and chestnut-covered hills; the river bounds down to a rocky little port below the village. Once there were as many watermills as houses at Pont-Aven, but only a few are left now. The village teems with people, cars and caravans and is very commercialised – galleries and souvenir shops as well as a museum with a history of the town's artists and a gallery of Breton landscapes. You won't see the greatest achievements on canvas of the Pont-Aven School, but you can still follow a signed walk through the Bois de l'Armour up on the hill above the Aven, where many of them were conceived.

Among schools of mostly mediocre artists from all over the world who were attracted by the picturesque Breton life and landscape, the village's most distinguished colonists were Paul Gauguin and Emile Bernard. These two, collaborating fruitfully in the late 1880s, went beyond the merely picturesque to evolve a new style of painting itself –

expressive of what Gauguin described as the 'great rustic, superstitious simplicity' of the Bretons. Pont-Aven is recorded in a 19th-century guidebook for English art tourists: 'The art student who has spent the winter in the Quartier Latin comes when the leaves are green and settles down for the summer to study undisturbed . . . his surroundings are delightful, everything he needs is to be obtained in an easy way . . . the climate is temperate and favourable to outdoor work. At the sunny end of the square the Hôtel des Voyageurs gets mostly Americans (some stay all year). Down by the bridge is the Pension Gloanec, the true Bohemian home also decorated with paintings.'

The Bélon River, which joins the Aven at the sea, is no less famous than its arty neighbour, because of the local type of oyster that bears its name. *Bélons* are the original edible oyster, flat as opposed to hollow (the so-called Portuguese oysters), and are now farmed all over Brittany and beyond; this is a good place to look at the exposure of oyster-beds in the muddy inlet at low tide. **Le Pouldu** was Gauguin's seaside home after he left Pont-Aven in 1889; it's a small port and resort at the mouth of the exotically named and attractively wooded Laita, with a good beach looking south. Gaugin and his artist friends stayed at the Maison Henri, where the inn has been reconstructed with period furniture and copies of the paintings which smothered the walls of the dining-room (the painter left a few paintings with the landlady – Marie Henri – as surety against rent he owed). **Quimperlé** has nothing to do with Quimper except that it too is at the junction of two rivers for which the local word is *kemper*. It has attractive old streets with ramshackle timbered houses, a colourful fish market and a beautiful cruciform Romanesque church, all close together at the heart of the town.

Morbihan and Loire-Atlantique

The south-east corner of Brittany is the land of megalithic monuments and the great lake which is the Gulf of Morbihan (which means little sea). Beyond it the Loire-Atlantique *département* is outside Brittany for administrative purposes, but historically it isn't – Nantes was the capital city of many of Brittany's most prestigious dukes, the Montforts – and for the tourist it is at least as Breton as it is Loire country.

Lorient was a custom-built port for the French East India Company, whence its name; now it's important for fishing. Like Brest it was unattractive even before the Second World War reduced it to rubble. The modern church of Notre-Dame-de-Victoire and the Palais des Congrès are, however, of interest. Across the estuary **Port-Louis** still has its own citadel and an interesting naval museum.

Even if you don't approach **Carnac** through its famous alignments (see page 408), there is no mistaking the *raison d'être* of this, the proud capital of prehistory, with its Hôtel Tumulus and many other establishments which it is to be hoped do not carry their prehistoric affiliations further than their names. In no other region of Brittany is there to be found such a variety of megalithic remains – menhirs, cromlechs, dolmens and tumuli – as around the once impressively wild and desolate coast of the Bay of Quiberon and the Gulf of Morbihan. Carnac has an important prehistory museum founded by the archaeologist James Miln. In a clear layout it displays a plethora of beautiful objects, while clever reconstructions provide edification. There is an interesting 17th-century church and a good view of the coast and alignments from the top of a tumulus called St-Michel.

Old Carnac almost merges with new **Carnac-Plage**, a pleasantly spacious beach resort in the garden suburb style, but with a characterless modern centre. It is sheltered from the open sea by the long **Quiberon peninsula**, once an island but now joined by the build-up of a low, sandy strip of land (the same is happening at Mont-St-Michel and Ile de Bréhat). The rocky west coast of this effective breakwater, the Côte Sauvage, seems rather misleadingly named if the weather is good and the sea calm. But bathing accidents do happen and there are warnings against swimming from the enticing sandy coves between the sharp rocks. Round the tip of the peninsula and along its sandy eastern shore, there is a succession of busy, rather unattractive resorts of which **Quiberon** itself is the biggest and by far the best choice.

With all its yachts and islands the muddy **Gulf of Morbihan** is very pretty at high tide, and the colour of its water famed for its brilliance. But when the tide is out there are enormous expanses of mud with oyster beds, and its beaches are correspondingly imperfect or even poor. At the lower entrance of the gulf, **Locmariaquer** is an attractive little resort as well as the site of very important prehistoric remains (see page 409). The road round the gulf is long and, especially between Auray and Vannes, not very interesting; it is much better to explore by boat.

At the head of its own river estuary, feeding the gulf, **Auray** has a very attractive old quarter (**St-Goustan**) down by the water, across the river from the main town. Nearby is the battlefield where, in 1364, the anglophile Montfort family won control of Brittany from the French. **Ste-Anne-d'Auray** is the most important pilgrimage centre in Brittany; a vast basilica was erected here in the last century.

Vannes is the old regional capital and one of the most favoured residences of the Montfort dukes. It is one of the best-looking old towns in Brittany, with well-preserved town walls, massive fortified gateways, beautiful gardens and the river at their feet. Within the walls cobbled pedestrian streets are overhung by timbered houses, many of them the object of careful restoration. The cathedral is interesting rather than

beautiful: there is a round Renaissance chapel with Saint Vincent Ferrier's tomb, and remnants of cloisters from the same period. In the old town there is an archaeological museum.

The road south of the gulf along the Rhuys Peninsula gives fine views of its scintillating waters, but neither the landscape nor the waterside villages are of particular interest. **St-Gildas-de-Rhuys** has memories of Abélard, who was miserable here as abbot and whose letters to Heloïse paint a now surprising picture of the desolation of the region, with its population of wolves and bears and scarcely more civilised humanity – the monks repeatedly tried to poison Abélard as they resented his attempts to impose discipline. The old abbey church is partly Romanesque and houses the tomb of the 6th-century Cornish missionary Gildas; it has a rich treasury. Along the coast eastwards the solid ducal castle of **Suscinio**, built in the 13th century, is a splendidly impressive empty shell; the sea, which used to fill its moat at high tide, is now half a mile away.

Excursions from the coast

• **Tours d'Elven** (north-east of Vannes) The two imposing granite towers of this château are romantic of aspect and association (Henry not yet the VII of England was imprisoned here); they were made famous in the 19th century by the enormously successful though now not undeservedly neglected novelist Octave Feuillet ('nothing more imposing, proud and sombre than this old *donjon*, impassive in the mists of time and isolated in the thick of these woods. Trees have grown to full stature in the deep moat and their highest branches hardly reach the lowest windows . . . In the solitude, faced with this abrupt mass of bizarre architecture it is impossible not to think of enchanted towers where beauteous princesses sleep away centuries').

● **Château de Josselin** This château stands substantially intact, marvellously situated, rising granite grey from the bank of the reflective River Oust and guarding the old town. Augustus Hare described Josselin as the Warwick Castle of France and the comparison is apt. Behind the forbidding round towers, built in the 14th century, the interior courtyard is over a century younger and beautifully decorated, a marvellous example of the intricate fantasy of late Gothic carving. Josselin's most glorious memory is the Combat of Thirty in 1351, when the English and French captains of Ploërmel and Josselin each led 30 knights into the field for a full day's set-to, to resolve their conflict. The French were victorious under Beaumanoir, whose widow, a Rohan, married Olivier de Clisson. The proud family – Clisson's motto was, roughly translated, 'because I feel like it', the Rohan's 'king I cannot be, prince I disdain to be, Rohan I am' – still own the château which is open in summer. Most of the interior is the work of 19th-century restorers, but no less interesting for that. Next door to the château is a wonderful doll museum which has some fine examples ranging from the 15th century to the present day. The large town church – Our Lady of the Brambles – contains the extremely beautiful double tomb of de Clisson and Marguerite de Rohan.

● **Ploërmel** This pretty old town has a remarkably ornate 16th-century church with fine stained glass as well as interesting sculptures. The pleasantly wooded valleys of the interior are worth exploring for churches:

Château de Josselin

- **Le Faouët** Near this attractive old village there are three chapels of interest: St-Fiacre and St-Nicholas have beautifully carved wooden screens full of humour; St-Barbe is an important *pardon* chapel.
- **Kernascléden** In a tiny village the surprisingly large, mottled grey church has wonderfully decorative architectural features, painted apostles in the porch, and a rare series of frescoes inside, including a gruesome depiction of Hell.
- **Guéhenno** This church has a fine Calvary, with an ossuary clearly representing the tomb of Christ, and a splendid statue of a cock crowing.

South of the Vilaine, the Guérande Peninsula, with its saltpans and the enormous beach of La Baule, gives a foretaste of the Atlantic coast. **Guérande** itself is a finely situated and remarkably preserved medieval walled town dominating the salt-pans reclaimed from the sea. There is an interesting local museum in the eastern fortified gateway illustrating, among much else, the how and why of the local salt industry, which originally had much to do with Guérande's status as a tax haven, exempt from the dreaded *gabelle* salt tax. The grey collegiate church of St-Aubin has some interesting features, including lively capital carving.

Narrow roads follow the banks between the salt-pans to the Grand Traict lagoon and the attractive old yacht, fish and crustacean port of **Le Croisic**. It has handsome 17th-century houses around the harbour, which is very animated and commercialised, partly because it's so near La Baule. On the quayside there is an exotic aquarium.

The drive round the Pointe back to La Baule follows the Grande Côte (rocky but not particularly impressive) and passes the old salt port of **Batz**, now, unlike Le Croisic, a resort with sandy beaches, retaining a late-Gothic church (St-Guénolé) whose belfry gives enormous views.

La Baule is unlike the Breton resorts of north or south coast; it resembles much more the long, modern seafront straggles of the Atlantic coast. The essence of the resort is an enormous crescent of fine sand which would probably win a French 'Best Beach' competition. Behind it stand anonymous apartment blocks, palatial hotels and villas with gardens (at the residential Baule-les-Pins end of the beach). It is not much younger as a resort than Dinard but the difference in atmosphere is one of generations. Dinard was fashionable with English and Americans when they were fashionable, La Baule is fashionable and popular with the French now, and is full of young people (as well as pampered pensioners who rarely leave the confines of their luxury hotels). There are golf courses, sailing schools, beach clubs, tennis clubs, cinemas, discothèques and nightclubs, an aero club, two yacht harbours, equestrian centres, a theatre festival, concerts, a *pardon* and a Breton Week (last week in August). There are thousands of hotel rooms, camping places, villas in the pines, apartments by the sea and 2,000 hours of sun a year, thanks apparently to the saltpans.

Megaliths

Alignments at Carnac

There can be few Breton words that have been adopted by other languages. Three that have are menhir, dolmen, and cromlech – different sorts of prehistoric stone monuments or megaliths, the work of unknown inhabitants of the area probably between 4,000 and 1,800 BC. They are to be found all over Europe and beyond but nowhere in such abundance as in Brittany. The area of greatest concentration is in the south-east, around Carnac and the Morbihan gulf, where there are several thousand stones, many of them aligned. The prodigious weight-lifting enthusiasm of the early Bretons (the largest menhir at Locmariaquer weighed some 340 tonnes), and the particular importance of Carnac remain something of a mystery, but the religious and often funerary significance of the megaliths is universally accepted – skeletons, in many cases dating from a much later period than the monuments themselves, have been found under many dolmens (flat-topped, table-like structures previously imagined to have been altars for human sacrifice) and within tumuli (the earth, or stones, which used to cover dolmens).

The following are the most important of Breton megalithic sites:

Carnac Nearly 3,000 menhirs in the fields on the edge of town arranged in three main alignments, two of which (the Ménec and Kerlescan alignments) end in semi-circular apse-like rings of menhirs, giving the alignments the look of foundations for enormous cathedrals. Of the numerous theories put forward to explain the significance of the Carnac lines, including the 'windbreak for Roman tents' suggestion, the most picturesque is the local legend of Saint Cornelius who was Pope in 3rd-century Rome but was expelled and chased by Roman soldiers all the way to Brittany. Here he found the inhabitants of Carnac sowing seeds; 'Tomorrow your corn will be ripe,' he told them. The next day the

Romans arrived and enquired as to Cornelius's whereabouts, and were told that he had passed through when the corn was being sown. Concluding from the advanced state of the crop that Cornelius must be many months ahead of them the Romans struck camp. The saint, hidden nearby, realised himself to be cornered with his back against the sea, and turned all the Romans to stone overnight. More recently it has been concluded from the precise orientation of Breton alignments towards the position of sun and moon at particular times of year (equinoxes and solstices) that these open-air cathedrals were indeed the temples of sun worshippers. A good view of the lines is to be had from the top of the tumulus St-Michel, whose passages (dug by archaeologists) and burial chamber you can visit.

Locmariaquer The so-called Witches' Stone must have been a staggering sight, over 20 metres high and 340 tonnes in weight, the largest menhir ever raised. Some time at the end of the 17th or beginning of the 18th century it was shattered, perhaps by lightning, into five pieces of which four remain in situ. Next door is a magnificent dolmen, the Merchant's Table, encased within a reconstructed cairn and composed of three granite slabs resting on 17 pointed supports, with some carvings in the stone.

Tumulus de Gavrinis The most impressive covered burial chamber in Brittany, on an island in the Morbihan Gulf easily accessible by boat from Larmor-Baden. There's a long gallery with patterned carvings on the supporting menhirs, and a funeral chamber.

Lagatjar Intersecting alignments of over a hundred stones near Camaret.

Brignogan-Plages Just one of many Christianised menhirs (the Miracle Stone) surmounted by one cross and inscribed with another.

La Roche-aux-Fées (Fairies' Rock) Between Le Theil and Marcillé-Robert, south-east of Rennes, this is an 18-metre covered gallery of purple slate stones.

Islands

Of the scores of islands around Brittany few are inhabited or easily accessible. The two islands that bear the brunt of the Atlantic storms are **Ouessant** (Ushant), and **Sein** just off the Pointe du Raz. These rugged outposts are full of legendary and historical interest, but bleak to visit.

Ushant is the westernmost point of France, an important staging post for sailors and migratory birds (access from Brest and Le Conquet). Little **Molène** lies between Ushant and the coast and is part of the Armorique Regional Park. There doesn't seem much to preserve except the primitiveness. It has an inn, a few creeks and room for some simple camping in summer (access from Brest and Le Conquet).

The little island of **Sein** was the last haven of paganism in Brittany, a Druidical burial site, and a renowned residence of wreckers. In 1940 the Germans found a community without any active males, all of whom had responded to General de Gaulle's appeal from London. The island was decorated for its devotion to duty (access from Audierne).

The islands off the south coast are more sheltered and clement and are busy in season. Well-named **Belle-Ile** has excellent beaches (east of Le Palais, and at Port-Donnant – this last dangerous for bathing), a choice of accommodation (at Le Palais, Sauzon or Port Goulphar), very fine rocky coastal scenery (the south-west coast), and a couple of attractive villages (Le Palais with Vauban fortifications, and Sauzon). The car ferry from Quiberon is in heavy demand in the summer months, and unless you are going for more than a few days it is cheaper to hire a car on the island, which improves your chances of getting off it when you want. The nearby islands of **Houat** and **Hoëdic** are also accessible from Quiberon and have good beaches.

Like Belle-Ile, the island of **Groix** has impressive rocky cliffs at one end, good sandy beaches at the other, and an attractive little port (access from Lorient).

The **Glénan Islands** have important schools for the instruction of sailing and skin-diving, and large colonies of seabirds (access from Benodet and half a dozen other nearby resorts).

Between the Vilaine and the Loire lies the **Brière Regional Park**, established in 1970 in an attempt to prevent the extinction of a unique way of life. The Brièrons traditionally punted around the canals and the marshes, shot the abundant wildlife, speared eels, cut peat, thatched cottages, and made their own clogs. Gradually the factories and shipyards of St-Nazaire claimed more livelihoods and the canals became overgrown. Now a complete old village (Kerhinet) has been restored, canals have been cleared, and cottage industries established. The most interesting and tourist-orientated part of the region is the island of **Fédrun**, which is separated from St-Joachim by a network of canals. You can take boat trips on the canals, and there is a small, marshy animal and bird park at Rosé nearby.

St-Nazaire is a busy modern shipyard and commercial port created in the 19th century to accommodate shipping which increasingly outgrew the stretch of the Loire up as far as Nantes; like so many other ports it was rebuilt after the Second World War and is without general appeal to the tourist. The maritime stretch of France's greatest river, between Nantes and St-Nazaire, is industrial.

Nantes's prosperity came principally from the sea, but it has historically been more than just a port: the capital of Brittany in the most brilliant years of the duchy (15th century), an important university city and an administrative centre. It is not immediately attractive, having suffered greatly in the Second World War. But if you are stuck in La Baule on a wet day there is no shortage of things to see in the city (except on Tuesdays).

Sights in Nantes

• **Ducal castle** Built by Anne of Brittany's father, Duke François II, in the mid-15th century, a splendid combination of military might and decorative richness, not unlike some early Loire châteaux. Two of the three museums housed here are worth seeing: one recalling the history of Nantes the port, with mementoes of the slave trade among many other nautical items, the other devoted to Breton art and folklore.

• **Cathedral** Although not finished until the 19th century this is basically a soaring late-Gothic church, distinguished above all by Michel Colombe's wonderful double tomb of Duke François II and his wife Marguerite de Foix, which was saved from Revolutionary demolition by a brave town architect.

• **Museums** The fine arts museum contains a varied collection of paintings, with more than a few masterpieces (including three Georges de la Tours). Just off the rue Voltaire is a cluster of four varied museums: natural history (an odd and quirky place), anthropology and ancient sculpture; local archaeology; and in the Palais Dobrée a rich collection of sculptures, *objets d'art*, and paintings.

• **Old houses** The former Feydeau Island in the Loire (between the bus station and Place Royale) retains its 18th-century elegance from the time of Nantes's greatest prosperity based on the slave trade.

HOTELS

> Key: ◆ = 0–250FF, ◆◆ = 251–450FF, ◆◆◆ = over 451FF; prices are per
> double room without breakfast, which costs around 35–60FF extra. Some
> hotels may insist on half-board during high season, some hotels or restau-
> rants may close at specific times during the week – it is always worth
> checking. Most hotels accept the major credit cards; we have indicated
> where a hotel takes no credit cards.

ARRADON

Les Vénètes

La Pointe
56610 Morbihan
TEL 97 44 03 11

Les Vénètes makes the most of its position right on the water's edge of the Golfe
du Morbihan; most of its rooms look out on a panoply of tree-covered islands
and an assortment of boats. All but one of the simple bedrooms, with modern
furniture and old-fashioned bathrooms, have this view; those on the first floor
have a balcony as well. The *patron*, dapper in his bow tie, fusses around the bar/
reception which opens on to a little terrace with yellow and blue awnings. The
rest of the ground floor is taken up with the restaurant, where flowers bedeck
the tables, ships' wheels are carved into the beamed ceiling and big windows
make the most of the nautical view. Dinner itself lacks a bit of sparkle.

OPEN Apr to end Sept ROOMS 12 (all with bath or shower)

AUDIERNE

Le Goyen

29770 Finistère
TEL 98 70 08 88; FAX 98 70 18 77

The turquoise shutters and geranium-covered balconies of Cap Sizun's most
stylish hotel overlook Audierne's harbour. The well-decorated bedrooms vary
greatly, though all are good value. But Le Goyen's fame rests primarily on its
adventurous fish restaurant, one of Brittany's best, a traditionally formal place
with a conservatory overlooking the harbour. Well-heeled yachters in jeans
make it more relaxed than you might expect. It is difficult to know whether to
cut costs and take the excellent-value half-board menu, or indulge in plates of
crustaceans and delicate pastry creations for which the restaurant is justly
famous. Breakfast is well above average.

OPEN All year exc. mid-Nov to mid-Dec ROOMS 26 (all with bath)

LA BAULE

La Palmeraie

7 allée des Cormorans
44500 Loire-Atlantique
TEL 40 60 24 41; FAX 40 42 73 71

Among the many similar hotels in Edwardian-style villas among the pine trees of the residential part of La Baule, between beach and high street, La Palmeraie stands out. The three-sided building encloses palms and a flush of pink and red roses. A short flight of steps leads up to a terrace bar under a creeper-covered trellis; behind it, big flower arrangements decorate the old-fashioned restaurant. By comparison, bedrooms are a little dour, perhaps with dull brown walls and carpets and old tiled bathrooms.

OPEN Early Apr to end Sept ROOMS 23 (all with bath or shower)

BENODET

Menez-Frost

4 rue Jean Charcot
29118 Finistère
TEL 98 57 03 09; FAX 98 54 84 25

Choose this as a base if your family wants to stay in Bénodet. It is a large, well-run, friendly hotel in its own grounds in the centre of the resort. The buildings, some modern, some old, overlook a pool and the colourful gardens, which include hydrangeas, roses, carnations, palms and cedars. The breakfast room (there is no restaurant) and bar occupy a modern extension. Bedrooms are generally large, though with dull décor – heavy floral patterns and solid wooden furniture. For longer stays there are well-equipped self-catering apartments.

OPEN May to end Sept ROOMS 40 (all with bath) FACILITIES Heated outdoor pool, sauna, solarium, tennis

BUBRY

Auberge de Coët-Diquel

56310 Morbihan
TEL 97 51 70 70; FAX 97 51 73 08

The surrounding conifers, the neatness of the grounds, the tinkling millstream and the design of the modern building makes you think more of Germany than of France when you arrive at this comfortable hotel deep in the countryside north of Lorient. The covered swimming pool, tennis court and generally relaxed attitude are bonus points to add to the small but well-equipped bedrooms. The dining room is large and rather impersonal, and friendly service compensates for the rather ordinary food.

OPEN Mid-Mar to end Nov ROOMS 20 (all with bath or shower) FACILITIES Heated indoor pool, tennis

CARANTEC

Pors-Pol

7 rue Surcouf
29226 Finistère
TEL 98 67 00 52

This large three-storey building, with a hedged garden leading to a small beach less than 50 metres away, is set in the quieter suburbs of Carantec. Its large, simple, rustic dining-room is packed to the gunnels in summer with locals and tourists alike. It is a no-frills place: food arrives soon after being ordered, and the wine bottle is plonked in your ashtray. The plainly but decently furnished bedrooms can be a little cramped.

OPEN Early Apr to mid-Sept ROOMS 30 (all with bath)

CARNAC

Lann-Roz ◆◆

36 avenue de la Poste
56340 Morbihan
TEL 97 52 10 48; FAX 97 52 29 93

This pleasantly ageing white and grey slate building with creepers, roses and a very flowery garden stands on the main road between Carnac-Ville and Carnac-Plage. Breton prints and furniture and the live parrot help give it a homely feel. The restaurant is popular with non-residents, and serves good food. Be prepared for a frenzy of pink in the bedrooms: pink wicker chairs, pink lampshades, pink-edged mirrors, pink bathrooms . . .

OPEN Mid-Feb to early Jan ROOMS 18 (all with bath or shower)

LE CONQUET

La Pointe Sainte-Barbe

29217 Finistère
TEL 98 89 00 26; FAX 98 89 14 81

The Pointe Sainte-Barbe is a good hotel in an area where they are thin on the ground. It is also a good staging post for trips out to Ouessant. The building is in a beautiful spot, overlooking the sea and harbour, but it is remarkably ugly, with concrete columns rising out of the rock. At the back of the hotel is a vast light and simple dining-room with windows everywhere. The seafood comes fresh, beautifully presented and in large quantities. Other dishes can be rather heavy or dull. Most of the functional modern bedrooms have a sea view, and these tend to be the most spacious and better equipped.

OPEN Mid-Dec to mid-Nov ROOMS 49 (37 with bath or shower)

DINAN

Hôtel de la Porte St-Malo

35 rue Saint Malo
22100 Côtes-d'Armor
TEL 96 39 19 76

The hotel lies only five minutes' walk from the centre of Dinan, but is outside the old ramparts and free from the tourist jostle. It is a simple place, with a large bar (which closes early) patronised by locals, and a sequence of comfortable, modern rooms, furnished without elaboration but with everything you need. There are one or two outside corners in which to sun yourself. No restaurant.

OPEN All year ROOMS 16 (12 with bath or shower)

DINARD

Emeraude–Plage

1 boulevard Albert 1er
35800 Ille-et-Vilaine
TEL 99 46 15 79; FAX 99 88 15 31

Hogging the corner plot of a terraced row in the centre of Dinard, just off the beach, Emeraude-Plage has an ideal location. It is a busy hotel, popular with families, and serves good food at affordable prices. Most of the rooms are well furnished, seaward-facing and bright and airy; avoid those on the ground floor because of traffic noise and late-night revellers.

OPEN April to early Oct ROOMS 60 (55 with bath or shower) (Credit cards not accepted)

DOUARNENEZ

Auberge de Kervéoc'h

route de Kervéoc'h
29100 Finistère
TEL 98 92 07 58

Some noise from passing traffic filters through to this amalgam of old farm buildings 5km south of Douarnenez. An old barn, a creeper-covered house and a converted stable block look on to the hydrangea and geranium-dotted court-yard. Behind it lies a large and pleasant garden with a pond and geese. Beams, low ceilings and stone floors make the sitting-room and dining-rooms cosy. Large fusty-smelling bedrooms, with dated furry wallpaper, wardrobes and chests of drawers, make up in character what they lack in style.

OPEN Easter to end Sept ROOMS 14 (all with bath or shower)

BRITTANY

FREHEL

Relais de Fréhel

route du Cap
22240 Côtes-d'Armor
TEL 96 41 43 02

Relais de Fréhel is a wonderful rustic hideaway, run by the same family for over 20 years. Deep in the countryside, it is a long, stone-walled house surrounded by trees, with a tennis court. Low wooden beams and heavy Breton furniture make it a snug place to stay. Rooms are basic, with partitioned shower rooms and separate toilets. Food is good – fish and meat are grilled on the fire that warms the room.

OPEN Apr to early Nov ROOMS 13 (7 with bath or shower) FACILITIES Tennis

LE FRET

Hostellerie de la Mer

le Port
Crozon
29160 Finistère
TEL 98 27 61 90; FAX 98 27 65 89

In this simple hotel in the tiny fishing village of Le Fret it is probably worth paying a little extra for a bedroom overlooking the calm waters of the Rade de Brest. All bedrooms are small but functional, with traditional wallpaper and tub baths. The large, popular restaurant is probably the best on the peninsula. Service is jovial but correct and the food good value.

OPEN All year exc. Jan ROOMS 25 (all with bath or shower)

JOSSELIN

Château les Cheminées

117 rue Glatinier
56120 Morbihan
TEL 97 22 29 97

Should you be yearning for an English-style B&B, full of familiar accents and familiar furniture, Lesley and Andy Robinson's splendid house on the outskirts of Josselin will oblige. But it is not recommended merely as a refuge for Francophobes; it is a good-natured and comfortable place to stay in this over-crowded town, with a relaxing garden and spacious rooms. Breakfast is included in the room price.

OPEN All year ROOMS 3 (all with bath or shower) (Credit cards not accepted)

LANDUJAN

Le Château de Léauville

route de Bécherel
35360 Ille-et-Vilaine
TEL 99 07 21 14; FAX 99 07 21 80

In deep countryside north-west of Rennes, this 16th-century, three-storey
château looks enchantingly untouched from the outside, with roses growing
against the walls and a peaceful old garden where chairs and a swimming-pool
promise relaxation, and friendly horses come to make your acquaintance. Inside
it is quiet, simple and comfortable, with large, if rather sparse bedrooms. It is
possible to eat here when there are enough guests, but check when you book.

OPEN Mid-Mar to mid-Nov ROOMS 7 (all with bath) FACILITIES Heated outdoor pool

LANNION

Porte de France

5 rue Jean Savidan
22300 Côtes-d'Armor
TEL 96 46 54 81; FAX 96 46 54 81

A rather eccentric hotel, this (you may stumble across pieces of junk, such as old
typewriters, in the corridor), but nevertheless a good choice in Lannion. It is a
stone's throw from the centre, with old-fashioned but comfortable rooms with
en suite bathrooms. a cosy bar with a huge stone fireplace lies opposite a gloomy
breakfast room. There is no restaurant.

OPEN All year ROOMS 9 (all with bath or shower)

LOCRONAN

Manoir de Moëllien

Plonévez-Porzay
29560 Finistère
TEL 98 92 50 40

Surrounded by farmland and reached by a sleepy country lane, this solid 17th-
century stone manor house makes an ideal rural retreat. It is just 3km from
Locronan and barely further from the sandy beaches of the bay of Douarnenez.
Coach parties come for lunch in the tiled and beamed dining-room; above,
reached by a spiral stone staircase, is an enormous room used to exhibit paintings. The bedrooms, all with pleasant countryside views, are side-by-side in the
stable block. They are less impressive than the public rooms, but comfortable.

OPEN End Mar to early Jan ROOMS 10 (all with bath)

BRITTANY

NANTES

Hotel Amiral

26 bis rue Scribe
44000 Loire-Atlantique
TEL 40 69 20 21; FAX 40 73 98 13

Close to the place Graslin, and with a secure car park nearby, this modern hotel is primarily kitted out for business people, but makes a friendly and unassuming spot for an overnight stay. The street is quiet and within easy walking distance of the shops and restaurants of the centre. Get a street map before trying to find your way by car or the one-way system will drive you to despair. No restaurant, but plenty in town.

OPEN All year ROOMS 49 (all with bath)

PAIMPOL

Le Repaire de Kerroc'h

29 quai Morand
22500 Côtes-d'Armor
TEL 96 20 50 13; FAX 96 22 07 46

Formerly a corsair's house, this large mansion overlooks the wide harbour of Paimpol. High-ceilinged rooms are named after the islands which lie off the coast. A formal restaurant serves expensive but delicious menus, each course preceded by a taster – one garlic oyster, a tiny portion of caramel custard, for example.

OPEN All year exc. first two weeks Feb, first week Jun, last 2 weeks Nov ROOMS 13 (all with bath)

PAIMPONT

Relais de Brocéliande

Bourg
Plélan-le-Grand
35380 Ille-et-Vilaine
TEL 99 07 81 07; FAX 99 07 80 60

Ideally placed for exploring the forest of Brocéliande, this hotel has the perfect combination of comfortable (indeed positively smart) rooms, a lively bar/restaurant with plenty of locals and a friendly and down-to-earth management. Most of the bedrooms are well tucked away from the bar, and some face onto a beautiful secluded garden. The food has no pretensions to grandeur, but comes in substantial and satisfying portions.

OPEN All year ROOMS 24 (12 with bath or shower)

PERROS-GUIREC

Le Sphinx

67 chemin de la Messe
22700 Côtes-d'Armor
TEL 96 23 25 42; FAX 96 91 26 13

This cliff-edge hotel, with direct access to the beach, is in a quiet, residential corner of town. Most bedrooms have a view over the sea, a couple have terraces. A smart open-plan dining room and bar also overlook the sea.

OPEN Mid-Feb to early Jan ROOMS 20 (all with bath)

Hermitage

rue des Frères le Montréer
22700 Côtes-d'Armor
TEL 96 23 21 22; FAX 96 91 16 56

Up the hill, some distance from the beach, the Hermitage is well placed for the shops, but separated from the main road by a private walled garden. The large family bedrooms are clean and reasonably priced.

OPEN Mid-May to mid-Oct ROOMS 23 (all with bath or shower)

PLOZEVET

Moulin de Brénizénec

route de Pont l'Abbé
29710 Finistère
TEL 98 91 30 33

The present owners of Moulin de Brénizénec also used to operate this 19th-century watermill, whose gears and wheels are still in place. 'I'm a miller, not a chef,' declares friendly Monsieur Le Guellec, explaining why B&B only is available. In summer, breakfast may be served in the garden to the sound of the river flowing beneath its willows. There is a small dining-room and a simple sitting-room, both with exposed stone walls. Sloping ceilings, beams, anterooms, big bathrooms and heavy-patterned floral wallpaper make bedrooms quirky; a couple have a kitchen unit.

OPEN Nov to end Sept ROOMS 10 (all with bath) (Credit cards not accepted)

Key: ◆ = 0–250FF, ◆◆ = 251–450FF, ◆◆◆ = over 451FF; prices are per double room without breakfast, which costs around 35–60FF extra. Some hotels may insist on half-board during high season, some hotels or restaurants may close at specific times during the week – it is always worth checking. Most hotels accept the major credit cards; we have indicated where a hotel takes no credit cards.

PONT-L'ABBE

Château de Kernuz

route de Penmarc'h
29120 Finistère
TEL 98 87 01 59; FAX 98 66 02 36

Down a track behind massive walls, the 16th-century château surrounded by tended lawns, dovecote and palm trees is surprisingly affordable. The delights to be found inside include a chandeliered bar with art deco mirrors, beautiful parquet floors and big soft-hued watercolours. The bedrooms are generally large and furnished with antiques; some elements of simplicity remain, however – for example, a curtain to separate bedroom from bathroom. The short and uninspiring menu may make B&B the best option.

OPEN Apr to end Sept ROOMS 19 (all with bath) FACILITIES Outdoor pool, tennis

QUIBERON

Gulf Stream

17 boulevard Chanard
56170 Morbihan
TEL 97 50 16 96; FAX 97 50 35 64

In an excellent position overlooking the town beach and a short walk from the town centre, the white frontage of the Gulf Stream, decorated with flower baskets, shutters and balustrades, is immediately attractive. Bedrooms have character and space, and many have balconies, with either a sea view (for which you pay more) or a view over the pretty garden. There is no restaurant, but there is a cosy bar and a breakfast room.

OPEN Apr to end Oct ROOMS 24 (all with bath or shower)

RAGUENES-PLAGE

Chez Pierre

Névez
29139 Finistère
TEL 98 06 81 06

This much-developed stone Breton building right on the roadside appears unprepossessing at first. Don't be put off: this unpretentious hotel is deservedly popular. People come here primarily for the good-value food; the cramped dining-rooms may be choc-a-bloc and the serving staff may be hard-pressed. The hotel, ever-expanding to cater for its popularity, is freshly and simply decorated. There is a tile-floored roadside café, a small sitting area doubling as a reception area, and an extensive garden scented by a giant honeysuckle. The modern annexe has the best of the bedrooms.

OPEN Apr to end Sept ROOMS 35 (28 with bath or shower)

LA ROCHE-BERNARD

Auberge des Deux Magots

place du Bouffay
56130 Morbihan
TEL 99 90 60 75; FAX 99 90 87 87

Standing in a pretty square on the edge of the old town, this stone building receives a lot of custom. Its café spills on to the square, and effectively adds an extra room to the restaurant's thick stone-walled dining-rooms, which are enlivened by colourful murals. The food is plain and very affordable, though unexceptional. Bedrooms are *fin-de-siècle*-styled with reproduction furniture and striped wallpaper, and, though rather dark, are quite comfortable.

OPEN Mid-Jan to mid-Dec ROOMS 15 (all with bath or shower)

ROSCOFF

Hôtel le Bellevue

rue Jeanne d'Arc
29680 Finistère
TEL 98 61 23 38; FAX 98 61 11 80

At the eastern end of Roscoff harbour, halfway to the ferry port, the Bellevue has clean, modern bedrooms with phones and TV. The restaurant, which overlooks the sea, serves good food at reasonable prices. The house specialities are lobster and fish dishes.

OPEN End Mar to early Nov ROOMS 20 (14 with bath or shower)

SABLES-D'OR-LES-PINS

Le Manoir St Michel

La Carquois
Fréhel
22240 Côtes-d'Armor
TEL 96 41 48 87; FAX 96 41 41 55

This 15th-century manor house surrounded by landscaped lawns lies just outside the resort and has views over stretches of beach. The public rooms are small but cosy, filled with Breton furniture and warmed by fires. Bedrooms are spacious. There is no restaurant.

OPEN Apr to early Nov ROOMS 20 (8 with bath)

ST-LYPHARD

Auberge de Kerhinet

Kerhinet
44410 Loire-Atlantique
TEL 40 61 91 46

Expect a friendly welcome to the vernacular buildings of this auberge in the thatched hamlet of Kerhinet, just south of St-Lyphard. They have been restored to the degree that, while they are picturesque, like the hamlet itself, they also feel rather artificial. Agricultural implements and black and white photographs adorn the walls of the large, beamed restaurant, where there is an extensive choice of set menus and dishes from the *carte*. All but one of the attractively plain bedrooms, with good-quality wooden furniture, sturdy tables and big cupboards, are housed in one separate thatched cottage. Room 7 takes up the whole of its own tiny building.

OPEN Mid-Jan to end Oct, early Nov to mid-Dec ROOMS 7 (all with bath or shower)

ST-MALO

La Korrigane

39 rue le Pomellec
35400 Ille-et-Vilaine
TEL 99 81 65 85; FAX 99 82 23 89

This is an elegant townhouse in St-Servan (a quiet suburb of St-Malo), which is beautifully decorated with antiques and souvenirs from around the world. The 12 guest bedrooms are comfortable and well equipped. There is no restaurant.

OPEN All year except mid-Nov to mid-Dec ROOMS 12 (all with bath or shower)

Hôtel le Valmarin

7 rue Jean XXIII
35400 Ille-et-Vilaine
TEL 99 81 94 76; FAX 99 81 30 03

This large mansion once belonged to a corsair and staying here is a treat. The park behind the house is beautifully kept and makes a peaceful suntrap on a sunny day. Rooms are huge – ask for one overlooking the back – with sizeable bathrooms. There's no restaurant.

OPEN All year, exc. mid-Nov to mid-Feb, by reservation only ROOMS 12 (all with bath)

TREBEURDEN

Ti-Al-Lannec

14 allée de Mézo-Guen
22560 Côtes-d'Armor
TEL 96 23 57 26; FAX 96 23 62 14

Perched on a hill overlooking the sea, the Ti-Al-Lannec is a smart, comfortable, but expensive hotel in a good position for exploring the Pink Granite Coast. Bedrooms are spacious and well equipped; the dining-room has sea-views and serves good food.

OPEN All year ROOMS 29 (all with bath)

TREGUIER

Kastell Dinec'h

route du Lannion
22220 Côtes-d'Armor
TEL 96 92 49 39; FAX 96 92 34 03

This is a converted farmhouse among fields, 2km outside Tréguier. The rooms, mostly in the former stables, are small, stylishly furnished and comfortable. A swimming-pool lies in the grounds, and dinners are served in a wooden beamed room, part of the main farmhouse. Excellent food is served in informal, child-friendly surroundings.

OPEN Mid-Mar to mid-Oct, end Oct to end Dec ROOMS 15 (all with bath or shower) FACILITIES Heated outdoor pool

VAL-ANDRE

Hôtel de la Mer

63 rue Amiral Charner
22370 Côtes-d'Armor
TEL 96 72 20 44; FAX 96 72 85 72

This small, unpretentious hotel lies on a road which runs parallel to the beach. Its rooms are newly furnished, clean, and smell of polish. The restaurant is casual with a busy atmosphere and friendly staff. There is also an annexe called Motel Nuit et Jour, which has eight studio rooms.

OPEN All year, exc. mid-Nov to mid-Dec and most of Jan ROOMS 21 (19 with bath or shower)

How came the flame-haired Norsmen to these lands of fattest pasture and brightest bloom, fresh-painted daily by a loving dewy brush? Bitter indeed, the north wind that filled their sails

[Fearne d'Arcy]

NORMANDY

Normandy is close to England geographically, historically and climatically. Even if the last can hardly be considered a point in its favour where holidays are concerned, it does account for a green and plentiful countryside which many visitors find comfortingly reminiscent of southern England. Of all France's northern coastal regions Normandy is the most varied. The north coast of Brittany has its popular resorts on the rocky and sandy seaside, but relatively little of more than seasonal interest. Artois and Picardy are well worth exploring for individual towns and monuments, but do not leave a visitor with any great sense of regional identity, and the coast is mostly drab. In Normandy the architectural and historical interest is great, the countryside – especially around the Seine Valley – has a prosperous domesticated charm, and there is a wealth of literary and artistic associations. The area has style: colourful manor houses quite different from those in other parts of France, lively and fashionable seaside resorts, and impeccably bred horses which embellish the countryside, and provide the focus of attraction in Deauville.

Scenically Normandy splits into two parts. The fertile chalky farmlands of Upper Normandy, north of the Seine and along the coast to the mouth of the Orne, have as their capital the fascinating ancient and modern city of Rouen. This area has more in common with the Ile-de-France than with Lower Normandy, which belongs geologically to Brittany, land of scrub and harsh granite. Within each part there is great diversity. In the north the spectacular chalky cliffs, shingle beaches and open farmlands of the Caux contrast with the sandy beaches and lush orchards of the Pays d'Auge. In Lower Normandy the bleak rocky north-west coast and flat interior of the Cotentin peninsula are far removed from the Mancelles Alps or the rolling hills and steep river valleys of the so-called Norman Switzerland.

The history of Normandy is a story of invasions, inward and – more characteristically of the bold seafaring race – outward. Adventurous Scandinavians (known as Norsemen, whence Normans) sailed up the Seine in the 9th century. Their right to the area around the lower Seine

Normandy

ENGLISH

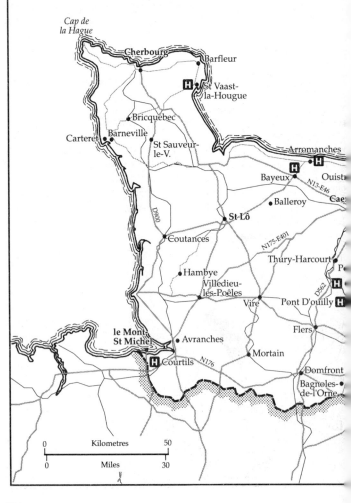

Cap de la Hague

Cherbourg

Barfleur

H St Vaast-la-Hougue

Bricquebec

Carteret ● Barneville

St Sauveur-le-V.

Arromanches

H **H**

Bayeux

N13-E46

Ouistr

Cae

● Balleroy

St-Lô

N175-E401

Coutances

Thury-Harcourt

● P

● Hambye

Villedieu-lés-Poêles

D562

H

Vire

Pont D'ouilly **H** **H**

le Mont St Michel

● Avranches

Flers

H Courtils

N176

● Mortain

● Domfront

Bagnoles-de-l'Orne

D900

| 0 | Kilometres | 50 |
| 0 | Miles | 30 |

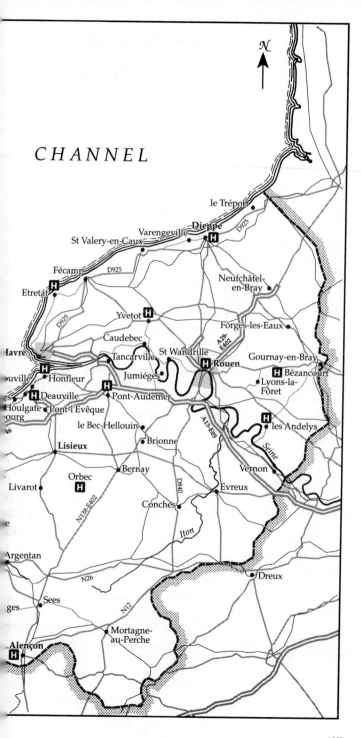

valley was recognised in 911, and 155 years later the first duke Rollo's great-great-great-great-grandson was well enough rooted to press his claim to the English throne. The conquest of England was only one of a glorious series of conquering excursions which brought the systematically structured Norman styles of government and architecture to remote parts of the known world, and at the same time relieved the primogenital system of landless younger sons. For today's tourist there are interesting historical associations between Normandy and Norman Britain, and a style of ecclesiastical architecture which the Normans took across the channel with them.

The D-Day invasion which began on 6 June 1944 did as much in a few months as church-building Normans did in generations to change the face of Normandy. The Allied landing on the sandy beaches of the Calvados coast and the east of the Cotentin peninsula was preceded and accompanied by intensive bombing which brought even more widespread devastation to Normandy than the First World War had inflicted on north-eastern France. Many of the 500 rebuilt towns and villages seem as cold and characterless as a Moscow suburb compared with the rambling timbered provincial towns elsewhere in France, but reconstruction has at least ensured that many of the old monuments are shown off to their best advantage. Along the coast there are a number of museums devoted to the history of the invasion and the subsequent battles, and in many places war debris still litters the dunes. As in north-eastern France, there are many war cemeteries, but because the events of the battle are more recent in Normandy there are more tourists who come here specifically to revisit invasion beaches or pay respects to lost friends and relations. Norman hotels are full of silver-haired Americans determined to tell every other inmate the full story of how they flew in over 'Arrowmoosh' (Arromanches) or 'Cayenne' (Caen).

Most of the coast cannot pretend to rival Brittany for beach holidays. The most popular stretch by far is the Côte Fleurie between the rivers Seine and Dives, an almost uninterrupted chain of resorts built in a characteristic neo-rustic architectural style after the railways brought the Normandy coast suddenly closer to Paris. The wide breezy beachscapes full of human interest provided perfect material for the fresh-air painters of the 1860s, and the pretty town of Honfleur is no less a painters' haunt now than it was in the time of Boudin and Monet. Honfleur – picturesque, old, and situated on the Seine estuary – is less typical of the coast than fashionable Deauville, which made its name by providing summer distractions in the days when the Riviera was considered tolerable only in the winter, and which is now a very horsy resort in season when crowds come to watch the races and to ride along the beach.

If you are susceptible to proud equine beauty – or if you want to take a mare to stud – the stud farms of inland Normandy (most heavily concentrated around L'Aigle and Alençon) will be of great interest and perhaps even fruitful. Those without a business interest should visit the national stud farms – originally for the provision of the army – to learn about breeding for perfection, and to feel the aura of hushed respect which still surrounds the noblest of God's creatures.

Normandy is excellent for a gastronomic tour, with a rich and varied larder. Its pride is dairy produce – France's best butter, milk and cream form the basis of Norman cooking, so you should respect rich creamy sauces and an array of luscious cheeses (of which the most famous is Camembert). Fécamp and Dieppe are important fishing ports for cod and sole respectively, and seafood of all varieties is plentiful.

Of the many aspects of Normandy that make you feel closer to home than in most areas of France, the most striking, after the rain, is the apple. The Normans produce not wine but cider, and although you don't have to drink it with meals many Normans do. Norman cider varies in sweetness and strength and is usually served from bottles corked and wired up like champagne. The apples are also used to produce Calvados (apple brandy) which varies too, not in strength but in quality. Normans drink 'Calva' with or in a morning cup of coffee, between courses in a big meal (*le trou normand* being the hole which a large gulp of Calvados blows in your stomach to create space) and afterwards.

The North and the Seine Valley

The **Pays de Caux**, along the Channel coast north of the Seine, is a featureless chalky agricultural region without much to tempt you inland except for the splendid beech forests (especially fine is Eawy forest, south-east of Dieppe). The Alabaster Coast gets its name from the succession of chalk cliffs which are losing their battle against the tide and the weather at the rate of up to two metres a year in some places. The disappearing cliffs tower over narrow shingle beaches (inaccessible for long stretches), and have been eroded into majestic forms of natural architecture. Fishing ports – and, since the 19th century, resorts – have grown up in the gaps between the cliffs. The short distance from Paris has assured the villages a busy summer, but outside July and August they are not particularly attractive places to come for a holiday.

Le Tréport and its neighbour across the mouth of the Bresle, **Mers-les-Bains**, are typical – grey of building and beach, with rows of white changing huts like sentry boxes along the shingle. The beaches here, as elsewhere along this part of the coast, shelve steeply. Le Tréport has an attractive little fishing harbour and a finely situated church looking down over the busy resort centre. The beach is backed by ugly blocks of flats, and the cable car which used to ferry people up to a panoramic Calvary at the top of a cliff is rustily redundant. **Mers** is quieter and nicer, with period boarding houses on the car-free promenade. A few miles inland, **Eu**, the marriage site of William-not-yet-the-Conqueror, has a very fine early Gothic church dedicated to the Virgin and St Lawrence O'Toole who died at Eu in 1180. The outside of the choir is ornate in the later Flamboyant style; inside there is a fine 15th-century sculpture of the Entombment.

Dieppe, the resort closest to Paris, is probably France's oldest seaside resort: thalassotherapy goes back to the 3rd century, but only in the 19th when sea bathing became a fashionable pleasure did Dieppe outgrow its long-established role as an important commercial and fishing port. It is now a busy weekend resort with a full panoply of casino, tennis courts and mini-golf stretched along the spacious grassy prom behind the shingle beach; but it's less interesting for all these than for the shabby old area behind the animated and colourful port. Dieppe is a popular gateway to and from France with good roads south and to Paris. The busy pedestrian shopping streets are full of tempting goodies for the returning British traveller.

Sights in Dieppe

- **Château** A characteristic although hardly enchanting feature of the sea front, this imposing 15th-century fortress contains a museum rich in ivories. Their carving was once a flourishing local craft, when ivory was imported from south and east. There is also a collection of works by Braque, model ships and old maps.
- **St-Jacques** A gloomy church of interesting parts from all Gothic periods (13th to 16th centuries).

Excursions from Dieppe

- **Arques-la-Bataille** An attractively situated village (south-east of Dieppe) in a hollow beneath the overgrown ruins of an 11th-century fortress which has suffered from being used as a quarry. Across the valley is a monument to Henry IV's remarkable victory, against heavy numerical odds and the forces of the Catholic League, in 1589.
- **Manoir d'Ango** West of Dieppe near Varengeville at the end of a splendid beech avenue, this graceful 16th-century manor house boasts, in the middle of the main courtyard, a remarkably beautiful and ornate dovecote.
- **Ailly lighthouse** Just off the coast road between Varengeville and Ste-Marguerite. Enormous views from the top down the coastline of cliffs.

Along the coast south and west of Dieppe there are numerous small and unremarkable resort villages. **Varengeville** and **Ste-Marguerite** are both set back from the sea in lush countryside, and have interesting churches.

Fécamp is a big fishing port and resort with very little charm, prospering on cod and Benedictine, distilled originally by the monks of the great monastery, of which now only the church survives.

Sights in Fécamp

● **La Trinité** This enormous, mostly early Gothic abbey church is one of the longest in France (some 117 metres). The overall impression of the church is rather less magical than its history. The abbey and its pilgrimages owe their importance to the drops of Precious Blood collected by Joseph of Arimathea, which were pushed out to sea in the trunk of a fig tree only to land here at Fécamp. Some centuries later at the consecration of a new church in 943 an angel pilgrim appeared to officiating bishops and left a footprint which can still be seen beside the beautiful 15th-century sculpture of the Dormition of the Virgin. The nave is impressively severe, the transept and chancel more interesting, with a number of beautiful works of art – tombs, screens and sculptures.

● **Distillery** 19th-century mock Gothic buildings house the former Benedictine distillery and a museum devoted to the old abbey, which you visit on a combined tour.

Etretat is a small resort in a magnificent setting between spectacularly eroded cliffs, which has attracted artists (notably Corot and Monet) as well as tourists. The village has lost much of its charm but it is still worth a visit for cliff walks and a boat trip for the best view of the grottoes, soaring arches and the solitary 60-metre chalk needle left stranded in the water. The church is mostly Romanesque.

The port and city of **Le Havre** were completely flattened in 1944, and the replacement town built after the war is an interesting example of post-war town planning from the days when reinforced concrete and grand conceptions were fashionable. Wide straight boulevards and tall featureless blocks are lightened by the seafront setting, and there is a curious charm beneath the surface ugliness. If you choose to linger, there are some interesting modern buildings.

Sights in Le Havre

● **St-Joseph** Set back from the yachting port this striking concrete church has a 98-metre tower and is brilliantly colourful inside on a fine day, thanks to stained glass squares and diamonds illuminating the hollow interior.

- **Fine Arts Museum** The steel and glass building is showing its age, but is well conceived for the display of the paintings. Boudin and Dufy came from Le Havre and they are still well represented here.
- **The Port** France's largest petroleum port is constantly busy with ships and fine views of the traffic are to be had from the pier opposite the Fine Arts Museum. Tours of the port are available.

On the hill between the Hève lighthouse (where the erosion of the coastline happens faster than anywhere else) and the city centre, Ste-Adresse is a more elegant seaside resort suburb (they call it 'le Nice Havrais') with some Norman-style villas, and cottages with flowers in the thatch.

The Seine carves deep horse-shoe bends through the Normandy countryside (its name is thought to be derived from the Celtic word for tortuous). The river is commercially important and much used for freight; in places it is lined with industrial buildings and refineries. But its winding course is mostly a very attractive one, with sightseeing interest in abundance – the museum city of Rouen, majestic ruined abbeys and castles, and very fine scenery especially on the outside of each loop where the river runs beneath tall white cliffs.

The road upstream from Le Havre passes the **Tancarville** suspension bridge, built in 1959 to bridge the Seine between Rouen and the sea for the first time (there are still about a dozen ferries across the river downstream from Rouen). From the terrace of the nearby château there's a fine view down the widening estuary.

Caudebec-en-Caux is the old regional capital, but no longer looks very old after extensive war damage. The church (Notre-Dame) survived; it's a fine Flamboyant Gothic building with many interesting and elegant details including a balustrade running round the roof made of letters forming Salve Regina Magnificat. Close by there is an interesting museum celebrating the river life on the Seine.

A couple of kilometres away from the river the old **Abbaye de St-Wandrille**, a Benedictine monastery founded in the 7th century, still has its community of monks who sing Gregorian chant, sell honey, sweets and wax, and give guided tours. There are a few ruined remains of the Gothic church and handsome cloisters, to which men only are admitted, with a remarkable Renaissance washbasin set in the outside of the refectory wall. The new church is a 15th-century barn which was recently imported stone by stone. It is attractively simple inside, with plain wooden beams supporting a tall pitched wooden roof. A short walk from the abbey entrance leads to the curious and very old chapel of St-Saturnin.

Upstream lie the much more extensive ruins of the **Abbaye de Jumièges**, beautifully set on a promontory almost encircled by a meander of the Seine. Jumièges is one of France's most majestic and atmospheric ruins, often compared to Fountains Abbey and Rievaulx in Yorkshire. Its setting is not as isolated, but architecturally Jumièges stands the comparison. The tall 11th-century towers flanking the central door are tremendously imposing and the ruined nave is hardly less fine.

The third great abbey church of the lower Seine is at **St-Martin-de-Boscherville**. The church, St-Georges-de-Boscherville, is lesser in dimension than the other two, but intact thanks to its continued use as a parish church; it is beautifully decorated with typically Norman geometric motifs and, less typically, with very entertaining capitals.

Surveying the Seine from on high the castle ruins named after the mythical Robert le Diable now house a wax museum, a deep well and a spooky underground passage. Below them, La Bouille is an attractive leafy port with a ferry across the Seine and lots of weekenders from Rouen.

Rather than following the Seine upstream directly from Rouen, head due east for the splendid beech forest of **Lyons**, former hunting playground of the Norman dukes. **Lyons-la-Forét** is a restful and attractive village (with accommodation) at the heart of the forest. Nearby there are two ruined abbeys to visit or admire as you pass: **Mortemer** is pleasantly pastoral, **Fontaine-Guérard** more romantically set beside the river Andelle at the foot of a steep wooded hill.

On the southern edge of the forest, **Ecouis** is grouped around the solid square towers of its collegiate church, whose single-aisled interior of plain red brick and stone is unusual and contains a variety of interesting statuary, and some splendid Renaissance carved panelling behind the choir stalls. The road south from Ecouis rejoins the Seine at **Les Andelys**, twin villages (Petit and Grand Andely) stretching up a narrow valley from a fine bend in the river, which is magnificently commanded by the ruins of Richard Coeur de Lion's **Château-Gaillard**. You can climb the steep hill from attractive riverside Petit Andely, or drive a long way round the back, stopping to admire Grand Andely's interesting church, a mixture of Flamboyant Gothic and classical Renaissance. Château-Gaillard itself was built in only a year, so legend has it, to defend Normandy from the unwelcome advances of the French king. Although considered impregnable, Château-Gaillard was taken from John Lackland by the French king Philippe Auguste in 1204, John having weakened the castle's defences by installing a vulnerably placed lavatory, with window, noticed and exploited by a French soldier called Bogis. In the Hundred Years' War the castle changed hands between French and English a few times, and was finally dismantled in the 17th century as it was proving too useful to the enemies of law and order. The ruins are partly overgrown, but still imposingly massive (some of the walls are five metres thick), and the view down over Petit Andely and the Seine is superb. Château-Gaillard is traditionally thought to have received its name – which means happy or laughing castle – from one of Richard Coeur de Lion's admiring comments when he saw the completed work. A less

Rouen

Rouen is more than a museum city: it is a busy industrial river port spreading on both sides of the Seine on the end of one of its meanders, with high-rise modern blocks looking down from the wooded hills which encircle the town. The open-work iron spire of the cathedral (the highest in France) soars gracefully above the old centre of town on the right bank. All the interesting monuments are concentrated nearby, as are fascinating narrow streets of tall houses whose timber frames survived intensive bomb blast; old Rouen has been meticulously restored, and is one of the most attractive and interesting city centres to explore in all France. Ruskin described it as 'a labyrinth of delight, its grey and fretted towers misty in their magnificence of height'.

Sights in Rouen

• **Cathedral (Notre-Dame)** One of the country's most beautiful Gothic cathedrals whose stylistic variety betrays construction over many centuries (mostly 13th to 16th); the lofty west end is a mass of intricate detail with ill-matched twin towers – one early and simple, the other (Butter Tower) Flamboyant and sumptuously decorated. Equally fine is the doorway outside the south transept. The inside has some remarkable features – above all, the tomb of Normandy's great Renaissance patrons of the arts, the cardinals of Amboise. There is also fine stained glass and a delicate staircase leading up to the libraries.
• **St-Maclou** At the centre of a very picturesque square with cobbles and timber-framed houses where a Brasserie Bavaroise hardly looks out of place, this very beautiful late-Gothic church climbs effortlessly to the tip of its see-through spire.
• **Aître St-Maclou** Not immediately obvious down a covered alley off the square behind the church of the same name, the old charnel house has a timbered cloister remarkably decorated with skulls, bones, scythes and other accessories of Father Time. The cloister gives a splendid view of the tower of St-Ouen.
• **St-Ouen** This large church, almost as long as the cathedral, is a magnificent achievement of Gothic architecture celebrated for the purity and harmony of its lofty interior proportions. There is very little ornament to detract from the overall impression, but there is fine stained glass and an excellent organ often used for concerts.
• **Old town** The famous 14th-century gilt clock, decorated with a wealth of symbolic animals, spans an attractive and animated pedestrian shopping street (the Rue du Gros Horloge) linking the Place du Vieux Marché to the cathedral. The rich decoration of the archway over the street, the nearby law courts, and the Hôtel Bourgtheroulde are the finest examples of the sumptuously ornate style of Rouen in the times of Cardinal Georges d'Amboise who brought the Italian Renaissance to Normandy.

- **Museums** The fine arts museum has a large and splendid collection of paintings, with the French 19th century (especially Géricault) particularly well represented. There are many other treasures including an interesting and lively collection of early 20th-century portraits of the social and artistic élite by Jacques Emile Blanche. Other museums are the Le-Secq-des-Tournelles with a well-presented display of ironwork; the Musée des Antiquités, whose very varied collection of works of art includes many treasures – among them enamels, icons, and tapestries; the Corneille museum, arranged in the house of the classical dramatist's birth in 1606; and a museum of medical history in the old hospital where the novelist Gustave Flaubert was born and his surgeon father practised. Flaubert's house at Croisset (where he wrote *Madame Bovary*) above the right bank of the Seine, downstream from the town centre, has also been turned into a small museum.
- **Saint Joan** The patron saint of France was burned to death on the Place du Vieux Marché on 30 May 1431. A tall cross marks the spot, and is flanked by a remarkable modern church, whose scaly roof is reminiscent of flames or waves. The interior, roofed like an upturned boat, is particularly beautiful on account of the 16th-century stained glass salvaged from a bombed church.

picturesque explanation is that the castle is named after the town of **Gaillon** on the other side of the Seine. It is not a very attractive town and the remains of Georges d'Amboise's château, once one of the great showpieces of the French Renaissance, are disappointing. Despite heavy war damage in 1940, **Louviers**, situated on the Eure just before its junction with the Seine, retains some attractive old wooden houses and an interesting church built in the 13th century and given a new exceedingly elaborate Flamboyant exterior 200 years later.

South-east towards the Ile-de-France and Paris, **Vernon** occupies a once-important strategic position on the Seine. Two towers remain of the old fortifications, and attractively leafy ruins of a fortified bridge across the river. The Gothic church of Notre-Dame stands over the town, tall and elegant. **Giverny**, where Monet's beloved Epte meets the Seine, preserves the painter's house and garden (of the hallucinatory water-lilies) as a museum. This is the most popular sight in the Seine valley, but it is well worth braving the crowds to admire the careful planting of the garden. The drive up the Epte valley, the Norman frontier, is a pretty one, with ruined fortresses at **Baudémont** and **Château-sur-Epte**. The Epte and the Seine nearly meet at **La Roche-Guyon**, where another hilltop castle was in function, if not in grandeur, the French equivalent of Normandy's Château-Gaillard. **Gisors** was the most important Norman bastion on the Epte, and still has extensive remains of the fortress, with handsome gardens inside the walls. The 13th- to 16th-century church (St-Gervais et St-Protais) is also worth a visit to admire its Renaissance decoration.

Central Normandy

The area between the Seine and the Dives is the most popular part of Normandy. Along its coast lie the most fashionable resorts, and inland Normandy's most attractive countryside, heavy with blossom or apples and thick with bright green pastures plundered by dairy cattle, which produce the raw material for Camembert, Pont-l'Evêque and Livarot. 'Even in Switzerland', wrote the delighted Ruskin, 'the green is blacker and not so soft.' To appreciate the intimate charm of the countryside with its colourful manor houses, cottages with flowers planted in the thatch and noisy farmyards, it is essential to branch off the main roads; the most rewarding area for exploration is between the Dives and the Touques valleys, west and south-west of Lisieux.

Honfleur is the most intrinsically attractive town of the Côte Fleurie and perhaps of all Normandy, quite different from the purpose-built 19th-century resorts. Tall slate-fronted houses are tightly packed around the yacht harbour with the 16th-century governor's house (la Lieutenance) guarding its entrance; across the water the church

(St-Etienne) has been turned into a local museum. The church of Ste-Catherine on the central square is a great curiosity – built entirely of wood by the Honfleur shipbuilders who are said to have been too eager to give thanks for the English departure after the Hundred Years' War to wait for the stonemasons. Honfleur has attracted painters for over a hundred years: a group of Impressionists (including Boudin and Monet) settled at the Ferme St-Siméon on the hill behind the village (now an expensive hotel) and are commemorated in the Boudin Museum in Honfleur. Sadly the view across the estuary from the top of the hill (the Côte de Grâce), which they so appreciated, is now full of tankers and refineries. Artists still jostle for position round the old port, and Honfleur's charm is enhanced by the numerous art galleries. The wealth of nearby Deauville has clearly overflowed, and there are shops selling furs and expensive carpets as well. But Honfleur is not yet too spoilt despite the new Pont de Normandie nearby, and still has its busy fishing fleet.

The rest of the Côte Fleurie, west to Cabourg, is a string of classy resorts on whose long sandy beaches the fashion for sea bathing was born in the mid-19th century. **Deauville** reigns supreme, with its turn-of-the-century neo-rustic villas and the smartest hotels, shops, night-life and people – they come for the yearling sales, racing, roulette, regattas, polo, bridge, golf, tennis and to be seen on the *planches* (a path of duckboards all the way along the back of the beach, which is traditionally as close to the water as it is seemly for the blazer and white flannel brigade to go). There is too much to do to spend time on the beach, at least in August which is the start and finish of Deauville's butterfly life of a season. Adjacent **Trouville** has more of a real-life

Sunshades on Deauville beach

atmosphere; **Blonville** and **Villers-sur-Mer** are little more than beach resorts. **Houlgate** is a quietly residential resort, rather more faded than **Cabourg** with its wide promenade, the Boulevard des Anglais, and tree-lined avenues fanning out from the spacious lawns in front of the overblown casino and the Grand Hotel which Proust, a frequenter of Cabourg in its heyday, described as a décor for the third act of a farce.

The social attractions and good (if polluted) beaches of the Côte Fleurie are complemented by the natural beauty of the green valleys and hills behind it. Of the hinterland towns **Pont-l'Evêque** suffered greatly in the last war, as did **Pont-Audemer**, which nevertheless has some interesting old houses, and Renaissance windows in the church (St-Ouen). **Lisieux** is the biggest industrial centre in the Pays d'Auge, and its biggest industry is Saint Teresa. The short and outwardly unremarkable life of this Carmelite sister, born in 1873 at Alençon, was an exemplary one of long-suffering and selfless perfection of the spirit. The main pilgrimage is in early October, but throughout the year the capacious Romano-Byzantine Basilica on the edge of town is crowded with pilgrims. Colourful mosaics illustrate the universal impact of Saint Teresa's autobiography, *The Story of a Soul*. All around town there are souvenir shops galore and a number of displays, with wax models telling the story – by definition unspectacular – of Saint Teresa's life, and of her subsequent miraculous achievements. In the middle of all this stands a fine, uncomplicated early Gothic cathedral.

The delightful manor houses of the **Pays d'Auge** are too numerous to list; they are all highly individual in design and decoration, many with moats, pitched roofs of red and coloured tiles, and walls of either timber frames filled with geometrically patterned tiles or chequerboard brick and stone squares. Two of the finest, south-west of Lisieux, are **St-Germain-de-Livet** (open to visitors; Renaissance frescoes and furniture) and **Coupesarte**, but there are many others to highlight your meander through the lanes of the Pays d'Auge, which may be given direction by the established cider and cheese routes – ask at any local tourist office for a map to lead you to farms which will open their doors for you to sample and buy their produce.

South-east of Pont-Audemer, in the soft green vale that Ruskin so admired, little remains (except a proud 15th-century tower) of the medieval **Abbaye du Bec-Hellouin**, academy of Christendom which produced a succession of distinguished theologians and church politicians following the example of its two great 11th-century abbots (both later to be archbishop of Canterbury) Lanfranc and Anselm. Today's abbey, which you can visit, is mostly a reconstruction of the 17th- and 18th-century buildings. There is also, strangely enough, a display of racing cars.

To the south and east of Le Bec-Hellouin lie the fertile Neubourg plain and the more wooded Pays d'Ouche. There are some châteaux to see and visit (most in summer only) – **Beaumesnil** and **Champ-de-Bataille**

Château de St-Germain-de-Livet

are majestic brick and stone 17th-century buildings, the one tall and imposing, the other low and spread around a spacious court. The moated medieval fortress of **Harcourt** is hidden in a vast arboretum of a park.

Evreux is a busy market town, thoroughly rebuilt since the War, but with two interesting churches and a good archaeological museum. The cathedral, repeatedly burnt and restored, displays many styles. Its north and west façades are richly decorated, respectively Flamboyant Gothic and Renaissance. Inside there are fine 15th- and 16th-century windows around the elegant choir whose chapels are all enclosed by remarkable and varied carved wooden screens. The old Benedictine abbey church of St-Taurin has a few Romanesque elements, and an elaborate silver gilt and enamel reliquary of the saint in the choir.

Conches-en-Ouche is set on a spur rising abruptly from a bend in the river Rouloir. There is a good view from the terrace beside the small church of Ste-Foy, whose interior is dominated by a very fine series of 16th-century windows illustrating the lives of Christ and the Virgin. The ruins of a medieval castle are set in a small park.

Once a strategic town on the borders of the Pays d'Ouche and the Normandy Perche, **Verneuil-sur-Avre** has lost most of its fortifications but retains two churches of interest. La Madeleine, on the spacious central square, is more distinguished outside than in, with splendid sculptures all around the tower and porch. Notre-Dame (follow signs to the Abbaye St-Nicolas) is full of sculptures of saints, varying greatly in date (from the 12th to the 17th centuries) and quality.

The South

The **Normandy Perche** is a very pleasant hilly and wooded area whose main interest lies in its manor houses and its horses (Percherons). The manors are quite unlike those of the Pays d'Auge – older, more forti-fied, and less colourful. Rural itineraries from the convenient and attractive bases **Mortagne-au-Perche** and **Longny-au-Perche** (maps from the tourist office) take you past some of the most interesting of them – **La Vove, L'Angenardière, Courboyer** and **Les Feugerets** (these are places to look at, not visit). Mortagne has some well-preserved old houses and a Gothic/Renaissance church with a massive 18th-century carved wooden altar-piece brought from a nearby monastery. On a small hill behind Longny stands the charming little Renaissance chapel of Notre-Dame-de-Pitié, with very delicate stone and wood carving outside.

Horses, and not just the sturdy local Percherons which are mainly good for pulling, grace the landscape all over the Perche. The most interesting stud (*haras*) to visit is the national one at **Le Pin**, founded by Louis XIV's minister Colbert for the provision of the army – originally there was a colony of mares as well. The stud farm itself has as good a pedigree as the stallions, for Mansart designed a château of appro-priately elegant sobriety, and Le Nôtre put in some terraced gardens which look out over the farm's domain of majestic avenues and fields of brilliantined beasts. A groom guides you for nothing more than a gratuity round the stables and expatiates in tones of due reverence on the technicalities of horse breeding, and the family trees and in many cases multitudinous progeny of France's finest stallions.

A few kilometres down the road the **Château d'O** could be in the Loire Valley, so delightful is the fantasy and ornament of its archi-tecture. It is not so much moated as built in the middle of a lake.

Sées is a handsome old town with a lofty and bright Gothic cathedral whose twin spires can be seen from the terrace at Le Pin many kilo-metres away. As well as the beautiful proportions of the choir and transept, you may admire the 13th-century stained glass and a very sweet statue of the Virgin and Child.

The **Ecouves** forest lies just off the main Sées to Alençon road, and is one of the finest of many in this part of Normandy. There are deer, and an extensive panorama from the Signal d'Ecouves (417 metres). The **Perseigne forest** on the other side of the road is smaller but hardly less attractive, with riding and walking paths and picnic areas.

Alençon is a busy market town on the Sarthe, with an illustrious past; elegant Flamboyant Gothic architecture in the churches of Notre-Dame and St-Léonard and the imposing 15th-century Maison d'Ozé (now a museum of local antiquities) date from the period when Alençon was the brilliant capital of an important duchy. In the 17th century the town became a very important lace-making centre; like so many local crafts, technological progress has reduced it to little more than a curiosity. When you see the price of the hand-made lace in the lace-making school you will understand why. In the fine arts museum, there's a good collection of lace, and some paintings of high quality.

South-west of Alençon the so-called **Alpes Mancelles** (Le Mans Alps) rise to a high point of 417 metres. Although not exactly alpine, the landscape is interesting, and charming with swiftly running streams and heathery hills. The most attractive villages in the small area, both on the steeply banked Sarthe, are **St-Léonard-des-Bois** and **St-Cénéri-le-Gérei**, the latter with a small frescoed Romanesque chapel.

Very similar in its appeal and in the exaggeration of its title is the area to the north called **La Suisse Normande** (Norman Switzerland). Here too the river (in this case the Orne) cuts through steep banks; tourists come for rock climbing and canoeing (the most popular centre for excursions is the resort village of **Clécy**) so perhaps the name is not so inappropriate. For quite spectacular views the vantage points are the **Roche d'Oëtre** and the **Pain de Sucre**.

These two regions contrast strikingly with the lush undulations and plains of Upper Normandy. They lie at the eastern edge of the granite Armorican Massif, and thus belong geologically to Brittany. **Bagnoles-de-l'Orne** is a good base between the two areas, provided you enjoy the inimitable atmosphere of spa resorts. It is attractively set in a forest beside a lake, with woodland walks and facilities for riding, boating and gambling, as well as healing waters from a hot spring in the rock, whose fame originated with the miraculous rejuvenation of an old nag. For sightseers there are interesting excursions to the **Châteaux de Lassay** and **Carrouges**. The first is a very impressive 15th-century military fortress, the second a vast brick and granite château of many periods with a fine collection of furniture, styles Louis XIII to XVI. Also within easy reach of Bagnoles-de-l'Orne, **Domfront** is an attractive little town whose old centre is splendidly situated hundreds of metres above the river Varenne. Looking down over the river, the ruins of a once mighty fortress are incorporated in the public gardens. By the side of the river there is a restored Romanesque church (Notre-Dame-sur-l'Eau) of great charm.

At **Falaise**, on the eastern edge of the Suisse Normande, there remains less of an old town than at Domfront but much more of a fortress, where Duke Richard II of Normandy's younger son consummated his passion for a tanner's daughter called Arlette. The fruit of the union was William the Bastard, later the Conqueror. The massive 12th-century keep and 15th-century round tower on a rock above the town are tremendously impressive. Two interesting churches (Notre-Dame-de-Guibray and St-Gervais) retain some Romanesque elements. Just off the road north from Falaise to Caen there are two beautiful châteaux (**Versainville** – now a youth centre – and **Assy**, both mostly 18th-century) and an impressive limestone gorge formed by the river Laison (La Brèche au Diable).

The West

This area includes most of Lower Normandy, the Cotentin peninsula and its hinterland. The Cotentin juts out north into the Channel, its coastal port **Cherbourg** as convenient a bridgehead for British tourists as it was an important one for the Allied Forces to conquer in 1944. It has little else to recommend it. The peninsula, joined to the mainland by a long strip of low-lying marshland no more than nine metres above sea-level, is not a particularly exciting welcome to France. For the transit traveller there are no spectacular and few interesting landscapes, but rather an only vaguely characterised succession of woods and scrubland. For the explorer there are few treasures (apart from some impressive rocky coastline around the north-west tip not unlike western Brittany), but plenty of deserted sand dunes and a series of small resorts. The best beaches in Normandy are to be found here. The flat east coast and the north-facing Calvados coast stretching as far east as Caen have few resorts of any charm, but they do have their interest, as this almost uninterrupted stretch of dunes and flat beaches was the toehold for the Allied invaders in June 1944. The invasion beaches are not only littered with memories, but also with the remains of gun batteries, and other debris of modern warfare – old mines are uncovered in the dunes from time to time. There are a number of other museums along the coast to complement the evocative remains. Especially good are those at Arromanches and Port-en-Bessin.

In this area as in so much of Normandy and Northern France most of the sightseeing interest resides in warfare and the religious buildings, from the great abbeys of the capital of Lower Normandy, Caen, at one end, to the mystical acropolis of France, Mont-St-Michel, at the other. **Caen** was one of the worst casualties of 1944, relentlessly softened up by the Allies and then shelled by the retreating ex-occupiers. It has risen again from the rubble, a thriving modern city with industrial zones sprawling without geographical constraint, and clean, broad streets in the city centre. Its great churches and even a few attractive old half-timbered houses survived the bombs. But for the most part Caen is, if not ugly, certainly less than picturesque; the bald modern buildings, built of the light local stone which was used in the construction of so many historic monuments in Normandy and England, fit in surprisingly well with the severely undecorative style of Norman architecture. Caen's three great landmarks are tributes to their builders, William the Conqueror and his wife Matilda, to whom the town owed its great importance. To win papal approval for their marriage, the cousins each founded an abbey.

Sights in Caen

● **Château** Damaged, but at least freed of surrounding later buildings by the last War, the impressive walls of this vast 11th-century fortress house two interesting museums – fine arts and local history.

● **Abbaye aux Hommes** William's abbey church (St-Etienne) is remarkable in its severe simplicity and lofty grandeur. Inside there are no side chapels, few capitals, and just a plaque to Guillelmus Conquestor, whose femur alone survived 16th-century Huguenot pillaging, but not the Revolution. The abbey buildings beside the great church date mostly from the 18th century, and their sober classical elegance in no way clashes with the Norman church. Inside you can see some splendid carved wooden panelling, the cloister which gives an excellent view of the church, and a remarkable display of photographs of Caen during the invasion, from 5 June to 15 August 1944, when St-Etienne sheltered thousands of inhabitants.

● **Abbaye aux Dames** Matilda's abbey church (La Trinité) is smaller, squatter, more damaged and not spared discordant additions to the original Norman architecture. But apart from this the main façade is handsome, as too are the interior and the crypt, both enlivened by some amusingly primitive carving on the capitals.

● **St-Pierre** The mostly Gothic church at the foot of the castle is chiefly remarkable for the exuberant Renaissance decoration of the interior and exterior of the east end. The features of Gothic architecture (hanging keystones and flying buttresses) are transformed into pure ornament, rich in fantasy. It would be hard to imagine a more marked contrast with the spirit of the abbey church of St-Etienne.

● **St-Nicolas** An unspoilt Romanesque church with a fine porch.

● **Old houses** The finest are to be admired on and off the Rue St-Pierre between St-Pierre and St-Etienne; the tourist office just opposite St-Pierre occupies one of the biggest and best.

● **Memorial museum** Excellent new museum dedicated to peace, on the outskirts of town. Films, photos, documents, all well displayed, chart the downfall of peace after the First World War to the end of the Second World War and beyond. There's a research and documentation centre, and a crèche.

Excursion from Caen

• **Fontaine-Henry** North-west of Caen, this 15th- and 16th-century château owes its character to the steep tiled roof over one wing, taller than the body of the building it shelters. The exterior is gracious; short guided tours of the main rooms of the inhabited interior reveal some interesting works of art, and a splendid Renaissance staircase and furniture. Nearby, just off the road and not immediately obvious, is the attractive deconsecrated Romanesque church of **Thaon**.

Being considerably smaller and much less affected by the Allied blitz than Caen, **Bayeux** is a popular alternative base for Lower Normandy, with picturesque old streets around the cathedral.

Sights in Bayeux

• **Bayeux Tapestry** Normandy's greatest historical and artistic treasure – the 70-metre long series of 58 embroidered episodes illustrating the Norman Conquest – is well displayed in the Centre Guillaume le Conquérant, rue de Nesmond. The interest of the tapestry is both documentary – it was almost certainly executed in England to the orders of the bishop of Bayeux not long after the events portrayed – and artistic; the audio guide in English is well worth having. The Barton-Gérard Museum, also near the cathedral, contains a fine collection of paintings, porcelain and lace.
• **Cathedral** Even without the Bayeux Tapestry, destined for the adornment of its chancel, this is a more decorative church than Caen's sober abbeys and characteristic in its mixture of Gothic and Romanesque styles, with some delightful geometric and simple figurative carving on the arches of the nave.
• **Museum of the Battle of Normandy** A comprehensive collection of battle hardware and good explanations of the tough fighting which followed the Allied invasion.

Excursions from Bayeux

• **Abbaye de Mondaye** (ten kilometres south) This abbey still functions and the monks sell their produce; the buildings and church are harmoniously classical, the abbey having been reconstructed in the 18th century.
• **Château de Balleroy** The grandeur of this imposing reddish-grey early 17th-century château is enhanced by the tributary nature of the village which lines the long straight drive down the hill to its gates, where splendid grilles and antler-like spikes discourage intruders. You can go inside to see the rich décor and royal portraits, a hot-air balloon museum, and attractive gardens designed by Le Nôtre.

- **Abbaye de Cérisy-la-Forêt** Across the forest from Balleroy, this great Romanesque abbey church stands alone in the fields on the edge of the village. The church has been much damaged (the nave was mostly amputated) but it is nevertheless simple, bright and beautiful. The abbey buildings (partly a farm) can be visited.
- **St-Lô** This large town needed almost total rebuilding after the War, but the mutilated ruins of the façade towers of Notre-Dame were left as an evocative reminder. On the Bayeux road, just outside the town centre, you can visit one of Normandy's biggest stud farms. South of the town the Vire cuts through rocky escarpments. There is good trout fishing and some fine viewpoints – especially Les Roches de Ham near Torigny-sur-Vire, where you can visit the recently restored château of the Breton family from which the princely dynasty of Monaco descends.

The Calvados coast west of Caen, and the east coast of the Cotentin, was the theatre for the D-Day Invasion of June 1944. In the east the British forces met with little resistance (whence the survival of Bayeux) pressing south from Sword, Juno and Gold beaches; so the coastline here, with its succession of busy resorts, shows few signs of desolation. The American forces, landing on Utah and Omaha beaches, had much more trouble establishing a foothold. Of the resorts, **Ouistreham-Riva-Bella** is the most substantial and popular, with a big yachting port near the ferry terminal. The area is well known for oysters, especially from Courseulles, and seaweed which imparts health-giving fumes to the air when exposed at low tide. War memorials are a bigger attraction; the most frequented and interesting of the museums commemorating the Invasion is at **Arromanches-les-Bains**, the small and busy resort where the Allies installed the famous mobile Mulberry Harbour (remains can still be seen out to sea) which for three months (before the port of Cherbourg could be made serviceable) made possible the disembarkation of millions of men and vehicles. The museum at the water's edge, with its models and Royal Navy films, gets extremely crowded. **Port-en-Bessin** is a busy and attractive fishing port tucked between chalk cliffs. A nearby museum exhibits tanks and other debris salvaged by divers from the invasion coast. The American landing beaches, which unlike Gold, Juno and Sword have retained their code names Utah and Omaha, are more exposed, emptier, and in many ways more evocative. There is a huge American war cemetery at **St-Laurent-sur-Mer** with nearly 10,000 white crosses, and at **La Cambe** just south of Grandchamp there are twice as many German graves. Utah beach is the most northerly, separated from Omaha, as the Cotentin peninsula is from the Calvados, by the deep and wide Baie des Veys and the rich pastures of the Carentan plain, origin of France's best dairy products. The dunes of Utah beach still yield rusty treasure from time to time, and tanks and amphibians stand as memorials beside a small museum devoted to the

American Invasion. Utah beach is hardly more hospitable now than it must have been when tens of thousands of American troops had to advance at dawn through a nightmare of barbed wire and mines on the mudflats exposed by the tide's retreat.

At the end of Utah beach, the rocky Cotentin promontory begins. Dark grey stone contrasts with the chalk of the Upper Normandy coast and gives the Cotentin and its buildings something of a Breton appearance. The north-eastern tip is relatively sheltered, and has two attractive fishing and yachting ports – **Barfleur** (with better beaches) and **St-Vaast-la-Hougue**. The Saire valley inland from St-Vaast is particularly green and pleasant.

The north coast is rocky and bleak; the east-end lighthouses of Gatteville (near Barfleur) and Cap Lévy give panoramic views of the coastline and peninsula. The west (especially the **Cap de la Hague** and the **Nez de Jobourg**) is more windblown and impressively rocky in the style of the Atlantic tip of Brittany. The attractively situated **Port-Racine** is allegedly France's smallest port. In the middle of the north coast, **Cherbourg** is no delight to the eye, having been thoroughly destroyed by the retreating occupiers in 1944, but has two museums of some interest – one devoted to the War and the liberation of Normandy, the other to fine arts.

The west coast of the Cotentin is a succession of sandy beaches with enormous low tidal retreat, and small family resorts with views of and ferries to nearby Jersey and Guernsey. **Granville** is a substantial town with a lively fishing and yachting port and an old (18th-century) upper-town within grey ramparts.

The main points of sightseeing interest on the Cotentin peninsula are churches. The **Abbaye de Lessay's** large church has been (→ page 449)

Coutances cathedral – looking up into the lantern tower

Mont-St-Michel

Abbey, fortress, village and natural curiosity, Mont-St-Michel proclaims itself France's premier tourist attraction. At its best it is an unforgettable vision of natural and man-made beauty; at its worst, Mont-St-Michel can be a nightmarish experience of suffocation in steep, narrow, over-crowded streets of souvenir shops.

The granite mound, crowned by monastic buildings, rises from the muddy mouth of the Couesnon river, whose main path runs west of the rock, thereby placing it in Normandy not Brittany. At high tide, sea surrounds the rock, and occasionally floods the car park at its gateway. At low tide the spire of the abbey church soars over miles of mudflats; record tides empty the bay for nearly 16km. In places the water rushes in and out at over 16km an hour, so wandering around the low tide sands can be very dangerous, especially as there are passages of trea-cherous quicksand (the Bayeux Tapestry records that Harold saved some Normans from the sands of the Couesnon). Partly because of the cause-way built across to the rock 100 years ago, the salt marsh coastline is advancing on the rock, and eventually high tide waves lapping at the gates of Mont-St-Michel will be no more.

The first hermits set themselves up on the so-called Mont-Tombe (thought because of its name to have been a Celtic burial ground) sometime around AD 500. The monastic community was founded in the 8th century and expanded as miracle stories were put about and pilgrims began to make their way to the rock. From the 10th century the dukes of Normandy patronised the monastery and made possible the remarkably ambitious expansion of the monastic buildings. The stone had to be brought from the Chausey Islands some 40km away and the summit had to be surrounded by support buildings; of the church now standing only the crossing itself is founded on rock. A natural strong-hold, Mont-St-Michel had fortifications from the earliest times, and still gives the impression of being as much a castle as a monastery. Many of its ramparts which survive today date from the 14th and 15th centuries, when it defied all English attempts at conquest, and came for a time under the captaincy of du Guesclin.

Like so many monasteries Mont-St-Michel's post-medieval history is one of disciplinary and architectural decay, here abetted by lightning – which accounted for half the nave. The buildings, including the church itself, were used as a prison and split up into several levels. Restoration was undertaken only about 100 years ago, and a few monks from St-Wandrille came back to Mont-St-Michel in 1966.

Seven hundred thousand visitors a year tramp up between the sou-venir shops and the restaurants of the Grande rue to the abbey build-ings. The commercialisation of the bottom half of the village, with its souvenir shops, crêperies and the horrific density of people, can be prohibitive at times; but the atmosphere was no doubt not very different 500 years ago. The great surprise that makes toiling up through the tumult worthwhile is that, unlike most pilgrimage places, the fortified monastery of Mont-St-Michel is made up of some of the most beautiful Gothic and Romanesque religious buildings in France. The church, cloister and refectory, the elements of greatest beauty, can in summer be visited only on a guided tour (some are conducted in English) which takes about an hour.

The church is a triumphant combination of amputated Romanesque nave, and a light, soaring, Flamboyant choir which was added in the 15th century and not completed until 1518. It has been described as the last heavenward rocket launched by the dying Middle Ages. The cloister and refectory form the upper of three layers of the so-called Merveille, built (like a gallery hanging in mid-air from the side of the rock) in the early 13th century. The cloister looks out to sea on two sides and has twin colonnades of great delicacy. The guided tour also covers the Gothic and earlier rooms in the nether parts of the monastery, including the original sanctuary (Notre-Dame-sous-Terre) incorporated in the support system for the enlarged church. There are magnificent views from the terrace in front of the church, from the cloister, and from the so-called lacework staircase built into a flying buttress outside the choir, which rises to 120 metres above the sea.

To see Mont-St-Michel at its best there is nothing to equal an overnight stay on the rock, which will enable you to wander around the deserted citadel by moonlight or at dawn with the abbey buildings looming above you and your own footsteps echoing on the cobbles. You can also do the abbey tour before the crowds arrive. If you do stay overnight, check on the tides before you leave your car unattended on the lower car park.

Boat trips around the rock are no longer possible, but when the tide is out it is well worth walking all the way around on the sand at its feet. If you are feeling very self-indulgent, consider hiring a small plane from nearby airfields for an exhilarating bird's eye view.

restored to its full beauty, bright, unadorned and harmoniously Romanesque. **Coutances** is an unprepossessing rebuilt town with a soaring slender Gothic cathedral, where very little decoration distracts your eye from the heavenward impulse of the architectural streamlines of the exterior. The interior is as light as it is lofty, thanks to a magnificent octagonal lantern tower over the crossing, which prompted Louis XIV's military architect Vauban to enquire who could be the sublime madman who dared throw such a monument to the skies. Further south, the picturesque ruins of the 12th-century **Abbaye de Hambye**, overgrown and complete with circling rooks, lie in the delightfully secluded Sienne valley. Almost contemporary with Hambye and in a similar setting inland from Granville is the **Abbaye de Lucerne** of which little remains except the church.

South of Granville the coast is lent interest by Mont-St-Michel, which stands up across the water, or mudflats, of Avranches Bay. At **Genêts** you can, indeed must, find a guide if you want to walk across to the abbey on foot in the steps of many millions of pilgrims. **Avranches** itself is a busy town with valuable manuscripts from Mont-St-Michel in its museum. Nearby the dammed river Vélune is popular for fishing.

HOTELS

Key: ◆ = 0–250FF, ◆◆ = 251–450FF, ◆◆◆ = over 451FF; prices are per double room without breakfast, which costs around 35–60FF extra. Some hotels may insist on half-board during high season, some hotels or restaurants may close at specific times during the week – it is always worth checking. Most hotels accept the major credit cards; we have indicated where a hotel takes no credit cards.

ALENCON

Château de St-Paterne

72610 Orne
TEL 33 27 54 71; FAX 33 29 16 71

On the outskirts of Alençon, this small château is gradually being done up by its enthusiastic owner, who takes in guests to help pay for the work. Sensibly, he has started on the bedrooms, and these are comfortable, have masses of character and are even sometimes a bit spooky; the salons are elegant rooms, traditionally decorated. Evening meals are available by arrangement, but whether you eat or not, you will find yourself warmly welcomed.

OPEN Mar to Dec ROOMS 6 (all with bath or shower)

NORMANDY

LES ANDELYS

La Chaîne d'Or

27 rue Grande
27700 Eure
TEL 32 54 00 31; FAX 32 54 05 68

In a prime position on the banks of the Seine, close to Monet's garden at Giverny, this hotel scores for its good food and the comfort of its renovated bedrooms alike. It is popular with Parisian weekenders and foreign visitors, so needs to be booked far in advance. While not cheap, it makes an ideal place from which to tour this part of the Seine Valley.

OPEN All year exc. Jan ROOMS 10 (all with bath or shower)

ARROMANCHES

Le Marine

14117 Calvados
TEL 31 22 34 19; FAX 31 22 98 80

A big white building on the sea-front, Le Marine is not only the most prominent hostelry in Arromanches, but it is usually the first choice for visitors to this stretch of the D-Day coast. It is simple – perhaps rather too simple for comfort in its annexe rooms – but with some big bedrooms, excellent sea views, and decidedly good seafood.

OPEN Mid-Feb to mid-Nov ROOMS 30 (most with bath or shower)

BAYEUX

Churchill

14–16 rue St-Jean
14404 Calvados
TEL 31 21 31 80; FAX 31 21 41 66

Right at the animated hub of Bayeux, this is a good, comfortable hotel with all the necessary virtues, including a friendly owner and a galleried breakfast room. Bedrooms (some of them at least) are on the small side, but are well furnished. There is ample parking space behind the hotel.

OPEN Mid-Mar to mid-Nov ROOMS 32 (all with bath or shower)

BEZANCOURT

Château de Landel

Gournay-en-Bray
76220 Seine-Maritime
TEL 35 90 16 01; FAX 35 90 62 47

On the eastern edge of the Fôret de Lyons, this is a family-owned property of mellow grandeur. While it is neither the most beautiful nor the most lavish of Normandy château hotels, you will find comfortable and well-designed bedrooms, some quietly formal public rooms, a friendly welcome and plenty of peace and quiet.

OPEN Mid-Mar to mid-Nov ROOMS 17 (all with bath or shower) FACILITIES Heated outdoor pool, tennis

CABOURG

Pullman Grand

promenade Marcel-Proust
14390 Calvados
TEL 31 91 01 79; FAX 31 24 03 20

Famed for its connections with Marcel Proust, the Grand is a classic of its kind – a turn-of-the-century seaside hotel built at the height of the fashion for sea-bathing, and planned as the most prominent building in the whole resort. To one side is the sea, to the other the centre of Cabourg. The hotel has been undergoing extensive renovation, but the magnificent lobby and the large bedrooms are likely to remain. It is not cheap, but it is magnificent.

OPEN All year ROOMS 70 (all with bath or shower)

CAEN

Le Dauphin

29 rue Gémare
14000 Calvados
TEL 31 86 22 26; FAX 31 86 35 14

Rebuilt Caen is not famous for fine hotels, but this one close to the centre is as good as any. It has boring but comfortable modern bedrooms, fair food, slick service and a small car park.

OPEN All year ROOMS 22 (all with bath or shower)

CLECY

Hostellerie du Moulin du Vey

Le Vey
14570 Calvados
TEL 31 69 71 08; FAX 31 69 14 14

This large hotel seems to have taken over much of Clécy (it has two annexes in the area). Its chief advantage is the wonderful position of the main building – an old mill on the Orne with the rush of water to soothe you to sleep and views of canoeists to keep you entertained by day. Food is served in the large bare restaurant, or outside if the weather is fine. It suffers slightly when the restaurant is full to capacity with visiting parties (which it often is).

OPEN All year exc. Dec ROOMS 25 (all with bath or shower)

COURTILS

Manoir de la Roche Torin

50220 Manche
TEL 33 70 96 55; FAX 33 48 35 20

This is the perfect hotel to use as a base for a visit to Mont St-Michel (9km away). A neo-Gothic building on the edge of the salt marshes, but well sheltered from the wind, it is quite a plush place inside. Rooms are furnished in tastefully sparse style and are comfortable. The food is very good; the menu features the local delicacy of salt-marsh lamb.

OPEN Mid-Mar to mid-Nov ROOMS 12 (all with bath or shower)

DEAUVILLE

Hôtel du Pavilion de la Poste

25 rue Fossorier
14800 Calvados
TEL 31 88 38 29

In fashionable Deauville, this is an unpretentious family-run place, remarkably well located. Bedrooms are often tiny, but a great deal of care has gone into their decoration, and they are made to feel larger than they are. There is no restaurant, but plenty of choice in the surrounding streets.

OPEN All year ROOMS 15 (all with bath or shower)

DIEPPE

Auberge du Clos Normand

22 rue Henri IV
Martin-Eglise
76370 Seine-Maritime
TEL 35 04 40 34

This small hotel makes an ideal stop for visitors to Dieppe – whether to spend the night in one of the small, quiet, rustic rooms which line the courtyard of the old farmstead, or whether simply to eat lunch from M. Hauchecorne's pleasingly simple and well-presented kitchen. Food and rooms alike are good value, and there is an excellent atmosphere of laid-back enjoyment.

OPEN All year exc. 1st week Apr and mid-Nov to mid-Dec ROOMS 8 (all with bath or shower)

ETRETAT

Le Donjon

chemin de St-Clair
76790 Seine-Maritime
TEL 35 27 08 23; FAX 35 29 92 24

A creeper-clad tower-turned-house of some antiquity, this family-owned hotel high above the seaside town of Etretat is a seductive place. The furnishings and atmosphere are turn-of-the-century, but bathrooms are well up to date and bedrooms interesting and comfortable. Food (mainly seafood) is excellent and comes in the shape of lavish six-course set dinners.

OPEN All year ROOMS 8 (all with bath or shower) FACILITIES Outdoor pool

HONFLEUR

Hostellerie Lechat

3 place Ste-Catherine
14600 Calvados
TEL 31 89 23 85; FAX 31 89 28 61

Of Honfleur's great variety of hotels (many of which are booked solid for most of the summer) this is probably the best if you want a room at fair value and good food into the bargain. The competently run town-centre inn is in a good position right beside the Eglise Ste-Catherine. Bedrooms are fair, if nothing to write home about. The food is a step or two up on its immediate rivals.

OPEN All year ROOMS 23 (all with bath or shower)

ORBEC

Hôtel de France

152 rue Grande
14290 Calvados
TEL 31 32 74 02; FAX 31 32 27 77

A very simple and pleasant hotel in one of Normandy's least damaged market towns, the France is very convenient for exploring the prettiest parts of the Pays d'Auge countryside. It has large, simply furnished bedrooms and good-value family cooking.

OPEN All year exc. mid-Dec to mid-Jan ROOMS 25 (17 with bath or shower)

PONT-AUDEMER

Auberge du Vieux Puits

6 rue Notre-Dame du Pré
27500 Eure
TEL 32 41 01 48

Weeping willows shade the cars parked in the courtyard of this well-known stop-off point, an old inn with modernised rooms around its internal courtyard. Bedrooms are comfortable enough, but perhaps less interesting than the food, which is lovingly served up by M. Foltz in the small country-style restaurant. Fish dishes are wonderful and there are few places in Normandy where the cheese is better kept.

OPEN End Jan to end Dec ROOMS 12 (10 with bath or shower)

PONT D'OUILLY

Auberge St-Christophe

14690 Calvados
TEL 31 69 81 23; FAX 31 69 26 58

A good place to stay on the edge of the Suisse Normande, and remarkable value, this small inn has modern, restfully decorated bedrooms and a small sitting-room. The food is not in the gourmet class, but is utterly satisfactory and there is a fine selection of Calvados to go with it.

OPEN All year ROOMS 7 (all with bath or shower)

ROUEN

Hôtel de la Cathedrale

12 rue St-Romain
76000 Seine-Maritime
TEL 35 71 57 95; FAX 35 70 15 54

Rouen is full of bland business hotels, where comfort is to be had for somewhat inflated prices. This hotel is by contrast old-fashioned and cheap (though clean), but unless you are extremely fussy you will find it more than adequate for a night or two. Its chief advantages are its central position, its shady internal courtyard and the fact that it has more character and a more interesting clientele than all of Rouen's other hotels put together.

OPEN All year ROOMS 24 (21 with bath or shower)

ST-VAAST-LA-HOUGUE

Hôtel de France et des Fuchsias

18 rue Maréchal Foch
50550 Manche
TEL 33 54 42 26; FAX 33 43 46 79

In spite of the fact that it is utterly swamped at times with English visitors, and consequently feels more as if it were in the home counties than in France, we are nevertheless including this hotel, since it struggles hard to remain French, serves excellent food and has supremely comfortable bedrooms for the price. The garden, full of scented shrubs and sunny tables, is another huge plus. Book well in advance in summer.

OPEN Mar to Dec ROOMS 32 (27 with bath or shower)

YVETOT

Auberge du Val au Cesne

76190 Seine-Maritime
TEL 35 56 63 06; FAX 35 56 92 78

A tiny restaurant-with-rooms lost in the lanes of the Pays de Caux, this has long been a favourite with visitors striking inland from Dieppe. A low half-timbered house contains the restaurant, where you can eat extremely well in a series of miniature rooms carved out around the old hearth. Bedrooms are in a separate building, and are pretty and rural. Animals abound.

OPEN All year ROOMS 5 (all with bath)

Grande Place, Arras

What war could ravish, commerce could bestow,
And he returned a friend, who came a foe
[Pope]

THE NORTH

Poor little rich girl. The North, France's unlovely industrial heartland, lays itself open to British advances but gets rough treatment from the tourists who storm impatiently through, their blinkered eyes fixed on the distant charms of other areas, their right feet relentlessly depressed. No more respectful is the behaviour of the rapacious hordes of day-trippers who descend on Calais and Boulogne for a few hours' merciless pillage in the supermarkets, bars and bistros before staggering back, sated and sick, to the white cliffs of perfidious Albion.

Northern France, plain as it is, deserves better than this. Only a small part of it – the strip between the coal-mining belt (Béthune to Valenciennes) and the Belgian border, and the port of Dunkerque – is heavily industrial and unsightly. Artois, Picardy and Champagne remain essentially rural and peaceful. The coast south of Calais has good birdwatching, fine chalk cliff scenery, enormous sandy beaches, and a couple of fashionable resorts. France north of Paris is the birthplace and spiritual home of the lofty Gothic architectural style, and despite the damage inflicted as everywhere else by anti-religious revolutionaries, and much more than anywhere else in both World Wars, this remains the best area of France for a Gothic cathedral crawl, appropriately crowned by a visit to the coronation city of Reims. In Flanders there are splendid examples of red brick Flemish town architecture, windmills and even modest little northern Venices with canals for streets. The big towns have very good art museums, Lille's being one of the most distinguished in provincial France. The countryside too is a museum in its way – a reminder of man's inhumanity, with countless war cemeteries and memorials to the sacrifice of the lost generation of 1914–18.

Rough treatment is no novelty to northern France. The nearest part of the country to the old enemy and rival, England, and France's only naturally defenceless border (excluding Alsace, which is not historically French and has suffered even more), this has been the great battlefield of Europe, the scene of the most glorious French victories – at Bouvines (1214) and Fontenoy (1745), both near Lille – and of some of the most inglorious defeats – Crécy (1346), Agincourt (1415) and Sedan (1870). During the First World War an uninterrupted battle front

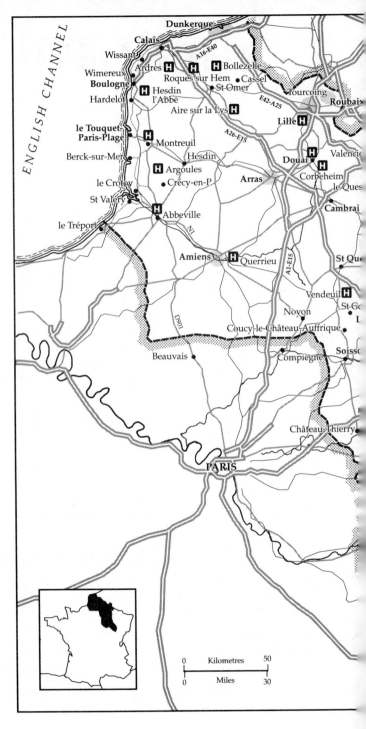

458

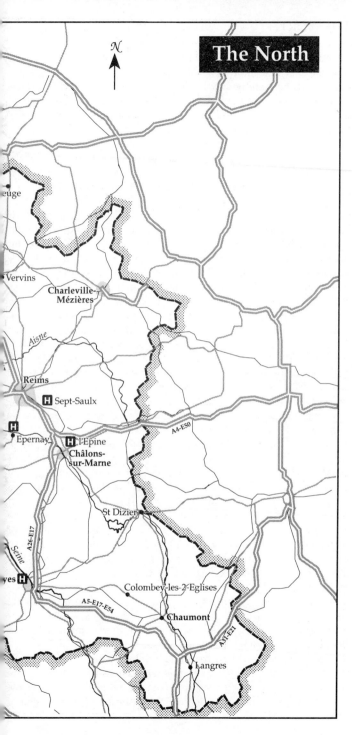

The North

N

euge

Vervins

Charleville-
Mézières

Aisne

Reims

H Sept-Saulx

H

Epernay

H l'Epine
Châlons-
sur-Marne

A4-E50

St Dizier

Seine

A26-E17

yes H

A5-E17-E54

Colombey-les-2-Eglises

Chaumont

A31-E21

Langres

459

extended from the North Sea to the Swiss border. The World Wars brought total desolation to whole tracts of land, and where villages once stood there are now only simple crosses and the woods which have grown up since the war to cover the scar tissue. In other places imposing monuments stand on strategic positions to commemorate the thousands who fell there in attack or defence. Châteaux, churches, and dwellings were destroyed indiscriminately, countryside laid bare. Earlier campaigns were hardly less devastating, for the general wreaking of havoc was as important a part of military strategy as the winning of set-piece battles. Such was the difficulty of leading a satisfactory life in the now green and peaceful Thiérache region, north of Laon, that the inhabitants fortified their churches (some 50 of which still stand) for community refuge in all periods from the 12th to the 16th centuries, when the frontier area was continuously plagued by invaders and by the mercenary armies which were often more of a nuisance in peace-time than in war. Shakespeare's description of the war-weary France of 1420, when 'naked, poor and mangled peace' had for too long been chased from this the best garden of the world, is the story of northern French life down the centuries: 'All her husbandry doth lie on heaps . . . her vine, the merry cheerer of the heart, unpruned dies; her hedges even-pleach'd like prisoners wildly overgrown with hair, put forth disorder'd twigs; her fallow leas the darnel, hemlock, and rank fumitory doth root upon, while that the coulter rusts, that should deracinate such savagery. Even our children . . . grow, like savages – as soldiers will that nothing do but meditate on blood – to swearing and stern looks, diffus'd attire, and everything that seems unnatural'.

After each war the resilient and industrious northern French people have risen from their knees, their towns prosperous owing to their situation on the edge of the economic nerve centre of Europe, the Low Countries. Long before the discovery of coal in the 19th century the towns of Artois and Flanders had grown rich, famous and coveted thanks to their skill in weaving rich cloth; Arras was the richest of the cloth towns, and today retains the finest architectural monuments of bourgeois pride. As early as the 11th and 12th centuries the northern cloth towns were far in advance of the rest of France, both economically and culturally, developing like north Italian city states until the monarchy extended its power to include them. Powerful merchant-family oligarchies ruled them, fought fiercely for their independence from any outside control, and raised civic buildings symbolic of their non-religious, non-aristocratic power. In the north, town halls and belfries are no less important buildings than cathedrals.

Champagne does not fit comfortably into northern France. It falls south of the great divide between the France of wine and the France of beer and cider, which runs approximately from the mouth of the Loire to the Ardennes. Wine is the great distinction and attraction of

Champagne. The chalky hills around Reims and Châlons-sur-Marne are pleasant without being the most beautiful of French vineyard country. Production is centred in the towns, mainly Reims and Epernay, not in vineyard châteaux. Nevertheless, the prestige of champagne, and the history and technicalities of its unique evolutionary process from grape to débutante's dancing slipper, make visiting the cellars in either or both towns extremely interesting and easy to accomplish in a short time. To all this is added the great historical and cultural interest of Reims.

Champagne does share with northern France its bad luck in being on the invasion route to Paris. The First World War front settled just outside Reims, which was largely destroyed like so many other northern towns. Southern Champagne contrasts strikingly in having been spared destruction – beyond the fire of First World War artillery and too rural to be worth bombing in the Second. So Troyes, for example, the once brilliant capital of the flourishing court of Champagne, has survived attractively old and wooden.

France claims only a fraction (and not the most interesting fraction) of the almost mountainous Ardennes forests, which are a popular recreation area for campers, Belgian bicyclists, wild boar and its pursuers (one of whom was Charlemagne). The steep and rocky hills which flank the Meuse as it runs north from industrial Charleville-Mézières towards Belgium are interesting as a contrast to the plains of much of northern France, but if you are tempted to stray far from your itinerary by the superlative-ridden landscape descriptions of over-sensitive romantic writers of the 19th century (George Sand was particularly impressed by the Ardennes) you are likely to be disappointed. The area is best combined with the more interesting Belgian Ardennes.

The main reason for a visit to northern France is because it is France: to stock up with wine perhaps, for which you need only go as far as the nearest supermarket in a port, or just to enjoy a weekend break to shorten the distance between holidays and to get a taste of France. And tasting, or more often making unrepentant pigs of ourselves, is what that means. Never mind the cathedrals, the museums and the war memorials; give us weekend break tourists a few good meals and we are content. Northern France's gastronomic links with the Low Countries are hardly less strong than its economic ones, and that is no culinary criticism – the Belgian taste for the best in food and wine goes back for many centuries; like England for claret, Brussels is the traditional export market for the best burgundies.

In many ways the northern French and especially the Flemings are a race apart. They drink beer, and they play darts. They go in for racing pigeons, archery and cock fighting; instead of *boules* they play skittles and for local folklore nearly every northern town has its giant mascots, brought out in annual festivities and processions.

The Coast

The long coast between Belgium and Normandy is punctuated by three of France's most important ports, all different in nature and aspect – Dunkerque is renowned for industry, Boulogne for fish, and Calais for humanity in transit (ten million a year). Being so close to our south coast Boulogne and Calais have also built up a thriving business in day trips, which the Channel Tunnel is likely to encourage further.

The day trip to France used to be a fairly dignified affair involving a flight to Le-Touquet-Paris-Plage for a quick gamble and gambol. In recent times the phenomenon has changed for a number of social and economic reasons, including the growing popularity of things previously of minority interest (basically French food and wine) and price wars among cross-channel operators, which have combined to turn Calais and Boulogne (mainly on Saturdays) into spectacles of mass gluttony and acquisitiveness.

The English are no strangers to Calais and Boulogne. After his victory at nearby Crécy in 1346, Edward III took possession of Calais after an eight-month siege marked by the futile heroism of its inhabitants and the reluctant clemency of the English king when the town eventually surrendered. The English held Calais for over 200 years, inscribing on one of the town gates, 'Then shall the Frenchman Calais win, when iron and lead like corks shall swim'. Boulogne was taken by Henry VIII in 1544 and held briefly but profitably – in 1550 Henry sold it back for 400,000 crowns. Napoleon massed troops on the hills beside Boulogne for years in preparation for his invasion of Britain, transformed the harbour to accommodate a fleet of flat-bottomed boats, and even struck medals in 1804 inscribed, 'Descente en Angleterre, frappé à Londres'. Trafalgar and the Austrians made him call off his plans to abolish the monarchy and the House of Lords.

After the outbreak of peace the two ports soon became havens for British people on the run (from creditors and others). In Murray's 1843 Handbook, Boulogne (where 5,000 out of 30,000 inhabitants were British) is described as 'one of the chief British colonies abroad. The town is enriched by English money, warmed, lighted and smoked by English coal; English signs and advertisements decorate every other shop door, inn, tavern and lodging house and almost every third person you meet is either a countryman or speaking in our language.' Things have not changed much. A traveller in the time of James I described Calais as 'a beggarly extorting town, monstrous dear and sluttish'. 'In the opinion of many,' commented Murray, 'this description holds good . . . a traveller will do well to quit Calais as soon as he has cleared his baggage from the Custom house.' In the opinion of many, Murray's advice is still the best. Calais is more convenient than Boulogne for the Paris motorway.

If you do feel like lingering, or if you have to, **Calais** has one of the best sandy beaches along the north coast of France, a reputation for good *croissants*, and Rodin's magnificent memorial to the sacrificial, but not sacrificed, Burghers of 1347, standing in front of the heavily ornate town-hall and belfry, modern but 15th-century Flemish in style. The town church is the only example of English Perpendicular Gothic architecture in Flamboyant France. There is also a fine arts museum with a section devoted to Calais's important lace industry, introduced in the 19th century by English industrialists. One of them was the father of the great seascape painter Richard Parkes Bonington who studied here and some of whose works can be seen in the museum.

Boulogne was about two-thirds destroyed in 1944 but nevertheless manages to look more interesting than Calais, because the two-thirds did not include the walled old town on a hill above the now rather ugly port and lower town. The walls themselves are impressively solid and enclose handsome 18th-century houses, a fine medieval belfry, and the great landmark of Boulogne – the soaring dome of the Basilica of Notre-Dame, uncharitably but not unreasonably described by the Victorian traveller Augustus Hare as 'pretentious and ill-proportioned with an absurd dome that outrages the older buildings beneath it'.

The municipal museum has a remarkable collection of Greek vases, Egyptian, Gallo-Roman and medieval antiquities and a Napoleonic collection including English cartoons satirising the planned invasion. There is also a collection of paintings. Apart from its sightseeing interest much of the fun of Boulogne derives from its being France's most important fishing port (over 100,000 tons of fish a year), a fact celebrated by the high technology displays in Nausicaä, a modern

Boulogne's Gothic belfry

463

combination of aquarium and museum of the sea. The modern town is always animated and smelly and there are fish restaurants for all pockets. It is also justifiably very popular with Channel-hoppers for day or weekend shopping trips; it has a variety of good shops to suit all tastes, as well as a large and colourful street market (the main one takes place on Saturday mornings).

The Opal Coast, named after its milky waves, is at its most handsome between Calais and Boulogne. At **Sangatte**, where the flat Flanders coast ends, the new Channel Tunnel terminal lies close to the site of earlier attempts to burrow under the sea, a project first planned in Napoleon's day. North Sea becomes Channel at Cap Griz Nez, where England and France are closest. Much better views are to be had from the higher Cap Blanc Nez at the other end of **Wissant's** excellent beach, which is thought to have been Caesar's point of departure for the conquest of Britain. **Wimereux** has a sandy beach and a period atmosphere – like Boulogne it was a fashionable bathing place in the early 19th century.

From Boulogne to the Somme the coast is one of shifting sands blown into dunes and stabilised in places by a forest of pines. The beaches are sandy, windswept and uninterrupted except by the Canche and Authie estuaries; they are therefore very popular for sand yachting – exponents gather for annual regattas at Berck-Plage.

Le Touquet-Paris-Plage was created by the British for the British at the turn of the century and was one of the most fashionable of pre-war resorts. Three golf courses remain, along with casinos, riding centre, luxury hotels and more than 2,000 villas in the forest which surrounds the geometric resort centre; although very lively in summer it's not conspicuously trendy anymore. Le Touquet has changed since the carefree Chelsea élite flew to France for the day but the Lydd/Le Touquet air link which took them there has been revived. **Hardelot** is more contemporary in its luxury, and more of an agglomeration of substantial villas hidden among the trees than a villagey resort. But there are hotels and splendid sports facilities, again including golf. The facilities at **Berck-Plage**, which originally attracted visitors because of its curative properties, are augmented by the nearby Parc de Bagatelle where the amusements vary from mini-zoo to riding, go-karting and aeroplane jaunts.

The Somme estuary is wide and muddy (you can walk across at low tide and fish in the pools) and distinguished most of all by the variety of its migratory bird life. There is a reserve on the north side of the bay. The beaches are not ideal, but **St-Valery** and **Le Crotoy** are both attractive old fishing ports facing each other across the bay. Neither of them has the important sea traffic they had before the estuary silted up and became mostly salt marshes, used for rearing sheep. In 1049 Harold son of Godwin was shipwrecked here and rescued from the local prison by Duke William of Normandy who later, on 27 September 1066, set sail from St-Valery to take from Harold the throne which William claimed had been promised him 17 years before.

South of the Somme the coast takes on a Norman character – cliffs of chalk and beaches of shingle, resorts of little charm. Just up the Somme from St-Valery the big town of **Abbeville** is skirted by most travellers on the Paris–Boulogne road. The town is no beauty now, having been all but obliterated in the Second World War, but from accounts and drawings it was one of the most attractive towns of northern France. 'Many of the houses are of wood, with a greater air of antiquity than I remember to have seen,' recorded the travelling farmer Arthur Young in May 1787. Abbeville was more to the taste of the Victorian John Ruskin, who wrote: 'I have wasted years in mere enjoyment of the Alps, but I never to my knowledge wasted an hour in Abbeville . . . for cheerful unalloyed unwearying pleasure, the getting in sight of Abbeville on a fine summer afternoon . . . rushing down the street to see St-Wulfram again before the sun was off the towers, are things to cherish the past for, to the end.' St-Wulfram still stands – with a marvellously carved late 15th- and 16th-century façade which is well worthy of admiration. There is also a museum (paintings and prehistory) and, on the south side of town, an exquisite pink and white 18th-century folly of a château aptly named Bagatelle (open to visitors in summer).

A few miles east of Abbeville **St-Riquier** has a squat belfry, and a very fine church (mostly Flamboyant Gothic), the remains of a Benedictine monastery of great antiquity and importance. Typically, for Picardy, the façade is covered with extremely delicate carving (the chalky stone being easy to work). The interior is clean and bright and pleasing; in the abbey buildings some old photos and farm tools are displayed. North of Abbeville, there is not much to see at the battlefield of Crécy, except a cross marking the bravery of the blind king of Bohemia who insisted on being led into battle (to be duly hacked up).

Rue is an attractive old village with a 15th-century belfry and a small chapel which presents a wealth of elaborate late Gothic carving inside and out (guided tours). **Valloires** is an old Cistercian abbey which remains preserved as it was rebuilt in the 18th century, sober and elegant in brick and stone, with superb woodcarving especially in the church.

The First World War

In terms of monuments no less than human life Northern France was tragically impoverished by two World Wars, which have given it a reputation for grim, grey and monotonous towns which add no joy to a journey through the region. Among the saddest casualties must be reckoned Coucy-le-Château, by all accounts and from old pictures one of the very finest old fortresses in France. Remarkably, most great buildings have been carefully and successfully restored; the great loss, which no restoration work can recover, is the charm and character of a flattened town. For all their sightseeing interest Amiens, Abbeville, Soissons, even Reims itself are unattractive towns which few tourists are sad to leave.

Yet, from the strictly tourist point of view, the effect of these wars, and especially the First World War, is not all negative. The War itself is the most compelling horror story of our time, and there is no better way to ponder the tragedy of those whom we have sworn never to forget than to visit the monuments that mark the battlefields along the Western Front. In many places battlefield sightseeing is a matter for those with a particular historical or family interest, and a powerful imagination. The First World War memorials provide more than this, partly because the War itself is thought-provoking beyond the issues of international politics, partly because of the grandeur of the memorials themselves. While there is very little nourishment for French national pride in the story of the Second World War, in the Great War France triumphed at the cost of a whole generation – in 1915 alone France lost more soldiers than Britain was to lose in the whole course of the war, and that was before Verdun – and the national achievement is appropriately commemorated. The most impressive and vividly evocative war memorials are in the areas where the French achievement was greatest, that is to say around Verdun, which now has something of the sacred aura of a national pilgrimage.

Once the front had been established, by the end of 1914, in an unbroken line of entrenchments from the North Sea to the Vosges through Flanders, Picardy, Champagne and Lorraine, the scope for tactical manoeuvres was reduced to suicidal offensives against well-defended positions. The Germans rightly identified Verdun as the symbolic bulwark of France, which the French could not afford to sacrifice, and where her forces would be spent under the weight of German artillery. This opened up, with a bombardment of unprecedented intensity, on 21 February 1916. Throughout the spring and summer the few square kilometres north and east of Verdun were completely laid waste as the row of concrete forts – which had been built after 1870 to defend the city – and the hills beside the Meuse were lost and retaken at appalling cost and in infernal conditions. By November, after a battle of eight months, the lines were back almost to where they had been in February, and well over half a million soldiers had died. After Verdun it was the British turn: on the first day of the

Somme offensive (1 July 1916) which took some of the pressure off Verdun, 19,000 British troops were killed, 37,000 wounded or missing.

Verdun In the town there is a memorial to the battle, a solemn knight in armour resting on his sword at the head of a great stairway. Underneath, the monument books containing all the names of the participants of the battle are displayed. In Vauban's old citadel you can visit the underground galleries which were used during the Great War to shelter troops exhausted from the battle. The battlefields around Verdun are fairly well signposted from the town, and there are organised tours. Of the many memorials around the battlefields east of the Meuse and north of Verdun, some of them no more than a small shrine where once there stood a whole village, the most evocative are the memorial museum, cemetery and ossuary at Douaumont; and two of the forts which were the most important strategic elements of the battle, Douaumont and Vaux.

The corners of French fields which are for ever England, Australia or Canada are in Flanders, Artois and Picardy. The memorials below are listed from north to south.

Notre-Dame-de-Lorette (near Arras) The summit of the Artois battlefields, with an orientation table, a huge cemetery and a museum.

Vimy Ridge (near Arras) An impressive Canadian memorial on a strategic hillside captured at heavy cost by Canadian forces in 1917.

Beaumont-Hamel (between Arras and Amiens) Scene of action of the British 29th Division, incorporating a battalion of the Newfoundland Regiment, where many of the elements of the battle landscape are preserved or have been reconstructed.

Thiepval (between Arras and Amiens) British memorial arch.

Péronne A well-presented museum of the First World War with weaponry, uniforms and memorabilia. It makes a good starting point for a tour of the Somme battlefields.

Chemin des Dames A ridge, offering a commanding defensive position between Laon and Reims, which the French tried to storm in Spring 1917. The failure and cost of the operation, the exhaustion of the French troops after Verdun and news of the Revolution in Russia combined to provoke a wave of mutinies.

Above the attractive green Canche valley a few kilometres inland from Le Touquet, **Montreuil-sur-Mer** (as it was once) is one of the most pleasant weekend bases in the north. The hill town is still contained within impressive brick ramparts with a splendid mostly 17th-century citadel at one end. Much of the charm of the place is attributable to the vegetation within and without the walls, which makes a walk round them much more pleasant than just any old rampart tramp, especially when there is a rustling autumnal carpet. It is worth pursuing the Canche up to **Hesdin** for the countryside and to wander around the town centre. The town hall has a lavishly decorated 17th-century porch and balcony. The road north from Hesdin to St-Omer passes the site of the battle of Agincourt; but not surprisingly there is little, apart from a small museum, to remind you of this, one of the most idiotic of French military catastrophes.

St-Omer is a sizeable town on the borders of Artois and Flanders but unlike most sizeable northern French towns it is quiet, interesting and good-looking. There are many elegant 17th- and 18th-century town houses. One of the finest is the Hôtel Sandelin, which houses a good museum (paintings, sculptures, ceramics and local history). The Gothic basilica of Notre-Dame has the dimensions and air of the cathedral it once was, and contains a number of interesting works of art, including a 16th-century astronomical clock and a 13th-century sculptural group which looks disproportionate until you realise that it was intended to be seen from far below. To the north-east of town the marshes between the Aa and the forest of Clairmarais have been canalised into 3,000 kilometres of waterways, and christened the Venice of the North – an overstatement of their beauty perhaps but aptly descriptive of the waterborne life of the communities beside the canals.

French Flanders and Picardy

Waterways, water-mills, windmills and belfries characterise maritime Flanders, reclaimed from the sea in the Middle Ages (much of it is below sea-level). There is little wood and little stone so the Flemings have built houses of brick and tile, low and long because of the wind that meets no natural resistance as it sweeps in from the North Sea. There aren't many windmills left now, but you can visit one, built in 1127, near the Flemish-speaking village of **Hondschoote. Bergues** is a more interesting town, with a modern replacement of what was until 1944 the finest belfry in northern France. It has attractive old streets, a good museum (paintings, natural history) and brick fortifications which are mostly the work of Louis XIV's military architect Vauban, who filled the ditches with water and the water with fish (boats for hire). **Cassel** is equally interesting as a typically Flemish little town perched on the isolated Mont Cassel (175 metres) which gives views far and wide of the flat surrounding countryside. Cassel too has its museum of history and folklore and a long central square of 17th- and 18th-century low painted brick houses.

Between the intensively cultivated maritime Flanders and the grimy slag-heaps of the coal-mining belt sprawls the great industrial urban agglomeration of Lille/Roubaix/Tourcoing, over a million strong. Cloth and beer are the traditional foundations of the town, but recently the basis of **Lille's** considerable prosperity has diversified. The citadel, separated from the old part of Lille by the Deule Canal, is one of Vauban's finest and the best preserved of all the fortresses built along the north-east, France's defenceless frontier. The fine arts museum and the museum of modern art are generally acknowledged to be among the best in provincial France and there are some good examples of Flemish town architecture of the 17th and 18th centuries. Outstanding among them is the Ancienne Bourse (Exchange), a heavily ornamented brick and stone baroque palace built around an arcaded courtyard. Other buildings of interest include the modern Palais de Justice and the Flamboyant church of St-Maurice.

Of all the northern towns **Douai** has perhaps the best known (thanks to Corot) and most handsome Gothic belfry, grey and spiky and topped by the proud flag-waving Flanders lion. The town also boasts a very fine museum of Old Master paintings in an old Carthusian monastery. **Cambrai** also has an art museum which is worth visiting, and two interesting 18th-century churches – there is a large painting by Rubens in the church of St-Géry. Cambrai's central square and belfry is mostly the work of restorers. At the nearby town of **Le-Cateau-Cambrésis**, birthplace of Matisse, there is a museum devoted to the artist. **Le Quesnoy** is remarkable as the only example of a Vauban citadel which remains intact as a complete system of town walls. The fortifications, heavily overgrown and surrounded by several lakes, are as attractive to walk around as they are interesting to the student of military architecture. In 1918 New Zealand troops had to take the town by climbing the walls with ladders. Camping, boating and sports facilities and even a small sandy beach are on hand. East of Le Quesnoy is some very attractive countryside, a striking contrast after the coalfields north of it. To the south lies **Maroilles**, origin of northern France's smelliest cheese, and the fascinating **Thiérache** region, bristling with fortified churches from hard times when this was the disputed frontier between France and Empire. Many of the red brick buildings are flanked by solid round towers and there are rooms in the space above the nave where the local inhabitants could take refuge. Some of the most interesting are near Vervins, at **Beaurain**, **Burelles**, **Prisces**, and **Plomion**.

Undoubtedly the pick of the northern towns, the most prosperous and culturally brilliant in the past, and the most beautiful and interesting today, is **Arras**, capital of Artois. Its splendid cobbled central squares – the Place des Héros and the Grande Place, dominated by

Windmill at Wormhoudt

Gothic town hall and lofty belfry – are the most complete and harmonious examples of brick and stone Flemish architecture in France. The 17th-century houses are arcaded at ground level, tall, thin and decorated with pilasters and elegant curving gables that could be part of a Dutch skyline. The old abbey of St-Vaast's classical church has become the cathedral, and its 18th-century monastic buildings house the town's art museum, with a fine collection of local, Flemish and Dutch paintings, and sculptures. As well as being the most interesting, Arras is also one of the most convenient of the northern towns to visit in transit, situated as it is beside the motorway to Paris and the south. It is also a good base for exploration of First World War battlefields and monuments at the northern end of the front line where most of the English fighting took place. The last hills of Artois looking out over Flanders Fields took on great strategic importance and were bitterly disputed (Notre-Dame-de-Lorette and Vimy Ridge; see page 467).

Exploring Flanders in France takes time and is best combined, without hurrying, with Flanders in Belgium (Bruges being the big attraction). It is not on an obvious route south or east of French Channel ports. If you are just passing through, and want to balance progress with interest, and especially if your sightseeing taste embraces Gothic churches, the route through southern Picardy to Reims is clearly the one you should take.

From the interesting churches of **Rue**, **St-Riquier** and **Abbeville** you follow the Somme upstream to **Amiens** – a big industrial town very severely damaged in both World Wars and unlikely as a whole to etch an image of enduring beauty on your memory. But its cathedral, which survived the bombings, is one of the very finest in France, the largest and least composite in architectural style, having been more or less completed in 50 years of the 13th century. The façade is richly adorned with sculptures of great beauty, which inspired Ruskin's Amiens Bible; the nave is France's longest, and impressively lofty; the 15th- and 16th-century carving in wood and stone within and around the choir is endlessly fascinating. Amiens also has a museum of considerable interest, outstanding among its collection of paintings being a series of the altar-pieces presented annually to the cathedral by a local literary and religious guild.

On the edge of Amiens beside the Somme is a network of canals and market gardens (*hortillonnages*) where until very recently punts full of vegetables being poled to market were a common sight on the water. The practice is dying out now but you can still explore the canals by boat.

Eastward roads lead alternatively to Noyon or St-Quentin. **Noyon** is a quiet town whose former importance as a religious centre is suggested by the scale of its cathedral, a very simple and beautiful example of the transition to early Gothic style from the Romanesque, well restored after severe damage in the First World War when Noyon was the closest occupied town to Paris and synonymous with the German threat. **St-Quentin** is much more industrial and its great Gothic basilica less noteworthy. But there is a butterfly and insect museum of rare quality and a large collection of 18th-century pastel portraits by the great flatterer of pre-revolutionary France – Maurice Quentin de la Tour – in the Lécuyer art museum.

Laon is one of the most attractive and interesting towns in northern France. The walled medieval city, capital of Carolingian France, crowns a lonely hill commanding the plains. Pedestrians can reach it by a funicular from the station. It is dominated by the openwork towers of its cathedral, like Noyon's a bright and beautiful mixture of the qualities of Romanesque and Gothic styles, dating from the late 12th century, and (unlike Noyon) with some fine stained glass. The most endearing of its features are the stone oxen which stand out from the top of the façade towers, eternal tributes to the heavy task of hauling all the stones uphill. There are a number of other old buildings of interest round the narrow streets of Laon, including a medieval lepers' hospital (the Salle Gothique) next to the Cathedral, a delightful octagonal Templar chapel and another interesting early Gothic church (St-Martin). There are several 14th-century fortified town gates and a path round much of the city ramparts. To the west of Laon **St-Gobain Forest** has some splendid 30-metre oaks and three old monasteries – Le Tortoir now a farm, St-Nicolas-aux-Bois part of a private estate, and Prémontré a mental hospital – all worth admiring. On the southern edge of the forest **Coucy-le-Château**, the setting for much of Barbara Tuchman's history of the 14th century, *A Distant Mirror*, was one of the most formidable citadels in France until the retiring Germans blew it up in 1917. The town walls and gateways are still impressive. In the woods at the foot of Coucy you can see the emplacement of Big Bertha, the gun which shelled Paris in 1918, one of its direct hits being the church of St-Gervais in the middle of mass.

Soissons lies a few kilometres south of Coucy, on the south bank of the Aisne. Apart from its interesting churches Soissons is an unattractive post-First World War reconstruction. Its cathedral is another very early Gothic one famed for the symmetrical beauty of its nave, something you would never suspect from its lop-sided exterior. A remarkable feature is the earliest part of the church, the south transept – round and arcaded like a second choir. On the edge of town the twin-spired façade of the old abbey of St-Jean-des-Vignes stands in isolation, its rose window a gaping hole, and is the more impressive for its desolate state. The rest of the great abbey church was pulled down at the beginning of the last century; you can still visit the splendid Gothic cellar and refectory and some of the cloister. There are two other ruined abbeys at Soissons – St-Léger, in town, provides an interesting setting for the varied contents of the municipal museum. Of St-Médard to the north of the Aisne there is little left to see except the very old crypt (9th-century).

The Ardennes

The French Ardennes, which are not on the way to anywhere in particular, have no monuments of interest and apart from wild boar pâté not much in the way of gastronomy. Nevertheless this is a frequented tourist area because of its status as an area of natural beauty – which it is, by the less than exalted standards of this part of France. The steep rocky hills which enclose the Meuse as it winds northwards from the twin towns of Charleville-Mézières to Belgium are a convenient recreation area for people from the industrial communities, with woods, rivers and lakes. Apart from the tortuous river valley itself, which is in places almost spectacular in its rocky severity, the main attraction is the great expanse of forest, not as wild and savagely inhabited as when Charlemagne hunted boar and wild ox here but still extensive – 346,000 acres. Some of the rocky crests are good walking goals and give fine views of the wild countryside. North of Charleville, **Monthermé** is well situated on a great loop in the river near its junction with the attractive Semois and a good base for excursions, but has no particular village charm. Finest of the peaks to see nearby are the Rocher des Quatre Fils Aymon, the Roche aux Sept Villages and the Roches de Laifour.

Although the French Ardennes are little more than pleasant, the Belgian part of the Massif is more interesting, with some châteaux and grottoes, varied countryside and the impressively situated town of Dinant. As a whole the Ardennes area is not so obviously avoidable as a description of its French section makes it sound.

On the southern edge of the Ardennes forests and hills, **Charleville-Mézières** is the capital of the *département*, the result of a merger of the two towns, whose inhabitants now rejoice in the name of Carolo-macériens. Set on two tongues of land between deep loops in the Meuse, the towns retain their separate characters.

In the centre of geometrically planned Charleville, the magnificent 17th-century Place Ducale is a fine achievement, despite the later town hall on one side, and is thought to be the work of Clément Métezeau, younger brother of Louis, creator of the Place Royale in Paris (now the Place des Vosges). The two squares are as closely related as the two architects. In an old mill built in the Meuse there is a museum devoted to Ardennes folklore and the memory of Charleville's most famous son, the late 19th-century poet Rimbaud who shot across the literary firmament with all the fleeting brilliance of a comet.

Further upstream, **Sedan** was a rich cloth town in the 16th and 17th centuries, and the site on 1 September 1870 of the battle between the French army of 100,000 men against two German armies totalling 240,000 men which ended in Napoleon III's capitulation. A few months later the Prussians were at the gates of Paris. Apart from the forbidding walls of one of the country's largest fortresses, there is not much to admire in the town.

Champagne

Any or all of three things may bring you to Champagne: Reims, bubbly, or a destination such as Alsace, Switzerland or Burgundy beyond its southern or eastern borders. Champagne is the *sine qua non* of celebration, 'its sparkling foam' in Voltaire's words, 'the brilliant image of our French people'. The unique manufacturing process, the welcome extended to the tourist by the manufacturers, and the charm of the landscape make a wine stop in Champagne (*le* champagne is the wine, *la* Champagne is the area) as fascinating and informative as it is delicious.

Champagne was famous long before it was fizzy. The Romans found vines when they arrived; popes Urban II and Leo XII, kings François I of France and Henry VIII of England stocked their cellars from the prestigious vineyards of Ay. The elaboration of the complicated double fermentation method to encourage the local wine's natural sparkle came later, and is traditionally attributed to the 17th-century Benedictine abbot of Hautvillers (near Epernay), one Dom Pérignon. Whatever the truth about the great oenophile's contribution, the result today of viticultural evolution in Champagne is an industry and a product quite different from other wines in France.

The vineyard area is called the **Montagne de Reims**. Its gentle slopes of vines crowned by tufty clumps of trees are well worth a leisurely tour, in spite of the fact that there are few places for wine tasting. Not surprisingly the villages are prosperous. **Ay** lies at the heart of some of the most distinguished vineyards, **Hautvillers** is splendidly situated at the top of a steep hill looking down over the Marne, but of the Abbey where Dom Pérignon had a sparklingly bright idea (now owned by Moët et Chandon, who have set up a private museum there) only the church remains to be seen for the time being.

Reims is one of the most important cities in the history of France, the main settlement of the Rémi tribe of Gallo-Belgians, who welcomed Caesar as an ally, and whose descendants saw their city grow in stature to become a major religious centre. On Christmas Day 496 it was the site of the baptism of the previously pagan Clovis, King of the Franks, by Saint Rémi himself. In memory of this, the first page in the history of France, coronations at Reims became an essential part of royal legitimacy; in 1359 the pretender Edward III of England headed straight for Reims to be crowned, but was repelled. Joan of Arc's mission was the coronation of Charles VII at Reims, and this she achieved on 17 July 1429. On 29 May 1825 Charles X was crowned in full ceremonial, Reims's last coronation.

Reims was once no doubt a fine old town, but even before the First World War Augustus Hare complained that wide straight boulevards had been laid down as in Paris. They were not to last long: (→ page 477)

Champagne

Three varieties of grape are grown in an area covering some 70,000 acres (only three per cent of French vineyard area), a region of chalky hillsides some 140km north east of Paris, consisting of three main districts. On the Montagne de Reims, between Reims and Epernay, most of the black **Pinot Noir** grape is grown; along the Marne valley between Epernay and Château-Thierry the black **Pinot Meunier** predominates; the delicate white **Chardonnay** grape is concentrated south of Epernay along the Côte des Blancs.

After harvesting, which usually takes place in early October, the grapes are quickly pressed to extract the juice with as little colour as possible. The first fermentation will normally terminate by Christmas time. In the New Year, after the malolactic fermentation, *assemblage* takes place, blending young wines, usually 75 per cent black and 25 per cent white grapes, from many different villages according to each producer's own individual formula. The *liqueur de tirage* (wine, sugar and yeast) is added and the wine is bottled. After the second fermentation, which creates the bubbles (or mousse), is complete, the bottles sit in cellars for two or three years before being placed in racks, necks tilted down, and for six weeks are given regular, short, sharp shakes by trained *remueurs* (who can manage over 30,000 bottles a day after a long apprenticeship) to encourage the sediment to settle on the temporary closure. When this is achieved, each bottle's neck is swiftly frozen so that the sediment adheres to the closure and the bottle can be re-inverted to an upright position without clouding the wine. The closure is quickly removed and the pressure of the mousse forcibly ejects the sediment in a pellet of slushy ice. A *liqueur d'expédition* (mature champagne and sugar) is used to top up the small amount of wine lost during the disgorgement process. Even a so-called 'brut' champagne will contain up to 15 g/l of sugar, but should taste dry because it is added not to sweeten the wine, but to round off the acidity, which is intrinsically high in champagne.

The big champagne houses own relatively few, but choice, vineyards (about 12 per cent of the total), whose yield they augment by buying from co-operatives of small-scale proprietors who retain sufficient grapes for their own champagnes, which account for 33 per cent of world sales. Each champagne house sells a variety of wines. The standard non-vintage champagne, which accounts for up to 80 per cent of all champagnes produced, is in theory at least unchanging from year to year thanks to careful blending and the use of old reserve wines. Some champagne is produced from white grapes only and is called *blanc de blancs*, and rosé champagne has been in particular vogue since the mid-1980s. In an especially good year some wine is not blended and is dated (*millésimé*). Most houses produce ultra-expensive prestige cuvées along the lines of Moët et Chandon's famous Dom Pérignon.

Visiting a champagne house is not like visiting a handsome old château in its vineyards, as you do in the Bordeaux regions, for example. The big champagne houses are mostly in Reims and Epernay and seem more like the headquarters of old-established firms, which, of course, they are. The avenue de Champagne in Epernay has a certain style – wide and straight and flanked on both sides by the most prestigious establishments, built in a suitably grand manner.

The dozen biggest champagne houses account for some 65 per cent of world sales, and they are the ones that lay on the best organised tours in a variety of languages, and tasting in the universal language of champagne. Mumm and Piper-Heidsieck in Reims and Moët et Chandon in Epernay are the obvious choices, but there are scores of other houses which will welcome you. Mercier has the most-up-to-date reception facility, which incorporates a laser light show. The heart of these places, indeed of Champagne itself, is the enormous extent of chalk galleries in the hillside where the wine evolves in ideal conditions of constant humidity and temperatures (about 10°C) whatever the external weather conditions. In Reims, these galleries connect a series of *crayères*, vast caverns hewn out in Gallo-Roman times to provide building material for the city itself. Ruinart has the most fantastic *crayères* – the only *crayères*, in fact, that are officially classified as a national monument. Everywhere you will be bombarded with statistics – how many hundreds of thousands of bottles are laid up in the cellars, representing how many tens of millions of francs' worth of stock and so on. One of the most surprising facts is that of world-wide sales of some 250 million bottles a year, less than 40 per cent is exported, yet it earns more revenue than any other French alcoholic product or region. Some 50 per cent more, in fact, than Bordeaux, even though the latter is just as famous and four times the size.

The largest champagne cask (it holds 200,000 bottles)

overrun by the Germans right at the beginning of the First World War, then relieved after a few weeks' pillage, the city was to suffer 49 months of relentless bombardment, for the front line was only a kilometre or two away. In the old centre of Reims 12,000 of the 15,000 houses were destroyed, leaving the great cathedral miraculously still standing although far from undamaged. The shells did uncover some Gallo-Roman remains. Only in Autumn 1918 was the town evacuated: until then many inhabitants had stayed, living in the 100km of underground galleries of the old chalk quarries, now champagne cellars. Reims was quickly rebuilt, without any frills, and escaped the Second World War more or less unscathed.

Sights in Reims

• **Cathedral** One of the big four with Paris, Chartres and Amiens, displayed to advantage by the arrangement of rebuilding and a radiant golden colour when the late afternoon sun hits the west façade, the cathedral's great glory. To the architectural framework of massive but graceful symmetry is added a wealth of sculpture – a row of 63 unidentified kings, each 3 metres tall and six tonnes in weight, and three deep doorways framed by the most beautiful examples of the most charming school of Gothic sculpture. Best loved of all is the smiling angel who stands next to the scalped St-Nicaise. More angels flutter in the flying buttresses along the north side of this the 'cathedral of angels'. Inside too the most striking feature is sculpture – the west end is covered with statues in niches, still marvellously detailed having been sheltered from the weather. Some of the original 13th-century stained glass was restored after the First World War; there is also some modern glass including a chapel with windows by Chagall.

• **St-Rémi** An enormous old Benedictine abbey church built in the 11th and 12th centuries; over the long dark Romanesque nave is suspended a gilt crown with 96 lights (once candles) symbolising the lifespan of Saint Rémi. The choir provides an elegant light Gothic contrast. The current version of Saint Rémi's tomb is an enormous 19th-century creation, but incorporates some fine statues from the 16th century.

• **Palais du Tau** The archbishop's palace, dating mostly from the 17th century but retaining a vaulted Gothic room, site of post-coronation banquets, which now contains two of the greatest treasures of a very rich museum, 15th-century Arras tapestries telling of the strong King Clovis.

• **St-Denis Museum** Paintings of the highest quality – Renaissance German (Cranach) to modern French (Matisse, Picasso and Corot).

• **Chapelle Foujita** Neo-Romanesque chapel designed and decorated by a modern Japanese artist.

• **Porte Mars** Damaged and dirty but still very impressive 3rd-century triumphal arch on the edge of the town centre.

Reims cathedral, west façade

Châlons-sur-Marne, not Reims, is the departmental capital. It is not a very attractive town, despite being crossed by the Marne and some tributary canals, but there are churches of some interest (mainly for their stained glass, of which Châlons was an important centre).

Rather more agreeable as an ecclesiastical pause (and a very good gastronomic one too) than a plunge into urban Châlons is **L'Epine**, little more than a string of houses along the straight road from Châlons towards Metz, which makes the basilica of Notre-Dame-de-l'Epine all the more surprising in its isolated domination of the surrounding expanse of corn fields. It is a late Gothic building with extremely intricate decorative tracery all over the golden façade and openwork spires. Although nearly all the statuary is missing, some splendid gargoyles remain. The interior is more simply elegant and contains an emotive sculpture of the Entombment.

Southern Champagne has neither the viticultural nor, quite, the cultural attractions of the north; but this peaceful, spacious landscape escaped devastation in the First World War, so its towns, even if they lack monuments of the first order, are more attractive as towns. The plains and woods seem off the beaten track, but in fact Champagne was Europe's most important medieval thoroughfare, and its capital **Troyes** an international trading and artistic centre. Even when merchants stayed put in Antwerp and Florence and Troyes lost its commercial importance, the Trojan school of sculpture and stained glass continued to flourish, particularly in the late 15th and early 16th centuries when local production was distinguished from the mainstream of the Renaissance by its simple realism. Today it is a quiet provincial town tucked into a loop in the young Seine. It still has narrow streets of timbered houses leaning over the cobbles, some rather grubby, and many interesting churches.

Sights in Troyes

- **St-Urbain** This church is a prodigious achievement for its time (the late 13th century), described by Viollet-le-Duc as 'certainly the last limit that construction in stone can reach'. It was built to the order of Pope Urban IV on the site of his father's shoe shop, much to the annoyance of the nuns who owned the land, and who did all they could to sabotage construction. Elegantly decorated outside with pinnacles, gargoyles, balustrades and flying buttresses, the interior is a dazzling expanse of coloured glass (mostly 13th-century) hardly interrupted by the spindly stone skeleton of the church.
- **Cathedral** Although lacking stylistic unity this church is richly decorated outside (especially the Flamboyant west façade and earlier north doorway). There is a wealth of stained glass from 13th-century (choir) to 17th-century, all of the highest quality.
- **St-Nizier** Renaissance church containing interesting stained glass and sculptures.
- **St-Madeleine** Splendid 16th-century stained glass around the choir and two masterpieces of 16th-century Trojan sculpture – the ornate roodscreen and the statue of Saint Martha in the south transept.
- **St-Jean** Scene of the marriage of Henry V of England to the heiress Catherine of France as agreed in the treaty of Troyes in 1420. The distorted nave pillars give the church a surreal aspect.
- **St-Pantaléon** A mostly Renaissance church with a wooden vault, turned into a museum of over 40 statues from deconsecrated and destroyed churches.
- **Museums** There are several near the cathedral: fine arts, modern art, archaeology and natural history. More unusual is the local history museum in the fine old Hôtel de Vauluisant near the church of St-Pantaléon; its varied contents include good local sculpture and a

separate section devoted to the knitwear industry (*bonneterie*) which has been the mainstay of the town since the 18th century.

• **Old Town** The most picturesque old streets with tall overhanging timbered houses are in the area around the church of St-Jean (especially the Rue des Chats and the Rue de Champeaux).

Here in central eastern France the beaches of Atlantic and Mediterranean are remote indeed. But the lucky Trojans and the Bragards – as the inhabitants of St-Dizier style themselves – have their local beaches, on the reservoirs created to regularise the course of the Seine (**Lac d'Orient**) and the Marne (**Lac du Der-Chantecoq**). Both are very extensive, full of weekenders and well provided with facilities for camping, swimming, fishing and water sports. There are some churches of interest in the Der region (sculptures and stained glass at **Chavanges**, unusual timber-framed construction in many village churches but most complete and attractive at **Lentilles**). Most of the forest to the east of the Lac d'Orient has been taken over by tourists (there are walks and rides and picnic areas) but the wildlife has been granted its reserves.

The Marne valley upstream from Châlons is not particularly interesting, but improves towards Chaumont. The village of **Vignory** is worth a pause to admire its very fine large church which has been little altered since its construction in the mid-11th century; its arches and pillars are pleasingly round and massive, its vault is still wooden. South-east of Vignory the empty rolling hills bear tributes to two great Frenchmen. A granite double-barred cross of Lorraine, symbol of French resistance and national spirit, crowns a hill on the edge of Colombey-les-Deux-Eglises, adopted home for nearly 40 years of General de Gaulle. Chez de Gaulle (La Boisserie) is a modest place, but you can visit it and see several of the general's rooms preserved as a memorial. Saint Bernard was no less of a colossus in his time, restoring expelled popes to Rome, launching crusades, reforming corrupt practices within the church, combating heresy, and still finding time to look after the Abbaye de Clairvaux which he founded in 1115 beside the Aube. Now this important monastery, once the capital of the Cistercian order, is a prison with more than a thousand inmates. South of Colombey, the market town of **Chaumont** enjoys a fine situation between two rivers, but offers the tourist little more than an impressive railway viaduct and a Gothic basilica with interesting sculptures.

Langres, at the gates of Burgundy, is an interesting old city of severe classical dignity, which still seems to be a world apart, enclosed within old walls and bypassed by main road and railway. Langres was an important stronghold for the Romans as it had been for the Gauls. Its site at the edge of a high plateau is a magnificent natural fortress, and until the attachment of Lorraine and the Franche-Comté to the Crown it was a major border town; so its fortifications were repeatedly improved from Roman times to the 19th century. From the 3rd century onwards Langres was also a very important episcopal see: the bishop of Langres had the right to strike his own coinage. Walking along or below the ramparts gives enormous views (including the Alps, they say) and reveals a succession of splendid gateways of which the oldest dates from the 2nd century and has been incorporated in the walls.

Sights in Langres

• **Cathedral** A beautiful, severe transitional Romanesque/Gothic building masked by a heavily inappropriate 18th-century façade.
• **St-Martin** A much altered Gothic church with a very fine wooden statue of Christ over the altar (16th century from Troyes).
• **St-Didier Museum** Gallo-Roman archaeological finds, and some paintings.

HOTELS

Key: ◆ = 0–250FF, ◆◆ = 251–450FF, ◆◆◆ = over 451FF; prices are per double room without breakfast, which costs around 35–60FF extra. Some hotels may insist on half-board during high season, some hotels or restaurants may close at specific times during the week – it is always worth checking. Most hotels accept the major credit cards; we have indicated where a hotel takes no credit cards.

ABBEVILLE

La Maison Carrée

Bois de Bonance
Port le Grand
80132 Somme
TEL 22 24 11 97; FAX 22 31 63 77

A small red-brick, creeper-covered mansion in open countryside near Abbeville, La Maison Carrée is the family home of Jacques and Myriam Maillard. The three comfortable and graceful bedrooms have oil paintings, antique furniture and large well-equipped bathrooms. For the excellent breakfast, guests sit together around a large mahogany table in the elegant yet homely dining-room (dinners are not served). The house is surrounded by a beautiful ornamental garden with immaculate lawns, an array of colourful flowers and a decent-sized swimming-pool.

OPEN Early Jan to Christmas ROOMS 5 (all with bath) FACILITIES Heated outdoor pool (Credit cards not accepted)

THE NORTH

AIRE-SUR-LA-LYS

Hostellerie des Trois Mousquetaires

Château du Fort de la Redoute RN43
62120 Pas-de-Calais
TEL 21 39 01 11; FAX 21 39 50 10

On the road between St-Omer and Béthune this mock-medieval mansion sits in splendid ornamental grounds with duck ponds, a putting green and a children's playground. The interior is notable for its panelling of rich Hungarian oak, grand stone fireplaces and attractive chandeliers hanging from high ceilings. Bedrooms in the main building tend to be grand in style (some have four-poster beds) with elegant furnishings; those in the newer extension are equally spacious and colourful but opt for more modern fabrics and furnishings. Well-prepared local dishes feature on the menu in the stylish restaurant which overlooks the rear lawns.

OPEN End Jan to end Dec ROOMS 30 (all with bath or shower)

ARDRES

Clément

91 esplanade du Maréchal Leclerc
62610 Pas-de-Calais
TEL 21 82 25 25; FAX 21 82 98 92

The Clément has long been a popular first stop for travellers fresh off the Calais ferry, and the quality of the place should be sufficient to ensure that it remains popular in the face of the Channel Tunnel. This is a solid village inn a few kilometres south of the port, typically French in the bustle which envelopes kitchen and dining-room at mealtimes, but with tranquil and comfortable bedrooms and a small garden. The restaurant – large, high-ceilinged and old-fashioned in the best sense, serves good, though not gourmet, food; the bar is lively and the welcome warm.

OPEN Mid-Feb to mid-Jan ROOMS 17 (all with bath or shower)

ARGOULES

Abbaye de Valloires

80120 Somme
TEL 22 29 62 33; FAX 22 23 91 54

Instead of staying in stylish accommodation and journeying to see the sights of Picardy you can do both at the same time by staying in the old monks' quarters, now charming *chambre d'hôte* bedrooms, of this Cistercian monastery. Founded in the 12th century and rebuilt in the 18th, the abbey is famous for the wrought-ironwork of its chapel and its elegant cloister. The rooms have views across landscaped gardens and offer an unrivalled sense of escape from the hustle and bustle. There is no restaurant.

OPEN All year ROOMS 6 (all with bath or shower) (Credit cards not accepted)

BOLLEZEELE

Hostellerie St-Louis

47 rue de l'Eglise
59470 Nord
TEL 28 68 81 83; FAX 28 68 01 17

The small salon in Hostellerie St-Louis gives an indication of how the house would have looked in its early days. Furnished in a late 18th-century style, it has a polished wooden floor, an ornate marble fireplace and a hidden door built into the wall. Otherwise, the period touches in the hotel seem understated against the bright pastel shades and modern fabrics, and certainly less eye-catching than the carved wooden figures that distinguish the public areas. Bedrooms have marble-effect walls adorned with thoughtfully chosen oil paintings.

OPEN Feb to Dec ROOMS 19 (all with bath)

CORBEHEM

Le Manoir de Fourcy

42 rue de la Gare
62112 Pas-de-Calais
TEL 27 95 91 00; FAX 27 95 91 09

The location, in a semi-industrial area outside Douai, is inauspicious, but shouldn't put you off this elegant turn-of-the-century manor house. The marble-floored smoking-room has a large vase in the centre with a profusion of brightly coloured flowers and also features a glass-case display of model vintage cars. The two adjacent, and equally stylish, dining-rooms have been separated for the benefit of non-smokers. Bedrooms are huge and employ numerous period flourishes without seeming pretentious, but those at the back of the building have an infinitely preferable view.

OPEN All year ROOMS 8 (all with bath or shower)

DOUAI

La Terrasse

36 terrasse St-Pierre
59500 Nord
TEL 27 88 70 04; FAX 27 88 36 05

Located in a quiet side street close to the centre of town, La Terrasse has a fine restaurant featuring a good-value set menu. Emile Hanique's passion for adventurous cuisine is matched by his taste in art, with almost every inch of wall hung with striking paintings. Bedrooms are more plain and functional than you might expect but they're spacious enough. Standards of service can range from the fastidiously correct to less so.

OPEN All year ROOMS 26 (all with bath)

EPERNAY

Auberge Champenoise ◆

Moussy
51200 Marne
TEL 26 54 03 48; FAX 26 51 87 25

In the heart of Champagne, where hotel prices are frequently as frothy as the wine their guests are here to sample, this is a useful hotel for those on a tight budget. It is a classic roadside auberge – very basic, but with promising food, a useful location and an enthusiastic and outgoing owner. There are bedrooms of all kinds; the cheapest are best avoided as they are also the most old-fashioned. The furnishing is very plain indeed, but most rooms have plenty of space and the largest are ideal for big families. All are clean and adequate. Downstairs there is a large local bar, usually full of villagers mingling with the guests. A couple of chairs serve as the lounge, but there is a cavernous restaurant, most of which is a dark function room, but which extends into a pleasant and peaceful canopied conservatory facing the garden. M. Arthozoul collects cheques, so bring him an unusual specimen.

OPEN All year exc. Christmas week ROOMS 39 (all with bath or shower) FACILITIES Tennis

L'EPINE

Aux Armes de Champagne ◆◆–◆◆◆

31 avenue du Luxembourg
51460 Marne
TEL 26 69 30 30; FAX 26 66 92 31

Six kilometres east of Châlons-sur-Marne, in the middle of a flat, almost deserted landscape, the huge basilica at l'Epine rises out of the empty fields. The old coaching inn opposite, by seemingly acquiring half the village to use as annexes and turning the spaces between the houses into flower beds, tennis courts and the chef's garden, has become a large, if rather disparate hotel. It is a place that runs like clockwork under the eyes of Denise and Jean-Paul Péradel, and feels a good deal smarter than it actually is, although the plush green and blue bar is distinctly posh. Bedrooms come in a huge variety of shapes, sizes and locations. Those in the annexe houses behind the hotel are the quietest, but among the smallest. The prices, as usual, depend more on facilities and location than on size, but all the rooms are beautifully kept – the standard of service here is especially high. Patrick Michelon's kitchen produces fine four- or five-course menus for the two dining-rooms, offering a local champagne as aperitif and concentrating on '*La fameuse cassolette d'escargots "Armes de Champagne"*'. The breakfast room, on a glassed-in first floor terrace, is a sunny and welcoming place to start the day.

OPEN Mid-Feb to early Jan ROOMS 37 (all with bath or shower) FACILITIES Tennis, mini-golf

HESDIN-L'ABBE

Hôtel Cléry

62360 Pas-de-Calais
TEL 21 83 19 83; FAX 21 87 52 59

This small, cream, 18th-century château stands in a vast park about nine kilometres from Boulogne, guaranteeing absolute tranquillity, despite being close to the busy N1. Inside, many original features remain, like the Louis XV wrought-iron staircase, and although the salon, with its parquet floor and large oil portraits, has a whiff of tradition, the overall feel is bright, breezy and decidedly unstuffy. The bedrooms, divided between the main building and a small annexe, have modern furniture and well-co-ordinated colour schemes. There is no restaurant.

OPEN Early Jan to end Dec ROOMS 19 (all with bath or shower) FACILITIES Tennis

LILLE

Grand Hôtel Bellevue

5 rue Jean-Roisin
59000 Nord
TEL 20 57 45 64; FAX 20 40 07 93

Grand indeed. The hallway of this 18th-century hotel is delightfully elegant with its marble floor, golden chandeliers, ornate plasterwork surrounding pretty roundels and period furniture. Mozart is said to have stayed here in 1765 when it was known as the Hôtel des Bourbons. The bedrooms are large and are decorated in a manner which is simple and modern, yet stylish. The Windsor bar, with its cluster of button-back leather sofas, seems a little out of place. There's no restaurant but plenty of choice in town.

OPEN All year ROOMS 61 (all with bath or shower)

MONTREUIL-SUR-MER

Auberge de la Grenouillère

La Madelaine-sous-Montreuil
62170 Pas-de-Calais
TEL 21 06 07 22; FAX 21 86 36 36

Within view of the ramparts of Montreuil, this charming Picardy-style farmhouse sits beside the river Canche. The original sideboards, wainscoting and copperware were augmented in the 1930s by the trademark canvas frescoes of frogs engaged in a spot of high living. Frogs are likely to crop up on the menu too and indeed it is the culinary expertise of Roland Gauthier which is the highlight of any stay, whether it's lunch on the riverside terrace or dinner in the intimate restaurant. The four bedrooms are simply furnished and have a rustic feel.

OPEN Mid-Jan to mid-Dec ROOMS 4 (all with bath)

QUERRIEU

Château de Querrieu

la route Nationale
80115 Somme
TEL 22 40 13 42; FAX 22 40 17 53

This château, 9km from Amiens, offers four *chambre d'hôtes* rooms at reasonable prices. The rooms are not in the château itself but in its converted stables, a courtyard of low, half-timbered buildings. The décor is beautifully rustic, and the split-level rooms also have small lounge areas with televisions. Breakfast is served in a long, high-ceilinged brick and timber room, at the far end of which the lounge has several sofas around a log fire.

OPEN All year ROOMS 5 (all with bath or shower) (Credit cards not accepted)

RECQUES-SUR-HEM

Le Château de Cocove

62890 Pas-de-Calais
TEL 21 82 68 29; FAX 21 82 72 59

Within easy striking distance of three port towns, it is not surprising that the 18th-century Château de Cocove has become an established favourite with the British, many of whom come to buy wines from the extensive cellars and stay for the weekend. Stone floors and open brick fires are characteristic of the public areas, of which the highlight is the restaurant, a converted stables, with its chalk walls, wooden beams and large arched windows. The bedrooms are spacious and have understated colour schemes and good views.

OPEN All year exc. Christmas ROOMS 22 (all with bath or shower) FACILITIES Sauna

---

Key: ◆ = 0–250FF, ◆◆ = 251–450FF, ◆◆◆ = over 451FF; prices are per double room without breakfast, which costs around 35–60FF extra. Some hotels may insist on half-board during high season, some hotels or restaurants may close at specific times during the week – it is always worth checking. Most hotels accept the major credit cards; we have indicated where a hotel takes no credit cards.

SEPT-SAULX

Le Cheval Blanc

rue du Moulin
51400 Marne
TEL 26 03 90 27; FAX 26 03 97 09

Half-way between Reims and Châlons-sur-Marne, so ideally placed for exploring Champagne, this is a peaceful hotel blessed with a good restaurant and an
extensive garden. The hotel and the restaurant are actually separated by a small
road, but the former is really just the bedroom annexe, and all the action goes on
in the restaurant. This is a hushed and fairly formal place served by a flock of
scurrying waiters who lead you to your table in procession. The food is worthy
of their attention – textures, as in their asparagus soufflé, are perfect, and the
flavours fairly bounce on the tongue. The selection of Champagne cheeses is
excellent too. Bedrooms are plain and soothing, with simple pink, white and
grey colour combinations in the palest shades. Ground floor rooms have access
to the garden – a shady expanse of grass with tennis court, putting green and
small river.

OPEN Mid-Feb to mid-Jan ROOMS 25 (all with bath or shower) FACILITIES Tennis, mini
golf

TROYES

Le Relais St-Jean

51 rue Paillot de Montabert
10000 Aube
TEL 25 73 89 90; FAX 25 73 88 60

Right in the centre of Troyes' medieval streets, the Relais is a half-timbered
ancient building, like its neighbours, but one which has been expensively and
imaginatively converted into a good example of French flair in modern interior
design. It is basically a hotel designed for business clients, and you perhaps pay
slightly over the odds for what are rather small bedrooms, but a weekend
discount makes it affordable. There is plenty of detail to enjoy in exchange for
the price – an internal tropical garden, brushed steel rodding formed into the
newel post of the stair, and a first-floor gallery. The lounge and bar are Cosa
Nostra chic, with smoked glass, lots of chrome, black leather armchairs and no
meretricious fakery. The breakfast room (there's no restaurant) by contrast
is small, square and floral. Bedrooms are virginal white, softened by polished
grey granite and set off by colourful modern prints. Best of all, this is not an
anonymous chain, but a family-run enterprise, and a friendly one at that. There
is an underground car park with direct access to the hotel, and bicycles for
guests to use.

OPEN All year exc. Christmas and New Year ROOMS 22 (all with bath)

VENDEUIL

L'Auberge de Vendeuil

R.N. 44
02800 Aisne
TEL 23 07 85 85; FAX 23 07 88 58

This is an ideally positioned hotel for an overnight stop close to the A26 Calais–Troyes autoroute. It stands on the edge of a small village, just out of earshot of the nearby N44, with views over the fields which lie behind. It is a curious-looking modern house, slightly German in style, with the bedrooms kept in a clever hexagonal extension on two floors. The bedrooms are something of a squash for two people, but are neatly designed, decorated in white and apricot, and have small modern bathrooms. The restaurant takes up most of the ground floor of the main building. It is big, bright and rural (though not rustic) with a wooden bar tucked into one corner and the kitchen in plain view beyond. The food is competent and satisfying without being outstanding – though cheeses are fine and there is a good-value, if unadventurous, wine list. Mme Ranson presides over her establishment with immense good humour and prides herself on the tranquillity of her hotel. The Auberge de Vendeuil also makes a good base from which to explore the hill-top town of Laon or the sights of Compiègne.

OPEN All year ROOMS 22 (all with bath)

Dambach-la-Ville

A blending of all beauties – streams and dells,
Fruit, foliage, crag, wood, corn-field, mountain, vine,
And chiefless castles breathing stern farewells

[Byron]

ALSACE, LORRAINE AND THE VOSGES

Two provinces could hardly be more different one from the other than Alsace and Lorraine, yet modern history has welded them in the collective consciousness. Estranged from France for nearly half a century after the national débâcle of 1870, Alsace-Lorraine or Elsass-Lothringen as it was renamed by the Prussian conquerors was an open wound in France's side and a cause of grief to every true patriot. The actress Sarah Bernhardt (not from Alsace despite her Germanic-sounding name) having performed to the same entrancing effect before a German admirer as Salome before Herod, and receiving the same offer, said without a moment of hesitation, 'Give back Alsace and Lorraine'.

The Lorraine of the Alsace-Lorraine issue is not the whole province but the modern *département* of Moselle in the north-east with Metz its principal town. The region is characterised, although less strongly than Alsace, by the widespread use of a Germanic local dialect; there are several of these, spoken regularly by approximately a million and a half people. Apart from this justification of the German territorial claim, and despite being one of the latest of crown acquisitions (the mid-18th century), Lorraine is a thoroughly French region, and encloses within its boundaries many of the most characteristic features of France: the heavy industry of the north (50 per cent of France's iron and 45 per cent of its coal), the supreme elegance of its 18th-century capital Nancy, the quiet spacious rolling farmlands and the seriously relaxing spa towns of its south. So it is not inappropriate that Lorraine should have become for historical reasons synonymous with patriotism. Lorraine is Joan of Arc, saviour of France at the time of her greatest need. The twin-barred cross of Lorraine was the symbol of the Free French Army of General de Gaulle, who told the French in 1940

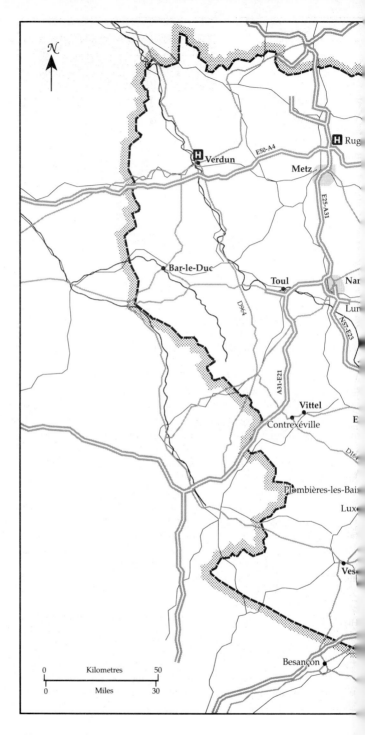

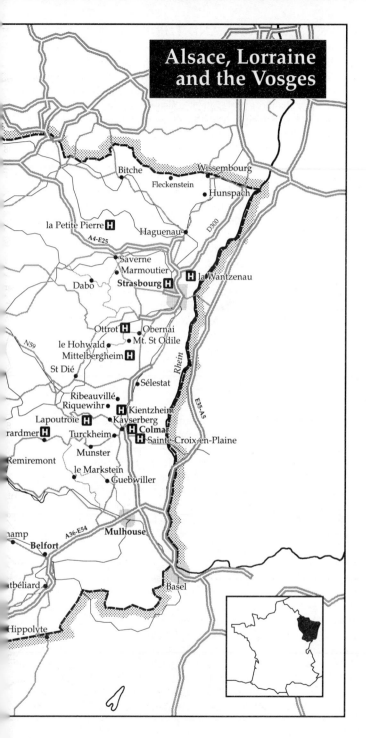

Alsace, Lorraine and the Vosges

Bitche
Wissembourg
Fleckenstein
Hunspach
la Petite Pierre **H**
Haguenau
A4-E25
D300
Saverne
Marmoutier
Dabo
Strasbourg H
H la Wantzenau
Ottrot **H**
Obernai
N59
le Hohwald
Mt. St Odile
Mittelbergheim **H**
St Dié
Sélestat
Rhein
Ribeauvillé
Riquewihr
H Kientzheim
E35-A5
Lapoutroie **H**
Kaysberg
rardmer **H**
Turckheim
H **Colmar**
H Sainte-Croix-en-Plaine
Munster
Remiremont
le Markstein
Guebwiller
namp
A36-E54
Belfort
Mulhouse
tbéliard
Basel
Hippolyte

493

that there was no question of doing a deal with the occupying Nazis. Lorraine is also Verdun, where 300,000 Frenchmen fell in a few months in 1916, the greatest battle in history according to the local propaganda, and certainly the most profligate (see also pages 466–7).

Alsace is the French side of the Rhineland Plain, separated from Lorraine by the natural barrier of the Vosges Mountains which run north-south parallel to the Rhine – the river which has brought the region commercial activity from the earliest times. Local art and architecture display some French and much German influence, but also some from the Low Countries and northern Italy, telling of the region's popularity with travellers between the Mediterranean and the North Sea. The local language is a dialect closely related to Old High German. Names of people and places sound Germanic, faces look Germanic, home-cooking and wines taste Germanic, and the spotlessly clean and colourful villages are reminiscent of parts of Germany too.

From the French point of view, the Alsace-Lorraine issue was resolved simply enough, once and for all, by Tacitus, who wrote that the Rhine divides Germany from Gaul. After the Roman departure the Germans moved in, and after the disintegration of the Carolingian Empire Alsace remained loosely attached to the anarchy that was the Holy Roman Empire. Towns guarded their freedom and formed a league (the Decapolis) of mutual assistance, and petty local lords in their hilltop strongholds bowed to no one. Only when the religious wars of the early 17th century brought unimaginable devastation to the province, whose population is conservatively estimated to have declined by half in less than half a century, did the Alsatians look to the French monarchy for protection. The French takeover was not complete until 1681 when Strasbourg yielded to the Sun King, but even so reserved its right to freedom of religious practice. Alsace, separated from France by the independent duchy of Lorraine until 1766, was so little affected by being French that when Arthur Young crossed the Vosges five days after the storming of the Bastille, he recorded: 'I found myself to all appearance veritably in Germany; here not one person in an hundred has a word of French . . . looking at a map of France and reading histories of Louis XIV never threw his conquest of Alsace into such light as travelling into it did: to cross a great range of mountains to enter a level plain inhabited by a people totally distinct and different from France, with manners, language, ideas, prejudices, and habits all different, made an impression of the injustice and ambition of such a conduct'. Even now the visitor will find Young's verdict easy to understand.

For reasons of its own, Alsace espoused the Revolutionary cause with enthusiasm. Mulhouse decided it would rather be French than Swiss in 1798, and the area contributed more than its share of dashing generals to the Napoleonic epic. It started to become much more

French, and much more French-speaking, so that when all but Belfort was lost to the Germans again in 1871 some 250,000 Alsatians voted with their feet to stay French and Belfort suddenly became a big town. For many of those who stayed, association with the booming prosperity of Germany grew acceptable with time, and the 'liberation' of Alsace in 1918 was not universally welcomed. However, the growing and uncomfortably close Nazi threat in the '30s (Alsace has a large Jewish population) and brutal measures of Germanisation during the occupation that followed – names had to be changed (for example from Claude to Klaus), Alsatians were drafted into the German army and deported to Poland, the speaking of French and even the wearing of berets was punishable with prison – all reinforced pro-French feeling. Since 1945 French Alsace and Lorraine have resumed their traditional role of Middle Kingdom between Germany and France. Strasbourg is now the symbol of supra-national politics. Tens of thousands of Alsatians and Lorrains commute to work in the cities of Sarrebrücken, Karlsruhe and Basle. German capital creates new jobs in France.

Of the two provinces, Alsace is by far the more attractive to the tourist. Strasbourg and Colmar are two of the most beautiful and culturally rich towns in France. Crisp, fruity and luscious Alsatian wines are produced on the foothills of the Vosges which rise abruptly from the narrow fertile plain. Delightful old villages break up the carpet of vines and are strung in a chain that makes the most pictur-esque wine tour in France. The Vosges themselves are mainly wooded with open grassy rounded tops – excellent for breezy picnics and not too arduous walking. There are scores of fortresses to admire and a few simple, relaxing mountain resorts. The climate is dry and in summer hot, especially down on the plain which is sheltered by the Vosges from France and its westerly rain-bearing winds. Not the least of the attractions of Alsace is its compact scale, which enables you to get from museum to vineyard to mountain top and back within a day, and to tour the whole region from no more than two or three bases.

The towns of Alsace

Capital of the province so often the cause of war in Europe, **Stras-bourg's** choice as the seat of the Council of Europe and one of the capitals of the EC has a symbolic value of determined hatchet burial. It is a thriving and cosmopolitan, commercial and industrial centre and an important Rhine port. It is also a lively and youthful university town, and in the old centre very picturesque and touristy.

Sights in Strasbourg

● **Cathedral** The characteristic dark greyish-pink façade crowned lopsidedly by a single soaring tower and open-work spire dominates Strasbourg and the Alsatian plain for miles around, and is one of the symbols of Alsace. From the completion of the spire in 1439 until the 19th century this was the tallest building in Christendom (142 metres). Its greatest glory, apart from the spire, is the magnificent sculpture adorning the doorways and on the pillar of angels (13th-century) in the transept which is often hard to see properly because of the crowds of people admiring the gaudy complexity of the 19th-century astronomical clock (guided tours).

● **Old Town** The area around the cathedral is very attractive, if crowded in summer, with cobbled pedestrian streets and timber-framed houses – of which the most decoratively carved is the Maison Kammerzell (on the Place de la Cathédrale). There are souvenir shops full of stuffed geese, storks, tins of foie gras and bottles of wine. At night the cathedral is lit up, there are *son et lumière* performances in French and German, and people sit up late outside the cafés entertained by street artists. From the Place du Marché aux Poissons behind the Rohan Palace you can take a boat trip on the River Ill.

● **Musée de l'Oeuvre Notre-Dame** This excellent museum, in a partly 14th-century town house, contains (as well as a large collection of local art and furniture) many of the originals of the finest cathedral sculptures which have been taken down in the interest of their own safety and replaced by copies.

● **Château des Rohan** Despite war damage this is one of Strasbourg's most beautiful buildings and one of the least Alsatian in character. The stone is white, the style that of the French 18th century, the effect expressive of the grand style of the four Rohan princes, cardinals and bishops who presided from 1704 to 1790. The Palace houses the city's fine arts, decorative arts, and archaeological museums, but the sumptuous and beautifully restored Grands Appartements are more worthy of your attention than any of these.

● **Historical Museum** and **Alsatian Museum** These are good examples of their kind and especially interesting because of the turbulent and often bitter history of Strasbourg and the peculiarities of local folklore and popular arts and crafts. The Historical Museum has a painting of one of the proudest moments in Alsatian history – Rouget de l'Isle singing in Strasbourg his patriotic song for the Rhine Army, composed on the moment of declaration of war with Austria in April 1792. Soon the song was to be known as the Marseillaise.

● **Ancienne Douane** Modern art collection and exhibitions (and a riverside restaurant) in the old Customs House.

● **St-Thomas** Handsome hall church (early 13th-century) with Pigalle's splendidly theatrical tomb of the Maréchal de Saxe, victor of Fontenoy.

• **Petite France** The most picturesque part of old Strasbourg, where the River Ill divides into four streams or canals spanned by covered bridges with towers and old watermills. It is fascinating to wander around the narrow alleys of this old tanning, fishing and milling quarter, banned to cars.

• **European Parliament** (Palais de l'Europe) This occupies an angular modern building in a residential area on the banks of the Ill between central Strasbourg and the Rhine. You can visit the building by prior appointment (tel 88 17 20 07), and what you see depends on whether or

Petite France, Strasbourg

not the parliament is in session. Nearby there is a fine park (Orangerie) with exotic plants, a little zoo and a boating lake.

Saverne lies at the foot of the natural gateway into Alsace across the mountains (the Col de Saverne – 410 metres). This strategically important fortress town was in the possession of the prince/bishops of Strasbourg for five centuries up to the Revolution; Prince Louis-René de Rohan was responsible for the imposing later-18th-century château.

From Saverne a good road leads up into the hills to the south, to the ruins (on three pink rocky outcrops) of the fortress of **Haut-Barr**, first built in 1170 by the Bishop of Strasbourg and known as the eye of Alsace. The views from the top justify the name. **Marmoutier**, a few kilometres on the Strasbourg side of Saverne, is a small town with a large and beautiful partly Romanesque church which survives from the period of the Benedictine monastery's greatest prosperity. The west end is the oldest part, massively solid with tiny windows like elephant's eyes in the greyish-pink façade which is unadorned except for a few isolated panels of decoration, and bands of simple low relief arch patterns (as elsewhere in Alsace, they reveal the Italian influence).

Colmar is the art-lover's main objective in Alsace. Its old town centre is as unspoilt as the prettiest of Alsatian country villages, with the added interest of richly decorated old town houses and even a 'Little Venice' quarter. It is very conveniently situated just a few kilometres from the heart of the wine road and only a short drive from Strasbourg and the Vosges; not surprisingly it's full of tourists in summer, especially around the time of the wine festival in mid-August. Colmar is a particularly good base for those relying on public transport, but for all its old-world charm not everyone's ideal place to stay: it is an important commercial and industrial town, which sprawls modern and unsightly across the fertile, pylon-scarred plain. Colmar prospered in the Middle Ages and headed the alliance of Alsatian towns known as the Decapolis. In the 15th and 16th centuries its burghers built themselves showy town houses decorated with Renaissance carving. All the arts prospered with the town, and like it benefited from Alsace's position on the great thoroughfares of Europe between Italy and Flanders, France and Germany. Colmar's great master was Martin Schongauer (late 15th-century), who had much to teach the young Dürer, and like his better-known pupil was first a draughtsman and engraver, second a painter. Schongauer's achievement in both media can best be seen in Colmar; indeed, there are hardly any of his paintings of any distinction anywhere else.

Sights in Colmar

• **Old Town** There are beautiful old houses and pedestrian streets around the Dominican church, the cathedral, and the splendid old Customs House, especially the commercial rue des Marchands. Look out particularly for the Maison Pfister (rue des Marchands) decorated with delightful medallions and ornamental religious paintings, and the Maison des Têtes (rue des Têtes), its loggia above the street elaborately carved with heads.

• **Unterlinden Museum** A large, varied and exceptionally rich museum housed in old convent buildings around a shady cloister. The star attraction, and for many tourists the single reason for a journey to Colmar, is the overwhelming Issenheim altar-piece, painted by Grünewald in the first years of the 16th century. The many panels of the work, which were opened and shut according to the religious season, include an anguished and gruesome Crucifixion and a Resurrection of corresponding brilliance. If you can tear yourself away from these hallucinatory images (which were intended to comfort those afflicted with the sickness called St-Anthony's Fire) there are plenty of other things to admire: Schongauer's paintings and prints; sections devoted to costumes, dolls, furniture, interiors, folklore, crafts; even an interesting modern art collection.

• **Dominican Church** Schongauer's greatest painting, 'The Virgin of the Rose Bush', is on show here (there's an entrance charge). It is a bittersweet masterpiece, with a densely symbolic decorative background.

• **St-Martin Cathedral** There are wood carvings all around the choir in the style of the 15th century, interesting sculpture round the west and south doorways and a fine wooden crucifixion group.

Neuf-Brisach is the most interesting remaining example of Vauban's fortification of the Rhine, a complete 17th-century new town geometrically laid out with a double system of walls and canals. The picturesque old town of Breisach (in French Vieux-Brisach) across the river in Germany is well worth a visit to admire its fine setting high above the river, a church with frescoes by Schongauer, and some fortifications. To the south **Ottmarsheim** has an unusual 11th-century octagonal church.

Between Colmar and Strasbourg, **Sélestat** is a partly old town with two large pink churches within the fragmentary old walls, one Romanesque, the other Gothic. You can visit a library, founded in 1542, which contains the precious books of a distinguished Renaissance scholar and friend of Erasmus, Beatus Rhenanus.

Mulhouse (roughly pronounced Moolooze) is Alsace's second city in size and economic importance, and puts money before beauty, perhaps a legacy from its 300-year attachment to the alliance of Swiss Cantons.

Sights in Mulhouse

- **Town Hall** This is the only building of interest in town; its walls are decorated with *trompe l'oeil* paintings from the late 17th century. Inside there is an interesting historical museum.
- **Textile Print Museum** (near station) A unique and fascinating museum devoted to the development of the industry which brought wealth and scores of thousands of new inhabitants to 19th-century Mulhouse.

Belfort plugs the wide gap between the Vosges and the Jura – a natural corridor into France from the east. Its strategic importance won it the attentions of Vauban, who did such a good job of building fortifications that the town was able to resist 40,000 German invaders in 1870 for nearly fourth months, and was awarded to France at the negotiating table, in recognition of its heroism. This separated Belfort from Alsace, and it has remained on its own ever since in charge of its own *département* or *territoire* – an appropriate term since the town's great feature is the monumentally barrel-chested lion carved in blocks of pink Vosges stone beside the walls of the defiant citadel.

A short drive west of Belfort, by the main road at the foot of the Vosges, lies **Ronchamp**. The town is pretty anonymous, in the style of this part of France, but that only adds to the impact of Le Corbusier's architecturally unorthodox chapel of Notre-Dame-du-Haut (1955), which stands as a memorial to soldiers sacrificed here in 1944. There are

Notre-Dame-du-Haut, Ronchamp

extensive views from the grassy knoll on which the new chapel stands, across the foothills and the forests of the Jura and Vosges mountains, whose bumps and hollows the architect wished his sanctuary to echo.

The Wine Road of Alsace

The Wine Road is the most attractive feature of Alsace. It is a sign-posted route, mostly along minor roads at the foot of the Vosges, from Marlenheim to Thann. Its character doesn't change much from one end to the other; if you want to visit only a bit of it the most picturesque section is at the heart of the vineyard area just north of Colmar (the villages Turckheim, Kaysersberg, Ribeauvillé and Riquewihr).

There is something strangely satisfying about vineyards, a tightly combed corduroy order imposed on nature. Vineyards in Alsace are much like vineyards anywhere else; what makes this wine road so special is their setting: the wooded mountains behind with fortresses in remarkable number surveying the plain, and the villages – pink, walled, cobbled and unspoilt although not undiscovered.

Vines press right up to the village walls and prevent any unsightly expansion of the community. In summer, their brilliant green contrasts richly with the dark pink Vosges stone cobbles. The substantial houses have carved and patterned dark timbers, and balconies decorated with boxes of bright scarlet geraniums. In village centres the little fountains pour forth wine at festival times as if this were some carefree modern-day Canaa. Local inhabitants, viticulturists for the most part, keep their wines in the village cellars, welcome the tourist to taste and buy, and are happy to talk for hours about their wines. Every village has some ingredients of the ideal wine village; Riquewihr comes closest to the model.

One traditional element of the Alsace wine village is now so rare that to describe it as typical would be an unfair concession to the power of nostalgia and tourist office mythology. Not so long ago the steeply tiled roofscapes and old towers bristled with the distinctive landmarks that are storks' nests, and the birds which returned summer after summer to the same nest were quite rightly considered part of the village population, and bearers of good fortune. But every year fewer and fewer storks return to Alsace, mainly because of massacre in their winter quarters. One of the few villages where your search for a stork may be rewarded is **Ostheim**, just north of Colmar; a handsome and often occupied nest sits on top of the ruined wall which acts as the war memorial. The Alsatians are now keeping storks cooped up in 'rein-troduction centres' for a couple of years to discourage their misguided migratory instinct. In these places at least you can see storks, but they don't look the same when they're not on top of a nest on top of a wine village. One such centre lies just south of Ribeauvillé.

Travelling south from Strasbourg, you first come to **Molsheim**, a sizeable town which has outgrown its old walls, parts of which remain and enclose interesting old streets. The focal point is the central square, with a fountain and the Renaissance Metzig (Butchers' Guild building) which has many interesting architectural features. **Rosheim** is an attractive small town, built unusually for this part of the world of a yellowish stone, with some impressive gateways, allegedly the oldest (12th-century) secular building in Alsace, and a very interesting Romanesque church which could almost have been transported from Pisa. Four man-eating lions surmount the façade.

At the foot of the much-frequented pilgrimage mountain of Ste-Odile, **Obernai** is an important and at heart very picturesque town with fine walls and towers, and a typically Alsatian main square with Renaissance public buildings and town houses, and a fountain. The pilgrimage trail from Obernai passes **Ottrott** (Haut- and Bas-), whence forest walks are rewarded by two medieval fortress ruins.

On the wooden summit of **Mont Ste-Odile** there's a popular pilgrimage convent and signed walks through the forest which generally lead you at some point to the massive so-called Pagan Wall whose remains still almost encircle the mountain top. The best section of the wall, which pre-dates the Romans by several centuries, is at the north end near the Dreystein Fortress.

Barr is an attractive and typical walled town with a fountain and a Renaissance town hall. The old village of **Andlau** lies beautifully situated beneath twin fortress-capped peaks. Not much of interest remains of its powerful and exclusive abbey except a Romanesque church with beautiful carvings on the west end, and a stone bear in the crypt, in memory of the real one which inspired the abbey's founder.

Dambach-la-Ville is another very attractive typical old wine village in the vineyards, with fortress ruins high above.

The colourful village of **Kintzheim** has a number of very popular tourist attractions nearby. The **Château de Haut-Koenigsbourg** is real film-set stuff, an eyrie 600 metres above the plain done up to the orders of Kaiser Bill in the early years of this century, to the disgust of purists and the delight of tourists. In the almost completely reconstructed citadel buildings there are eagles painted on the vaults and skulls of wild beasts hanging from ceiling lamps, a full-blown souvenir shop and an Alsatian tavern with trad-clad barmaids. The narrow stairways can be crowded in high season. The owner of the **Château de Kintzheim** itself has got the commercial spirit too: he shows off some 50 birds of prey (including eagles) in free-flying displays several times a day. Nearby there's a monkey park, and a stork reintroduction centre.

For those who deplore the imaginative restoration of old castle ruins, there are literally scores of them on the craggy peaks above the vineyards which stand untouched in all their romantic overgrown raven-circled splendour, making excellent goals for stiff walks up through the vines and woods from the villages below. Two of the finest old ruins are **Franckenbourg** and **Ortenbourg**.

Overlooked by no fewer than three ruined fortresses, and finely set in the pit of a theatre of vineyards, **Ribeauvillé** is an important tourist and wine centre which is busy and commercial but still very typically attractive. The town's most striking monument is the 13th- and 16th-century Metzgerturm which straddles the main street at the head of the square, and its greatest attraction is the Pfiffertag folklore festival in early September, with costumed processions, dancing and free wine. In summer there are numerous local bus tours which include tasting.

The village of **Hunawihr** has a fortified church and a stork reintroduction centre. **Riquewihr** is the most charming and harmoniously unspoilt of all the old wine villages, in the midst of Alsace's highest quality vineyards. It's the home of many prestigious wine firms. Much of it dates from the 16th century: the town walls are almost complete, with gateways, rampart walk, and torture chamber; there are many interesting buildings and an old Jewish ghetto. **Sigolsheim** has an early Gothic church, and the Blutberg (mountain of blood) memorial, necropolis of the thousands killed in the bitter fighting which preceded the liberation of Colmar in January 1945.

The delightful small town of **Kaysersberg** is situated between vineyard hills, and overlooked by castle ruins which form part of the town walls. Its Gothic church contains a remarkably carved 16th-century altar-piece. There's a small museum devoted to Albert Schweitzer who was born here. Nearby **Kientzheim** is quieter in high season and gently appealing. The pretty village of **Turckheim** has many old houses of which the most notable is the splendid olde-worlde inn, the Hôtel des Deux Clefs (1620). Fortified **Eguisheim** is the last of the typically pretty wine villages.

High up in the mountains between Turckheim and Kaysersberg **Les Trois Epis** is a summer resort and pilgrimage destination, with substantial hotels. The dull aspect of the place – heavily damaged in 1944 – is all the more striking for the contrast it offers with the wine villages. **Munster** lies at the heart of a deep valley and is a convenient, although not very charming, base for walks and drives into the Vosges. The local tourist office can give information about a 'cheese route' which takes you to rustic auberges and farms to taste and buy the extremely potent local cheese.

The southern section of the wine road lacks the charm of the north but is well worth pursuing to admire some splendid churches from the most individual period of Alsatian church building (the 12th and 13th centuries): at **Rouffach** (Notre-Dame-de-l'Assomption), at dull and industrial **Guebwiller** (St-Léger), and along the beautiful **Lauch Valley** which leads from here into the mountains from **Lautenbach** and **Murbach**, both of which have beautiful churches. **Thann**, the terminal point of the wine road, suffers like Guebwiller from the influence of industrial Mulhouse; but it too has a richly interesting church, one of the few important ones in Alsace in a fully developed Gothic style (15th-century). Its bell tower is tall and of celebrated beauty, its west doorways are teeming with sculpture, and the choir has lively and in many cases comic carved stalls.

The Vosges and the North

Despite their modest elevation (the Grand Ballon or Ballon de Guebwiller is the highest peak in the range at 1,424 metres) the Vosges have been an important mountain range historically, forming as they do the eastern rim of the wide Paris Basin and France's natural frontier. The mountains rise gently from the west to culminate in a ridge rather than in specific peaks, then drop abruptly down to the Rhine plain.

North of the river Bruche, which runs from near St-Dié to Strasbourg, the Vosges hardly rise above 1,000 metres, or break through the thick covering of forest. Unaffected by the action of glaciers, the northern Vosges have kept their dark-pink sandstone, which characterises the architecture of Alsace from Wissembourg to Belfort. In the south, glaciers have worn away the sandstone, leaving grey granite. Above the tree line there are open pastures with rounded mountain tops (called *ballons*). There are many attractive glacial lakes, and valleys which cut deeply into the mountain range. For all these reasons, and because of the panoramic **Routes des Crêtes** which runs along the ridge at the very top of the Vosges, the southern part of the range is of greater interest to tourists. As well as being a magnificent evergreen

fortress-topped backdrop to the wine road it is excellent walking territory where even the most leisurely stroller can reach the finest viewpoints, which will disappoint only those who hope to see as far as the
Alps in summer – Mont Blanc is about 240 kilometres away and hardly
ever visible between April and October. The serious walker can use the
exemplary large-scale maps and guidebooks produced by the Club
Vosgien. There are a few resorts in the mountains, of which
Gérardmer, Le Hohwald and Les Trois Epis are the only three of any
size, and Gérardmer the only one of any animation.

The Vosges drop almost as abruptly down to the Belfort Gap which
separates them from the Jura as they do to the east. The **Ballons d'Alsace** and **de Servance** are the two southern bastions of the range, easily
explored from the Upper Moselle Valley on the Lorraine side, or from
the southern end of the wine road in Alsace.

From **Thann** the Thur Valley leads up into the heart of the mountains
through some fine scenery, with easy access to the peaks of the **Petit
Drumont** beside the source of the Moselle, and the **Grand Ventron**. A
more frequented road is the **Route des Crêtes** itself which climbs from
Cernay, which has a steam train circuit. The Hartmanswillerkopf, or
Viel-Armand, was one of the most bitterly disputed strongholds on the
Vosges Front in the First World War. There is an appropriately solemn
memorial to more than 30,000 men who died here.

Soon after breaking through the tree-line into the high pastures
(*chaumes*), the Route des Crêtes passes beside the unremarkable culmi-
nation of the Vosges, the **Grand Ballon**. There are long views from the
top, and an orientation table. Beyond **Le Markstein**, a modest ski resort
at the junction of the Route des Crêtes with the road up from the Lauch
Valley, the Route des Crêtes lives up to its name by following the open
ridge at the top of the mountain range with views steeply down to the
lakes and valleys below. For much of the way the road is just west of
the crest itself, so as to be out of sight of the enemy – it was built to
improve communications behind the front in the First World War.
Some of the finest excursions in the region are to be made from
Munster and other points along the Fecht valley (to the **Petit Ballon**,
and the lakes of **Schiessrothried** and **Fischboedle**). From Munster one
road climbs through the quiet balcony resort of **Hohrodberg**; another
joins the Route des Crêtes at the **Col de la Schlucht** (1,139 metres).
Nearby there are several lakes; the Lac Blanc has a particularly
impressive rocky setting.

Five hundred metres below the peaks and some 16km beyond them
into Lorraine, **Gérardmer** is the main Vosges resort. It owes its long-
established popularity (it has the oldest tourist office in France) to the
nearby lakes and forests – strewn with moss-covered boulders known
locally as Gérardmer sheep – and to its convenience as a base for
exploration of both the Alsace and Lorraine sides of the Vosges. The
popularity is certainly not attributable to the town itself, which was

systematically burnt and blown up in November 1944 and rebuilt without style. **Lake Gérardmer**, on the end of which the resort and textile town is built, is the largest in the Vosges, finely surrounded by hillsides of pine, and provided with all manner of amenities, including casino, campsites, boating, bathing and fishing.

North of the **Col du Bonhomme** the Vosges are less individually distinctive. **Le Hohwald** is a tranquil resort (high up in the woods, as its name suggests) and a good walking base. The highest peak in the area is the **Donon**; from the top the view is extensive and it includes, just across the Bruche Valley, the concentration camp of **Le Struthof** where over 10,000 prisoners were exterminated between 1941 and 1944.

To the north of the Bruche, the Little Vosges, as they are called, present interestingly varied landscapes with the soft sandstone eroded into many impressively weird rocky shapes and cliffs, nowhere better admired than around the small woodland villages of **Dabo** and **Wangenbourg** (which have some accommodation). The ruined fortress and cascade of **Le Nideck** is a short walk from the road south from Wangenbourg to **Niederhaslach**, which has a large and harmonious Gothic church with splendid 18th-century choir-stalls. North of Dabo the attractive wooded Zorn valley is the easiest way through the Vosges via the **Col de Saverne**.

Alsace north of Strasbourg and the Col de Saverne is different. There are no more high mountain pastures, vineyards are outnumbered by hop fields – Haguenau is the great beer production centre – and the traditional old Alsatian villages are spacious and ordered, unlike the wine villages south of Strasbourg, huddled within their fortifications.

The old villages between Haguenau and the border town of Wissembourg are the most interesting feature of the area, as picturesque as the wine villages and considerably less affected by tourism. Local costume is sometimes worn by old village folk, and not just to satisfy the coachloads. **Hunspach, Seebach** and **Hoffen** are the pick of the villages: Hunspach is especially spotless, colourfully best-kept, and ordered with the regularity of a garden suburb, but the others show rather more character.

Wissembourg is a border town much frequented by German shoppers. Its old centre is cobbled and attractive with bridges over the several branches of the Lauter which thread through the town. The building of greatest interest is the Vosges-stone former abbey church of Saint Peter and Saint Paul, Gothic except for a single Romanesque tower, and with an enormous 14th-century wall painting of Saint Christopher. Just opposite the church beside the river stands the so-called Salt House (15th-century) whose enormous roof is broken up by layers of windows like gills in a fish's scaly side.

The drive west along the German frontier is an attractive one, through vineyards (around Cleebourg) and steep wooded hills with occasional dramatically perched fortresses – **Fleckenstein** and **Falkenstein** are the most impressive. **Niederbronn** is a substantial spa, appreciated by the

Romans, but altered since, notably during the Second World War. It is a reasonable base for the area and has extensive accommodation. **Bitche** marks the end of the attractive landscape with some sombre Vauban fortifications.

Lorraine

For most tourists Lorraine (excluding its flank of the Vosges already described) is a region to cross with open eyes rather than to explore meticulously. The main points of interest are Nancy, a brilliant highlight of any journey through eastern France, and Verdun with its great battle-fields and memorials (see page 467). The spas of the south also have some appeal. This large and varied province is crossed by three major rivers running northwards – the Meurthe, the Moselle, and the Meuse.

From its source very close to the Col de la Schlucht on the Route des Crêtes, the younger **Meurthe** runs down through the Vosges Forest, powering sawmills as it goes. **St-Dié** is a substantial town which would be ugly but for its surrounding wooded hills. In 1944 it was burned down like Gérardmer, and is not beautiful to behold in its new form. But there is a trio of religious buildings of considerable interest: the cathedral is a handsome mixture of Romanesque, Gothic and Classical styles; and a mostly 14th-century cloister connects it to the simple and beautiful 12th-century church of Notre-Dame.

Etival-Clairefontaine has a mostly Romanesque and early Gothic former abbey church, and a summer weekend steam railway which covers the short distance to Senones. **Lunéville** lies near the confluence of the Meurthe with the Vézouse, whose course was diverted to enable the 18th-century duke Leopold of Lorraine to embellish the magnificent gardens of his equally magnificent palace, a small-scale Versailles in its day. It now houses a local museum with a fine collection of local 18th-century faïence and an audio-visual tribute to the local artist Georges de la Tour, one of the great masters of the French 17th century. The town retains an 18th-century atmosphere; the church of St-Jacques is a rare and curious example of the Rococo style in France.

As it approaches Nancy the Meurthe becomes heavily and malodorously industrial. Chemical industries predominate to the south-east of town and the magnificent pilgrimage basilica of **St-Nicholas-de-Port**, a masterpiece of late Gothic architecture from the early 16th century, languishes in the dismal surroundings of an industrial suburb.

At the heart of this wide industrial basin, its flanks marked by bucket lifts for the transport of iron ore, lies **Nancy**. This historic capital of Lorraine is chiefly remarkable for the magnificent 18th-century architectural ensemble in the city centre, the Place Stanislas and the Place de la Carrière, one of the great artistic achievements of the period. The Place

Place de la Carrière, Nancy

Stanislas is spacious and harmonious, with gracious palaces, a triumphal arch, leafy baroque fountains worthy of Rome, and wonderfully ornate gilt iron-work gateways and grilles and lanterns adorning the square like jewellery. The effect, especially when the square is lit up at night, is magical. Beyond the triumphal arch the Place de la Carrière forms a noble complement to Nancy's brilliant centrepiece, and beyond that the medieval town with an old gateway and the Gothic ducal palace. Apart from these elements, most of Nancy is severe and characterless, having been laid on an ordered grid in the 16th century. It was left unfortified in the 19th century to save it from bombardment. Miraculously it escaped serious damage in both World Wars.

Sights in Nancy

● **Fine Arts Museum** A good collection of 18th-century French paintings, housed in one of the palaces on the Place Stanislas with some big names from other periods. A sombre canvas by Delacroix depicts the Battle of Nancy (1477) where Charles the Bold, or more accurately Rash, of Burgundy, met his death trying to recapture rebellious Nancy, after attempting a siege of the town in mid-winter with no more than a few thousand ailing troops.

- **Museum of Lorraine History** A dauntingly large museum housed in the old ducal palace and covering all aspects of regional geography, prehistory, history, art, costumes and folklore. Items of particular interest include several paintings by Georges de la Tour, and his studio, etchings and copper plates of another celebrated local artist, Jacques Callot (illustrator of the religious wars in all their horror), and a series of 16th-century Flemish tapestries.
- **Church of the Cordeliers** A deconsecrated and dilapidated old church next to the ducal palace, which contains much beautiful funerary sculpture.
- **Nancy School Museum** A fascinating presentation of furniture, glasswork and ceramics in the organic style of the turn of the century – called the Modern Style by the French – pioneered by Nancy craftsmen, especially the glassmaking family of Daum.

Just north of Nancy the Meurthe runs into the Moselle, setting it off on the least attractive section of its long and mostly pleasant course. The **Moselle**, the most important tributary of the Rhine, springs from the southern peaks of the Vosges and descends north-west through the unremarkably pleasant hillsides and woods of southern Lorraine, passing east of the area of spas. Each of these has its own particular curative speciality, and its own attraction as a quiet and peaceful town with extensive and in most cases comfortable accommodation in pleasant surroundings. **Vittel** is by far the largest and most developed of the spas, and especially restful thanks to the separation of thermal Vittel on one side of the railway line from the town on the other. The spa establishment itself has a casino and extensive sporting facilities (18 holes of golf; tennis; polo) which are set in a beautiful and spacious park. Nearby **Contrexéville**, its waters cold like those of Vittel, shares the pre-eminence and curative properties of its neighbour, but is distinguished from it by some lurid modern fountains. **Plombières** and **Bains-les-Bains** are two smaller spas whose hot waters were exploited by appreciative and over-indulgent Romans. **Luxeuil-les-Bains** is larger, and of more varied interest. The waters of Luxeuil were known to Romans too and Gauls before them, but in the Dark Ages the town grew famous because of the great abbey founded there by the Irish missionary Columba among the ruins of the old Roman spa. For centuries it was among the most prestigious establishments in Christendom. The old abbey church is a handsome 14th-century building with a pink stone Gothic cloister, and there are a number of medieval town houses.

The waters of the Moselle itself have none of the mineral richness which have brought the sick and the merely languorous to Vittel and Contrexéville, but the river's course is pleasant enough to follow. **Remiremont** is worth a pause: the main street is lined with arcaded houses, some of them dating from the 13th century. **Epinal** is a large and unattractive town which was very badly damaged in the Second World War. But it has a very interesting museum with a varied and distinguished collection of works of art from Gallo-Roman sculpture to Georges de la Tour paintings.

After Epinal the Moselle is finished with the Vosges, and it is no great sadness to deviate from it to visit the magnificent and sumptuously furnished **Château d'Haroué** built shortly after Lunéville in 1720 by the same architect. A few kilometres further west an isolated horseshoe ridge, the **Colline Inspirée**, rises hundreds of metres above the plateau from Sion to Vaudémont. For thousands of years it has been a place of defence and worship; Notre-Dame-de-Sion still attracts pilgrims in large numbers.

Toul is an important old town, one of the three great eastern bishoprics (the other two are Metz and Verdun), situated between the Moselle and the Marne-to-Rhine Canal. Despite war damage, Toul's tightly packed old centre has some houses of interest, and two splendid Gothic churches both with beautiful cloisters. The glory of the cathedral is its majestic Flamboyant façade from the late 15th century, still richly decorated despite the mutilation of its sculptures during the Revolution.

Between Nancy and the Luxembourg frontier the Moselle runs through attractive country which has however become one of France's most important industrial regions, with coalfields to the east and iron ore deposits and steel industry installations to the west. There is not much here for the tourist.

Metz (pronounced Mess) is the very old regional capital of this partly German-speaking area of Lorraine, annexed in 1871. It has always been a crossroads and is one still, with motorway, railway and river junctions. Quite a lot of the town is high-rise from the post-war reconstruction, but all the waterways (the Moselle splits into several branches) give Metz a pleasantly spacious feeling, enhanced by the very attractive gardens beside the river. By the cathedral, the Place d'Armes is an imposing 18th-century ensemble with an arcaded town hall.

Sights in Metz

• **Cathedral** This splendid cathedral is remarkable for the height of the nave (only surpassed by Beauvais and Amiens), and memorable for its wealth of brilliantly colourful stained glass from the 14th, 15th and 16th centuries.

• **Museums** Archaeology, painting, natural history, coin, prehistory, and frequent temporary exhibitions all in the same building near the Place d'Armes. The most important section is the archaeological one, full of beautiful pieces, and imaginatively presented to suggest many aspects of Gallo-Roman life.

The **Meuse** is born in border country between Lorraine, Champagne and Burgundy, not far north of Langres. Leaving the spas of Vittel and Contrexéville to the east it runs down into Joan of Arc territory, where there isn't much to see – a fact which doesn't stop many thousands coming to see it. Joan was born in January 1412, the daughter of a fairly well-to-do Jacques d'Arc of Domrémy (now Domrémy-la-Pucelle). She started hearing the voices of saints Michael, Margaret and Catherine in her father's wood – the Bois-Chenu – during the summer of 1424, and by summer 1428 was convinced of her mission to deliver the kingdom from despondency and the English. By February 1429 she had convinced the locals and the lord of Vaucouleurs who equipped her, and she set off dressed like a man with her hair cut short and with a six-strong escort on the road to Chinon, Reims, Rouen, and very rough treatment at the hands of the English and George Bernard Shaw. You can visit the simple peasant's house where Joan is said to have been born, beside which there is a small museum.

From the glorious patriotic associations of quiet rolling farmlands which seem hardly to have changed since the days over 500 years ago when the ringing of the church bells, the waters of the fountain, and the rustling of the leaves in the forest all spake the same message to young Joan, the Meuse runs northwards to a land of less romantic if hardly less glorious associations, the battlefields of the Meuse hills where hundreds of thousands of Frenchmen laid down their lives to save their country in a war where heroism was anonymous, and where new limits of human endurance were discovered.

St-Mihiel occupies a key position on the river, tightly enclosed between hills. The German possession of the town from 1914 reduced Verdun's supply lines to one, the road north-east from Bar-le-Duc. As a town St-Mihiel is no beauty spot, but its past is illustrious. The town produced an eminent school of artists, of whom the greatest genius was the sculptor Ligier Richier (1500–1567); two of his works can be seen in the churches of St-Michel and St-Etienne, both featuring a swooning Virgin rendered with great pathos. To see the most celebrated example of Richier's work a short diversion westwards to **Bar-le-Duc** is necessary. In the church of St-Etienne Prince René de Châlon is represented, at his own macabre dying suggestion, as a skeleton; the artist's brutal treatment of the decomposition of the body contrasts with its heroic pose, an intriguing mixture of artistic traditions.

The N35 road from Bar-le-Duc to Verdun is the famous Sacred Way, a crucial supply route in 1916 to the beleaguered city of **Verdun**. This road is the appropriate way to approach Verdun, whose great interest is almost exclusively related to the battle where the fate of Europe was decided (see pages 466–7). The cathedral is a strange mixture of Romanesque, Gothic and Classical and has an elegant cloister and a Romanesque crypt, blocked up for centuries but unearthed by bombardment in 1916. Where there were no decorated capitals new ones were carved, with war the theme.

Considering what it has witnessed, and the grim face of devastation of the battlefields, cloaked by forests, nearby, the Meuse Valley north of Verdun is surprisingly pretty. It is the sort of spacious and fertile river valley you might describe as smiling if it did not seem insensitive to do so. Along the river there is an interesting church at **Mont-devant-Sassey**, a large and beautiful one at **Mouzon** in the style of Laon Cathedral and Notre-Dame de Paris and a kind of safari park with boars and bears at **Bel-Val** (near Beaumont-en-Argonne). East of the river there are interesting remains of Vauban's old citadel town of **Montmédy** and the pilgrimage church of **Avioth**. This is the most distinguished of the monuments in the area, a delightful building from the 14th and 15th centuries, built of a warm golden stone and set in a secluded valley.

HOTELS

> Key: ◆ = 0–250FF, ◆◆ = 251–450FF, ◆◆◆ = over 451FF; prices are per double room without breakfast, which costs around 35–60FF extra. Some hotels may insist on half-board during high season, some hotels or restaurants may close at specific times during the week – it is always worth checking. Most hotels accept the major credit cards; we have indicated where a hotel takes no credit cards.

COLMAR

Le Maréchal

4–6 place des Six Montagnes Noires
68000 Haut-Rhin
TEL 89 41 60 32; FAX 89 24 59 40/89 23 73 61

An extravagantly decorated and expensive hotel right in the prettiest area of Colmar, with views of a small canal framed by painted half-timbered houses. Two salons, two restaurants and a shaded outside terrace make up the public areas; all are furnished with high-quality heavy wooden pieces and expensive fabrics. The bedrooms share the same standard of decoration, which only occasionally approaches the florid, and all have air-conditioning. The price is largely determined by the bathrooms – you can have every kind of bathing experience imaginable, at a cost. The menus are extensive and there are some mouth-watering proposals.

OPEN All year ROOMS 30 (all with bath or shower)

GERARDMER

Hostellerie des Bas-Rupts et Chalet Fleuri

route de la Bresse
88400 Vosges
TEL 29 63 09 25; FAX 29 63 00 40

Michel Philippe's well-known hotel on the mountain slopes above Gérardmer is a curious combination of unpleasant tower-block and pretty chalet. The two are linked by a covered gangway, and a small swimming-pool nestles under the chalet walls. For once, the most expensive rooms (in the chalet) are the best value – large, very comfortable, and beautifully decorated in the Austrian style, with hand-painted flowers. The cheaper rooms in the tower block are also nicely decorated, but nothing can disguise their fundamental functionality. Public rooms are largely open-plan, with reception, bar, salon and restaurant (large, with glassed-in extension) all running into one another. The food is unlikely to disappoint, and the hotel runs like clockwork.

OPEN All year ROOMS 32 (all with bath or shower) FACILITIES Heated outdoor pool, tennis

KIENTZHEIM

Abbaye d'Alspach

2/4 rue Foch
Kientzheim
68240 Haut-Rhin
TEL 89 47 16 00; FAX 89 78 29 73

Close to popular Kaysersberg, but in a much quieter if not quite so pretty village, this small, sunny hotel was once part of a convent, and boasts a wonderful stone spiral staircase in the main building. Two further houses, containing bedrooms and breakfast rooms, are linked by *passerelles* around a courtyard, and there is a small terrace under a trailing vine by the car park. Bedrooms vary in size, and the furnishing is a little sparse, but they are comfortable enough places. The basement restaurant serves only light meals, but there are plenty of other options nearby. Friendly owners, a cool, peaceful atmosphere, and reasonable rooms at reasonable prices make this a good 'wine route' base.

OPEN Mid-Mar to mid-Jan ROOMS 29 (all with bath or shower)

LAPOUTROIE

Les Alisiers

5 Faudé
68650 Haut-Rhin
TEL 89 47 52 82; FAX 89 47 22 38

This is a wonderful place, an old farmhouse high up on a mountainside close to the Col du Bonhomme. The views, the tranquillity of the location and the general sense of well-being which this hotel induces combine to make it extremely popular, especially with British visitors. The star attraction is the glassed-in restaurant, which has plunging views into the valley far beneath. There is also a sun-terrace for fine weather, a comfortable salon with squashy sofas and a traditional and pretty breakfast room. Bedrooms are relatively plainly furnished, and most are fair-sized rather than huge. Service is swift and attentive and the food is good.

OPEN Feb to Jun, early Jul to Dec ROOMS 10 (all with bath or shower)

MITTELBERGHEIM

Winstub Gilg

1 route du Vin
67140 Bas-Rhin
TEL 88 08 91 37; FAX 88 08 45 17

Mittelbergheim is a solid, quiet wine village towards the northern end of the Alsatian wine route, not overrun by tourists. The Gilg family owns an adjacent *cave* as well as this hotel, so the establishment is very much in the centre of village life. The *winstub* is a large traditional building with a lovely internal stone staircase. It is a friendly, typical local inn, without frills – all the life of the place lies in the big beamed bar/restaurant. Bedrooms are reasonably priced, and comfortable, though this is not a place to seek style or modernity. Room 3 is the biggest and best.

OPEN Early Feb to end Jun, mid-Jul to early Jan ROOMS 10 (all with bath)

OTTROTT

Beau Site

place de l'Eglise
67530 Bas-Rhin
TEL 88 95 80 61; FAX 88 95 86 41

At the upper end of a pretty, steep little village on the edge of the Vosges, this hotel has long been a favourite. The terrace restaurant is a wonderful room – a kind of massive conservatory with a successful stained glass mural to one end. A second restaurant is more traditional, and there is now a small *winstub* as well, with a separate menu of light dishes. Bedrooms are fresh and attractive, with much natural wood, and with tiled bathrooms. Some have balconies. This is a comfortable hotel in a good spot for exploration of the nearby mountains. There is a useful, shaded garage.

OPEN All year ROOMS 15 (all with bath or shower)

LA PETITE PIERRE

Aux Trois Roses

19 rue Principale
67290 Bas-Rhin
TEL 88 89 89 00; FAX 88 70 41 28

La Petite Pierre is a holiday village high in the northern Vosges close to the German frontier. Steep forested slopes and old fortresses attract walkers and those in search of mountain air. Many stay at this excellent family hotel right in the centre of the village. There's a bustling air to the ground floor, where a whole series of small sitting-rooms and larger dining-rooms are done up in dark wood and patterned chairs. A new terrace enables diners to eat outside on warm nights. Bedrooms in the basement or on the first floor are in two different styles – pine or modern darkwood. Many have balconies with extensive views and there are some good family rooms. The menu is fairly unexciting and heavily biased towards German tastes, but the service is friendly and willing. The indoor swimming-pool is a big plus point.

OPEN All year ROOMS 43 (all with bath or shower) FACILITIES Heated indoor pool, tennis

Auberge d'Imsthal

route Forestière d'Imsthal
67290 Bas-Rhin
TEL 88 70 45 21; FAX 88 70 40 26

Downhill from the village in a quiet valley with a lake (swimming in summer, geese all year round) in front, this is a quieter spot than Aux Trois Roses. A sympathetically extended farmhouse now houses three different styles of bedroom, a small salon, larger restaurant and an extensive fitness centre which includes a Turkish bath. Some bedrooms are a little small, but most are prettily decorated.

OPEN All year ROOMS 23 (all with bath or shower)

Key: ◆ = 0–250FF, ◆◆ = 251–450FF, ◆◆◆ = over 451FF; prices are per double room without breakfast, which costs around 35–60FF extra. Some hotels may insist on half-board during high season, some hotels or restaurants may close at specific times during the week – it is always worth checking. Most hotels accept the major credit cards; we have indicated where a hotel takes no credit cards.

PLOMBIERES-LES-BAINS

Hôtel de la Fontaine Stanislas

1 Fontaine Stanislas
88370 Vosges
TEL 29 66 01 53; FAX 29 30 04 31

This family hotel is in a good, tranquil location in wooded country above a small spa town on the western edge of the Vosges. The building, a curious mix of local farmhouse and chalet hotel, looks rather decrepit from the outside, but inside everything is well kept, if old-fashioned. This is a simple, good-value place with compact, plain bedrooms redolent of the 1950s, and exhibits the best features of the traditional small French country hotel. Mme Lemercier runs it in friendly fashion; her son does the cooking. There is a wide range of menus and plenty of regional dishes; all are served in the big bright restaurant with its glassed-in side galleries.

OPEN Apr to end Sept ROOMS 19 (all with bath or shower)

RUGY

La Bergerie

15 rue des Vignes
57640 Moselle
TEL 87 77 82 27; FAX 87 77 87 07

This excellently located stopover, just off the motorway north of Metz, is a converted farmhouse where the business is obviously kept on its toes by the lunchtime and conference trade from Metz. The bedrooms are comfortable but unexceptional and linked by institutional corridors, but there's a very comfortable sitting-room where model Afghan hounds lounge before the piano, and a bright restaurant across the courtyard with a vaguely tropical feel to it.

OPEN All year ROOMS 42 (all with bath or shower)

SAINTE-CROIX-EN-PLAINE

Hôtel Au Moulin

route de Herrlisheim
68127 Haut-Rhin
TEL 89 49 31 20; FAX 89 49 23 11

For exploring Colmar, this old mill 5km south of the city makes a tranquil and good-value base. The countryside around is featureless, but the old four-storey corn mill with its small courtyard and large willow tree is a building full of character. The bedrooms are excellent, with clean white or creamy decoration and modern bathrooms. Some rooms are in a cottage annexe on the far side of the courtyard from the main building. The Woeffles do not speak English, but are as welcoming as you could wish. There is no restaurant, but there are places to eat in the nearby villages if you do not want to go as far as Colmar.

OPEN End Mar to early Nov ROOMS 17 (all with bath)

STRASBOURG

Hôtel du Dragon

2 rue de l'Ecarlate
67000 Bas-Rhin
TEL 88 35 79 80; FAX 88 25 78 95

About ten minutes' walk from the town centre, in a quiet area with no parking problems, this is a large peach-painted undistinguished-looking building, once a dependency of a local manor house. M. Iannarelli now runs it as one of the most distinctive of Strasbourg's otherwise bland or overpriced hotels. It is distinctive because of its 'contemporary' style – the interior is grey and white in its entirety, with masses of white-pigmented oak, arches, triangles and metal and fabric chairs. The overall effect is very soothing – if already looking a little dated. Bedrooms are comfortable and those on the third floor have the advantage of some old beams and pretty windows. The breakfast room is in striking black and white. There is no restaurant.

OPEN All year exc. 1 week end Dec ROOMS 32 (all with bath)

VERDUN

Hostellerie Coq Hardi

avenue de la Victoire
55100 Meuse
TEL 29 86 36 36; FAX 29 86 09 21

This hotel has gone up in the world since it was first in the *Guide*, and is now perhaps a little pricey for what is effectively a town-centre inn, but it remains a solid, reliable and friendly place right in the middle of Verdun, and is the obvious place to stay. Bedrooms are either Louis XIII or modern. The former have heavy dark furniture and wall hangings, the latter round-backed chairs, big mirrors and small colourful prints. The heart of the hotel is the large, formal, rather over-decorated restaurant, which is busy and bustling at meal times. Medieval bric-a-brac in the reception area and small salon contrasts oddly with the large-calibre shells which act as door-stops, but symbolise Verdun's long and troubled history.

OPEN Feb to Dec ROOMS 40 (all with bath or shower)

LA WANTZENAU

Moulin de la Wantzenau

2–3 empasse du Moulin
27 route de Strasbourg
67610 Bas-Rhin
TEL 88 59 22 22; FAX 88 59 22 00

This prettily converted mill about 15km north-east of Strasbourg makes an excellent place to stay for those who do not wish to be in the city itself. Bedrooms in the five-storey building are linked to the ground floor by lift, and are of very high quality, with plenty of room, some lovely old country tables and pretty wallpaper. Bathrooms are modern and sparkling. There's a small sitting area by the reception, and a separately run restaurant across the yard (there are some other interesting places to eat in the nearby villages). Beatrice Wolff runs the hotel with admirable efficiency. All in all, excellent value.

OPEN Early Jan to end Dec ROOMS 20 (all with bath or shower)

Mountains are the beginning and the end of all natural scenery
[Ruskin]

THE ALPS

Characteristically French, Mont Blanc looks down on all Europe, from a height of 4731 metres. At its shoulders the French Alps stand guard on the Italian frontier from the waters of Lake Geneva and Evian's Quai de Blonay to the Mediterranean and Nice's Promenade des Anglais, over 320km to the south. The area is one of outstanding natural beauty, which amply compensates for its relative lack of cultural and historical interest; high mountain roads and cable cars make the spectacular mountain scenery, flora, and wildlife accessible to the least energetic sightseer.

A driving tour around the Alps can be very rewarding (given good weather), but you may be made to feel that there is more to holidaying in the mountains than mere absorption; and you may be stirred by the feeling that mountains exist not simply to be looked at but as a challenge. As you negotiate the steep hairpin bends of some lofty alpine pass your sense of achievement may be dulled by all the toiling cyclists you pass on the way up. For them the climb means much more than a pretty view. And as you stand in a cable car, with no more than a single lens reflex slung round your neck, you may find that you are squashed physically and morally by a cabin-load of heavily booted climbers with ice axes poking accusingly out of heavy packs. They use the dizzy cable car station as a point of departure, the mechanical transport as a way of missing out the tedious part of their trip.

The Alps are also a favourite playground for sports people who are no more than keenly recreational. High up in the mountains the mostly modern and functional ski resorts try to make up for their intrinsic lack of charm by laying on all manner of sports facilities for summer tourists. In a few it is possible to ski all the year round on glaciers. In other resorts you can ride, swim, play tennis, hang-glide, sail, boardsail, walk on marked paths and of course take mountaineering lessons. Bungee jumping is the current craze. At the foot of the range, resorts on the big alpine lakes are no less well equipped.

For many tourists the great outdoors of the Alps does not mean pushing the body to new limits of endurance, nor spending all day every day for two weeks on the polyathletic facilities of highly organised resorts. It means getting away from other people, to enjoy nothing more sophisticated than clean air, beautiful flowers, birds and

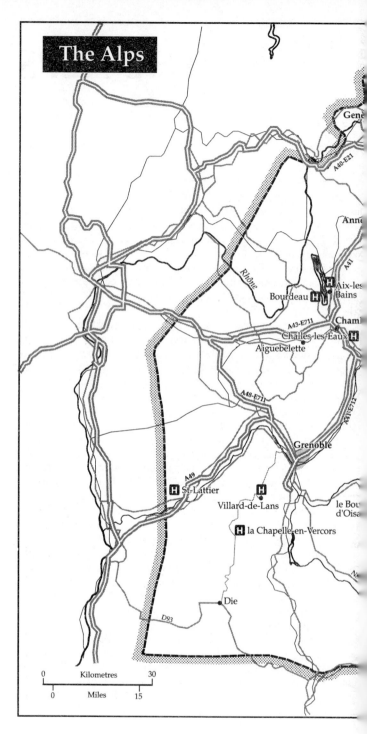

The Alps

Genè

Annè

A40-E21

A41

Rhône

Aix-les-Bains

Bourdeau

Cham

A43-E711

Challes-les-Eaux

Aiguebelette

A48-E711

A41/E712

Grenoble

A49

St-Lattier

Villard-de-Lans

le Bou
d'Oisa

la Chapelle-en-Vercors

Na

Die

D93

Kilometres   30

Miles   15

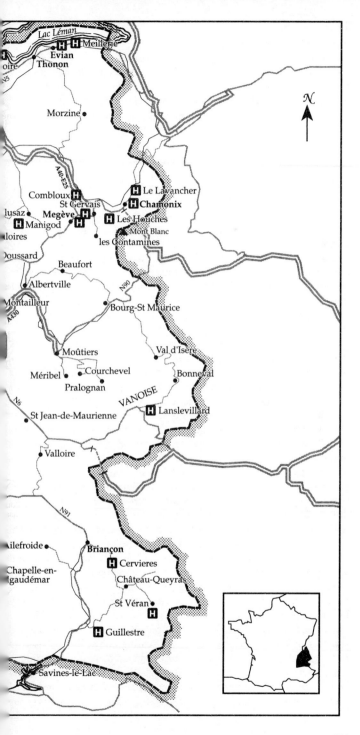

beasts – and of course the sublime landscape. Two of the highest mountain areas have never been inhabited by man and they are now preserved from all development as national parks; here it is possible to walk for days, staying in refuges, and to appreciate the environment not so much unspoilt as almost unsoiled by the intrusion of humanity. Alternatively you can stay in greater comfort in one of the resorts at the gates of the park and make short forays into the interior. If you're not such an ecological purist, and actually like the trappings of civilisation – meadows, farms, rustic villages, cowbells – you can more rewardingly and comfortably explore the countryside outside the national parks. Regional parks present a balance of protected environment, including traditional architecture and crafts, controlled development for the comfort and pleasure of tourists and, of course, for the prosperity of the locals.

If one side of the alpine coin bears the image of an iron-calved practitioner of the cult of physical and thus moral well-being, the obverse shows a wheezing invalid, gazing at the mountains from afar in the hope that some of their natural strength and vigour might rub off, breathing the pure mountain air and bathing in the richly impure mountain water for the alleviation of all manner of ills. Ironically, perhaps, the Alps have a much longer history as a resort for the sick than for the fit. Spa towns such as Aix-les-Bains, where Romans came to take the waters, and St-Gervais have in the past been as full of the infirm as the ski resorts are now of the emphatically firm. But it is possible to exaggerate the proto-funereal quality of the important Alpine spas; the surrounding area is so full of natural beauty that the abundant tourist facilities in the spas themselves attract large numbers of holidaymakers with no interest in the cure. Evian and Aix-les-Bains in full summer season are fashionable lakeside pleasure grounds – with concerts, theatres, regattas, galas and sporting events – as much as they are spas. St-Gervais is situated on the shoulder of Mont Blanc so the scenery and excursion possibilities are superlative. Even the infernally dull Brides-les-Bains, which specialises in the treatment of obesity and which is a match for any spa in France for cheerless institutional architecture and atmosphere, is not a bad place to stay for exploration of high valleys on the edge of the Vanoise National Park – although it would be unfair to expect too much of its gastronomic resources.

Many people choose to go to the Alps simply to tour around and look. The mountain massifs themselves differ greatly, and the transition from north to south can be remarkably abrupt. The north (the old duchy of Savoie and part of the Dauphiné) has glaciers and eternal snow-fields with brilliant white peaks soaring above the lushest and most colourfully floral of alpine pastures, grazed by plump bell-ringing dairy cows. Communications are good via the main valleys – steeply walled, with fast-flowing rivers, main roads and sizeable industrial towns exploiting hydro-electric power. The valleys of the Arve, the

Isère, the Arc and the Romanche are all (in parts at least) much more industrial than you might expect of the Alps, and the unpleasant contrast with nature undefiled in the higher mountain areas is often accentuated by the thick smoggy cloud which hangs around in the valleys when the peaks are in brilliant sun. But there are towns of charm and interest – Grenoble, Chambéry and Annecy – and at the feet of the high mountains the deep glacial lakes – Geneva, Annecy and Le Bourget – are beautiful in colour and context.

In contrast the snowless, grey and rocky southern (Dauphiné) Alps seem harsh and forbidding although hardly less impressive. The south is crossed by fewer deep river valleys; communications are less good and development much less advanced. Many of the high valleys remain extremely isolated. The southern Alps may not be the place to go for comfort and the most charming alpine scenery, but it is a fine region for escaping and exploring, and has more reliable weather than the north.

The two areas differ historically, too. In the north, the counts, later dukes, of Savoie established control in the early Middle Ages, and exploited the strategic value of their dominions – which they soon extended into modern Italy – to maintain their independence of French sovereignty until 1860. The Savoyards then voted overwhelmingly to join France, probably because the ruling house of Savoie, from the 15th century onwards, had gradually shifted its power base towards Italy, to the neglect of Savoie proper. Only in 1946 with the abdication of the last king of Italy, called Humbert like the first count of Savoie in the 11th century, did Europe's most durable dynasty yield the reins of power. The Dauphiné was sold to the French crown in 1349 by its profligate rulers the dauphins de Viennois, in a deal whereby the heir to the French throne ruled in Dauphiné with the title of dauphin.

Until the late 18th century, nature in its mountainous manifestation was considered unfriendly. Then, in the romantic period, a radical change of taste in landscape in favour of the awe-inspiring coincided with increasing glacier exploration in search of crystals and for reasons of scientific curiosity. The Geneva scientist de Saussure reached the summit of Mont Blanc in 1787 (without a rope and in a long-tailed silk coat) and spent four hours there conducting experiments. Wordsworth was at Chamonix admiring the glaciers in 1790, Shelley in 1816. The race to conquer new peaks and more and more difficult rocky needles gathered speed, with intrepid British Victorians setting the early pace; many peaks still bear their names. Throughout the 19th century thousands of tourists followed royalty to the spas (Queen Victoria went to Aix) and pushed on up into the mountains to see nature's cathedrals. They didn't explore much further than the Mont Blanc massif, with Chamonix and St-Gervais at its feet being easily accessible and offering such spectacular mountain scenery. In de Saussure's words, 'majestic glaciers, separated by great forests, crowned by granite rocks to an astonishing elevation, carved into gigantic obelisks and intermixed with snow and ice, offer one of the grandest and most remarkable spectacles that it is possible to imagine. The cool, pure air that one breathes, the high cultivation of the valley and the pretty hamlets one passes, gives the idea of a new world, a sort of earthly paradise'. Chamonix and Aix-les-Bains – witnesses to this period of discovery – still have a Victorian style and charm.

Style and especially charm are qualities notable for their absence in the majority of French alpine villages, in contrast to the abundance of traditional rustic houses and painted wooden chalets in Austria and Switzerland. Houses are more often built of rough stone than timber, and their balconies are more likely to be piled high with winter fuel than with colourful flowers. Old wooden villages high up in the pastures do not exist in many places in France; where they do they have rarely developed into resorts; where they have (for example at Val d'Isère) the development has been neither well thought out nor sightly. More typical has been the creation of new resorts out of nothing (as at Courchevel, Tignes, Les Arcs) situated and planned for the maximum convenience of winter sports people, but with little apparent thought given to the sheer ugliness inflicted on the summer visitor by careless siting of ski equipment and by dreary functional architecture. Indeed, so pervasive has been the spread of skiing development that it is hard to find a panoramic view without a ski tow crowning the distant peak. Since the summer season is so short in the Alps, most of the purpose-built ski resorts are simply boarded up and abandoned outside July and August, leaving a bizarre scene for visitors who make their way in by mistake: silent streets, rusting lifts and cableways, and Christmas decorations hanging over the sunny footpaths.

Because of the hardy outdoor nature of alpine holidays, accommodation in most places caters for tourists of simple tastes, with the notable exceptions of some hotels in Evian, Talloires, Megève and Chamonix. Sadder and more surprising than this shortage of expensive luxury hotels is the rarity of homely and welcoming chalet-style establishments with cheerful window boxes, chamois heads over the log fire and cowbells ringing in the background. The region does not rank high for gastronomic tourists, either, though again there are some notable, if expensive, exceptions.

To enjoy the Alps in the summer, good weather is no less essential than it is on the Côte d'Azur. It is also considerably less predictable because of the meteorological effects of abruptly high mountains. In general the northern Alps are colder and wetter than the southern, but there are remarkable local variations of microclimate. It is not unusual for one side of Mont Blanc to be cloudy and wet, the other bathed in sunshine.

The unpredictability of the weather, with not infrequent summer snowfalls at high altitude, can affect the practicalities of driving around the Alps. You can be fairly sure that all roads will be open from late June to late September, but at any other time there's a risk that high passes may be impassable because of snow. Remember that even in midsummer melting snow may freeze on the highest roads overnight. But motoring is generally more tiring than actually dangerous or frightening.

The Savoie Lakes

Banana-shaped **Lake Geneva** (Lac Léman) is by far the largest and deepest of the alpine lakes. It is too big to be really attractive (you very often cannot see across it except at the thin Geneva end). On the south (French) shore the mountains of the Chablais climb steeply from the waterside behind **Evian** – of which the 19th-century poet Gautier wrote, 'no decorator ever set a scene with such a marvellous understanding of effect than Evian is set by pure chance'.

The town which climbs the wooded hills behind the lake is one of France's most important spas, producing three hundred million bottles of water every year, and one of its most lively. The beneficial properties of the local water supply have been known for centuries, but private ownership of the château and waterside prevented the growth of a resort until the late 19th century. In place of the château they built an exotic domed casino and spread a handsome spacious promenade (the Quai de Blonay) in front of it. In nearby gardens the thermal spring, particularly noted for its effect on the temperamental imbalances of middle age, is clad in mock-Japanese architecture; behind, a few crowded streets are squashed into the small space between lake and pre-alpine hillsides. Villas and palatial hotels (in size at least) in spacious gardens climb the slopes in a rather suburban way. To stay full, Evian hotels have had to court conference business which has inevitably detracted from such elegant exclusiveness as the resort may once have had. But at least it's full of active people; there are all kinds of sports facilities including riding, tennis, golf and sailing (with annual regattas and tournaments), and there is plenty going on in the evenings. Evian is also a very good place for boat trips around and across the lake and coach excursions into the mountains and even as far afield as Venice.

East of Evian towards Switzerland stretches the most interesting section of rocky *corniche* road. **Meillerie** is a particularly attractive unspoilt old fishing village situated below impressive cliffs celebrated by Byron and Rousseau. On a clear day you can see right across the deepest part of the lake (over 270 metres), where Byron nearly perished in a storm, to the picturesque turrets of the 13th-century Château de Chillon on the Swiss shore, where the dukes of Savoie imprisoned many of their enemies.

From Evian to the Swiss border a few kilometres east of Geneva the lakeside flattens and the main road, not cramped beside the water's edge, passes through prosperous farmland and vineyards; some of the most prestigious and picturesque of these surround the handsome turrets of the first duke Amadeus's château/monastery of **Ripaille**, which is open to visitors, but is best admired from outside. **Thonon** is another spa familiar to mineral water drinkers. It is the main town of the region, set high on a platform above the lakeside, and has more everyday life than Evian. Of the two adjacent churches in the busy town centre, the basilica of St-François de Sales is the more interesting for its series of huge canvases illustrating the Passion painted by Maurice Denis in 1943. Nearby in the old château looking out over the lake a local folklore museum has been installed. Below the town is an attractive grassy promenade and port, and a small beach along the road to Ripaille. West of Thonon there are some more bathing resorts, Excenevex and Sciez, and the exceptionally pretty and meticulously kept walled and fortified village of **Yvoire**, a very popular destination for Swiss boat trips and usually crawling with admirers. Most of the old chalets are crêperies and souvenir shops.

Lake Annecy must be one of the most perfect landscape compositions anywhere. Its colour is a deep milky azure. The twists and turns of its shoreline give constantly changing views as you drive or sail round. Its size is just right too: not big enough to present a monotonous expanse of water, not so small that the variety of rocky cliffs, snowy peaks (usually), and wooded ridges seem oppressive. Elegant residences, classy restaurants and hotels (which depend more on their position than quality for custom) are strung around the leafy lakeside. Decorative, unconvincingly fortified castles jut out into the water and survey the whole from on high. The lake's water is renewed only very slowly, and a lot of work has been necessary to clean it up; strict controls have been imposed on the use of motorised boats.

At the head of the lake lies **Annecy** itself, one of the most attractive old towns in the Alps, and certainly a showpiece of the French part of the range. It's a busy and prosperous town whose recent rapid growth has luckily not spoilt the look of the lake. Not surprisingly it's a very popular place to live in as well as visit for a holiday. Annecy town has a delightful old (mostly 15th-century) centre, with a powerful castle looking down over the waterways, arcaded streets and bridges gaily decorated with flowers. Beside the lake itself there are spacious lawns and gardens and a majestic avenue of venerable plane trees. Swans usually do their bit to complete the scene. From the town you can take boat trips round the lake as well as swim, boardsail and pedalo.

Talloires is the lake's quality resort. Its situation is superb, looking across the narrowest part of the lake (which was originally split into two at this point) at Duingt's castle in the water at the foot of the elegant Taillefer mountain ridge. The village itself is pretty, and celebrated for the cluster of prestigious hotels along the waterfront.

Annecy

Excursions around Lake Annecy

● **Tour round the lake** Menthon, overlooked by its splendidly situated castle (open to the public), is mostly residential and peaceful and has a good grassy beach. The climb up behind Talloires to the **Col de la Forclaz** and down the other side to Vesonne just south of the lake is not one of the most spectacular climbs in the Alps but it is certainly one of the most attractive, giving splendid views of the lake (especially if you come from Vesonne to Talloires), and passing through such charming high pastures (alps, to give the word its proper meaning) that you wouldn't be surprised to see Julie Andrews come tripping and trilling over the brow of the hill. Due south of the lake a forest road leads down the dark wooded **Combe d'Ire**. Apart from the **Château de Duingt** the west shore is less interesting, but gives good views of the more spectacular mountains on the other side of the lake. Even better ones are to be had by driving up through the woods which clothe the Semnoz mountain to the **Crêt de Chatillon**. From the top there is a wonderful panorama of the highest peaks of the French Alps, and from further down of the lake itself. There are a number of paths for woodland walks on the mountains.

● **Aravis Massif** The mountains between Annecy and the Mont Blanc massif offer some of the most restful pastoral scenery in the French

Alps, with attractive wooded chalets, their balconies brilliant with geraniums. **Thones** is a good base for not too strenuous woody walks, and is also the odorous market place for Reblochon (the creamiest of alpine cheeses). **Manigod** higher up in the mountains is quieter and equally charming. From the **Col des Aravis** there is an excellent view of the nearby Mont Blanc massif. Some of the most attractive scenery in the area can be enjoyed by taking the indirect route from Thones to La Clusaz via the **Col de La Croix-Fry** and the Manigod valley.

The largest and deepest lake that is entirely French, **Lac du Bourget**, suffers by comparison with Lake Annecy although it was much more celebrated in the 19th century because of the popularity of Aix-les-Bains. The lake is surrounded by less interesting mountains than Lake Annecy but is none the less a very pleasant place for a holiday: as well as boat trips on the lake and climbs up into the neighbouring mountains there are beaches and a variety of sports facilities arranged in a number of places around the lake, notably at **Aix-les-Bains**. The great spa, traditional peak of luxury and fashion in the Alps, now seems more traditional than fashionable or even luxurious, but it does not merely live off the memory of its illustrious visitors (two French empresses and Queen Victoria): in season there are open-air plays and concerts, sporting events including golf, regattas and racing, and even nightlife outside the portals of the inevitable casino. Along the lake spacious gardens are laid out behind the beaches (admission charged at some) and port. This is the area of play, popular at weekends with the inhabitants of nearby Chambéry. The serious heart of the spa, with its heavily grand casino and hotels and the ghastly 1930s architecture of the thermal establishment (open to the public), is set some way back from the water, and is also pleasantly laid out with gardens at the foot of Mont Revard. The hill isn't appreciated by all *curistes*, and many hotels lay on special bus shuttles to the baths. For the uninitiated a visit to the baths is of great interest, and there are some Roman remains within. Nearby there is the interesting Dr-Faure museum, with 19th-century paintings of high quality and Lamartine memorabilia.

Excursions from Aix-les-Bains

• **Abbaye de Hautecombe** Splendidly situated on the edge of the lake, this large abbey and necropolis of the Savoyard dynasty is most attractively accessible by boat from Aix-les-Bains (several trips daily). It was extensively redecorated in the 19th century in an entertainingly extravagant romantic Gothic style with sugary sentimental monuments to the princes and princesses, so it clashes in no way with the atmosphere of Aix. It is, however, very crowded and commercialised.
• **Tour round the lake** The western side is the more interesting. From

the quiet waterside resort village of **Le Bourget-du-Lac** the route climbs up the side of the Mont du Chat; after you turn off the main road to cross the **Col du Chat** it winds high above the lake through rustic and panoramic farmland.

● **Mont Revard** From Aix to the small resort of **La Féclaz**, there's a delightful drive through wooded mountains with views of the lake on one side and the highest Alps on the other.

● **Chambéry** Animation in this dignified old capital of Savoie is centred on the elegant arcaded main shopping street (Rue de Boigne): a fountain of elephants stands at one end and the old ducal château at the other. Chambéry's shops, many of which line the narrow alleyways of the old town, make one good reason for a visit. The bizarre interior of the cathedral, where the Gothic tracery reveals itself to be a master-piece of trompe l'oeil, makes another.

● **Lac d'Aiguebelette** A popular and relatively small, clean lake south-west of Chambéry with good bathing and fishing.

The Savoie Alps

South of Lake Geneva the pre-alpine mountains of the Chablais climb steeply from foothills of vineyards. The highest peaks of this region are modest by alpine standards (under 2,500 metres) and unspectacular. But the region is a pleasant one of green valleys and wooded slopes, fairly characterised by the name of the local breed of dairy cattle, *Abondance*. **Morzine** is the most important winter and summer resort, unexciting but not unattractive and enjoying a very pleasant spacious setting at the meeting place of several high valleys. There are very extensive possibilities for walking and motoring excursions all round, and good sports facilities. The best drive of all from here is over the mountains to Samoëns, splendidly varied with its succession of ever-green woods, high pastures, the sudden appearance of Mont Blanc at the pass, and the steep descent down through orchards. **Samoëns** is an attractive old village and resort in the valley with a worthy collection of alpine plants on a steep hill. From here it's only a short drive up the river to its head – the soaring jagged **Cirque du Fer à Cheval** (horse-shoe). From the café at the bottom of this spectacular amphitheatre riding excursions are organised.

No less rewarding but certainly not for the faint-hearted is the long walk over the mountains from Sixt to the Arve valley between Sallan-ches and Chamonix. Most tourists take the road, which leads to the industrial and often smoky section of the Arve at Cluses. A motorway relieves you of the need to spend long down here, but it is worth stopping at **Sallanches** for one of the most celebrated views of Mont Blanc, which towers over 4,000 metres above you at a distance of no

more than 22km. From Sallanches there are some very attractive excursions up into the hills which flank the Arve on both sides. The north side is more frequented, with lots of holiday institutions around the **Plâteau d'Assy**, which has an exceptional modern church consecrated in 1950 (Notre-Dame-de-Toute-Grace) – the product of a collaboration between many of the world's leading artists.

Until recently the road up the steep mountainside to the narrow gateway into Europe's most spectacular valley, de Saussure's 'earthly paradise', was one of the most tedious in the Alps, a constant nose-to-tail of labouring juggernauts on their way up to the Mont Blanc road tunnel and Italy. Now a motorway, built in dramatic projection from the mountainside, lifts you out of the industrialisation as if your car were suddenly capable of flight. As you approach Chamonix the summit of Mont Blanc is obscured by the nearer peaks which rise so steeply from the widening valley floor that you are not surprised to learn that this is the world capital of *alpinisme*, the parochial French word for climbing, even in the Himalayas. It is no longer Mont Blanc itself that brings climbers here. Its ascent, as any alpinist will tell you, is really just a long walk. Chamonix's pre-eminence as a climbing centre is owed rather to the spectacular array of jagged spindly rock needles (*aiguilles*) which line up at the shoulders of the serene, rounded white peak and divide Italy from France like a wall crowned with deterrent spikes. No less spectacular are the glaciers that cascade from on high like frozen waterfalls. Since the last century they have been in retreat, but one – the glacier des Bossons – still descends well through the tree line towards the valley floor.

Apart from a few modern buildings **Chamonix** still looks very Victorian, and although the atmosphere is in no way old-fashioned it remains as it has been for over a hundred years – an unpretentious, bustling resort, full (often very full) of climbers and mere tourists.

It is impossible not to be infected in Chamonix by the spirit of adventure which must have reigned in the town in the last century when mountaineering was pioneering, rather than the search for technical difficulty for its own sake, which it has subsequently become. A fascinating and entertaining companion is the guidebook to Chamonix and the range of Mont Blanc, first published in 1896 and recently reissued, written by the great Victorian mountaineer and explorer Edward Whymper, who died in Chamonix on 16 September 1911 and who lies buried in the English church there. There is also a museum devoted mainly to the history of alpinism and the conquest of local peaks, with old equipment and fascinating photographs – including one of the aged Professor Janssen who had an observatory built on the very summit of Mont Blanc (it soon disappeared in the snow and ice) and was carried up to the peak by bearers. In the old days tourists were borne up the hillsides on donkeys to the most famous viewpoints. The favourite viewpoint of one of Chamonix's most enthusiastic devotees, John Ruskin, on the way up the Brévent, is still commemorated. Nowadays there are all sorts of mechanical ways of getting uphill, many of them almost as breathtaking as the panoramas they unveil.

Excursions from Chamonix and nearby resorts

• **Aiguille du Midi** This astonishingly engineered cable car climbs from Chamonix at about 1,000 metres to over 3,800 metres in two stages, the second of which is spectacularly precipitous. From the middle station there are walks down to Chamonix. The top, where you will notice the sudden change of altitude and temperature, is for views across the chain and down to Chamonix, and the sight of climbers setting off further upwards towards Mont Blanc – still over 1,000 metres higher. In good weather a further gondola will take you across the glaciers of the Vallée Blanche to the Italian side of the chain and thence down to the Aosta valley. Most tourists go as far as the Helbronner point and then return by lift; you can also go as far as Courmayeur in Italy (don't forget your passport) and then return by bus to Chamonix through the Mont Blanc tunnel, though this is time-consuming and not really worth it.

• **Brévent** A two-stage cable car from Chamonix's north side giving the most famous view of Mont Blanc itself. The top half is worthwhile for the excitement of the ride alone: the cable car spans an enormous chasm. From the half-way station there are good walks down to Chamonix and along the Balcon de Merlet to La Flégère.

• **Flégère** A two-stage cable car from Les Praz (to the east of Chamonix). There are splendid views from both the half-way station and the snowy top (which has some summer skiing) of the most famous of all the Mont Blanc glaciers, the Mer de Glace, which snakes languorously down from the Vallée Blanche towards Chamonix. There are good walks from the half-way station.

- **Montenvers** From the middle of Chamonix a rack railway climbs to the very edge of the Mer de Glace, the classical excursion into glacier territory for over a century. You can wander around on the ice and admire its grubby blue colour, visit a grotto (fun, with furniture carved out of ice) within the glacier itself, and see a small zoo where alpine fauna are rather sadly cooped up.
- **Nid d'Aigle** Accessible by rack railway (Mont Blanc Tramway) from St-Gervais or indirectly from the cable cars which link up with it from Les Houches in the Chamonix valley. This is the beginning of the easy way up Mont Blanc, a mere two days' walk (return) from here. There are shorter walks from the top of the railway to the Glacier de Bionnassay, with extremely impressive high mountain scenery and more gentle walking terrain around the Col de Voza where the St-Gervais and Les Houches lifts meet.

The trouble with Chamonix is that it is always crowded, even in the months when the rest of the Alps are very empty. The Swiss end of the valley is no less beautiful and much more peaceful, although **Argentière** and **Le Tour** are not the quiet undeveloped villages they once were. **Le Lavancher** is a particularly relaxing hamlet of old chalets with a couple of hotels and superb views. The name, a common one in the Alps, means that this is a place for avalanches. The head of the valley is surprisingly gentle; a road leads over the hills to Switzerland and gives magnificent views back down the Chamonix valley with the towering Aiguille Verte in the foreground above Argentière, and Mont Blanc behind. An excellent nature trail with a rich array of local flora is tucked under the shoulder of the Aiguilles Rouges.

Unless you catch the lifts up and over from Les Houches, you have to descend from this 'earthly paradise' to reach the old spa resort of **St-Gervais** on Mont Blanc's western shoulder. It is of the same vintage as Chamonix but much less lively. On all sides of St-Gervais there are splendid excursions on foot, by car or cable car or railway. Among the finest is the road up to **Le Bettex** and the cable car onward up the Mont d'Arbois. From St-Gervais the Montjoie valley leads up to the pleasantly spacious resort of **Les Contamines**, steeply overlooked by the glaciated mountains on the Mont Blanc side, but green and pleasant on the west. A track leads on up to the **Col du Bonhomme**, once a frequented route across to Italy. It's a long walk from Les Contamines to the Italian resort of Courmayeur but there are refuges to stay in on the way in the summer months. This is just one section of the classic walk all the way around the Mont Blanc massif (the *Tour du Mont Blanc*). Whymper describes it and says that a sturdy pedestrian can achieve the walk round the range in no more than four days. Today's *Guide Michelin* says that you should allow between ten and 12 days, and advises allowing three days to get from Les Contamines to Courmayeur. So much for the evolution of species.

Still benefiting from splendid views of the Mont Blanc range, **Megève** enjoys a relatively gentle setting. It's one of the earliest and still one of the most fashionable of French ski resorts, and has sprawled far and wide, with substantial chalet-style villas and hotels.

From Megève the river Arly leads down into the cheese country of the **Beaufortin**, through dark wooded gorges. At the bottom of the road, at the junction with the busy commercial and industrial artery of the Isère valley, **Albertville** is still living off its memories of the 1992 Winter Olympics. Photographs, videos and displays of costume and a post-modern central square, which ends abruptly, like a film set, are lovingly cherished. Otherwise, the town is without interest. Opposite, the walled town of **Conflans** has been heavily restored and transformed into an enclave of craft shops and cafés.

The main road along the deep Isère valley gives access to the new generation of French ski resorts high up in the Tarentaise and Vanoise regions south of the river. From each town along its course a road leads steeply up to one of the mountain playgrounds – Méribel, Courchevel, La Plagne, Les Arcs, Val d'Isère. Apart from the extremely attractive rough stone Romanesque basilica beside the road at **Aime**, the road itself reveals little of interest. Of the larger towns which punctuate it, **Moutiers** is the most animated and pleasant, with a large dirty cathedral by the market place. From here roads lead up to the Trois Vallées area of Courchevel, Méribel and Les Menuires/Val Thorens. This, according to its own publicity, is the largest ski domain in the world, but isn't much frequented in summer when the only skiing is at the dismally functional resort of **Val Thorens**.

Much more suitable as a summer base for pedestrian exploration of the **Vanoise National Park** is **Pralognan**, a steeply enclosed climbers' and hikers' village just on the edge of the park. Guided excursions, from stiff walks to glacier ski tours and rock climbs, are graded and priced according to difficulty so there is something for nearly everyone. The church at nearby **Champagny-en-Vanoise** contains a richly carved and painted altar-piece dating from the early 18th century.

Steeply pitched above the Isère valley and Bourg St-Maurice, **Les Arcs** is a carefully planned modern resort catering for all needs unless you require the place to have character. The little old villages of **Peisey** and **Nancroix**, on the other hand, have hardly any facilities but charm and character in abundance and a local costume festival in August.

From **Bourg-St-Maurice** one road winds up to the **Col du Petit St-Bernard** and Italy; buildings of an old hospice, founded according to legend by Saint Bernard in the 10th century, stand as tribute to the former importance of the pass and still show the damage inflicted when the border was disputed in the Second World War. A long steep and stony scramble gives access to the **Pic de Lancebranlette** and splendid views of the south side of Mont Blanc and its attendant *aiguilles*. An easier way to enjoy the same view, although from a much greater distance, is to explore the mountainsides (with the help of cable cars) above the neighbouring resorts of **Val d'Isère** and **Tignes**, also accessible by road from Bourg St-Maurice. The two villages together constitute one of the world's most famous and extensive ski areas. Val d'Isère is definitely no beauty spot, but at least it has the old rough stone houses of the original village, grouped around the handsome belfry of its typically Savoyard church. Since skiers moved in though, Val – as it is known to its habitués – has spread up and down the narrow valley apparently without the expenditure of much planning effort. Tignes has been built from nothing, up in a desolate bowl high above the tree line and a large reservoir (where the old Tignes used to be), at the foot of the graceful Grande Motte, one of the Vanoise's highest and finest peaks (3,656 metres). However unfriendly the skyscraper colonies may seem, Tignes is much frequented in summer as the best place in France for summer skiing, and has an enormous range of sports facilities on land, in the air and on water. It is also a convenient base for access to the Vanoise National Park. One of the few roads within the park itself climbs from Val d'Isère up across bare mountainsides to Europe's highest pass, the **Col de l'Iseran** (2,770 metres). There are high banks of snow by the road in early summer (it usually opens in late June) and glacier skiing near the top of the pass.

At the foot of the steep and awesome descent to the Arc valley, **Bonneval** is one of the most attractive villages in the Alps, whose primitive charm has been carefully preserved. Rough, rusty-coloured stone houses huddle close together as if for warmth beneath the towering treeless mountainsides. Firewood is stacked thick on the balconies. It is not difficult to imagine the severity of the winters here. Just outside Bonneval, there is a new village offering accommodation to climbers and hikers who explore the mountains on the Italian side of the valley from here. There are several equally attractive villages along

Ibex, sure-footed on the highest rocks

the Avérole valley which joins the Arc near the substantial farming village of **Bessans**, whose church and nearby chapel contain wood-carvings and frescoes, both of which are particularly interesting features of this valley. The decorative richness of the churches of the Arc valley have much to do with its traditional importance as a route across the Alps via the Mont Cenis pass to Susa and Turin. Napoleon was responsible for building the present road in the early 19th century; it replaced a mule track which had borne so many Grand Tourists towards Italy and the art treasures of Rome, just as many years earlier it had brought Italian artists north. The pass was celebrated for the local custom of sending travellers downhill by sledge, which clearly didn't die out with the engineering of the road. Murray's Handbook of 1838 describes the thrilling downhill service which enables travellers to descend 600 vertical metres in less than ten minutes, probably about one-tenth of the time they would spend going up the same distance.

At the bottom of the Mont Cenis road, the isolated chapel of St-Sebastien in **Lanslevillard** has remarkably vivid and melodramatic frescoes depicting the martyrdom of Saint Sebastian and the Life of Christ. Further down the valley, **Termignon**, **Freney** and **Aussois** give access to the Vanoise National Park, and have some accommodation. Near Aussois, the narrow steeply walled valley is blocked by the grimly powerful fortifications built by the Savoyards in the early 19th century as defence against the French. Other local aggressors included wolves: near Modane in the late 18th century, one pounced out of the forest, and carried off Horace Walpole's dog while he was on his way to Italy with the poet Thomas Gray. **Modane** itself is a dull town, and the Arc, as it grows, gets increasingly industrial. Rather than following it down to where it joins the Isère many kilometres from their adjacent birthplaces, take one of two splendid mountain drives south to the Dauphiné and the Romanche valley.

From **St-Michel-de-Maurienne**, it's about 32km to the high and barren **Col du Galibier** (2,645 metres) past **Valloire**, a traditional alpine village, which has managed the transition into a well-equipped summer and winter resort without the sacrifice of too much character. Its church is remarkable for the richness of its decoration, and the surrounding mountains are both shapely and only minimally spoilt by pylons. Local costumes are occasionally to be seen, notably for a procession on 15 August. By alpine standards the cathedral at **St-Jean-de-Maurienne** is of great interest; the decorative carving of the late 15th-century choir stalls and panelling is notable. From St-Jean one of the most varied and attractive drives into the Alps climbs through narrow wooded gorges to emerge into spacious grassy high pastures. The adjacent **Col de la Croix de Fer** and the **Col du Glandon** give very fine views respectively south to the peaks of the Ecrins and north to Mont Blanc. There are dramatic gorges (the **Combe d'Olle** and **Défilé de Maupas**) on the way down from the Glandon to Bourg d'Oisans.

The Dauphiné Alps

Grenoble, the most important city within the Alps, owes its development to the space afforded by the confluence of the wide valleys of the Drac and Isère, and also to the boom of alpine industry fuelled by hydro-electric power. Its dynamic period culminated in the '60s with the build-up to the Winter Olympics of 1968, when it was *the* French town for whizz-kid engineers and planners. Grenoble has a rare combination of high-rise modern building and impressive mountain backdrop, perhaps more characteristic of Denver, Colorado, than European Alps; most of the modern building is on the edge of town, bounded by motorways and ring roads. The old centre is tall and 18th-century in aspect, and much more busily commercial than Chambéry. Grenoble's big university, and its convenience for winter sports, have assured the town's popularity with foreign students and kept it young and up-to-date. The most interesting monument of avant-garde Grenoble is the fine arts museum, which as well as some old masterpieces contains a varied collection of modern art. The other image of dynamic Grenoble – ancient and modern – is the gondola cable car system which spans the Isère from the old part of town and whisks you up to a rocky citadel built by Vauban. Just outside Grenoble, the **Château de Vizille** is less renowned for its contents (mostly 19th-century) than for the memory of the meeting of the Dauphiné estates which took place here on 21 July 1788. The resolution passed at the meeting, objecting to Louis XVI's autocratic government, set something of a trend for the rest of France.

South-west of Grenoble the wooded slopes of the Chamrousse massif climb steeply from the green and peaceful spa suburb of **Uriage**. **Chamrousse**, custom-built at the tree line, is Grenoble's ski resort, and has little attraction in summer, except to masochistic weekend cyclists.

The pre-alpine massif of the **Vercors** is fairly tame by high mountain standards but climbs with impressive and forbidding steepness from the Isère Valley. Once you penetrate these outer walls, the Vercors (citadel of the resistance in the last war and theatre of bitter fighting) is green and gentle for the most part, full of cyclists and coffee-coloured cows. **Villard-de-Lans** is the most important resort: sprawling and unsophisticated, but pleasant and not too purpose-built, catering for recreational tastes both leisurely and energetic. Cable cars take you up towards fine viewpoints over the whole Vercors range and eastwards to the high Dauphiné Alps. Near Villard-de-Lans there is a particularly fine series of gorges which make a practicable circuit for a day's round-trip in a car. The limestone massif has scenery very different from the high Alps, enclosed and dark with views more often down to roaring torrents than up to the open sky. Most spectacular of all the gorges are the **Grands Goulets** where river and road squeeze through what seems like a crevasse in the mountains, barely penetrated by the light of day, and the **Combe Laval**, a hair-raising 600-metre drop to the river Cholet from the **Col de la Machine**, with a road precariously cut into a gallery in the apparently overhanging cliff face. Before these remarkable roads were created in the 19th century, the only route in or out for the region's chief export of charcoal was by mule train over the high passes. At the western end of the **Gorges de la Bourne**, the houses of **Pont-en-Royans** are built into a rock face dropping down to the water.

Seen from Grenoble, the sharp ridges of the **Chartreuse Massif** rear up like an angry sea. Unlike most of the Alps, the area is one of dense and partly deciduous woodland, which means that the autumn landscape is particularly beautiful. Like the Vercors it is a favourite weekend retreat for the Grenoblois, but there are few resorts or places to stay. **St-Pierre-de-Chartreuse** is attractively situated and has some accommodation. Nearby, the crest of the **Charmont Som** rises above the trees to give an extensive panorama. The famous **Grande Chartreuse** monastery was founded in the late 11th century by one Bruno, in what he considered to be a safe isolation from the world. The monks comforted themselves in their chilly solitude by brewing up the famous Chartreuse liqueur – using over a hundred herbs. The recipe remains secret and the monks (there are still about 40) maintain their isolation. But you can visit a small museum about monastic life at the entrance to the grounds, and at **Voiron** you can visit the distillery and taste. The circuit round monastic territory (called the Desert), from St-Pierre-de-Chartreuse via St-Laurent-du-Pont and St-Pierre-d'Entremont, passes through some of the finest and most varied scenery in the massif.

Leaving the Vercors southwards by the **Col du Rousset**, you experience an abrupt landscape transition from the lush green domestication north of the tunnel to the comparatively barren hillsides which extend southwards. A long way below lies **Die**, less distinguished by its old ramparts than by the local sparkling wine (*Clairette*). In contrast to the dry and stony mountainsides, the land down in the valleys around Die itself and along the road to Châtillon is pleasantly shady and fruitful, with vineyards and orchards. **Archiane** is a tiny rustic hamlet in the pit of a deep theatre of mountains, excellent for strenuous walks.

One of the most extraordinary peaks in the Dauphiné and one of its traditional seven wonders is the **Mont Aiguille**, admirably seen from the road north to Clelles. In 1429 the ascent of its stubby chimney-like summit was achieved with the aid of ropes and ladders, at the express command of Charles VIII, to discover whether there really were angels on top, as was reported. This remarkable and apparently isolated early rock-climbing feat revealed only chamois and flowers. Eastwards the increasingly austere mountain countryside is relieved by the V-shaped **Sautet reservoir**. Here you encounter the route Napoléon – a mostly fast main road which commemorates the Emperor's return from Elba in 1815. Although the road is rarely spectacular it is a quick and interesting route from the Mediterranean coast to Grenoble.

The long, steeply enclosed **Valgaudemar** joins the Drac just below the Sautet reservoir, and gives access to the Ecrins National Park and the highest French peaks outside the Mont Blanc massif. The walls of the valley are so steep that from most of its floor you can't see very much (the village of **Les Andrieux** is said to be deprived of sun for a hundred days a year) but it's certainly impressive and a popular base for climbers. **La-Chapelle-en-Valgaudemar** is the place to stay; there are fine walks as well as climbs. To the west of the Drac valley, the **Dévoluy** is a little-frequented area with some fine walking. In the high basin ringed by jagged limestone there's some self-catering development. The valley of the **Drac Blanc** is comparable to the Valgaudemar in steepness and rocky severity. On the more vegetated Drac Noir, **Orcières** has some accommodation and wide open walking territory high above it, if you don't mind the pylons and scarred hillsides of ski resorts in summer. The country over the **Col de Manse** towards Gap is altogether more open and pastoral.

Gap itself is aptly named for any itinerary, but being an important crossroads it is difficult to avoid. The Gap/Briançon (and thence Italy) road, which is busy with lorries and caravans, skirts and crosses the large and impressive **Sierre-Ponçon reservoir**. The small resort of **Savines-le-Lac** is charmless but well organised for water sports and camping. A quiet road runs down the west side of the lake, giving good views of it and a curious local phenomenon of *Demoiselles Coiffées* (bonneted maidens) – pillars of soft rock each saved from total erosion by a boulder which still sits on top. South of Savines the splendid forest of Boscodon is rich in elusive chamois; failing a glimpse of these, there's an old abbey to visit and panoramic belvederes. **Embrun**, an important old town long before the damming of the Durance, is impressively situated on a ledge above the river. The 12th-century cathedral of Notre-Dame is interesting and Italianate, with its black and white stone and marble columns supported by lions.

Beneath Vauban's disturbingly empty geometric fortifications at **Guillestre** you must choose whether to pursue the Durance up to the Vallouise and the **Ecrins National Park**, or the Guil into the no less attractive Queyras Regional Park. **Vallouise** is relatively full of tourists and climbers. **Ailefroide** is a good and attractive place to stay at the foot of the mighty Pelvoux, and gives easy access to the glaciers and lofty peaks of the Ecrins.

The **Queyras Regional Park** is a beautiful dead-end corner of the French Alps, closed off from Italy and Briançon by a wall of 3,000-metre peaks. The attractions of the region are its good sunshine record, exceptional floral richness and peaceful high pastures which make excellent starting points for high-altitude walks. At **St-Véran**, one of the highest villages in Europe (2,000 metres), the air is rarefied and the combination of resort and delightful rustic village of wooden chalets rarer still. The chalets are set in south-facing tiers to maximise their

St-Véran

sunlight; the walks and views across the valley and up it to Italy are excellent, with grassy slopes full of horses and cows.

In the Aiguilles valley, **Aiguilles** and **Abriès** are lower and attractively situated winter and summer resorts. A good road up into the bare hills around **L'Echalp** launches walkers towards the Monte Viso. Lower down, the valley is plugged emphatically by the **Château-Queyras**, which despite Vauban's restoration still looks like a medieval fortress on a hillock complete with turrets, rocky backdrop and village cowering at its feet. The drive over the **Col d'Izoard** to Briançon is one of the most exciting in the Alps – though it's not hair-raising, unless that is how you react to the sudden transition from familiar pine woods to the savage, stripped desolation of the upper slopes of the Queyras side of the Col, the Casse Déserte. The Briançon side of the pass is hardly less fine.

Briançon, sitting on a hill at another strategic river junction, has been an important stronghold since pre-Roman times. Vauban built the impressive walls and gateways which still surround and guard the substantial old town and defy you to attempt to drive round its maze of narrow streets. Vauban was also responsible for the cathedral, which is hardly more decorative than the ramparts.

The road back to Grenoble from Briançon is a major one. The winter and summer resort of **Serre-Chevalier** is a long, barely characterised sprawl beside the road giving access to extensive wooded and higher mountainsides; there is plenty of potential for walkers and for sports (including riding and tennis) down on the valley floor. As you drive up towards the **Col du Lautaret** (where there is a beautiful alpine garden and several craft shops) the hillsides gradually shed their forest clothing and open out into spacious green pastures with magnificent views of the glaciated Ecrins Massif, which now shows its most famous profile, the Meije, towering above the village of **La Grave**. The setting, more than anywhere else in the French Alps, is comparable to Mont Blanc/Chamonix, but La Grave – although an important climbing resort – isn't an endearing place. A cable car goes up the shoulder of the Meije to over 3,000 metres and the glacier's edge. Ski touring is possible from the top; walking is best from halfway. The classical view of the Meije is from an oratory at **Le Chazelet** just behind La Grave. A more extensive if less picturesque panorama is revealed from the **Col du Galibier** (2,645 metres), well worth the detour.

Another favourite base for climbers in the Ecrins is **La Bérarde**, at the end of the road up the overbearingly enclosed Vénéon valley which takes you deep into the heart of the massif. La Bérarde was the top recommendation of the celebrated American conquistador of alpine peaks, W A B Coolidge, who appreciated the variety of climbs that can be accomplished from it without having to spend the night under the chilly stars. From the valley and from La Bérarde itself there are a number of walks suitable for the merely hearty (notably the Tête de la Maye).

On a high plateau above the Vénéon, reached by road from the Chambon reservoir in the Romanche valley, **Les Deux Alpes** is one of the Dauphiné's few custom-built ski resorts, which like those in the Vanoise attracts some summer tourists for sports, including skiing, riding, tennis, archery and swimming. Another is **L'Alpe d'Huez** across the Romanche valley, accessible by means of a hairpin road up the almost sheer valley wall from Bourg d'Oisans. There isn't much to choose between the two resorts. From Bourg d'Oisans back to Grenoble the Romanche valley is very industrial.

HOTELS

> Key: ◆ = 0–250FF, ◆◆ = 251–450FF, ◆◆◆ = over 451FF; prices are per double room without breakfast, which costs around 35–60FF extra. Some hotels may insist on half-board during high season, some hotels or restaurants may close at specific times during the week – it is always worth checking. Most hotels accept the major credit cards; we have indicated where a hotel takes no credit cards.

AIX-LES-BAINS

Le Manoir

37 rue Georges 1er
73100 Savoie
TEL 79 61 44 00; FAX 79 35 67 67

This is a flowery country house, with lattice windows and a pleasant bar/terrace. It is pretty throughout, with lots of wood, stone walls and floral fabrics; bedrooms are attractive and modern, if a little on the small side. The restaurant gets busy, so book your table by the window terrace in advance.

OPEN Mid-Jan to mid-Dec ROOMS 73 (all with bath or shower)

ANNECY

Palais de l'Isle

13 rue Perrière
74000 Haute-Savoie
TEL 50 45 86 87; FAX 50 51 87 15

In the hub of old Annecy near the canals and shops, and only a short walk to the lake, this building, with its grey shutters, and traditional appearance, belies the modern stylish interior. Bedrooms are a striking peach and black. The lack of public rooms is not depressing as you have everything on your doorstep. A little street noise.

OPEN All year ROOMS 26 (all with bath or shower)

Hôtel Carlton

5 rue des Glières
74000 Haute-Savoie
TEL 50 45 47 75; FAX 50 51 84 54

A comfortable 1930s town hotel, simple and a little business-like, but rooms are adequate, bright and modern. Plus points are the central location and friendly staff.

OPEN All year ROOMS 55 (all with bath or shower)

BOURDEAU

Hôtel de la Terrasse

73370 Savoie
TEL 79 25 01 01; FAX 79 25 09 97

Built into the mountainside, overlooking the Lac du Bourget, this hotel is simple, cheap and scenic. The main appeal is the restaurant, which has panoramic views of the lake and surrounding area. Bedrooms are less inspiring, but the location is quiet with a little path leading down to the lake.

OPEN Early Mar to early Oct ROOMS 12 (all with bath or shower)

CERVIERES

L'Auberge Napolèon

Col d'Izoard
05100 Hautes-Alpes
TEL 92 21 17 42

L'Auberge Napolèon is situated in a dramatic, isolated location on the Col d'Izoard in the Queyras mountains, surrounded by a landscape of barren orange and grey mountains. Furnishings are simple and solid; the dining-room/lounge, where guests are watched by the stuffed chamois in the corner, is quite bare and wooden. Copper ornaments add warmth. The views make up for the lack of *en suite* facilities and the price makes it worth an overnight stop.

OPEN Only accessible during winter by ski depending on snow; closed May, Oct to Dec ROOMS 6 (none with bath or shower) (Credit cards not accepted)

CHALLES-LES-EAUX

Hôtel du Château

73190 Savoie
TEL 79 72 86 71; FAX 79 72 83 83

This is a grey stone castle in a tiny spa town just outside Chambéry. Bedrooms are a good size and without pretension. Depending on the weather, choose whether to eat in the sophisticated restaurant with its peach walls and grand fireplace or go for candle-lit romance on the terrace overlooking the parkland. Service is attentive at dinner, less so at breakfast, which is a help-yourself affair.

OPEN All year ROOMS 65 (48 with bath or shower) FACILITIES Outdoor pool, tennis

CHAMONIX-MONT-BLANC

Hermitage

rue des Cristalliers
74400 Haute-Savoie
TEL 50 53 13 87; FAX 50 55 98 14

This good three-star hotel has reasonable rates and is in a quiet location less than a ten-minute walk from the centre of Chamonix. The welcome is warm and friendly and the restaurant provides good local traditional food. Bedrooms are light and simply decorated.

OPEN Mid-Dec to end Sept ROOMS 30 (all with bath or shower) FACILITIES Fitness room, sauna

LA CHAPELLE-EN-VERCORS

Hôtel Bellier

26420 Drôme
TEL 75 48 20 03; FAX 75 48 25 31

One of the nicest hotels in the Vercors, the Bellier is a chalet-style building at the entrance to the village, raised far enough above the road to be free from noise. The interior is simple – bedrooms in alpine style with a lot of wood are cosy (though small) and equipped with welcome chocolates and a plug-in mosquito deterrent. The great advantage here is the garden, which is shady, peaceful and has a swimming-pool for hot days (you can also eat in the garden). It makes a good, family-run base from which to explore the Vercors, and the food has a good reputation too.

OPEN Mid-Jun to end Sept ROOMS 12 (all with bath or shower) FACILITIES Outdoor pool

COMBLOUX

Au Coeur des Prés

74920 Haute-Savoie
TEL 50 93 36 55; FAX 50 58 69 14

Rooms here are fairly standard, with simple wood furnishings; the ones at the top have more character but no balconies. A scenic location set above the village of Combloux with a friendly hotelier.

OPEN End May to end Sept, mid-Dec to Easter ROOMS 34 (all with bath) FACILITIES Sauna, jacuzzi, tennis, small fitness room

THE ALPS

DOUSSARD

Hôtel Marceau

Bout du Lac
74210 Doussard
Haute-Savoie
TEL 50 44 30 11

Well and truly off the bumpy beaten track, but worth finding for its friendly service and the breakfast terrace overlooking Annecy's lake, this is a traditional, family-run hotel of the 'they don't make them like this any more' variety. Bedrooms are interesting with antiques and gilt mirrors, all *en suite* except for number 39.

OPEN Early Feb to early Oct ROOMS 15 (all with bath or shower) FACILITIES Tennis

EVIAN

Hôtel le Savoy

17 quai Charles Besson
74500 Haute-Savoie
TEL 50 70 70 81; FAX 50 75 68 07

Le Savoy is an excellent central location, and its crumbly exterior belies the surprisingly modern interior. The bedrooms verge on the nondescript, but are modern, spacious and clean – most with balcony, so ask for a lake view. The restaurant is light and airy with a high ceiling and lots of plants and pictures.

OPEN All year ROOMS 24 (all with bath or shower)

La Verniaz

route d'Abondance
74500 Haute-Savoie
TEL 50 75 04 90; FAX 50 70 78 92

This tasteful and refined country house with a warm welcoming atmosphere is set above the town of Evian and surrounded by fields and meadows. The bedrooms are in a large cream house with bay windows, separate from the main building and restaurant. They are large and luxurious with good balconies and antique furniture.

OPEN Mid-Feb to mid-Nov ROOMS 35 (all with bath or shower) FACILITIES Heated outdoor pool, tennis, horse riding

GUILLESTRE

Les Barnières (I and II)

05600 Hautes-Alpes
TEL 92 45 05 07/92 45 04 87; FAX 92 45 28 74

These two hotels opposite each other make good bases for the Queyras mountains, with superb views from almost every angle. Bedrooms are simple and effective with dark wood carved furnishings and lacy white bedspreads. Public rooms are plentiful and restful, most with alpine views. Dining in the restaurant can be intoxicating if you go for the heavy local syrup-type apéritifs. The colour scheme is predominantly pink with high-backed chairs lending sophistication.

OPEN (I) Jun to end Sept (II) End Dec to mid-Oct ROOMS (I) 35, (II) 45 FACILITIES Both have outdoor swimming pools and tennis

LES HOUCHES

Peter Pan

Les Chavants
74310 Haute-Savoie
TEL 50 54 40 63

Peter Pan consists of two chalets camouflaged in the woods above the village with fine views from the terrace. Public rooms with wooden floorboards and ceilings are homely, with a clutter of flowers and ornaments and a collection of owls. Bedrooms vary in size and have character, slanting ceilings and more flowers. A popular place to have lunch.

OPEN Mid-Dec to mid-Oct ROOMS 14 (6 with bath or shower) (Credit cards not accepted)

LANSLEVILLARD

Les Prais

Val-Cenis
73480 Savoie
TEL 79 05 93 53; FAX 79 05 97 60

Simple and without airs and graces, the main attraction of this hotel is its central location. Rooms are basic, spacious and fresh with good bathrooms. Reasonably priced dinner menus are served in the cheerful, busy restaurant with friendly service and huge portions. Breakfast, a hearty help-yourself affair, is taken in a room where the hospital-waiting-room look is alleviated by goat skins and wooden skis hanging on the wall.

OPEN Mid-Jun to mid-Sept, mid-Dec to mid-Apr ROOMS 30 (all with bath or shower) FACILITIES Outdoor pool

LE LAVANCHER

Hôtel Beau Soleil

74400 Chamonix Mont Blanc
TEL 50 54 17 34; FAX 50 54 17 34

If you don't want to stay in Chamonix itself, but would prefer to be conveniently nearby, this simple Logis chalet hotel is a good place to choose, and in a good setting too, away from the busy valley road. The restaurant overlooks a pretty meadow and terrace, and the bedrooms, though on the small side, smell of fresh pine and are adequately comfortable.

OPEN Christmas to late Sept ROOMS 15 (all with bath or shower) FACILITIES Tennis

Hôtel du Jeu de Paume

705 route du Chapeau
Chamonix
74400 Haute-Savoie
TEL 50 54 03 76; FAX 50 54 10 75

This is a good-quality chalet-style hotel. Bedrooms are modern and bright with pine furnishings and thick carpets. The two lounges are pleasant places to relax; a stone fireplace, stone floors strewn with thick rugs, leather armchairs and antiques add to the overall impression of tasteful luxury. The restaurant is a small, simple and sophisticated affair with fine food and professional service; only the rather miserly breakfast lets it down. Not cheap.

OPEN Mid-Dec to early Nov ROOMS 24 (all with bath) FACILITIES Heated indoor pool, sauna, tennis

MANIGOD

Hôtel de la Croix Fry

Thones
74230 Haute-Savoie
TEL 50 44 90 16; FAX 50 44 94 87

This is about as perfect a chalet hotel as you can get. High up on the shoulder of the Col, with startling views of the Aravis chain, it is an utterly cosy, good-humoured place. The ground floor is largely open-plan with the space cleverly broken up by fleecy sofas and dozens of different artefacts salvaged from bygone alpine life. There's a bar, a huge picture window and a restaurant. Bedrooms, reached through a labyrinth of small stairs and passages, are universally comfortable, with old country furniture and rugs. Some are large; some are not; many have balconies.

OPEN Jun to end Sept, mid-Dec to end Apr ROOMS 12 (all with bath or shower) FACILITIES Heated outdoor pool, tennis

MEGEVE

Le Fer à Cheval

36 route du Crêt d'Arbois
74120 Haute-Savoie
TEL 50 21 30 39; FAX 50 93 07 60

Le Fer à Cheval is a traditional hotel with lots of character and a warm ambience. Bedrooms are in excellent condition with colourful matching fabrics and carved wood furniture, stylish yet unobtrusive. The lounge is made up of nooks, crannies and alcoves. Good food and impeccable service.

OPEN End Jun to early Sept, mid-Dec to Easter ROOMS 41 (all with bath) FACILITIES Outdoor pool (summer only), sauna, jacuzzi, solarium

MEILLERIE

Les Terrasses

74500 Haute-Savoie
TEL 50 76 04 06; FAX 50 76 05 95

Les Terrasses is a no-frills Geneva lakeside hotel just outside Meillerie – basic and priced accordingly. Bedrooms are small but those overlooking the lake have big balconies. Fine for an overnight stop.

OPEN Early Feb to mid-Jan ROOMS 13 (all with bath or shower)

MONTAILLEUR

La Tour de Pacoret

73460 Savoie
TEL 79 37 91 59; FAX 79 00 55 63

In a region where you can become a little bored with chalets, this is a hotel with a difference – an old watchtower in the Isère Valley not far from Albertville. It is at its best outside, for the stone building is a haunting old place; from its terrace (where you can eat spankingly good dinners in fine weather) there are excellent views over the valley. Inside, bedrooms are simply furnished, not large – the tower was built in a less lavish era than our own – but more than adequate. Steep stairs and a tiny sitting-room take up most of the rest of the interior. Extremely hard-working staff keep the place spotless and do everything possible to please.

OPEN Easter to early Nov ROOMS 10 (all with bath or shower)

THE ALPS

ST-GERVAIS

Chalet Rémy

Le Bettex
74170 Haute-Savoie
TEL 50 93 11 85; FAX 50 93 14 45

High on the shoulder of the mountain above St-Gervais, and with an enviable view of Mont Blanc, this is a very simple hotel – with a single open-plan ground floor, where the kitchen, bar and restaurant seem to melt into one another around the heavy timbers. Bedrooms are reached by a ladder stair and open off a first-floor gallery. Mostly, they are small, and you may well have to trundle down the passage in search of shower or lavatory, but they are entirely adequate. The food is substantial, with soups and casseroles featuring heavily on the menu. The mountainside starts right outside the hotel – this is an ideal spot for families.

OPEN All year ROOMS 19 (No baths or showers in rooms)

ST-LATTIER

Le Lièvre Amoureux

38840 Isère
TEL 76 64 50 67; FAX 76 64 31 21

This is a creeper-covered house opposite a field of sugar cane, where guests can take apéritifs and, if they choose, eat on the terrace at the unusual brightly coloured tables of chipped stone and tiles. The main house contains public rooms – quite stylish with beamed ceilings and antique furnishings. The bedrooms are in two separate buildings, old-fashioned and interesting in the old house, modern, fresh and spacious in the new annexe.

OPEN Mid-Feb to mid-Oct ROOMS 12 (all with bath) FACILITIES Outdoor pool

ST-VERAN

Les Chalets du Villard

05350 Hautes-Alpes
TEL 92 45 82 08; FAX 92 45 86 22

The nicest hotel in St-Véran offers breakfast on a little suntrap of a wooden terrace overhanging the valley. Each room has its own cooking facilities, making it ideal for families or the budget-conscious. All is simple and rustic with effective use made of wood. The restaurant is an atmospheric place to eat, with food cooked before you on the brick grill.

OPEN End Dec to Easter, end Jun to end Sept ROOMS 25 (all with bath or shower) FACILITIES Tennis

TALLOIRES

Hôtel Beau Site

74290 Haute-Savoie
TEL 50 60 71 04; FAX 50 60 79 22

There is no shortage of choice when it comes to hotels in Talloires, but if you want somewhere comparatively inexpensive, and with good food, then this is your best bet. In actual fact the hotel is made by its location rather than by the intrinsic merit of the building or its rooms, for the long garden slopes straight down to Lake Annecy and the views from the lake-facing rooms are superb. Bedrooms are modern and bland; there is, dare one say it, a certain lack of golden youth among the clientele, but the food is not to be sniffed at (nor the well-chosen wine list) and the welcome is friendly.

OPEN Early May to early Oct ROOMS 18 (all with bath or shower) FACILITIES Tennis

VILLARD DE LANS

Hôtel Eterlou

38250 Isère
TEL 76 95 17 65; FAX 76 95 91 41

Situated in a sleepy location in an otherwise lively resort, the Eterlou has a certain charm though it is not particularly stylish. The furnishings and colour schemes are a bit of a mish-mash and the public rooms cluttered but cosy. Bedrooms are a good size and pleasant, if a little dated. The pool area and grassy verge make a peaceful place to park your sun-lounger.

OPEN Early Jun to early Sept, mid-Dec to end Mar ROOMS 24 (all with bath) FACILITIES Heated outdoor pool, sauna, tennis

YVOIRE

Hôtel Restaurant du Port

74140 Haute-Savoie
TEL 50 72 80 17; FAX 50 72 90 71

Hôtel Restaurant du Port is in a superb location next to the port and Lake Geneva. The four rooms are modern, clean and comfortable, and the lake views make up for the lack of atmosphere. The terrace is panoramic and has reasonably priced food.

OPEN Mid-Mar to end Oct ROOMS 4 (all with bath or shower)

Bonifacio

Nor stones, nor timber, nor the art of building constitute a state; but wherever men are who know how to defend themselves, there is a city and a fortress

[Alcæus]

CORSICA

Over 150km of Mediterranean separate Corsica from mainland France: once or twice a year in certain weather conditions a mirage of its mountains can be glimpsed from high points of the Riviera. Superb mountain scenery rising to great peaks (the highest over 2,700 metres) takes up much of the area and its centre is a Regional Park. Geology made its western coast more beautiful than that to the east, and divided it into many distinctive areas. Geography gave it a coveted position in the busiest part of the western Mediterranean, and history brought successive invaders, driving its inhabitants inland or abroad in a pattern that formed the extremes of Corsican character.

Greeks, Etruscans, Carthaginians and Romans were followed by Vandals, Byzantines and Saracens before Christian powers disputed possession in the early Middle Ages. The Papacy gave it to Pisan bishops, but after a century or so of gentle rule the naval supremacy of the Genoese took over. They encircled the island with fierce little watchtowers and created citadel towns which were effectively Italian colonies. The Genoese shook off invasions by the king of Aragon (another Papal protégé) and the French (involved in a struggle with Charles V), and had comparatively little trouble with the Corsicans themselves, who suffered (or ignored) a feudal regime of their own. The Corsican seigneurs' idly autocratic habits of aggrandisement and vendetta finally produced a rebellious national consciousness, born of poverty and frustration. If Napoleon Bonaparte had never existed, Corsica's most famous man would be Pascal Paoli, who returned from exile in Italy with plans for a coup, a constitution and a Corsican democracy. He inspired and directed Corsican energies, and for 14 years the island achieved a beleaguered independence. By 1768 the Genoese had had enough; preoccupied elsewhere, they ceded Corsica to France. French troops defeated Paoli, but nationalism was unsuppressed: the English sent a supporting fleet, and the future admiral Nelson learnt a lot of strategy (and lost an eye) in subsequent events. But in 1796, post-Revolutionary France settled Corsica in two *départements* following the old Genoese division of *'en deça des monts'*, ruled from Bastia, and *'au delà des monts'* under Ajaccio. Later, Napoleon made the island a single unit

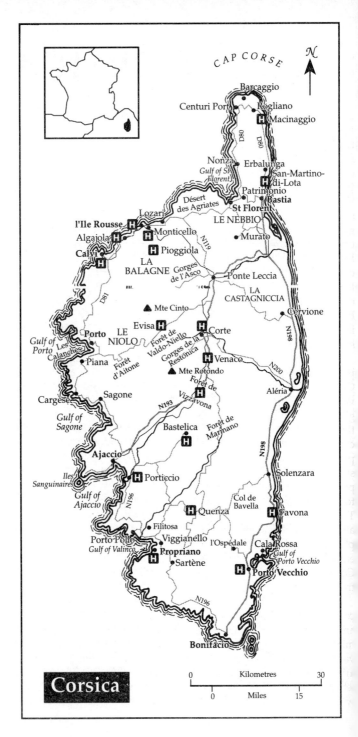

CAP CORSE

N

Barcaggio
Centuri Port
Rogliano
Macinaggio

D80
D80

Nonza
Erbalunga
Gulf of St
Florent)
San-Martino-
di-Lota
Patrimonio
Bastia
St Florent
LE NEBBIO

Désert
des Agriates
Lozari
Murato
l'Ile Rousse
Monticello
Algajola
N119
Calvi
Pioggiola
LA
BALANGE
Gorges
de l'Asco
Ponte Leccia
LA
CASTAGNICCIA
D81
Cervione
Mte Cinto
Evisa
Corte
N198
Porto
LE
NIOLO
Forêt de
Valdo-Niello
Gulf of
Porto
Les
Calanches
Gorges de la
Restonica
Piana
Forêt
d'Aitone
Venaco
Mte Rotondo
Forêt de
Vizzavona
Cargese
Sagone
Aléria
Gulf of
Sagone
N193
Bastelica
Forêt de
Marmano
N198
Ajaccio
Iles
Sanguinaires
Porticcio
Solenzara
Gulf of
Ajaccio
N196
Col de
Bavella
Favona
Quenza
Filitosa
l'Ospédale
Cala Rossa
Porto Pollo
Viggianello
Gulf of Valinco
Propriano
Gulf of
Porto Vecchio
Sartène
Porto Vecchio
N196
Bonifacio

Corsica

0   Kilometres   30

0   Miles   15

with Ajaccio as its *préfecture*; since 1975 it has been divided back again, into Haute-Corse and Corse-du-Sud.

Nearly half the islanders are corsophone, although few are exclusively so; there are two dialects, the north-eastern one more Latin, and the south-western one closer to the primitive Pyrenean languages. During the last 30 years the Corsicans' strong sense of regional identity has sharpened into angry and frequently violent separatism, as local feeling has in so many places. Whether the increasingly violent modes of expression are signs of increasingly widespread separatist feeling in the population as a whole is doubtful. An opinion poll in 1975, at the height of the troubles, indicated that over half the population was satisfied with Corsica's constitutional status, a large minority wanted a greater degree of autonomy within the Republic, and only three per cent wanted independence. The clandestine *Front National pour la Libération de la Corse*, responsible for most of the acts of terrorism, was estimated to have numbered no more than a few score activists and a few hundred supporters. In 1982 Corsica was duly granted a greater degree of autonomy than it had previously enjoyed, and than any other French region. A couple of FNLC attacks made the British newspapers in 1991 and 1992, but most tourists are only likely to see the graffiti on signposts.

Corsica is a collection of landscapes, each with its own characteristics. In the north-east, rugged grey schist rock forms the long spine of Cap Corse and the complex relief of the Castagniccia's ridges and valleys. The larger central mountain mass is many-coloured granite in giant tilted blocks; powerful rivers have gouged out valleys through the parallel ridges, and erosion has produced dramatic distorted configurations. In the west the ridges slope to a coast of bays and promontories; to the east they drop down to a flat plain behind a much straighter shoreline. There are alpine pastures among the high central peaks, above slopes of magnificent pines; lower down, rich chestnut forests and fertile valleys where vines, olives and orchards can flourish. The famous Corsican *maquis* covers over half the island – an evergreen and often impenetrable mass of low-growing trees, shrubs, climbing plants and fragrant herbs, scented all year and flowering brilliantly in early summer. A less attractive, but now all too frequent, feature of Corsican landscapes is the black stubble and skeletal shapes of lifeless trees produced by forest fires.

For centuries, the Corsicans retreated inland from their invaded coasts. They lived in mountain communes, shepherding huge flocks up and down according to the season, farming land only to provide for minimal needs and building from local materials the villages which vary so attractively from region to region. Poverty, pride and what amounted to imprisonment in their own country produced both lethargy and the high tension of internal vendettas. Those who could went abroad – emigration was the only route to fortune. Despite their resentment at being handed over to the French, the Corsicans took full advantage of their new status – Napoleon was among the first to benefit from French education and opportunities for advancement. The island grew ever poorer and more neglected as its younger talent departed to careers in France, particularly in the police, the army and the colonial service. After the Second World War much coastal land was cleared of its malarial mosquitoes, but government grants to develop Corsican agriculture chiefly benefited immigrants from Algeria, able and willing to apply modern methods to farming the fertile eastern plain.

Tourism in Corsica is a comparatively recent phenomenon, concentrated round the tiny fishing villages (*marines*) of the coast and further depopulating the interior – except when expatriate Corsicans return for summer family reunions. Fine beaches and the Mediterranean climate have attracted increasing crowds over the last 30 years, and holiday accommodation is now crammed to capacity each season. French and Italian visitors predominate, but an increasing number of British too are discovering the wild beauty of the island. Development is still low-key; the cost of importing materials and consumer goods is high, and holidays in Corsica are not cheap. *Cuisine*, though mainly French, is not *haute*. Food in the resorts is more often basic and international – steak, spaghetti, pizzas, ice-cream. Fish is varied but expensive. Corsican food includes game in season, sheep and goat cheeses, chestnut-flavoured sweetmeats, pâté made from blackbirds and a variety of *charcuterie* from the island's small native pigs. Wines range from fruity whites to powerful reds, and there are local *eaux-de-vie* and liqueurs like *cédratine*, made from Corsica's variant of the lemon. Shops under the name '*Produits Corses*' sell ethnic eatables, while '*Maisons Artisanats*' promote the island's traditional crafts.

Unless you are content to stay on your idyllic beach, you need a car for exploring. Public transport is limited, and coach trips inadequate. There is, however, a narrow-gauge railway that runs from Ajaccio through the natural park to Calvi and Bastia, worth taking for some spectacular views.

Roads inland are plentiful, but driving is a test of skill and patience; even the central artery from Ajaccio through Corte to Bastia has its steep hairpin bends, and the lesser narrow roads are tortuous and very tiring. Watch out for local pigs straying onto the road! Corsicans seem to drive with the venom once reserved for vendettas, and use signposts for target practice and graffiti. The tourist must crawl with caution, and on a long excursion carry spare petrol. The scenery is ample reward.

The West

Corsica's biggest bay, the **Golfe d'Ajaccio**, is the arrival point for many British visitors whether by boat or into the island's biggest airport. The great curve of busy blue water with a backdrop of mountain slopes is best seen from the point at **Porticcio**, a bright little modern beach resort on one of the sandy coves spreading south; the rocky north shore of the Golfe ends at the Pointe de la Parata and its Genoese tower. Out to sea are the little **Iles Sanguinaires**, the largest topped by an old light-house: they are a popular boat excursion, though there's nothing much to see.

Ajaccio is tucked into the north-west corner of the Golfe on its own bay, with a citadel – built by the French when the town was predomi-nantly Genoese – as menacing to landward as over the sea. The high blocks of Ajaccio's modern skyline give it an air of urban sophistication rare in Corsica, and its busy streets are lively and commercial by day, illuminated and conversational at night. The division of Corsica in 1975 into two *départements*, giving Bastia equal status, has not diminished the pride of a town that takes its name from Homer's Ajax and bred the greatest modern Frenchman. Napoleon confronts you everywhere. Near the port in place Maréchal-Foch his statue, classically robed, is guarded by four lions drooling into the fountain below – the surrounding palm trees and café life are less reminiscent of Trafalgar Square. In the vast place Général de Gaulle, Viollet-le-Duc's monument (locally known as The Inkstand) has him on horseback in his toga, above his four (unmounted) brothers; and further west he surveys the town from a long flight of steps, in the familiar cutaway coat and bicorne hat. The main shopping street (the cours Napoleon) borders Ajaccio's Old Town, a small appealingly shabby area of tall houses, cafés and pizzerias below the citadel – which is an army barracks and not open to the public. The 16th-century cathedral is unremarkable; the Buonaparte tombs were moved to their own 'Imperial Chapel' near the Palais Fesch.

Sights in Ajaccio

● **Maison Buonaparte** Empire-style rooms with genealogy, busts, photographs of portraits: little of interest.
● **Musée Fesch** Notable collection of Italian paintings from five centu-ries assembled by one of Napoleon's uncles: includes Bellini, Botticelli, Titian, Raphael.

From Ajaccio the N193 heads off into the island's interior, the inland route to Bastia on the north-east coast followed also by one of the most scenic railways in the world. For drivers, the first 20km up the river Gravona is an untypically fast introduction to Corsican mountain roads; another ten kilometres brings you up to the **Col de Vizzavona**, where there is a ruined Genoese fort and tremendous views. Beyond lies the **Forêt de Vizzavona**, where the steep slopes below the snowline are covered with *laricio* pines. Immensely tall, straight and strong, their trunks were used for ships' masts – and at one time imported by England to be chopped into railway sleepers. Before the watershed of the Col, the spreading hamlets of **Bocognano** among pines and beautiful chestnut trees formed one of the last bandit strongholds. In a domain called 'the green palace' the Bonelli dynasty spanned the 19th century. Bonelli *père* had three 'wives' and 18 children – a variant on the family name was Bellacoscia, 'beautiful thighs' – and controlled miles of valley pasturage. His eldest sons were the blackest of his sheep, with a huge price on their heads for many murders. Unbetrayed, and under official amnesty, they raised a company of musketeers and fought in the war of 1870 – only to take to the *maquis* again when it was over. Antoine (the eldest) was caught at the age of 75, but allowed to return to Bocognano where he died in 1912, aged 99, honoured as 'royalty in the *maquis*'.

A road runs 20km south from Bocognano to Bastelica over the **Scalella Pass**. It is very narrow, tortuous and steep, but it brings you close to the superb mountain landscape – gorges twisting on all sides, valleys dropping sheer below, cliffs soaring skyward – and about four kilometres from Bocognano it passes Corsica's highest waterfall, a slim torrent spreading into a wide delicate shimmer named the Bridal Veil. From the bleak top of the Col there are views far over the northern peaks; a less hazardous southern descent brings you to the hospitable little community of **Bastelica**, a favourite summer excursion from Ajaccio, surrounded by walks and climbs. Sampiero Corso was born here in 1498: during a melodramatically heroic career he succeeded in briefly liberating Corsica from Genoese rule, but was betrayed and murdered by relatives of his wife. Years before, Sampiero had killed her for suspected treason and infidelity; the family vendetta overruled patriotism. In Bastelica a bronze statue brandishing an urgent sword catches the fiery spirit of the man. From here, the D27 runs down through meadows and vineyards back to the coast; a more spectacular but much more difficult loop through **Tolla** follows the river Prunelli's gorges to its 1950s dam.

North of the Gulf of Ajaccio, the **Golfe de Sagone** has a number of small resorts scattered round it. Near **Calcatoggio** at the mouth of the river Liscia a small development straggles along a rather scruffy beach with few facilities, one or two simple but pleasant quiet hotels and some self-catering. Further north lies **Sagone**. The nearby ruins of a 12th-century cathedral, a menhir, and a Genoese watchtower indicate former settlements, but this little seaside resort is entirely modern and not particularly appealing. At the northern tip of the gulf lies the pretty red-roofed village of **Cargèse**, its houses rising in neat tiers on the steep hillside. A tiny port lies far below at the foot of the hill. Formerly a Greek colony for refugees from Turkish persecution, Cargèse still has a Greek Orthodox church, which stares gravely across at its Catholic counterpart on the other side of the valley. There are sandy beaches – notably the lovely and long Pero, with hotels and some self-catering. These resorts are good for very peaceful beach holidays, but there's little to do; a car is essential even for beach-hopping.

The only coastline included in Corsica's Regional Park, the **Golfe de Porto** with its northern bay the **Golfe de Girolata** is varied, beautiful and spectacular. Its most celebrated stretch is to the south, where the corniche road runs along **Les Calanche**: not sea-inlets like the Calanques of the Midi, but red granite cliffs eroded into a chaos of fantastic forms, with twisted needles rising above the pine trees in a glowing backdrop particularly wonderful at sunset. Two small but very popular resorts, Porto and Piana, monopolise this glorious scenery. **Piana** is just a small scattered village, a short but tortuous drive from two pretty beaches. **Arone**, back across Capo Rosso, is a crescent of gently shelving pale sand; and the **Anse de Ficajola**, approached by a precipitous series of hairpin bends and a steep walk, contains an exquisite cove of pink sand with steep red cliffs all around and a stream flowing through it – an idyll discovered by motorists, who crowd there in season. **Porto** is a small modern resort at the bottom of a steep lane. Its buildings are constructed from a version of the local stone, but somehow they lack charm, and have a curiously barrack-like appearance from above. The street leading down to the port is lined with shops, cafés and hotels; more hotels and fast-food restaurants cluster round the harbour area. The beach, divided from the port by a tall rock with a Genoese tower and approached by an arched footbridge, is grey shingle and pebbles, uncomfortable to walk on and shelving steeply at the waterline. Facilities are surprisingly poor for such a popular resort. Further round the gulf are several more sand-and-shingle beaches, but most are difficult to get to. The scenery on the local roads is magnificent – red rocks and eucalyptus trees.

The red granite of Les Calanche continues inland to the savage splendour of the **Gorges de Spelunca**; from Porto, small roads each side of the river run high along the mountainside to meet at the point where the Aitona torrent and its tributary the Lonca form the river Porto. A footpath from the crossroads (many cliff steps) leads down nearer the rushing waters, which are invisible from the roads. Upstream, the D84 continues a winding course to the little town of **Evisa**, set on a high terrace of chestnut trees overlooking the dramatic peaks and cliffs. From this peaceful spot walkers can explore in many directions; one footpath leads to a celebrated viewpoint down into the Spelunca, another descends to follow its bed. Beyond Evisa, chestnuts and red rock give way to immense *laricio* pines in the **Fôret d'Aitone**, climbing to the **Col de Vergio** which is the highest road in Corsica, kept open with snow ploughs in the winter.

Over the ridge, another great forest begins. The towering pines of the **Valdo-Niello** stretch down to the high plateau region called Niello or **Niolo**, enclosed and isolated among the mountain tops. In the range to the north, **Monte-Cinto** (2,710 metres) rises highest of all Corsica's peaks. The river Golo runs through the plateau, disappearing northeastward down its own spectacular gorge, the **Scala di Santa Regina**: for centuries this 'staircase' was the only way in or out of the region when the Col de Vergio was snowed up. The Niolin shepherds would bring enormous flocks of sheep and goats down to the western coast for the winter, and each summer return to the high mountain pastures dotted with grey stone shepherds' huts. The fertile Golo valley grew chestnuts in abundance and sufficient food for each flock-owning family; the pastoral economy required only a small labour force, and a mere handful of villages lie around the little 'capital', **Calacuccia**. The 20th century has brought changes. Flocks are smaller, shepherds fewer; ewes' milk goes to 'the Continent' to make Roquefort cheese instead of being processed in the *cave* under each neat stone house. Farming, like forestry, has become more organised. In the 1960s a massive dam, part of a hydro-electric scheme and reservoir system, created a large peaceful lake south of Calacuccia. The Niolo remains an area strong in Corsican crafts and traditions. The three-day *Fête de la Santa* each September, when the miraculous statue of the Virgin is carried in procession from the church at Calacuccia, keeps alive the chanting songs of the shepherds.

Back on the coast, the D81 twists and climbs north across the western slopes of the Regional Park's mountains, and on behind an inhospitable rocky shoreline. The bay of Galéria is an exception: there's a village with simple accommodation near a couple of good beaches, one naturist. **Calvi** is one of Corsica's historic citadel towns and now one of its most crowded summer resorts. The long sandy beach lies east of the town, gently shelving and safe, well-supplied with cafés and water sports, looking past the harbour to the mighty Citadel on its jutting promontory. The newer part of town stretches along the busy port: Quai Landry is palm-lined and pretty, much congested with traffic and animated (especially at night) with open-air restaurants and cafés. The streets behind hold all the requirements of a modern resort – noisy nightlife is concentrated in the Rue Clemenceau – and also considerable charm. Among the red roofs and creamy-grey façades rises the Baroque tower of the lower town's plain white church, begun in 1744 but not completed until 1938; below the Hôtel de Ville are vivid terraced gardens of palms and flowering shrubs. The Citadel on its high rock dominates all. Massive walls of ochre granite blocks slope up to the tall clustered buildings of the enclosed Old Town – another world, of ancient grey houses, twisting cobbled streets and a splendid rampart walk. The

Calvi

Genoese and their financiers fortified it in the 15th century; the town had been completely Genoese in loyalty for 200 years. It stood out against the French in two sieges in the 1550s, the women of Calvi joining their menfolk on the ramparts; it resisted the Corsican patriotism of Pascal Paoli, who in 1758 founded another town up the coast – L'Ile Rousse – as a centre of opposition. In 1794 it finally capitulated to the bombardment of the English fleet. After several weeks of this 'siege of 30,000 bullets' the defenders could only throw stones – one of which cost Nelson his right eye. Two years later the English left, and Calvi became as French as the rest of Corsica. Among the houses reduced to rubble was the alleged birthplace of Christopher Columbus in 1441, a time when to be Corsican was not so different from being Genoese; Calvi has as fair a claim as Genoa and marks the spot with a plaque. The Genoese Governor's Palace is today occupied by the Foreign Legion.

Sights in Calvi

● **Eglise St-Jean-Baptiste** The old Cathedral's octagonal cupola rises above the jostle of red-tiled roofs and its austere white 16th-century façade dominates the sloping Place d'Armes. The airy interior, a Greek cross, contains various treasures: notably an ebony Christ (credited with the miraculous lifting of one French siege) and a robed Spanish Virgin. Both are carried in festival processions – indeed throughout Corsica the portage of sheer weight seems to earn penitential merit points.

561

• **Oratoire St-Antoine** Elegant 15th-century chapel overlooking the bay, a storehouse for religious objects and works of art from the 16th to 19th centuries.

To the north **Algajola** is a small, mainly modern resort set on a long sandy beach, with small simple hotels. There's not much to see, apart from some unconvincingly restored Genoan fortifications in what little is left of the old town, but there is easy access to Calvi and L'Ile-Rousse on the little railway line that runs along this part of this coast. Close by, the little **Marine de St-Ambroggio** has self-catering complexes and villas, a Club Med village, water sports and several small sandy beaches.

L'Ile Rousse is a major resort and sizeable town which takes its name from the reddish rocks of the promontory, La Pietra, that juts out to sea beyond the port. Popular with French visitors, it gets very crowded in high season. There's a lively main square with open-air cafés under shady trees, *pétanque* players, a church at one end and a market place like a Hollywood mock-up of a Greek temple to one side. The main beach is of very fine, gently shelving white sand, with plenty of sports and facilities; the town has a number of nightspots. If you speak reasonable French, it is worth visiting the Océanographic Museum, whose curator, Pierre Pernod, gives talks about underwater life, scooping live lobsters and crabs from tanks and encouraging the audience to handle them. East of L'Ile-Rousse lie more sandy beaches, notably at **Lozari**, a peaceful area with a holiday village at one end. This is the last of Corsica's western holiday coast: the island's north-west corner is the arid, empty **Désert des Agriates**, a region of bare mountain slopes, blistering summer heat and almost no vegetation. A few dry-stone huts, the only signs of habitation, remain from the days when herds of goats were brought here for the winter; now a goat would starve, and even the *maquis* has given up.

The railway services between Calvi and L'Ile-Rousse and inland through the mountains, the plentiful coach and boat excursions, and the interest of Calvi itself make this one area where you might holiday without a car; yet it would be a pity not to explore the region behind the coastal strip. The **Balagne** is a green and fertile area of wooded hills, lush valleys and many charming villages, threaded with little roads and ideal for leisurely touring. Throughout Corsica's history her invaders have enjoyed this region: the Romans first cultivated it, the Moors in the Middle Ages left some flat-roofed cubic villages among the more characteristic red tiles and huddled grey walls, and the Papal forces who expelled the Moors built scores of pretty churches. This 'garden of Corsica' flourished like nowhere else in the island, growing olives, oranges, figs and almonds as well as the vines which still produce good wines. As the coast developed, it grew rather neglected and depopulated. But there was a deliberate revival in the 1960s, concentrating also on re-establishing local crafts: woodcarving, pottery, baskets and recently glass. Each village has an individual appeal: sometimes a splendid setting against a mountain forest (**Zilia, Speloncato**); sometimes perched with panoramic views (**Lumio, Montemaggiore**); many nestle in a valley or cling half-hidden to a sheltered hillside. The churches too have their own individual appeal and a variety of general style: at **Aregno** the green and white chequerboard building with strange little carved figures on the façade is Pisan Romanesque, while at **Corbara** the 18th-century choir is ornamented with splendidly Baroque carved marble columns. One of the tiniest villages, **Pigna**, is a thriving centre both of crafts – in its official *maison d'artisanat* – and of local gastronomic specialities. Its Casa Musicale holds concerts every Tuesday during the tourist season.

The North

The **Golfe de St-Florent**, between the Désert des Agriates and Cap Corse's mountain ridge, is deep and sheltered: the little town on a rocky outcrop in its inner curve enjoys an almost lakeside setting. **St-Florent** was built by the Genoese in the 1440s below a fine fortress tower (later the Gendarmerie) and kept its strategic value through Corsica's history of conquest. In 1793 when the conquerors were briefly the English, Nelson was moved to declare, 'Give me the Gulf of St-Florent and two frigates, and not a single ship could leave Marseille or Toulon' – but was never given the chance to prove his point. In the 18th and 19th centuries, the town became neglected and almost depopulated because of the malaria-breeding marshlands round the river Aliso; in the 20th it has new life – tourist development spreads along the road to Bastia and the harbour is enlarged for pleasure craft. Hotels, villas and campsites are overwhelmed by the high-season crowds. A pebble beach stretches east along the bay, and sand west of the reedy rivermouth; but the life of this tiny, pretty resort is concentrated in its shaded central square, the harbour and the oldest streets. Alleys and steps wind between tall houses of faded honey-grey, shuttered and crumbling, along the water's very edge. The port is lined with restaurants and souvenir shops, and in the sandy square open-air eating surrounds the games of *pétanque* and the strolling crowds.

Sights in St-Florent

• **Cathédrale de Nebbio** Nearly a kilometre away among the vineyards this 12th-century Pisan church (collect the key from the town tourist office) alone remains of the former Nebbio capital. It is built of pale limestone blocks in a serenely graceful design of tall blind arches; the interior capitals are intricately carved with curious animals, entwined snakes and snail-like motifs. Among the gilded wooden figures, Saint Flor is preserved under glass.

The **Nebbio** is the compact region immediately behind the Golfe de St-Florent, a landscape of fertile hills and valleys encircled by mountains; the Col de Teghime and the more impressive **Défile de Lacone** cross the bridge to Bastia and the east coast. Like the Balagne, the Nebbio has vineyards, orchards, meadows and picturesque villages; local characteristics are houses built of the same thin brownish stone slabs as the many dry-stone walls, and green-tiled roofs. **Oletta** and tiny **San-Pietro-di-Tenda** are the most beautifully set. Of many attractive churches, that of **Murato** is outstanding (literally too, on its own ridge less than a kilometre from the village). The Eglise St-Michel is a remarkable concentration of Pisan Romanesque and more barbaric decorative elements. Its simple rectangle has a tall western bell tower (added in the 19th century), half supported on fat round columns of alternating white and green slabs; the entire church is motley, but not always in regular layers – in places the green and white looks like some haphazard crossword. Around windows and blind arches, and in less likely places, there is a mass of carving – symbolic beasts, enigmatic figures and Biblical themes (such as Eve being tempted by the serpent with the apple in its mouth). To the north of the Nebbio, at **Patrimonio**, a south-facing amphitheatre of vines produces white, red and particularly rosé wines of some reputation. The local *vignerons* formed a co-operative in the 1960s, and visitors are welcome to taste.

St-Michel at Murato

The long narrow peninsula of **Cap Corse** stretching north of the island is a distinctly different part of Corsica. Its dorsal ridge, dropping steeply to the west and more gradually to the east, is grey schist and slate and sometimes serpentine rock; beaches are mostly grey-green shingle; buildings are weathered and grey, roofed with green tiles or heavier stone. Despite the cool colours, the north of the island is hot: the climate here produces good vines, olives, and the Corsican version of the lemon called the *cédrat*. The peninsula is ringed with Genoese watchtowers and old villages. Even before tourism turned each *marine* into a budding resort, the inhabitants of Cap Corse took more interest in the sea than was habitual in the rest of the island: rather than shepherds they were historically fishermen, sailors and (by economic necessity) traders. Their ports still thrive, while the villages up in the interior are inevitably becoming depopulated. The confident corniche road marked on the maps is narrow in the west and more pot-holed – look out for roadworks.

Almost every village seems to have its watchtower: that at **Nonza** is proudly perched on a vertiginous black rock, and lichen-grey houses cluster at the edge of a cliff round the central square and the Eglise Ste-Julie. Far down zig-zagging cliff steps is Ste-Julie's marble shrine and 'fountain'. Twin jets of water represent the two miraculous springs that rose at her grisly martyrdom, when before strangling her the Roman soldiers cut off her breasts and tossed them away. Nonza's other story concerns the tower: after a noisy siege its Corsican commander relinquished it to the French in 1768 only after demanding that its garrison be allowed to depart with full military honours, banners flying, transport provided . . . the French accepted the conditions, but only one man emerged to receive their ceremony. The patriots had prudently abandoned Nonza, and a solitary veteran had put up a splendid bluff.

The dark grey beach beyond the town is vast but deserted. North at **Albo**, asbestos mines were opened after the Second World War and abandoned in 1965; waste matter from the old workings became deposited along the shore. Albo itself has a tiny cluster of shops and houses and a greenish-pebbled beach. Then comes a succession of prettier villages among vines and olives, fruit and flowers. **Pino**, where a road heads east to the other coast, is an attractive little centre with a petrol station as well as pretty houses; tall cypresses shade a cemetery, and the village seems full of chapels. **Centuri-Port** on its small bay has now been thoroughly discovered, and pleasure boats share its pretty harbour with the lobster-fishers. In a setting of utter charm below the *maquis*-covered hills it has old pink and grey houses green-roofed with serpentine, plus hotels, restaurants and a disco.

The D80 swings east from the Col de Serra, but lesser roads lead to the northern extremity of Cap Corse where **Tollare and Barcaggio** are tiny clusters of fishermen's houses looking out to the **ilot de la Giraglia**, a huge rock of serpentine with a lighthouse on top. Winding across the peninsula, the D80 reaches the outskirts of **Rogliano**, a commune of hamlets, churches and a ruined seigneurial château up a short mountain detour – it has a particularly beautiful setting of olives, vines and splendid chestnut trees. The first village on the east coast, **Macinaggio**, is its *marine*; there are water sports in the shingly bay, and a *Produits Corses* shop selling local wine, delicacies and souvenirs. The beach at **Porticciolo** is much more attractive. **Sisco** has its little *marine*, but the hamlets inland up a green windswept valley are more interesting. In the Middle Ages, Sisco was a commune of metal-workers, and at Balba the Eglise St-Martin (limited opening hours) contains a famous hidden treasury including a saint's skull encased in silver-gilt. Further up the valley are more churches, and cypress-shaded cemeteries; but the *maquis* is gaining ground in the meadows, and many of the people have gone.

To reach **Erbalunga** you turn seaward off the corniche road, down to a venerable huddle of picturesque houses lapped by the waves on their tongue of schist rock, protected behind the remains of a massive watchtower. Fishing boats still use the colourful harbour that attracts painters, photographers and – inevitably – crowds of tourists in summer. Behind, there are ranks of terraced houses and appealing little squares. Erbalunga retains both charm and tradition: at Easter, a processional march takes in all the nearby villages and churches, culminating in a torchlit *Granitola*.

South of here the *marines* come into the magnetic field of Bastia, Corsica's big industrial town. **Lavasina** has a celebrated shrine to the Virgin, and **Miomo** a particularly well-preserved Genoese tower complete with machicolations. A much more pleasant (but longer) drive takes you through the leafy villages of San Martino di Lota, with some prosperous houses of Bastia's 'stockbroker belt'. In the flatter terrain of the cape's east coast, on a road double the width of that in the west, it is easy to speed up, declare the villages dull (which, comparatively, they are) and miss Erbalunga altogether. For a day's tour of Cap Corse it is in fact much better to drive anti-clockwise, saving the west coast for the afternoon sun. The round trip is 180km.

The East

At the foot of Cap Corse and the beginning of Corsica's long east-coast plain, **Bastia** faces Italy across the islands (Elba, Capraia) of the Tuscan Strait. Here in 1380 the Genoese built their first *bastiglia* (donjon), to protect the only natural harbour on this coastline exposed to the stormy south-easterly *libeccio*. A century later they set a Governor's Palace inside their Terra-Nova and fortified their stronghold with citadel walls. Non-Genoese residents were mostly kept out: around the harbour, Corsicans lived in the more accessible Terra-Vecchia. As garrison town,

Bastia harbour

commercial port and administrative capital Bastia held almost uninterrupted supremacy until, after Corsica became part of France in 1811,
bourgeois Ajaccio was made its capital. Bastia – still the vital centre of
commerce and industry – continued to expand as far as the inland
mountains allowed, and in separate phases, the most intensive after the
Second World War. Now its main industrial zone is to the north, its
newest residential development spreading south. Ajacciens (and other
Corsicans) still tend to think of it as an Italian city planted on their
island, but its vital function in the economy was recognised when in
1975 Bastia regained equal status, as the Préfecture of Haute-Corse.

British tourists arriving here by air or sea can (and do) look with
dismay at its teeming charmless sprawl and leave immediately for the
island's interior or the west coast. The town is not well endowed with
hotels, and the new-sprung resorts along the sandy beaches to the
south lack scenic appeal. But Bastia is an agglomeration of distinctive
zones: its older quarters, shabby through long neglect, have historic
appeal and some lively atmosphere. Behind the modern harbour the
vast tree-shaded place St-Nicolas is the town's social centre, animated
day and night and lined with café terraces. From its southern end you
reach Terra-Vecchia, a dense network of decaying narrow lanes whose
18th-century houses rise to eight storeys above the street-level
commerce and crafts, around the Hôtel de Ville's colourful market
square. The Vieux Port beyond is the most picturesque part, where the

network becomes a maze of shuttered façades linked Naples-style by lines of washing, behind the quayside cafés and boutiques. Walk round to the harbour's southern Jetée du Dragon for the classic view of Bastia's ancient waterfront across the yachts and fishing boats: out to sea are the islands and (on a clear day) the mountains of Italy. Above here the Citadel, Terra-Nova, is reached through the green-terraced Jardin du Romieu and a postern gate in the refurbished ramparts. Within, the crenellated fort that was the Genoese governors' palace dominates the Place du Donjon, and Bastia's oldest houses fill the twisting alleys round the peaceful little place Guasco.

Sights in Bastia

• **Terra-Vecchia churches** The twin towers of St-Jean-Baptiste's classical 17th-century façade rise high above the houses; its vast interior displays quantities of 18th-century stucco, statues and paintings. The Chapelle de la Conception holds religious works of art luxuriously surrounded by Genoese velvet; the Chapelle St-Roch has copious Florentine carving.

• **Terra-Nova churches** A cathedral from 1570 to 1801, the Eglise Ste-Marie is grandiloquent Genoese Baroque. Its Assumption of the Virgin, a massive 18th-century group of chiselled silver, is somehow carried round all the old streets in procession each 15 August. The modest little Chapelle Ste-Croix has an astonishing interior resembling a Louis XVI theatre: golden arabesques and little angels frolic across its sky-blue ceiling. A curtained niche holds a dramatically contrasting crucifix, the blackened wooden Christ des Miracles found floating in the sea in 1428.

• **Musée d'Ethnographie Corse** Inside the former governors' palace; successive rooms trace Corsica's animal and mineral history, from arsenic ore to Napoleon's death mask.

South of Bastia a vast expanse of desolate grey sand stretches for miles between the sea and a huge reed-fringed lake, which dries to a shallow marsh in summer, but is full of bird life. A number of hotels and resort facilities have grown up along the sand-bar and its hinterland of eucalyptus trees. Beyond the Etang de Biguglia is the Bastia-Poretta airport, and under the flight-paths the site of Roman **Mariana** – the marshes were once cultivated, and the emperor Augustus set a port on the river Golo. Hardly a vestige remains of the Roman settlement but the site was occupied later by others: in the 12th century the Pisans built a cathedral here. **La Canonica** was abandoned in the 14th century when the bishopric was moved inland, and its campanile has gone, but its pure Romanesque style is the prototype of Corsica's Pisan churches – three simple naves and an elegant apse. In shape it resembles the cathedral at Nebbio, but here the walls are warmer shades of stone –

amber, gold and grey, their colours cleverly harmonised by the builder. The red tiles of the roof are a modern aberration. Vivid animals form the carved frieze above the tympanum. Among nearby excavations are some 4th-century mosaics carved with Christian symbols, and not far away to the south-west the (restored) cemetery church of San Parteo is a small pretty replica of La Canonica.

The N198 from Bastia down the east coast is the fastest road in Corsica, and local drivers exploit it with zest. As far south as Solenzara it runs mostly through a flat plain, the only extensive one on the whole island. For many years it was ravaged by malaria, but recently its agricultural potential has been realised with the help of government funding. Much of the land is now under maize, vines, orange groves and peach orchards. Long sandy beaches run almost continuously down this part of the coast, and many small resorts have sprung up, but there are few facilities and many of the beaches are rather charmless and dull. The land between the main road and the sea is mostly not cultivatable, because it consists of marshland (lakes in winter) at the mouths of the rivers that flow east from the mountainous interior. The east coast is particularly popular with naturists and there are quite a number of holiday villages and campsites for them, especially near **Bravone**. There isn't much potential for sightseeing on the coast itself, except at **Aléria**, where there are the excavated remains of an important Graeco-Roman town, and a good museum.

Inland, however, there is some of Corsica's finest touring countryside. The N193 swings west to Ponte Leccia, Corte and the high granite mountains: between this route and the coast lies a continuation of Cap Corse's grey schist rock, the large region called the **Castagniccia** after its chestnut forests. Chestnuts have been its livelihood since the Middle Ages – made into flour for the Corsicans' staple diet, and feeding the pigs that wander freely throughout the region, eventually to be rendered into rich and varied *charcuterie*. Vines and olives on the lower slopes, and goats in the *maquis* above, once made up a self-sufficient economy for the scores of villages in this region of rugged hills and valleys. It is a natural fortress, a stronghold of Corsican independence over many centuries, birthplace of several famous men. Still the most characteristically Corsican of all the regions, it is today rather neglected and (except in high summer) depopulated: since the Second World War took its heavy toll of manpower many more inhabitants have moved away – to the plain, the coast, the Continent – returning to their native villages for holidays or for retirement. Only in the north-east corner, in the little area called **La Casinca**, are the villages above the plain as prosperous as in the days when they were a retreat from the malarial marshes. A short but intricately winding loop road from the N198 takes you through **Vescovato**, the 'capital' deep in a valley, where the fountain in the shady square bears a black Imperial eagle and the tall grey houses climb to a large Baroque church. Here the (→ page 572)

Napoleon and Corsica

Napoleon's birthday is a matter of no little national importance. Had the future Emperor been born in early 1768, as he registered when he married Josephine de Beauharnais in Paris, he would have been born nominally a Genoese subject but effectively an independent Corsican under the rule of General Pascal Paoli, freedom fighter and enlightened dictator.

It is rather more likely, and much more satisfactory from the French point of view, that Napoleone Buonaparte saw the light of day on 15 August 1769. Genoa had sold its claim to Corsica to the French in May 1768, and a few months before the birth of her second son, Letizia Buonaparte had fought on the losing side of the decisive confrontation in the French takeover campaign. Paoli had taken flight to sustain the cause of freedom in London, and Carlo Maria Buonaparte, one of his leading supporters, had returned from the mountains to Ajaccio and insinuated himself into the good graces of the new rulers with what must have seemed indecent haste to Letizia, whose staunch Corsican patriotism ran much deeper than Carlo's opportunism. So Napoleon was born French, as national historians have taken pains to emphasise.

Although Napoleone always held his father in contempt and was proud to have inherited all his qualities from his mother, the neatness with which Carlo (now 'Charles') trimmed his political sails to catch the prevailing French wind suggests that the inheritance was not entirely one-sided. By befriending one of the French Governors of Corsica and providing evidence of poverty and noble lineage, Charles secured a free military education for Napoleone in France. In 1779, when he was (probably) nearly ten, the boy started at military school in Brienne and from there went on to Paris. He did not return to Corsica for seven years, but far from alienating him from his native land, his education had quite the opposite effect; reading accounts of the curiously dark-skinned youth whose first task was to learn French (the way he pronounced his own name earned him the nickname *'paille au nez'*), it is easy to understand how he became more rather than less conscious of being a foreigner in France. Rather than make a determined effort to conform, he took pride in his isolation: 'I will never forgive my father for having concurred in the reunion of France and Corsica' he said to one of his few friends at Brienne; and 'I will make your French people suffer as much as it is within my power to do'.

As a serving junior officer in the French army Napoleone lost none of his obsession with Corsican affairs. In July 1786 he ordered from a Genevan bookseller all the books about Corsica the man could obtain, and in June 1789 he wrote to Paoli in London requesting information for a history of Corsica that he planned to write. To Napoleone's grandiloquent words ('slavery the price of our submission . . . island bound by the triple chain of lawyer, soldier and tax collector . . .') the general, who by now nourished no great affection for the Buonaparti and their style of Corsican patriotism, replied dustily that writing history books was no business for young soldiers. The dramatic events in revolutionary France, which might have seemed the natural theatre for an ambitious young soldier with grand ideas of his destiny, seem to have interested Napoleone hardly at all, except as an opportunity to agitate in Corsica where he spent as much time as he could manage. Of the $7\frac{1}{2}$ years up to June 1793, he spent a total of $2\frac{1}{2}$ years in France with his regiment; for nearly all the rest of the time he was in Corsica on extended periods of leave which went unpunished thanks to invented pretexts and the laxity of army discipline.

In Corsica Napoleone looked after his clan (his father died in 1785), and led its political activity, which was too revolutionary in character for the taste of the Paolist majority of Corsicans; they successfully kept him out of office in local elections until 1792 when, by means of intimidatory tactics, he managed to secure himself a position as lieutenant-colonel in charge of the battalion of *'Volontaires de la Garde Nationale'*. Shamelessly diverting this body from its intended purpose, he was the acknowledged leader of a mutinous outbreak of fighting at Ajaccio. The failure of this initiative sent him scurrying to Paris to plead a case which at other times would have been heard in court martial. Such was the shortage of officers at the time (thousands had fled the country rather than swear allegiance to the National Assembly) that he got away with it, and was soon promoted. A letter to his brother in August 1792 gave the first hint that he was beginning to sense that things in Corsica were getting too hot for the clan's comfort, and that he would do its prospects no harm by firmly establishing himself in France where, as he had discovered, military advancement was easily won. This concern, which turned out to be well founded, did not prevent Napoleone from returning to Corsica in September 1792 (accompanying his sister). He remained there at a time when the Revolutionary Army was fighting, and losing, an international war, and Paris itself was under threat. Napoleone's contribution to the national struggle was limited to participation in a disastrous attack on the Sardinian island of la Maddalena.

Although both were originally anti-French in their aims, the Buonaparte and Paoli factions had become increasingly antagonistic. Early in 1793, Napoleone's younger brother Lucien saw fit to denounce Paoli to the National Convention which duly gave orders for the general's arrest. if it was intended to strengthen his family's position, Lucien's action was gravely miscalculated. In May a Paolist Assembly at Corte passed a resolution condemning the Buonaparte family 'to perpetual execration and infamy', and Napoleone went into hiding. His mother was persuaded by a friendly voice to evacuate her Ajaccio home with the rest of her family, and escaped just before the house was invaded by a furious band of looters and no doubt would-be murderers. Letizia camped rough on the coast until Napoleone appeared in a small vessel with a simple message for his mother: 'this country is not for us'. They embarked on a stormy crossing to France, and the rest, as the saying goes, is history.

In 1803, when Napoleon Bonaparte (as he now styled himself) assumed absolute power as First Consul for life, it was decreed in

---

Napoleon and Corsica continued

Corsica that 15 August, elsewhere the Feast of the Assumption, should be the feast of the little-known Saint Napoleon. It is still the occasion of a firework display in Ajaccio, and the town is full of tributes to the glory of its greatest son. In reality, Corsica had little cause to thank the inflammatory subversive who had been chased from the island by the force of popular execration. Napoleon set foot on the island only once again, a fleeting visit on his way back from Egypt, and his style of ruling the island consisted of a measured alternation of neglect and, when necessary, harsh repression of the uprisings against foreign control, which continued much as they had before. So loathsome was French rule that the people of Bastia appealed to the British for help in 1811, and when the emperor abdicated the Ajacciens threw his statue into the sea.

---

bishops of La Canonica spent a century or two before moving their see to Bastia; here in 1557 a Corsican Assembly accepted integration with France, only to be handed back to the Genoese two years later. La Casinca's other villages – from **Loreto**, highest up, to **Castellare**, nearest the plain – are perched on a narrow ridge above their cultivated terraces, looking out over Bastia to the sea.

La Castagniccia too has sea views: from the village of **St-Jean-de-Moriani** they extend to the islands of the Tuscan strait. **San-Nicolao**, close by, is splendidly set on a sea-facing terrace among chestnut forests, and the elegant campanile of its Pisan church can be seen for miles. At **Cervione**, just south, the corniche road ends in a sweeping curve and the church is Baroque. For visitors with spare time and energy there is a half-hour walk down a rough path to the Romanesque Chapelle Santa-Christina; inside are frescoes, their delicate colours excellently preserved.

The D71 meanders right through the region, under the dappled shade of the chestnuts. Animals and provisions traditionally occupy the ground floors of the local houses, built of grey schist stone and roofed with heavy slates (*lauzes*). Many are empty these days, and the *maquis* encroaches on neglected terraces of vines and olives; but the dozens of hamlets recall the region's crowded history. Those round **Valle-d'Alesani** – one of several communities described as 'the heart of the Castagniccia' – produced Gross-Minuto, Corsica's only known humorist. He was a puny but spirited travelling pedlar of the 18th century, who in later life grew fat and famous for his misfortunes and his untranslatably sardonic quips. In this same locality the one and only king of Corsica was crowned Théodore I in 1736, and reigned improbably for eight months. An adventuring German baron, he had some efficient ideas, including proclaiming 'liberty of conscience' in

Corsica to attract Jewish financiers who might revive the island's economy. He even had his own coinage struck. At the old convent where he was crowned (two or three kilometres south towards Piazzali) the church holds some vivid paintings, including a pensively charming *Vierge à la Cerise* of the 1450 Sienese school.

Carcheto and **Piedicroce** each have fine Baroque churches, their towers visible from afar above the trees; but the one at **La Porta**, up a series of hairpin bends, outclasses them completely. Free-standing beside the relatively restrained façade and twice its height, the tawny-ochre campanile resembles an extravagantly sculpted candle with five mellow tiers of scrolls and pilasters, arches and pediments. In the north-west of the region, **Morosaglia** is the home village of the Paoli family – Pascal by far the most famous, but his father and brother also honoured patriots. Pascal Paoli's ashes were retrieved from Westminster Abbey and lie under a flagstone in the family house, whose rooms contain many mementoes. His bronze statue was erected in 1953, financed by Corsicans world-wide.

West of the Castagniccia, in Corsica's central geological division, grey schist rock ends and red crystalline granite begins. The change is not dramatic at **Ponte Leccia**, railway junction and crossroads village in a valley: routes lead off quite gently, later to climb and twist up the mountain passes. A kilometre and a half up the N197 towards L'Ile-Rousse, the **Vallée d'Asco** heads some 32km south-west between the towering ranges of **Monte Padro** and **Monte Cinto**, the island's highest peak. In the fertile lower Asco valley the road runs almost straight through olives and fruit trees, until the *maquis*-covered slopes close in and the little brown village of **Moltifao** comes into sight, perched high on a northern spur. Soon after, the **Gorges d'Asco** begin: the river dashes down its boulder-strewn bed between outcrops of colourful jagged rock and ever more dramatic heights. At the head of the gorge, the solitary village of **Asco** clings to steep terraces, and a Genoese bridge spans the stream below. Further up, the **Fôret de Carrozzica** clothes the mountainsides with great pines, and the peaks above stay under snow for almost all the year. At the end of this alpine defile, ringed by superb mountain vistas, **Haut-Asco** caters for skiers and summer climbers: mere walkers can scale Monte Cinto, but it takes several hours. The valley is rapidly losing its isolated mystique, but still has its own wildlife. Among the peak there used to be eagles, and you may still see *gypaétes*, huge bearded vultures with wingspans of over two metres; and lower down, the *maquis* has its own varieties and fragrance. A rare type of juniper gives Asco honey its special flavour, and is said to account for the 'manna' phenomenon – a sweet and sticky white deposit that appears each year for a day or two in midsummer.

From Ponte Leccia the N193 south runs smoothly up the Golo valley for several kilometres, and then begins a swinging climb round spurs of mountain to arrive at **Corte**, spiritual capital of Corsica, its citadel perched high and proud above a meeting point of mountain routes. This is a logical touring centre, but not a tourists' town. New suburbs spread along the valley roads; the university, founded here during the years (1755 to 1769) when Corte was capital of independent Corsica, was re-established in 1977 and the student population adds youthful energy missing elsewhere inland; but only the Old Town attracts, and its appeal is history rather than charm. Sombre ranks of dark, grey-schist houses heap themselves up the steep slope below the citadel rock. The place looks stern and grim – it was a stronghold emotionally defended, never re-taken by the Genoese, but lost to the French with Corsica's hopes of independence.

From the busy central place Paoli where traffic surges round the bronze statue of Pascal Paoli, *père de la nation*, a steep lane leads up to the place Gaffori where the statue of Jean-Pierre Gaffori, *général de la nation*, stands before his bullet-scarred house. Here, at a critical stage of the War of Independence, Gaffori's redoubtable wife held a lighted fuse over a powder barrel, threatening to blow the partisans to hell if they surrendered to the Genoese before her husband's reinforcements could arrive. In a third square, the place du Poilu, is a house briefly lived in by the Buonaparte family, and the Palais National: originally occupied by Genoese administrators, seat of the parliament of independent Corsica, then successively a prison, a college and a minor museum. The great grey citadel was built under the Aragonese viceroy in the early 15th century; it was large enough to make a vast barracks for the troops of Louis XV. Now it contains an information centre on the natural park. Visitors can admire the view from the terrace on its spur of rock.

Excursions from Corte

- **Venaco** South of Corte over the Col de Bellagranajo, this is a favourite destination of Corsicans, half-way between Bastia and Ajaccio by road or rail. It is surrounded by walking, fishing and hunting country – except for an area just south, where moufflons have been reintroduced and are protected in the Parc de Verghetto.
- **Gorges de la Restonica** The river descends from the Lac de Melo, among 1,800-metre peaks, to join the Tavignano south-west of Corte. A sinuous little road climbs rapidly through chestnut forests to the pine belt. The road runs close beside the tumbling river full of pools and miniature cascades; conical Corsican pines rise from a landscape of great rounded boulders below the higher rugged outcrops. After crossing the river at Pont de Tragone, the road mounts through much wilder scenery to end near deserted dry-stone shepherds' huts, the *bergeries de Grotelle*, in alpine terrain. A footpath continues to the head of the valley, and serious walkers can scale Corsica's second highest

peak, Monte Rotondo – five hours up and four hours down, ideally with an intervening bivouac, to wake and watch the sunrise from the island's central ridge.

● **Gorges de Tavignano** Only a footpath follows this beautiful forested gorge, but a ten-minute walk gives a wonderful view back over the town to the citadel rising against its green mountain backdrop.

● **Monte Cecu** The D18 running north-west skirts the summit of Monte Cecu, from whose flat top (with television mast) the view is spectacular all round. To the south, the curious formations called the **Aiguilles Rouges** can be seen more closely by following the same road to Castiglione and Popolasca, the village perched below them.

● **Omessa** North of Corte about 16km down the N193, a side road winds east up to this delightful village perched above the valley, topped by the tall Baroque campanile of its church. The plane-shaded square is approached through a vaulted alleyway; beyond the fountain, the Chapelle de l'Annonciade has a pretty marble Virgin and Child.

From Corte back to the east coast, the N200 follows the pleasant wooded Tavignano valley to the Plaine d'Aléria, where concentrated government enterprise has replaced the encroaching *maquis* with abundant vineyards, maize, fruit trees and sunflowers. It is the most productive area of Corsica, but not of great scenic interest. **Aléria** itself, on an isolated hill, originated as a Greek colony and was later the capital of a Roman province; there is a vast area of excavations, initiated by Prosper Mérimée, and a museum housed in a 16th-century fort. Exhibits come from hill villages and inland lakes, as well as from the immediate vicinity; they include some interesting drinking vessels in the shape of dogs and a mule's head, and a reconstruction of a prisoner's tomb from AD 50.

The South

Between the developing resort of **Solenzara** ribboning along the main coast road, and the lovely seascape of the Golfe de Porto-Vecchio, a rocky stretch of coastline with a few little rivermouth *marines* is christened the **Côte des Nacres**, after its deep-water shells – huge elaborate shapes called *jambonneaux* and *plumes de mer*. **Favone** has a better beach than Solenzara; there are also stretches of sand at **Tarco** and **Parata**, between ridges of rock running out to sea. Inland, there is another route: it is longer and infinitely more difficult – often badly surfaced as well as narrow, especially at the Solenzara end – but one of the most spectacular in Corsica. It winds up to the **Col de Larone**, and on to the **Bavella** – a forest, a gorge, a pass and an extraordinary landscape of towering peaks and rocky chaos, coloured pink and red and ochre under the sun, purple in shadow, all on a heroic scale. Relentless hairpin bends climb to the **Col de Bavella**, between the fantastically twisted and eroded **Aiguilles** and the vast depression, littered with heaps of rock, known as the **Trou de la Bombe**. From the Col, range upon range stretches away into the Regional Park. In this age-old hunting territory there has been much fire damage; chestnuts and cedars have been planted among the soaring pines, and on the high slopes the moufflons are now protected. Tourist traffic explores here all summer; red-roofed little Zonza at a crossroads has cafés. The route south-east to the coast descends more gently through the trees, past spectacular crags around the great Pointe du Diamant.

The sheltered **Golfe de Porto-Vecchio** is fringed by fine sandy beaches and peaceful lagoons. Its hinterland is a gently undulating forest of cork oaks. When the cork is first stripped from the trunks, to a height of over two metres, the bare wood beneath appears a brilliant russet colour, eventually fading to a softer brown. Holiday developments spread round the Golfe: Sogno, Cala Rossa and St-Cyprien to the north all have excellent beaches. **Sogno** has extensive shallow lagoons in idyllic surroundings – small children can paddle safely, and the horses from the nearby riding school love splashing through. There are a number of sandy beaches, some quiet and secluded, the main one (backed by a large campsite) offering water sports, boat trips, and entertainments. **Cala Rossa** has one of Corsica's most pleasant hotels, some private villas, and a self-catering complex. **St-Cyprien**, further north, has some luxurious villas.

Porto-Vecchio itself, set deep in the Golfe, has ancient origins – it was founded by the Greeks, and Roman ships took away cork as a form of tax. The Genoese built fortifications but succumbed to the local malaria. For centuries the town was neglected and largely depopulated, and very little of historic interest remains. Today, it is a major centre of Corsica's tourist trade, rapidly provided with facilities begun in 1965, agreeably planned and still expanding. Streets full of small shops, restaurants and travel agents lead from the small central square with its church and open-air cafés. There are some small hotels in town, but most are some way outside: a car is essential. There is no good beach in the town itself – only a dismal patch of gritty sand near the saltpans by the harbour – but within easy driving distance lie many of the finest beaches in Corsica. The **Plage de Palombaggia**, south of the rocky headland of La Chiappa, is one of the best. Backed by a ridge of pines and dunes, this long beach is split by red rocks into several sheltered shallow coves, and delightfully secluded parts can be reached by walking. Further south lie the sandy beaches of **Santa-Giulia**, with many villas, and **Rondinara**, a very peaceful beach, though difficult to get to.

There are also a couple of prehistoric sites close to Porto-Vecchio. **Torre**, a few kilometres north on the N198, is a small hamlet with the remains of a Torréen fortress tucked away behind some back gardens. **Castello d'Arraggio** is more spectacular – and more inaccessible: a hard 20-minute uphill trek over rocks and tree-roots to reach the thick-walled chambered ramparts with great views over the gulf.

At the southern tip of Corsica, hard crystalline rock gives way to porous limestone, creating an aridly exotic landscape more like parts of Provence. In **Bonifacio**, only a few sea-miles from Sardinia, the Corse dialect is markedly different and the inhabitants speak of 'going into Corsica' as other Corsicans say 'going to the Continent'. An easy drive from Porto Vecchio, this *'petit pays à part'* is unique. Crumbling creamy bluffs, precipitous and overhung, face the troubled Sardinian strait, but behind them a long inlet enters from the west: the Goulet de Bonifacio, parallel to the sea and completely sheltered. On the narrow promontory the citadel and Haute-Ville rise high, white and seemingly impregnable. A line of steps scores a 45-degree angle up the rockface from the sea: 'The King of Aragon's Staircase', reputedly cut by Aragonese soldiers in an unsuccessful siege in 1420. From the Ville Basse round the port at the eastern end of the inlet it's a steep walk up, or you can go by road. Vantage points with breathtaking views are Capo Pertusato to the east – or the Col St-Roch up a footpath nearer the encircling ramparts. The cafés and restaurants round the crowded marina can supply energy for a hot but worthwhile climb.

Bonifacio reputedly took its name from a Tuscan marquis of the 9th century. It became a pirate stronghold: the Genoese gained their first foothold in Corsica here only by surprising the pirates drunk at a wedding feast. By the late 12th century, Bonifacio was a Genoese colony. The whole place is built to resist siege: ramparts immensely thick, grain silos below the Place Grandval, houses designed like mini-fortresses with storage chambers on the ground floor and access originally by ladder to the first. The 'flying buttresses' crossing the cobbled alleys were part of a system of canals and gutters, carrying water from a communal cistern under the loggia of the town church. The layout of the promontory town was necessarily compact, a dense little network of streets, shadowed by tall narrow buildings. Today there are trippery souvenir or craft shops and crowded cafés, all with somewhat inflated prices. Half the site is taken up by the citadel, guarding the western point – rather a desolate wasteland apart from an army barracks and single hotel.

It is worth taking a 50-minute boat trip for the best views of the houses overhanging the cliffs. The boat also visits various caves – most interesting is Sdragonatu, lit by sunlight coming in through a hole in the ceiling shaped like Corsica. There are also longer trips, lasting a whole day, to the Iles de Lavezzi, part of a nature reserve.

Sights in Bonifacio

- **Eglise St-Dominique** Built by the Templars at the end of the 13th century, the citadel church is Provençal Gothic with rare ogive vaulting. The choir, however, was rebuilt in the 18th century. Among many decorative Baroque pieces are two massive religious groups carved in wood, which in true Corsican fashion are manhandled through the streets in the Easter procession.
- **Eglise Ste-Marie Majeure** Most interesting is the big arcaded loggia fronting the Haute-Ville church, where all manner of town business was transacted. The church itself is a medley of styles from the 13th century to the 18th. The bottom tier of the campanile is Romanesque, the three above Gothic.

Corsica's deep south is not well supplied with beaches: around the Golfe de Santa Manza they are strips of gritty sand extensively used for rough camping, and west of the cape a succession of rocky coves, increasingly inaccessible after Tonnara Plage. But at the **Golfe de Valinco** the fine west-coast beaches begin: spacious and sandy along its southern curve, smaller and quieter to the north. This is one of Corsica's developed holiday areas – hotels and self-catering villages have sprung up all round the Golfe. **Porto Pollo** to the north is a peaceful little resort; **Propriano** in the middle is popular with the British. The tourist centre of the bay is thoroughly modernised now, the harbour area crowded with restaurants, cafés and souvenir shops. It's not of any great appeal except as a base from which to explore some interesting places inland.

Excursions from Propriano

- **Sartène** This thoroughly atmospheric little hill town of narrow streets and gaunt granite houses has a history of fierce resistance to outsiders and savage vendettas among its inhabitants. The strangest Easter rite in Corsica is Sartène's *Procession du Catenacciu*; 'the chained one' is both Christ-symbol and town penitent, anonymous, and chosen by the priest from a waiting list of sinners. Hooded and robed in red, he carries a cross (heavy, of course) through the streets while the crowd attempts to unmask him. His stumbles and falls are not all ritual. An exhibition in Eglise Ste-Marie evokes the creepy atmosphere well. There's also a small Musée Prehistoire in an old prison.
- **Castello de Cucuruzzu** Further inland, off the winding D268 that passes through the pretty village of Ste-Lucie-de-Tallano, a circular walk of about an hour through shady woods takes you past two sites. The Castello de Cucuruzzu sits on a rocky spur overlooking the wooded valley around – you can clamber over huge rounded boulders

flecked with moss and lichen to explore the small chambers within the walls. Capula is a medieval castle built on top of a former dolmen, the brick walls incorporating the circular boulders.

• **Spin' a Cavallu** Corsica is full of medieval bridges built by the Genoese, but they are usually glimpsed far down a ravine. This one is not only well preserved but accessible, a few kilometres north of Sartène up the D268. The design is a single humped arch of shaped granite blocks, supporting a narrow but secure path in the form of a graduated causeway.

• **Filitosa** North of the Golfe de Valinco, the biggest prehistoric site in Corsica is still being explored (and somewhat commercialised). A whole Torréen village has been excavated; there are complex mounds of rock constructed for religious ceremony or defence. Most striking are the menhirs carved with faces – stylised, impassive and strange, but each distinct and human (from the front – from behind they look more phallic).

Filitosa

HOTELS

> Key: ♦ = 0–250FF, ♦♦ = 251–450FF, ♦♦♦ = over 451FF; prices are per double room without breakfast, which costs around 35–60FF extra. Some hotels may insist on half-board during high season, some hotels or restaurants may close at specific times during the week – it is always worth checking. Most hotels accept the major credit cards; we have indicated where a hotel takes no credit cards.

ALGAJOLA

Hôtel l'Ondine

7 rue A Marina
20220 Haute-Corse
TEL 95 60 70 02; FAX 95 60 60 36

This hotel, not far from Calvi and l'Ile Rousse, stands right on the beach, with the sound of the sea the only noise. Its gardens are pretty and the pine trees offer plenty of shade. There is a bright and airy restaurant overlooking the sea, as well as an outdoor terrace and grill area. Bedrooms are fairly small, simple and fresh.

OPEN Early Apr to end Oct ROOMS 56 (all with shower) FACILITIES Outdoor pool, windsurfing

BASTELICA

Le Sampiero

20119 Corse-du-Sud
TEL 95 28 71 99; FAX 95 28 74 11

Surrounded by mountains and in the centre of the village, Le Sampiero is a fine little family-run establishment. The creamy pebble-dash building with brown shutters has a café terrace shaded by a reed cover. The feel of the public rooms is old-fashioned and comforting; the bedrooms are modern.

OPEN All year exc. Oct ROOMS 26 (all with bath or shower)

CALVI

Hostellerie l'Abbaye

BP 42 route de Santore
20260 Haute-Corse
TEL 95 65 04 27; FAX 95 65 29 26

Rebuilt on the ruins of a 17th-century abbey, the stone building is covered in creepers and flowers and has a terrace and patio, as well as a very pretty garden. Inside, the restaurant, with its beamed ceiling and large stone fireplace, is particularly enticing. Bedrooms are individually furnished with a variety of period-style pieces and have all mod-cons. The overall atmosphere is solid and respectable, and the owner friendly.

OPEN Apr to Oct ROOMS 46 (all with bath or shower)

La Caravelle

La Plage
20260 Haute-Corse
TEL 95 65 01 21; FAX 95 65 00 03

This is a modern low-rise hotel in an excellent right-on-the-beach position, a quarter-of-an-hour's walk from the town centre. Tiled floors, whitewashed walls and bright paintings make a tasteful cool décor. The courtyard garden is full of creepers and palms.

OPEN Early Apr to mid-Oct ROOMS 35 (all with shower)

CORTE

Auberge Restonica

Vallée de la Restonica
20250 Haute-Corse
TEL 95 46 20 13; FAX 95 61 03 91

Restonica is a quiet retreat near the gorges of the same name, with plenty of character as well as lots of cats and dogs around the place. The interior is nicely rustic: wood panelling, a galleried staircase and stags' antlers on the wall. Rooms vary in size and decoration – number 2 has good views of the gorge. In warm weather, breakfast is taken on the terrace. The modern hotel opposite is under the same ownership – not much character but comfortable.

OPEN All year ROOMS 7 (all with bath or shower) FACILITIES Outdoor pool

EVISA

L'Aïtone

20120 Corse-du-Sud
TEL 95 26 20 04; FAX 95 26 24 18

A very friendly hotel, with good facilities, in a popular walking-base village in the wooded mountains behind Porto. The bedrooms in the newer part are better equipped than those in the old part, which are more old-fashioned and cramped (but also cheaper). There are fine views across a steep valley from most of the bedrooms and from the terrace. The food in the woody, bright dining-room is simple and the wine robust.

OPEN Jan to early Nov ROOMS 32 (all with bath or shower) FACILITIES Outdoor pool

FAVONA

U Dragulinu

20144 Corse-du-Sud
TEL 95 73 20 30; FAX 95 73 22 06

The main attractions of this hotel include its position on the beach and the pleasant surroundings, with small bedroom blocks set in grounds of trees and bushes. Rooms are very simple and small, but each has its own terrace.

OPEN Mid-May to mid-Oct ROOMS 38 (all with bath or shower)

L'ILE ROUSSE

La Bergerie

route de Monticello
20220 Haute-Corse
TEL 95 60 01 28; FAX 95 60 06 36

This old converted stone farmhouse covered in greenery is close to the beach, on the road up to Monticello. The outdoor courtyard restaurant is well shaded by trees and the bedrooms are rustically comfortable, if a little small.

OPEN Mid-Mar to end Nov ROOMS 19 (all with bath or shower) FACILITIES Outdoor pool

MACINAGGIO

U Libecciu

20248 Haute-Corse
TEL 95 35 43 22; FAX 95 35 46 08

In a quiet spot on Cap Corse, U Libecciu is a modern pink building near the beach and harbour, which makes it a good overnight stop when touring. It is comfortable and clean, has a terrace and garden and, best of all, is good value.

OPEN Apr to end Oct ROOMS 30 (all with shower)

MONTICELLO

A Pasturella

20220 L'Ile Rousse
Haute-Corse
TEL 95 60 05 65; FAX 95 60 21 78

In the main square of a medieval stone village which stands on a steep hill 3km inland from l'Ile Rousse, this small hotel is run by a friendly, cheerful family and is the focal point of village life. The furnishings are traditional, the bedrooms old-fashioned and smallish (some with stupendous views) and the cooking of the wholesome, generous, country variety.

OPEN All year exc. Nov ROOMS 14 (all with bath or shower)

PIOGGIOLA

Auberge Aghjola

20259 Haute-Corse
TEL 95 61 90 48; FAX 95 61 92 99

If you want to relax completely for a while, make for this tiny village and auberge off the beaten track where you can horse ride, walk or swim in the pool. The comfort and décor are suitably country style, with plenty of wood and stone, solid dark colours, painted furniture and a big open fireplace in the dining-room, which is known for its excellent food.

OPEN Apr to Oct ROOMS 12 (all with bath or shower) FACILITIES Outdoor pool

PORTICCIO

Hôtel Kallysté Maquis

route du Vieux Molini
Agosta Plage
20166 Haute-Corse
TEL 95 25 54 19; FAX 95 21 79 00

This is a converted beige villa – small scale, clean and quiet, but with enough features, such as the lovely wrought-iron staircase, to make it special. It's some way out of Porticcio along the coast road and a steep trek down to the Plage d'Agosta if you do not have transport.

OPEN Apr to Oct ROOMS 10 (all with bath or shower)

PORTO VECCHIO

San Giovanni ◆◆–◆◆◆

route d'Arca
20137 Corse-du-Sud
TEL 95 70 22 25; FAX 95 70 20 11

This hotel can be found amid a forest of cork-oaks, 3km inland from Porto Vecchio. The gardens are particularly lovely, full of palm trees and bright flowers, and the bedrooms are in a bungalow-style block with little patios and rockeries. They're comfortable and well decorated. Cooking is homely and good.

OPEN Apr to Nov ROOMS 29 (all with bath or shower) FACILITIES Heated outdoor pool, tennis, jacuzzi, sauna

PROPRIANO

Loft Hotel

3 rue Jean-Paul Pandolfi
20110 Corse-du-Sud
TEL 95 76 17 48; FAX 95 76 22 04

If you are looking for a base in Propriano from which to explore the south-east corner of the islands, the Loft is the best value of the cheaper hotels we've seen here – spotlessly clean, with a modern but not too stark feel. It's behind the resort's main street, so close to lots of restaurants, bars and the marina.

OPEN All year exc. Feb ROOMS 25 (all with shower)

QUENZA

Auberge Sole e Monti

20122 Corse-du-Sud
TEL 95 78 62 53; FAX 95 78 63 88

Quenza is a little mountain village to the north-east of Porto Vecchio in good walking country; the Sole e Monti is its only auberge, with a good reputation for well-cooked regional food (we had a delicious rabbit casserole with tortellini on the night we visited). The slightly cramped bedrooms are a drawback.

OPEN Mid-Mar to end Sept ROOMS 20 (all with bath or shower)

SAN MARTINO DI LOTA

Hôtel de la Corniche

Bastia
20200 Haute-Corse
TEL 95 31 40 98; FAX 95 32 37 69

This is an excellent out-of-the-way spot overlooking leafy valleys near Bastia, though it takes a little effort to get there along a narrow twisting road. The hotel has a charming and friendly proprietor and comfortable old-fashioned bedrooms, which have chestnut-wood furniture.

OPEN Feb to mid-Dec ROOMS 15 (all with bath or shower)

VENACO

Paesotel E Caselle

20231 Haute-Corse
TEL 95 47 02 01; FAX 95 47 06 65

There is not much that is run-of-the-mill in this hotel, starting with its stone-dash (as opposed to pebble-dash) exterior. More stone can be found on the floor and walls of the bar, though the ceiling is sheepskin – brown and white fur. Bedrooms continue the rustic mountain theme. The hotel makes a good base for walking holidays, or you can just laze by the pool and enjoy the mountain village peace.

OPEN May to early Oct ROOMS 47 (all with bath or shower) FACILITIES Heated outdoor pool, tennis, sauna, jacuzzi

VIZZAVONA

Hôtel du Monte d'Oro

Col de Vizzavona
20219 Haute-Corse
TEL 95 47 21 06; FAX 95 21 82 28

This is yet another mountain hotel in lovely surroundings right in the centre of the island. It's a particularly good base for walkers, with good, friendly service. There is only one set menu so no choice at dinner, though what you get is excellent home cooking.

OPEN May to end Sept ROOMS 57 (16 with bath or shower) FACILITIES Tennis

Practical information

TRAVEL

Crossing the Channel

The opening of the Channel Tunnel (see below) is likely to change the pattern of Channel crossing in the future, but for the time being the car ferry operators are fighting fit with a whole new generation of plush super-ferries. Ultimately, your choice of cross-channel route depends on your UK departure point, your destination in France and preference for sea or land travel.

Cross-channel operators and routes:

- Brittany Ferries, tel (0752) 221321 or (0705) 827701; Plymouth to Roscoff (6–7 hours), Portsmouth to St-Malo (9–10$\frac{1}{4}$ hours) and Caen (6–7 hours)
- Hoverspeed, tel (0304) 240202; Dover to Calais (35 mins on hovercraft, 55 mins Seacat); Folkestone to Boulogne (55 mins Seacat only)
- P&O Ferries, tel (0304) 203388; Dover to Calais (1$\frac{1}{2}$ hours), Portsmouth to Cherbourg (4$\frac{3}{4}$–9$\frac{3}{4}$ hours) and Le Havre (5$\frac{3}{4}$–7 hours)
- Sally Line, tel (0843) 595566; Ramsgate to Dunkerque (2$\frac{1}{2}$ hours)
- Stena Sealink UK, tel (0233) 647047; Dover to Calais (1$\frac{1}{2}$ hours); Newhaven to Dieppe (4 hours); Southampton to Cherbourg (5–9 hours)
- Truckline (part of Brittany Ferries), tel (0705) 827701; Poole to Cherbourg (4$\frac{1}{4}$–6 hours)

Channel Tunnel

The Channel Tunnel due to open in May 1994 will run a vehicle shuttle service from Folkestone to Calais, 24 hours a day, every 15 minutes at peak times. The journey will take 35 minutes and you need not book. You can purchase your ticket from the toll booths on arrival at the terminal and take the next available service, or book through a travel agent or from Le Shuttle customer service centre on (0303) 271100. The price varies seasonally and is based on the cost of the car regardless of the number of passengers. A three-hour non-stop rail service between Waterloo and Paris is due to start in summer 1994.

Motoring

Route planning

Both the AA and the RAC can tailor-make route plans for you for a standard fee – apply at least three weeks in advance. Call (0272) 308242 for the AA, and (0345) 333222 for the RAC.

Maps showing alternative routes, and how to avoid the worst traffic jams, are produced annually by the French Ministry of Transport. They're called *Bison Futé* (wily buffalo) and are available free at petrol stations, roadside information centres and from the French Government Tourist Office. Some roads are labelled *Bison Futé* and are marked with green and yellow signs.

For a recording of European traffic information call either the AA on (0336) 401904 or the RAC on (0891) 500241.

Breakdown insurance

Called 'vehicle security' or 'vehicle protection', the purpose of this insurance is to protect you from some of the expense and inconvenience which can result from a car breakdown, and also cover other risks. You claim back from the insurer costs which you have had to meet, and most policies also claim to offer practical help and advice at the time of the incident. If your car is out of action, the policies have provisions for either accommodating you while it's being repaired or continuing your holiday by other means. Some policies cover incidents other than breakdowns – for example, the insurance comes into effect if your car is stolen, or if injury or illness strikes the driver. None of the policies covers the cost of parts needed to repair the car, and you may have to pay a labour charge. Policies on offer include the AA 5-star, Europ Assistance, RAC Eurocover, National Breakdown and Mondial Assistance.

The RAC and AA policies are available to non-members as well as members for a small extra charge (members who buy ferry tickets through the RAC can get a reduced-rate insurance).

It's worth getting hold of a list of dealers for your car: the red Michelin guide to France lists garages for most towns, with details of makes of car, but not of opening times.

Driving regulations

Seat belts must be worn by the driver and front-seat passenger; under-tens may not travel in the front seat unless the car has no back seat.

If your car breaks down, you must place a red warning triangle on the road 30 metres behind the car if it is not fitted with hazard warning lights.

Driving with side-lights only lit is not allowed; it is advisable to have headlight beams adjusted for right-hand drive, or to buy a headlamp converter (the clip-on-type also changes the light to amber). You should carry the car's registration document with you (if you've hired it in Britain, you need a certificate from the AA or RAC; if the vehicle is not owned by you, you need a letter authorising you to drive it).

• For more details on driving regulations in Europe ring the AA, tel (0336) 401869 or the RAC (0891) 500243 (recorded).

Speed limits

Built-up areas 50kph (31mph); outside built-up areas, 90kph (56mph) on normal roads, 110kph (68mph) on dual carriageways and toll-free motorways, 130kph (80mph) on toll motorways. Speed limits are lower when wet: 110kph (68mph) on toll motorways, 100kph (62mph) on dual carriageways and toll-free motorways, 80kph (50mph) on other roads. There is a new minimum speed limit of 80kph (50mph) for the outside lane on motorways, during daylight, on level ground and with good visibility. The minimum age for driving a car is 18, and for a year after passing the test drivers may not exceed 90kph (56mph). Speeding offences may be fined on the spot.

Priority

The *priorité à droite* rule, under which, in the absence of any indications to the contrary, traffic coming from the right has priority, no longer holds. Major roads outside built-up areas now have right of way, called *passage protegé*, and are indicated by a yellow and black diamond-shaped sign. The rule no longer applies at roundabouts, either, where traffic entering from approach roads gives way, as it does in Britain. In built-up areas, though, priority still applies and you must give way to cars coming out of a side turning on the right. If a car flashes its headlights, it is indicating that it has priority and you should give way.

Roads and road signs

Toutes directions (all directions) in towns means the route for through traffic; *centre ville* indicates the town centre. *Poids lourds* is the route for heavy traffic (lorries); *sens interdit* means no entry; *sens unique* one way. Other common roads signs include:

Absence de glissière no crash barrier; *Absence de marquage* no road markings; *Cédez le passage* give way; *Déviation* diversion; *Marquage effacé* no road markings; *Parking gratuit* free parking; *Péage* pay-booth on motorway; *Ralentir* slow down; *Priorité aux piétons* give way to pedestrians; *Rappel* literally 'remember' (usually under speed signs); *Route barrée* road closed; *A (autoroute)* motorway; *N (route nationale)* main road; *D* secondary road.

Parking

Regulations are similar to those in the UK. Yellow marks (usually on the kerb rather than on the road) indicate that parking is prohibited. Some areas – called grey zones – have parking meters or automatic ticket machines; you have to pay between 9am and 7pm (with occasional clearly marked exceptions, such as in August in some parts of Paris, and in certain streets elsewhere at weekends, where a yellow disc marked *P* is displayed on meters). Most large towns also have blue zones where you have to display a time disc – which allows up to an hour's parking – between 9am and 12.30pm, and 2.30pm and 7pm. Discs are available free from tourist offices.

Motorways

Most are toll roads (*autoroutes à péage*); some are expensive, even for relatively short distances. The tolls from Calais to Nice return amount to about £45 for a car, £64 for a car and caravan. Payment may be made by Access (Mastercard) and Visa credit cards. There are 24-hour service areas every 30 to 50km and more frequent rest areas with toilet facilities. Free emergency telephones are sited every 2km on most motorways. If you break down, it is compulsory to display a warning triangle. A useful leaflet, *Bienvenue en France par l'autoroute*, available from the French Government Tourist Office, gives information and translations of relevant vocabulary.

Accidents

Police should be informed, particularly if someone is injured. A *constat à l'ami- able* (an accident statement form) must be completed in all cases and signed by both parties (if appropriate); any disputes should be taken to a local bailiff who will prepare a report (*constat d'huissier*).

Emergency telephone numbers

Police and ambulance 17; fire 18.

Car hire

Major car rental companies have offices in almost all towns. You can usually arrange to collect the car in one place, and leave it in another at no extra charge (provided the company has an office there). It is sometimes worth booking in advance (from 24 hours to seven days, depending on the company) from this country to obtain a special reduced rate – 'super saver'. French Railways, SNCF, also offer car hire, with cars available at more than 2,000 stations throughout the country. Fly-drive arrangements are available in conjunction with airlines or tour operators, and many deals can prove good value. Some rates are fully inclusive, others have extras such as insurance and collision damage waiver.

PRACTICAL INFORMATION

Petrol
Petrol in France is a few pence dearer per litre than in the UK. There are surprisingly few petrol stations on N- and D-roads – fill up in towns. Petrol in supermarket stations can be 15 per cent cheaper than on autoroutes. Eurocard/Mastercard (e.g. Access) and Visa are the most widely accepted credit cards for petrol. Unleaded is *sans plomb* in French.

Fines
You can be stopped and fined up to 2,500FF on the spot for driving offences. Fines for not wearing a seatbelt range from 230–600FF, for speeding 600–4,000FF, and for drink-driving (alcohol limits are the same as in the UK) 2,000–30,000FF.

Air

There are direct scheduled flights from the UK to many regional airports in France, including Biarritz, Bordeaux, Caen, Dijon, Lille, Lourdes, Lyon, Marseilles, Montpellier, Nantes, Nice, Perpignan, Rennes, Rouen, Strasbourg and Toulouse, as well as Paris. Schedules, airlines and destinations served can change from season to season, so check with a good travel agent for the most up-to-date information.

Fly-drive
Inclusive deals covering air fare and hire car are offered by major airlines and many tour operators who specialise in French holidays. These can be better value than if you book flights and car separately. Prices are quoted differently depending on the operators – per person, per car, with or without insurance and/or collision damage waiver.

Rail

French Railways (SNCF) operate a good network of services, with many lines using the comfortable, modern, air-conditioned Corail trains; some major lines have the 1st-class only Trans Europe Express trains (TEE). The high-speed train (TGV), with 1st and 2nd class, operates from Paris to Annecy, Avignon, Besançon, Chalon-sur-Saône, Chambéry, Dijon, Geneva, Grenoble, Lille, Lyon, Mâcon, Marseille, Montpellier, Nîmes, Nice, and St-Etienne, and from Nantes, Rouen or Lille to Lyon. Paris to Lyon takes 2 hours, to Geneva $3\frac{1}{2}$ hours, to Lille 1 hour 20 minutes. The TGV has also been extended to the west and south of France and the final section of line has opened between Lille and Calais, making the Paris to Calais journey only 1 hour 50 minutes. The new TGV Atlantique operates west to Brest and Nantes, and south-west to Bordeaux, Toulouse and the Spanish border. SNCF at 179 Piccadilly, London W1V OBA; tel 071–493 9731 (to arrange a personal visit only). For information call (0891) 515477. For credit card bookings only call (0345) 300003.

If you intend to fly to France and continue your journey by rail, it may be worth booking an inclusive fare (through Air France offices or travel agents), or combining the flight with a rail rover ticket (see below).

Sleeper
On the longer routes there are sleeper trains like those in Britain – with single, two-berth or three-berth compartments; and also cheaper couchettes, compartments for four or six with bunks.

Tickets

When buying a ticket in France you must validate it (*composter*) by using the orange automatic date-stamping machine at the platform entrance. If you fail to do so, you will have to pay a surcharge of 20 per cent of the fare. There are various reduced tickets: rail rover (*Euro domino*) for 3, 5, or 10 days' unlimited travel; holiday return (*séjour*) tickets, which allow a 25 per cent reduction on fares (with certain conditions).

Motorail

There are several car-carrying train services which might be useful: from Calais to Biarritz, Avignon, Bordeaux, the Dordogne (Brive), Toulouse, the Alps and the Mediterranean coast, more services from Paris. Information and bookings from French Railways on 071–409 3518.

Bus

Eurolines operate services between London and most major tourist destinations in France, tel 071–730 0202. There are very few long-distance bus services in France. Coach tours operated by French Railways are organised in the major tourist areas in summer; there are half-day, day and longer excursions. Local buses in rural areas are few and far between – some have only one or two services a week, usually coinciding with local markets. Local tourist offices have timetables.

Cycling

Bikes travel with their owners on the overnight rail service. Otherwise, bikes can be carried on many (but by no means all) other trains. French Railways will undertake to carry your bike unaccompanied as luggage; there is no guarantee that the bike travels with you on the same train, and a delay of up to five days is possible in high season.

You can hire a bike at 250 railways stations (and at some you can make arrangements to leave it at another station). The Cyclists Touring Club, Cotterell House, 69 Meadrow, Godalming, Surrey GU7 3HS, tel (0483) 417217, has a French touring information sheet and touring notes compiled by members, information on recommended routes and advice leaflets. They also organise tours. Specialist tour operators offer cycling holidays in France – details from the French Government Tourist Office.

Yachting and boating

Inland waterways are extensive and, with a few exceptions, no charge is made for the use of waterways and locks. Yacht holidays are becoming increasingly popular as new marinas spring up. The French Government Tourist Office has information on maps, rules and regulations, organisations that can be of help, and a suggested reading list. For inclusive yacht and boat holidays, consult its list of 'special interest' tour operators.

ACCOMMODATION

Hotels

In France, hotels are graded from one to four stars and four stars luxury, depending on their level of facilities.

Local tourist offices with a reservation service (called *Accueil de France*) can help with bookings up to a week ahead for a small charge if visited in person. There are numerous hotel chains in France. Two of the more interesting, with accommodation at opposite ends of the price spectrum, are the *Fédération de Logis de France*, which has over 4,000 small family-run establishments throughout France, and *Relais et Châteaux*, which incorporates 150 luxury hotels. Guides listing hotels in both schemes are available from the French Government Tourist Office. The *Logis* guide is also available in bookshops.

Some useful tips:

- hotels in popular tourist areas, particularly the Brittany and Mediterranean coasts, are often fully booked in July and August: book well in advance
- prices are usually quoted per room. Singles often lose out. Specify if you want a single when you book
- most hotels have a bewildering range of prices for all types of room, with varying degrees of bathroom facilities – if you don't mind a corridor walk to the bathroom you can save a lot of money. A room with bath usually costs more than a room with shower (*douche*), and the bath may be half-size anyway
- most hotels have a half- and full-board rate (*demi-pension* or *pension*) that invariably works out cheaper, but you may be saddled with less interesting meals
- breakfasts are often much tastier and fresher in a café than in the hotel dining-room. You pay separately for breakfast in hotels. If you don't eat it, make sure the hotel doesn't charge you for it
- some resort hotels in high season insist on half-board – even though French law states that a hotelier should provide accommodation without meals.

Gîtes

Gîtes are houses, often converted farmhouses or cottages, in rural spots. They are classified by ears of corn – from one to four depending on how well equipped they are: the emphasis is on simplicity rather than sophistication. For popular areas in high summer, you should book as early as possible – the preceding September is the best time, particularly if you want a place by the sea. There are two ways of booking a *gîte*: the French Government Tourist Office can provide addresses and phone numbers for booking offices in any *département* in France, as can the *Fédération Nationale des Gîtes de France*. Each office has a complete guide to *gîtes* in the area; you can then book direct with the owner, or in some cases the local office will act as a booking agent. A simpler alternative, especially if you are concerned about your linguistic abilities, is to leave all the arrangements to *Gîtes de France* in this country, and choose a *gîte* from their more limited brochure selection (which still details 2,500 establishments countrywide). The cost of the package includes discounted ferry rates but also the price of a 15–25 per cent commission. Other tour and ferry operators include *gîtes* in their selection of accommodation. *Les Nouveaux Gîtes Ruraux* is a booklet, on sale in bookshops in France, that gives details on *gîtes* that have surfaced after the local offices have compiled their annual lists. In UK bookshops you can buy *The Gîtes Guide* (FHG Publications), which lists a large number and gives details of booking procedures.

- Gîtes de France, 178 Piccadilly, London W1V 9DB, tel 071–493 3480
- Fedération Nationale des Gîtes de France, 35 rue Godot de Mauroy, 75009 Paris, tel (1) 49 70 75 75

Chambres d'hôtes

Chambres d'hôtes – similar to B&B in the UK – come in all shapes and sizes, from grand châteaux downwards. In some, you will be provided with an evening meal and may be expected to do a bit of socialising. In others, everything may be much more relaxed. Local tourist offices have lists of *chambres d'hôtes*. Almost all are marketed through the *Gîtes de France* group. Their guides, available from bookshops or from their London office (phone to be sent a copy – see phone number and address above), are called *French Country Welcome* (which lists 12,000 B&Bs) and *Chambres d'Hôtes de Prestige* ('magnificent country homes in rural France'). *Gîtes de France* also offers a selection of *chambres d'hôtes* on a package deal. The *Château Acceuil* is a chain of the grandest private houses. The booklet listing them is available from the French Government Tourist Office.

Camping

The French regard themselves as the most sophisticated campers in Europe. The French Government Tourist Office publishes a useful booklet *The Camping Traveller in France*. Each region publishes a complete list of campsites; some of the best are to be found in the grounds of châteaux and are often members of the chain *Castels et Camping Caravaning*.

Campsites in France are graded from one to four stars. All are required by law to have a source of purified water, are expected to have running water (some one-stars don't have to offer hot running water), a daily refuse collection and a public phone. The main differences and improvements, as you progress through the ratings, relate to the general range of amenities, how crowded they might get and the minimum size of pitch. Many French campsites are municipal; these are often simpler than privately owned sites, but just as likely to be well maintained. Some sites now have *campeollettes*, Swiss-style chalets.

A package camping holiday provides you with a tent in a three- or four-star site and a courier to look after you. The site is likely to be the 'fun-camp' style. You can pay up to twice as much for this service than for making your own arrangements, but if you are new to camping you obviously save on buying your own equipment.

A cheaper option is using a reservation agency (a service offered by some tour operators and by membership organisations): you are expected to be self-equipped, but bookings are taken care of and you may get a wider choice of smaller sites.

One of the main advantages of camping independently is that you can choose a pitch away from other people. To book, write (or phone) direct to the sites. Some sites will not accept an independent booking without a camping *carnet*, others offer a reduction if you have one. The *carnet* is available (for a fee) to members from the AA, RAC, the Caravan Club, tel (0342) 326944, the Camping and Caravanning Club, tel (0203) 694995 and the Cyclists Touring Club, tel (0483) 417217. If you are not a member of any of these organisations, you can also get a *carnet* from the GB Car Club, tel (0794) 515444, for a small fee.

If you want to stay at *any* site in July or August, book in advance. In May, June or September many advertised facilities (e.g. bar or shop) are shut. If you are camping independently, the Michelin Guide *Camping Caravaning France* is indispensable; also *Camping à la ferme* (Gîtes de France).

Package holidays

Independent travel to France is straightforward and often cheaper than taking a package. All the same, there are a large number of tour operators offering a wide range of packages, including special interest holidays – from battlefields to gastronomy.

For a complete list of tour operators, get *The Traveller in France Reference Guide* from the French Government Tourist Office (address on page 605).

RECOMMENDED BOOKS

Accommodation and restaurants

The red Michelin *Guide France*, which appears annually, is very useful for practical information, with town maps indicating hotels, restaurants and much besides; it selects and gives judgements (in symbol form) on hotels, gives accolades for excellent food and quotes prices. What it does not do is give you much impression of what a place is like. A guide book which does is the *Gault Millau Guide France*, also annual, which is not always easily bought in Britain. It is much stronger on food (its authors started the *nouvelle cuisine* fashion) than on hotels; it is written (in French) in an amusingly idiosyncratic and linguistically demanding style.

Paris (useful reference)

Michelin *Paris Atlas*; street atlas and comprehensive municipal index of everything from embassies to swimming pools

Gault Millau, *Le Guide de Paris* (French only); lists and descriptions of hotels, restaurants, bars, nightlife, shops, and services

Officiel des Spectacles, weekly publication listing events and what's on at theatres, cinemas, nightclubs; *Une Semaine de Paris – Pariscop* is similar

Food

Charcuterie and French Pork Cookery, Jane Grigson (Penguin)
French Provincial Cooking, Elizabeth David (Penguin)
Mediterranean Seafood, Alan Davidson (Penguin)
The Taste of France, Fay Sharm (Macmillan, out of print)

Wine

French Wine Atlas, Hubrecht Duijker and Hugh Johnson (Mitchell Beazley)
Regional Guides to the Wines of France (series), ed. Simon Loftus (Octopus, out of print)
Guide to French Wines, Steven Spurrier (Mitchell Beazley)
Sainsbury's Pocket Wine Book, Oz Clarke (Webster's)

Specialist

Access Guides (for disabled travellers) to *Paris*, available from RADAR, 12 City Forum, 250 City Road, London EC1V 8AF.

Inland Waterways of France, D. Edwards-May (Imray)
Walking in France, Rob Hunter (Oxford Illustrated Press)
Walks and Climbs in the Pyrenees, Kev Reynolds (Cicerone Press, out of print)

Historical background

The Conquest of Gaul, Julius Caesar (Penguin)
Astérix le Gaulois (and many sequels, some translated), Goscinny and Uderzo (Dargaud)

PRACTICAL INFORMATION

The Distant Mirror, the Calamitous 14th Century, Barbara Tuchman (Penguin, out of print)

The Sun King and *Madame de Pompadour*, Nancy Mitford (out of print)

When the Riviera Was Ours, Patrick Howarth (Routledge & Kegan Paul)

A History of Modern France, 1715–1962, Alfred Cobban (Penguin)

The Pelican History of Art, founding editor Nikolaus Pevsner. Relevant titles include *Carolingian and Romanesque Architecture; Gothic Architecture; Art and Architecture in France, 1500–1700; Art and Architecture of the 18th Century in France; Painting and Sculpture in Europe, 1780–1880; Painting and Sculpture in Europe 1880–1940; Architecture: 19th and 20th Centuries.*

Pages from the Goncourt Journal, edited by Robert Baldic (out of print)

Travel and literature

Alain-Fournier, Henry, *Le Grand Meaulnes* (Loire/Berry)

Balzac, Honoré de, *Les Chouans* (Brittany); *Le Curé de Tours* and *Le Lys dans la Vallée* (Loire); *Les Illusions Perdues* (Paris)

Carrington, Dorothy, *Granite Island: Portrait of Corsica*

Fitzgerald, Scott, *Tender is the Night* (South)

Flaubert, Gustave, *Madame Bovary* (Normandy); *Education Sentimentale* (Paris)

Hugo, Victor, *Les Misérables* (Paris)

Hóias, Pierre Jakez, *The Horse of Pride* (Brittany)

Loti, Pierre, *Pêcheur d'Islande* (Brittany)

Miller, Henry, *Tropic of Cancer* (Paris)

Mauriac, François, *Thérèse* (Atlantic Coast)

Orwell, George, *Down and Out in Paris and London*

Oyler, Philip, *The Generous Earth*

Rowe, Vivian, *The Loire*

Smollett, Tobias, *Travels Through France and Italy*

Stendhal, *Mémoires d'un Touriste*

Stevenson, Robert Louis, *Travels with a Donkey in the Cévennes*

White, Freda, *Three Rivers of France; Ways of Aquitaine;* and *West of the Rhône*

Whymper, Edward, *Chamonix and the Range of Mont Blanc*

Young, Arthur, *Travels in France During the Years 1787, 1788, 1789*

Zola, Emile, *Les Rougon Macquart* series (France under Napoleon III) including *Germinal, L'Assommoir, Nana* and *La Terre*

MAPS

All of France on one sheet

Michelin 1:1,000,000 Clear, detailed, accurate and easy to use. One of the cheapest maps available. The only drawback is the use of solid yellow blobs for big cities, obscuring through routes. You can also buy this map double-sided or as two separate sheets – northern and southern France.

Hallwag 1:1,000,000 More expensive than Michelin, but attractive and very well printed, with a useful index booklet.

IGN 1:1,000,000 A very strikingly designed map, with heavily emphasised mountains; main roads clear and accurate.

Three other national maps worth looking out for are the **IGN Artistic Treasures** and **Long Distance Footpaths** maps, which use the IGN 1:1,000,000 map as a base for overprinted detail of places of artistic and historic interest and long distance footpaths respectively – useful for planning your trip; and the *Bison Futé* (wily buffalo), a map issued free every year by the French Ministry of Transport (see Travel, page 587).

Individual regions on one sheet

Michelin 1:200,000 These familiar yellow-covered maps are available in narrow, strip-shaped sheets covering quite a small area, as well as in a much larger (and more convenient) 'Regional' format, covering the whole country. Both series are admirably clear, easy to follow and comprehensive.

IGN Red Series 1:250,000 Some detail a bit difficult to read, but a very attractive general-purpose map which gives a good idea of the terrain. Covers the whole country, with index and lists of major events and festivals.

Recta-Foldex Cart' Index 1:250,000 Very nearly as good as Michelin for navigating, and better for touring information (e.g. campsites and places of interest). Has an index printed on the back. Covers seven areas of France, mainly the coasts and the Pyrenees.

Local maps

IGN Green Series 1:100,000 A good choice for really detailed local exploring by car. Shows contours and some footpaths, but not really detailed enough for walking. Covers the whole country in a number of large sheets.

IGN Orange Series 1:50,000 The equivalent to the British Ordnance Survey Landranger Series. Sheets are much smaller than with the British OS equivalent and it takes over 1,000 of them to cover the whole of France. There are also some large-sheet special editions based on IGN maps, but overprinted with walking and touring information, which can work out cheaper and more convenient than the Orange series if they cover an area you're interested in. These include the *Didier Richard Series* (30 maps of the Alps, the Rhône Valley, the Jura and Corsica at 1:25,000 and 1:50,000); the *Randonnées Pyrénéennes* (11 maps of the Pyrenees at 1:50,000); and the *Club Vosgien series* (17 maps of the Vosges at 1:50,000 and 1:25,000).

PRACTICAL INFORMATION

IGN Blue Series 1:25,000 Equivalent to the British Ordnance Survey Pathfinder Series. Covers the country in 2,000 sheets, and gives tourist, walking and climbing information. Selected Blue Series maps of popular climbing areas are available overprinted with footpaths in the IGN Top 25 Series.

City maps

For navigating in larger towns and cities, it's well worth buying the **Michelin** Red Guide which contains many excellent town plans.

Where to get maps

The following shops will supply to mail order as well as to personal callers:

Edward Stanford Ltd, 12–14 Long Acre, London WC2E 9LP, tel: 071–836 1321

The Map Shop (A T Atkinson and Partner), 15 High Street, Upton-upon-Severn, Worcs. WR8 0HJ, tel: (0684) 593146

Heffers Map Shop, 19 Sydney Street, Cambridge CB2 3HL, tel: (0223) 358241

McCarta's Maps obtainable from World Leisure Marketing, PO Box 17, Matlock, Derbyshire DE4 4XP, tel: (0629) 826262

The following publisher has a mail-order catalogue:

Roger Lascelles, 47 York Road, Brentford, Middlesex TW8 0QP, tel: 081–847 0935

WEATHER

The table below compares the temperature and sunshine record of representative towns on the coasts and inland – the average daily maximum temperature, and bright sunshine as a percentage of daylight hours. There is more to the French climate than the general truth that the further south you go the hotter and sunnier the weather. The main climatic influences are oceanic (along the Atlantic coast), continental (the further east the more continental the climate), and Mediterranean. The oceanic influence is cooling in summer, warming in winter and gently rain-bearing. The continental influence is more extreme – hotter summers, colder winters, and storms. The Mediterranean influence is warm and sunny. These factors account, for example, for harsher winters in Lorraine than Anjou and much drier and sunnier weather in the eastern than western Pyrenees.

	April		July		October	
	TEMP °C	SUN %	TEMP °C	SUN %	TEMP °C	SUN %
Caen	13	50	22	47	15	39
Nantes	15	49	23	52	16	40
Biarritz*	16	50	23	42	18	38
Montpellier	18	62	29	79	20	54
Nice	17	60	26	77	21	58
Paris	16	47	25	49	16	37
Le Puy	13	47	24	60	15	41
Grenoble	16	48	26	61	16	40
London	13	38	22	39	14	30
Ilfracombe	12	43	19	40	14	30

*Biarritz sunshine figures based on only 2 years' data

Coasts The Gulf Stream gives the Cap de la Hague on the northern tip of the Cotentin peninsula (Normandy) the same average temperature in January as Nice, the famous warm winter resort. Brittany too is mild in winter as it is in summer. What the Gulf Stream cannot do is to make the sun shine, in which respect the Côte d'Azur has more than an edge on Normandy. Cherbourg has about 50 hours a month of midwinter sun, Nice about 150 hours. Mountains by the sea mean atmospheric turmoil, often in the form of the unpleasant *mistral*, a cold north wind which howls down the Rhône valley into Provence for days on end. Less often there are warm winds, dry or damp, from the south, bringing North African dust and sand with them.

Mountains Mountain ranges are important influences on the weather. The Alps shelter a small section of the Mediterranean coast near the Italian border where the winter is particularly warm and fruit ripens. The annual average temperature in Monaco is 16°C; there is about one frost per decade. Pau, just to the north of the western Pyrenees, is wetter, but also very mild in winter. The formidable natural

PRACTICAL INFORMATION

barrier of the Alps disrupts all normal weather patterns and local variations in climate are remarkable. Mont Blanc in particular is a meteorological law unto itself. The Vosges shelter the Rhineland plain, often resulting in stifling summer weather in Alsace. The Massif Central, the huge mountain area of central southern France, has a variety of climates sharing all influences; as a whole, it is stormy in summer. The southern Massif's climate is one of extremes, the dryness of the summer accentuated by the poor water-retentive power of the limestone sub-soil. The Cévennes region (in the southern Massif) is where all sorts of air currents converge and is more rained on than anywhere else in France (two metres of rain a year, and on 30/31 October 1963 608mm in 24 hours, on Mont Aigoual). The northern Massif (Auvergne) is characterised by extreme variations of temperature – an astonishing 41°C minimum/maximum spread was recorded on 10 August 1885 – and chilly midsummer days are not rare.

PRACTICAL INFORMATION

Beaches and bathing

Sea water temperature varies surprisingly little along the length of France's Channel and Atlantic coasts – in midsummer, for example, the northern French sea is only a couple of degrees cooler than the Basque and Landes coasts (high 'teens C, mid-60s F). The Mediterranean is significantly warmer; and the waters of the Côte d'Azur are warmer than those of the Languedoc coast.

On the Mediterranean coast, public beaches are free (but more generally litter-strewn and lacking in facilities); most resorts have a more attractive fee-paying stretch with facilities including sun-loungers, sun-shades, showers and cafés. On the Atlantic and Channel coasts, beaches are almost always free.

Almost all resorts beaches have a lifeguard, or notices and warning signs about dangerous currents and tides. Most resorts have a supervised children's activity area (often called Mickey Club) for which there is a daily charge.

To find out which beaches meet the standards of the EC Bathing Water Directive call at the local tourist offices which hold up-to-date results, available during and after the summer season.

Customs and duty free

From 1 January 1993 the restrictions on the allowances for duty-paid goods (i.e. purchased from local shops) brought from any EC country into the UK were greatly increased. However, these goods should be carried personally and intended for your own use. If you bring back more than the suggested UK guide limits (10 litres of spirits, 20 litres of fortified wine, 90 litres of table wine, of which 60 litres may be sparkling, 110 litres of beer, 800 cigarettes, 400 cigarillos, 200 cigars) you may have to prove that your shopping is for you.

Duty-free shopping – at airports or on ferries – will continue until 30 June 1999. Duty-free allowances will still apply, but will be controlled at point of sale, not at customs.

Electricity

In most areas of France the electricity supply is very similar to that in Britain, i.e. 220 volts (including graded campsites). You will need an adaptor as British plugs will not fit into French sockets. It is important not to use a two-pin socket to power an appliance which needs an earth and consequently a three-pin plug at home (travel iron, water heater).

Health and Insurance

EC member states have reciprocal health agreements which entitle you to receive urgent medical treatment and care in a state-run hospital within the EC. In theory, you need the form E111 to prove your entitlement. The E111 and information about it is contained in the leaflet T2, *Health Advice for Travellers*, available from main post offices. The E111 does not entitle you to repatriation and should not be considered as an alternative to taking out a holiday insurance policy.

PRACTICAL INFORMATION

When arranging insurance cover for France:

• make sure that you are insured for medical expenses up to £250,000 and that the insurance includes cancellation or curtailment of your holiday
• make sure any valuable individual items are covered
• always check the exclusion clauses in the small print
• if you hire a car, be sure to take out collision damage waiver; personal accident cover is only necessary if not already covered by your general holiday insurance.

Metric conversions

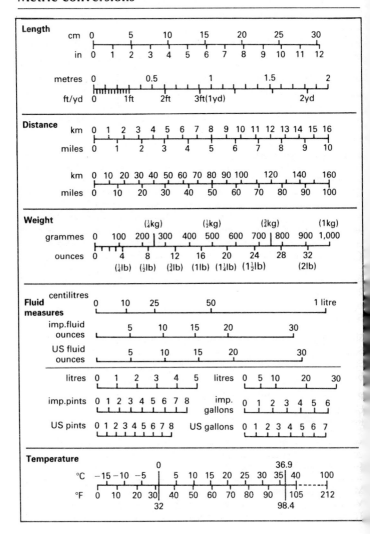

Money

Hotel deposits (*arrhes*) Usually demanded especially for high-season bookings. Use a credit card, a Eurocheque (bi-annual charge for a Eurocheque card, then a small charge per cheque) or a banker's draft (available from your bank at a fixed rate per draft, or an amount per £100).

Changing money Before you go, buy some francs in cash from a bank. On top of that, you'll probably need some travellers' cheques. French franc-denominated cheques generally give you slightly better value than sterling ones – despite their greater initial cost – as the exchange rates French banks offer for sterling cheques tend to be rather poor. But you may still find yourself asked to pay commission for changing French franc cheques. If that happens, try another bank. Some hotels accept French franc travellers' cheques at face value, though you cannot rely on it; and some exchange cash and sterling travellers' cheques, usually at fairly unfavourable rates.

Eurocheques are very convenient, as you can use them to pay bills in hotels, shops and restaurants, as well as to obtain cash in banks. Apply to your bank at least a fortnight before you go for a supply of cheques and the necessary bank card, which cost £4 to £8 every two years. There is a small handling charge for each cheque.

Credit cards Major credit cards (Mastercard and Visa) are widely accepted. On average, you're likely to get a better exchange rate by using them rather than changing money in a bank – but exchange rate fluctuations between the date when you use your card and the date when your bill is calculated can work either way.

Charge cards such as American Express and Diners Club are quite useful for hotels, restaurants and smart shops, though using them will normally work out more expensive than Mastercard or Visa.

Opening hours

Banks Normally open at 9 am, close at lunch (12 noon or 12.30 pm to about 2 pm) and close at about 4 pm. All close on Sunday; some close on Monday and open for Saturday markets. Crédit Agricole branches sometimes open on Saturday in towns where there is no Saturday market.

Shops Food shops open about 7 am to 6.30/7.30 pm; they usually open on Saturday morning, and often on Sunday morning, but may close on Monday. Supermarkets and hypermarkets open until 9 or 10 pm Monday to Saturday, but may close Monday am. Many shops close between noon and 2 pm.

Restaurants Almost all small town and rural restaurants open for Sunday lunch, but many close on Sunday evening, and on another day in the week. In large towns and cities, many close on Sunday.

Museums and châteaux Many are shut on either Monday or Tuesday.

Public holidays

Most shops and banks are shut on the following days: **New Year's Day**; **Easter Monday** (moveable); **Labour Day** 1 May; **VE Day** 8 May; **Ascension Day** 6th Thursday after Easter; **Whit Monday** 2nd Monday after Ascension; **Bastille Day**

14 July; **Assumption** 15 August; **All Saints** (*Toussaint*) 1 November; **Armistice Day** 11 November; **Christmas Day**. If any fall on a Sunday, the holiday is taken on the following day. If they fall on a Tuesday or Friday, the day between it and the nearest Sunday is also taken as a holiday.

Telephoning

French telephone numbers are all 8-figure. The only dialling extra is for calls between Paris (*Région Parisienne*) and the rest of France (*Province*). From Paris to the rest: dial 16, wait for a tone change, then dial the 8-figure number. To Paris from the rest: dial 16, wait for a tone change, then dial 1 followed by the 8-figure number (note that Paris numbers are also preceded by a 1 when calling from the UK). For calls to the UK, dial 19, wait for a tone change, then dial 44 followed by the UK area code (but omit the first 0 – for example, the code for inner London will simply be 71) followed by the number. For directory enquiries, dial 12; operator 13; police 17; fire 18.

Most telephone booths now take cards (*télécarte*) which can be bought from post offices or tobacconists.

Tipping

Restaurants Most restaurants include a service charge in their prices; a few exclude it from their prices but mention it in small print on the menu and add it on before the final addition.

Cafés Service is nearly always included in the price of drinks if you sit down, usually excluded if you stand at the bar.

Hotels Porters hover.

Taxis Tip expected.

Public lavatories Very often guarded by fierce women who do not expect tips, simply charge an entrance fee, however agonised your plea.

Cinemas Tip the usherette.

Garages *Pompistes*, even in the motorway service stations, very often clean windscreens and check oil. Tips are welcomed, but not expected.

FESTIVALS AND EVENTS

January	Monte Carlo Rally
February	Lemon Festival, Menton Nice Carnival
March	Black Pudding Festival, Mortagne-au-Perche, Normandy 'Foire à la Ferraille et au Jambons'; (Junk Fair), Châtou, near Paris
April	Daffodil Festival, Gérardmer, Alsace
May	Paris Marathon Monaco Grand Prix Cannes Film Festival Gipsy Festival, Stes-Maries-de-la-Mer, Camargue
May–June	International Tennis Championship, Paris
June	Le Mans 24-hour car race
July	Bastille Day Tour de France French Grand Prix Nice Jazz Festival Antibes Jazz Festival Aix-en-Provence International Festival of music and opera
July–August	Avignon Festival of music and drama 'Chorégies d'Orange' (opera and recitals in the Théatre Antique)
August	Deauville Grand Prix Cannes Fireworks Festival Blue Fishing Nets Festival, Concarneau Assumption Day celebrations, Brittany
September	Wine and beer festivals in Alsace
October	Grand Prix de l'Arc de Triomphe, Longchamp
November	Dijon Gastronomic Fair
December	Christmas crib festivities (especially in Provence)

Further information

The French Government Tourist Office, 178 Piccadilly, London WIV 0AL, has a public information service; you can call at their office (open Monday to Friday from 9 am to 5 pm), or telephone (0891) 244123 (36p per minute cheap rate, 48p peak rate).

In France, there are local *Offices de Tourisme* and *Syndicats d'Initiative* in almost every town and resort. They can advise on accommodation, restaurants, entertainments and local transport.

Glossary of food

Abricot Apricot
Agneau Lamb; **de pré-salé** pastured on salt meadows
Aiglefin Haddock
Aiguillettes Long slices, usually poultry or game
Ail Garlic
Aile Wing
Aïoli Garlic mayonnaise
Alose Shad
Alsacienne (à l') Usually with sauerkraut, ham and sausages
Amuse-gueule Appetizer served with aperitif
Ananas Pineapple
Anchois Anchovy
Andouille, andouillette Pork sausage of chitterlings and tripe
Aneth Dill
Anglaise (à l') Plain boiled
Anguilles au vert Eels with white wine and herbs
Armoricaine (à la) With sauce of tomatoes, herbs, white wine, brandy
Artichaut Artichoke
Asperges Asparagus
Avelines Hazelnuts

Ballottine Boned, stuffed and rolled
Bar Sea-bass
Barbeau Barbel (river fish)
Barbue Brill
Basilic Basil
Baudroie *lotte*, monkfish
Bavarois Custard cream dessert, often flavoured or with fruit
Béarnaise Sauce flavoured with tarragon and vinegar
Beignet Fritter
Bercy Sauce with wine, shallots and bone marrow
Berrichonne (á la) With bacon, cabbage, onions and chestnuts

Betterave Beetroot
Beurre blanc Butter sauce with shallots and dry wine or vinegar
Beurre noir Browned butter with vinegar
Bigarade Bitter orange sauce
Bigorneau Winkle
Bisque Thick cream shellfish soup
Blanchaille Whitebait
Blanquette Thickened white stew
Boeuf à la mode Beef braised in red wine with vegetables
Bonne femme Poached in white wine with onions and mushrooms
Bordelaise Sauce of red wine and bone marrow
Bouchée Tiny filled puff pastry
Boudin Large fat sausage
Bouillabaisse Provençal fish soup with wine, garlic, tomato and saffron
Boulangère (à la) Braised or baked with onions and potatoes
Bourgeoise (à la) With carrots, onions and bacon
Bourguignonne (à la) Cooked with burgundy, onions and mushrooms
Bourride Creamy Provençal fish soup with aïoli
Brandade de morue Creamed salt cod with oil and garlic
Brème Freshwater bream
Bretonne (à la) Served with haricot beans, sometimes as a purée
Broche (à la) Spit roasted
Brochet Pike
Brugnon Nectarine
Bruxelloise (à la) Served with Brussels sprouts and chicory

Cabillaud Cod
Caille Quail

Calmar Inkfish, squid
Canard Duck
Caneton Duckling
Capoum *Rascasse*, scorpion fish
Carbonade de boeuf Beef braised in beer, onions and herbs
Cardinal Rich, red fish sauce with mushrooms, truffles (usually for lobster)
Cargolade Snails cooked in wine
Carré d'agneau Rack of lamb
Carrelet Plaice
Cassis Blackcurrant
Cassoulet Casserole of beans and varied meats, e.g. pork and goose
Céleri Celery
Céleri-rave Celeriac
Cèpes Fine, delicate mushrooms
Cerfeuil Chervil
Cerise Cherry
Cerneau Green walnut
Cervelle Brains
Champignons Mushrooms
Chanterelles Mushrooms
Chapon Capon
Chateaubriand Thick centre cut of fillet of beef
Chausson Puff pastry turnover
Chemise (en) Wrapped, generally in pastry
Chevreuil Venison
Chicorée Curly endive
Chipirons à l'encre Squid, stuffed and stewed in their ink
Choron Béarnaise sauce with tomato purée
Choucroute garnie Sauerkraut with various sausages and potatoes
Choufleur Cauliflower
Ciboule Spring onion
Ciboulettes Chives
Citron pressé Fresh lemon juice
Citron vert Lime
Civet Rich game stew
Civet de lièvre Jugged hare
Civettes Chives
Clafoutis Batter cake with fruit
Cocotte Small cooking dish
Coing Quince
Colin Hake
Confit(e) Preserved or candied

Confit de canard (d'oie) Potted duck (goose) cooked and preserved in its own fat
Contrefilet Part of the sirloin
Corbeille de fruits Basket of fresh fruit
Coque cockle
Coquillages Shellfish
Coquilles St-Jacques Scallops
Cornichon Gherkin
Côte de côtelette Chop
Cou (d'oie) Neck (of goose)
Coulibiac Fish cake (usually salmon) in pastry
Coulis Thick sauce or purée, of vegetables or fruit
Court-bouillon Aromatic poaching liquid
Crécy (à la) With carrots
Crème anglaise Light custard
Crémet Fresh cream cheese eaten with sugar and cream
Crêpe Pancake
Cresson Watercress
Crevettes grises Shrimps
Crevettes roses Prawns
Croque-monsieur Toasted cheese sandwich with ham
Croustade Mould or puff pastry shell with various savoury fillings
Croûte (en) Pastry case (in a)
Cru Raw
Crudités (Pieces of) raw vegetables
Crustacés Shellfish

Darne Large fish steak
Daube Meat slowly braised in wine and herbs
Daurade Sea bream
Daurade rose Red sea bream
Diable Highly seasoned sauce; also type of cooking pot
Dijonnais (à la) With mustard sauce
Dinde (dindon) Turkey
Doux (douce) Sweet
Duxelles Stuffing or seasoning of cooked minced mushrooms

Ecrevisses Freshwater crayfish
Endive Chicory
Entremets Desserts

GLOSSARY OF FOOD

Epaule Shoulder
Epinards Spinach
Epis de maïs Sweetcorn
Escargots Snails
Espadon Swordfish
Estouffade As *daube*; meat is first marinated and browned
Estragon Tarragon

Faisan Pheasant
Farci(e) Stuffed
Faux-filet Part of the sirloin
Fenouil Fennel
Fève Broad bean
Flageolets Kidney beans; fresh green, dried white
Flétan Halibut
Foie Liver
Foie gras Goose liver
Fonds d'artichauts Artichoke hearts
Forestière (à la) With bacon and mushrooms
Four (au) Baked
Fourré Stuffed
Frais Cool
Fraises des bois Wild strawberries
Framboise Raspberry
Frappé Iced or chilled
Fricadelles Small balls of minced meat
Fricandeau Topside of veal
Fricassee Creamy stew of white meat
Friture Small fried fish
Fruits der mer Seafood
Fumé Smoked

Galantine Cold pressed poultry, meat or fish in jelly
Gamba Large prawn
Garbure Thick vegetable soup
Gardons Small roach
Garni With vegetables
Gaufre Waffle
Genièvre Juniper
Gésier Gizzard
Gibier Game
Gigot Leg of lamb or mutton
Gingembre Ginger
Girolles/chanterelles Mushrooms
Gougère Cheese-enriched choux batter

Goujon Gudgeon
Goujonnettes Small fried fillets
Gourmandise Sweetmeat
Grand Veneur Sauce for game with wine, redcurrants, pepper
Granité Grainy water ice
Gratin/gratiné Browned topping, often with breadcrumbs or cheese
Gratin dauphinois Sliced potatoes baked with cream and garlic (eggs and cheese often added)
Grecque (à la) Vegetables cooked and marinated in wine, spices and herbs
Grenade Pomegranate
Grenouilles (cuisses de) Frogs (frogs' legs)
Griotte Bitter red cherry
Groseille, groseille à maquereau Gooseberry
Groseille rouge Redcurrant
Groseille noire Blackcurrant

Hareng Herring
Hareng fumé Kipper
Hareng salé Bloater
Haricots blancs Dried white beans
Haricots rouges Red kidney beans
Haricots verts French (string) beans
Hochepot Thick casserole
Hollandaise Sauce with butter, egg yolk and lemon juice
Homard Lobster
Hongroise (à la) With paprika, tomato, onions and cream
Huile Oil
Huître Oyster

Ile flottante Dessert of poached egg whites in vanilla custard

Jambon Bayonne/à la bayonnaise Mild ham cooked partly in wine
Jambon persillé Cold pressed ham and parsley in white wine jelly
Jambonneau Small ham, knuckle of pork
Jardinière With diced mixed vegetables
Julienne With matchsticks of vegetables

Laitue Lettuce
Lamproie River lamprey, eel-like fish
Langouste Spiny lobster, crayfish
Langoustine Scampi
Langue Tongue
Lapin Rabbit
Lapereau Young rabbit
Lavaret Lake fish of salmon type
Lièvre Hare
Limande Lemon sole
Lotte de mer Monkfish, anglerfish
Lotte de rivière Burbot, river fish
Loup de mer Sea-bass
Lyonnaise (à la) With onions

Macédoine Mixture of diced fruit or vegetables
Magret (de canard) Fillet, breast (of duck)
Mangetout Young peas in the pod, eaten whole
Maquereau Mackerel
Marcassin Young wild boar
Marchand de vin In a red wine sauce
Marengo (poulet) Fried chicken, eggs, and tomatoes with garlic, brandy and crayfish
Marjolaine Marjoram
Marmite Tall cooking pot
Marron glacé Candied chestnut
Matelote (d'anguilles) Wine stew of freshwater fish and eel
Merlan Whiting (hake in S. France)
Mérou Bland Mediterranean fish
Mesclun Mixture of salad leaves
Meunière (Fish) cooked in butter with lemon juice and parsley
Mirabelle Small golden plum
Moelle Bone marrow (usually beef)
Montmorency With cherries
Morille Type of mushroom
Morue Salt cod
Mouclade Mussels in creamy sauce with saffron, turmeric and wine
Moules (à la) marinière Mussels cooked in white wine with shallots
Mousseline Hollandaise sauce with whipped cream

Mulet Grey mullet
Mûres Mulberries
Myrtilles Bilberries

Nage (à la) (Shellfish) poached in *court bouillon* with herbs
Nantua Cream sauce for fish with crayfish purée
Navarin Mutton or lamb stew with potatoes and onions
Navet Turnip
Noisette Small round steak
Noix (de veau) Topside of leg (veal)
Normande (à la) With cream and any or all of: Calvados, cider, apples
Nouilles Flat noodles

Oeufs Eggs
  brouillés Scrambled
  en cocotte Baked in oven
  à la coque Soft boiled
  durs Hard boiled
  mollets Soft boiled
  à la neige See *île flottante*
  sur le plat Cooked in butter in a shallow dish in the oven
  pochés Poached
  poêlés Fried
Oie Goose
Omble chevalier Freshwater char, type of salmon
Ombre Grayling
Omelette Norvégienne Meringue-covered sponge and ice-cream; like baked Alaska
Orange (jus d') Usually canned or bottled orange juice
Orange pressée Fresh orange juice
Oseille Sorrel
Oursin Sea-urchin

Palmier (coeurs de) Palm hearts
Palourdes farcies Cooked stuffed clams
Pamplemousse Grapefruit
Panais Parsnip
Pan bagnat Large bread roll filled with salad, olive oil, anchovies
Papillote (en) Baked in a packet of grease-proof paper or foil

GLOSSARY OF FOOD

Parfait (de) Creamy iced mousse
Pastèque Watermelon
Pâte brisée Shortcrust pastry
Paupiette Thin slice (of meat or fish) stuffed, rolled and braised
Pavé (Slab) thick slice
Pêche Peach
Perdreau Young partridge
Persil Parsley
Petite marmite Individual pot of consommé
Pétoncle Queen scallop
Pieds de porc Pigs' trotters
Pigeonneau Young pigeon, squab
Pignons Pine kernels
Piment doux Sweet pepper
Pintade Guinea-fowl
Pipérade Scrambled mixture of eggs, onions, green peppers and tomatoes
Pissaladière Dough-based tart of onions, tomatoes, anchovies, black olives
Pissenlits Dandelion leaves
Pistaches Pistachio nuts
Pistou (soupe au) Strong vegetable soup with garlic, basil and thick vermicelli
Plie Plaice
Pochouse Stew of eel and other freshwater fish in white wine
Poire Pear
Poireau Leek
Poivrade Peppery sauce served with game (roebuck)
Poivre Pepper
Poivron Sweet pepper, pimento
Polonaise (à la) With browned breadcrumbs, chopped hard-boiled eggs, parsley and butter
Pommes Apples
Pommes de terre Potatoes
  à l'anglaise Boiled
  à la vapeur Steamed
  allumettes Matchsticks, fried
  boulangère, rôtie Roast
  frites Deep fried (chips)
  lyonnaise Sautéed with onions
  nature, au naturel Boiled
  purée de Mashed
Porc (carré de) Loin of pork

Porcelet Suckling pig
Portugaise (à la) Includes tomatoes
Potage Thick soup
Pot-au-chocolat Chocolate cream dessert
Pot-au-feu Boiled beef, vegetables and broth
Potée Heavy soup of various meats, cabbage, beans/lentils
Poulet Chicken
Poussin Small baby chicken
Praires Small clams
Printanière (à la) With mixed spring vegetables
Provençal (à la) With tomatoes, oil and garlic
Prune Plum
Pruneau Prune

Quenelle Light poached dumpling of fish, veal or poultry
Quetsche Small, purple plum
Queue de boeuf Oxtail

Râble de (lièvre/lapin) Saddle of (hare/rabbit)
Ragoût Stew, usually meat
Raie Skate
Raifort Horseradish
Raisin Grape
Rascasse Scorpion fish
Ratatouille Stew of aubergines, courgettes, tomatoes, green and red peppers and onions in oil
Reine-claude Greengage
Rémoulade Sharp-flavoured mayonnaise
Rillettes Potted pork seasoned with herbs or spices
Ris (d'agneau/de veau) Sweetbreads (lamb or veal)
Riz Rice
Rognon Kidney
Romarin Rosemary
Rôti Roast
Rouget Red mullet
Roulade (de) Roll (of)
Rouille Strongly flavoured creamy sauce served in/with fish soups

Royan Large sardine
Rutabaga Swede

Sabayon French version of zabaglione
St-Germain With peas
St-Jacques See *coquilles*
St-Pierre John Dory
Saisons (suivant) Depending on season
Salade niçoise Substantial salad including eggs, green beans, olives, anchovies, sometimes tuna
Salade panachée Mixed salad
Salade verte Green salad
Salmis Roast joints of game or poultry in a red wine sauce
Sandre River fish; pike-perch
Saucisse Fresh raw sausage (sold uncooked)
Saucisson Larger sausage for slicing (sold cooked)
Sauge Sage
Scarole Endive
Selle Saddle
Selon grosseur/grandeur Priced according to size (*sg* on menus)
Soissonnaise (à la) With white haricot beans
Sole:
　à la Dieppoise Fillets with sauce of mussels, shrimps and white wine
　Dugléré With tomatoes, onions, herbs and cream sauce
　Marguéry With mussels, shrimps and rich egg sauce
　Véronique Poached in white wine with grapes
Soubise With purée of onions and sometimes rice

Suprême Boneless breast or wing of poultry
Tartare (steak) Finely minced steak served raw with raw egg yolk, onions and capers
Tarte Tatin Substantial upside-down apple tart
Thon Tuna fish
Thym Thyme
Tiède Lukewarm
Topinambour Jerusalem artichoke
Tournedos Fillet steak
　chasseur With shallots, mushrooms, tomatoes
　Rossini Topped with pâté in a madeira sauce
Tourte Covered savoury tart
Tourteau Large crab
Tripes Tripe
Truffes Truffles
Truite (au bleu) Trout poached in vinegar *court bouillon*, giving a blue tinge to skin
Ttoro Basque fish stew

Vacherin Meringue ring filled with whipped cream, ice-cream and fruit
Vallée d'Auge With Calvados, apples and cream
Veau Veal
　pané Breadcrumbed escalope
　à la Viennoise Escalope with chopped egg, capers and parsley
Velouté Cream sauce/soup
Volaille Poultry

Waterzooi Freshwater fish or chicken stew

Hotels index

Paris (including restaurants)

HOTELS INDEX

HOTELS INDEX

Out of Paris (by hotel)

HOTELS INDEX

Hotel	Town	(Chapter)	Page

HOTELS INDEX

HOTELS INDEX

Out of Paris (by town)

HOTELS INDEX

HOTELS INDEX

HOTELS INDEX

Index

INDEX

INDEX

INDEX